Race, Culture, Psychology, & Law

To our children, Sarah, Sonora, and Henry.

—KHB & WHG

To my parents and grandparents, Rosemary Holt and Philip Holt, Nellie Halton and Howard Huntley, and Agnes Haggerty and Walter Haggerty. And for the Halton sisters who crossed the Atlantic from Ireland, children alone: Nellie, Annie, Tessie, and Mary.

—KHB

To my parents and grandparents, Lillie B. George and Will Henry George, Claude Brantley and Jimmie D. Brantley, and Campbell George and Gertrude George. And for ancestors known and unknown—African, African American, and Native American Indian—who contributed in spirit.

—WHG

Race, Culture, Psychology, & Law

Editors

Kimberly Holt Barrett
University of Washington, Seattle

William H. George
University of Washington, Seattle

SAGE Publications
Thousand Oaks ▪ London ▪ New Delhi

For information:

Sage Publications, Inc.
2455 Teller Road
Thousand Oaks, California 91320
E-mail: order@sagepub.com

Sage Publications Ltd.
1 Oliver's Yard
55 City Road
London EC1Y 1SP
United Kingdom

Sage Publications India Pvt. Ltd.
B-42, Panchsheel Enclave
Post Box 4109
New Delhi 110 017 India

Printed in the United States of America

Library of Congress Cataloging-in-Publication Data

Race, culture, psychology, and law / Kimberly Holt Barrett and William H. George, editors.
    p. cm.
Includes bibliographical references and index.
ISBN 0-7619-2662-3 (cloth: alk. paper)
ISBN 0-7619-2663-1 (pbk. : alk. paper)
   1. Discrimination—Law and legislation—United States. 2. Discrimination in justice administration—United States. 3. United States—Race relations. I. Barrett, Kimberly. II. George, William, 1954-
KF4755.R33 2005
342.7308'73—dc22

          2004008315

04   05   06   07   08   09   10   9   8   7   6   5   4   3   2   1

Acquiring Editor:	Jerry Westby
Editorial Assistant:	Vonessa Vondera
Typesetter:	C&M Digitals (P) Ltd.
Indexer:	Pam Van Huss
Cover Designer:	Michelle Lee Kenny

CONTENTS

FOREWORD

What is our culture when America is not a homogeneous society? The U.S. population includes people with many origins and ancestries. More than 11% of the people now living in the United States were not born here, an estimated 32.5 million people. More than 150 languages and dialects are spoken here.

In addition, ever-changing world politics trigger further immigration, creating even greater cultural and ethnic diversity challenges. Since 1970, the composition of our foreign-born population has changed dramatically. Between 1970 and 2002, the estimated share of foreign-born U.S. residents from Europe dropped from 62% to 15%. Over the same period, the share of foreign-born residents from Asia grew from 9% to 25%. The share from Latin America also increased significantly, from 19% to 52%. We live in a culturally dynamic society.

When it comes to our legal system, however, our deep-rooted goals of "equality and justice for all" often are not reached, due greatly to our perception that our system of justice must be "colorblind" and "race neutral." This often means that judges, lawyers, and other professionals involved in legal proceedings may discount relevant and important information that a person "brings to the table." Recognition of cultural values and customs, ethnic traits, prior social structure, and even religion may give us greater insight into what happened and what can be done.

We live in interesting times. Memories of the civil rights movement are fading into history. Our aggressive foreign policy has created negative feelings toward some ethnic, social, and religious groups. And it appears that our own issues of race, culture, and ethnicity are being placed "on the back burner."

Our legal system is slow to bring culture, race, and psychology into our courtrooms—first, for fear of delving into these sensitive areas and, second, because of the perceived inconsistency with the very foundation of our legal system—equal justice and fairness. Perceptions of treating people differently, affording greater resources, or looking at things through different lenses are some of the factors that perpetuate such resistance. Coming to terms with diversity and culture is one of the greatest challenges that the law in this country now faces. And with the increased urgency of global conflict resolution, the intersection of American culture, race, psychology, and law becomes even more important.

The chapters collected by editors Kimberly Holt Barrett and William H. George cover a broad range of issues and topics, and yet all address an even more fundamental concern, that is, "equal access to justice." *Race, Culture, Psychology, and Law* is a substantial step toward opening our eyes and leveling the playing field. Irrespective of ethnicity, national original, and physical or mental impairment, everyone is entitled to the "opportunity to effectively participate" in legal proceedings. This book gives the reader a greater understanding of what that truly is.

Ron A. Mamiya
Municipal Court of Seattle

FOREWORD

Why is this book concerning race, culture, psychology, and the law necessary or important? Isn't psychology as well as law applicable to all? The contributors to this book illustrate how psychology and law cannot be understood or applied without a fundamental grounding in race, ethnicity, and cultural experiences. The U.S. surgeon general, in his supplemental report (U. S. Department of Health and Human Services, 2001), noted how culture "counts" in explaining mental health outcomes. The same is true in psychology and law. Culture counts in at least two ways. First, cultural issues are intimately involved in explaining human behaviors and outcomes in our judicial system. Second, psychology and the law each have a culture. Unfortunately, these cultures have in the past been largely biased in an ethnocentric direction. They have perpetuated a colorblind philosophy, when the reality is that there are racial and ethnic disparities in the dispensing of justice and in the protection and security that are experienced. In fact, given the reality, a colorblind philosophy allows racism to flourish by denying the existence of prejudice and discrimination and by de-emphasizing the search for remedies.

Editors Kimberly Holt Barrett and William H. George have brought together an impressive array of contributions that demonstrate how critical it is to understand race, ethnicity, and culture in forensic psychology. There is an extraordinary range of topics that include the importance of race relations, psychological testing and evaluation, racial "profiling," disparities in death penalty convictions, immigration and domestic violence, asylum seekers, deportations and civil rights, juvenile justice, cross-cultural lawyering, and cultural competency in the administration of justice. In presenting the topics, the contributors vary in the use of theories and models, case examples, empirical research grounding, and practical guidelines on addressing dilemmas involving cultural issues (e.g., assessment and use of interpreters). The presentations will be particularly appealing and useful to practitioners, researchers, and forensic specialists in both psychology and the judicial system.

In appreciating the significant contributions of the authors, it is important to understand that the chapters are not intended simply to advocate that something be done for ethnic minority groups. Though one major effect of this book is to highlight the need to address the plight of ethnic groups, the real implication is to bring us back to the notion of "equal justice under the law" and its true meaning.

Stanley Sue
University of California, Davis

REFERENCE

U.S. Department of Health and Human Services. (2001). *Mental health: Culture, race, and ethnicity—A supplement to mental health: A report to the surgeon general.* Rockville, MD: U.S. DHHS, Office of the Surgeon General.

ACKNOWLEDGMENTS

I want to acknowledge numerous individuals. The development of this book involved the contributions of many professionals who dedicate their lives to the pursuit of justice for all. I wish to thank them for their work on this book and for their work in the world. In meeting all of them through this project, I greatly value the sense of camaraderie I have developed with those who fight a good fight—a common fight—in the words of the late Fred Hampton, "For the People." I especially want to thank the professionals who mentored me along the way and who provided encouragement at times when I was shocked and discouraged at the injustice that I observed in our legal system, including that which is perpetrated and perpetuated by those within the discipline of clinical psychology. For this mentorship and encouragement, I wish to thank Judge Ron Mamiya, who encouraged me to write about my experiences in the courtroom and who contributed to the Foreword in this book; tireless and steadfast federal public defenders Carol Koller and Jay Stansell; those who work in civil rights and criminal justice, Tony Alfieri, Thad Martin, Jack Connely, Gary Gaer, Kristine Koy, and Heather Spencer; and all of the dedicated attorneys and staff at the Northwest Immigrant Rights Project, past and present, including Kate Laner, Jeanette Zanipatin, Bina Hanchinamani, Jonathan Moore, Ann Benson, and Delila Leiber. From my own discipline, I wish to thank Dr. Maria Root, Dr. Joseph Trimble, Dr. Stanley Sue, Dr. David Sue, Dr. Felipe Castro, Dr. Cynthia Garcia Coll, Dr. William Cross, and Dr. James Jones for their listening ears, consultation, advice, and outstanding work as teachers and researchers in the field of ethnic minority psychology and multicultural competence. This book would not have been possible without the knowledge that they contributed to its development. The research and production efforts for this book were assisted by Kimberly Moore, a former undergraduate in our department, who is now working toward an advanced degree in public health. In her work as a victim advocate, she brings significant contributions to our community, and her coauthorship of Chapter 28 in this volume will assist others in that field. Most of all, I wish to thank all the clients I have served, for they have been my most important teachers. I will always remember and respect the African American children and families of Puyallup, Washington, who had the courage to fight for civil rights in times that make it a lonely battle. I wish to thank my beloved husband, colleague, and coeditor, Bill George, for his love, wisdom, intellect, and patient all-night efforts at editing.

Kimberly Holt Barrett

I want to acknowledge several people who supported my contributions to this volume and my work in general. I want to acknowledge the far-reaching and powerful mentoring influences of Dr. Alan Marlatt, Dr. Stanley Sue, and Dr. Claude Steele for their impact on my career path and my scholarship. I want to thank all of my former and current graduate students and all students who have taken my race-related courses; their insights and teachings have been invaluable. I want to thank numerous people who lend moral support and tolerate my absences, overcommitments, and attentional lapses with grace and substitute coverage. This includes my current postdoctoral fellows—Dr. Kelly Cue Davis, Dr. Joel Martell, and Dr. Susan Stoner—and graduate students—Kari Stephens, Jean Yi, Kristen Lindgren, Rebecca Schacht, and Christian Hendershot. This also includes members of the REASONS lab—especially Kelly Kajumulo and Dr. Tina Zawacki—and the SIS/WIN lab—especially Dr. Jeanette Norris and Tatiana Masters. I am thankful for the love and support of my siblings Wanda, Derrick, and Mark. My greatest thanks go to Kim Barrett, my wife, colleague, and coeditor, for love and support that defies description. I am also grateful for her leadership on this project; her vision, energy, intelligence, and dedication made this happen.

William H. George

We both want to extend love and a special thanks to our children Sarah, Sonora, Henry, and our newest "son" Charmarke Aden, who all listened, learned, and gave us their patience and cooperation so that we could work toward making theirs a better world. We are thankful for the support of our family in Mexico: Juan and Nieve Lucero and their children, and Carlos and Celia Burgoine. We give many thanks to former and current students who have worked with us on race matters, especially Carol Wong, Jean Yi, Kari Stephens, Karen Chan, Robert Ochoa, Roxana Nourizi, Na'ila Mued, Dr. June LaMarr, Dr. Loraine Martinez, Dr. Jennifer Watson, Dr. Jennifer Wheeler, Dr. Barbara Dahl, and Dr. Jaslean LaTaillade. We wish to thank our contributors for their work and perseverance, which made this book possible, and for their commitment to this field. We are extremely grateful to Stan Wakefield—the agent who sent the proposal to Sage Publications, to Jerry Westby and others at Sage who brought this project to fruition—especially Denise Santoyo and Vonessa Vondera, and to Mary Tederstrom for magnificent copyediting. We are indebted to the mentoring of Dr. Alan Marlatt and Dr. Nathaniel (Ned) Wagner (who never knew he set the two of us on converging paths, bound to merge). Finally, we are exceedingly grateful for the contributions and influences of Dr. bell hooks, the Honorable Robert Nesta Marley, Dr. Martin Luther King Jr., Malcolm X, Kwame Ture (Stokeley Carmichael), Dr. Angela Davis, Dr. Cornell West, and Dr. Ronald Takaki.

Kimberly Holt Barrett
William H. George

THE NEED FOR CROSS-CULTURAL COMPETENCE IN PSYCHOLOGY AND THE LAW

Introduction and Overview

This book was developed to fill a critical void in the field of psychology as it intersects with the legal profession and the justice system of the United States. We each began working with the courts several years ago because of particular professional skills and personal background characteristics. Kimberly Barrett entered this domain for several reasons, such as her language proficiency in Spanish, the university courses she taught on race and culture, her research on racism and racial identity, and her professional skills in working with ethnic minority individuals and families. William George entered this domain because of his expertise in teaching about race and minority mental health, his professional experience in corrections, and his research expertise about cross-cultural issues and alcohol involvement in sexual violence. Our personal background as a mixed racial couple and parents of multiracial children has also been a source of insight in our thinking about race and society.

Upon entering the world of forensic psychology, we were shocked and amazed to find a professional climate that largely ignored issues of race and culture, even when racial and cultural dynamics were strongly related to the legal case at hand. At times, we worked with well-intentioned professionals who were aware that race and culture were important in their work with clients and the courts, but they were uncertain about how to address race and culture in their approach to the case. At worst, we found a high degree of stereotyping, poor cultural communication skills, and the imposition of professional biases that maligned cultural values and practices and that masked the true identity and life history of the client. Too often we encountered the inappropriate use of testing with individuals who had minimal English skills and low levels of acculturation to the United States. Being new to the forensic field, we sought literature to guide us regarding cross-cultural psychological-legal work and discovered almost nothing. We determined it to be an important mission to continue to teach ourselves and to educate others about the diversity of cultural groups that pass through our courts each day. The racial and cultural background, the psychological and legal needs, and the history and sociopolitical circumstances of minority individuals must be considered by all professionals involved in order to provide appropriate and adequate services.

American ethnic and racial minority groups, immigrants, and refugees to this country are disparately impacted by the justice system of the United States. This is evident beginning with the net cast by racial profiling and continuing with disproportionate incarceration, deportation, and capital punishment. Racial and cultural minorities are also at the forefront of the individuals and groups needing legal protection. For instance, immigrant women victimized by domestic violence, African American and Latin American children whose civil rights are violated by school systems, biracial and bicultural children who lose one side of their cultural heritage through divorce, refugees seeking asylum from torture and religious or political persecution, and the victims of hate crimes all exemplify situations in which the legal system must attend to matters of race and culture in a competent and humane fashion.

Unfortunately, the published scholarship seemed virtually devoid of guidance about providing culturally competent psychological and social services within the legal arena. As we became more fully aware of the enormity of this void and the need for guidance, we embarked on writing this book. It was clear that professionals needed more informational and instructional resources regarding how to work with cultural competence in the intersection of psychology and law. This book is broad in its scope and effort to cover the domains of knowledge and practice that are crucial in providing comprehensive services to ethnic, racial, and cultural minorities.

CULTURAL COMPETENCE

We recognize that cultural competence is a construct that is difficult to define with conclusive precision. This book was prepared with a working definition of cultural competence in mind. We see a culturally competent professional as someone who has made substantial progress yet continues to strive toward

1. Developing an awareness of personal, professional, and cultural biases that may adversely impact minority groups, immigrants, and refugees

2. Developing an awareness of the definitions and dynamics of racism, discrimination, and cultural oppression; this includes an understanding of personal racial socialization processes that foster prejudice and an understanding of the meaning and impact of stereotypes

3. Acquiring knowledge about the history (especially sociopolitical), culture, norms, and traditions of diverse groups; this especially encompasses cultural views and beliefs about health, mental health, and treatment processes. This also includes assessing the client's psychosocial environment with a focus on culturally relevant stressors and support systems

4. Understanding the importance of ethnic, cultural, and racial identity processes as they impact human development; one's sense of well-being; and one's familial, social, and intergroup relationships. An understanding of such identity processes is important regarding the lives of the clients as well as the lives of professional service providers

5. Developing relevant interpersonal skills and effective methods for working with diverse groups. This includes gaining an understanding of how race, culture, and language affect interactions with professionals, the expression of emotion, parenting styles, spirituality, and family organization. This also includes becoming knowledgeable about the cultural and linguistic limitations of using standardized assessment instruments with diverse groups

6. Taking action in the service and advancement of equality and justice. Professionals working with marginalized and oppressed groups should contribute to addressing injustice and discrimination in the lives of their clients. This helps the client to become aware of the role that cultural, societal, and political bias and discrimination play in the problems that they face and helps the client to address injustice through social and institutional channels

GOALS

Our overall goal for this book is deliberately broad and wide ranging. We aim to provide a compendium of knowledge, historical background, case examples, guidelines, and practice standards pertinent to the delivery of psychological, legal, and social services to individuals and families—from racial minority, ethnic minority, immigrant, and refugee groups—who are involved in legal proceedings. To pursue this goal, we have drawn together contributing authors from several disciplines including law, psychology, sociology, social work, and family studies. Our intended audience includes psychologists, lawyers, social workers, and graduate students in these and related disciplines involved in providing services for minority, immigrant, and refugee clients in the legal arena.

The chapters are divided into six distinct but overlapping sections. The first section, Race and Justice, considers a range of background, philosophical, and general issues characterizing the interface of race, culture, and the American justice system. The second section focuses on the use of evaluation and assessment procedures for legal proceedings. The third section is devoted specifically to immigration issues and topics. The fourth and fifth sections address matters related specifically to working with children, families, and juveniles, including understanding racial and cultural identity processes. The final section focuses on violence victimization, particularly domestic violence and sexual violence. Collectively the coverage explores minority versus majority perceptions of justice, documents racial injustice and cultural disparities, identifies contemporary legal challenges and dilemmas, highlights critical service needs, and describes assessment and treatment procedures. The coverage also presents the background of the law and legal circumstances that surround particular sorts of cases—for example, deportation, asylum, human trafficking, and unaccompanied minors. History is also a cross-cutting theme that radiates throughout the chapters: Knowledge about the background and history of particular groups at the hands of our society and its legal institutions is important for fully appreciating the current plight and dynamics of people caught in the web of American law. We hope that the references used in each chapter can serve to guide readers in their professional endeavors and to enhance the studies of those hoping to increase their knowledge base. The book itself is a template of the culturally comprehensive coverage that is warranted by a culturally diverse clientele.

PART I

RACE AND JUSTICE

1

PSYCHOLOGY, JUSTICE, AND DIVERSITY

Five Challenges for Culturally Competent Professionals

KIMBERLY HOLT BARRETT

University of Washington

WILLIAM H. GEORGE

University of Washington

The use of psychological evaluation and psychological testimony in the courts creates an interface between the disciplines of psychology and law. Perhaps nowhere can we find a lack of cultural competence to be more devastating than when it interferes with the service of justice. The need for cultural competence at the junctures of law and the study of human behavior is paramount.

In law, as in many other disciplines (medicine, psychology, education), minimal attention has been devoted to the importance of providing culturally competent services (Sue & Sue, 2003; U.S. Department of Health and Human Services, 2001). Despite well-published demographic information that points to the rapidly increasing diversity of America and the publication of the American Psychological Association's (APA)

"Guidelines for Providers of Psychological Services to Ethnic, Linguistic, and Culturally Diverse Populations" (1993), a review of the major texts and journal articles in the area of forensic psychology reveals a paucity of literature that addresses the importance of culture and race in forensic assessment.

Dramatic increases in ethnic minority populations in the United States are leading to a demographic shift that will place whites in the minority racially, while collectively, people of color will become the majority. In the past 20 years, immigration trends led to a shift in the racial and ethnic composition of the United States not seen since the late seventeenth century, when Africans were brought to America in the bonds of slavery (U.S. Department of Health and Human Services, 2001). Asians,

3

Latinos, and other ethnic and linguistic minority groups make up the bulk of this new immigrant population. Interracial marriage and a baby boom of biracial and multiracial children, plus a decline in white birthrates, are also trends contributing to the development of a highly diverse American society. Our racial, ethnic, and cultural diversity create an urgent demand for professional service provisions that meet the needs that arise for people of particular racial and cultural backgrounds.

The dynamics of racism and discrimination impinge broadly on the lives of minority individuals. Addressing these dynamics must occur on multiple levels in evaluations or interventions that take place in legal contexts. The APA's "Guidelines for Providers of Psychological Services to Ethnic, Linguistic, and Culturally Diverse Populations" (1993) directs clinicians to address issues of bias, prejudice, and discrimination in the practice of psychology and in the lives of their clients. We open this book with a focus on this critical need for professionals to develop the requisite knowledge bases and skill sets. For professionals pursuing development of an effective cross-cultural practice in the interface of psychology and the law, we have identified five key challenges: (a) preparing for work in a diverse society, (b) understanding racism and discrimination in clients' lives, (c) eliminating personal and professional biases, (d) understanding the power and impact of the justice system for minority clients, and (e) debunking judicial "colorblindness" and "race neutrality" to help courts understand race matters.

CHALLENGE 1: PREPARING TO WORK WITH A DIVERSE SOCIETY

Immigration Patterns

As you read this book, you will encounter demographic information that appears in various chapters. The statistics point to the increasing diversity of our population and the flow of people throughout the world who are victims of human trafficking, war, and the atrocities of ethnic conflict. Immigration trends have also brought newcomers who are searching for a way to provide a decent livelihood for their families.

The United States has experienced enormous growth due to immigration in the past three decades. Although immigration policies have become more open to non-European countries, there are increasing anti-immigrant sentiments in the public. Congressional legislation in the 1990s and state initiatives, such as proposition 187 in California, also point to an overall national climate that is hostile to immigrant groups. More than 8 million immigrants remain undocumented, despite the fact that our economy, especially the multi-billion-dollar agricultural economy, is deeply intertwined with undocumented labor. In addition, many legal actions are now being taken against immigrants, and against U.S. citizens who are mistaken for immigrants, due to post–September 11 homeland security measures and the absorption of the Immigration and Naturalization Service (INS) into the Department of Homeland Security (DHS). With the merger of the INS into the DHS, immigration has become equated with terrorism (American Civil Liberties Union [ACLU], 2002; National Council of La Raza [NCLR], 2003). Overall, the present social and legal climate in the United States renders immigrant groups a frequent target of law enforcement agencies. Immigrants that are unfamiliar with our laws and court systems need guidance to navigate their way through this complex institution. Our court systems must also be prepared to assist them and to understand the role that language and culture play in ensuring equal justice for immigrant clients (Moore 1999).

Minority Groups Need Legal Protection

Immigrant groups and people of color are often in need of the protection of the law. Immigrant women—because of their noncitizen status—are more vulnerable to domestic violence than are women who are U.S. citizens (American Bar Association Commission on Domestic Violence, 2001). Refugees from around the world, including unaccompanied children, seek asylum in the United States, and tens of thousands of women and children come here in slavery as victims of human trafficking. Civil rights violations impact minority groups in the workplace and in schools. Hate crimes motivated by bias against ethnicity and national origins more than doubled between 2001 and 2002, and religious bias hate crimes against Islamic groups in the United States grew by 1,600% between 2000 and 2001, with 546 incidents of hate crimes occurring against Islamic people (Federal Bureau of Investigations [FBI], 2002).

Children from diverse backgrounds become involved with the courts as a result of child abuse, juvenile delinquency, the need for foster homes or residential placements, and custody proceedings in divorce scenarios. Children require services that take into account their racial, ethnic, cultural, religious, and linguistic background in order to preserve their cultural/ethnic heritage and native language abilities. Research has shown that a strong and positive sense of racial and ethnic identity is a protective factor in child development, buffering the impact of racism and helping the child to establish a sense of belonging in society. With the rise in children of multiracial, multicultural heritage, we must be prepared to understand and facilitate the developmental processes of children with dual or multiple racial/ethnic backgrounds in order to preserve all sides of their heritage. Racial, cultural, and ethnic identity processes are important dynamics to consider in regard to divorce-custody arrangements, juvenile rehabilitation, dependency, and foster-care situations.

Racial Profiling

In addition to the legal issues that confront immigrants, racial profiling directed toward African Americans and Latino Americans, and the disproportionate impact of the "war on drugs" on blacks and Latinos, is well documented at all levels of our legal systems. This includes evidence of disproportionality in the administration of the death penalty (Amnesty International, 2003; Building Blocks for Youth [Web site]; Human Rights Watch, 2002, 2003).

Who Needs Services—
Demonstrating the Need for
Cross-Cultural Service Provision

When it comes to diversity, the fields of forensic psychology and law must be prepared to work effectively with persons of color and immigrants who are in great need of competent and sensitive services. The following statistics tell the tale of who needs services.

- There are currently 11.9 million Asian Americans in the United States, or 4.2% of the U.S. population.
- "There are approximately 3 million Muslims in the United States. . . . Globally, Islam is one of the fastest growing religions, with about 1.3 billion adherents" (Sherif-Trask, Chapter 18, this volume).
- There were 11,451 hate crime incidents reported in 2001 (FBI, 2002).
- The U.S. population of Latinos grew 58% between 1990 and 2000. Latinos are intraethnically very diverse and now compose the largest minority—12.5% of the total U.S. population—surpassing African Americans.
- Students of color now constitute 45% of the population in our public schools (Sue & Sue, 2003).
- The birthrate for American Indian groups increased as much as 50% between the 1960s and the 1980s (U.S. Department of Health and Human Services, 2001).
- Worldwide, at least 4 million people are victims of human trafficking, with conservative estimates showing that 45,000–50,000 women and children are trafficked to the United States each year (Basu, Chapter 15, this volume).
- Every year, 5,000 children come to the United States without parents or guardians. With the imposition of the Patriot Act, most of these children are now being incarcerated, sometimes with youth who are dangerous criminals, rather than being placed in appropriate foster care or residential settings. International child advocate agencies and Human Rights Watch have denounced policies used by the United States as violations of U.S. and international law. Immigrant and refugee children are often denied hearings and legal representation and may languish in jail for months or years, repeating the types of trauma that they have fled. Unaccompanied children are discussed by Dana Chou in Chapter 19.
- Nearly 22 million people throughout the world are asylum seekers or refugees (Burnett and Thompson, Chapter 14, this volume).
- Estimates are that 1.5 to 4 million women experience intimate partner violence annually

in the United States. Immigrant women are more likely to be victims of domestic violence than are women who are U.S. citizens (American Bar Association Commission on Domestic Violence, 2001).

- According to the U.S. Department of Justice, more than 2 million men and women are now behind bars in the United States. The United States now incarcerates more of its people than any other country, despite patterns that indicate declining or stable rates of violent crime in the past two decades. Human Rights Watch points out that even more troubling than the large numbers of people in jail or prison is the extent to which those men or women are African American. Although blacks account for 12% of the U.S. population, 44% of all prisoners in the United States are black. In some states, the incarceration rate is even higher than the national rate; for example, in Illinois, the black population is 15.1%, yet the percentage of blacks in Illinois prisons is 62.9% (Human Rights Watch, 2003).

- By the end of July 2003, the 300th execution of an African American prisoner since 1977 took place. Although African Americans make up 12% of the U.S. population, they account for 40% of the country's death-row inmates (Amnesty International, 2003).

- In 10 states within the United States, Latino men are incarcerated at rates from five to nine times greater than white men; in 8 states, Latina women are incarcerated at rates from four to seven times greater than white women; and in 9 states, Latino youth are incarcerated in adult prisons at a rate two to three times that of white youth (Human Rights Watch, 2003).

- In 2002, the U.S. district court system awarded 7.5 million dollars in a civil rights lawsuit to 36 African American students in the Puyallup, Washington, school district. The students had endured racial violence, death threats, the frequent use of the word *nigger* in their classroom, disparate disciplinary practices, and discriminatory treatment by teachers and school administrators for a number of years, at all levels of the educational system, K–12th grade (Barrett, Chapter 2, this volume).

- The Bureau of Justice Statistics has estimated that 28% of black men will be sent to jail or prison during their lives (Amnesty International, 2003).

- Between 1990 and 2001, the federal prison incarceration rates of immigrants for civil or immigration offenses increased 610%, from 1,728 to 12,266 (NCLR, 2002).

- Since the Patriot Act (post–September 11), more than 1,000 people have been detained and many deported in secret with little or no due process. The government now has far-reaching powers to track and monitor the telephone and e-mail communications of Americans, banking transactions, and charitable contributions that jeopardize the civil liberties of all Americans, especially immigrants (ACLU, 2002; NCLR, 2003).

CHALLENGE 2: RACISM AND CULTURAL DISCRIMINATION IN THE LIFE OF THE CLIENT

In *Counseling the Culturally Diverse* (Sue & Sue, 2003), the most cited text in the field of ethnic minority psychology, the authors urge practitioners to study history, to attend to the political nature of mental health practice, and to see the potential for cultural bias that is inherent in psychology's models and definitions of mental health. "Mental health practitioners must realize that racial/ethnic minorities and other marginalized groups (women, gays/lesbians, and the disabled) in our society live under an umbrella of individual, institutional, and cultural forces that often demean them, disadvantage them, and deny them equal access and opportunity. Experiences of prejudice and discrimination are a social reality for the culturally different and affect their worldview of the helping professional who attempts to work in the multicultural arena" (p. 68). "It should come as no surprise that our racial/ethnic minority citizens may view Euro-Americans and our very institutions with considerable mistrust and suspicion" (p. 74).

The APA's "Guidelines for Providers of Psychological Services to Ethnic, Linguistic, and Culturally Diverse Populations" (1993) are an important guide for clinicians in conducting assessments and in designing treatment interventions for clients of diverse backgrounds.

The guidelines point out that social, cultural, economic, and political factors significantly impact the lives of members of diverse groups. The clinician is asked to attend to prejudice, discrimination, adverse socioeconomic factors, and sociopolitical events in the client's environment and to "work within the cultural setting to improve the welfare of all persons concerned, if there is a conflict between cultural values and human rights" (p. 47).

The American Psychiatric Association's *Diagnostic and Statistical Manual of Mental Disorders* (DSM-IV-R, 2000) also instructs the clinician to note cultural explanations of the individual's illness, cultural factors related to the psychosocial environment and levels of functioning, and the cultural elements or differences that exist between the client and the individual. The *DSM-IV-TR* cautions clinicians not to confuse behaviors that arise as a result of sociocultural conflicts with paranoia, noting that the process of clinical evaluation may reinforce guarded or defensive behaviors in minority group members due to experiences of "perceived neglect or indifference of the majority society" (p. 692).

Learning About Racism and Cultural Discrimination

In order to understand the racial and cultural terrain of their clients, clinicians must work to become familiar with the workings of prejudice and discrimination in the United States. This includes learning to define and appropriately use the "language of race and racism"—words and terms that are used to describe and define race, culture, and ethnicity, as well as racism, discrimination, and prejudice. It is also important for the practitioner to understand and recognize the differences between individual, institutional, and cultural racism and to explore and understand the "everyday racism" and cultural challenges that are faced by groups other than one's own. We can suggest the use of well-known texts on race and racism, including Jones (1997), Feagin and Feagin (2003), Feagin (2001), Farley (2000), Marger (2003), Wu (2002), Tatum (1997), and Aguirre and Turner (2003), as guides for learning the basics. Texts that are more specific to particular ethnic groups can usually be found in the ethnic studies, history,

and cultural studies sections of bookstores and through online catalogues. Documentaries and films that portray the stories, political movements, and histories of American ethnic groups, immigrants, and refugees are also useful and informative. In addition, becoming familiar with the use of cross-cultural fiction and biography, poetry, music, film, and art as a means of cross-cultural exploration is a rewarding process. Keeping up with current events in the media, particularly in the independent press, radio, and television, will reveal social, political, and legal trends that affect diverse groups in American society and in their countries of origin. The study of the U.S. Constitution and the Civil Rights Acts are also important for professionals who work with minorities, as well as the study of Critical Race Theory (Crenshaw, Gotanda, Peller, & Thomas, 1995; Delgado & Stefancic, 2001). Thus, with study and ongoing experience, culturally competent clinicians can identify and describe racism and cultural bias when it emerges and can be more effective at documenting the influence of adverse circumstances in the lives of their clients that are related to discrimination and prejudice. Clinicians who are cognizant of and comfortable with racial issues are better able to help their clients recognize and confront racism and bias when it occurs in their lives or in their cases.

In the APA's "Guidelines for Providers of Psychological services to Ethnic, Linguistic and Culturally Diverse Populations" (1993), psychologists are also asked to help the client to determine whether or not a problem stems from racism or bias in others so that the client does not needlessly personalize the problem. Psychologists who counsel people involved in the legal system may need to educate their clients about racism if it arises during the course of litigation and help them find the means to cope with racial/cultural stressors. Evaluators may also find it appropriate to discuss racial or cultural bias with clients that they evaluate if the evaluator is going to address racial or cultural discrimination in the context of testimony or written evaluation.

One should not assume that the client will always recognize or understand how prejudice or discrimination may be operating in his or her life or in the context of his or her legal case. As an example, we can present the case of the Mendoza family, who were fighting an order for deportation because one of Mr. Mendoza's letters of recommendation for permanent residency status had come from an employer who had been found to write fraudulent letters. (However, his letter, and all other letters written for Mr. Mendoza, had been legitimate.) The attorney for the family had requested a psychological evaluation to assess the hardship/impact that deportation to Mexico would have on the Mendozas' 4-year-old daughter, who had been born in the United States and who had been raised in a loving extended family environment, with aunts, uncles, grandparents, and cousins. All of the Mendozas' extended family now resided in the United States. Mr. Mendoza brought in volumes of records to the evaluation—10 years' worth of bank statements, records of his work as an electrician in the United States (all under legal circumstances), pay-stub receipts, various mail, electric bills, employer recommendations, letters that validated good nature and character, and picture albums of his wife, child, and extended family. Mr. Mendoza seemed highly stressed and confused about the deportation order. He repeatedly stated that he did not understand why he was not seen as "good enough" to become a citizen of the United States. He approached the appeal process with the perspective that if he could prove his personal "worth" in terms of hard work and good character, then he would be accepted by the government as a permanent resident. The sense of rejection and confusion was heightened by the fact that the rest of his family had become legal residents or citizens several years before. Sensing his misplaced anxiety and distress, the evaluator discussed the current climate of immigration in the United States with Mr. Mendoza, including the political and economic variables that were contributing to a climate of restrictiveness and fear for immigrants who worked in the United States, either with or without legal status. Once Mr. Mendoza was able to see his own status difficulties in a broader context, he was relieved of the burden of personalizing the rejection of his application. He expressed his relief to the evaluator at the end of the evaluation, and later in court. His new

level of understanding had helped him regain his dignity, reduced his anxiety, and assisted him in approaching his struggle from a sociopolitical rather than a personal perspective.

How Are Issues of Racism and Discrimination Likely to Arise in Legal Settings?

There are a number of ways that the sociopolitical dynamics of individual, cultural, and institutional racism become important in the provision of psychological evaluations and social or mental health services to minorities (racial, ethnic, cultural, linguistic) who are involved in the legal system. The clinician may need to address discrimination and racism in the following contexts:

1. Discovering how experiences with prejudice or discrimination have influenced the current mental health status of the client being evaluated or treated, as well as assessing for the influences of racism and cultural bias on child and adult development, identity formation, language use, personality, behavior, support systems, stresses, and coping. For example, Mr. Kim, a refugee from Cambodia, was evaluated in a case that involved domestic violence. Mr. Kim experienced extreme symptoms of post-traumatic stress disorder (PTSD) following years of hard labor, starvation, and witnessing the torture and murder of family members and other children while he was in child-labor camps under the Khmer Rouge. However, his symptoms worsened, resembling a paranoid psychosis, because of experiences with racism that occurred while working with white Americans in canneries and sawmills.

2. Determining and addressing how the dynamics of race and culture may impact the relationship between the client and the clinician and the treatment or evaluation process, especially if the client is from a minority group and clinicians/ evaluators are from the white majority. *DSM-IV-TR* instructs the clinician to document this aspect of the evaluation as part of the cultural formulation process. Mr. Drew, a 45-year-old African American bus driver, complained of racial harassment and physical problems as a

result of this stress experienced on his new bus route, after having worked successfully for the metro bus service for 20 years. The evaluating psychiatrist, a white male, diagnosed Mr. Drew with a paranoid personality disorder. He did not acknowledge the racial differences, dynamics, or difficulties inherent in this evaluation with the client nor in his report. He ignored the possibility that Mr. Drew could be encountering racism and that he had worked without complaint for more than 18 years. A second evaluator arranged to have an observer ride the bus with Mr. Drew. The observer concluded that Mr. Drew was indeed experiencing racial slurs and harassment on his route. Mr. Drew experienced added, undue racial stress as a result of the first evaluation and contact with a professional who ignored the reality of his experiences as a black man.

3. Reviewing and addressing, within the scope of psychological practice, how the dynamics of racism, culture, and cultural politics may impact legal proceedings in areas such as encountering bias and prejudice in other professionals related to the case; discovering the financial exploitation of clients who are culturally unaware of appropriate fees, charges, and so on; the violation of the civil rights of clients who are unaware of their rights at the time of arrest or who—due to cultural and linguistic reasons— do not understand the legal processes in which they have become involved; the misuse of interpreters; the misapplication of psychometrics; and the inappropriate use of traditional models of evaluation and diagnosis with individuals from particular cultures and so on.

4. Determining and documenting the extent to which the client is able to participate fully in his or her own legal proceedings due to issues of acculturation, linguistic background, and/or mental health difficulties; making recommendations designed to help the client to become more active in his or her own behalf.

5. Revealing and correcting racial and cultural stereotypes, misrepresentations, and omissions that may appear in other evaluations in regard to the client's identity, culture, and behavior— while also presenting the psychological profile of the client in the appropriate social, racial, and cultural context.

6. Providing educational information to attorneys and the court about racism, discrimination, culture, and ethnicity—using scholarly research, definitions, and terms (see Aguirre & Turner, 2003; Feagin & Feagin, 2003; Jones, 1997; Root, Chapter 9, this volume; Sue & Sue, 2003).

7. In respect to cases where children are involved, providing instruction to the court as to the impact of race and culture on child development, identity formation, physical and mental health, academic performance, and so on (Berry, 1998; Castro, Chapter 22 of this volume; Coll et al., 1996; LaFrambois, Hardin, & Gerton, 1998; Gibbs & Huang, 2003; Leadbeater & Way, 1996; Phinney, 1998; Root, 1998; Steele, Spencer, & Aronson, 2002; Trimble & LaDue, Chapter 23, this volume).

8. Documenting and describing the particular vulnerabilities of women who, as a result of racism, sexism, and cultural variables, may fall victim to abuse in cases of domestic violence, sexual assault, sexual exploitation, oppressive labor practices, and trafficking.

Clinicians who work with attorneys in the process of conducting evaluations or providing expert testimony in cases that intersect with race, culture, and racism and discrimination should take care to gain an understanding of the attorney's level of expertise and comfort with the topic areas. It is not uncommon to encounter legal professionals who are uninformed and/or uncomfortable in discussing matters of race and culture. In such instances, the psychologist is wise to review his or her findings and testimony with the attorney, providing instruction and consultation, if necessary, to help the legal professional become familiar and at ease with the pertinent racial issues of the case.

CHALLENGE 3:
ELIMINATING PERSONAL AND
PROFESSIONAL BIASES IN PRACTICE

The APA diversity guidelines state that psychologists should recognize ethnicity and culture as significant parameters of psychological processes, including how their own cultural backgrounds, experiences, attitudes, and values influence their practice. "They make efforts to correct any prejudices and biases" (Guideline 3a, p. 46).

How does the professional embark on a process of eliminating his or her bias and prejudice? A good beginning takes place through a process of reviewing the major influences and processes in one's racial socialization—the role that family, friends, media, and the broader sociohistorical, cultural environment have played in influencing one's views of groups other than one's own. Autobiographical work in this case is useful, as is the study of societal stereotypes. The study of the history of minority groups in the United States from a cross-cultural perspective (Takaki, 1993) is likely to reveal the historical stereotypes, myths, and omissions that have helped to construct negative views of minority groups throughout history. The professional is also advised to assess the demographics of his or her personal and professional familiars. A lack of contact with diverse groups leaves one much more open to the impact of stereotypes, while also reducing the chances for developing a sense of comfort and familiarity with people who are different from oneself. As discussed earlier, building knowledge about and familiarity with other cultures also is a way of reducing bias and prejudice. Reading cross-culturally based fiction and nonfiction; participating in community activities related to art, music, and film; traveling to other parts of the world—or to other parts of your city; second or third language acquisition; and social activism and community outreach all can assist the professional in breaking through cultural barriers, biases, and misunderstandings.

The professional should also become aware of the cultural biases contained in the formal professional training that he or she has received, including review of assessment instruments and practices that may be inappropriate for particular groups (see Castillo, 1997; Dana, 2000; Gopaul-McNicol & Thomas-Presswood, 1998; Samuda, 1998; Samuda, Feuerstein, Kaufman, Lewis, & Sternberg & Associates, 1998; Sue & Sue, 2003). Practitioners should review models of social and racial identity development and understand how their own level of racial identity may influence their interactions with clients,

professionals, and race-sensitive subject matter (Sue & Sue, 2003; Thompson & Carter, 1997). White practitioners will benefit from reading books and articles that review the study of whiteness (Frankenberg, 1997; Goodrich & Mills, 2001; Helms, 1995; Kivel, 2002; Tatum, 1997). We strongly recommend that students and professionals seek specific training in the development of cultural competence as part of increasing their understanding of racism in society, as well as gaining perspectives on personal and professional biases and stereotypes that might interfere with their work.

CHALLENGE 4: UNDERSTANDING THE POWER AND IMPACT OF THE JUDICIAL SYSTEM IN THE LIVES OF MINORITIES IN THE UNITED STATES

We are nothing to the white people; we are a few Hopis, but they are Americans, millions of them. My father told me that their leader, whoever he is, ends his speech by saying that God is on their side; then he shakes his fist and says to all the other nations: you had better pay attention, because we are big, and we will shoot to kill, if you don't watch out. My mother says all the big countries are like that, but I only know this one. We belong to it, that is what the government of the United States says. They come here, the Bureau of Indian Affairs people, and they give us their orders. This law says . . . another law says . . . And soon there will be a new law. In case we have any objections, they have soldiers, they have planes. We see the jets diving high in the sky. The clouds try to get out of the way, but they don't move fast enough. The water tries to escape to the ocean, but can only go at its own speed.

—The words of a 12-year-old Hopi child (*The Political Life of Children,* Robert Coles, 1986, p. 43)

Although it is beyond the scope of this book, we urge practitioners to become familiar with court decisions, both historical and contemporary, that continue to have a major impact on minority groups of the United States. Most major texts on racism and discrimination will summarize this information. In recent years, the Supreme Court has made several important decisions that have adversely impacted minorities who seek legal relief and remedies for societal discrimination. These decisions have created setbacks for those who seek minority-based scholarships for college, for those who want an education in a desegregated environment, for those who promote programs to assist in minority business development, and in regard to creating a government with greater minority political representation through the process of redrawing congressional district lines (Parker, 1996). Despite the favorable decision toward affirmative action policies in graduate programs at the University of Michigan in 2003, the court still prohibited the use of race in determining undergraduate admissions. In his 1996 article that appears in the *American University Law Review,* legal scholar Frank Parker concludes,

> The Court's goal may not be to resegregate American society, but resegregation may be the effect of its decisions. By limiting the remedies available to minorities to overcome discrimination and gain equal opportunity, the Court's new constitutional jurisprudence foreshadows increased divisions of society along racial lines between the better educated, richer, politically empowered white "haves" and the uneducated, poorer, unrepresented minority "have nots." Thus, instead of reducing racial polarization, these decisions may contribute to heightened racial tensions and polarization.

How do minority groups see the courts—as sources of liberation or as sources of discrimination? As mentioned earlier in this chapter, both Human Rights Watch and Amnesty International, among numerous other groups, have documented disparate treatment of minorities by law enforcement officials, as well as at every step of the judicial process (see also Farley, 2000). Examination of the sociopolitical role played by our court systems, past and present, reveals swings between patterns of racial domination and the potential for racial liberation and the advancement of democracy. Following the progressive rulings and programs of the civil rights movement, the judiciary branch of government and our courts have enacted racial domination and power through the institution and prosecution of the war on drugs and mandatory sentencing requirements, leading to the incarceration of millions of blacks and Latinos and, in most cases, also leading to the termination of their voting rights ("Prison and Beyond," 2002). Increased use of the death penalty and three-strikes laws also heavily impact minority groups (Farley, 2000).

In regard to immigrants and the law, we can also consider trends that favored Asians, Latinos, and refugees through the opening of borders with the Immigration Act of 1965 and the Refugee Act of 1980. We also saw progressive decisions in the institution of laws that protected farmworkers following the work of Cesar Chavez and the founding of the United Farm Workers Union. However, these liberal policies were quickly followed by laws and courts that are tough on immigrants, leading to a climate of fear among immigrant workers who are unlikely to challenge the low wages and poor working conditions that they face as they work each day. These conditions are allowed to exist due to poor enforcement of the labor laws that were designed to protect farmworkers and urban laborers alike (Massey, 2003; Rothenberg, 1998). Refugees seeking asylum are now being incarcerated in large numbers, even though they are not guilty of any crime, and the U.S.–Mexico border has become a militarized zone, with the border patrol having become the largest arms-bearing branch of the U.S. government with the exception of the military itself (Massey, 2003).

The tension that exists between the polarities of court-sanctioned injustice and the potential for progressive action in the legal system is keenly felt by clients who are in the midst of litigation. In addition, police brutality, and the failure to prosecute police brutality nationwide, has led to widespread distrust of our legal system by minority groups. Minority and other citizen outcries of injustice were publicized during the events surrounding the O. J. Simpson and Rodney King cases, and more recently the Louima and Diallo cases in New York. Social scientists have found (Farley,

2000; Feagin & Feagin, 1999; Feagin, 2001; Steinhorn & Diggs-Brown, 2000) that many blacks, including those in the middle class, see white police officers as a source of danger and death and that minorities report high rates of bad personal experiences with the police.

Race, Law, and Culture: A Call for Change

In a paper that calls for new thinking, leadership, and action in regard to race, law, and culture, Arkansas Court of Appeals judge Wendell Griffin (1999) states that "most Americans are in denial about racism and its pervasive influence on the legal system." Griffin cites the need for drastic changes that involve ending a succession of eras of public amnesia when it comes to race. He calls for new leadership, thinking, and action in our justice system that breaks through centuries of denial and that acknowledges the racial history of America, "otherwise we will continue following the leadership that produced past and current racial injustices" (p. 903). Judge Griffin cites broken treaties with Native Americans; the Chinese Exclusion acts; Japanese internment; the swindles that resulted in the loss of millions of acres for Mexican landowners in Texas, Arizona, Colorado, and New Mexico; and the Supreme Court's sanctioning of slavery as evidence of racial injustices that had come from a "mindset that has produced so much of what we deem legitimate about American law and culture" (p. 905). He invokes the vision of Dr. Martin Luther King, of a society and world where people of diverse languages, cultures, religions, and races would live and work together. Judge Griffin urges us to seek leadership among people whose worldview is informed by those who have been the victims of injustice, rather than by those who have created and perpetuated the unjust systems that have served the interests of whites. He engages all people in the task of making "diversity pronouncements and policies [that] must become institutional practices and personal patterns," guided by principles of racial pluralism, rather than by "color blindness" (p. 925).

Gaining knowledge about the history of and current affairs relating to the institutional oppression of racial, ethnic, and cultural groups is a step toward cultural awareness that lends itself well to practice within the scope of the judicial system. It is also a step toward curing the "amnesia" about race that is discussed by Judge Griffin. African American, American Indian, and American-born Asian and Latino clients are likely to hold expectations of unjust outcomes, based on collective knowledge of discrimination that has developed over time. In contrast, many new immigrants are unaware of the adversarial nature of legal proceedings and hold images of the U.S. justice system as representing the world's pinnacle of justice and fairness. This naïveté can lead to a trust of professionals from the opposing sides of the case and a lack of self-protective action or advocacy on their own behalf. I have worked with immigrant clients who literally entrust themselves to the system with complete confidence that the outcome will be just.

Fear of the courts, or the disappointment that comes as a result of realizing that the rules are not golden, will contribute to additional emotional distress in an inherently stressful process. Recently, I (KB) spoke with a high-ranking federal judge to protest another judge's treatment of a fragile young refugee who at the age of 10 had been traumatized by torture and witnessing the rape and murder of his family members. In his asylum hearing, the local judge had repeatedly screamed accusations and insults at the client, who was 18 at the time of his hearing. In my conversation with the judge that was higher in rank, I remarked that this treatment had not only been unduly stressful, but that it shattered the client's image of American justice, an image that I find is held dear by many immigrants and refugees. The judge's response was protective of the local judge who had behaved so cruelly in the courtroom. This judge, in fact, expressed concern for our immigration judges "who are under tremendous pressure in their courtrooms, trying to determine if the person in their courtroom is really Osama Bin Laden." I was shocked by the degree of sensationalism and stereotype that was expressed in this comment. In regard to my comment about the shattered image of justice, the judge's cheerful response was, "Don't forget, that justice is 'just–us!'"

Who Is "Just Us"?

This judge's "just us" retort is shockingly ironic. It is ironic because this exact utterance is often used by African Americans to remark tragicomically on the justice system's seeming predation on black people: Justice in America means it's "just us" (immigrants and people of color) being arrested, prosecuted, incarcerated, and supervised by the system. An African American civilian visitor need only walk through a criminal courtroom, correctional center, or probation/parole office to be stung by the meaning of the phrase "it's just us." The overrepresentation of African Americans in the system becomes staggeringly obvious to the eye, wounds the soul, and mocks the ideal of equal justice. This is not, of course, what the judge meant. The judge's subtext reads: Remember, "justice" is concretized into a phalanx of imperfect human beings ("just us") serving as authorities and functionaries charged with the impossible task of dispensing justice in a clogged, overburdened system. This is a different "just us"! The judge's use of this phrase turns the African American colloquialism on its head because it implies that it is the people running the system who are somehow put upon or victimized in their righteous yet imperfect efforts to mete out society's just outcomes.

"Just us" (empowered authorities administering the system) is not "just us" (disempowered people of color and immigrants disproportionately represented as defendants, inmates, and supervisees). Therefore this comment, made by a judicial official who serves primarily minority groups, reveals a lack of conscious consideration of the dynamics of race and culture in the justice system. It also reveals a form of cultural bias that refuses to acknowledge the discriminatory impact created by the lack of minority group representation and how this lack of representation sways the distribution of power in legal and political institutions. Since the founding of the American colonies, our systems of government and law have been controlled nearly exclusively by white males. This guarantees the maintenance of a cultural ideology that upholds the supremacy of the white Anglo majority, while enforcing notions of the inferiority of people of color, assumptions that have been used to justify economic exploitation and cultural oppression (Aguirre & Turner, 2003). Compared with other societal institutions (education, health care, media, religious), legal and political systems wield the most power over the lives of minority groups, with little or no representation from the groups that are being influenced or controlled. Very few people of color or immigrants make up the judge's "just us" in our legal systems. Thus professionals involved with the legal system, especially white professionals, will often be seen as representatives of that system, distant and apart from the individuals and groups whose lives are sometimes held in the balance (or imbalance) of legal decision making. Those who work with minorities in the courts must be acutely aware of the resulting degrees of estrangement and mistrust associated with historical and contemporary meanings of law and justice in the United States. Amnesty International (2003) quotes Senator Russ Feingold, speaking on civil rights and the death penalty: "We simply cannot say that we live in a country that offers equal justice to all Americans when racial disparities plague the system by which our society imposes the ultimate punishment."

Knowledge, Awareness, and Practice

How does this knowledge of history, awareness of oppression, and consideration of client mistrust translate into practice? First, professionals, especially white, majority-culture professionals, should not be taken aback if they encounter guardedness, mistrust, suspicion, and defensiveness on the part of the minority client. Self-disclosure may come slowly. These situational stylistic habits are survival skills, not pathology (Sue & Sue, 2003). Tendencies toward seeing the client as resistant, noncompliant, defensive (in psychological terms), angry, or paranoid should be guarded against on the part of the clinician or legal professional. Second, the practitioner should understand that client perceptions of psychological and legal professionals will be influenced by sociopolitical and historical forces. How the client attributes credibility, expertise, competence, trust, and sincerity to the professional will also be influenced by dynamics of race and culture. In cross-cultural professional–client relationships, the practitioner should not presume either trust or faith in their abilities until they have proven otherwise to their clients. The professional should not take this personally and should not become defensive, angry, or accusatory with the client. A spirit of openness, a willingness to be "tested," and being honest about one's level of contact and experience with groups other than one's own are important attributes in enhancing effectiveness. In addition, developing knowledge about the particular culture and cultural values of the client that you are seeing and sharing a little information about your own personal background will help to reduce mistrust and establish credibility.

Credibility, Gift Giving, and Normalization

Sue and Zane (1987) presented a formulation of elements of the practitioner–client relationship that enhance the effectiveness of treatment and help to improve retention rates. The techniques presented in their article can also be applied to evaluations in order to achieve a more open, respectful, culturally informed, and effective exchange of information between client and evaluator. Two key elements of successful interactions are presented in Sue and Zane's article—credibility and "gift" giving. Credibility is more likely established with the client if the clinician's interactions and interventions are informed by knowledge of the client's culture, so that the structure, form, and style of the communications and interventions to take place will better "fit" within the client's worldview or belief systems.

For example, in the case of Mr. Kim, the Cambodian refugee, the evaluator's development of knowledge regarding Cambodian culture, religion, and the horrors of life under the Khmer Rouge helped to establish trust and credibility quickly and also helped to alert the evaluator to identify symptoms of PTSD that had been misperceived as paranoia by his attorney and family members. The evaluator was also able to normalize his extreme sensitivity to the hard physical work and racial harassment that he had experienced in the sawmill and cannery, as his work environment had so greatly

resembled the suffering that he had endured as a child in Khmer Rouge labor camps. Mr. Kim was grateful for this perspective, and it also helped to reduce tensions in the family.

CHALLENGE 5: DEBUNKING JUDICIAL COLORBLINDNESS AND RACE NEUTRALITY: HOW PSYCHOLOGISTS CAN HELP THE COURTS BETTER UNDERSTAND RACE MATTERS

Race and culture are controversial topics in contemporary society. We are working in a social climate in which the white majority is in disagreement with people of color regarding the forms and severity of racism in America (Dovidio, 2001; Dovidio, Gaertner, Kawakami, & Hodson, 2002; Feagin, 2001; Steinhorn & Diggs-Brown, 2000). Programs designed to enhance the socioeconomic opportunities and civil rights of minorities are under fire, and in the 1990s and post–September 11, we have seen a dramatic increase in anti-immigrant sentiments and legislation. These societal processes and attitudes in regard to race and culture can also be found in many court systems, including in the rulings of the Supreme Court over the last decade (Crenshaw et al., 1995; Delgado & Stefancic, 2001; Parker, 1996; Wu, 1996).

Discussion of race and culture in the courtroom is complex and controversial for a number of reasons. From the judicial perspective, contemporary concepts of race neutrality and colorblindness represent an American cultural value that stems from early constitutional premises of equality and justice for all, combined with liberal integrationist sentiments drawn from the civil rights movement. In addition to colorblindness, the courts may at times reflect current societal notions and themes that hold that racism is over for the most part, and that if discrimination occurs, it is not likely to be intentional. Civil rights law has shifted in the area of discrimination. Individuals who seek remediation for damages caused by discrimination now must prove that the discrimination was intentional. Previously, disparate outcomes alone—rather than intentionality—constituted sufficient evidence that discrimination could be taking place.

Psychologists and attorneys who work with racial, cultural, and ethnic minorities very likely will need to discuss racial/cultural issues in presenting the dynamics and context of the client's case, identity, and character. Thus a dilemma is posed when legal or psychological professionals oppose the use of race or culture in testimony, under the guise of colorblindness, or even through calling the use of culture or race "racist" if examples or testimony stand in opposition to supposed principals of neutrality or in challenge to the status quo of white society. The next chapter offers a comprehensive discussion of colorblindness and how psychologists might provide alternatives to race-neutral ideology in the courts.

In regard to the challenges presented in this chapter, colorblindness (Markus, Steele, & Steele, 2002) is raised as a challenge in order to help professionals prepare for the possibility of controversy when they offer testimony in regard to race and culture. Objections can arise when lawyers, judges, or experts object to or nullify the importance of race and culture as part of legal proceedings by calling forth as justification the principles of colorblindness, racial and cultural objectivity, universality of the human condition, and the "end" of racism. Psychologists should not be discouraged by these objections and should strive to present their findings as part of (a) presenting empirical data and scholarly research in the area of race, culture, and ethnicity; (b) presenting developmental, diagnostic, and race/culture/identity-based information in the narratives of psychological reports with assessment and diagnostic procedures that are in accordance with the APA diversity guidelines; and (c) utilizing the APA diversity guidelines, APA ethnic guidelines, plus *DSM-IV-TR* racial/cultural recommendations to illuminate and emphasize issues of race, racism, cultural bias, and misrepresentation of the client's identity and behaviors.

CONCLUSION

We have established the severe need of culturally competent professional service providers to work with minority clients caught up in the tentacles of the legal system. We have reviewed in detail five key challenges that face mental-health professionals working in this domain. As is evident by these challenges, this is not an easy mission. One should expect to encounter difficulties from all sides of a case: clients, their families, judges, attorneys, and other mental-health professionals. However, also expect that a high integrity investment in developing these competencies will yield intangible rewards of intellectual, personal, cultural, and sociopolitical enrichment.

REFERENCES

Aguirre, A., & Turner, J. H. (2003). *American ethnicity: The dynamics and consequences of discrimination.* New York: McGraw-Hill.

American Bar Association Commission on Domestic Violence Continuing Legal Education Teleconference Civil Legal Assistance for Battered Immigrants, May 23, 2001. Accessed from http://www.abanet.org/domviol/textualmaterials.pdf

American Civil Liberties Union. (2002, September). ACLU Chart on Homeland Security Bills in the House and Senate. Legislative Update. Washington, DC: American Civil Liberties Union. Accessed from http://www.aclu.org/SafeandFree/SafeandFree.cfm?ID=10667&c=206

American Psychiatric Association. (2000). *Diagnostic and statistical manual of mental disorders* (4th ed., Text revision). Washington, DC: Author.

American Psychological Association. (1993). Guidelines for providers of psychological services to ethnic, linguistic, and culturally diverse populations. *American Psychologist, 48,* 45–48.

Amnesty International. (2003, April). *United States of America: Death by discrimination—The continuing role of race in capital cases.* Amnesty International Reports. Available from http://web.amnesty.org/library/index/ENGAMR510462003

Berry, J. W. (1998). Acculturative stress. In P. O. Organista, K. M. Chun, & G. Marin (Eds.), *Readings in ethnicity psychology* (pp. 117–122). New York: Routledge.

Building Blocks for Youth. Report: Donde está la justicia? Michigan State University Institute for Youth Children and Families. Accessed from http://www.buildingblocksforyouth.org/research.html

Castillo, R. J. (1997). *Culture and mental illness: A client centered approach.* Pacific Grove, CA: Brooks/Cole.

Coles, R. (1986). *The political life of children.* Boston: Houghton Mifflin.

Coll, C. G., Lamberty, G., Jenkins, R., McAdoo, H. P., Crnic, K., Waski, B. H., et al. (1996). An integrative model for the study of developmental competencies in minority children. *Child Development, 67*(5), 1891–1914.

Crenshaw, K., Gotanda, N., Peller, G., & Thomas, K. (Eds.). (1995). *Critical race theory: The key writings that formed the movement.* New York: New Press.

Dana, R. (2000). *Handbook of cross cultural assessment.* Mahwah, NJ: Lawrence Erlbaum Associates.

Delgado, R., & Stefancic, J. (2001). *Critical race theory.* New York: New York University Press.

Dovidio, J. F. (2001). On the nature of contemporary prejudice: The third wave. *Journal of Social Issues, 57*(4), 829–849.

Dovidio, J. F., Gaertner, S. E., Kawakami, K., & Hodson, G. (2002). Why can't we just get along? Interpersonal biases and interracial distrust. *Cultural Diversity and Ethnic Minority Psychology, 8*(2), 88–102.

Farley, J. E. (2000). *Majority-minority relations.* Upper Saddle River, NJ: Prentice Hall.

Feagin, J. R. (2001). *Racist America.* New York: Routledge.

Feagin, J. R., & Feagin, C. B. (1999). *Racial and ethnic relations.* Upper Saddle River, NJ: Prentice Hall.

Feagin, J. R., & Feagin, C. B. (2003). *Racial and ethnic relations.* Upper Saddle River, NJ: Prentice Hall.

Federal Bureau of Investigation. (2002). *Hate crime statistics, 2001.* U.S. Department of Justice, Federal Bureau of Investigation. Washington, DC: National Press Office.

Frankenberg, R. (1997). *Displacing whiteness: Essays in social and cultural criticism.* Durham, NC: Duke University Press.

Gibbs, J. T., & Huang, L. M. (2003). *Children of color: Psychological interventions with culturally diverse youth* (2nd rev. ed.). Indianapolis, IN: Wiley.

Goodrich, P., & Mills, L. G. (2001). The law of white spaces. *Journal of Legal Education, 51*(1), 15–38.

Gopaul-McNicol, S. A., & Thomas-Presswood, T. T. (1998). *Working with linguistically and culturally different children.* Needham Heights, MA: Allyn & Bacon.

Griffin, W. L. (1999). Race, law, and culture: A call to new thinking, leadership, and action. *University of Arkansas at Little Rock Law Review, 21,* 901–926.

Helms, J. (1995). An update of Helms's white and people of color racial identity models. In G. Ponterotto, J. M. Casas, L. A. Suzuki, & C. M. Alexander (Eds.), *Handbook of multicultural counseling* (pp. 181–198). Thousand Oaks, CA: Sage Publications.

Human Rights Watch. (2002, February 27). Race and incarceration in the United States. *Human Rights Watch Briefing.*

Human Rights Watch. (2003, April). Incarcerated America. *Human Rights Watch Backgrounder.*

Jones, J. (1997). *Prejudice and racism.* New York: McGraw-Hill.

Kivel, P. (2002). *Uprooting racism: How white people can work for racial justice.* Gabriola Island, BC: New Society Publishers.

LaFrambois, T., Hardin, L. K., & Gerton, J. (1998). Psychological impact of biculturalism: Evidence and theory. In P. B. Organista, K. M. Chun, & G. Marin (Eds.), *Readings in ethnic psychology* (pp. 123–156). New York. Routledge.

Leadbeater, B. J., & Way, N. (Eds.). (1996). *Urban girls: Resisting stereotypes, creating identities.* New York: New York University Press.

Marger, M. (2003). *Race and ethnic relations: American and global perspectives.* Belmont, CA: Thomson Wadsworth.

Markus, H. R., Steele, C. M., & Steele, D. M. (2002). Color blindness as a barrier to inclusion: Assimilation and non immigrant minorities. In R. A. Scweder & M. Minow (Eds.), *Engaging cultural differences: The multicultural challenge in liberal democracies* (pp. 453–472). New York: Russell Sage Foundation.

Massey, D. (2003). Closed door policy. The American Prospect Online. Retrieved July 19, 2003, from http://www.prospect.org

Moore, J. (Ed.). (1999). *Immigrants in courts.* Seattle: University of Washington Press.

National Council of La Raza. (2002, July). Latinos and the federal criminal justice system. Statistical Brief No. 1.

National Council of La Raza. (2003, June). Counterterrorism and the Latino community since September 11. NCLR Issue Brief No. 10.

Parker, F. (1996). The damaging consequences of the Rehnquist court's commitment to color-blindness versus racial justice, the essay. *American University Law Review, 45* (book 3), 763-773.

Phinney, J. (1998). Ethnic identity in adolescents and adults. In P. B. Organista, K. M. Chun, &

G. Marin (Eds.), *Readings in ethnic psychology* (pp. 73–99). New York: Routledge.

Prison and beyond: A stigma that never fades. (2002). *Economist, 364*(8285).

Root, M. P. (1998). Resolving "other" status: Identity development of biracial individuals. In P. B. Organista, K. M. Chun, & G. Marin (Eds.), *Readings in ethnic psychology* (pp. 100–112). New York: Routledge.

Rothenberg, D. (1998). *With these hands: The hidden work of migrant farmworkers.* New York: Harcourt.

Samuda, R. J. (1998). *Psychological testing of American minorities: Issues and consequences.* Thousand Oaks, CA: Sage Publications.

Steele, C. M., Spencer, S. J., & Aronson, J. (2002). Contending with group image: The psychology of stereotype and social identity threat. In M. P. Zanna (Ed.), *Advances in experimental social psychology* (Vol. 34, pp. 379–440). San Diego: Academic Press.

Steinhorn, L., & Diggs-Brown, B. (2000). *By the color of our skin: The illusion of integration and the reality of race.* New York: Plume.

Sue, D. W., & Sue, D. (2003). *Counseling the culturally diverse.* New York: John Wiley & Sons.

Sue, S., & Zane, N. (1987). The role of culture and cultural techniques in psychotherapy. *American Psychologist, 42,* 37–45.

Takaki, R. (1993). *A different mirror: A history of multicultural America.* Boston: Back Bay.

Tatum, B. D. (1997). *"Why are all the black kids sitting together in the cafeteria?" and other conversations about race.* New York: Basic Books.

Thompson, C. E., & Carter, R. T. (1997). *Racial identity theory.* Mahwah, NJ: Lawrence Erlbaum Associates.

U.S. Department of Health and Human Services. (2001). Mental health: Culture, race, and ethnicity—A supplement to mental health: A report to the surgeon general. Rockville, MD: U.S. DHHS, Office of the Surgeon General.

Wu, F. (1996). Changing America: Three arguments about Asian Americans and the law. *American University Law Review, 11,* 811–822.

Wu, F. (2002). *Yellow: Race in America beyond black and white.* New York: Basic Books.

2

CASE EXAMPLES

Addressing Racism, Discrimination, and Cultural Bias in the Interface of Psychology and Law

KIMBERLY HOLT BARRETT

University of Washington

DISPUTING RACIAL AND CULTURAL STEREOTYPES IN CRIMINAL CASES

There are times when psychological evaluation may serve to confirm personality and behavior patterns that may contribute to the assessment of culpability in the commission of a crime. Sometimes the understanding of racial and cultural features of a case may contribute to this sort of assessment, especially in regard to addressing stereotypes, cultural confusion, and racial profiling in the context of criminal proceedings. Clinicians may contribute to the culpability assessment in three ways: understanding the offense, understanding the offender, and understanding the victim (Melton, Petrila, Poythress, & Slobogin, 1997). Exploration and discussion of racial and cultural variables may contribute to better understanding of the offense, of those accused of crimes, and of the victims. Any information that helps the judge or jury understand limitations in the development of an offender's psychological controls or that

identifies factors that may have undermined the offender's controls may be of use in their determination of the individual's culpability (Melton et al., 1997).

The Case of Salvador Diego

Mr. Diego was a 25-year-old Mexican national who had lived in the United States for 2 years (undocumented status). He was arrested with another man by federal law enforcement officials and charged with the possession and sale of 3 kilos of cocaine. In his arrest records and in papers filed by the federal prosecutor, Mr. Diego was portrayed as a hardened, sophisticated, business-oriented drug dealer. In contrast, his public defender had noted an innocent, "childlike" quality about Mr. Diego, particularly in regard to his openness and style in admitting to undercover officers on two occasions to his participation in the sales of drugs. "I was there in the car. . . . I know that there were drugs. . . . I handed him the drugs," and so forth. The public defender, suspecting cognitive or psychological impairment, requested a psychological evaluation of Mr. Diego.

In the evaluation, the psychologist learned that Mr. Diego worked as a dishwasher and had worked at a number of menial jobs since his arrival in the United States. Mr. Diego was not able to supply the evaluator with several basic facts or developmental events in regard to his past or present life. He was not able to give his address, was not able to read or write, and was not able to remember more than four digits at one time. The evaluator learned that he relied on "friends" to help him buy clothing and food. In the context of attempting to trace his migration patterns to and within the United States, Mr. Diego vaguely described getting in a car with a stranger near his home in Mexico and traveling to the United States. In regard to his local residency patterns, the client recalled once living in "el centro" of the city (which would have been downtown Seattle), near a place where he was once hospitalized in "the hospital where you could see the big mountain," for a head injury that occurred after he had been physically assaulted on the street. The description of the hospital with a mountain view led the evaluator to check for hospital records at Harborview Medical Center in Mr. Diego's name. Hospital records included a CT scan that revealed significant scarring and lesions of the brain, caused by a parasitic infection, cysticercosis, which had occurred during Mr. Diego's childhood. A neuropsychologist was then called in to provide testing and examination as to the degree and areas of neurological impairment that had been suffered by Mr. Diego. It was determined that Mr. Diego did not have the cognitive capacity to have participated in drug dealing, and it came to light that he had been asked to go along on the deals to enhance the sense of safety of the person who was indeed selling drugs. Mr. Diego was released and escorted to his parent's home in Mexico.

This case is presented here in light of the possible durability of stereotype and racial profiling that leads to the arrest and prosecution of Latino individuals suspected of drug trafficking. In addition, on a superficial level, communication difficulties with cultural and linguistic minorities in the legal system are often dismissed as artifacts of cultural and language differences. It is important for law enforcement and legal officials to note that it is common for psychologically and intellectually vulnerable people such as Mr. Diego to be victimized by criminals who use them to assist in illegal activities. In the prosecution's attempt to convict Mr. Diego of this crime, obvious signs of cognitive impairment were ignored or overlooked. Mr. Diego was not even able to carry out basic living skills, much less carry out the level of involvement with drug sales that he was accused of. A thorough examination also helped to determine that the client would require special services on the return trip to his country of origin, as he would not have been able to return home on his own if simply left at the border.

The Case of Jose Lopez

Jose Lopez was a 16-year-old, undocumented Mexican migrant laborer at the time of his arrest for the murder of a 19-year-old youth at a migrant labor camp. Jose maintained that he had left his cabin at the camp one evening on hearing that his younger cousin had become involved in a fight with a group of youth who had arrived at the camp from a local town. He found his cousin struggling and being beaten by several older youth and stated that he feared for his cousin's life. Jose claimed that he and his cousin had then been surrounded by a number of older youth who had driven up in a car, yelling insults and racial slurs at the cousin and at other people in the camp. Jose reported that he then returned to his cabin and grabbed a gun that had been left there by another migrant worker who had left the gun in Jose's care. Jose said that he returned to the scene of the fight and shot the gun into the woods in order to "scare everyone away." The group quickly returned to their car and drove away. Jose and his cousin returned to their cabin, and Jose put the gun in a closet.

The next day, officers arrived at the cabin and questioned Jose about the fight and asked if he had a gun. Jose told the officers about the fight and showed them the gun. While at his cabin Jose said that he was told by the police that "one of the youths in the car had died that night." Jose was surprised, as he had not seen any injuries occur. (The youth that had been shot had not realized that he had been hit until several minutes after getting into the car; he died later that night at a local hospital.) Jose was arrested at his cabin, although he stated that he did not realize at the time that he was being arrested, much less accused of murder. He went with the officers to the police station, where he was questioned and charged. A review of the videotape of his interrogation, which took place in very inadequate Spanish, revealed that Jose did not clearly understand what he had been charged with. (Jose answered "Yes" to the question "You know somebody died that night?" without understanding that this phrase was used to implicate his admission to the shooting death of one of the youths.) Jose also did not understand that he was about to be tried for murder as an adult. The Latino officers who conducted the interview, using very poor Spanish, were friendly with Jose and were very indirect and unclear about the serious charges that they were discussing as they spoke with him. One officer smiled and winked at the camera when he had succeeded in getting Jose to sign papers that indicated that he knew his rights, indicating that he knew what he was charged with, and indicating that he had agreed to a trial as an adult. (The officers had told him in the taped interview that the facilities were much better for adults than for juveniles and that it was to his advantage to consent to legal proceedings as an adult rather than as a juvenile.) At the time, Jose was not clear about or aware of the true nature of the proceedings that he was participating in. He later stated that at the time of his interrogation, and for some time afterward, he never really understood that it was the bullet from the gun that he had fired that night that had killed the young man. Even several weeks later, the evaluator found that it was difficult for Jose to believe that anyone had died that night.

Jose's public defender requested a psychological evaluation, based on his feelings that Jose was "a good kid," and that he had wanted to further investigate Jose's life story. He wanted to learn "what happened out there that night," as Jose was not able to clearly describe to him what had happened. The public defender also hoped to learn about any possible intellectual or psychological circumstances that might shed light on Jose's case. (I have found that it

is common for legal professionals to infer intellectual deficiencies in their clients due to difficulties with language and cross-cultural communication.) The prosecutor had portrayed the fight as gang related and tried to establish that Jose was a violent adult. Jose's cooperative and open manner during the police interrogation, plus the way that he had answered the manipulative and poorly phrased questions used during the police interview, was implicated as evidence that Jose had admitted to committing the crime and showed no remorse.

After interviewing Jose and reviewing the tape of his being formally charged by the police, it became clear that Jose was not able to fully explain what had happened on the night of the shooting because he was very unclear about the circumstances of the death of the youth who had been shot. A great deal of this confusion had been created by the police, who had told him that there had been a death, but never directly stated that they thought that the death was a result of the shots fired by Jose. Jose had difficulty for many weeks associating the death with his gunfire because everyone had walked or run away from the fight and gotten into the car, seemingly without injury.

The psychological evaluation, conducted in Spanish, revealed that Jose had traveled with his father from Mexico to work in the United States 1 year before the shooting. Jose had later been abandoned by his father in the migrant camp, living there alone for several months while his father had gone to work in another state. Jose had continued to work to support himself, helped to take care of the 13-year-old cousin that was in his charge, and also sent money home to his mother and sisters in Mexico on a regular basis. A risk and protective factors assessment of his years as a child in Mexico revealed strong family relationships, with the exception of inconsistency on the part of his father in supporting the family. Jose described positive peer relations, and, as is the case with many Mexican migrant children, Jose had taken on odd jobs at a young age to help to support the family. Jose said that he had been a good student in Mexico, and his mother had objected to his leaving school for work purposes. Intelligence testing showed that Jose was a bright and intellectually capable young man, working at or above grade level for his age. The Spanish version of the adolescent Minnesota Multiphasic Personality Inventory (MMPI-2) also revealed a normal profile.

During the course of the assessment, in order to gain an understanding of the community and juvenile social/racial climate in regard to Mexican farmworkers, the evaluator spoke with many Mexican residents in the town where Jose had been charged and was incarcerated. Farming was the main industry of the area, and the local growers, almost exclusively of European American background, were reliant on Mexican labor for the cultivation and harvesting of crops. Several Mexican residents interviewed reported a great deal of discrimination and prejudice held toward Mexicans who lived and worked in the area. One Mexican American postal worker reported being regularly questioned and screened in regard to the legitimacy of his presence at the post office, despite his badge, uniform, and 7 years of work there. A white merchant in the town, who owned a grocery store and had been familiar with Jose's case, had expressed concern about bias toward Mexicans by police and city officials. The store owner went so far as to discuss the fact that her teenage son had recently killed a pedestrian in a drunk driving incident, stating that there had not been much of a penalty for his crime. Her son had been given 1 year of community service in lieu of incarceration. She stated that it was her opinion that the laws were much more severe when applied to Mexicans in the community. Both Mexican and white storekeepers described a frequency of adolescent tensions and conflicts between white and Latino youth. It also seemed as though there were tensions between Mexican immigrant farmworkers and the more long-standing Mexican residents the community. Many of the police were Latino but did not speak Spanish as their first language. One of the prosecutors was also of Latin American heritage, but spoke disparagingly about the linguistic dialect and cultural background of Jose. It seemed conceivable that child protective services might have been interested in intervening in cases of migrant children like Jose, living alone; however, it appeared as though there was a great deal of separation between the local social services and the migrant community.

Assessment of acculturation tasks and hurdles showed that Jose had been isolated within the migrant community, with no assistance in adjusting to U.S. culture. He had experienced taunting and threats of assault from white youth in the local town and was marginalized in the broader community context. He was fearful about seeking help for his situation and sought shelter in the familiarity of other migrant farmworkers, who also showed him how to find new jobs as the seasonal labor shifted. Jose missed his family in Mexico and continued to keep in contact with his mother and sisters, as well as sending money to them.

Projective methods of assessment were also used in Jose's evaluation. Themes gleaned from several early recollections recounted by Jose revealed a strong degree of caring and worrying about the well-being of his family and the need to work hard to help to care for his mother and sisters. A thematic appreciation test (TAT) was also administered, with the use of a psycho-cultural approach to TAT scoring and interpretation (Ephraim, 2000). TAT themes also revealed an extremely strong ethic of caring, work, and family responsibility. A sense of competence, optimism, and achievement-oriented goals was also revealed. Some degree of sadness and disappointment was also reflected, arising in relationship to the inconsistencies and lack of nurturance on the part of his father. Although Jose was capable and resourceful, he was not able to totally mask his fears and vulnerabilities as a child who had been left alone in a foreign country. He was an eager learner and was visibly very appreciative of the schooling, food, and shelter that he had been given while in detention. Residential staff in the detention facility noted that Jose did not associate with deviant youth and that he spent his time reading, learning English, and performing other constructive activities while in the jail.

The profile of Jose Lopez that emerged from the evaluation was one of a sensitive, bright, responsible, and highly prosocial youth. He was resourceful and capable, but also frightened and lonely, as he struggled to survive on his own in a strange land, without the benefit of adult guidance or supervision. According to Jose, he had fired the gun in an attempt to protect his cousin, who he believed to be in grave danger. This explanation was consistent with impressions formed about Jose as a result of the evaluation. The image of a young man trying to save the life of a younger family member stood in stark contrast to the prosecutor's image of a heartless, violent gang member, a young man not seen as a teenager but as an adult who had been hardened by a difficult life of farm labor.

The events surrounding the shooting had been difficult to piece together because of the shroud of confusion created by law enforcement officials who attempted to manipulate Jose and trick him into signing away his civil rights. This deception came about as a result of his youth and cultural and linguistic vulnerabilities. Because of the psychological evaluation and important ballistics evidence that proved that the death had been caused by a ricocheted bullet, the prosecutor's office returned the case to the juvenile court level, and Jose accepted a plea for second-degree reckless manslaughter and was sentenced to 18 months in a juvenile detention center.

PSYCHOLOGICAL TESTIMONY IN LEGAL SITUATIONS WHERE "RACELESSNESS," RACE-NEUTRALITY, CULTURAL OBJECTIVITY, AND THE END OF RACISM IS CLAIMED

The Case of Olive Chan

It is also important to note that, as discussed in Chapter 5 of this book, it is common for those who claim "racelessness" or race neutrality in evidence or testimony to still use racial information in legal cases when it is in their best interest. For example, in biracial or bicultural child custody cases, there are sometimes great objections raised in regard to the consideration of the child's ethnic and cultural background in making placement decisions, based on the grounds that such information is "racist" or that it defies principles of racial equality, regardless of the cultural differences that exist between the divorcing parents. In one such custody case, where racial and cultural objectivity was claimed and racial and cultural testimony was objected to, attorneys for a white American father, who sought custody of his biracial

children, demeaned the cultural traditions and norms of the children's Asian immigrant mother. A parenting evaluation was conducted, and all family members were interviewed. The psychologist who conducted the evaluation omitted and ignored important cultural information, based on claims of the "universal" nature of good parenting. Despite such claims of cultural irrelevance, the same psychologist recommended that placement be made with the father, because he could provide a "more democratic, American household" for his children, as compared with their mother, portrayed as a rigid and strict "traditional Asian mother, who overly valued the educational success of her children."

Despite the numerous cultural, racial, and linguistic dynamics inherent in the case, and the fact that the children had been raised in an Asian country until middle childhood, the parenting evaluation and assessment process had been devoid of critical information about the family's racial and cultural background. A cross-cultural critique of the first parenting evaluation cited the cultural bias that was blatant in the case, despite claims of racial and cultural equality on the part of evaluating psychologists, the father, and the father's attorney. A second, culturally conscious evaluation raised important issues such as balancing the racial and cultural identity development in the children, who were biracial, providing research on the importance of ethnic identity in the development of minority children. It was pointed out that access to their mother's traditional culture was dependent on the maintenance of the children's continued ability to speak Mandarin as their first language and their observance of Buddhism, the religion that the children had been raised in. Observance of their father's side of their heritage and English usage would be reinforced as part of daily life in American schools and culture and in spending time with their father and his extended family. Both parents were encouraged to help their children maintain a strong sense of their ethnic and cultural heritage.

The mother's parenting practices were assessed within the context of her own culture, with the inclusion of collateral interviews with professionals who were familiar with these parenting norms and with people who had observed the mother with her children. The mother demonstrated strong and healthy parenting skills, appropriate in either American or Asian countries. It was pointed out that in most Asian cultures education is highly valued and that Asian parents are quite successful in helping their children to be successful in school. Additional aspects of the assessment included consideration of acculturation stresses, an expected degree of cultural conflict as part of the adjustment process for the immigrating children and family, and the newness of racial prejudice that was encountered by the phenotypically Asian children at school.

Critiques of the first evaluation addressed the problems created by a lack of consideration of cultural dynamics and the cultural biases inherent in the use of a traditional Western assessment model and English-language instruments with persons from an Asian culture and language background. Child protective services had also been called by a court-appointed observer when she found out that the mother regularly bathed her daughters, ages 8 and 10, a practice that was a routine part of the mother's culture and traditions. This presented a terrible assault to the mother, to her culture, and to her relationship with the children. To summarize, in this case, the racial and cultural dominance imposed by the father, by legal and psychological professionals, and for a time by the courts, who had separated the mother from her children, was addressed and discussed in light of a culturally comprehensive psychological evaluation. Assumptions of racial objectivity and cultural neutrality were countered and challenged. Culturally relevant data provided the court with information that could lead to a more informed decision-making process when it came to making decisions about custody arrangements for the children. The importance of biracial and bicultural identity development in child-custody decisions was considered by the judge to be important information for the family courts to consider, despite objections grounded in race neutrality that had been posed by the father's attorney.

School Discrimination and Civil Rights

In a civil rights case, 36 African American children sought judicial relief and reparations as the victims of racism and discrimination in a school district in the northwestern United States. From Grades K–12, in several schools, black students experienced physical assaults, bomb threats, regular exposure to KKK symbols and pictures of black lynchings placed in student lockers, and the use of racial taunting and slurs in the hallways. On occasion, black athletes found their uniforms covered in human feces. African American students were also stereotyped by teachers and administrators as being unintelligent individuals, poor students, drug dealers, and gang members. Disparate discipline was common, especially when conflicts involving blacks and whites were brought to the attention of teachers or school bus drivers. Then, punishment was usually given to the black students, with few consequences for the whites. This led to an escalation of student conflicts as a means of leading black students into disfavor with the school. Teachers gave white students license to use the word *nigger* in classrooms through the use of discussions around texts such as *Huckleberry Finn* and *The Grapes of Wrath.* The social exclusion of black children by white children and families was open and blatant. If black children sought support and solace in one another's company at school, they were accused of gang activity and were often separated. Parent requests for a more diverse curriculum, requests for districtwide diversity training, and pleas for the protection of their children's safety at school went unheeded.

The psychological consequences of exposure to multiple forms of racism resulted in a diagnosis of posttraumatic stress disorder for many of the children, some also with co-occurring major depression. Others suffered from anxiety disorders, digestive problems, and hypertension, despite their youthful ages. A few of the youth attempted to fight back and were thus labeled as delinquents and antisocial gang members. Children who were resilient suffered just as much as those who developed problems, and in their case, many of them worked excessively hard in order to succeed and be accepted. Many of the students hoped to grow up and be teachers, attorneys, or youth workers, so that they might help minority children to never experience what they had experienced. Several children expressed the desire to be paramedics or disaster workers, symbolic of the life-threatening nature of their situation.

In the case, experts for the school district including several psychologists and psychiatrists used tactics that are emblematic of modern racism and race neutrality to prove the innocence of the district. Claims that the types of events experienced by the children occurred in a normal, everyday context of peer conflicts and playground controversies were made. Claims were also made that it was a normal or universal aspect of development for minority children to experience some degree of prejudice and discrimination while growing up. Some experts even went so far as to say that experiencing prejudice was a healthy experience for the children, preparing them for life in a world where prejudice abounds. In regard to the use of racial slurs and harassment, one expert stated that school officials must determine the intent of racial harassment before punishing the harassing student. He also stated that policies that punished racial harassment would actually "foster racial tension" and disturb elements of free speech. He emphasized that learning environments that promote the "free exchange of ideas" and expression of "feelings" would act to reduce racial tension. He discouraged school districts from prohibiting racial harassment as a form of student expression.

Conservative minority "celebrity" experts were used in this case. The defense also attempted to dispute the existence of the children's claims of racism, through the use of rationale from modern racism, such as "racism is over" (there was no racism in this school) and that blacks use racism as an excuse for laziness or poor performance. In psychological and other evaluations for the school district, most of the children in question were reported to be poor students, drug users, or gang members, or they were antisocial, lazy, or prone to violence, or else were they diagnosed with paranoid personality disorders. White experts for the plaintiffs who cited examples of white racism in the district were accused of harboring stereotypes and other racist notions against whites by one expert, who also claimed that African American sensitivity to racism "leads them to see racism where it is not intended or where none exists." Poor attendance that resulted from student fears

of school was dismissed by many as cultural deficiencies in black Americans. Even when a white student came in blackface to the school's senior picture day, the student was seen to "have had no racial animus behind the behavior."

Psychological evaluation and testimony that countered these claims made by evaluators and witnesses for the defense (the school district) focused on research which demonstrates that racism is a stressor that injures the health of minorities and that impedes the academic performance of minority students, as well as leading to the social marginalization of minority youth. Research on stereotype threat, academic disidentification, and the consequences of perceived injustice in academic settings was also presented (McKown & Weinstein, 2003; Schmader, Major, & Gramzow, 2001; Steele, Spencer, & Aronson, 2002). Articles that noted the importance of race in identity development were also included in a summary that accompanied the children's psychological evaluations. Assessment and diagnosis of the children with consideration of the racial incidents that took place demonstrated serious mental health and physical consequences for most of the children. Surveys of black families (Hill, 1999) were cited that discuss the methods that black parents use to help protect their children from racism, as well as other studies that dispute the "universality" of racist experiences across school and community cultures. The Schedule of Racist Events (Landrine & Klonoff, 1996), an instrument that assesses the forms, prevalence, and severity of racism in various environments and settings, was used to provide a more detailed and comparative description of the types of experiences encountered by the children and their resulting emotional consequences. The Phinney multiethnic identity measure was used to assess the children's level of ethnic identity development and feelings about their own group. The mental health problems that were revealed in psychological evaluations were tied to specific incidents of racial violence—the use of repeated racial slurs and taunting, social exclusion, the application of stereotypes by teachers, and continual disparate discipline by teachers and administrators.

Developmental assessment included surveying the risk and protective factors (Mash & Wolfe,

2002) that were present in the children's lives (biological, family/parenting, academic, social/peer, personality, socioeconomic). Risk and protective factors were also discussed in refuting or supporting conclusions drawn by other mental health evaluators.

Critiques of other psychological evaluations noted the absence of information, data, or contexts of discussion about issues of racism and discrimination in African American life, which are cited as critical dynamics in the mental health of African Americans (see Gilliam, 2002; Sue & Sue, 2003; U.S. Department of Health and Human Services, 2001). Despite numerous cautions in the *Diagnostic and Statistical Manual of Mental Disorders* (American Psychiatric Association, 2000), and other psychological literature about African Americans that cautions the use of diagnosis of paranoia, several children were diagnosed with paranoid personality disorders. Neither of the defense evaluators was found to have had significant experience or expertise in working with African American clients; in fact, one of the evaluators admitted in his deposition that in the more than 20 years of practice he had only treated one black client for a mild phobia. He had no black colleagues or acquaintances. A lack of professional or personal experiences with black Americans possibly contributed to the appearance of many stereotypes in their reports. One evaluator even mistakenly used Michael Jordan's name in a report when referring to an African American person involved with the case.

When counsel for the defense attempted to dismiss racism as "a cry of wolf" or general complaint by the plaintiffs, alluding to the fact that racism was passé, it became important to avoid using racism as a general term and to focus on the specific forms and operating structures of racism that had taken place. The specific forms of racism were broken down into typologies and described using the appropriate terms and definitions. Thus the differences between events of dominative, aversive, modern, and everyday racism were described and categorized as they had occurred, as were the differences between and manifestations of individual, institutional, and cultural racism. We also identified incidents in which various forms of stereotyping, prejudice, and discrimination had taken place. The

more specific the claims were, the more difficult it became for the defense to dismiss them by pooh-poohing the idea of "racism" in the case.

It was a great psychological victory for the children and families to win this case. It took a great deal of courage to stand up to racism in a societal climate where racism is labeled extinct. Once again, hard work and sacrifices made by African Americans who fought to uphold the constitution of our country brought a victory for civil rights.

Case Example—Child Abuse and Child Custody: The Case of Andrea Garcia

Ms. Garcia was a Latin American mother of three children. The white American father of her youngest child, Andrea, left the home when Ms. Garcia became pregnant with Andrea. Ms. Garcia did not hear from him again until he appeared to request visitation with Andrea when she was three years of age, following Ms. Garcia's filing for assistance of child support. At first, Andrea was reluctant to visit with her father because he was a stranger to her. After a few visits, she became even more reluctant to see him and began screaming and clinging to her mother when he approached the house. At one point, Ms. Garcia's neighbors called the police to report the child's distress when her father took her from her home. After about three months of visits with her father, Andrea told her older sister that her father "hurt" her when she was with him. Ms. Garcia reported this to Child Protective Services (CPS). When CPS began to investigate the complaint, Andrea's father hired an attorney, who accused Ms. Garcia of alienating the child's affection and turning her against him. CPS ordered an evaluation from a team of psychologists who also conducted parenting evaluations in divorce-related child custody cases. The team requested that Andrea be placed in foster care in order to find a "neutral setting" for her while they evaluated the parents and determined whether or not Ms. Garcia was fabricating her complaints against Andrea's father. While she was in the custody of the state, Andrea's father filed a petition for full custody of his daughter.

Parenting evaluations of both parents were conducted. Although Ms. Garcia spoke mostly Spanish, had limited English skills, and spoke only Spanish with her children, the evaluation was conducted in English. Non-Spanish-speaking observers watched her play with her child from behind a one-way mirror. She was asked to speak only in English to her child in order to accommodate the observers. An English version of the MMPI was administered, and it took Ms. Garcia several hours and more than one visit to complete the instrument. She reported several times that she did not understand many of the questions, not only because they were in English but from a cultural perspective. The MMPI was administered more than once before a valid profile was obtained, and eventually it was given to her again in Spanish. The playroom observers noted that Ms. Garcia was overly directive and overly instructive with her daughter as she played and that Ms. Garcia did not follow an "appropriate" child-centered manner of play with Andrea. In addition, in her history, Ms. Garcia had been previously married, and her ex-husband had been arrested for rape after their divorce. At another time in the family history, one of her older daughters had been molested by a neighbor. The evaluator determined that Ms. Garcia had tendencies toward being self-centered and intrusive and thought that she had deliberately turned her child against her father. It was also determined that perhaps Ms. Garcia was not able to protect her children from dangerous men, in that there were two connections in her life to sex offenders. Custody was awarded to Andrea's father, and limited visitation was afforded to Ms. Garcia, as Andrea's father lived several hours away. Within a few months, Andrea's father seriously physically abused Andrea, and she was hospitalized for several weeks. Andrea was then placed in foster care in the town where her father lived, and far from her mother. Without going further into voluminous details in a case that involved both the family court and the state in regard to child protective services, Ms. Garcia had to fight for several years before regaining custody of her daughter.

Andrea was placed in foster care with a non-Latino family. Ms. Garcia requested that Andrea continue to worship in the Catholic tradition and hoped that she would have some way to maintain her Spanish-language skills. Neither of these requests was granted, and Andrea became active in the foster family's fundamentalist Christian church. The court still considered the psychological evaluation of Ms. Garcia to be valid (that she might not be able to "protect" her child from sex offenders and that she might still try to turn Andrea against her father, despite the fact that the child was already terrified of him). Supervised visitations were ordered.

Ms. Garcia was forbidden to see Andrea alone or speak to her in Spanish or write her letters in Spanish. Her letters to her daughter were examined before delivery by CPS. She was allowed to see her only once a month, early on a Saturday morning, so that she was forced to drive many hours on Friday night or very early Saturday morning, across a mountain range, with snow in winter months. There were many conflicts of interest in regard to connections among the therapists who saw Andrea, her father, and the foster family for counseling following the abuse. The therapist for Andrea had been the marital therapist at one time for the foster family. She put negative evaluations of Ms. Garcia in her case notes. Because she had been accused of being intrusive in the original evaluation, Ms. Garcia tried to be more "detached" in her visits with Andrea, which were stilted anyway because they did not take place in her first language. Observers then criticized Ms. Garcia for being cold and estranged from her daughter.

A judge finally ordered that Ms. Garcia could receive therapy to make sure that she was a fit mother. Over the years, Ms. Garcia struggled to get help in a legal system that overwhelmed her because of linguistic and cultural disadvantages. She had been given interpreters that did not speak Spanish well, and she had had two ineffective attorneys. Andrea was in foster care in an area with large numbers of Latino farmworkers, and prejudice against Latino people ran high. Ms. Garcia had received overwhelming support in her case from her employer, who was a physician; the Hispanic community; her church; the staff of her older children's school; and people in her neighborhood. Her older children were well-adjusted, excellent students, who received awards at school. Her daughter had been granted a college scholarship when she was a junior in high school. Despite these efforts, Ms. Garcia continued to struggle until she eventually found a good attorney, an effective

Spanish-speaking therapist, and a parenting evaluator who also was Latin American, who were able to help her eventually regain custody of her daughter.

Commentary: Cultural Politics and Cultural Bias in the Case of Ms. Garcia

I was a treating therapist in this unfortunate case, and as I write about it several years later, I ask, how did this ever happen? I will try to touch on the major issues at hand, as this was a very complex case that involved issues of both child abuse and child custody between the child's parents.

We can begin by examining the disadvantages posed by being a woman, an immigrant, and a member of an ethnic minority. This woman then found herself in a conflict with an abusive white male in a system that was strange to her and dominated by professionals who were from the majority culture and of a different racial and linguistic background from her own. Chapter 25 contains useful information to illuminate the vulnerability of women like Ms. Garcia. Majority culture status, combined with professional status and familiarity with our judicial system, afforded the evaluators a great deal of power and control in the lives of Ms. Garcia and her daughter. This power and control afforded the evaluators the power to determine which language and method would be used in the evaluation; the power to determine the "right" way to parent and play with her child, despite cultural differences; and the power to determine that Ms. Garcia was not trying to protect Andrea from child abuse, but rather that she was "really" attempting to alienate her from her biological father. The evaluating group also had the power to have the evaluation respected by the courts, even though it was highly faulty in both process and content.

The evaluating psychologist who conducted the parenting evaluation, who saw both parents, did not interact with Ms. Garcia in her first language, and neither did the professionals who assisted with the administration and scoring of testing or in conducting play observations. When I read the evaluation and case notes, it seemed to me that the first evaluator found it much easier to converse with and gain information from Andrea's father, who was English speaking and

of the same cultural background. The play observation used with Andrea and her mother involved looking for a form of "appropriate" play and interaction between parent and child that was bound in the biases and values of Anglo-American psychologists who favor "child-centered" play—a form of play that probably would have been seen as inappropriate in Ms. Garcia's culture. In reading the notes on the play sessions, it was clear to me that Ms. Garcia was trying to "teach" Andrea how to use many of the toys and materials available and also wanted Andrea to perform well while being observed, which would have been consistent with the cultural norms and behavior of a Latina mother. It is also critical to note that the communication that takes place between a parent and child in their first language provides a far more accurate representation of their relationship than does interaction in a language they never use with one another. The MMPI data should not have been used, given the degree of linguistic and cultural difficulty that Ms. Garcia demonstrated in using the instrument.

There was hesitation on the part of many professionals involved in this case to seek the support and services of mental health professionals who were Latino, even on the part of Ms. Garcia's attorney. The reason for this hesitation was due to prejudicial fears that a Latino professional would be biased in favor of Ms. Garcia. Witnesses and support efforts given by the Latino community were largely ignored, despite the testimony of well-known community figures on Ms. Garcia's behalf. Despite the fact that many grave errors were made, ultimately leading to the abuse of Andrea, the original psychological evaluation still carried the weight necessary to keep Andrea away from her mother. My observations led me to believe that racial and cultural bias played a major role in favoring the white father over the Latina mother, despite the abuse that had occurred. There was also bias in this case in regard to language use and cultural identity. English was used throughout the proceedings for a number of years. It was only in the last months of the case that Ms. Garcia was given the opportunity to work with Spanish-speaking professionals. The town in which Andrea lived had a high number of Latino residents that could have served to translate letters from her mother to CPS, could have served as observers of parent–child visitation, and potentially could have provided culturally consistent foster care. The social welfare professionals involved were all white and felt that anyone who was Latino would be biased in favor of Ms. Garcia. I heard many disparaging remarks made about Latinos by the social workers involved in the case. Over a number of years, Ms. Garcia was prohibited from using her first language with her child, which muddied the evaluation process, stilted her interactions with Andrea, and prevented genuine emotional communication between mother and daughter. Andrea also lost her ability to speak Spanish and was robbed of her cultural heritage for many years. It was a sad irony that during her years apart from her daughter, Ms. Garcia had worked as a nanny for a family of two physicians, who trusted her with the care of their children, even to the point of allowing their children to have overnight visits at her home.

During my testimony, I reviewed the history of my therapy work with Ms. Garcia and emphasized her capability as a mother. I had observed her with her other children and discussed her children's progress in school with their teachers. I found no evidence of danger toward the children and had sought collateral interviews with others who could have expressed opinions to the contrary (teachers, clergy, community contacts). I described to the court a list of cultural errors that were made in the evaluations and observations of Ms. Garcia. I also presented information about the importance of ethnic identity in the child development of biracial and bicultural children like Andrea, who had been kept away from the Latino side of her heritage for a number of years. In addition, I stated that I thought that a great deal of racial and cultural bias and conflicts of interest among professionals who knew Andrea's father and foster family had been at play in this case.

The nature of this testimony was welcomed by some and met with outrage by others. There were numerous objections made in the hearing when it came to the discussion of the dynamics of race, ethnicity, and culture as they intersected with the case, as well as how culture and ethnicity were important in Andrea's development. Research was presented that supported the

importance of ethnic and bicultural identity in child development (LaFrambois, Hardin, & Gerton, 1998; Phinney, 1998; Root, 1998). The parameters of cross-cultural assessment (Castillo, 1997; Dana, 2000; McClure & Teyber, 1996; Gopaul-McNicol & Thomas-Presswood, 1998; Sue & Sue, 2003) and the APA (1993) cultural diversity guidelines were also outlined for the court. While on the witness stand, one of the attorneys for the state asked me to tell the court the race of my husband. The attorney that had been assigned to Andrea objected to this question, but the judge overruled the objection and asked me to answer the question. When I stated that my husband was African American, the attorney for the state, and later the attorney for Andrea's father, tried to make the point that I was blindly championing people of color because I was married to a black man.

The testimony of two Latina psychologists who had evaluated Ms. Garcia, the testimony of other professionals, and others who knew Ms. Garcia painted a portrait of an excellent parent. The judge finally ordered Andrea returned to the home of her mother, after more than 7 years of separation. Andrea was still required to visit her father on a regular basis, supervised at first, but eventually with supervision removed.

I later received a letter from the judge, admonishing me for raising issues of race and culture in his courtroom. He stated that in cases of child welfare, culture was not important and that I should be embarrassed for having raised the issue. He also reminded me that the rule of the court called for colorblindness. This judge, however, had not thought it inappropriate for an attorney to ask me the race of my husband in his courtroom, and ultimately, he failed to see how race, culture, and language had been critical factors in the case.

REFERENCES

American Psychiatric Association. (2000). *Diagnostic and statistical manual of mental disorders* (4th ed., Text revision). Washington, DC: Author.

American Psychological Association. (1993). Guidelines for providers of psychological services to ethnic, linguistic, and culturally diverse populations. *American Psychologist, 48,* 45–48.

Castillo, R. J. (1997). *Culture and mental illness: A client centered approach.* Pacific Grove, CA: Brooks Cole.

Dana, R. (2000). *Handbook of cross cultural assessment.* Mahwah, NJ: Lawrence Erlbaum Associates.

Ephraim, D. (2000). A psychocultural approach to TAT scoring and interpretation. In R. H. Dana (Ed.), *Handbook of cross cultural and multicultural personality assessment* (pp. 427–445). Mahwah, NJ: Lawrence Erlbaum Associates.

Gopaul-McNicol, S. A., & Thomas-Presswood, T. T. (1998). *Working with linguistically and culturally different children.* Needham Heights, MA: Allyn and Bacon.

Hill, S. H. (1999). *African American children: Socialization and development in families.* Thousand Oaks, CA: Sage Publications.

LaFrambois, T., Hardin, L. K., & Gerton, J. (1998). Psychological impact of biculturalism: Evidence and theory. In P. B. Organista, K. M. Chun, & G. Marin (Eds.), *Readings in ethnic psychology* (pp. 123–156). New York: Routledge.

Landrine, H., & Klonoff, E. A. (1996). The schedule of racist events: A measure of racial discrimination and a study of its negative physical and mental health consequences. *Journal of Black Psychology, 22*(2), 144–168.

Mash, E. J., & Wolfe, D. A. (2002). *Abnormal child psychology.* Belmont, CA: Wadsworth.

McClure, F. H., & Teyber, E. (1996). *Child and adolescent therapy: A multicultural-relational approach.* Orlando, FL: Harcourt Brace.

McKown, C., & Weinstein, R. S. (2003). The development and consequences of stereotype consciousness in middle childhood. *Child Development, 74*(2), 498–515.

Melton, G. B., Petrila, J., Poythress, N. G., & Slobogin, C. (1997). *Psychological evaluations for the court: A handbook for mental health professionals and lawyers.* New York: Guilford.

Phinney, J. (1998). Ethnic identity in adolescents and adults. In P. B. Organista, K. M. Chun, & G. Marin (Eds.), *Readings in ethnic psychology* (pp. 73–99). New York: Routledge.

Root, M. P. (1998). Resolving "other" status: Identity development of biracial individuals. In P. B. Organista, K. M. Chun, & G. Marin (Eds.), *Readings in ethnic psychology* (pp. 100–112). New York: Routledge.

Schmader, T., Major, B., & Gramzow, R. H. (2001). Coping with ethnic stereotypes in the academic domain: Perceived injustice and psychological disengagement. *Journal of Social Issues, 57*(1), 93-111.

Steele, C. M., Spencer, S. J., & Aronson, J. (2002). Contending with group image: The psychology of stereotype and social identity threat. In M. P. Zanna (Ed.), *Advances in experimental social psychology* (Vol. 34, pp. 379–440). San Diego: Academic Press.

Sue, D. W., & Sue, D. (2003). *Counseling the culturally diverse.* New York: John Wiley & Sons.

U.S. Department of Health and Human Services. (2001). *Mental health: Culture, race, and ethnicity—A supplement to mental health: A report to the surgeon general.* Rockville, MD: U.S. DHHS, Office of the Surgeon General.

3

JUDICIAL COLORBLINDNESS, RACE NEUTRALITY, AND MODERN RACISM

How Psychologists Can Help the Courts Understand Race Matters

KIMBERLY HOLT BARRETT
University of Washington

WILLIAM H. GEORGE
University of Washington

I know what the world has done to my brother and how narrowly he has survived it. And I know, which is much worse, and this is the crime of which I accuse my country and my countrymen, and for which neither time nor history will ever forgive them, that they have destroyed and are destroying hundreds and thousands of lives and do not know it and do not want to know it. One can be, one can indeed one must strive to become, tough and philosophical concerning destruction and death, for this is what most of mankind has been best at since we have heard of man. (But remember: most of mankind is not all of mankind.) But it is not permissible that the authors of devastation should also be innocent, it is the innocence which constitutes the crime.

—James Baldwin (*The Fire Next Time,* pp. 6, 7)

Discussion of race, ethnicity, and culture in the courtroom is complex and controversial for a variety of reasons. However, the discussion becomes increasingly complex if the philosophy of the courts does not allow the consideration of race, ethnicity, and culture as identifying or contextual variables in cases involving minority clients. From the judicial perspective, contemporary concepts of race neutrality and colorblindness represent an American core cultural value that supersedes the importance of considering race, ethnicity, and culture as significant factors. This viewpoint stems from early constitutional premises of equality and justice for all, combined with liberal integrationist sentiments drawn from the civil rights movement. This state of affairs creates a conflict for professionals representing minority clients.

On the one hand, psychologists and attorneys who work with racial, cultural, and ethnic minorities very likely will need to discuss racial/ethnic/cultural issues in presenting the dynamics and context of the client's case as well as the client's identity, personality, and character. On the other hand, the judicial system embraces a race-neutral colorblind stance. Thus, a dilemma is posed when legal and psychological professionals representing the client are poised against counterparts who—under the guise of race-neutral colorblindness—oppose the use of race or culture in testimony. In the extreme, legal and psychological professionals representing the other side have called it "racist" to use legal arguments or testimony based on culture or race because such arguments are seen as contradicting the imposed principles of neutrality or as challenging the status quo of white society (Crenshaw, Gotanda, Peller, & Thomas, 1995). After a discussion of colorblindness and its dangers, we will offer some suggestions as to the role that psychologists might play in better illuminating and remediating the problems posed by ignoring race and culture in the courtroom.

WHAT IS COLORBLINDNESS?

"*In the eyes of the government, we are just one race here. It is American.*" This statement, as quoted by Wu (1996, p. 813), was made by Supreme Court Justice Antonin Scalia in 1995 regarding a decision on affirmative action. This comment reflects the principle of race neutrality or colorblindness as enacted in the courts. The notion of race neutrality in today's courts translates in lay terms to an amalgam of erroneous but politically popular ideas that undermine one's effectiveness in representing minority

clients in the legal arena. These ideas include the following points: (a) The days of overt prejudice and discrimination are over and therefore racism is no longer a problem; (b) everyone is treated equally and objectively in the legal system, regardless of race or national origins; (c) there are no built-in system biases working methodically to disadvantage minority individuals; (d) race, culture, and ethnicity are not important identifying factors in the eyes of the law; (e) justice cannot and will not be derailed because of racial or cultural discrimination; and (f) race-based programs, such as affirmative action, scholarships for minority students, and funds for minority business development, are unnecessary and are unconstitutional because they violate the premise of equal treatment under the law.

Legal scholar Frank Wu (1996) cites the ineffectiveness of this model in light of demographic evidence pointing to a society rapidly becoming more multiethnic. Wu charges our current legal system with ineffectiveness in responding to the rise in multiculturalism. He states that it is only recently that legal scholars have begun to respond to issues that are created by a diverse population, suggesting that race-neutral colorblindness is a less than appropriate metaphor at the turn of the millennium.

POLICY SHIFT: DISCRIMINATORY INTENT TRUMPS DISCRIMINATORY OUTCOMES

Closely connected to race neutrality in the courts is a major shift in civil rights law. Title VI of the Civil Rights Act of 1964 prohibits discrimination based on race, color, or national origin. In 2001, the Supreme Court ruled that individuals cannot sue public agencies for discrimination unless an *intent to discriminate* is shown (see ruling *Alexander v. Sandoval,* 2001). This need for proof of intent will have a negative impact on minorities who suffer from disparate negative outcomes in particular areas of public life, such as in systems of higher education or in the disproportionate confinement of blacks, Latinos, and immigrants in the U.S. prison system. One example that illustrates the difficulty of proving intent to discriminate is in comparing the discriminatory outcomes versus intent to

Box 3.1

Modern Racism	Colorblind Courts
Overt racism is bad, but it is mostly over.	Race as an identifier is unnecessary.
Equality is valued.	Everyone is equal in the eyes of the law.
Whites no longer see themselves as racist.	The courts are objective, and the law does not discriminate based on race/ethnicity/culture.
The playing field is now equal.	Special minority programs such as affirmative action are deemed as no longer necessary.
Special programs or services are deemed unnecessary and undeserved and unfair to whites.	Such programs violate the equal protection clauses of the Constitution, thereby discriminating against whites.
If racism occurs, it was unintentional because "I am not a racist."	In order to seek protection from discrimination, one must prove intent to discriminate.

discriminate in the use of standardized test scores such as the Scholastic Aptitude Test (SAT), which has a disparate negative impact on the college admissions of black and Latino students. It would be difficult to prove that the use of the SAT scores in college admissions represents a deliberate intent to discriminate, yet the use of these tests systematically reduces the chance of admission for minority students, who as a group tend to score lower than the majority culture applicants.

It is important to emphasize that this policy shift lies in the difference between proving discriminatory intent—a nearly impossible criterion—versus proving disparate outcomes. We can compare this shift from outcome to intent with one of the dynamics of modern racism, where intentional or overt racism is seen as bad, but as mostly over and in the past. Real but nonovert racism, by contrast, is simply seen not to exist. See Box 3.1 (Dovidio, Gaertner, Kawakami, & Hodson, 2002; McConahay, 1986).

CONVERGENCE BETWEEN THE JUSTICE SYSTEM AND SOCIETAL VIEWPOINTS: AGAIN

If we combine issues of intentionality, criticism of special minority programs, endorsement of

equality and racial objectivity, and the belief that racism is over, then we can see a convergence. The contemporary philosophy of the present judicial system converges with the racial climate of the society at large—a spirit of liberal egalitarianism characterized by the following points: overt racism is over; people are no longer racist; we (whites) endorse principles of equality and do not openly discriminate; the playing field is level for all; if prejudice or discrimination occurs, it is not intentional; and special programs for minorities are no longer necessary. Demands for affirmative action, minority scholarships, and the like are proof of minority demands for undeserved resources and special attention.

By examining and highlighting these parallels between societal and court processes in regard to equality, objectivity, and intentionality, we can find that once again this convergence is not new. As before in history, the most current form of racism has been sanctioned and institutionalized by the highest court in the land. In the past, our courts have sanctioned slavery, segregation, broken treaties, exclusion acts, and internment. And in each historical instance the blatantly racist policies were sanctioned by Supreme Court decisions (e.g., *Scott v. Sandford,* 1856, and *Plessy v. Ferguson,* 1896). Likewise, in the present, the Supreme Court has sanctioned and institutionalized America's most contemporary evolutionary manifestation of racism: modern racism or "new" racism.

Modern or new racism has been identified and described by psychologists and sociologists who are dedicated to the empirical study of race relations (see Feagin, 2001; Feagin & Feagin, 2003; Feagin & O'Brien, 2003; Feagin, Vera, & Batur, 2001; Jones, 1997). James Jones, a social psychologist and scholar of race relations, described the situation aptly:

> The new racism takes on a self-congratulatory "objectivity" about race. But rather than exalting the very best of our traditions of freedom and liberty, these new traditionalists conjure up the bigotry and bias that we seek to eliminate. . . . In sum, the new racism isn't new. It is the same old values and beliefs, spun anew in a different time. . . . The new racism proclaims us to be closer to fairness than those members of minority racial groups—and many others who wage antiracism warfare—believe us to be. (1997, p. 502)

Jones (1997) links modern racism to an analysis of cultural and *racial hegemony*—how one group in power continues to adopt various practices and values that serve to perpetuate their group's domination and control. As overt forms of control have become less viable—such as legally enforced segregation—newer, more subtle forms of domination have arisen. Jones cites the work of Winant (1994) to support the notion that these modern or newer forms of racism can be construed as part of a system of hegemonic domination. Winant describes the mechanism by which this evolving process unfolds, stating that power is maintained by incorporating contemporary "oppositional currents" (Winant, 1994, p. 29) that stand in the way of progress toward the development of an egalitarian society. Therefore racial themes, conflicts, and controversies from contemporary public and political discourse are incorporated into and utilized in the concurrent attempts at maintaining power and control. If we examine the shift in the high court's positions on race relations over time, from the legal sanction of slavery to rulings on "separate but equal," and then leap ahead to their contemporary interpretation of the Civil Rights Acts, we can trace

patterns and shifts in the court's participation in the system of hegemonic control and dominance of the white majority. This shift unfolds utilizing contemporary themes (such as affirmative action) that place racial discrimination in the past and that tout our society as egalitarian and free of color-based prejudice. As a consequence, nonegalitarian outcomes are relegitimated and solidified: Thus, the existing power differential—racial hegemony—is again preserved.

THE DANGERS OF COLORBLINDNESS

A major danger posed by the convergence of modern racism with colorblindness in the courts is that all elements of race and culture are negated through proclamations of objectivity and neutrality. By eliminating race as a concept, we ignore the role of race (and that of ethnicity and culture) as a central aspect of the development, cognitions, behavior, identity, socioeconomic status, social relationships, worldview, and daily life of minorities in the United States. Ignoring race is also to ignore the role played by whites, who created race as a concept and who used self-defined classifications and perceptions to craft mythical and stereotypical images of people of color (called the "normative gaze" by Cornell West, 1999). These images and myths are called up in the assertion of white superiority and are used as justification for the economic exploitation and subjugation of minority groups within society.

Wishing race away is a timeworn trend and tactic used by whites in order to "forget" or claim innocence for racial crimes and inequities while continuing to foment newly disguised racial crimes and inequities. This irony was poetically referred to by Russell Banks as "beads on a string to us, bubbles of blood on a barbed steel strand that stretches from the day the first enslaved African was brought ashore in Virginia to today, and we have not reached the end of it yet" (Banks, 1999, p. 8). Adoption of race-neutral colorblindness offers whites absolution for their sins, past and present, without the requirement of confession or penance. At the fantasy level, it is perhaps an attempt to wish away people of color altogether, for undoubtedly, even the most naive of whites knows that the reality of race is inescapable for people of color in America.

We contend that a doctrine of race-neutral colorblindness is in itself a form of racism. It negates the reality of life for millions of people who experience prejudice and discrimination in most aspects of daily living because of the color of their skin. Griffin (1999) and Parker (1996) cite colorblindness as evidence of pathology, dysfunction, and impairment. Judge Griffin stated that "color awareness is essential if institutional racism and its injustice is to be corrected" (p. 907). Wu (1996) reminds us that race has been used historically by the government to establish seemingly race-neutral public policies that disfavor nonwhite racial groups and could very well be so used again. Likewise, scholars of Critical Race Theory (see Crenshaw et al., 1995; Delgado, 2001) charge that by eliminating consideration of race, we actually foster white racial domination because we eliminate the social and historical contexts of racial oppression and subjugation.

It is important to note, however, that there is dissention within the judiciary. As we see from quotes from Judge Griffin (in this chapter and in Chapter 1), colorblindness and ignorance of the role of culture and ethnicity in the courts is not supported by all judges and court systems. Professionals who work with people of color and immigrants on a daily basis become acutely aware of the impact of culture in human life and of the need for cultural awareness in our court systems. In the foreword to the text *Immigrants in Courts* (Moore, 1999), Washington State Supreme Court Justice James M. Dolliver writes,

> Contributions to this book from all over the United States indicate that the crisis of misunderstanding in cases involving immigrant parties is widespread. Addressing this fundamental problem requires ongoing efforts by judges, attorneys, and court officials to secure the rights of persons who, because of their linguistic, and cultural backgrounds, are unable to participate fully in their own court proceedings. (Dolliver, 1999, p. viii)

In the same text, Judge Paul DeMunhiz writes,

> [A] culturally responsive justice system is one in which the key players have the education, training,

and sensitivity necessary to identify the linguistic needs of a diverse population of immigrants, and to have some understanding of the legal and cultural forces that may have contributed to the immigrants behavior. (DeMunhiz, 1999, pp. 6–7)

COLORBLINDNESS FROM A MEDICAL AND PSYCHOLOGICAL PERSPECTIVE

By comparison, it is important to note that in the health arena—as opposed to the legal arena—doctrines of race-neutral colorblindness are no longer deemed philosophically or pragmatically tenable. Some health dilemmas systematically affect some groups more than others, and such patterns can be rectified only by deliberately attending to—and not ignoring—cultural factors. Also, considerable attention has been recently devoted to racial disparities in health care and health outcomes (Cohen, 2003; Ren, Amick, & Williams, 1997). Such disparities persist despite practitioner claims of nondiscriminatory policies and practices. In the health arena, it is becoming increasingly understood and acknowledged that—apart from intention and design—discriminatory polices and practices exist and drive racially disparate outcomes (Smedley, Stith, & Nelson, 2002). Thus again we see that in the world of health and health care deliberate attention to racial, ethnic, and cultural factors is encouraged and embraced rather than rejected or pathologized and is fast becoming the Zeitgeist (U.S. Department of Health and Human Services, 2001).

From a psychological perspective, race, ethnicity, and culture are powerful influences that shape and influence human thought, behavior, identity, communication, and social relationships. In addition, according to the surgeon general's report (U.S. Department of Health and Human Services, 2001), race, culture, and ethnicity have also been found to affect the health, mental health, coping mechanisms, and socioeconomic status of minority groups in the United States. The quality of service provision in mental health and medical services and the utilization of these services by minority groups are also affected by race and culture (Sue & Sue, 2003; Sue & Zane, 1987). The surgeon general notes that minority groups lack trust in mainstream institutions and service providers because of historical mistreatment, stigma, and clinician bias and stereotyping.

If we were to apply colorblindness to the fields of health and mental health, we would be overlooking the epidemiological, etiological, and environmental factors that are related to health problems and mental illness. We would also be hampering our abilities to provide the most effective treatments and our ability to deliver those treatments.

Likewise, colorblindness in the law prevents us from investigating and remedying the sociocultural and economic "illnesses" that plague our society and that disproportionately attack people from minority groups. Colorblindness handicaps our ability to review standards of care and masks the differential, lower quality of treatment that is given to minorities within our law and justice programs (Markus, Steele, & Steele, 2002).

For the psychologist, race, ethnicity, and culture are critical domains for exploration when it comes to the study of numerous areas and issues. These areas include the study of child development; the study of personality and identity formation; the tracking and treating of emotional, physical, and behavioral problems that arise as a result of the stress of prejudice, discrimination, and socioeconomic marginalization; the diagnosis of mental illness within particular cultural groups; understanding cross-cultural patterns of assimilation, adaptation, and acculturation stress; evaluating the quality of family, peer, and social relationships; exploring and explaining the "goodness of fit" between the individual and his or her interactions within academic and occupational settings; understanding values, emotions, behavior, and communication in the context of culture, ethnicity, and spirituality; and understanding social norms that relate to gender roles, family hierarchy, and sexual behavior.

Any description or diagnosis of a person of color, or a person of ethnic or cultural minority status, without consideration of the previously mentioned domains within a sociocultural context is inadequate and incomplete. Similarly, descriptions and diagnoses would also be incomplete without examination of the role that white Anglo culture plays in influencing the development and functioning of minority individuals

within the context of mainstream society. Judge Scalia's "American" race represents none other than white, Anglo-Saxon culture, dragging its long chain of cultural hegemony, defining the norms of the legal system, and maintaining the status quo (Goodrich & Mills, 2001).

For better or for worse, culture is the primary aspect of humanity. Race and ethnicity are constructions of culture. To ignore race is also to ignore culture and all that has gone before us. To ignore racial, ethnic, and cultural factors in the interface of psychological services and the legal system amounts to a massive collective dereliction of professional duty.

THE ROLE OF PSYCHOLOGY IN ADDRESSING COLORBLINDNESS

What role then can psychology play in helping to clear the murky waters that are created by claiming objectivity, neutrality, and equality in the area of race, when in both the law and American society it is well demonstrated that rules of bias, stereotype, inequality, and prejudice prevail? How can psychologists clarify the meaning of race, ethnicity, and culture as they relate to identity processes and as they connect to the biases and prejudices of the dominant race and culture? The following list outlines how and why the testimony of psychologists in race-based cases is of value to the court and the legal system.

1. Definitions

Definitions undergird any accurate understanding of the dynamics of race and culture. Defining and clarifying racial terminology and nomenclature falls within the disciplines of social, clinical, and cross-cultural psychology (as well as sociology and other disciplines). In addition, empirical research in social and clinical psychology scientifically dismantles, demonstrates, and documents the mechanisms and impact of racism in contemporary society.

We lack a common language in which to discuss matters of race and culture, and no one can understand racism or the basics of culture without the requisite defining knowledge. Our lack of a vocabulary and educated discourse creates an atmosphere of confusion that can lead to avoidance, defensiveness, intimidation, and/or irrational expressions of emotion. More extremely, this void can enable the creation of self-serving definitions that actually subvert or mock our understanding of racism, as in the following prototypic claims: "Affirmative action is the only form of racism that exists in America today." "Reverse discrimination against whites violates Dr. Martin Luther King's hope that individuals be judged by the content their character rather than the color of their skin." Such claims illustrate the urgency of the need for common ground in defining racism and related constructs.

Our experiences as professors teaching courses and seminars on racism, ethnicity, and cultural psychology for the past 14 years have taught us that most people cannot accurately define the words and terms that we use about race and culture on an everyday basis. Understanding the difference between race, ethnicity, and culture can be critical to understanding the identity of particular individuals. Grasping the sociocultural historical roots of the concept of *race* is an important beginning to tracing the development of racist ideology from systems of colonial dominance and slavery to the sociopolitical uses and misuses of the word today. In addition, words such as *racism, prejudice, discrimination,* and *stereotypes* represent distinctive processes and require accurate definition and understanding of their qualitatively different forms and meanings. For example, in one of the most authoritative texts on racism, Jones (1997) devotes three chapters and close to 150 pages to defining and explaining the mechanisms of racism. In order to move away from the colorless world created by race neutrality, we need an accurate and adequate language that can provide us with the words to illustrate more clearly and vividly the concepts, contexts, and processes that are involved in explaining and representing the experiences of racism and discrimination in the lives of racial, ethnic, and cultural minorities who so deeply understand the terrain of American race relations. As a scientific and scholarly discipline, psychology is well positioned to shed light on rigorously defining race, ethnicity, racism, and related constructs.

2. The Subtlety of Current Race Dynamics

The dynamics and processes of contemporary race relations and racial discrimination are complex, subtle, and difficult to isolate. Psychologists can educate the court about the various forms that racism takes. This information is crucial in addressing questions of intentionality and in exploring and explaining the factors that are inherent in racially hostile environments. An abundance of scientific studies within the disciplines of psychology and sociology have demonstrated various mechanisms, forms, and consequences of racism, prejudice, and stereotyping. The subtleties of modern racism have been captured (e.g., Bonilla-Silva, 1997; Bonilla-Silva & Forman, 2000; Dovidio, 2001, Dovidio et al., 2002; Feagin, 2001; Gaertner & Dovidio, 1986; Jones, 1997; McConahay, 1986) as well as the unintentional and unconscious forms of prejudice (e.g., Greenwald & Banaji, 1995).

As a society and in the legal system, we moved abruptly yet subtly from recognizing racism to being blind to it. We went from seeing and acknowledging racism in its most overt and dominative forms (Jones, 1997), such as segregation, overt and intentional discrimination, lynchings, the KKK, and the like, to not seeing and not acknowledging the more subtle, persistent, aversive (Jones, 1997), and more modern forms of racism, which have been hidden or denied through illusions of integration and the endorsement of egalitarian beliefs. Speaking to the controversial issue of discrimination within the criminal justice system, Alfieri (see Chapter 5 of this book) addresses the importance of revealing and understanding the less-than-overt forms of racism: "Limiting racialized narrative to intentional discrimination cabins the regulatory ambit of ethics rules to conscious bias and prejudice, leaving unconscious forms of prosecutorial bias and prejudice safely beyond the reach of bar supervision and court sanction" (p. 67, this volume).

Again, in the courts, as in society at large, the inability to distinguish between the various forms of racism, old and new, compounded with the refusal to acknowledge and understand the evolutionary course that racism has taken, has led to an increasing perception gap between whites and people of color as to the existence and severity of racism today (Bonilla-Silva & Forman, 2000; Doob, 1999; Gilliam, 2002; Jones, 1997; Pinkney, 2000; Steinhorn & Diggs-Brown, 2000). Several emerging instruments and studies pave the way for documenting the realities and consequences of prejudice and discrimination in the daily life of American minorities (e.g., Clark, Anderson, Clark, & Williams, 1999; Cross, 2002; Essed, 1991; Feagin, 2001; Landrine & Klonoff, 1996; McKown & Weinstein, 2003; U.S. Department of Health and Human Services, 2001).

One way to break down the monolithic duality of is-it-racism-or-is-it-not and to sort out the subtleties that confuse and cloud the question of intentionality is to educate both jurors and professionals in the legal system about the many facets, faces, and consequences of racism that have been explored and explained by scholars and empirically investigated through the rigors of research. If attorneys are to demonstrate discrimination in the courts or to establish evidence of hostile racial environments, it is necessary to have the terminology, categories, and patterns of racism available for description and documentation in a cohesive, categorical format, along with the empirical research that documents the empirical validity of these patterns and categories. This educative process becomes exceedingly important as we enter the 21st century, as the demographic changes of the coming decades mandate the need for social dialogue and intercultural skills with which to facilitate the development of a cohesive multiracial and multicultural society.

3. Deliberate Attention Versus Deliberate Inattention to Race and the Role of Stereotypes

Psychologists can assist legal professionals through providing the court with racially and culturally conscious narratives that accurately describe the identity of the client across life domains and contexts. Narrative and identity are central themes described by legal scholars in critical race theory (Crenshaw et al., 1995; Delgado, 2001). Alfieri (Chapter 5 in this book) calls attention to the need for an accurate and race-conscious representation of the identities of defendants and victims, as well as of the collective identities of their families and communities. According to Alfieri, in race trials, this representation of identity must be inclusive of descriptions of "racial identity, racialized narrative, and color-conscious advocacy." Without a direct and deliberate race-conscious representation, the colorblind objectives of "impartiality" contained within the concepts of race neutrality are met on the surface by a primary, direct avoidance of racial discourse in criminal justice cases. This avoidance leaves jurors, legal professionals, experts, witnesses, and so on ill equipped for grappling constructively with racial matters. Instead they are open to creating and responding to racialized "color-coded" messages and meanings at a secondary indirect level—"a racial identity molded by legal agents and litigation, and further, declared as truth" (Alfieri, Chapter 5, this book).

Given the nature of racial discourse in American culture, which is ill informed and grounded in myth and stereotype, this indirect casting of identity is potentially fraught with bias and prejudice, both conscious and unconscious. Clinicians trained in cross-cultural competence are able to identify and describe societal stereotypes as they are applied to minority groups in various settings, including legal discourse and testimony and psychological evaluations. Once revealed for what they are, and how they may be misused in a legal case, a skilled evaluator then replaces the stereotype with accurate information about the character and personality of the individual involved.

An example of the identification of stereotypes in a psychological evaluation can be found in a psychological report that was presented to the court in a custody contest involving a white American father and a mother who was an immigrant from Southeast Asia. In gathering data for his report as part of making a determination about the placement and parenting plan for the couple's 7-year-old daughter, the evaluating psychiatrist spent several hours talking with the father and only about 2 hours with the mother because of his "difficulties in communicating" with her. In the report, the woman, who was in her mid-thirties, was described as being young, uneducated, from a "poor village," and the daughter of a farmer. The psychiatrist noted her physical beauty and made two negative comments in the body of his report, including that she had worn skirts that were above her knee to the evaluation. He noted that her style of dress was inappropriate for a play session with her daughter. He described her as looking younger than her years, also in a disparaging tone. In reality, the woman had been educated in top private schools, and had received a master's degree in business administration. Her father was the mayor of a midsized but rural town. He owned many properties and a great deal of land, some of which he sublet to farmers. In addition, even though the young woman had only lived in the United States for about 7 years, she had started and owned two successful businesses. Her manner of dress was tasteful and expensive. Although her skirts were "above the knee," they were part of a very tailored business ensemble (skirt, vest, jacket). In writing the report, the psychiatrist had crafted an image of a young, poor, uneducated, but sexually attractive and provocative Asian girl. The stereotype most known for this image is the one of "Suzy Wong." The evaluator also criticized the mother for leaving her child in a "communal setting" rather than in a daycare center when she was at work. In fact, the child was in an excellent private school, and at times was cared for by her mother's sisters in their homes along with her young cousins while her mother was at work.

When questioned in court about his gross inaccuracies and misrepresentations of this highly professional and competent mother, the psychiatrist admitted that he was drawing his own conclusions without the benefit of having gathered information from the client. He, however, did not seem to be remorseful or apologetic about describing the client with the use of his own biases and stereotypes about Asian women and culture. A second, culturally comprehensive evaluation portrayed an accurate representation of the client and provided the court with a critique of the other parenting evaluation that revealed numerous stereotypes and signs of cultural bias that appeared in the psychiatrist's report and that were inherent in the process of his evaluation.

Psychologists have also documented the impact of stereotypes on perceptions, cognitive structures, information processing, and behavior as related to prejudice and discrimination (see Jones, 1997). The impact of stereotypes on unconscious processes reveals that there are aspects of prejudice and discriminatory actions that may take place beyond the conscious knowledge of the individual who harbors the stereotypes (Greenwald & Banaji, 1995). Stereotypes can lead to societal impressions regarding the violent behavior of blacks (Cross, 2003). They play an important role in the identification of criminal suspects and, most recently, in judgments about whether or not African American individuals are mistakenly identified as carrying a gun (Greenwald, Oakes, & Hoffman, 2003). The consequences of being stereotyped as a racial or ethnic minority have also been demonstrated, particularly in regard to *stereotype threat* and its impact on academic performance (Steele, Spencer, & Aronson, 2002) and in regard to children's awareness of being a member of a stigmatized group (McKown & Weinstein, 2003), even as early as elementary school. Psychologists can provide the courts with education regarding the power and complexity of stereotypes in contemporary society, as they are applied to the case at hand.

A major tool of the clinical psychologist, often used in legal settings, is the psychological evaluation. Through interviewing and assessment the psychologist gathers data with which to construct a story or narrative about the life and background of the client across the domains of development, from prenatal life through adulthood. The narrative includes the influences of biology, personality, and temperament, including interactions with family, peers, and community; educational and training experiences; occupational endeavors; culture; spirituality; and personal talents and interests.

The psychologist who is cognizant of the importance of race, ethnicity, and culture as critical factors in assessment, evaluation, and reporting may utilize principles from the American Psychological Association's (APA's) "Guidelines for Providers of Psychological Services to Ethnic, Linguistic, and Culturally Diverse Populations" (1993). These guidelines instruct psychologists to consider race, ethnicity, and culture as significant parameters in understanding psychological processes. The roles of family and community and cultural and religious beliefs and the adverse impact of sociocultural and political marginalization and discrimination are also key aspects of the assessment process according to the APA guidelines. Culturally comprehensive evaluations debunk stereotypes and provide a more "humanized" view of clients as they live their lives in the context of family and community.

Information that is gathered about clients through the use of contemporary models of racial, ethnic, and cultural identity (Cross, 1995; Helms, 1995, LaFramboise, Hardin, & Gerton, 1998; Leadbeater & Way, 1996; Phinney, 1998; Root, 1996, 1998; Sue & Sue, 2003; Thompson & Carter, 1997) can be incorporated into the psychological evaluation and in the presentation of narratives that describe the client in question. Discussion of racial identity helps to illustrate the role that race, culture, and ethnicity play in regard to how the individual develops a view of self within the context of a multiethnic/multiracial society, including explaining the degree of efficacy and success with which the individual moves about in both mainstream and minority group cultures in various social and occupational settings.

4. Deliberate Consideration of Racial Identity

There is a large and growing literature on racial identity. Racial identity refers to "a sense of group or collective identity based on one's perception that he or she shares a common heritage with a particular racial group" (Helms, 1990, p. 3). Thus identity is linked with a sense of belonging to one's own group, as well as being influenced by a sense of being included or excluded by other groups in society. Berry (1998) discusses the costs and consequences of social marginalization for minority individuals who lack a sense of belonging to their own racial group, as well as to mainstream society. His model helps to explain the stresses of assimilation and acculturation for immigrants and minorities, associating psychological, social, and cultural marginalization with potential pathways to deviance. It is a model that is useful in illuminating risk factors for juvenile delinquency and understanding pathways to deviance

for minority individuals who are disassociated from positive social influences.

Understanding the tasks inherent in the identity development of minority individuals presents a vivid picture of the challenges faced by immigrants and people of color as they struggle to find their place in mainstream society: "The closer one comes to resolving the moral dilemmas associated with race, the nearer one comes to achieving a fuller, integrated identity" (Thompson & Carter, 1997, p. 2).

The presentation of a racially and culturally comprehensive evaluation in the courts can provide the case with a life story of the client that is portrayed with contextual accuracy and complexity, documenting mental health problems or aversive life circumstances while also utilizing empirical research as it applies to developmental pathways, diagnosis, and prognosis. Such an evaluation includes the role played by race and culture in the life of the individual and as applied to the particulars of the case. A brief example is an evaluation of a young Latino immigrant facing deportation for juvenile gang-related charges.

Carlos was 19 years old, raised in a rural agricultural area of Washington State by parents who worked in the fields as farmworkers. He was a minority in the public schools and did well academically until the 6th grade, when discrimination from peers and teachers began to take a toll. His father suffered an injury on the job, which led to chronic pain and irregular work patterns, after which he began to drink heavily, behaving abusively to his family. His father, who had become a U.S. citizen, did not assist his wife or children with the residency process, and they thus remained undocumented, even though they were eligible for legal status. When Carlos reached the age of 14, he became involved with a gang, which helped him to gain a sense of his identity and belonging as a Latino youth within the white community that had rejected him. The affiliation also helped him to ward off frequent physical and verbal attacks from his white peers. Carlos described a great deal of caring and mutual support that took place among the youth that he spent time with. Although he later regretted the illegal nature of their activities, he stated that his gang friends had helped him to cope with his problems at home and at school.

Carlos had been arrested as a juvenile on three occasions for fighting. Despite his gang activity, he was the primary caregiver for his younger siblings while his mother worked, often skipping school in order to care for them. He revered his mother and became her protector when his father was drinking. When he was 18, Carlos was caught in an immigration raid and quickly deported to Mexico, even though he was eligible for legal remedies that would have prevented his deportation. He returned to the United States within a week of his deportation and was once again arrested. He spent a year in prison for violation of deportation before he was able to gain competent legal help. When asked about the most difficult aspects of life in prison, he reported that he had felt a great deal of anguish about how his mother and siblings were coping without him, because they had become so reliant on his care and support.

Carlos should not have been deported because of eligibility circumstances. He was eligible for status as a legal resident because his abusive father had refused to document his children. However, the Immigration and Naturalization Service (INS) still sought to deport Carlos because of his previous juvenile charges.

The evaluation of Carlos was presented before the judge. Carlos had received a diagnosis of post-traumatic stress disorder (PTSD) due to symptoms suffered following physical abuse by his father and due to witnessing domestic violence in the home. The racial and cultural contexts of his life were presented in a developmental trajectory, outlining the risk and protective factors in his childhood. Also documented and presented were the developmental pathways described in the psychological research that were predictive of gang involvement for youth like Carlos, including the "positive" or adaptive aspects of joining an ethnically based youth gang for a child who faced being marginalized and discriminated against as a member of a child of Mexican American farmworkers. Critical to the description of Carlos as a person was a discussion of his identity struggles as a member of a racial and cultural minority in a hostile community environment. Another aspect of his life that was connected to culture was a portrayal of Carlos as a youth who observed traditional Mexican family values and norms that led him to care for his mother and siblings at a cost to his own education. Carlos had sought support and counseling on occasion with his local Catholic priest, who also served as a collateral contact who could describe the community environment and Carlos's prosocial behavior.

Without a race-conscious, culturally comprehensive narrative about his life as part of the evaluation, Carlos would have fallen prey to stereotypes of his identity as a gang member. Structured interviewing did not reveal developmental signs or symptoms of conduct disorder or any antisocial tendencies. Carlos had grown up with many risk factors for gang involvement. However, these risk factors were environmental rather than endogenous. In the view of the INS, he was an immoral person, of poor character, and a danger to the community. However, in light of the evaluation, Carlos became a youth who had lived through difficult circumstances, rather than a teenage hoodlum out of *West Side Story*. His deportation was canceled, he was referred for psychotherapy, and he is currently a college student who hopes to become a teacher.

5. Deliberate Attention to Whiteness

Critical race theorists have also called attention to whiteness (Feagin et al., 2001; Frankenberg, 1997; Harris, 1995) in terms of white racial privilege and dominance, whiteness as property, and whiteness as national identity. The perceptions that whites bring to the justice system in regard to minorities are a product of their racial socialization experiences and how they integrate, make sense of, and incorporate these experiences in their cognitions, judgments, and behavior toward minority groups and individuals. Scholars have known for years that racialized images permeate society and penetrate minds, such that most whites experience their perceptions and judgments of nonwhites as completely factual rather than as they truly are—by-products of widespread prejudice.

However, because whites often lack a conscious awareness of the role that being white plays in their lives, they are often oblivious to the impact of their own thoughts and behavior on the collective racial atmosphere of the society (Greenwald, Rudman, Farnham, Nosek, & Mellot, 2002). They are also likely not aware of how their own biases and stereotypes influence their perceptions and judgments in regard to racial stimuli. This lack of awareness contributes to the overall atmosphere of confusion about race. Confusion about the role one plays in race relations can be seen in massive contemporary efforts by whites to prove that "I am not a racist!" (Bonilla-Silva & Forman, 2000). This defensiveness lies close to the surface and is easily activated in conversations about race and diversity. A lack of vocabulary, factual information, and understanding of the contemporary racial terrain contributes to unproductive emotions and arguments when problem solving and sound decision making are required. Confusion, misunderstanding, mistrust, and ignorance about the true dynamics of race and racism often lead to feelings of guilt, shame, anger, and defensiveness on the part of whites who commonly feel accused and blamed for historical and present racial injustices. This type of guilt and defensiveness is a major contribution to racial tension and can lead to avoidance of engagement in intellectual and interpersonal endeavors to understand how and why the problems of racism still persist today.

Whites vary in their degree of readiness and ability to understand racism and to interact comfortably with people of diverse backgrounds. Helping whites to understand that racial views are a product of socialization, that they are learned, and that they can be unlearned can lead to more productive interactions and decision making in matters associated with race. Reducing the mystery and mythology that surrounds contemporary racism and educating whites about the various forms and mechanisms involved in creating a racist society can lead to a framework for taking responsibility for understanding and reducing racism (Tatum, 1997) rather than becoming stuck in a quagmire that leads to a vicious cycle of "white guilt," shame, and backlash.

6. White Racial Identity

In order to help white professionals and laypersons involved with the judicial system better grasp the meaning of whiteness in American culture, the theories and research of a number of psychologists (Feagin & O'Brien, 2003; Helms, 1995; Kivel, 1995; Rowe, Bennett, & Atkinson,

1994; Tatum, 1997; Thompson & Carter, 1997) can illuminate the impact and outcomes of racial socialization processes as they are manifested in particular forms of racial consciousness and racial behaviors in white individuals. Models of white racial identity development explore the various forms and levels of awareness held by whites in regard to how they view themselves and others through the lens of race. In racial identity models, race is examined as a primary feature of social life and culture and is seen as a central feature of identity.

> Race can take on different meanings to different people, but a "system of racial meanings stereotypes of racial ideology (exists and) seems to be a permanent feature of U.S. culture" (Omi & Winant, 1986, p. 7). Through racial socialization, individuals are imbued with messages that determine the appropriateness or inappropriateness of their roles as racial beings. (Thompson & Carter, 1997, p. xv)

In the model developed by Helms (perhaps the most well-known of the white identity models), one is found to be at a specific status of awareness regarding the racial self and others, due to differential racial socialization experiences and one's reactions to that socialization, plus the "ongoing management of racial stimuli within oneself" (Helms, 1995, p. 183). One important use of the concepts inherent in white racial identity models is in examining how one's level of racial awareness impacts one's response to racial stimuli. For example, for people who are quite unaware of racism or of the dynamics of white privilege and power, a story about white police brutality toward a person of color might be met with disbelief, defensiveness, or with the thought that somehow the person of color had lied about the story. Another alternative would be to consider that the police had acted in self-defense. A person with a high degree of awareness about racism, and who does not feel threatened as a white person discussing the racism of other whites, would likely be aware of statistics about police brutality and racial disparities in our legal system (see Farley, 2000; Feagin, 2001; Human Rights Watch, 2002, 2003). Such a person would be able to comfortably discuss issues of racial injustice and perhaps how whites could help to reduce racial abuses in law enforcement in their own community.

Helms's model begins with three statuses (contact, disintegration, and reintegration). The first level, contact, finds white individuals to be (perhaps selectively) unaware of their position of privilege or power in their country, viewing nonwhites as "different, other, or exotic" (Thompson & Carter, 1997). People at the contact status are naive about the realities of racial inequality and are comfortable with the racial status quo. When a white person becomes more consciously aware of racial inequalities, he or she is likely to become aware of the role of whites in bringing about racial oppression and disparities. This leads to confusion, dissonance, and ambivalent feelings about being part of the white racial group, or disintegration. For a time, the disintegration status person may become outspoken and active against racism, seeking friendships with people of color. However, if the white individual encounters mistrust from people of color and is questioned about his or her motives or genuineness, or if one is criticized or rejected by friends, family, and other whites for one's new views or associations with people of color, then one may choose to retreat back into the white community. Once back into the fold of whiteness, or reintegration, the need to rationalize racial inequalities leads to blaming minorities for their own misfortunes and to an endorsement of selective stereotypes about people of color. Whites are seen as deserving of the privileges and benefits accrued to them in society as the dominant group. Reintegration status whites may seek friendships with people of color who also have conservative, critical views of minorities (a la Shelby Steele, Dinesh D'Souza, or Ward Connerly), which helps to affirm the stereotypes or prejudice of whites. Whites who have retreated back into the white community also may become very avoidant of contact with minorities. In the extreme, whites in the reintegration status may be highly protective of white privilege, resulting in more active forms of discrimination or aggression.

The three advanced statuses in Helms's model represent more mature and thoughtful views of race (pseudo-independent, immersion-emersion, and autonomy) and involve increased efforts to understand and come to terms with racism and with what it means to be white in a racist society. For these more advanced levels of consciousness and understanding to occur, Helms and others posit requisite dissonance experiences or events (Rowe et al., 1994), which shatter or shake up one's worldview and feelings about self: "Maturation is triggered by a combination of cognitive-affective complexity within the individual and race-related environmental stimuli" (Helms, 1995, p. 184). Such events might involve witnessing racial violence, becoming involved with a romantic partner of color, developing a close friendship with someone of color, taking a class, or undergoing a training experience. In our teaching experiences, we have found that white college students who were at the more "advanced" status levels had become very aware of racism as a result of watching and listening to parents who stereotyped and disparaged people of color and/ or who were patently hypocritical by teaching "egalitarian" values to their children and then contradicting those values through forbidding interracial dating and other social taboos. The dissonance created by this experience with parents (or sometimes grandparents) led the young person to seek educational experiences, which helped to explain racist behavior.

As white individuals move forward in self-awareness and in their understanding of racism, they become more aware of their position of social and cultural control and privileges as members of the dominant group. They also gain knowledge about the mechanisms and elements of white racism on individual, institutional, and cultural levels. At first, they may try to stop racism by "helping" people of color to do better in mainstream culture, until they realize that this is actually perpetuating white standards and cultural dominance (pseudo-independence). They may also be stricken with emotions of sadness and guilt as they examine the inherent values and tactics of white culture that have led to the exploitation and oppression of people of color. As these values are revealed, white individuals will work toward abandoning the negative aspects of whiteness and notions of white superiority. They strive to learn more about the mechanisms of racism while combating racism in their environment (immersion-emersion). A further examination of their own identity may lead to a search for lost ethnic roots and a realization that they are also part of a racial group, rather than being without classification, or "just normal" (see Tatum, 1997). In the autonomy status, there is no longer need for guilt, and there is a solid sense of self as a white individual, and perhaps ethnic identity has been established. The person seeks opportunities for increased awareness about racism, race, and culture; is comfortable with people of diverse backgrounds; and works toward eliminating racism in society.

Psychological theories, research, and models that explore white racial identity and whiteness are useful in a number of settings, particularly in regard to professional training that addresses work with diverse populations (Sue & Sue, 2003). Identity models help students and professionals involved in continuing education to develop a better understanding about the sources and influences of their own racial socialization and how that socialization has culminated in a particular form of cognitions and behaviors in regard to individuals and groups other than their own. These models also help whites to better understand their position of power and privilege in society and to realize that they as a group are not beyond classification—they too have ethnic roots and a racial identity that has been influenced and formed as a result of living in a highly racialized society.

The professional who has a solid understanding of racial identity can more skillfully identify, understand, and interact with individuals and professionals who behave in a racist manner, or who respond to racial material through their own particular lens of racial identity. The psychological study of whiteness sets forth goals and directions for whites, providing guidance as to how one might (with time, social interaction, and study) reverse the negative influences of racism in one's own life, develop ways of interacting sensitively and competently in a multicultural society, and work toward combating racism in the community and in the lives of one's clients.

CONCLUSIONS

The Supreme Court cited the work and testimony of psychologists and other social scientists, including the social psychologist Dr. Kenneth Clark, in determining that segregation had a "detrimental effect on colored children" in Brown v. Board of Education, when it struck down the separate but equal doctrine from Plessy v. Ferguson. A panel of three judges was also presented with psychological testimony regarding the school environment of African American children in *Briggs v. Elliot.* Historically, with this work and the pioneering studies of prejudice put forth by Dr. Gordon Allport, psychologists have had a profound impact on providing perspectives on how racism can destroy equality, opportunity, and justice in this nation.

In contemporary society, the work of psychologists must be directed toward a continued effort to overturn the myths and fallacies that are raised when the principles of racial equality, objectivity, and neutrality are co-opted by those who—as in *Plessy v. Ferguson*—use constitutional philosophy to mask racist practices. We can continue to look to the field of psychology and many of the authors who have contributed to this book to help us expose and explain the contemporary manifestations of racism and to help us to continue to put up the good fight in promoting the development of a society where race, ethnicity, and culture are recognized, understood, and honored.

REFERENCES

Alexander v. Sandoval, 532 U.S. 275 (2001).

American Psychological Association. (1993). Guidelines for providers of psychological services to ethnic, linguistic, and culturally diverse populations. *American Psychologist, 48,* 45–48.

Banks, R. (1999). *Cloudsplitter.* New York: Harper Collins.

Berry, J. W. (1998) Acculturative stress. In P. O. Organista, K. M. Chun, & G. Marin (Eds.), *Readings in ethnicity psychology* (pp. 117–122). New York: Routledge.

Bonilla-Silva, E. (1997). Rethinking racism: Toward a structural interpretation. *American Sociological Review, 62*(3), 465–480.

Bonilla-Silva, E., & Forman, T. A. (2000). "I am not a racist but . . .": Mapping white college students' racial ideology in the USA. *Discourse and Society, 1,* 50–85.

Clark, R., Anderson, N. B., Clark, V. R., & Williams, D. R. (1999). Racism as a stressor for African Americans. *American Psychologist, 54,* 805–816.

Cohen, J. J. (2003). Disparities in health care: An overview. *Academic Emergency Medicine, 10,* 1155–1160.

Crenshaw, K., Gotanda, N., Peller, G., & Thomas, K. (Eds.). (1995). *Critical race theory: The key writings that formed the movement.* New York: New Press.

Cross, W. E., Jr. (1995). The psychology of nigrescence: Revising the Cross model. In J. G. Ponterotto, J. M. Casas, L. A. Suzuki, & C. M. Alexander (Eds.), *Handbook of multicultural counseling* (pp. 93–122). Thousand Oaks, CA: Sage Publications.

Cross, W. E. (2002, August). *The psychology of buffering in black children.* Paper presented at the meeting of the American Psychological Association, Chicago, IL.

Cross, W. E., Jr. (2003). Tracing the historical origins of youth delinquency and violence: Myths and realities about black culture. *Journal of Social Issues, 59*(1), 67–82.

Delgado, R., & Stefancic, J. (2001). *Critical race theory.* New York: New York University Press.

DeMunhiz, P. (1999). Introduction. In J. Moore (Ed.), *Immigrants in courts.* Seattle: University of Washington Press.

Dolliver, J. M. (1999). Foreword. In J. Moore (Ed.), *Immigrants in courts.* Seattle: University of Washington Press.

Doob, C. B. (1999). *Racism: An American caldron* (2nd ed.). New York: Addison Wesley Longman.

Dovidio, J. F. (2001). On the nature of contemporary prejudice: The third wave. *Journal of Social Issues, 57*(4), 829–849.

Dovidio, J. F., Gaertner, S. E., Kawakami, K., & Hodson, G. (2002). Why can't we just get along? Interpersonal biases and interracial distrust. *Cultural Diversity and Ethnic Minority Psychology, 8*(2), 88–102.

Essed, P. (1991). *Understanding everyday racism: An interdisciplinary theory.* Newbury Park, CA: Sage Publications.

Farley, J. E. (2000). *Majority-minority relations.* Upper Saddle River, NJ: Prentice Hall.

Feagin, J. R. (2001). *Racist America.* New York: Routledge.

Feagin, J. R., & Feagin, C. B. (2003). *Racial and ethnic relations.* Upper Saddle River, NJ: Prentice Hall.

Feagin, J. R., & O'Brien, E. (2003). *White men on race.* Boston: Beacon Press.

Feagin, J. R., Vera, H., & Batur, P. (2001). *White racism: The basics* (2nd ed.). New York: Routledge.

Frankenberg, R. (1997). *Displacing whiteness: Essays in social and cultural criticism.* Durham, NC: Duke University Press.

Gaertner, S. L., & Dovidio, J. F. (1986). The aversive form of racism. In J. F. Dovidio & S. L. Gaertner (Eds.), *Prejudice, discrimination, and racism* (pp. 61–91). Orlando, FL: Academic Press.

Gilliam, F. D. (2002). *Farther to go: Readings and cases in African-American politics.* Orlando, FL: Harcourt.

Goodrich, P., & Mills, L. G. (2001). The law of white spaces. *Journal of Legal Education, 51*(1), 15–38.

Greenwald, A. G., & Banaji, M. R. (1995). Implicit social cognition: Attitudes, self esteem, and stereotypes. *Psychological Review, 102,* 4–27.

Greenwald, A. G., Oakes, M. A., & Hoffman, H. G. (2003). Targets of discrimination: Effects of race on responses to weapons holders. *Journal of Experimental Social Psychology, 39,* 399–405.

Greenwald, A. G., Rudman, M. R., Farnham, L. A., Nosek, S. D., & Mellot, D. S. (2002). A unified theory of implicit attitudes, stereotypes, self-esteem, and self concept. *Psychological Review, 10*(1), 3–25.

Griffin, W. L. (1999). Race, law, and culture: A call to new thinking, leadership, and action. *University of Arkansas at Little Rock Law Review, 21,* 901–926.

Harris, C. I. (1995). Whiteness as property. In K. Crenshaw, N. Gotanda, G. Peller, & K. Thomas (Eds.), *Critical race theory: The key writings that formed the movement.* New York: New Press.

Helms, J. (1990). *Black and white racial identity: Theory, research, and practice.* New York: Greenwood Press.

Helms, J. (1995). An update of Helms's white and people of color racial identity models. In G. Ponterotto, J. M. Casas, L. A. Suzuki, & C. M. Alexander (Eds.), *Handbook of multicultural counseling* (pp. 181–198). Thousand Oaks, CA: Sage Publications.

Human Rights Watch. (2002, February 27). Race and incarceration in the United States. *Human Rights Watch Briefing.*

Human Rights Watch. (2003, April). Incarcerated America. *Human Rights Watch Backgrounder.*

Jones, J. (1997). *Prejudice and racism.* New York: McGraw-Hill.

Kivel, P. (1995). *Uprooting racism: How white people can work for racial justice.* Gabriola Island, BC: New Society Publishers.

LaFramboise, T., Hardin, L. K., & Gerton, J. (1998). Psychological impact of biculturalism: Evidence and theory. In P. B. Organista, K. M. Chun, & G. Marin (Eds.), *Readings in ethnic psychology* (pp. 123–156). New York. Routledge.

Landrine, H., & Klonoff, E. A. (1996). The schedule of racist events: A measure of racial discrimination and a study of its negative physical and mental health consequences. *Journal of Black Psychology, 22*(2), 144–168.

Leadbeater, B. J., & Way, N. (Eds.). (1996). *Urban girls: Resisting stereotypes, creating identities.* New York: New York University Press.

Markus, H. R., Steele, C. M., & Steele, D. M. (2002). Color blindness as a barrier to inclusion: Assimilation and non immigrant minorities. In R. A. Scweder & M. Minow (Eds.), *Engaging cultural differences: The multicultural challenge in liberal democracies* (pp. 453–472). New York: Russell Sage Foundation.

McConahay, J. B. (1986). Modern racism, ambivalence, and the modern racism scale. In J. F. Dovidio & S. Gaertner (Eds.), *Prejudice, discrimination, and racism* (pp. 91–126). Orlando, FL: Academic Press.

McKown, C., & Weinstein, R. S. (2003). The development and consequences of stereotype consciousness in middle childhood. *Child Development, 74,* 498–515.

Moore, J. (Ed.). (1999). *Immigrants in courts.* Seattle: University of Washington Press.

Omi, M., & Winant, H. (1986). *Racial formation in the United States from the 1960s to the 1980s.* New York: Routledge & Kegan Paul.

Parker, F. (1996). The damaging consequences of the Rehnquist courts commitment to color blindness versus racial justice. *American University Law Review, 45*(3), 763–773.

Phinney, J. (1998). Ethnic identity in adolescents and adults. In P. B. Organista, K. M. Chun, & G. Marin (Eds.), *Readings in ethnic psychology* (pp. 73–99). New York: Routledge.

Pinkney, A. (2000). *Black Americans.* Upper Saddle River, NJ: Prentice Hall.

Plessy v. Ferguson, 163 U.S. 537 (1896).

Ren, X. S., Amick, B. C., & Williams, D. R. (1997). Racial/ethnic disparities in health: The interplay between discrimination and socioeconomic status. *Ethnicity and Disease, 9,* 151–165.

Root, M. P. (Ed.). (1996). *Multiracial experience: Racial experience as the new frontier.* Thousand Oaks, CA: Sage Publications.

Root, M. P. (1998). Resolving "other" status: Identity development of biracial individuals. In P. B. Organista, K. M. Chun, & G. Marin (Eds.), *Readings in ethnic psychology* (pp. 100–112). New York: Routledge.

Rowe, W., Bennett, S., & Atkinson, D. R. (1994). White racial identity models: A critique and alternative proposal. *The Counseling Psychologist, 22,* 120–146.

Scott v. Sandford, 60 U.S. 393 (1856).

Smedley, B. D., Stith, A. Y., & Nelson, A. R. (Eds.). (2002). *Unequal treatment: Confronting racial and ethnic disparities in health care.* Washington, DC: Institute of Medicine, National Academy Press.

Steele, C. M., Spencer, S. J., & Aronson, J. (2002). Contending with group image: The psychology of stereotype and social identity threat. In M. P. Zanna (Ed.), *Advances in experimental social psychology* (Vol. 34, pp. 379–440). San Diego: Academic Press.

Steinhorn, L., & Diggs-Brown, B. (2000). *By the color of our skin: The illusion of integration and the reality of race.* New York: Plume.

Sue, D. W., & Sue, D. (2003). *Counseling the culturally diverse.* New York: John Wiley & Sons.

Sue, S., & Zane, N. (1987). The role of culture and cultural techniques in psychotherapy. *American Psychologist, 42,* 37–45.

Tatum, B. D. (1997). *"Why are all the black kids sitting together in the cafeteria?" And other conversations about race.* New York: Basic Books.

Thompson, C. E., & Carter, R. T. (1997). *Racial identity theory.* Mahwah, NJ: Lawrence Erlbaum Associates.

U.S. Department of Health and Human Services. (2001). *Mental health: Culture, race, and Ethnicity—A supplement to mental health: A report to the surgeon general.* Rockville, MD: U.S. DHHS, Office of the Surgeon General.

West, C. (1999). *The Cornell West reader.* New York: Basics Civitas Books.

Winant, H. (1994). *Racial conditions.* Minneapolis: University of Minnesota Press.

Wu, F. (1996). Changing America: Three arguments about Asian Americans and the law. *American University Law Review, 45,* 811–822.

4

FIVE HABITS FOR CROSS-CULTURAL LAWYERING[1]

SUE BRYANT

CUNY School of Law

JEAN KOH PETERS

Yale Law School

Practicing law is often a cross-cultural experience. The law, as well as the legal system in which it operates, is a culture with strong professional norms that give meaning to and reinforce behaviors. The communication style of argument predominates, and competition is highly valued. Even when a lawyer and a non-law-trained client share a common culture, the client and the lawyer will likely experience the lawyer–client interaction as a cross-cultural experience because of the cultural differences that arise from the legal culture.

In addition to these cultural differences, we know that the global movement of people, as well as the multicultural nature of the United States, creates many situations where lawyers and clients will work in cross-cultural situations. To meet the challenges of cross-cultural representation, lawyers need to develop awareness, knowledge, and skills that enhance the lawyers' and clients' capacities to form meaningful relationships and to communicate accurately.

This chapter, and the habits it introduces, prepares lawyers to engage in effective, accurate cross-cultural communication and to build trust and understanding between themselves and their clients. Section 1 identifies some ways that culture influences lawyering and the potential issues that may arise in cross-cultural lawyer–client interactions. Section 2 identifies the principles and habits that are skills and perspectives that can be used to identify our own cultural norms and those of our clients and to communicate effectively, knowing these differences. As one anthropologist has recognized, there is "a great distance between knowing that my gaze transforms and becoming aware of the ways that my gaze transforms."[2] To help lawyers identify the ways their gaze transforms and the cultural bridges that are needed for joint work between lawyers and clients, we have developed five habits for cross-cultural lawyering.

CULTURE AND THE ROLE IT PLAYS IN LAWYERS' WORK

To become good cross-cultural lawyers, we must first become aware of the significance of culture in the ways in which we make sense out of the world. Culture is like the air we breathe; it is largely invisible, and yet we are dependent on it for our very being. Culture is the logic through which we give meaning to the world.[3] Our culture is learned from our experiences, sights, books, songs, language, gestures, rewards, punishments, and relationships that come to us in our homes, schools, religious organizations, and communities.[4] We learn our culture from what we are fed and how we are touched and judged by our families and significant others in our communities. Our culture gives us our values, attitudes, and norms of behavior.

Through our cultural lens, we make judgments about people based on what they are doing and saying. We may judge people to be truthful, rude, intelligent, or superstitious based on the attributions we make about the meaning of their behavior. Because culture gives us the tools to interpret meaning from behavior and words, we are constantly attaching culturally based meaning to what we see and hear, often without being aware that we are doing so.[5]

In this chapter, when we talk about cross-cultural lawyering, we are referring to lawyering where the lawyer's and the client's ethnic or cultural heritage comes from different countries, as well as where their cultural heritage comes from socialization and identity in different groups within the same country. By this definition, everyone is multicultural to some degree.[6] Cultural groups and cultural norms can be based on ethnicity, race, gender, nationality, age, economic status, social status, language, sexual orientation, physical characteristics, marital status, role in family, birth order, immigration status, religion, accent, skin color, or a variety of other characteristics.

This broad definition of culture is essential for effective cross-cultural lawyering because it teaches us that no one characteristic will completely define the lawyer's or the client's culture.[7] For example, if we think about birth order alone as a cultural characteristic, we may not see any significance to this factor. Yet if the client (or lawyer) comes from a society where "oldest son" has special meaning in terms of responsibility and privilege, identification of the ethnicity, gender, or birth order alone will not be enough to alert the lawyer to the set of norms and expectations for how the oldest son ought to behave. Instead, the lawyer needs to appreciate the significance of all three characteristics to fully understand this aspect of the client's culture.

A broad definition of culture recognizes that no two people have had the exact same experiences and thus no two people will interpret or predict in precisely the same ways. People can be part of the same culture and make different decisions while rejecting norms and values from their culture. Understanding that culture develops shared meaning and, at the same time, allows for significant differences helps us to avoid stereotyping or assuming that we know that which we have not explored with the client. At the same time that we recognize these individual differences, we also know that if we share a common cultural heritage with a client, we are often better able to predict or interpret, and our mistakes are likely to be smaller misunderstandings.

When lawyers and clients come from different cultures, several aspects of the attorney–client interaction may be implicated. The capacities to form trusting relationships, to evaluate credibility, to develop client-centered case strategies and solutions, to gather information, and to attribute the intended meaning from behavior and expressions are all affected by cultural experiences. By using the framework of cross-cultural interaction, lawyers can learn to anticipate and name some of the difficulties they or their clients may be experiencing. By asking ourselves as part of the cross-cultural analysis to identify ways in which we are similar to clients, we identify the strengths of connection. Focusing on similarities also alerts us to pay special attention when we see ourselves as "the same" as the client so that we do not substitute our own judgment for the client's through overidentification and transference.

Establishing Trust

Lawyers and clients who do not share the same culture face special challenges in developing a trusting relationship where genuine, accurate communication occurs. Especially where the culture of the client is one with a significant distrust of outsiders[8] or of the particular culture of the lawyer, the lawyer must work hard to earn trust in a culturally sensitive way. Similarly, cultural difference may cause the lawyer to mistrust the client. For example, when we find the client's story changing or new information coming to light as we investigate, we may experience the client as "lying" or "being unhelpful." Often this causes us to feel betrayed by our client's sanctions.

Sometimes when a client is reacting negatively to a lawyer or a lawyer's suggestions, lawyers label clients as "difficult." Professor Michelle Jacobs has warned that white lawyers interpreting clients' behavior may fail to understand the significance of racial differences, thereby erroneously labeling African American clients as "difficult." Instead, the lawyer may be sending signals to the client that reinforce racial stereotypes, may be interpreting behavior incorrectly, and therefore may be unconsciously failing to provide full advocacy.[9]

In these situations, lawyers should assess whether the concept of insider-outsider status helps explain client reactions. Where insider-outsider status is implicated, lawyers must be patient and try to understand the complexities of the relationship and their communication while building trust slowly.

Accurate Understanding

Even in situations where trust is established, lawyers may still experience cultural differences that significantly interfere with lawyers' and clients' capacities to understand one another's goals, behaviors, and communications. Cultural differences often cause us to attribute different meanings to the same set of facts. Thus one important goal of cross-cultural competence is for lawyers to attribute to behavior and communication that which the actor or speaker intends.

Inaccurate attributions can cause lawyers to make significant errors in their representation of clients. Imagine a lawyer saying to a client, "If there is anything that you do not understand, please just ask me to explain" or "If I am not being clear, please just ask me any questions." Many cultural differences may explain a client's reluctance to either blame the lawyer for poor communication (the second question) or blame himself or herself for lack of understanding (the first question). Indeed clients from some cultures might find one or the other of these results to be rude and therefore be reluctant to ask for clarification for fear of offending the lawyer or embarrassing themselves.

Cultural differences may also cause lawyers and clients to misperceive body language and judge each other incorrectly. For an everyday example, take nodding while someone is speaking. In some cultures, the nodding indicates agreement with the speaker, whereas in others it simply indicates that the listener is hearing the speaker. Another common example involves eye contact. In some cultures, looking someone straight in the eye is a statement of open and honest communication, whereas a diversion of eyes signals dishonesty. In other cultures, however, a diversion of eyes is a sign of respect. Lawyers need to recognize these differences and plan for a representation strategy that takes them into account.

Organizing and Assessing Facts

More generally, our concepts of credibility are very culturally determined. In examining the credibility of a story, lawyers and judges often ask whether the story makes "sense" as if "sense" were neutral. Consider, for example, a client who explains that the reason she left her native country was that God appeared to her in a dream and told her it was time to leave. If the time of leaving is a critical element to the credibility of her story, how will the fact finder evaluate the credibility of that client's story? Does the fact finder come from a culture where dreams are valued, where an interventionist God is expected, or where major life decisions would be based on these expectations or values? Will the fact finder, as a result of differences, find the story incredible or evidence of a disturbed thought process or, alternatively, as a result of similarities, find the client credible?

The way different cultures conceptualize facts may cause lawyers and clients to see different information as relevant. Lawyers who experience clients as "wandering all over the place" may be working with clients who categorize information differently than the lawyer or the legal system. If a lawyer whose culture is oriented to hour, day, month, and year tries to get a time line from a client whose culture is not oriented that way, she may incorrectly interpret the client's failure to provide the information as uncooperative, lacking intelligence, or, worse, lying.[10] A client who is unable to tell a linear time-related story may also experience the same reaction from courts and juries if the client's culture is unknown to the fact finders.

Individual and Collective

In other settings, the distinction between individual and collective cultures has been called the most important concept to grasp in cross-cultural encounters.[11] Understanding the differences between individual and collective cultures will help lawyers see how they and clients define problems, identify solutions, and determine who important players are in a decision.[12]

Lawyers who explore differences in individual and collective cultures may see different communication styles, values, and views of the roles of the lawyer and client. In an individualistic culture, people are socialized to have individual goals and are praised for achieving these goals. They are encouraged to make their own plans and "do their own thing."[13] Individualists need to assert themselves and do not find competition threatening. By contrast, in a collective culture, people are socialized to think in terms of the group, to work for the betterment of the group, and to integrate individual and group goals. Collectivists use group membership to predict behavior. Because collectivists are accepted for who they are and feel less need to talk, silence plays a more important role in their communication style.

Majority culture in the United States has been identified as the most individualistic culture in the world.[14] Our legal culture reflects this commitment to individualism. For example, ethical rules of confidentiality often require a lawyer to communicate with an individual client in private if confidentiality is to be maintained and may prohibit the lawyer from representing the group or taking group concerns into account to avoid potential conflicts.[15] Many client-empowerment models and client-centered models of practice are based on individualistic cultural values.

Here is an example of how a result that appeared successful to the lawyers can nevertheless be unacceptable when taken in the context of the client's collective culture. In this case, lawyers negotiated a plea to a misdemeanor assault with probation for a battered Chinese woman who had killed her husband and who faced a 25-year sentence if convicted of murder. The client, who had a strong self-defense claim, refused to plead to the misdemeanor charge because she did not want to humiliate herself, her ancestors, her children, and their children by acknowledging responsibility for the killing. Her attorneys did not fully comprehend the concept of shame that the client would experience until the client was able to explain that the possibility of 25 years in jail was far less offensive than the certain shame that would be experienced by her family (past, present, and future) if she pled guilty. These negative reactions to what the lawyers thought was an excellent result allowed the lawyers to examine the meaning of pleas, family, responsibility, and consequences within a collective cultural context that was far different than their own.[16]

Legal Strategy and Decision Making

In another case, attorneys—whose client was a Somalian refugee seeking political asylum—had to change their strategy for presenting evidence in order to respect the client's cultural and religious norms. Soldiers had bayoneted her when she resisted rape, and she was scarred on a breast and an ankle. To show evidence of persecution, the plaintiff would have had to reveal parts of her body that she was committed, by religion and culture, to keeping private. Ultimately the client developed a strategy of showing the injury to the INS lawyer who was also female.[17] This strategy, challenging conventional legal advocacy and violating cultural norms of the adversarial system, allowed the client to present a case that honored her values and norms.[18]

Immigrant clients often bring with them prior experiences with courts or interactions with governments from their countries of origin that influence the choices they make in their cases. Strategies that worked in their country of origin may not be successful here. For example, clients from cultures that punish those challenging governmental action may be resistant to a lawyer's suggestion that a Supplemental Security Income (SSI) benefits appeal be taken, challenging the government's decision to deny a claim. Conversely, those who come from societies where refusal to follow government requirements is a successful strategy may be labeled as belligerent by the court when they consistently resist or challenge the court.

Finally, cultural differences may cause us to misjudge a client or to provide differential representation based on stereotype or bias. Few lawyers engage in explicit open racial or cultural hostility toward a client. However, if recent studies in the medical field have relevance for lawyers, we need to recognize that even lawyers of goodwill may engage in unconscious stereotyping that results in inferior representation. Studies in the medical field show that doctors are less likely to explain diagnoses to patients of color and less likely to gather significant information from them or to refer them for needed treatment.[19] Although no studies of lawyers to our knowledge have focused on studying whether lawyers engage in discriminatory treatment, two recent studies have identified differential treatment by the legal system based on race. One study done by Child Welfare Watch shows that African American children are far more likely to be removed from their home, put in foster care, and left there longer than similarly situated white children.[20] Another study showed that African American juveniles received disproportionate sentences when compared with similarly situated white youths. In each of these legal studies, lawyers—as prosecutors, representatives, and judges—were deeply implicated in the work that led to the differential treatment.

Once a cultural difference surfaces, we can see stark cultural contrasts with clear connections to lawyering choices. In hindsight, it is easy to see the cultural contrasts and their effect on the clients' and lawyers' challenges to find acceptable accommodations to the legal system. In the moment, however, cases are more difficult, and the differences and similarities are more subtle and, at times, invisible. The following sections give you some insights into how to make this more visible.

Culture-General and Culture-Specific Knowledge

In addition to developing awareness of the role that culture plays in attributing meaning to behaviors and communication, a competent cross-cultural lawyer also studies the specific culture and language of the client group the lawyer represents. Culture-specific knowledge, politics, geography, and history, especially information that might shed light on the client's legal issues, relationship with the lawyer, and process of decision making will assist the lawyer in representing the client better. As the lawyer develops culture-specific knowledge, he or she should apply this knowledge carefully and examine it on a case-by-case basis. Finally, a lawyer will have a greater capacity to build trust and connection if he or she speaks the client's language even if they do not share a common culture.

If the lawyer represents clients from a multitude of cultures, the lawyer can improve cross-cultural interactions by acquiring culture-general knowledge and skills. This culture-general information is also helpful to lawyers who are beginning to learn about a specific culture. Because learning any new culture is a complex endeavor (remember the number of years that we spent learning our own), the lawyer can use culture-general knowledge and skills while learning specifics about a new culture.

HABIT 1: DEGREES OF SEPARATION AND CONNECTION

The first part of Habit 1 encourages lawyers to consciously identify the similarities and differences between their clients and themselves and to assess their impact on the attorney–client relationship. The framework of similarities and differences helps assess lawyer–client interaction, professional distance, and information gathering.

The second part of the habit asks the lawyer to assess the significance of these similarities and differences. By identifying differences, we focus consciously on the possibility that cultural misunderstanding, bias, and stereotyping may occur. By focusing on similarities, we become conscious of the connections that we have with clients as well as the possibility that we may substitute our own judgment for the client's.

Pinpointing and Recording Similarities and Differences

To perform Habit 1, the lawyer brainstorms, as quickly as possible, as many similarities and differences between the client and himself as he can generate. This habit is rewarded for numerosity—the more differences and similarities the better. A typical list of similarities and differences might include the following:

Ethnicity	Economic Status	Marital Status
Race	Social Status	Role in Family
Gender	Language	Immigration Nationality
Sexual Orientation	Religion	Education
Age	Physical Characteristic	Time
Individualistic/ Collective	Direct or Indirect Communication	

With each client and case, you may identify different categories that will influence the case and your relationship. These lists will change as the relationship with the client and the client's case changes. Exhaustive lists help the lawyer make conscious the less obvious similarities and differences that may enhance or interfere with understanding.

Consciously identifying a long list of similarities and differences allows lawyers to see clients as individuals with personal, cultural, and social experiences that shape the clients' behavior and communications. In asking you to create long lists, we do not mean to suggest that all similarities and differences have the same order of importance for you or your client. For example, in interactions involving people of color and whites, race will likely play a significant role in

the interaction given the discriminatory role that race plays in our society.[21] In some cases, such as rape or domestic violence, gender differences may also play a greater role than in others. The connections that cause a lawyer to feel connected to a client may be insignificant to a client.

The most important thing is to make this list honestly and nonjudgmentally, thinking about what similarities and differences you perceive and suspect might affect your ability to hear and understand your client's story and your client's ability to tell it.

Another way to illustrate the degrees of connection and separation between client and lawyer is through the use of a simple Venn diagram. Draw two circles, overlapping broadly if the worlds of the client and of the lawyer largely coincide, or narrowly if they largely diverge. By creating a graphical representation of Habit 1, the lawyer can gain insight into the significance of the similarities and differences. For example, the list of similarities may be small, and yet the lawyer may feel "the same" as the client because of one shared similarity, or the lawyer may have many similarities and yet find herself feeling very distant from the client.

Analyzing the Effect of Similarities and Differences on Professional Distance and Judgment

After creating the lists and diagrams, the lawyer can identify where the cross-cultural challenges might occur. By naming the things that unite and distance us from our clients, we are able to identify relationships that need more or less professional distance because they are "too close" or "too far." No perfect degree of separation or connection exists between lawyer and client. However, where the list of similarities is long, the lawyer may usefully ask, "Are there differences that I am overlooking? Am I developing solutions to problems that may work for me but not for my client?" By pondering these questions, we recognize that even though similarities promote understanding, misunderstanding may flow from an assumption of precise congruence. Thus, in situations where lawyers and clients have circles that overlap, the lawyer should ask herself, "How do I develop proper professional distance with a client who is so similar to me?"

In other cases, where the list of differences is long, the question for the lawyer is "Are there any similarities that I am missing?" We know that negative judgments are more likely to occur when the client and lawyer see the other as an "outsider." Thus the lawyer who identifies significant cultural differences between the client and herself will be less likely to judge the client if she also sees herself as similar to the client. Where large differences exist, the lawyer needs to consciously address the question "How do I bridge the huge gap between the client's experiences and mine?"

What does the analysis of connection and difference indicate about what we ought to share with clients about ourselves? Lawyers usually know far more about their clients than the clients know about the lawyers. Some information of similarity and difference will be obvious to a client, and other significant information will be known only if the lawyer chooses to tell the client. In thinking about establishing rapport with clients, lawyers often think about revealing information that will reveal similarities and establish connections to clients. Of course, exactly what information will cause the client to bond with the lawyer is difficult to know, as the significance of specific similarities and differences may be very different for the lawyer and the client.

Analyzing the Effect of Similarities and Differences on Gathering and Presenting Information

Differences and similarities or assumptions of similarity will significantly influence questioning and case theory. One example of how differences and similarities in the lawyer–client dyad may influence information gathering can be seen in the way lawyers probe for clarification in interviews. Lawyers usually ask questions based on differences that they perceive between their clients and themselves. Thus a lawyer, especially one with a direct communication style, tends to ask questions when a client makes choices that the lawyer would not have made or when he perceives an inconsistency between what the client is saying and the client's actions. A lawyer tends not to ask questions about choices that a client has made when the lawyer would have made the same choices;

in such a situation, the lawyer usually assumes that the client's thought processes and reasoning are the same as his own.

For example, in working with a client who has fled her home because of spousal abuse and is living with extended family members, a lawyer might not explore the issue of family support. In contrast, had the client explained that she could not go to her family for support, the same lawyer might have explored that and developed housing alternatives. The probing occurs when the lawyer perceives the client's choices as different from the ones the lawyer might make, and therefore she tries to understand in this case why the client has failed to involve her family. The same lawyer might ask few questions about family support when she assumes that a client living with family had family support, because the lawyer would expect her own family to support her in a decision to leave an abusive spouse.

In her failure to ask questions of the first client, the lawyer is probably making a host of assumptions about cultural values that relate to the client's and the lawyer's family values. Assumptions of similarities that mask differences can lead the lawyer to solutions and legal theories that may not ultimately work for the client. For example, in assuming that the first client has family support, the lawyer in the previous example may neglect to explore other housing arrangements or supportive environments that the client needs. Family relationships are incredibly rich areas for cultural misunderstanding, and thus assumptions of similarity are perhaps even more problematic when issues of family are involved.

To identify the unexplored cultural assumptions that the lawyer may be making, the lawyer should ask what she has explored and what she has left unexplored. Reflection on the attorney–client interview allows the lawyer to identify areas where the lawyer may have missed relevant explanations of behavior.

HABIT 2: RINGS IN MOTION

If the key to Habit 1 is "identifying and analyzing the distance between me and my client," the key to Habit 2 is identifying and analyzing how cultural differences and similarities influence the interactions between the client, the legal decision makers, the opponents, and the lawyer.

Lawyers interview clients to gain an understanding of the client's problem from the client's perspective and to gather information that will help the lawyer identify potential solutions, particularly those that are available within the legal system or those that opponents will assent to. What information is considered relevant and important is a mixture of the client's, opponent's, lawyer's, and legal system's perspectives.

If these perspectives are different in material ways, information will likely be presented, gathered, and weighed differently. Habit 2 examines these perspectives explicitly by asking the lawyer to identify and analyze the similarities and differences in different dyads and triads to assess the various cultural lenses that may affect the outcome of a client's case.

Like Habit 1, the lawyer is encouraged to name and/or diagram the differences and similarities first and then to analyze their effect on the case.

Pinpoint and Record Similarities and Differences in the Legal System–Client Dyad

The lawyer should identify the similarities and differences that may exist between client–law and legal decision maker–law. As in Habit 1, the similarities and differences can be listed or can be put on a Venn diagram. In many cases, multiple players will influence the outcome and should be included when identifying the similarities and differences. For example, a prosecutor, a prospective jury, a presentence probation officer, and a judge may all make decisions that influence how the client charged with a crime will be judged and sentenced. Or a forensic evaluator in a custody case may play a significant role in deciding the outcome of a case. Therefore, at various points in the representation, different, important players should be included in the diagram of similarities and differences.

For example, a forensic evaluator in examining a capacity to parent may look for signs of the parent's encouragement of separation of parent and child. In cultures that do not see this kind of separation as healthy for the child, the evaluator may find little that is positive to report. For example, the parent may be criticized for overinvolvement, for practices such as sharing beds with children, or for failing to tolerate "normal" disagreements between child and parent. Lawyers should identify the potential differences that exist between the client and decision makers and focus on how to explain the client's choices where they differ from the evaluator's norms.

In thinking about how differences and similarities might influence the decision makers, lawyers often try to help clients make connections to decision makers to lessen the negative judgments or stereotyping that may result from difference. To the extent that lawyers have choices, they may hire or suggest that the court use expert evaluators that share a common culture or language with the client. Cross-cultural misunderstandings and ethnocentric judgments are less likely to occur in these situations. By checking with others that have used this expert, lawyers can confirm that, despite their professional education, the expert has retained an understanding and acceptance of the cultural values of the client. When the client and decision makers come from different cultures, the lawyer should think creatively about similarities that the client shares with the decision makers. By encouraging clients and decision makers to see similarities in each other, connections can be made cross-culturally.

In addition to focusing on the decision makers, the lawyer should identify the cultural values and norms implicit in the law that will be applied to the client. Does the client share these values and norms, or do differences exist?

Pinpoint and Record Similarities and Differences in the Legal System–Lawyer Dyad

The lawyer should also focus on the legal system–lawyer dyad and assess the similarities and differences between herself and the legal system. To what extent does the lawyer adopt the values and norms of the law and legal decision makers? How acculturated to the law and legal culture has the lawyer become? In what ways does the lawyer see the "successful" client the same as the law and legal decision makers, and to what extent does the lawyer have different values and evaluations? Understanding the differences and similarities between the lawyer and the legal system players will help the lawyer assess whether her evaluation of the case is likely to match the legal decision maker.

Again the lawyer can list or create a diagram that indicates the similarities and differences. By studying these, the lawyer can develop strategies for translation between the client and the legal system that keeps the client and her concerns central to the case.

Pinpoint and Record Similarities and Differences of Opponents to Legal Decision Makers/Clients/Lawyers

The cultural background of an opposing party may also influence the outcome of a case. By listing or diagramming similarities and differences of the opponent with the various other players involved in a case, the lawyer can assess a case and design creative solutions. Often in settling cases, lawyers look for win-win solutions that meet the needs of clients and their adversaries. For example, in assessing the possibility of resolving a custody case, a lawyer may want to know what the norms of custody are in the opposing party's culture and the extent to which the opposing party still embraces these values. How might gender norms about who should have custody influence the opponent's capacity or willingness to settle the case? Will the opponent be the only decision maker in resolving the case, or might the extended family, especially the grandparents, be the people who need to be consulted for the settlement to take place. All these factors and more should be included in a lawyer's plan for negotiation.

Reading the Rings: Analyze the Effect of Similarities and Differences

After filling in the diagrams and/or making the lists of the different dyads, the lawyer can interpret the information to look for insights about the impact of culture on the case and potential successful strategies. The lawyer's goal in reading the rings is to consciously examine influences on the case that may be invisible but will nonetheless affect the case.

The following questions may help identify some of those insights:

Assessing the legal claim: How large is the area of overlap between the client and the law?

Assessing cultural differences that result in negative judgments: What are the cultural differences that may lead to different values or biases, causing decision makers to negatively judge the client or the opponent?

Identifying similarities that may establish connections and understanding: What does a successful client look like to this decision maker? How similar or different is the client from this successful client?

Assessing credibility: How credible is my client's story? Does it make "sense"? To what extent is knowledge of the client, her values, and her culture necessary for the sense of the story? How credible is my client? Are there cultural factors influencing the way the client tells the story that will affect her credibility?

Identifying legal strategies: Can I shift the law's perspective to encompass more of the client's claim and desired relief? Do my current strategies in the client's case require the law, the legal decision maker, or the client to adjust perspectives?

Identifying bones to pick with the law: How large is the area of overlap between the law and myself?

Identifying how my biases shape the inquiry: How large is the area of overlap between the lawyer–client, lawyer–law, and client–legal system circles? Notice that the overlap is now divided into two parts: the characteristics relevant to the legal case that the lawyer shares with the client and those relevant characteristics that the lawyer does not share with the client. Does my client have a plausible claim that is difficult for me to see because of these differences or similarities? Am I probing for clarity using multiple frames of reference—the client's, the legal system's, the opponent's, and mine? Or am I focused mostly on my own frame of reference?

Identifying hot-button issues: Of all the characteristics and perspectives listed on the rings, which loom largest for me? Are they the same ones that loom largest for the client? For the law?

Habit 2 is more cumbersome than Habit 1 and requires looking at multiple frames of reference at once.[22] However, lawyers who have used Habit 2 find that it helps them to focus when a case or client is troubling them. The lawyer can identify why she has been focusing on a particular aspect of a case even when that aspect is not critical to the success of the case. She may gain insight into why a judge is bothered by a particular issue that is presented in the case. In addition, lawyers might gain insight into why clients are resisting the lawyer's advice or the court's directive and are "uncooperative." Lawyers might also begin to understand why clients often see the lawyer as part of a hostile legal system when a high degree of overlap between the lawyer and the legal system is identified.

What can the lawyer do with the insights gained from reading the rings or lists? Lawyers can ask whether the law and legal culture can be changed to legitimate the client, her perspective, and her claim. Can the lawyer push the law or should she persuade the client to adapt? Hopefully, by discovering some of these insights, the lawyer may be better able to explain the client to the legal system and the legal system to the client.

HABIT 3: PARALLEL UNIVERSES

Habit 3 helps a lawyer identify alternative explanations for her client's behavior. The habit of parallel universes invites the lawyer to explore multiple alternative interpretations of any client behavior. Although the lawyer can never exhaust the parallel universes that explain a client's behavior, in a matter of minutes the lawyer can explore multiple parallel universes to explain a client's behavior at a given moment.

For example, if a lawyer has a client in a custody dispute who has consistently failed to follow a court order to take her child for a psychiatric evaluation, the lawyer might assume that her client has something to hide. Although the client tells the lawyer she will do it, it remains undone. A lawyer using parallel universe thinking can imagine many different explanations for the client's behavior: the client has never gone to a psychiatrist and is frightened; in the client's experience, only people

who are crazy see psychiatrists; going to a psychiatrist carries a lot of shame; the client has no insurance and is unable to pay for the evaluation; the client cannot accept that the court will ever give the child to her husband, who was not the primary child caretaker; the client may fear that she will be misinterpreted by the psychiatrist; or the client simply did not think that she needed to get it done so quickly.

Using parallel universe thinking, the lawyer for a client who fails to keep appointments can explore parallel universe explanations for her initial judgment that "she does not care about the case." The behavior may have occurred because the client lacked carfare, failed to receive the letter setting up the appointment, lost her way to the office, had not done what she promised the lawyer she would do before their next appointment, or simply forgot about her appointment because of a busy life.

The point of parallel universe thinking is to get used to challenging oneself to identify the many alternatives to the interpretations to which we may be tempted to leap on insufficient information. By doing so, we remind ourselves that we lack the facts to make the interpretation, and we identify the assumptions we are using. The process need not take a lot of time; it takes only a minute to generate a number of parallel universe explanations to the interpretation to which the lawyer is immediately drawn.

Parallel universe thinking would cause the lawyer in the introductory example to try to explore with the client why she is resistant or to talk to people who share the client's culture to explore possible cultural barriers to her following the court's order.

Parallel universe thinking is especially important when the lawyer is feeling judgmental about her client. If we are attributing negative inferences to a client's behavior, we should identify other reasons for the behavior. Knowledge about specific cultures may enlarge the number of explanations that we can develop for behavior. Parallel universe thinking lets us know that we may be relying on assumptions rather than facts to explain the client's behavior and allows the lawyer to explore further with the client or others the reasons for the behavior. This exploration may also be helpful in explaining the client's behavior to others.

By engaging in parallel universe thinking, lawyers are less likely to assume that they know why clients are doing what they are doing when they lack critical facts. Parallel universe thinking also allows the lawyer to follow the advice of a cross-cultural trainer who suggests that one way to reduce the stress in cross-cultural interactions is to ask, "I wonder if there is another piece of information that, if I had it, would help me interpret what is going on."[23]

HABIT 4: RED FLAGS AND REMEDIES

The first three habits focus on ways to think like a lawyer, incorporating cross-cultural knowledge into analyzing how we think about cases, our clients, and the usefulness of the legal system. Habit 4 focuses on cross-cultural communication, identifying some tasks in normal attorney–client interaction that may be particularly problematic in cross-cultural encounters as well as alerting lawyers to signs of communication problems.

Good cross-cultural interaction requires mindful communication where the lawyer remains cognitively aware of the communication process and avoids using routine responses to clients. In cross-cultural communication, the lawyer must listen deeply, carefully attuned to the client and continuously monitoring whether the interaction is working and whether adjustments need to be made.

Habit 4 is accomplished in the moment and requires little planning for the experienced lawyer. The lawyer can identify ahead of time what she will look for to spot good communication and "red flags" that will tell her that accurate, genuine communication is probably not occurring.

In addition to paying attention to red flags and corrective measures, culturally sensitive exchanges with clients should pay special attention to four areas: (1) scripts, especially those describing the legal process; (2) introductory rituals; (3) client's understanding; and (4) culturally specific information about the client's problem.

Use Scripts Carefully

The more we do a particular activity, the more likely we are to have a "script." Lawyers often have scripts for the opening of interviews, explaining confidentiality, building rapport, explaining the legal system, and other topics common to the lawyer's practice. However, a mindful lawyer uses scripts carefully, especially in cross-cultural encounters, and instead develops a variety of communication strategies to replace scripts and explore understanding.

Pay Special Attention to Beginnings

A lawyer working with a client from another culture must pay special attention to the beginnings of communications with the client. Each culture has introduction rituals or scripts as well as trust-building exchanges that promote rapport and conversation. A lawyer who is unaware of the client's rituals must pay careful attention to the verbal and nonverbal signals the client is giving to the lawyer. How will the lawyer greet the client? What information will be exchanged before they "get down to business"? How do the client and lawyer define "getting down to business"? For one, the exchange of information about self, family, status, or background is an integral part of the business; for another, it may be introductory chitchat before the real conversation takes place. If an interpreter who is familiar with the client's culture will be involved with the interview, the lawyer can consult with the interpreter on appropriate introductory behavior.

Use Techniques That Confirm Understanding

Both clients and lawyers in cross-cultural exchanges will likely have high degrees of uncertainty and anxiety when they interact with someone they perceive to be different. The lack of predictability about how they will be received and their capacity to understand each other often leads to this uncertainty and anxiety. To lessen uncertainty and anxiety, both the lawyer and the client will be assisted by using techniques that consciously demonstrate that genuine understanding is occurring. Active listening techniques, including feedback to the client rephrasing his or her information, may be used to communicate to the client that the lawyer understands what the client is saying.[24]

In addition to giving the client feedback, the lawyer should look for feedback from the client that she understands the lawyer or is willing to ask questions if she does not understand. Until the lawyer knows that the client is very comfortable with a direct style of communication, the lawyer should refrain from asking the client if she understands and instead probe for exactly what the client does understand.

Gather Culture-Sensitive Information

How do we gather information that helps us interpret the client within her cultural context? In the first instance, the lawyer should engage in "deep listening" to the client's story and voice. For reasons identified in Habit 1, the lawyer, in question mode, will often be too focused on his or her own context and perspective. When exploration of the client's values, perspective, and cultural context is the goal, the lawyer needs to reorient the conversation to the client's world, the client's understandings, the client's priorities, and the client's narrative. Questions that get the client in narrative mode are usually the most helpful.

Questions that ask the client how or what she thinks about the problem she is encountering may also expose differences that will be helpful for the lawyer to understand the client's worldview. What are the client's ideas about the problem? Who else has the client talked to and what advice did they give? What would a good solution look like? What are the most important results? Who else besides the client will be affected? Consulted? Are there other problems caused by the current problem? Does the client know anybody else who had this problem? How did they solve it? Does the client consider that effective?

If the client has come from another country, the lawyer should ask the client how this problem would be handled in the client's country of origin. For example, in many legal cultures, the lawyer is the "fixer" or the person in charge. In contrast, most law students in the United States are taught client-centered lawyering, which sees the lawyer as partner, and our professional code puts the client in charge of major decisions about resolving the case.

Look for Red Flags That the Interaction Is Not Working

What are the red flags that mindful lawyers pay attention to in assessing whether the conversation is working for the client and lawyer? Red flags that the lawyer can look for include the following:

The client appears bored, disengaged, or even actively uncomfortable;

the client has not spoken for many minutes, and the lawyer is dominating the conversation;

the lawyer has not taken any notes for many minutes;

the client is using the lawyer's terminology instead of the lawyer using the client's words;

the lawyer is judging the client negatively;

the client appears angry; or

the lawyer is distracted and bored.

Each lawyer and client and each lawyer–client pair will have their own red flags.

The first step is to see the red flag and be shaken out of complacency. "Uh-oh, something must be done." The next step is the corrective one. This must be done on the spot, as soon as the red flag is seen. The general corrective is to do anything possible to return to the search for the client's voice and story.

Explore Corrective Measures

In creating a corrective, the lawyer should be careful to use a different approach than the one that has led to the red flag. For example, if the client is not responding to a direct approach, try an indirect approach. If the call for narrative is not working, ask the client some specific questions or ask for narrative on a different topic.

Other suggested correctives include

turning the conversation back to the client's stated priority;

seeking greater detail about the client's priority;

giving the client a chance to explain in greater depth her concerns;

asking for examples of critical encounters in the client's life that illustrate the problem area;

exploring one example in some depth;

asking the client to describe in some detail what a solution would look like; and

using the client's words.

Again, these are only a few examples of many correctives that can be fashioned. Encounter by encounter, the lawyer can build a sense of the red flags in this relationship and the correctives that "work" for this client. Client by client, the lawyer can gain self-understanding about her own emblematic red flags and correctives that specifically target those flags. Red flags can remind the lawyer to be aware of the client and to be focused on the client in the moment. With reflection, the red flags can help the lawyer avoid further problems in the future.

HABIT 5: THE CAMEL'S BACK

Like the proverbial straw that breaks the camel's back, Habit 5 recognizes that, in addition to bias and stereotype, there are innumerable factors that may negatively influence an attorney–client interaction. A lawyer who proactively addresses some of these other factors may limit the effect of the bias and stereotyping and prevent the interaction from reaching the breaking point. Once the breaking point has been reached, the lawyer should try to identify why the lawyer–client interaction derailed and take corrective actions or plan for future corrective action.

Consider the case of a woman client with a horrible story of torture, whom the lawyer had very limited time to prepare for in an asylum trial (she lived out of town). During their conversation, the woman spoke in a rambling fashion. The lawyer, just back from vacation, was thinking angry thoughts toward the client. In the extreme stress caused by time pressure and by listening to the client tell about some horrible rapes that she had suffered, the lawyer fell back on some awful, old conditioning: against people who are of a different race, people who are overweight, and people who "talk too much."

In the midst of these feelings, which were causing the lawyer shame, what can the lawyer do to put the interview back on track and prevent a collision? This lawyer, like all lawyers,

had biases and stereotypes that he brought to this attorney–client interaction. Research on stereotypes indicates that we are more likely to stereotype when we are feeling stress and unable to monitor ourselves for bias. By identifying the factors contributing to the negative reactions and changing some of them, the lawyer could prevent himself, at least sometimes, from acting on the basis of his assumptions and biases.

For example, the lawyer in the previous situation can take a break, have some food and drink, and identify what is interfering with his capacity to be present with the client before he resumes the interview. This, however, requires that the lawyer accept his every thought, including the ugly ones, and find a way to investigate and control those factors that are simply unacceptable in the context of lawyering. Knowing oneself as a cultural being and identifying biases and preventing them from controlling the interview or case are keys to Habit 5 thinking.

Over time, lawyers can learn to incorporate the analysis that they are doing to explore bias and stereotype into the analysis done as part of Habit 1. In addition to biases and stereotypes, straws that break the lawyer's back frequently include stress, lack of control, poor self-care, and a nonresponsive legal system. Final factor analysis identifies the straws that break the lawyer's back in the particular case and corrective steps that may work to prevent this from happening.

For example, assume that a lawyer, after working with a few Russian clients, begins to stereotype Russians as people who intentionally communicate with a lack of candor with lawyers. Habit 5 encourages this lawyer to be extra mindful when interviewing a Russian client. Given her biases, there is a higher likelihood that the lawyer will not find herself fully present with this client. In addition to using the other habits, the lawyer can improve the communication by controlling other factors (hunger, thirst, time constraints, and resource constraints), knowing that she is at greater risk of misunderstanding this client.

The prudent lawyer identifies proactively factors that may impede full communication with the client. Some she cannot control: pressure from the court, lack of resources, bad timing, excessive caseload. But some she can: the language barrier (through a competent interpreter), her own stress (through self-care and adequate sleep, food, and water), and the amount of time spent with the client (increase as needed).

Habit 5 thinking asks the lawyer to engage in self-analysis rather than self-judgment. A lawyer who has noticed a red flag that recurs in interactions with clients can brainstorm ways to address it. Likewise, a lawyer who has noticed factors that tend to be present at particularly smooth encounters with clients can brainstorm ways to make more use of these advantages. By engaging in this reflective process, the lawyer is more likely to respond to and respect the individual clients.

NOTES

1. This work grows out of a joint collaborative process that was conceived in conversations in the early 1990s and began as a project in fall 1998 with a concrete goal of developing a teaching module about cross-cultural lawyering. Ultimately that project resulted in these materials for use in clinical courses, which we first presented at the 1999 CUNY Conference, "Enriching Legal Education for the 21st Century, Integrating Immigrant Perspectives Throughout the Curriculum and Connecting With Immigrant Communities." This work has also contributed to a chapter written by Jean Koh Peters in the supplement to her book, *Representing Children in Child Protective Proceedings: Ethical and Practical Dimensions*.

Many wonderful colleagues, students, and staff from CUNY and Yale aided us in the development of this work. The Open Society Institute, Emma Lazarus Fund, provided support for the conference, our work, and the publication of these materials.

2. R. Carroll, *Cultural Misunderstandings* 3 (University of Chicago Press 1988). Others have referred to this as "conscious incompetence," where the individual recognizes that cross-cultural competence is needed, but the person has not yet acquired the skills for this work. See W. S. Howell, *The Empathetic Communicator* 30–35 (1982).

3. Carroll, *Cultural Misunderstandings* 2. Objective culture includes that which we observe including artifacts, food, clothing, and names. It is

relatively easy to analyze and identify its use. Subjective culture refers to the invisible, less tangible aspects of behavior. People's values, attitudes, and beliefs are kept in people's minds. Most cross-cultural misunderstandings occur at the subjective culture level. See K. Cushner & R. Brislin, *Intercultural Interactions* 6 (Sage Publications 1996), p. 6.

4. Those who grew up in cultures in the United States that prized individualism and self-reliance can identify specific experiences from their childhood that helped them develop these traits, such as paper routes and baby-sitting jobs and proverbs such as "God helps them who help themselves" and "The early bird catches the worm." Cushner & Brislin, *Intercultural Interactions,* p. 7. Not all who grew up in the United States share this commitment to individualism; significant cultural groups in the United States prize commitment to community. They might have heard "Blood is thicker than water."

5. Ethnocentrism occurs when a person uses his own value system and experiences as the only reference point from which to interpret and judge behavior.

6. Cushner & Brislin, *Intercultural Interactions,* p. 10.

7. Critical feminist race theorists have established the importance of intersectionality in recognizing, for example, that women of color have different issues than white women or men of color. The intersectionality of race and gender gives women of color different vantage points and life experiences. Angela P. Harris, *Race and Essentialism in Feminist Legal Theory*, 42 Stan. L. Rev. 581 (1990); Kimberlé Crenshaw, *Mapping the Margins: Intersectionality, Identity Politics, and Violence Against Women of Color*, 43 Stan. L. Rev. 1241, 1249 n. 29 (1991); see also Melissa Harrison and Margaret E. Montoya, *Voices/Voces in the Borderlands: A Colloquy on Re/Constructing Identities in Re/Constructed Legal Spaces*, Columbia Journal Of Gender and Law (1996), 387, 403. Professors Montoya and Harrison discuss the importance of seeing multiple and changing identities.

8. The insider/outsider group distinction is one of the core themes in cross-cultural interactions. K. Cushner & D. Landis, The Intercultural Sensitizer, in *Handbook of Intercultural Training* 189 (2d ed.; D. Landis and R. Bhagat eds., 1996). Historical struggles between native countries of the lawyer and client or situations where lawyer's or client's native country has dominated the other's country can create difficult power dynamics between lawyer and client.

For example, racial discrimination both historical and current by Anglo-Americans against African Americans can have significant influences on the lawyer–client relationship. *Infra*, note 32.

9. Michelle Jacobs, *People From the Footnotes: The Missing Element in Client-Centered Counseling,* 27 Golden Gate U.L. Rev. 345, 372 (1997).

10. Harrison and Montoya, *supra* note 4, at 160. For example, after discussing the scholarship on lawyer as translator or ethnographer, Professor Zuni Cruz invited Esther Yazzie, a federally certified Navajo translator, to describe and enact the skills necessary to work successfully with language inter-preters. "Ms. Yazzie's presentation debunked for all of us the idea that languages are transparent or that representations of reality somehow exist apart from language. One of several examples cited by Ms. Yazzie involved different conceptualizations of time: 'February' translated into Navajo as 'the time when the baby eagles are born.' Certainly, this is a temporal concept more connected to nature and to place than a word such as 'February' and, as such, is a different construct."

11. Cushner & Brislin, Intercultural Interactions, *supra* note 14, at 302.

12. Christine Zuni Cruz, *[On the] Road Back In: Community Lawyering in Indigenous Communities,* 5 Clin. L. Rev. 557, 580–584 (1999), *supra* note 5, at 580–584, tells a number of stories illustrating difference in individualistic and community-focused lawyering and how culture influences the choices that lawyers make.

13. Cushner & Brislin, *Intercultural Interactions, supra* note 4 at 302.

14. Hofstede 1980 and 1991 as cited in Cushner & Brislin, Intercultural Interactions, *supra* note 4, at 302. Other nations that rank high on this dimen-sion are Australia, Canada, Great Britain, the Netherlands, and New Zealand. Nations that score high on collectivism are primarily those in Asia and South America.

15. See also Kimberly O'Leary, Using "Difference Analysis" to Teach Problem-Solving, Clin. L. Rev. 65, 72 (1997), at 72. Professor O'Leary points to both the ethical rules and concepts of standing as limiting lawyers' conceptions about who is involved in a dis-pute. Following our presentation at the 2000 AALS Clinical Teacher's conference, Peter Joy alerted us to a contemplated change in California professional responsibility rules on confidentiality, allowing the privilege to be maintained when family members or others were part of the interview process.

16. This scenario was told to me by Professor Holly Maguigan, who for years has represented a number of battered women in criminal cases. In this case, her students worked with a lawyer from the Legal Aid Society. These lawyers were significantly aided by the advocates of the New York Asian Women's Center who perform both language and cultural translations. The New York Asian Women's Center is a community-based organization that works with a diverse group of Asian women in assisting them to deal with issues of intimate violence. For a more detailed analysis of the difference between individualism and collectivism, see Cushner & Landis, *Handbook of Intercultural Training,* note 11 *supra*, at 19.

17. Peter Margulies, *Re-framing Empathy in Clinical Legal Education*, 5 Clin. L. Rev. 605 (Spring 1999). Margulies also presented this case at the 1999 CUNY Conference, "Enriching Legal Education for the 21st Century, Integrating Immigrant Perspectives Throughout the Curriculum and Connecting With Immigrant Communities."

18. The classic fact finder, the judge, never saw the evidence. The adversary learned about the evidence not from the lawyer, but from the client, and the adversary, not the advocate, presented the evidence to the court.

19. See Jacobs, *People From the Footnotes*.

20. *Race, Bias & Power in Child Welfare*, Child Welfare Watch, Spring/Summer 1998, Number 3. Child Welfare Watch is funded by the Child Welfare Fund and produced by City Limits Community Information Services, Inc.

21. The legal system's focus on the protection of individual rights and personal liberties reflects the essential and pervasive cultural value of individual-ism. The American values of free-market competition, decentralized and minimized government interven-tion, and laissez-faire economics are mirrored in the adversarial process. The American legal model, including the "rules of the game," fosters competition between largely autonomous and self-interested, zeal-ous advocates in a winner-take-all scheme.

22. Because Habit 2 requires the exploration of multiple frames of reference, Jean came up with the rings as a way to assess the perspectives and analyze where there was overlap of all three perspectives and where there were differences. Not everyone comfortably uses the diagrams or thinks in the visual

ways that diagramming encourages. Habit 2 can be done with lists, filled-in Venn diagrams, or other imaginative ways that help the lawyer concretely examine the cultural differences and similarities that are involved in a case.

23. R. Brislin and T. Yoshida, *Intercultural Communication Training: An Introduction* (Sage Publications, 1994).

24. I do not know how the recommendation that we engage in active listening by identifying the emotional content of the client's communication works for clients from more indirect cultures. One might hypothesize that a client who would be reluctant to directly name the way she is feeling may feel uncomfortable with the lawyer giving feedback of the emotional content of the message.

5

RACE, COMMUNITY, AND CRIMINAL JUSTICE

ANTHONY V. ALFIERI

University of Miami School of Law

For more than a decade, I have searched for the place of identity, narrative, and community in the ethics of the lawyering process, initially looking to poverty law practice and more recently turning to criminal law representation.[1] From the outset, race figured prominently in this search. During the last 5 years, the figurations of race have grown to occupy a central part of what is now an ongoing study of lawyers and ethics in cases of racially motivated violence. The purpose of this continuing project is to understand the nature and meaning of racial identity, the sound and substance of racialized narrative, and the form and ethical content of race-neutral representation for both prosecutors and defense lawyers in the criminal justice system.

To that end, the project has focused, perhaps errantly, on high-profile criminal race cases drawn from contemporary American legal history. Constructed from transcripts, court records, and media reports, these trials of racial violence bristle with the rhetoric of race. The discourse and imagery infusing the prosecution and defense of racial violence revive the controversy over our vision of the good lawyer in race trials. At stake in this controversy are the status of racial dignity and community in American law and the norms of moral non-accountability and race-neutrality in legal advocacy and ethics. Instead of the promise of resolution, the project proposes the modest accommodation of reconciling racial dignitary and community interests with the duties of effective representation in criminal prosecution and defense by curbing the use of racialized narratives in race trials.

This midcourse essay seeks to advance the purposes of both jurisprudential and practical reconciliation through an investigation of race-conscious, community-regarding methods of representation culled from conventional and alternative models of criminal prosecution and defense. The essay is divided into three parts. The first part examines the current posture of prosecutors and defenders in race cases. The second part analyzes the prosecution of racial violence. The third part evaluates the defense of racial

Author's Note: This chapter is based on a prior essay. See Anthony V. Alfieri, *Race Prosecutors, Race Defenders,* 89 Geo, L.J. 2227 (2001). This essay is dedicated to Robert Alfieri, a Christmas uncle.

violence and puts forward a race-conscious defense ethic of representation. The essay concludes with a meditation on harnessing advocacy and race in legal theory and practice.

PROSECUTORS AND DEFENDERS

Like prior endeavors aimed at the profession, this essay attempts to uproot the normative and empirical premises underlying the settled traditions of legal representation and ethical responsibility. Uprooting the theoretical and practical foundation of legal advocacy tests the logic and value of lawyering traditions dominant in the fields of private and public law. The field of criminal justice develops out of the practice traditions of prosecutors and defense lawyers. Dense with penal statutes, punitive norms, and disciplinary institutions, and crosscut by the adversary system, the field provides the context for the prosecution and defense functions. Neither function receives full exposition in isolated acts of advocacy. Only the accumulation and intertwining of such acts amid the adversarial tension of everyday representation give whole expression to the meaning of prosecutorial and defense conduct. That meaning is enmeshed in culture and society.

The actions of prosecutors and defense lawyers reflect and refashion cultural artifacts (caste and color) and social norms (character and community). Acting as sociolegal agents, prosecutors and defenders infuse legal discourse with images and tropes gleaned outside the law, inscribing cultural and social meaning into law. At the same time, they apply a juridical gloss to such images and tropes, restyling popular meaning by force of law. Through this semiotic and iterative process, prosecutors and defense lawyers acquire the role of double signifier. Not only do they translate social meaning into law, but they also construct social meaning out of law. Whether inside the courtroom or outside the courthouse, prosecutors and defense lawyers are interpretive agents engaged in sociolegal construction.

The scope of lawyer interpretive engagement in the criminal justice system is far-reaching. The boundaries of that engagement are laid down by constitutional text, statutory provision, and common-law doctrine. Within those boundaries, lawyers exercise substantial discretion. For prosecutors, discretion is ubiquitous and profound, for example, in charging and plea bargaining. For defense lawyers, less pronounced discretion survives, flourishing in pretrial tactics (suppression and venue motions) and trial strategies (jury selection and cross-examination). For both interpretive agents, the discretion captured in narrative and storytelling serves to mold the individual identity of defendants and victims, as well as the collective identity of their families and communities.

Recognition that the discretion of prosecutors and defenders exerts an impact beyond the courtroom challenges the practice traditions that historically insulate the prosecution and defense functions from interpretive and, consequently, moral accountability. Prosecution traditions claim a narrow realm of interpretive discretion familiar to the jurisprudence of legal formalism, confining interpretation to the discovery of fact and the application of law. Defense traditions, by comparison, claim a broader domain of interpretive discretion resembling the freewheeling policy and sociological machinations of legal realism. Under this more modern framework, interpretation employs public policy and social science to reassess fact and revise law.

Two jurisprudential developments in liberal theory challenge these long-standing practice traditions. The first comes out of the law and narrative movement in the form of discourse ethics.[2] The second originates in the civil rights and critical race movements in the figure of race ethics.[3] Discourse ethics demands the moral accountability of legal actors when the voice or figure of the "other" (defendant, victim, or community) is portrayed in narrative and story. The actors include lawyers and judges. Their performative narratives and stories encompass trial arguments, appellate briefs, and judicial opinions. Derived from the liberal mandate to enlist and respect the "other" in dialogue, discourse ethics asserts that legal translation and textual reinscription carry truth-telling responsibility. That responsibility is partially encoded in procedural and regulatory rules.[4] It extends to adversaries, courts, clients, and third persons.

Race ethics enlarge the discursive responsibility encased in procedural and regulatory rules to take account of reconciliation and reparation norms. Deduced from the American experience of racial violence, the ethics system contends that dignitary and equality norms impose a heightened responsibility in advocacy to honor the racial identity of the defendant and victim and, moreover, to promote interracial community participation through education and outreach. This responsibility is likewise partly entrenched in procedural and regulatory rules.[5] It also runs to adversaries, courts, clients, and third persons.

Burdening the prosecution and defense functions with normative, indeed transformative, responsibilities challenges the traditional place of legal advocacy in the criminal justice system. Allied with that system, the prosecutor customarily stands as public sentinel, and the defense lawyer as constitutional guardian. Assignment of the additional onus of textual accountability for word and image compels changes in prosecution and defense habits of interpretation and advocacy. Here, as elsewhere, race-conscious change provokes controversy and often condemnation. The cry of heresy leaps quickly when the intrinsic commitments and the instrumental rationales of advocacy fall under attack. Yet out of that same provocation sometimes comes reform.

The instant project sounds a call for reform in the hope of racial progress. Progress is judged not by the measure of prosecutorial conviction or defense acquittal rates but by the normative standards of racial dignity and interracial community. To be sure, these standards are undeveloped and sharply contested. In fact, their very vagueness invites quarrel. The quarrel is cast in deontological terms. It concerns the nature of a lawyer's duty in race trials.

Unlike more conventional treatments of the prosecution and defense functions in the criminal justice literature, prior works in this project addressed the duty of race-trial representation in terms of racial identity, racialized narrative, and color-conscious advocacy. That multifaceted inquiry is absent from the surprisingly sparse literature discussing the roles of prosecutors and defenders in local communities. Sketched impressionistically rather than empirically, the instant inquiry discloses lawyer tendencies to construct racial identity, deploy racialized narrative, and configure race-coded modes of representation deeply entrenched in criminal advocacy.

Lawyers operating inside the criminal justice system construct racial identity in the routine acts of daily advocacy. Prosecutors, for example, compile investigative targets, rank jury profiles, estimate flight risks, formulate sentencing recommendations, and pronounce judgments of wrongdoing in indictments, trial statements, and appellate arguments. Granted, these acts establish neither a clear racial imprint nor a deliberate racial intent. But taken together and accrued over time, they evoke images of color and character that bear the mark of race and the inference of racial consciousness. For example, between 1991 and 1997, racialized legal tactics pervaded the successive New York state criminal and federal civil rights prosecutions of Lemrick Nelson and Charles Price for the 1991 killing of Yankel Rosenbaum and the incitement of four days of interracial violence in Crown Heights, Brooklyn.[6] Additional tactics and imagery permeated the federal criminal civil rights prosecution of five white New York City police officers on charges of assaulting Abner Louima at a Brooklyn station house in 1997.[7] They also saturated the 1990–1991 Central Park Jogger sexual assault trials in New York City and the 1998–1999 James Byrd murder trials in Texas.[8]

Criminal defense lawyers similarly exploit the imagery and rhetoric of race in advocacy. Race informs their arguments and objections, direct and cross-examinations, and proposed jury instructions. The symbolic and rhetorical presence of race is magnified in cases of racially motivated violence, both black on white and white on black. The defense of Damian Williams and Henry Watson on charges of beating Reginald Denny and others during the 1992 South Central Los Angeles riots, for example, demonstrated that black criminal defense stories present historically pernicious as well as transformative visions of racial identity and racialized narrative.[9] Likewise, the criminal and civil trials of the Alabama Ku Klux Klan in the 1981 lynching of Michael Donald showed that white criminal defense stories embody identity claims and narrative constructions that mimic and thereby reinforce racial caste structures of inequality.[10]

The interconnection of race, law, and legal representation is unsurprising in a nation founded on de jure and de facto racism. The historical presence of race and racism in American law gives rise to claims of color and character that shape reputation and endow privilege through image, interpretation, and narrative. The upshot is a racial identity molded by legal agents and litigation and, further, declared as truth. Whatever the alchemy of advocacy and adjudication, identity remains unstable, disrupted by class, gender, sexuality, and the multiple racial categories of culture and society. Despite its unsteady quality, racial identity subjects individuals and whole communities to suspicion, notwithstanding state affirmative intervention, speech regulation, and hate crime legislation. Combating suspicion in the spirit of diversity, multiracial coalition, and goodwill falters against the force of criminal law advocacy.

The traditional function and structure of criminal law persist in spite of quarrels over procedure, inequality, crime, and federal intercession. Criminal law organizes and legitimates state authority to enforce debts of wrongdoing through violence. In the post hoc reconstructions of the courtroom, state violence and legal authority are social facts of coercion and punishment.

Reexamination of the advocacy roles of prosecutors and defenders in the criminal justice system requires an analysis of punishment as an instrument of violence. Intimately tied to punishment, violence is basic to American politics, culture, and society. Both punishment and violence harbor competing values: justice, liberty, atonement, rehabilitation. When linked to deterrence, punishment demands blame, commensurate with common sense and public morality.

In accounting for the victims and agents of private and public violence, the norms of criminal responsibility and punishment usually overlook differences in culture and community. Merely acknowledging the interrelation among difference, crime, and community, however, fails to eradicate bias in the criminal justice system and in advocacy, adjudication, or policing. Racial contamination of the criminal law in the sway of bias and discrimination is well documented. Neither hate-crime legislation nor affirmative action posits a corrective. Furthermore, resort to the deliberative judgment of the

nullifying jury or to alternative jurisprudential movements provides little recompense. The quandary of race contamination vexes the prosecution of racial violence.

PROSECUTING RACIAL VIOLENCE

First-blush analysis of the prosecution of racial violence suggests an upsurge in high-profile criminal and civil-rights trials at federal and state levels. The significance of this first impression is augmented by a mounting literature on the prosecution function, criminal justice norms, and federal-state regulatory authority. The prosecutorial literature tends to focus on the scope of lawyer discretion, though the import of race and narrative and the realms of hate crimes, capital punishment, and domestic violence attract growing attention. Increasingly the spotlight of attention shifts to the victim and community rather than to prosecutorial misconduct or civil-rights enforcement.

The prosecution of racial violence typically tramples the defendant and victim, as well as their affiliated communities. In the status distinctions and hierarchies of race trials, defendant, victim, and community become enshrouded in racial identity, racialized narrative, and race-coded representation. On the surface, the shroud is colorblind. In fact, the prosecution of race trials adheres to a colorblind narrative of law and policy. Allegations of factual guilt and innocence join this narrative. Although its content may veer from the covert color-coded insinuation of racial animus to the overt race-conscious assertion of invidious stereotype, still the narrative appeals to neutrality. Narrative neutrality differs from nonpartisanship. Within the adversarial system, prosecutors serve as partisan representatives of the state but strive to maintain the pretense of race-neutrality. The formality of trial and appellate procedures, and the physical impartiality of the courtroom, fortify this pretense.

Rationalizing racialized modes of civil and criminal advocacy as race neutral depends on naturalist and necessitarian justifications. These twin justifications rely on three overlapping modes of reasoning: objectivity, form, and process. The logic of objectivity fastens racialized narrative to empirical fact, suggesting that a racialized narrative merely describes a naturally racialized world. Description in this sense is a simple, value-neutral activity undisturbed by the histories of racial caste and conflict. As such, it is a dispassionate means of rendering discoverable the world of race.

Prosecutors routinely apply the logic of objectivity in charging, pretrial motions, and trial argument. In the case of Charles Price, for example, federal prosecutors charged Price with incitement in fueling black community protest and violence against Hasidic Jews in Crown Heights, Brooklyn.[11] By definition, the charge of incitement asserts both the individual power to control or manipulate others and a group receptivity to exhortation or impassioned plea. On these terms, the charge implies the universal corruptibility and vulnerability of human nature. That sense of universality appears colorblind, extending equally to white and black. Applied to the conduct of a black man in the context of a race-religious riot, however, the charge acquires a color-coded meaning that signifies race and racial character. Historically situated, the charge against Price demonizes the black insurgent, alluding to the antebellum culture of slave suppression and revolt. It also caricatures the black mob, evoking the antebellum culture of primitive slaves in tribal frenzy. Inured to the racial tropes of naturalist objectivity and convinced of their own conscious neutrality, federal prosecutors regarded their cultural performance in charging and trying Price as colorblind and impartial.

The logic of form links racialized narrative to overt bias and prejudice. This linkage requires proof of discriminatory intent. Without proof of intent, there can be no bias. Limiting racialized narrative to intentional discrimination cabins the regulatory ambit of ethics rules to conscious bias and prejudice, leaving unconscious forms of prosecutorial bias and prejudice safely beyond the reach of bar supervision and court sanction.

Prosecutors likewise employ the logic of form in their charging, pretrial, and trial practices. In the case of Lemrick Nelson, for instance, New York state prosecutors charged Nelson with four counts of second-degree murder and manslaughter.[12] At trial, in their opening statement and closing argument, the prosecutors contended that Nelson "got caught up in the frenzy of the moment."[13] Nelson, they insisted, "was exactly the type of person who you would expect to get caught up in the mindless mob violence."[14] At the time of his arrest, Nelson was a 16-year-old black male with no prior arrest record.[15] Like millions of young black juveniles in impoverished, segregated communities, he suffered the physical and mental privations of a childhood wrought by deficient public education, inadequate health care, and family dysfunction.[16] Yet none of these circumstances clearly predisposed Nelson to racial "frenzy."[17] In fact, nothing in the evidentiary record rendered him "exactly the type of person who you would expect to get caught up in the mindless mob violence."[18] State prosecutors, however, charged and treated Nelson as a blackfaced sociopath, even though medical evidence of pathology and disorder appeared sparse and vague.[19] The conflation of race and deviance in the charging and trial narratives of the Nelson case prosecutors occurred within a logic of form that provided succor to bias and prejudice. Absent proof of conscious motive and discriminatory intent, that logic offered ethical safe harbor for unconscious racial transgression in the prosecution of Nelson's case.

The logic of process attributes racialized narrative to instrumental forces outside the law and the adversary system. On this premise, it is unruly external forces (politics, economics, culture, and society) that intrude on the impartiality of the law and the legal process. Left to operate under the rule of liberal legalism, so the argument goes, the internal structure of the law (its rules, agents, and institutions) would maintain a race-free, or at least race-neutral, environment.

Prosecutors utilize the logic of process in charging and trial practice as well. In the case of James Byrd, for example, Texas state prosecutors charged three young white male defendants, two of them Klansmen, with capital murder under the legal process dictates of equal treatment.[20] Adverting to the egalitarian symmetry of liberal legalism, the prosecutors interpreted Texas criminal law to compel the charge of capital murder even in the setting of white-on-black racial violence.[21] Their admission that "no Klansman had ever been convicted of harming a black man"[22] bolstered the egalitarian logic and constitutional neutrality of the charging process in the Byrd trials.[23] "Now they see," the prosecutors exclaimed in a paean to the rule of law, "that a white man can be given a death sentence for killing a black man."[24]

The logics of objectivity, form, and process apply equally under naturalist and necessitarian rationales. The naturalistic justification of racialized prosecution leans heavily on claims of objectivity and form. For the naturalist prosecutor, race and racial hierarchy constitute incontrovertible facts. In this view, the race-ing of facts in pleadings, trial arguments, and appellate briefs is an evidentiary compulsion instead of an invention. At successive phases of trial and sentencing in the Byrd case, for example, Texas state prosecutors referred to one Klan defendant as a "racist psychopath"[25] and to another as "satanic" in his "racist views."[26] For the naturalist prosecutor, these views are found inlayed in the social reality of racial hierarchy.

The necessitarian justification for racialized prosecution rests more acutely on adversarial process values. At race trials, those values combine with the logics of objectivity and form to accomplish the goals of representation, even if the end goals bend to racial stereotype. Trafficking in stereotypes reduces objectivity to an adversarial exchange of evidentiary proffer and objection. Out of this exchange, already compromised by inconsistent rules of admission and the ad hoc determinations of local triers of fact, comes an artificial sense of courtroom objectivity. Immersed in this sensibility, prosecutors rebuff claims of external objectivity, accepting the contingent nature of evidentiary rulings and fact-findings.

The tight embrace of internal objectivity misleads both prosecutors and courts into a stance that devalues racially subordinate communities. In the Central Park Jogger case, neither the prosecutors nor the courts realized that the construction of the juvenile defendants in the guise of racial predators not only denied but also defaced the larger reality of the defendants' families, schools, and communities located outside the courtroom.[27] Nor did they realize that the disparagement and obliteration of that social reality would offend communities of color throughout New York City, thereby causing an irreparable breach of faith in the criminal justice system.[28]

Similarly, for the necessitarian prosecutor, form fulfills a crabbed function specific to the adversary system. Prosecutorial forms of investigation, indictment, and trial strategy match racialized narratives to the substantive purposes of prosecution: black on white and white on black. Conformity legitimates claims of constitutional, statutory, and common-law wrongdoing. In the trials of Lemrick Nelson and Charles Price, for instance, prosecution claims of civil-rights statutory violations accompany racialized narratives of individual pathology and "vigilante mob" revenge to advance the retributive punishment of black-on-white violence.[29] The exploitation of racialized norms and narratives in prosecution signals a loss of faith in objective judgment, neutral form, and fair process.

The justification of racial prosecution under naturalistic and necessitarian rationales ensnares prosecutors in the widening debate over the place of race in lawyering and ethics. This debate strikes at the core of the prosecutorial duty to embrace a colorblind constitutional faith despite state and public pressure to deploy color-coded stereotypes in the interests of justice. The temptation to breach the higher duty of color-blind constitutionalism in race trials for reasons of individual or collective justice recommends recalibrating the moral baseline of prosecution.

The trials of Lemrick Nelson and Charles Price on charges of unprovoked murder and mob incitement illustrate the prosecutorial moral imagination distorted by racial identity and narrative.[30] The narrative of Lemrick Nelson heard from prosecutors speaks in natural and neutral tones about a born-out-of-wedlock, ill-schooled, 16-year-old black juvenile deserving of adult trial and sentencing. This portrait, engulfing a generation or more of young black men, confirms the symbolic caste of race and the narrative status of racial inferiority. In race trials, the precept of inferiority taints prosecutorial speech and conduct, reducing the defendant to an object of hate. Here Nelson, presumptively guilty of the sin of blackness, is pushed beyond the redemptive powers of law and society.

The Nelson and Price prosecutions reinstate a vision of blackness as original sin. At trial, prosecutors depict Nelson and Price in the bonds of deviant pathologies of race hatred and mob violence without hope of rehabilitation. This totalizing version of irredeemable black racial inferiority causes individual and community harm in the experience of stigma. The concept of stigma injury derives from civil-rights doctrine in affirmative action, school desegregation, and voting rights. The injury of stigma ensues from state-enacted racial classification. Like harm flows from state-sanctioned racial regulation of the electoral process as exemplified by gerrymandering. Predicated on color-blind principles of participatory citizenship, the notion of expressive or representational harm stems from the perception of institutionalized racial bias.

Theories of stigma injury and expressive or representational harm fashion a new ethic of prosecution based on social-contract and group-defamation precepts. Animated by legal and political responsibility to the "other" (individual, group, or community), the ethic binds racial groups in a reconfigured social contract respectful of the dignity of racial identity and the integrity of racial community. This reimagined ethic of prosecutorial responsibility leads to provocative conclusions about the importance of group and community representation in race trials. These conclusions risk the amendment and sometimes the abandonment of the liberal norms governing representational autonomy and loyalty.

Uncovering alternative norms sufficient to mediate the tension between individual and collective autonomy and obligation starts with reciprocity. By reciprocity, I mean a shared sense of equitable exchange. The cultivation of this sentiment and openness to an exchange of pluralistic views are basic to deliberative democracy. Here, the concept of reciprocity is grounded in the idea of mutual state, victim, defendant, and community accountability. It is realized in the practice of deliberative democracy. Local democratic practices afford no guarantee of individual-collective or state-community interest mediation. By force of training and culture, prosecutors elevate state interests over community, defendant, and victim considerations. But reciprocity at least introduces the dialogue of community restoration.

Restorative dialogues of agreement must anticipate the protest of individual and group divergence and conflict. Rooted in the customs of radical individualism, pluralistic dissent, and adversarial competition, that protest may defeat the interest convergence needed to implement a race-conscious, community-guided model of prosecution.

Consider this race-conscious model in the Abner Louima case.[31] During August 1997 in New York, the Brooklyn district attorney indicted four arresting officers on state charges of assault and sexual abuse. Subsequently, the U.S. Attorney for the Eastern District of New York, Zachary W. Carter, commenced a federal investigation, convening a federal grand jury to conduct a criminal inquiry. In February 1998, Carter filed a superseding federal indictment charging five officers with criminal civil-rights violations. Simultaneously he referred the Louima incident to the Civil Rights Division of the U.S. Department of Justice for a citywide police brutality investigation of the New York City Police Department.

The Louima federal criminal prosecution and civil-rights investigation present a race-conscious, community-oriented model of prosecutorial discretion. The prosecution and investigation demonstrate that a race-conscious approach to prosecutorial decision making may not only meet but invigorate the requirements of conventional ethics rules. In addition to rule compliance, the Louima prosecution and investigation exhibit the state's normative reaffirmation of racial dignity and equality. Together, dignitary and equality norms protect individuals and communities of color against group- or state-sanctioned racial violence.

Race-conscious, community-oriented duties to investigate and prosecute cases of racially motivated violence correspond with the public purposes of criminal justice: positive law sanction, moral retribution, and instrumental deterrence. They also coincide with the prosecutorial tradition of heroic moral witness. The ideal of bearing historic witness to confront injustice impels advocacy in other areas of the criminal law—for instance, in death penalty defense practice. In the Louima case, the ideal urges a sympathetic view of federal prosecutors as modern abolitionists in the struggle for

American racial dignity and equality. Too often prosecutors buttress racial hierarchy instead of equality.

The reinforcement of hierarchies of white dominance and black subordination in the prosecution of racially motivated violence occurs in the symbolic and rhetorical representation of the body—its color, its caste, and its racial character. For the prosecutor, race talk and racial imagery surround the public defense of the victim and the interrogation of the defendant. The disjunction of the body from personhood, from the corpus of the victim and the defendant, and from the ethos of their respective families and communities alienates prosecutors and the public. Alienation in criminal and civil-rights prosecution prevents dignitary redemption of the person and community reconciliation of segregated groups.

The tendency toward victim, defendant, and community estrangement in race trials is embedded in the tradition of criminal prosecution. In the Louima case, this practice was overcome by affirmative and sustained prosecutorial intervention. Observed throughout communities of color in New York, that intervention instigated and gained momentum from political organization and mobilization over claims of criminal and civil-rights injustice. The speed and scope of that mobilization points to the potential for broader community organization around the norms of criminal and civil justice.

To prevail in theory and practice, a race-conscious community ethic of prosecution must meet objections from epistemology, ethics, and practicality. A threshold objection challenges the claim of prosecutor, defendant, and victim community consensus. The claim of consensus, and the weaker contention of goal correspondence, applies at three levels. At the highest level of generality, the claim refers to relationships among prosecutors, defendants, victims, and associated communities. At an intermediate level, the claim concerns the relationships between defendant-communities and victim-communities. At a threshold level, the claim pertains to the relationships between defendants and their communities, and between victims and their communities. Empirically, the claim of consensus and goal correspondence among prosecutor, defendant, and victim fares poorly at

each level of interaction. This failure deepens in racial settings. In fact, since the advent of the civil rights movement and the war on crime, communities of color have been beset by internal conflict and fragmentation. Less battered jurisprudentially, the claim of consensus still may be unobtainable. Racially constricted dialogue may prove inadequate to reach consensus. The tautness of racial conversations and relations renders the claim further indefensible. The saving presumption of collective reciprocity and voluntary deference seems counterfactual in race cases.

The adversarial system elicits a second objection alluding to structural barriers blocking prosecutor, defendant, and victim-community consensus. Both liberal and critical scholars of the legal profession mention the endemic adversarial tendencies to sequester opposing litigants as combatants and to divide class litigants into competing groups. Systemic isolation and conflict undermine consensus-making agreement between individuals and among groups otherwise allied or in opposition. Striving for mutual agreement among the parties to race-conscious community prosecution thus seems not only futile but also likely to subordinate and silence defendants, victims, and communities too weak to overcome prosecutorial power.

The scope of prosecutorial authority brings forth a third objection pointing to the imbalance of power among prosecutors, defendants, and victims in negotiating consensus. Entering into community dialogue or collective deliberation seems far-fetched in the context of hierarchical relationships. Hierarchy suppresses dialogue and skews deliberation. Although the impulse for cross-racial dialogue and deliberation may carry on, it appears misplaced in circumstances of unequal standing and paternalism.

The circumstances surrounding the prosecutor-led negotiation of consensus among defendants, victims, and their affiliated communities prompt a fourth objection relating to culture and society. Insofar as cultural and socioeconomic circumstances and prevailing political currents manufacture the shape of race trials—situating identity, designating narrative, and stipulating color-coded representation—reform of lawyering and ethics regimes seems unavailing. Indeed, on the strength of this objection, neither lawyering nor ethics can rescue the participants of race trials. For critics, rescue must come from politics, culture, and society, not law. The erosion of civil rights and the disintegration of biracial coalitions support the turn away from lawyering solutions.

The facial incompatibility of a race-conscious, community-based ethic of prosecutorial discretion and colorblind constitutional tradition sparks a fifth objection. Undeniably, race-conscious standards of prosecutorial discretion may run afoul of strictly read equal protection principles. But strict construction is nowhere compelled by equal protection. Surely equality principles often oblige more expansive readings. Like state-enacted, race-conscious procedures and remedies, prosecutor-espoused, race-conscious standards confront the tension of constitutional contraction and expansion. That confrontation saps the axioms of liberal jurisprudence and the constitutional tradition of colorblind adjudication.

The mutability of racial identity and the inconsistency of racialized narratives further pummels prosecutorial standards of race-conscious discretion, thereby providing a sixth objection. The Louima case shows racial identity wrenched by categories of color, race, ethnicity, nationality, and sexuality. It also demonstrates the variation in racialized narrative when enunciated by prosecutors, defense lawyers, defendants, victims, and judges. In addition to categorical overlap and discrepancy, racial identity and narrative suffer the inscription of a white-black dichotomy. Reiterated in both high- and low-profile trials, this inscribed dichotomy misapprehends mixed-race classification and racial gradation for the duality of black and white.

Stubbornly fixed in race-conscious prosecutorial discretion, that duality leads to a seventh objection based on the claim of white-majority harm. This expressive or representational harm occurs when state prosecutorial action appears to favor minority interests. Theories of expressive and representational harm apply equally to white-majority and black-minority communities, though the race-conscious standards proposed here anticipate injury only to the dominant racial group. The theories project the harm of community stigma and the loss of public faith in government.

Public faith is crucial to the success of race-conscious, community-oriented prosecutorial discretion. Loss of faith conjures a last objection tied to the predicted decline of voluntary cross-racial community. Decline results from prosecutorial intervention that displaces alternative community-based, citizen-led modes of racial reconciliation. This mode of reconciliation fuses collective action with diversity and legal rights with political mobilization. To satisfy the norm of equal citizenship, mobilization must revere racial inclusion. Private market forces and American populist histories are barren of such reverence. The crude conception of community-based, popular justice unleashed by the antebellum and postbellum forces of history, together with concerns about constitutional incompatibility, practical unmanageability, expressive and representational harm, and compromised voluntary cross-racial community, tarnish the prospects of a race-conscious, community-oriented model of prosecutorial discretion.

DEFENDING THE VIOLENCE OF RACE

Impediments to the installation of a race-conscious, community-oriented model of prosecution in the current framework of the adversarial system rise up as well in the criminal defense context. Because the defense function evolves from the moral obligation to shield the poor from state-inflicted violence, the impediments to formulating a race-conscious defender approach to race trials seem even more formidable. The conventional approach to the defense process deems guilt and innocence irrelevant to criminal trials. More germane is the historic inequity and rationing of state resources in the defense of the accused. These scant resources produce models for indigent defender systems sparing of innovation. Entrapped by the political economy and custom of unequal adversarial engagement, defense lawyers fall prey to plea bargaining and paternalism. Neither plea bargaining nor paternalism supplies a race-conscious, community-oriented approach to defenders in trials of racially motivated violence.

The prior criminal defense cases surveyed in this project yield precisely such an approach, albeit inchoate and haphazardly tried. The cases glean a race-conscious, community-oriented approach to advocacy from the disparate trials of Damian Williams and Henry Watson,[32] the Alabama-based United Klans of America,[33] and Lemrick Nelson and Charles Price. Although the trials reveal different conceptions of racial identity, racialized narrative, and race-neutral representation, they point to a basic mutability of identity, instability of narrative, and color-coding of neutrality. The fluctuations of identity, narrative, and color-coded advocacy stem from the interchanges of procedural and substantive laws, judges and juries, defendants and victims, prosecutors and defenders, and culture and society. Unconfined by law and the adversarial system, the interchanges feed on stereotypes of color to fix a secure sense of racial hierarchy and status. In race trials, this sense of caste security is ephemeral. Repeatedly the case studies demonstrate that identity, narrative, and color-coded advocacy shift in an ongoing contest of accommodation and resistance to well-entrenched racial hierarchy.

Criminal defenders reproduce white-black racial hierarchies in race trials. They veil hierarchy in constitutional interpretation, statutory construction, and common-law application. The colors of black and white adorn the discourses of constitutionalism, legislation, and common law. Evoked in speech and symbolic conduct, those discourses naturalize color-coded inferences and color-conscious stereotypes about racial identity. Both inference and stereotype equate black racial identity with moral inferiority. The precept of inferiority is rhetorically encoded in the defense of racially motivated violence.

Race trial defenses assemble color-coded claims that overtly and covertly appeal to demeaning racial stereotypes. The stereotypes contain racial identity judgments of moral inferiority. Criminal defenders stand unaccountable for expressing judgments of inferiority in narrative and story. Earmarks of the adversary system, narrative partisanship, and nonaccountability receive widespread acceptance in criminal defense advocacy. Jurisprudentially, they also obtain the freely given assent of defendant clients.

Liberal theories of moral agency decree the treatment of clients as subjects. Subjectivity enables defendant-client assent to racialized narrative, even when it is demeaning. Contingent on instrumental lawyer strategy and voluntary client self-construction, the narrative forms part of a natural or a necessary racial order. The ranking of this order bottoms on a naturally defective black moral character or a deprivation-induced black moral deficiency. This strategic ranking of racial inferiority legitimates subordinating narratives about black character and conduct under the aegis of race-neutral representation. The stance of race neutrality in this way shields color-coded criminal defense advocacy.

The case of Damian Williams and Henry Watson illustrates the color-coded defense of race trials.[34] To defeat charges of attempted murder and aggravated mayhem in the beating of Reginald Denny and others, the Williams-Watson defense lawyers controverted evidence of intent and voluntary conduct. They sparked controversy by introducing a "group contagion" theory of mob-incited diminished capacity.[35] Mounted as an exculpatory defense, the social psychology-based theory intimates that young black males as a group, and the black community as a whole, share a pathological tendency to commit acts of violence in collective outings.[36] Both Williams and Watson were young, male, and black. The defense team supplemented this evidence with defendant-inspired narratives of deviance and defiance.[37]

The Williams-Watson trial record is replete with interlacing and sometimes dissonant deviance and defiance narratives.[38] The narratives construct the identity of young black males in antebellum terms of bestial pathology and insurrectionist rage, projecting images of good and bad young black men. This identity projection re-creates the racial dichotomy of virtue and sin. Under its distended terms, to be born black is itself an act of original sin fatal to moral character. Distilling racial identity into an objective, unalterable quality of human nature robs blacks of liberal subjectivity in the making of identity and in the crafting of community. The tendency of white and black criminal defense lawyers to mix deviance and defiance narratives in race trials imprints bestial pathology into the sociolegal texture of racial identity and community. This tendency reemerges in the defense of white-on-black violence.

Defenders of the 1981 Ku Klux Klan lynching of Michael Donald recapitulated the identity-making function of legal narrative in the context of race and community bias.[39] Employing several lynching defenses (jury nullification,[40] victim denigration,[41] and diminished capacity[42]), they spun narratives of cloaked racial invective and hatred seeking to captivate the white imagination and its sympathy. The narrative defenses of jury nullification and victim denigration appeal overtly to racial hierarchy. Nullification narratives invoke white racial supremacy. Denigration narratives restate black racial inferiority. The narrative defense of diminished capacity implores hierarchy by more covert reference, remarking favorably on the psychological disfigurement of a rightly segregated community.

Resonant of hierarchy, the racialized narratives accompanying the lynching defenses of nullification, denigration, and diminished capacity denote difference in sociolegal status. The defense of nullification, for example, petitions community members of a jury to affirm their commitment to racial difference and subordination by overriding the course of law and the weight of evidence. The affirmation encapsulates the moral sentiment of antebellum and postbellum community to rectify superficial alterations in racial status. For defenders of Klan lynching, jury-featured race trials provide a forum for disenfranchised white citizens to participate in overturning the temporary realignment of racial hierarchy.

The defense of victim denigration also confirms racial status hierarchy by imparting narratives of black deviance. Deviant imagery degrades the worth of the black victim, thereby elevating the status of the white lawbreaker. Validating the debased status of black victims bolsters claims of moral, physical, and mental inferiority. The claims compose the moral rationale for lynching, segregation, and jury-granted white clemency.

The defense of diminished capacity reinforces racial status hierarchy by absolving white lawbreakers of moral and criminal culpability. Absolution recognizes and rewards the overwrought, almost delusional commitment to unalloyed white dominance. Defenders contend that the depth of white commitment to racial

supremacy induces an emotional state of rage. Swept up in a populist battle to reverse private and public advances in political, cultural, and socioeconomic integration, white lawbreakers commit acts of racial violence without individual or collective remorse. Discarding the image of white savagery, the defense revitalizes the exculpatory narrative of distraught white innocence.

The exculpatory narrative of racial innocence extends to the defense of black defendants. The race trials of Lemrick Nelson and Charles Price for the 1991 murder of Yankel Rosenbaum and the incitement of interracial violence both alluded to the racialized defense of diminished capacity.[43] Noteworthy for dueling race-contaminated narratives in opening statements, witness examinations, and closing arguments, the trials sparkled with defense claims of white hierarchical bias, manifested in the acts of police officers and prosecutors, and shared prosecutorial and defense assertions of black deviant pathology demonstrated in family dysfunction, juvenile delinquency, and drug abuse.[44] These commingled narratives triggered prosecution and defense motions (defendant adult transfer and judicial recusal)[45] that concurrently asserted the defective, indeed irredeemable, state of white and black moral character.

Race-neutral ethics codes tolerate color-coded criminal defense narratives. Tolerance of color-coded advocacy rests on makeshift contractarian and communitarian accounts of liberal theory. The contractarian account builds on the presuppositions of moral agency and rational individualism. In this code-ratified account, the defendant-client independently decides the objectives and collaboratively consults on the means of representation. On this account, the client's autonomous embrace of racialized defenses accords with the rational and voluntary decision making of a liberal agent.

The communitarian account weaves deliberative and third-party considerations customarily relegated to the periphery of the codes. In this similarly rule-sanctioned account, the defendant-client approves racialized defense strategies as a result of client-lawyer colorblind deliberative counseling. Standing alone, code deliberation may be inclusive or exclusive of public or third-party interests. The by-product of deliberative inclusivity is accommodation; for exclusivity, the end result is preclusion. These distinct outcomes limit the influence of communitarian counseling. Code-encouraged discretionary dialogue in counseling affords little moral incentive to boost that influence in race trials.

The roughly cobbled contractarian and communitarian accounts deduced from current ethics codes condone the deformity of client and community racial identity constructions advocated in race trials. The codes countenance this deformation by allowing the marshaling of color-coded deviance and defiance defenses. The defenses acquire their legitimacy from the presumption that a defendant-client may freely adopt a self-abasing narrative. Adoption retains its legitimacy only when the client arrives at his subordinating self-description independently or through consensual counseling.

Ethical forbearance of this destructive defender practice rests in part on the rhetoric of colorblindness that drapes the prejudicial undergirding of race trials. It rests in comparable part on the belief that the desecration of race in the public sphere of law bears no relation to subjective racial identity in the private sphere of family and community. This separation of public and private spheres partitions law and legal discourse from society and shared subjectivity. That division excises the discursive cause of racial harm, thereby erasing the taint of stigma injury for defendants, their families, and their communities. Equally important, the division shelters defenders from any accountability for voicing racialized defenses.

Two centuries of defender-facilitated racial stigma, however, are not erased by the sleight-of-hand partitioning of social reality. Defenders' approving stance toward racialized defenses, and its ethical correlates, works to preserve racial status boundaries in law and society. For defendants, the boundaries of racial caste traverse public and private spheres. Denial of the conjunction or the merging of public and private spheres in law and legal advocacy permits criminal defenders to maintain a colorblind stance of nonaccountability. This stance dominates lawyer appraisal of the moral consequences of defendant self-subordination for law and society. It also governs measurement of the harm done to the defendant and third-party or public interests.

Remedial regulation of criminal defense advocacy under an alternative race-conscious community ethic of professional responsibility hinges on the principle of lawyer moral accountability. This accountability extends to racial harm that disfigures the character of individual defendants and tarnishes the integrity of third parties or communities. The ethic combines both liberal and postmodern precepts. The initial precept, race-consciousness, posits race and racial difference as fundamental to a client's identity and therefore central to his moral decision-making process. An additional precept, contingency, asserts that a client's moral character and identity develop in contexts enlivened by family, friends, and community. A final precept, collectivity, conceives lawyers and clients as collaborators in devising strategies of representation that are equally effective in defending the client from state violence and in preventing harm to his own dignitary and community interests.

Interweaving this cluster of alternative precepts into a feasible ethic entertains two rule-based approaches. A strong version of the ethic winnows from long-standing traditions of lawyer independence and moral activism. It requires criminal defense lawyers unilaterally to refuse deployment of deviance-based racialized strategies, except to nullify a racially discriminatory prosecution. A weak version borrows from well-known lawyer advisory and counseling traditions. It encourages client–lawyer counseling dialogue on the meaning of racial identity and community and on the potential harm posed by racialized defense strategies. This type of dialogue tests defendant-deviance narratives against the background norms of dignity and integrity, weighing the risk of harm to personhood and to community.

Denunciations of these unilateral and bilateral remedial prescriptions stretch widely, finding fault with the abandonment of the public-private distinction, the validation of identity-based harm to dignitary and community interests, and the curtailment of the criminal defense lawyer's duty of zealous advocacy. To confess fault in the tempering of classical defender commitments is to point out fault in the disaggregation of the conjoined public and private experience of law, in the negation of dignity and community norms, and in overstepping the limits of loyalty and zealous advocacy. Staging the antisubordination politics of Critical Race Theory in the theater of criminal justice, where it might explode racial hierarchies and enhance equality in law and society, presents an opportunity to temper the bloated principles of criminal defense advocacy. This stab at a theory of racial conciliation nowhere demands the abdication of professional role or the wholesale repudiation of ethical duty. The proposed ethic of race-conscious community representation merely seeks to reopen and to reincorporate the suppressed normative premises of liberal legalism in fashioning an enlarged vision of lawyer duty and client or third-party injury in race trials.

The ethic of race-conscious responsibility transforms the liberal regime of colorblind criminal defense practice by revitalizing the foundational norms of dignity and community in the context of racial violence. The transformative race-ing of defense practice challenges the identity-making rituals of criminal lawyers, especially the tendency to construct racial difference out of the image of deviance and out of the narrative of inferiority. Recapitulated in the instant case studies, this tendency reenacts racial subordination in advocacy. Halting that reenactment in the criminal justice system requires the reintegration of dignitary and community values in legal ethics.

The call for the restoration of values in the legal profession resounds in contemporary ethics literature. Defender codes sustain a weak normative conception of ethics deficient in the valuation of dignity, community, and equal citizenship. This deficiency encourages the traditional routine of identity disfigurement in defending cases of racial violence. Allegiance to that advocacy routine emphasizes the primacy of a private, contractarian client–lawyer relationship and the priority of lawyer technique and tactical gambit.

Code emphasis on the private, contractarian nature of the client–lawyer relationship is not fatal to a public, community-oriented ethic of race-conscious responsibility. Adverting to a contractual relation in fact exposes certain background regulatory norms, such as reciprocity, that apply with equal vigor to a public ethic. Derivative of the norms of rational bargaining, reciprocity sanctions racialized defenses as the efficient, transactional product of client–lawyer consensus. The claim of efficiency plainly discounts the external costs of character and community harm. More troubling, the contention of moral or instrumental consensus falls overboard. Too often in the turmoil of criminal defense representation, reciprocity proves counterfactual, and consensus collapses into fallacy. Insistence on neutral tactics and colorblind technique in the racialized routine of the criminal justice system seems likewise false.

The falsity of client–lawyer reciprocity and consensus under the traditional ethic of defender representation in no way diminishes the value of moral dialogue in advocacy. Instead, it underlines the normative importance of dialogue commensurate with the preservation of individual dignity and community integrity. The task of value preservation converts defenders into moral custodians. Their custodial responsibility entails race-conscious dialogue with clients and communities in jointly opposing racial violence. Equivalent to an ethic of care applauded in emerging alternative ethics regimes, race-conscious dialogue brings other-directed empathy and solidarity to criminal advocacy.

The facile rhetoric of empathy and solidarity and the disavowal of entrenched tradition spur multiple objections to the ethic of race-conscious community responsibility. A starting objection condemns the blithe imposition of constraints on a criminal defendant's freedom of defense. Protesting anticipated encroachments on a defendant's strategic prerogative overlooks the code-endorsed limitations on a client's liberty to decide the means of his own defense. Under the ethics codes, defensive strategy effectively rests on the discretionary judgments of counsel, not the client.

Critics also claim that race-conscious constraints encumber a criminal defendant's right to trial. Without more, disquiet over hindering a defendant's right to trial seems exaggerated. Nothing in the proposed ethic of race-conscious community responsibility curbs a criminal defendant's Sixth Amendment right. The ethic merely limits the racialized tactics available at trial, a limitation already erected from equal protection principles in the areas of jury selection and peremptory challenge.

Further objections bemoan the implementation of a race-conscious ethic for fear of lawyer bad faith in counseling and negotiating cases of racial violence. Proponents of this objection fear that the newfound ethical disdain for the traditional conduct of race trials heightens the danger of plea-bargaining agreements and accelerated dispositions inimical to the interests of defendants. Absent evidence of past abuse or misconduct, conjecture about the danger of lawyer bad faith in race-case counseling and negotiation seems premature. To the extent that race-case counseling introduces additional variables for deliberation, it is fair to speculate that the risk of error increases proportionately. By definition, legal decision making in advocacy, adjudication, and legislation carries the risk of error. Mitigating the chance and effect of such error in race-conscious counseling for defendants facing mandatory sentencing or capital punishment urges a review of counseling protocols in race cases.

Additional objections go to the principle of collectivity guiding client-lawyer character and community deliberation. Practitioners warn that this principle erodes client-centered rights and loyalties, skewing the individualist logic of the adversarial system. But practitioners cling to a truncated version of such rights and loyalties. The partisan duty they profess relegates other-directed third-party rights and community obligations to secondary consideration even when collective fidelity serves to enrich the adversarial system by purging it of bias and prejudice.

The racial cleansing of adversarial rights and duties may strike some practitioners as enfeebling. Deprived of righteous zealotry, defenders may feel enervated. Coupled with role confusion, this sense of weakness and ineffectuality may re-create the ethical ambivalence and moral anxiety experienced under the traditional defender practice of color-coded advocacy. Salvaging that defender tradition may come from the claimed right to racial injustice. This sullied claim of zealous advocacy views injustice as sometimes vital to client liberty. On this accounting, fostering or simply exploiting racial injustice may enhance personal autonomy to the detriment of social equality. The claimed right to long-run racial justice augments this logic. It maintains that short-run incidents of racial injustice prevent greater aggregate injustice. Even if empirically verifiable, the systemwide

costs of overweening partisanship of this sort seem pernicious, depleting the morality of the defender role and public respect for law. The lynching defenses of jury nullification, victim denigration, and diminished capacity provide a case in point. Championed as zealous advocacy, the defenses privilege sociolegal norms of white supremacy. That act of racial privileging dissipates norms of racial community and equal citizenship. State-focused claims of oppression and corruption raised to excuse such aggressive racialized defenses furnish no rescue when they fail to vindicate intrinsic client rights or extrinsic emancipatory policies.

CONCLUSION: RACE IN THEORY AND PRACTICE

Constructive engagement in legal advocacy and ethics demands a liberal faith in reason and reform. Part of that faith entails a tolerance for experimentation and imperfection in the hard march toward attaining racial equality and community. For many criminal defenders and lay activists, the march of civil rights and civic reconstruction long ago abandoned the liberal ideals of individual dignity and collective good. What is left of that derelict march is a kind of rear-guard action aimed at stanching the retreat from basic procedural and substantive safeguards and at adjusting the recurrent imbalance of the adversarial system. For prosecutors, the march serves a disciplinary rather than an emancipatory function. Its civic purpose is punitive, not reconstructive. That purpose overrides rehabilitative and therapeutic objectives in the urgency to enforce law and legal sanction.

Albeit practical, neither the prosecutor's nor the defender's sense of purposive professional commitment exhibits the other-regarding faith or risk-taking tolerance found in the dialogic and communitarian strands of liberal legalism. Oddly, the postmodern sensibility—so impatient with the practical and so indulgent of abstraction—displays a receptivity to the higher aspiration of dialogue and community, even as it belittles the liberal faith. The postmodern sensibility also shows an adroitness in mapping the twisting flow of discursive practices, institutional procedures, and social relations within law and lawyering. Critical Race Theory demonstrates a similar acuity and vigor of analysis, particularly in parsing the color-coded meaning of constitutional, statutory, and doctrinal materials. But both postmodernist and critical race sensibilities stall in pursuing and resolving the tensions bearing on the liberal-postmodern and theory-practice divides. Partially spawned by identity and community conflicts, those tensions challenge legal theorists and practitioners to revisit conventional standards of discursive and symbolic speech, narrative interpretation, and social construction to better understand and aid subordinated clients, victims, and communities in the criminal justice system. Because the standards prevail at multiple sites—courtrooms, law offices, and police precincts—the struggle to reform prosecution and defender practices ranges widely across public and private fields of advocacy. This confluence of sites and convergence of public-private spheres hinders the navigation of this project through liberal and critical theory.

It is my hope that in time this project will persuade race prosecutors and defenders to reconsider their ethical responsibilities in racially and politically charged cases such as the recent state murder trial of four New York Police Department (NYPD) officers for the shooting death of Amadou Diallo and the federal investigation of that killing, and the current federal and state investigation of police brutality in the Los Angeles Police Department's (LAPD's) Rampart Division. Both the NYPD and LAPD officers under scrutiny participated in neighborhood-based, anticrime units within impoverished communities of color—communities that were represented by public defenders as well as private criminal defense lawyers. Furthermore, both investigations have involved U.S. Justice Department lawyers, local U.S. attorneys, and state prosecutors. Whether this project can convince prosecutors and defenders in such circumstances to adopt a race-conscious community ethic of representation remains unanswered. Until an answer is found, the project will prod practitioners and scholars to reevaluate the place of racial identity, racialized narrative, and race-neutral representation in law, lawyering, and ethics.

NOTES

1. See Anthony V. Alfieri, *Defending Racial Violence,* 95 Colum. L. Rev. 1301 (1995); Anthony V. Alfieri, *(Er)Race-ing an Ethic of Justice,* 51 Stan. L. Rev. 935 (1999); Anthony V. Alfieri, *Lynching Ethics: Toward a Theory of Racialized Defenses,* 95 Mich. L. Rev. 1063 (1997); Anthony V. Alfieri, *Prosecuting Race,* 48 Duke L.J. 1157 (1999); Anthony V. Alfieri, *Prosecuting Violence/Reconstructing Community,* 52 Stan. L. Rev. 809 (2000); Anthony V. Alfieri, *Race Trials,* 76 Tex. L. Rev. 1293 (1998); Anthony V. Alfieri, *Race-ing Legal Ethics,* 96 Colum. L. Rev. 800 (1996).

2. The law and narrative movement enlivens clinical and nonclinical scholarship. See generally Thomas Ross, Just Stories: How the Law Embodies Racism and Bias (1996); Law Stories (Gary Bellow & Martha Minow, eds. 1996); Law's Stories: Narrative and Rhetoric in the Law (Peter Brooks & Paul Gewirtz, eds. 1996).

3. Critical race movements include Critical Race theory, LatCrit theory, and Native American and Asian American theory. See generally Critical Race Theory: The Cutting Edge (Richard Delgado, ed., 2d ed. 2000); Critical Race Theory: The Key Writings That Formed the Movement (Kimberlé Crenshaw et al., eds. 1995); Race and Races: Cases and Resources for a Diverse America (Juan F. Perea et al., eds. 2000).

4. Both ethics and procedural rules codify the muted forms of lawyer truth-telling responsibility. See Fed. R. Civ. P. 11 (requiring reasonable inquiry and evidentiary support behind factual allegations); Model Rules of Prof'l Conduct R. 3.1 (2000) (requiring meritorious claims and contentions based on nonfrivolous good-faith argument).

5. See Model Rules of Prof'l Conduct R. 8.4 (2000); see also *Edmonson v. Leesville Concrete Co.,* 500 U.S. 614 (1991) (regulating civil peremptory challenges); *Batson v. Kentucky,* 476 U.S. 79 (1986) (regulating criminal peremptory challenges).

6. See Alfieri, *Race Trials,* supra note 1, at 1323–1339.

7. See Alfieri, *Prosecuting Race,* supra note 1, at 1164–1185 (discussing the feasibility and legitimacy of a race-conscious model of federal prosecution).

8. See Alfieri, *Prosecuting Violence,* supra note 1, at 818–831 (exploring the nature of prosecutorial norms and narratives, their cultural and social significance, and their impact on interracial community in the aftermath of racial violence).

9. See Alfieri, *Defending Racial Violence,* supra note 1, at 1301–1320 (proposing a race-conscious ethic of professional responsibility appropriate to the defense function in race cases).

10. See Alfieri, *Lynching Ethics,* supra note 1, at 1063–1065 (investigating subordinating racialized defense strategies in criminal and civil trials of white-on-black violence).

11. See Alfieri, *Race Trials,* supra note 1, at 1335.

12. See id. at 1329.

13. Id. at 1334.

14. Id.

15. See *United States v. Nelson,* 921 F. Supp. 105, 108 (E.D.N.Y. 1996).

16. See *Nelson,* 921 F. Supp. at 109–13 (discussing Nelson's education, environment, and family).

17. See Alfieri, *Race Trials,* supra note 1, at 1334.

18. Id.

19. See *Nelson,* 921 F. Supp. at 109–117 (reviewing Nelson's intellectual development, personality disorder, and psychological maturity).

20. See Alfieri, *Prosecuting Violence,* supra note 1, at 820–821, 826.

21. See id. at 849.

22. Richard Stewart, *Jasper Trial Site Undecided: Venue Arguments to Be Heard Today,* Houston Chronicle, Nov. 8, 1999, at A1.

23. See Alfieri, *Prosecuting Violence,* supra note 1, at 841.

24. Stewart, supra note 22.

25. *Jury in Jasper Case Weighs Man's Fate, Jurors Weigh Fate of Byrd's Convicted Killer,* Austin Am.-Statesman, Sept. 23, 1999, at B6.

26. Court TV, *Texas Dragging Death Murderer Sentenced to Death* (Feb. 25, 1999), http://www.courttv.com/trials/jasper/022599_am_ctv.html.

27. See Alfieri, *Prosecuting Violence,* supra note 1, at 818–819, 830.

28. Id.

29. See Alfieri, *Race Trials,* supra note 1, at 1334–1335.

30. See Alfieri, *Race Trials,* supra note 1, at 1330–1332. See generally *United States v. Nelson,* 921 F. Supp. 105 (E.D.N.Y. 1996).

31. See Alfieri, *Prosecuting Race,* supra note 1, at 1172–1183.

32. See Alfieri, *Defending Racial Violence,* supra note 1, at 1301–1320.

33. See Alfieri, *Lynching Ethics,* supra note 1, at 1074–1084.

34. See Alfieri, *Defending Racial Violence,* supra note 1, at 1301–1320.

35. See Record at 8628–29, *People v. Williams* (Cal. Super. Ct. 1993) (No. BA058116) [hereinafter Record].

36. See Alfieri, *Defending Racial Violence,* supra note 1, at 1304.

37. See id. at 1309.

38. See, e.g., Record, supra note 35, at 5124, 5131. One witness, a police officer, testified that Williams confronted him prior to the outbreak of violence, stating: "Fuck you. You ain't shit. If you was any kind of nigger, you would be out here with us." Id.

39. See Alfieri, *Lynching Ethics,* supra note 1, at 1074–1084.

40. See id. at 1077–1079.

41. See id. at 1079–1081.

42. See id. at 1081–1084.

43. See Alfieri, *Race Trials,* supra note 1, at 1323–1339.

44. See id. at 1332–1339.

45. See id. at 1323–1324.

6

TRIALS AND TRIBULATIONS OF AFRICAN AMERICANS IN THE COURTROOM

Refuting the Myths

RUDOLPH ALEXANDER JR.

Ohio State University

Many individuals—private citizens and public figures alike—endorse and support the mythic belief that America is a colorblind society. These supporters of a colorblind society often lament and criticize professionals who insist that racial discrimination currently exists in American institutions (D'Souza & Edley, 1996). Further, these supporters tend to reject the inclusion of racial and cultural considerations in the political and legal arenas (Kennedy, 1997), even though reports from the 2000 presidential election emerged that a significant number of African Americans in Florida were unfairly prevented from voting (Dahlburg, 2002; Holland, 2002; Lichtman, 2002). According to their viewpoint, the United States Constitution, the highest law in the land, is colorblind. Symbolically, the picture of the blindfolded lady justice epitomizes the idea that justice is colorblind: The courts do not see race, sex, national origin, or social class and treat everyone the same.

Yet polls show that endorsement of the colorblindness myth varies with race, with whites believing this view of America more than African Americans (Sack & Elder, 2000). For instance, 58% of whites believe that the playing field is level, compared with 39% of African Americans. Moreover, about 67% of African Americans state that they have been treated less equitably by the police, compared with 25% of whites (Sack & Elder, 2000). Thus African Americans—who are most likely to be victimized by prejudice and discrimination—appear much less likely to endorse the view that racism has abated and colorblindness has been achieved.

As if adding insult to injury, supporters of the colorblindness view of the criminal justice system often retort with the ironic claim that racism is a myth (Wilbanks, 1987). Criminal justice professionals of this persuasion insist that the belief that the criminal justice system is racist is flatly incorrect and is a myth promoted by liberals and African Americans who seek to play the "race card." Conservative pundits argue that African Americans engage in a disproportionate amount of violent crimes and that this disproportionality in crime perpetration accounts for their disproportionate involvement in the justice system.

Critics of the colorblindness viewpoint argue that race and culture are inescapable factors in the legal system (Butler, 1995, 1997, 1998). They note that research shows African Americans' odds of social control increase significantly at each stage of the criminal justice process from arrest to incarceration (Chiricos & Crawford, 1995; Humphrey & Fogarty, 1987; Steffensmeier & Demuth, 2000).

This chapter adopts the latter viewpoint and is therefore based on the assumption that racial problems are extant. In Part 1 of this chapter, I will discuss the prominent myths concerning African Americans and the justice system, and I will provide argumentation refuting those myths. These include the myth of colorblindness, the myth that African Americans cause crime, and the myth of equal treatment in sentencing outcomes. In Part 2, I will consider two special topics where race and culture influence justice proceedings: adoption and mental health diagnoses. Last, I will present conclusions and offer a few recommendations.

PART 1: PROMINENT MYTHS ABOUT AFRICAN AMERICANS AND THE JUSTICE SYSTEM

Refuting the Myth of a Colorblind Court

Historical Evidence Refuting the Colorblindness Myth

As noted at the outset, a central and overarching myth about African Americans and the legal system is the colorblindness viewpoint. According to this myth, the justice system is fair, unbiased, and nonpartisan; therefore all individuals regardless of race will be treated equally and fairly. This myth can be refuted by both historical and contemporary evidence.

Unlike other minority groups, the first African Americans were brought to the United States as slaves. In America, the dehumanization of Africans surpassed that of any other group, including the Irish, the Chinese, the Japanese, Native Americans, Jews, and Italians. Of course, these groups were targeted for discrimination and oppression too, but nothing on the scale of what was done to the descendants of African people. For instance, most political science textbooks discuss the Dred Scott legal decision in 1856 in reference to how the U.S. Supreme Court considered Scott's claim of being a free man. He claimed that because he had lived in Illinois as a free person, he was a citizen of Missouri upon his return to that state, but the U.S. Supreme Court ruled against him (McClenaghan, 1988; O'Connor & Sabato, 1993; Watson, 1985).

However, the U.S. Supreme Court did more than rule against Dred Scott. Consisting of 240 pages, which numbered more pages than most other U.S. Supreme Court decisions, the Dred Scott decision consisted of a lengthy, hateful diatribe discussing why African Americans were the lowest group on Earth. The author of the decision wrote that all white Americans and institutions endorsed this view, including the president and members of Congress. The U.S. Supreme Court justice, a formerly prominent attorney from Massachusetts who wrote the majority decision, stated that the United States would accept American Indians as citizens before accepting African Americans, provided that the American Indians gave up their savage ways (*Dred Scott v. Sandford,* 1856). This U.S. Supreme Court justice in effect portrayed African Americans as being beyond savages. Many of the political science textbooks that discuss Dred Scott omit this legal denunciation of African American personhood (e.g., see McClenaghan, 1988; O'Connor & Sabato, 1993; Watson, 1985).

Following the emancipation of the slaves, some laws were passed to assist African Americans because of the virulent racism in the southern states and the patent lack of protections from the courts and law enforcement— particularly, the Fourteenth Amendment was passed in 1868, and a Civil Rights Act was passed in 1871. The U.S. Supreme Court led the way in weakening these laws such that they were mostly ineffective (Kaczorowski, 1985).

Moreover, the U.S. Supreme Court was highly inconsistent in its rulings in cases where

African Americans were plaintiffs or defendants. In one case, the U.S. Supreme Court held that Chinese laundry owners were being discriminated against in San Francisco, California, although a city ordinance never referred to the Chinese. The court ruled that even if a law is neutral in wording, but officials apply the law discriminatorily for similarly situated persons, the affected group is denied equal protection in violation of the Fourteenth Amendment (*Yick Wo v. Hopkins,* 1886).

However, a few years later, the U.S. Supreme Court held that an African American was not being discriminated against in a case in Mississippi. An African American was on trial for a capital offense and objected to the composition of the all-white jury that convicted him and sentenced him to die. Particularly, jurors were selected from the voter rolls. Previously, about 190,000 African Americans were eligible to vote compared with 69,000 whites. After passing discriminatory laws such as the poll tax, literary requirements, and other disqualifying criteria to vote, the number of African Americans eligible to vote dropped to near zero. In a specious explanation, the U.S. Supreme Court concluded that the Chinese were discriminated against in San Francisco, California, but not African Americans in Mississippi (*Williams v. Mississippi,* 1898).

In the late 1800s and early 1900s, Alabama and Mississippi developed strategies for wholesale oppression of African Americans, which other states adopted. What these states decided was to not refer to African Americans particularly in laws and instead use other criteria that were correlated with race (Alexander, 2000). Laws were passed, for instance, that stated one could not vote unless his grandfather had voted. Because slaves did not vote, the children of slaves, though barely citizens, could not vote. In another strategy, Alabama searched the records of the "Negro courts" to determine which crimes African Americans were more likely to commit and then used those crimes as disqualifying factors in voting. In a related strategy, officials added another criterion for voter disqualification: moral turpitude. All African Americans were considered to be immoral and thus ineligible to vote. Many of these laws stayed on the books for decades, and many were not declared

unconstitutional until the 1960s. In fact, many of the criteria that were codified in law to prevent and impede African Americans from voting are still in use, although some of the criteria have been amended. For instance, persons convicted of a felony may vote only if they have been pardoned or had their civil rights restored by the governor (Florida Statute § 97.041; Kentucky Revised Statutes Annotated § 116.025; Official Code of Georgia Annotated § 21-2-216; Virginia Constitutional Article II, § 1).

In sum, the historical record reflects a legacy of political sentiment, legislative actions, and court rulings that refute the colorblindness myth. From its inception—at a time when slavery was legal in America—the system has used skin color as a pivotal factor not only in administering justice but also in determining whether a person is a citizen. This legacy has not dissipated and remains deeply ingrained in the subtext of American judicial culture.

Contemporary Evidence
Refuting the Colorblindness Myth

The colorblindness myth is sometimes refuted on the basis of its past tense. Such rebuttals acknowledge past systematic racism but assert that it has been corrected and that the system has evolved to be currently colorblind. However, there is ample contemporary evidence to the contrary. This can be illustrated by considering court decisions about affirmative action, where it appears that race drives systematically different decisions than gender.

Currently, several U.S. Supreme Court justices, such as Justice Clarence Thomas, declare that the Constitution is colorblind and have made it extremely difficult for African Americans to prove racial discrimination and to obtain courts' approval of affirmative action programs. When an affirmative action program exists involving African Americans, the program must survive the strict scrutiny test (Alexander, 2000; Strolovitch, 1998), the highest legal test in the law (Alexander, 2002). Law (1999) noted that the U.S. Supreme Court did not approve a single affirmative action program involving race from 1990 to 1999. At the same time, in cases involving women and affirmative action, the U.S. Supreme Court has permitted a lower legal standard—intermediate scrutiny (Alexander, 2000; Strolovitch, 1998).

Often, African Americans are attacked for endorsing quotas, and the courts have been quite hostile to any suggestions that, for instance, African Americans should constitute 30% of police officers if they represent 30% of a city's population. Yet this very same principle is legally endorsed when women plaintiffs assert it. Statistics presented by women plaintiffs are viewed differently from statistics presented by African Americans and other racial minorities. At one time, both women and minorities were denied opportunities to participate fully in the American workforce. Numerous jobs were reserved for white males. As cities and counties were sued and affirmative action plans implemented, some white males responded with lawsuits contending that they were the innocent victims of reverse discrimination. In reviewing these affirmative action plans, women and minorities legally splintered in separate directions.

To determine whether an affirmative action plan for African Americans was constitutional, the U.S. Supreme Court has mandated use of the strict scrutiny test (*Adarand Constructors, Inc. v. Pena,* 1995). In addition, general statistics regarding the composition of African Americans in a community and the composition in skilled positions provide little support for their cases. However, there is a different legal standard for women. Following a case in which the U.S. Supreme Court upheld the use of general statistics (*International Bd. of Teamsters v. United States,* 1977), the Eleventh Circuit Court of Appeals held that reliance on general statistics is appropriate in gender-only cases when other anecdotal evidence exists (*Ensley Branch, NAACP v. Seibels,* 1994).

General statistics about the percentage of women in the community and in skilled positions are probative. This difference between women and African Americans was highlighted in several cases. One case involved an affirmative action plan for women in the Dade County, Florida, Fire Department, where one judge wrote that it was easier to rule for women in affirmative action cases than racial minorities (*Danskine et al. v. Metro Dade County Fire Department et al.,* 1999). Statistics showed that women made up 52% of Dade County but only 1% of the fire department workforce. The court determined that this evidence was probative. This was convincing evidence to support an affirmative action plan for women. However, similar statistics offered by African American plaintiffs were not viewed equally. Although African Americans could also show that they made up a significant percentage of citizens in Dade County and that stark racism kept them from holding jobs in the fire department, African Americans would not be treated the same as women plaintiffs. African Americans seem to have a more difficult legal burden to satisfy in affirmative action cases.

The courts, including the U.S. Supreme Court, have permitted quotas for women in athletic programs. If women constitute 50% of a university, then they are currently entitled to 50% of athletic scholarships. Some universities have taken extreme measures to meet their quotas. Ohio State University created a crew team, then announced that it was going to create another crew team of smaller women (Powers, 1998). In effect, there was intent to create weight divisions in order to meet its quotas and to give more athletic scholarships to women. Several universities have announced that they plan to create equestrian teams for women (O'Toole, 2002). One of the noticeable aspects of these creations is that these sports attract white women. Ohio State crew team was all white. Few African American women participate in equestrian events, and there were no suggestions of recruiting African American women for an equestrian team.

The reason for differential treatment of African Americans in the courts compared with women is that the law is not colorblind, and judges, who are mostly white, reflect many of the attitudes of other whites. For instance, Strolovitch (1998) conducted a multivariate analysis of support for affirmative action programs, gender, and race. According to Strolovitch, the general public perceives women as being white women. When affirmative action is seen as benefiting women, particularly white women, white men and white women are more supportive of affirmative action programs. White men and white women are significantly less supportive when affirmative action programs are seen as benefiting African Americans. She found that whites play favorites. The attitudes of whites about affirmative action are reflected in the courts' current decisions regarding African Americans. Linked to Strolovitch's findings, Law (1999) documented that white privilege and affirmative action have always existed. For African Americans, the playing field is not level.

A final contemporary example refuting the colorblind myth is reflected in an affirmative action decision by the Fifth Circuit Court in *Hopwood v. Texas* (1996). Although the judges in the majority felt that they were addressing and eliminating race from the admission process at the University of Texas Law School, what they did instead was to reaffirm the use of race. For instance, Circuit Judge Jerry E. Smith in the Hopwood case wrote the following:

> While the use of race per se is proscribed state-supported schools may reasonably consider a host of factors—some of which may have some correlation with race—in making admissions decisions. The federal courts have no warrant to intrude on those executive and legislative judgments unless the distinctions intrude on specific provisions of federal law or the Constitution. A university may properly favor one applicant over another because of his ability to play the cello, make a downfield tackle, or understand chaos theory. An admission process may also consider an *applicant's home state* or *relationship to school alumni.* Law schools specifically may look at things such as unusual or substantial extracurricular activities in college, which may be atypical factors affecting undergraduate grades. Schools may even consider factors such as *whether an applicant's parents attended college* or the *applicant's economic and social background.* (*Hopwood v. State of Texas,* 1996, p. 946)

While Circuit Court Judge Smith was laying out reportedly constitutional ways of making admission decisions, he was also laying out ways to discriminate against some applicants. Criteria such as relationship to alumni, home state or residential area, whether an applicant's parents attended college, and economic and social background can all favor white applicants. This is no different than what white supremacists did to disenfranchise black voters

in Mississippi and other states during the late nineteenth century.

Judge Smith's blueprint can have nefarious objectives, although race is not used. For instance, a criterion stating that an applicant can receive favoritism because his or her parents went to college benefits whites. A number of factors correlate with race, as Judge Smith intimated. Voting, home ownership, participation in the stock market, and membership in country clubs are associated with race, economics, and social background. According to Judge Smith, a law school can favor an applicant who plays the cello. If that is true, then it can favor applicants who play golf and tennis, activities that whites engage in significantly more often than African Americans. Today, several of these race-neutral factors can eliminate most African Americans from colleges and universities, just as white supremacists eliminated the opportunity to vote for African Americans in the nineteenth century.

Refuting the "African Americans Cause Crime" Myth

Many persons believe that African Americans cause most crime in America, and this belief is often fueled by the news media, coupled with stereotypes held by whites of African Americans (Oliver & Fonash, 2002; Robinson, 2000). Whites tend to misidentify African Americans in crime stories (Oliver & Fonash, 2002) and believe that the mere presence of African Americans in a neighborhood is associated with crime (Quillian & Pager, 2001).

Dorfman (2001) conducted a content analysis of articles published in professional journals to learn, in part, how news coverage depicts minorities and crime, and the extent to which news coverage disproportionately depicts youth of color as perpetrators of crime. Dorfman's conclusion was that television news unduly connected race and crime, and the news overrepresented African Americans as perpetrators of violent crimes and underrepresented African Americans as victims. African American youths, through the phrase "young black males," had become synonymous with criminals, and as a result, any discussion of crime is essentially a discussion of race. Dorfman reported that the unbalanced and inaccurate discussion of race and crime affected the public perception and often led to punitive legislative policy. Undoubtedly, social control agents, such as law enforcement officers and judges, are not immune to the news media's reporting. Hence the media, in part, fuel the public view of African Americans as dangerous.

For a number of years researchers have stated quite regularly that African Americans are overrepresented in crime statistics. African Americans constitute 12% of the U.S. population, but their representation in crime statistics is considerably higher (Allen & Simonsen, 2001). Lost in the discussion is that being in the lower class has traditionally been correlated with some crime, whether the group is Italian, Irish, Jewish (O'Kane, 1992), or black. As a group moves out of the lower social class, crime for that group goes down (O'Kane, 1992). Breaking out of the lower class has been tougher for African Americans.

There is little doubt that African Americans are overrepresented in crime statistics. But this has come to be viewed by many whites as a fact that African Americans commit *all* the crimes, which is not the case. The rate and proportion for African Americans are high, but whites commit more crimes overall.

For instance, crimes are ranked according to the degree of seriousness. These index, or Part One, crimes include murder, forcible rape, robbery, aggravated assault, burglary, larceny-theft, motor vehicle theft, and arson. Within this group, African Americans were more likely to be arrested for two of the eight index crimes—murder and armed robbery. Whites constituted 56% of those persons arrested for rape, 60% of those persons arrested for aggravated assault, 68% of those persons arrested for burglary, 65% of those persons arrested for larceny, 57% of those persons arrested for motor vehicle theft, and 74% of those persons arrested for arson. When crimes are divided by violent and property crimes, whites were arrested for 55% of violent crimes and 65% of property crimes. For a couple of Part Two offenses, which constitute all crimes that are not classified as Part One, whites made up 60% of those persons arrested for drug offenses and 58% of those persons arrested for property offenses (Maguire & Pastore, 1998).

Despite these statistics, whites, including police officers and judges, have come to believe that African Americans commit more of the serious crimes. Based on the erroneous belief that African Americans commit all crimes or all the serious crimes, police officers thus feel justified in stopping more African Americans, and judges feel justified in incarcerating more of them.

The Myth of Equal Treatment in Sentencing Outcomes

A number of researchers have found that African Americans tend to receive harsher sentences compared with whites (Austin & Allen, 2000; Spohn & DeLone, 2000). Immediately when such studies are reported, judges and conservative professionals involved in the legal process will point out that African Americans commit more of the serious crimes and have lengthier criminal records, which explains why African Americans receive the more serious sanctions and are incarcerated in high numbers. However, a group of researchers in the 1980s were the first to question this defense as it related to juveniles (Krisberg et al., 1987).

Looking at the portion of African American juveniles who commit serious offenses and their incarceration rates, these researchers found that a serious mismatch existed and that the argument that African American juveniles are more likely to be incarcerated because African American juveniles commit more of the serious crimes cannot be accepted. Simply, what these researchers (e.g., Poe-Yamagata & Wordes Noya, Chapter 21 of this volume) and other subsequent researchers said is that if African Americans commit 55% of the armed robberies, then they should constitute roughly the same percentage of persons imprisoned for armed robbery. But if African American juveniles commit 55% of the armed robberies, and they constitute 90% of the persons incarcerated for armed robbery, then discrimination is occurring.

Although critics will argue with statistical studies that show discrimination, qualitative data, in the form of official admissions, will sometimes confirm the impact of race in the courtroom and sentencing. For instance, as an undergraduate criminal justice major, I took a course in criminal law, which was taught by a practicing prosecutor. Before the course began, this prosecutor, as he related to the class, asked his boss, the district attorney, if could he tell students how the criminal justice system actually operated. He was told yes, but he could not be too specific about some situations. Among the comments he made to the class were that there were *always* racial and social undercurrents operating during a trial, but he could not publicly say so. Hence, if he were being interviewed by a reporter from the news media, he would give the politically correct response, which was that race and social class have no bearing on a trial and that everyone is treated the same (Alexander, 2001).

These racial and social undercurrents were not elaborated on, but they can be logically construed. Race, social class, and social standing matter in the courtroom. They are factors whether one is a victim or a defendant in the criminal justice system or a plaintiff or a defendant in the civil process. A perception exists that African American males constitute the most significant criminal element in American society. When a police officer sees an African American male, he or she sees a criminal, and judges see the same when an African American male is sitting in the defendant's chair in a criminal trial (Sartwell, 2001). Criminal trials become more aggravated when the defendant is a minority and the victim is white than when the situation is reversed. As an illustration, George and Martinez (2002) studied attitudes about racism and rape, and among their findings were that subjects recommended longer sentences for African American rapists than white rapists. A white police officer who kills an African American and who goes on trial is treated differently than an African American who kills a white police officer.

A dramatic illustration of unequal treatment is the differential punishment for crack and cocaine offenses in the federal system. African Americans and some whites bitterly complained about differences in punishment between crack use and cocaine use, with crack being punished more harshly. Congress, prosecutors, and judges denied that race had anything to do with the laws. However, Butler (1997, 1995, 1998), an African American and a former prosecutor in Washington, D.C., stated that African Americans

constituted 70% of the offenders imprisoned for drug offenses, whereas whites made up the majority of drug offenders. Butler has stated quite forcibly that racial discrimination exists in the criminal justice system and that imprisoning many African Americans simply for possessing drugs is immoral.

Human Rights Watch (2000) has studied this issue extensively. It noted that, beginning in the 1980s, the United States has been quite aggressive in reducing drug abuse. While learned people might disagree about the feasibility of the war on drugs, no person can refute that this war has had a devastating effect on African Americans, though African Americans do not constitute the majority of the drug abusers in this country in terms of percentages or actual numbers. Nevertheless, 63% of offenders sent to prison for drugs are African Americans (Human Rights Watch, 2000). In seven states, African Americans constitute 80% to 90% of the persons sent to prison for drug offenses (Human Rights Watch, 2000).

Further, the U.S. Supreme Court has made legal challenges to unequal laws and punishment virtually impossible for African Americans to contest in the courts. In *McCleskey v. Kemp* (1987), a Georgia death row prisoner contended that he was denied equal protection of the law because Georgia had a penchant for giving African Americans the death penalty when they had been convicted of crimes against whites. He produced a study by Baldus, which showed that Georgia prosecutors sought the death penalty 70% of the time when an African American was accused of murdering a white person, compared with 32% of the time when a white person was accused of murdering a white person, 15% of the time when an African American was accused of murdering an African American, and 19% of the time when a white person was accused of murdering an African American. However, the U.S. Supreme Court rejected these findings and ruled that a defendant must show that the Georgia legislature enacted and maintained the death penalty because of an anticipated racially discriminatory effect and that prosecutors evinced discrimination in the defendant's case (*McCleskey v. Kemp,* 1987). In short, an empirical study demonstrating a clear pattern of racial discrimination is useless in the courts.

One can see the myth of equal treatment more easily in the way that cases involving juveniles are handled. For example, one Ohio juvenile justice professional explained why about 90% of the youths referred to juvenile court for drug offenses in Cuyahoga County (Cleveland and surrounding suburbs), Ohio, were African Americans. The 90% came from three areas of the county, constituting one tenth of the county (Berens, 1992). White youths who were arrested for drug offenses were taken to suburban community groups, and these groups determined whether the problem would be addressed in juvenile court or by the community group (Berens, 1992). These suburban youths were not taken to juvenile detention. As one minority judge stated, this practice was illegal (Berens, 1992). But more interesting, the practice revealed a conspiracy among white community leaders and white police officers to protect white youths and keep them out of the juvenile justice system.

Similarly, Michigan wanted to get tough on juveniles and passed a law making them eligible for life imprisonment without parole for some crimes. However, when three cases emerged in which all the defendants were white and from good homes, a debate ensued whether the law was too harsh and unconstitutional. One judge went so far as to declare the law unconstitutional. Another trial judge cried as he was forced to sentence one of the youths in a murder case. But the debate surrounding the harshness of the law did not ensue until the system was threatening to incarcerate some white juveniles from good homes. The debate never occurred when juveniles from the inner city of Detroit were sentenced under the same laws.

PART 2: SPECIAL TOPICS—
EXAMPLES OF CURRENT
RACIAL BIAS OPERATING IN COURTS

Adoption

Following these principles of a colorblind society, numerous judges and some social workers, for example, now believe that African Americans are racists when African Americans denounce interracial adoption of African American children by white parents. Without a discussion of whether interracial adoption is harmful or beneficial, several researchers have eloquently stated how racism still exists in the child welfare area and that judges and Congress are only interested in one-way interracial adoption—whites who want to adopt African American children (Kupenda et al., 1998). One Mississippi judge, according to Kupenda et al. (1998), without any explanation quickly ordered social workers to remove a white female child from the household of an African American couple who took the child in foster care.

This incident caused Alexander (2002) to speculate further that the white systems throughout the country would always take race into account when placing white children who need adoptive families. These children overwhelmingly are going to, and will always go to, white families, regardless of whether the state is Mississippi, New York, Minnesota, California, or Washington.

If the country is colorblind, and race and culture should have no effect on child placement decisions, then one should see children randomly going to couples seeking adoption. If 100 white babies are available for adoption and all 100 babies go to white couples, then race is a factor. The white system will certainly take race and culture into consideration when a blonde, blue-eyed white female infant is available for adoption, and these infants will have very little chance of going to an African American or Latino couple. Simply, race and culture are important factors in the courtroom depending on whether these factors are perceived as detrimental to white culture.

Race and culture are condemned when these factors are raised within the context of African American, Latino, or other minority populations. However, race and culture, as they apply to whites, are certainly factors in a courtroom, and these factors do not need to be discussed. As Kupenda et al. (1998) stated, the Mississippi judge in the previously mentioned decision never gave his reasons for the little girl's removal from the home of an African American couple, but he did not need to state those reasons. His silence was quite illuminating.

Unfavorable Mental Health Diagnosis of African Americans

Often, the negative views that judges have of African Americans in the courtroom come from court personnel, including probation officers, psychologists, and psychiatrists. Bridges and Steen (1998) conducted a study of probation officers' written recommendations to juvenile court judges in Washington, D.C. Probation officers' recommendations to the judges often were affected by the juvenile's race. African American juveniles were perceived to be more dangerous than white youths. Moreover, African American juveniles' problems were assessed as being caused by personality factors, whereas white juveniles' problems were assessed as being caused by their environment. As a result, African American juveniles were perceived to be in greater need of control and intervention, which meant more incarceration (Bridges & Steen, 1998). In Bridges and Steen's study, none of the variables involved mental health assessments, but mental health professionals are an integral part of the assessment process for the courts.

Several professionals in the psychiatric department of the University of Cincinnati studied the charts of 1,001 children who had been admitted to the Adolescent Psychiatry Unit at Cincinnati Children's Hospital Medical Center. African American adolescents, particularly males, were significantly more likely to be diagnosed with conduct disorder than white adolescents. On the other hand, white adolescents were diagnosed more frequently than African American juveniles with alcohol disorder and major depression. These researchers concluded that race and sex might have influenced clinical psychiatric diagnoses (DelBello, Lopez-Larson, Soutullo, & Strakowski, 2001).

Probably the most negative diagnoses in the psychological and psychiatric classification system are conduct disorder for adolescents and antisocial personality disorder for adults (Kaplan & Sadock, 1998.) African Americans tend to receive these diagnoses more often than whites (Kaplan & Sadock, 1998), and mental health professionals convey this information to the legal system.

CONCLUSION AND RECOMMENDATIONS

Although courts have discussed race when forced to decide a case, the practice is to avoid discussing race as much as possible. Take, for example, the death penalty in rape cases, a practice that was halted by the U.S. Supreme Court in 1977. All the men executed for rape were African Americans, and all the victims were white females. In Virginia, African Americans were executed for attempted rape. Yet the Virginia Supreme Court maintained that race had nothing to do with these laws and executions. When the U.S. Supreme Court ruled on the constitutionality of the death penalty for rape, it avoided the race issue. When the U.S. Supreme Court ruled on the famous Miranda case, a draft opinion was circulated among the justices, and references were made in the decision to an FBI report that documented common police practices of beating confessions from African Americans. However, the justices decided to leave race out of the actual decision (Schwartz, 1983). In 2001, Washington, D.C., judges were accused of sidestepping race and religion in a murder appeal when a juror wearing a bow tie, which prosecutors believed identified the prospective juror as a member of the Nation of Islam, was struck without being asked any questions (Schoenberg, 2001).

A significant number of whites are willing to lie, deny, reject, hide, protect, reinterpret, and ignore racial issues. It began in the postslavery era and continues today (Alexander, 2000). As the Strolovitch study showed, whites have discriminatory attitudes regarding affirmative action. Take, for example, the issue of capital punishment for rape in the United States. There was not one white male who was executed for rape or one rape case that resulted in an execution when the victim was a minority woman. Yet a significant number of whites will deny even today that race was a factor in rape executions. Although some studies have shown that extralegal punishment of African Americans for rape was tied to economic conditions (Myers, 1995), the facts still remain that race was a critical factor and other groups were not scapegoated for economic downturns.

Similarly, if whites had stated in large numbers that the punishment for possessing crack cocaine should be the same as that for powder cocaine, a major effort would have been made in providing equal protection and fair treatment. But whites will continue to explain away the differences when they know that the differences in punishment are due to the fact that powdered cocaine users are likely to be their sons, daughters, relatives, friends, or colleagues, and crack attracts many African Americans from the lower class.

When judges claim that race and culture are not relevant in a courtroom involving a minority, they are being either naive or dishonest. Judges and juries come to court with their life experiences, biases, prejudices, and stereotypes. These simply are not dropped at the courthouse door. When they are led to believe by the news media that African Americans commit all the crimes, this is what they are going to see when an African American is a defendant in a criminal trial. Race and culture are always relevant and extant when middle- or upper-class white persons are defendants in a courtroom. A psychiatrist or psychologist is more likely available to this group to explain to the judge and jury the pressures impinging on a privileged group and to offer a nonstigmatizing label.

Dorfman (2001) discussed a number of recommendations to advocates on how they can work with the news media to lessen the problems of how African Americans are depicted in the news. Undoubtedly, these recommendations, if successfully implemented, will affect how African Americans are viewed in the courtroom. However, other strategies are needed.

While Dorfman called for challenging and educating the media in order to change how African Americans are depicted, a similar challenge should be made to mental health professionals, especially those mental health professionals whose evaluations are heard by judges and juries. Psychologists and psychiatrists should reexamine and reconsider the diagnoses that tend to be applied to African Americans and how these diagnoses are used by the legal system. A diagnosis of antisocial personality disorder or conduct disorder for an African American male likely means prison or detention. Perhaps the seriousness of conduct should be part of the consideration of a diagnosis, with the result that minor conduct would not facilitate imprisonment.

Another reconsideration that may need to be harbored by mental health professionals is that a diagnosis of antisocial personality disorder or conduct disorder in an African American may not be in and of itself bad. Perhaps, it is "normal" to rebel and not acquiesce to racism, oppression, discrimination, squalid living conditions, and dimmed futures. Perhaps being antisocial and displaying a conduct disorder is a sign of strength and resiliency that is fertile ground for reshaping and growth.

As a means of lessening the racism in laws and the courtrooms, Professor Paul Butler has advocated African Americans using self-help tactics by refusing to convict and send to prison African Americans for victimless crimes, such as drug possession. Butler advocates jury nullification, which "occurs when a jury acquits a defendant who it believes is guilty of the crime with which he is charged. In finding the defendant not guilty, the jury refuses to be bound by the facts of the case or the judge's instructions regarding the law. Instead, the jury votes its conscience" (Butler, 1995, p. 9). He contends that he has witnessed jury nullification as a federal prosecutor in Washington, D.C., and he contends white jurors have consistently engaged in this practice.

Butler stated that African Americans should engage in jury nullification when African Americans are tried for drug offenses and there is no violence. Although jury nullification would not be appropriate in capital cases, concerned persons who are sensitive to racism in the death penalty issue can have an impact. African Americans who oppose capital punishment should consider changing their views to support capital punishment in appropriate cases. A change in view is needed in order to qualify as a juror. Anyone who is adamantly opposed to capital punishment under all circumstances is ineligible to serve on a jury in a capital case. Once seated on a jury, a juror who believes that the defendant is guilty can vote to convict but later vote not to execute. The alternative sentence is likely life without parole, which protects the community from the offenders. It would be better for one person to sit on a jury and vote no to capital punishment than to have a dozen persons writing letters to governors and protesting at prisons on the eve of an execution.

Given the people, many of whom are African Americans, who have been released from death row after a determination of their innocence, voting for life without parole serves justice. Until society does more to acknowledge and alleviate race in the courtroom, other strategies to lessen the impact of racism should be used.

REFERENCES

Adarand Constructors, Inc. v. Pena, 515 U.S. 200 (1995).

Alexander, R., Jr. (2000). *Race and justice.* Huntington, NY: Nova Science Publishers.

Alexander, R., Jr. (2001). *To ascend into the shining world again.* Westerville, OH: Theroe Enterprises.

Alexander, R., Jr. (2002). *Understanding legal concepts that influence social welfare policy and practice.* Pacific Grove, CA: Brooks/Cole.

Allen, H. E., & Simonsen, C. E. (2001). *Corrections in America: An introduction* (9th ed.). Upper Saddle River, NJ: Prentice-Hall.

Austin, R. L., & Allen, M. D. (2000). Racial disparity in arrest rates as an explanation of racial disparity in commitment to Pennsylvania's prisons. *Journal of Research in Crime and Delinquency, 37,* 200–220.

Berens, M. (1992, May 20). Racial imbalances glaring inside youth services: Blacks make up 54.1 percent of inmates in 9 counties. *Columbus Dispatch,* p. 5C.

Bridges, G. S., & Steen, S. (1998). Racial disparities in official assessments of juvenile offenders: Attributional stereotypes as mediating mechanism. *American Sociological Review, 63,* 554–570.

Butler, P. (1995). Essay; Racially based jury nullification: Black power in the criminal justice system. *Yale Law Journal, 105,* 677–725.

Butler, P. D. (1997). The role of race-based jury nullification in American criminal justice: Race-based jury nullification: Case-in-chief. *John Marshall Law Review, 30,* 911–922.

Butler, P. (1998). Review of the book *Race, crime, and the law. Harvard Law Review, 111,* 1270–1288.

Chiricos, T. G., & Crawford, C. (1995). Race and imprisonment: A contextual assessment of the evidence. In D. F. Hawkins (Ed.), *Ethnicity, race, and crime: Perspectives across time and place* (pp. 281–309). Albany, NY: University of New York Press.

Dahlburg, J. (2002, June 23). Group aims to have every vote counted. *Los Angeles Times,* p. 15.

Danskine et al. v. Metro Dade County Fire Department et al., 1999 U.S. Dist. LEXIS 12890.

DelBello, M. P., Lopez-Larson, M. P., Soutullo, C. A., & Strakowski, S. M. (2001). Effects of race on psychiatric diagnosis of hospitalized adolescents: A retrospective chart review. *Journal of Child & Adolescent Psychopharmacology, 11,* 95–103.

Dorfman, L. (2001). *Off balance: Youth, race & crime in the news.* Building Blocks for Youth. Washington, DC: Youth Law Center.

Dred Scott v. Sandford, 60 U.S. 393 (1856).

D'Souza, D., & Edley, C., Jr. (1996). Debate: Affirmative action debate: Should race-based affirmative action be abandoned as a national policy. *Albany Law Review, 60,* 425–464.

Ensley Branch, NAACP v. Seibels, 31 F.3d 1548 (11th Cir. 1994).

Florida Statute § 97.041.

George, W. H., & Martinez, L. J. (2002). Victim blaming in rape: Effects of victim and perpetrator race, type of rape, and participant racism. *Psychology of Woman, 26,* 110–119.

Holland, J. J. (2002, June 8). Justice Department: Nothing we could do about most Florida election 2000 complaints. *Associated Press.*

Hopwood v. Texas, 78 F.3d 932 (5th Cir. 1996).

Human Rights Watch. (2000). *Punishment and prejudice: Racial disparities in the war on drugs.* Retrieved June 29, 2003, from http://www.hrw.org/reports/2000/usa/Rcedgr00.htm

Humphrey, J. A., & Fogarty, T. J. (1987). Race and plea bargained outcomes: A research note. *Social Forces, 66,* 176–182.

International Bd. of Teamsters v. United States, 431 U.S. 324 (1977).

Kaczorowski, R. J. (1985). *The politics of judicial interpretation: The federal courts, department of justice and civil rights, 1866–1876.* New York: Oceana.

Kaplan, H. I., & Sadock, B. J. (1998). *Synopsis of psychiatry: Behavioral sciences/clinical psychiatry.* Baltimore: Williams & Wilkins.

Kennedy, R. (1997). *Race, crime, and the law.* New York: Pantheon Books.

Kentucky Revised Statutes Annotated § 116.025.

Krisberg, B., Schwartz, I., Fishman, G., Eisikovits, Z., Guttman, E., & Joe, K. (1987). The incarceration of minority youth. *Crime and Delinquency, 33,* 173–205.

Kupenda, A. M., Thrash, A. L., Riley-Collins, J. A., Dukes, L. Y., Lewis, S. J., & Dixon, R. R. (1998). Law, life, and literature: Using literature and life to expose transracial adoption laws as adoption on a one-way street. *Buffalo Public Interest Law Journal, 17,* 43–69.

Law, S. A. (1999). White privilege and affirmative action. *Akron Law Review, 32,* 603–627.

Lichtman, A. J. (2002, March 5). Race was a big factor in ballot rejection. *Baltimore Sun,* p. 11a.

Maguire, K., & Pastore, A. L. (1998). *Sourcebook of criminal justice statistics.* Washington, DC: U.S. Government Printing Office.

McClenaghan, W. A. (1988). *Magruder's American government.* Needham, MA: Prentice Hall.

McCleskey v. Kemp, 481 U.S. 279 (1987).

Myers, M. A. (1995). The new South's "new black criminal": Rape and punishment in Georgia, 1870–1940. In D. F. Hawkins (Ed.), *Ethnicity, race, and crime: Perspectives across time and place* (pp. 146–166). Albany, NY: University of New York Press.

O'Connor, K., & Sabato, L. J. (1993). *American government: Roots and reform.* New York: Macmillan.

Official Code of Georgia Annotated § 21-2-216.

O'Kane, J. M. (1992). *The crooked ladder: Gangsters, ethnicity, and the American dream.* New Brunswick, NJ: Transaction.

Oliver, M. B., & Fonash, D. (2002). Race and crime in the news: Whites' identification and misidentification of violent and nonviolent criminal suspects. *Media Psychology, 4,* 137–156.

O'Toole, T. (2002, June 17). Equestrian makes Title IX horse sense. *USA Today,* p. 1C.

Powers, S. (1998, December 9). The gender trends: The law requiring gender equity in college sports has been called both a blessing and a curse, but OSU has embraced it. *Columbus Dispatch,* p. 7A.

Quillian, L., & Pager, D. (2001). Black neighbors, higher crime? The role of racial stereotypes in evaluations of neighborhood crime. *American Journal of Sociology, 107,* 717–767.

Robinson, M. (2000). The construction and reinforcement of myths of race and crime. *Journal of Contemporary Criminal Justice, 16,* 133–156.

Sack, K., & Elder, J. (2000, July 11). Poll finds optimistic outlook but enduring racial division. *New York Times,* pp. A1, A23, A24.

Sartwell, C. (2001, April 10). Commentary: Racism disguises itself as the natural order. *Los Angeles Times,* p. B9.

Schoenberg, T. (2001, July 20). Race, religion in Washington juries: Judges sidestep a sensitive issue. *Legal Times.*

Schwartz, B. (1983). *Super chief: Earl Warren and the Supreme Court.* New York: New York University Press.

Spohn, C., & DeLone, M. (2000). When does race matter? An analysis of the conditions under which race affects sentence severity. *Sociology of Crime, Law, and Deviance, 2,* 3–37.

Steffensmeier, D., & Demuth, S. (2000). Ethnicity and sentencing outcomes in U.S. federal courts: Who is punished more harshly? *American Sociological Review, 65,* 705–729.

Strolovitch, D. Z. (1998). Playing favorites: Public attitudes toward race- and gender-targeted antidiscrimination policy. *NWSA (National Women's Studies Association) Journal, 10,* 27–53.

Virginia Constitutional Article II, § 1.

Watson, R. A. (1985). *Promise and performance of American democracy* (5th ed.). New York: John Wiley & Sons.

Wilbanks, W. (1987). *The myth of a racist criminal justice system.* Monterey, CA: Brooks/Cole.

Williams v. Mississippi, 170 U.S. 213 (1898).

Yick Wo v. Hopkins, 118 U.S. 356 (1886).

7

WORKING WITH AFRICAN AMERICAN CHILDREN AND FAMILIES IN THE CHILD WELFARE SYSTEM

MARIAN S. HARRIS

University of Washington, Tacoma

ADA SKYLES

University of Chicago

The survival of African American families from slavery to contemporary times in this country has hinged upon their strength and resilience in coping with the multitude of problems emanating from the larger society. One of the most perplexing problems encountered by African American families today is the proliferation of African American children in the child welfare system. Race continues to be a very important factor in child welfare policy and practice today. "In a recent report on racial characteristics of children served by the child welfare system, African-American children comprised 40.5 percent of children in care, 42.8 percent awaiting adoptive placement, and 29.2 percent of children in finalized adoption" (Prater, 2000, pp. 98–99). Although African American families have survived and demonstrated their resilience for centuries, many of these children and families spend a large part of their lives involved with the child welfare system, especially poor children. Therefore, in order to work with African American families, one needs to have a strong knowledge base regarding these families as well as a high degree of cultural competence and sensitivity.

FEDERAL POLICY AND CHILD WELFARE

There are decades of prejudicial and discriminatory treatment of African Americans in the history of the child welfare system. Until the end of World War II, African Americans were virtually excluded from child welfare services, and when they did receive them they were limited to segregated institutions (Billingsley & Giovanni, 1972). From the mid-nineteenth century through the Great Depression, most dependent children in the United States were cared for in orphanages. By the time of the 1923 census, 31 northern states reported a total of more than 1,000 child-caring agencies; 35 were only for African American children, 234 accepted children of all races, 60 took non-Caucasian children except for African Americans, and 711 were exclusively for Caucasian children (Billingsley & Giovanni, 1972). It was more likely than not that African American children who were in need of care were classified as delinquent and sent to "prison" as their caregiving institution (Billingsley & Giovanni, 1972, p. 80). African American families who could not provide primary care for their children relied on extended family networks and community resources such as churches, women's clubs, and benevolent societies (Roberts, 2002).

In the 1930's, African American children were finally recognized by the child welfare system when services shifted from private institutions to public agencies that provided foster care (Billingsley & Giovanni, 1972). Yet religious charities, which provided the majority of child placement services in urban cities, continued the pattern of segregation and discrimination against African American children. The growth of African American children in placement continued after World War II and increased dramatically in the following decades (Roberts, 2002).

Federal policy is influential in the participation of African American families in the child welfare system. Welfare policies are fundamentally linked with child welfare policies. Families must qualify for public assistance (formerly Aid to Families With Dependent Children [AFDC], now Temporary Assistance to Needy Families [TANF]) before they are eligible for Title IV-E funds, Subpart 2 of the Social Security Act, which supports foster care and adoption assistance services. In 1996, Congress passed welfare legislation that substantially changed the 60-year-old AFDC program. The Personal Responsibility and Work Opportunity Reconciliation Act (PRWORA) shifted the responsibility for public assistance from the federal government to the states and required that public

assistance be time-limited and conditioned on the individual's participation in work activities. Moreover, it limited eligibility for the AFDC program as of July 16, 1996. PRWORA further required that the states place greater emphasis on family, in contrast to nonrelative caregivers, as resources for placing children. Although the impact of the 1996 welfare reform act is still unknown, some research studies revealed that the law has contributed to increases in the foster care rolls in several states (Shook, 1999; Slack, 2002).

The Adoption and Safe Families Act (ASFA) of 1997 amends the Adoption and Child Welfare Act of 1980, Title IV-B, Subpart 2 of the Social Security Act, and changes the name of the program that has funded general child welfare services to Promoting Safe and Stable Families (PSSF). ASFA placed greater emphasis on child safety and permanency. It shortened the time frame for achieving permanency for children from 18 months to 12 months, required states to file petitions to terminate parental rights of parents whose children have been in foster care for 15 of the previous 22 months (there are provisions for cases involving kinship care, where to do so is not in a child's best interests and where agencies have not made reasonable reunification efforts), and allows states to engage in "concurrent planning" to arrange for adoptive homes at the same time they are making reasonable efforts to reunify the family. ASFA also provided for family preservation services, family support services, and adoption promotion and support services. The implementation of PSSF is guided by the principles that are intended to support a family-focused approach based on an appreciation of cultural and community strengths. Further research is needed to determine the extent to which African American families are receiving these services and how the time-limited reunification services are affecting children and their families.

Federal policy that affects the juvenile justice system, the Juvenile Justice and Delinquency Prevention Act of 1974 (PL93-415) as amended in 1988, 1992, and 2002, requires the reduction of the disproportionate minority confinement and disparate treatment of minorities at all stages in the juvenile justice system and is also linked to the child welfare system. The pattern of greater participation of African Americans in the child welfare system is similar to what occurs for African Americans in the juvenile justice system. In 1992, the reduction of disproportionate minority confinement (DMC) became one of the priorities for the Office of Juvenile Justice and Delinquency Prevention, and in the 2002 amendments, the legislation required states not only to address and reduce DMC but also to address the disparate treatment of minorities at all stages of the juvenile justice process. In contrast, there is no mandate in any child welfare legislation to address the disproportionate participation of African Americans in that system.

The juvenile justice system is an important pathway to and from the child welfare system for African American youth. Each system is a recruitment source for the other (Green, 2002). Research has found that maltreated children are more likely than nonmaltreated children to engage in behaviors that lead to incarceration, and many youth who age out of the foster care system end up in correctional facilities (Jonson-Reid & Barth, 2000; Wiebush, Freitag, & Baird, 2001).

Further research is needed to determine how these new policies and practices that are mandated in the law will affect the well-being of African American children and the reduction of their overrepresentation in the child welfare system.

UNDERSTANDING AFRICAN AMERICAN FAMILIES

A clear definition of the African American family is a precursor to any work with African American children and their families in the child welfare system. For African Americans, the legacy of racism and oppression cannot be ignored or forgotten in the examination of family. Martin and Martin (1978) defined the African American family as

> a multigenerational, interdependent kinship system which is welded together by a sense of obligation to relatives; is organized around a "family base" household; is generally guided by a "dominant

family figure;" extends across geographical boundaries to connect family units to an extended family network; and has a built in mutual aid system for the welfare of its members and the maintenance of the family as a whole. (p. 1)

The basis of the African American family is interdependence. The family is a system of blood and fictive (nonblood) kin. The kinship networks of most African American families include relatives as well as individuals not related by blood or marriage. Extended family systems are usually large and constantly growing. Family connotes many generations.

The extended family has always been a viable system in the African American culture. Its roots can be traced back to Africa. "In Africa, close-knit families and kinship groups were the foundations of the larger social structure of the tribe and the nation" (Black, 1996, p. 59). Inherent in this system for African Americans are the blood relatives and nonblood relatives who are bound together through reciprocal support as well as a strong sense of caring and responsibility. Loyalty and responsibility to others is instilled in one at an early age. African Americans have a responsibility to their family of origin as well as a responsibility to their community. Family means community. "This is evident in the fact that in the African American community the meaning of the term *parents* includes natural parents and grandparents as well as others who, at different times, assume parental roles and responsibilities" (Locke, 1992, p. 25). In times of crisis or need family members have a responsibility to help family members (Carter & McGoldrick, 1998; Hines & Boyd-Franklin, 1996). It is quite common for family members to make sacrifices for the sake of the family; this is one of the strengths often demonstrated by many African American families. These strengths must be identified and supported in work with African American families in the child welfare system. It is a crisis when African American children come into the child welfare system. According to Williams (1991), the child welfare system has a "funnel effect" on African American children; it is easy for these children to enter and remain in the system, but hard for them to exit the system.

PROBLEM OF OVERREPRESENTATION: WHAT IS KNOWN

African American children are overrepresented in America's child welfare system. Although African Americans constituted 15% of the child population of the United States in 1999, they accounted for 45% of children in out-of-home care (U.S. DHHS, 1999). In contrast, white children constituted 60% of the child population and only 36% of the children in substitute care (Morton, 1999). An entry into the child welfare system begins with an investigation and then a substantiated report of child abuse, neglect, or abandonment by child protective services (CPS). Throughout the various stages in the system, there are decision points for the professionals involved to make decisions regarding permanency planning for African American children.

Research studies show that African American and white children follow dissimilar paths and have disparate experiences in the child welfare system (Courtney et al., 1996; Garland & Besinger, 1997; Hampton, 1987; Wulczyn, Brunner, & Goerge, 1999). African American children are significantly more likely than white children to be reported to child protective services (Chasnoff, Landress, & Barrett, 1990; Hampton & Newberger, 1985; Rolock & Testa, 2001). According to Fluke, Yuan, Hedderson, and Curtis (2002), they appear to be investigated disproportionately more than whites, particularly children who are emotionally maltreated or physically neglected, or who have suffered serious or fatal injuries. There was also evidence of disproportionality in investigations when the reports came from mental health or social service professionals and when the children's parents abused substances (Sedlak & Schultz, 2001). Also, most studies examining substantiation rates of child abuse and neglect conclude that African Americans are overrepresented (Ards, Myers, Malkis, Sugrue, & Zhou, 2003; Cappellari, Eckenrode, & Powers, 1993; Hampton, 1987; Hill, 2003).

Once maltreatment allegations are substantiated, child welfare agencies have three options: to close the case without any services, to provide services in the home, or to place the child in out-of-home care. Nationally, for those children receiving child welfare services, 56% of African American children were placed in foster care, whereas 72% of white children received services in the home (U.S. Children's Bureau, 1997). More recent studies have found that African American children are more likely than white children to be placed in foster care (Barth, Green, & Miller, 2001; Goerge & Lee, 2001); this is true even when controlling for differences in factors such as age, maltreatment reason, and neighborhood poverty (Needell, Brookhart, & Lee, 2002). Studies that examined children exiting out-of-home care reveal that African American children remain in foster care longer, with much lower probabilities for becoming adopted or reunified with their families (Barth, Courtney, & Berry, 1994; Barth, Webster, & Lee, 2000; McMurtry & Lie, 1992; Wulczyn et al., 1999). Although the slower rates of reunification and adoption of African American children contribute to their overrepresentation in the child welfare system, research on the reentry of children into foster care does not show a higher return rate for African American children and is not considered a contributory factor to their overrepresentation (Baird, 2001; Terling, 1999; Wulczyn et al., 1999).

EXPLANATIONS OF OVERREPRESENTATION

There is ongoing debate about the disproportionate presence of African American children in the child welfare system relative to their numbers in the general population (overrepresentation) and in relation to other racial groups (disproportionate participation). The most common explanations include the following:

- African American children and their families have higher levels of risk factors (such as poverty, single-parent families, unemployment, substance abuse) that are associated with child maltreatment, which in turn results in greater need for services (Bartholet, 1999; McCabe et al., 1999).
- Overrepresentation is the result of a failure to understand African American families and the inappropriate placement of African American

children in the child welfare system (Hill, 2003; Roberts, 2002).

- Overrepresentation is the product of racial discriminatory practices and policies both societal and institutional (Roberts, 2002).

Research studies of community factors and delivery of services are informative in understanding the overrepresentation of African American children in the child welfare system. Studies that examine the importance of community factors consistently suggest that overrepresentation has much more to do with the disadvantaged and impoverished characteristics of the communities in which the families live than with their race (Garbarino & Kostelny, 1992). These researchers found a strong relationship between reports of child maltreatment and socioeconomic conditions of communities. For example, in neighborhoods where child abuse and neglect were higher than expected, the research informants had a difficult time saying anything positive about the community, assumed the lack of formal or informal support systems, described the physical environment as depressing, perceived extensive gang activity, and knew less about available community services. In the communities where maltreatment was less than expected, the informants expressed more positive attitudes toward the community. Korbin, Coulton, Chard, Platt-Houston, and Su (1998) also concluded that child maltreatment was explained more by the characteristics of the community than by race of the residents, with findings of somewhat lower rates of child maltreatment among African American communities than in white communities. A recent study of poor Chicago communities revealed that the neighborhoods occupied by African Americans were the same neighborhoods with high maltreatment when European immigrants occupied them almost 100 years earlier (Testa, 2001).

Research on delivery of services to the children and their families in the child welfare system consistently demonstrates that African American children are at a disadvantage regarding the range and quality of services provided, the type of agency to which they are referred, the efficiency with which their cases are handled, the support their families receive, and their eventual outcomes (Courtney et al., 1996; Daniel, Hampton, & Newberger, 1983; Fanshel, 1981; Jeter, 1963; Maluccio & Fein, 1989; Olsen, 1982). Close (1983) examined a national survey of social services and concluded that African American children had fewer visits with their families, less contact with workers, and fewer services overall than white children. A later study by Saunders, Nelson, and Landsman (1993) reported that the child welfare system is less responsive to the needs of African American families than to those of white families by delaying intervention until their problems are perceived as chronic; the child welfare system fails to address the most pressing problems such as poverty, ill health, inadequate housing, and unsafe neighborhoods. Further, African American children in foster care consistently receive fewer or poor quality mental health services, even after controlling for factors such as need, income, insurance status, maltreatment type, and severity of mental health problem (Garland, Landsverk, & Lau, 2002). Courtney et al. (1996) concluded in their extensive review of research pertaining to race and child welfare that there was "a pattern of inequity, if not discrimination, based on race and ethnicity in the provision of child welfare services" (p. 112).

THE ASSESSMENT PROCESS

Strengths of each African American family should be identified during the assessment process. A pathology-based assessment will do nothing to promote culturally sensitive practice in working with African American families in the child welfare system. "African American families are complicated, strong, weak, multidimensional, similar, and dissimilar. While contributing to their diversity, individuality and collectivism, these characteristics make each person a unique African American who is also a member of an African American family" (Brisbane & Womble, 1992, p. 4).

According to Hill (1997), the strengths of African American families are as follows: "strong achievement orientation; strong work orientation; flexible family roles; strong kinship bonds; and strong religious orientation" (p. 50). The strengths of African American families have been ignored in many earlier studies; these studies have pathologized African American families and described them as disorganized, deprived, and disadvantaged (Deutsch & Brown, 1964; Frazier, 1966; Moynihan, 1965). However, several contemporary researchers have focused on the strengths of the African American family (Billingsley, 1968, 1992; Boyd-Franklin, 1989; Hill, 1972, 1997; Hines & Boyd-Franklin, 1982, 1996; Hines, Garcia-Preto, McGoldrick, Almeida, & Weltman, 1992; McAdoo, 1981; Staples, 1985; White, 1972).

It is imperative to work with the entire family system when African American children are in the care and custody of the child welfare system. This work includes understanding the relationship of the child to his or her family of origin. However, prior to work with any African American family, it is important to do a thorough assessment of the family. All family members should be included in each phase of the assessment and service planning process.

Development and implementation of a good service plan is a key component in the permanency planning process for African American families in the child welfare system. The family of origin should be involved in the development of the service plan. For the purpose of this chapter, family of origin is defined as

> that family of blood ties, both vertical (multigenerational) and horizontal (kinship), living or dead, geographically close or distant, known or unknown, accessible or inaccessible, but always in some way psychologically relevant. Also included in the family of origin are adopted members and fictive kin, people who, although not related by blood, are considered and have functioned as part of a family. (Hartman & Laird, 1983, pp. 29–30)

This definition is biologically, socially, and psychologically based. Inherent in this definition is the fact that most individuals are concurrent members of more than one family. This is especially true for the large number of African American children who are in the care and custody of the child welfare system today. These concurrent family memberships can be used to

help rather than hurt children in the child welfare system. Yet, once children come into the care and custody of the child welfare system, it seems as though the child welfare system forgets and/or negates the fact that these children have families of origin. Although there is some emphasis today on family continuity and family preservation, there is agreement that the number of children entering the foster care system has escalated dramatically in recent years. At the same time that caseloads were growing, foster care resources were shrinking. The child welfare system has turned to relatives of abused, neglected, and dependent children for help in managing this increasing demand for services in the midst of decreasing resources. In the African American culture, many children have been cared for by extended family members (Martin & Martin, 1978; Stack, 1974). However, the care of children by extended family members was an alternative to the child welfare system (Gleeson & Craig, 1994). Today, care of children by the relatives of their birth parents also operates as a government-funded and -regulated type of substitute care for abused, neglected, and dependent children.

KINSHIP CARE

The kinship networks of most African American families include relatives as well as individuals not related by blood or marriage. This frame of reference is certainly in accord with kinship care as defined by the Child Welfare League of America (2004).

> Kinship care may be defined as the full-time nurturing and protection of children who must be separated from their parents by relatives, members of their tribes or clans, godparents, stepparents, or other adults who have a kinship bond with a child. (p. 2)

During the 1980s and 1990s, there was a dramatic surge in kinship care because of the increase in substance abuse problems by birth parents (Harris, 1997, 1999; Johnson, 1994). Several studies have shown that children who are removed from the care of their birth parents because of parental substance abuse are less likely to be reunified with their birth parents, and this is even more apparent for children of color (Besharov, 1989; Fanshel, 1975; Feig, 1990; National Black Child Development Institute, 1989; Walker, Zangrillo, & Smith, 1991).

Placement of children in kinship care is a frequent child welfare practice in large, urban states such as New York, California, Maryland, and Illinois; the majority of these children are members of economically disadvantaged families of color (Barth & Berry, 1990; Kusserow, 1992; Testa, 1992, 1993; Wulczyn & Goerge, 1992). For example, in the state of Illinois, the growth in kinship care placements is largely a Cook County and an African American phenomenon. The percentage of African American children from Cook County in kinship foster care placements increased from 33% in fiscal years (FY) 1977–1978 to 65% in FY 1991–1992 (Testa, 1993). Over one half (56%) of the kinship care placements in Illinois in FY 1991–1992 included initial placements of African American children with relatives in Cook County (Testa, 1993). Children in kinship care placements have lower rates of reunification or other types of discharge from the child welfare system than children placed in nonrelated foster care placements (Testa, 1993; Wulczyn, Harden, & Goerge, 1997).

Several lawsuits affected formalized kinship care. In *L. J. v. Massinga,* a class-action suit brought against Maryland by the Baltimore Legal Aid and the Children's Defense Fund, the primary focus was on the failure of the system to protect foster children from neglect and abuse while in the system. A consent decree, approved in 1988, focused on systemic reform in a number of issues. It established the principle that children in kinship care should have access to specialized services formerly only provided to children in licensed foster homes. In *Miller v. Yoakim,* a case originally filed in federal district court in Illinois and later appealed in the U.S. Supreme Court, the principle was established that states cannot discriminate against kinship caregivers under the federal foster care program. In essence, foster care payments should be provided to kinship caregivers when the following conditions are met: (a) The child is eligible for federal Title

IV-E assistance by being eligible for TANF, (b) there is judicial determination of abuse and neglect, (c) the kinship home meets state licensing requirements, and (d) the child is under the custody of the agency (Downs, Moore, McFadden, & Costin, 2000, p. 346).

Some of the policies in kinship care have been problematic for many African American families and children. For example, there has been a strong push in recent years to use relative adoption as a permanency goal for children in kinship care; some kinship caregivers, especially grandmothers, have been reluctant to adopt their grandchildren. "There has always been informal adoption of children in many African American families, however, in contemporary times kinship caregivers are strongly encouraged by child welfare practitioners to formally adopt children in their care or to become the subsidized guardian of children in their care" (Harris, in press). One grandmother asked, "Why should I adopt my grandchild? I am her grandmother and will always be her grandmother." In traditional kinship care in African American families, relatives expect and accept reliance on one another whenever the need arises. Grandparents, aunts, cousins, sisters, and brothers share responsibility for child care. In fact, it is not unusual for a child or children to be informally adopted and reared by extended family members who have the necessary resources that the birth parents do not have (Hill, 1997). This practice is viewed as a very positive aspect of extended family support. According to Stack (1974), this process is called "child keeping"; it is viewed as a survival method that evolved in the African American culture as a reaction the problems and stressors inherent in rearing children with few economic resources. Many grandparents have expressed their reluctance to accept the termination of parental rights in order for them to be able to adopt their grandchildren. These grandparents hope that the birth parents will eventually be able regain custody of their children and assume their parenting role. Although kinship care continues to be the placement of choice for many African American children in the child welfare system, research is still limited regarding this widely used type of placement. Berrick, Barth, and Needell (1994) stated:

A careful comparative assessment of the well-being of children placed in kinship care as compared to other alternatives would be informative, but it is impossible as long as kinship foster parents receive fewer services and less financial support than other providers. Kinship foster parents in this sample suggested that their relationship to the child was warm and close; their expectations that the child would experience a bright and promising future attest to the potential strength of family raising children. Kinship foster parents maintain close ties to birth parents and indicate that they consider the child to be family. They love the children they take into their homes. A family's love is certainly not enough, but is there a better place to start? (p. 83)

African American families have very extensive and intensive kin networks. These kinship networks play a major role in helping to sustain African American family life when African American children are in the child welfare system.

CULTURAL COMPETENCE

It is imperative for one to have a high degree of cultural competence when working with African American children and families in the child welfare system. Cultural competence is an ongoing process. One cannot simply attend one or two workshops, seminars, classes, and the like and think that he or she is culturally competent. One has to be continuously committed to this developmental process, because it is a lifelong process. Cultural competence is a "set of congruent behaviors, attitudes, and policies that come together in a system, agency, or among professionals and enable that system, agency, or professionals to work effectively in cross-cultural situations" (Cross, Bazron, Dennis, & Isaacs, 1989, p. 13). The term African American includes a diverse group of people (African Americans who were born in this country and Africans as well as individuals from Central and South America and the West Indies). In working with African American children and families in the child welfare system, it is imperative to remember that slavery, racism, and oppression have defined the experience of African

Americans in this country; yet there is much diversity in these families.

It is significant to have self-awareness when working with African American children and families in the child welfare system. One cannot work effectively with children and families who are racially, ethnically, or culturally different than oneself if one lacks self-awareness. Self-awareness will increase sensitivity to African American children and families in the child welfare system. "Knowing one's own personal biases, values, and interests—which stem from culture—as well as one's own culture will greatly enhance one's sensitivity toward other cultures" (Locke, 1992, pp. 1–2). A lack of self-awareness will greatly hamper the service delivery process for African American children and families in the child welfare system.

There are two elements of culture that encompass cultural competence. "Culture is both subjective and objective in that it is comprised of a meaning system (subjective) that dictates how and why to behave in a certain way, the objective component" (Hogan-Garcia, 1999, p. 11). Culture is dynamic and exists at several levels. African American children and families in the child welfare system are affected at all of these levels.

Culture also needs to be thought of as operating on *several levels simultaneously*.

It exists at the *micro level* of the individual—in the person's values, beliefs, explanatory systems, and behaviors, which are learned in the family and other basic social groups. Culture, however, also exists at the *macro level* in organizations and institutions encompassing schools, workplaces, media, government, the criminal justice system, and the like. The policies, procedures, and programs of these organizations and institutions embody the culture in which and through which we live. (Hogan-Garcia, 1999, p. 12)

The culture of the child welfare system frames the daily lives of the African American children and families in this system. The decisions made by individuals in this system can affect the lives of these children in a positive or negative way. The system has enormous power over the lives of the disproportionate number of African American children who are constantly entering this system. Therefore, cultural competence is required to conceptualize their problems and develop permanency plans that are congruent to the culture of African American children and families. Professionals in the child welfare system must be able to assess the role of all significant family members, their cultural values and belief systems, and how these will affect permanency planning for African American children and families in the child welfare system. Finally, cultural competence entails integration of knowledge about the African American culture and the impact of all social, political, economic, and environmental stressors and their relationship to the entry and exit of African American children and their families in the child welfare system. Racial, ethnic, and cultural differences can adversely affect African American children and families in the child welfare system if professionals do not have cultural sensitivity and a high degree of cultural competency.

professionals in the child welfare system to mobilize around concerns that affect African American children and their families (Rooney, 2002). Professionals in the child welfare system must start to develop cultural competence, including a knowledge base regarding the following: (a) structure of African American families; (b) history of African American families including issues of racism, discrimination, and oppression; (c) formal and informal kinship care practices; (d) culturally sensitive family assessment; (e) reasons for overrepresentation of African American children in the child welfare system; and (f) policies that affect African American children and families in the child welfare system. This knowledge base and ongoing development of cultural competency and sensitivity will go a long way in eliminating many of the discriminatory practices currently affecting African American children and families in the child welfare system.

CONCLUSION

There are many unanswered questions about why there is an overrepresentation and disproportionate number of African Americans in the child welfare system. However, decades of research show that children in similar circumstances are treated differently, whether the discrimination was intentional or not (Ards et al., 2003; Courtney et al., 1996).

Roberts (2002) admonishes professionals not to forget that race matters in our society when considering policies and practices that affect African American children and their families. "All else is not equal. And all else is not equal because of a continuing legacy of racial discrimination. Racism allows us to predict with absolute certainty the color of families you will see if you walk into any urban juvenile court or child welfare agency" (p. 94). She emphasizes that "[t]he racial disparity in the child welfare system—even if related directly to economic inequality—ultimately results from racial injustice" (p. 95).

Focusing on change and opting for the future as guiding principles in the helping process for African American children and their families are also important when considering policies in the child welfare system; these principles allow

REFERENCES

Ards, S., Myers, S., Malkis, A., Sugrue, E., & Zhou, L. (2003). Racial disproportionality in reported and substantiated child abuse and neglect: An examination of systematic bias. *Children and Youth Services Review, 25*(5–6), 375–392.

Baird, C. (2001, January). *The impact of risk assessments and their relationship to maltreatment recurrence across races.* Paper presented at the Race Matters Forum sponsored by the University of Illinois at Urbana-Champaign.

Barth, R. P., & Berry, M. (1990). A decade later: Outcomes of permanency planning. In North American Council of Adoptable Children (Ed.), *The Adoption Assistance and Child Welfare Act of 1980: The first ten years* (pp. 7–39). St. Paul, MN: North American Council of Adoptable Children.

Barth, R. P., Courtney, M., & Berry, M. (1994). Timing is everything: An analysis of the time to adoption and legalization. *Social Work Research, 18*(3), 139–148.

Barth, R., Green, R., & Miller, J. (2001, January). *Toward understanding racial disproportionality in child welfare services receipt.* Paper presented at the Race Matters Forum sponsored by the University of Illinois at Urbana-Champaign.

Barth, R. P., Webster, D., & Lee, S. (2000). *Adoption of American Indian children in California.* (Unpublished manuscript available from the author at UNC-CH School of Social Work, 301 Pittsboro Street, Chapel Hill, NC 27599–3550.)

Bartholet, E. (1999). *Nobody's children: Abuse and neglect foster drift and the adoption alternative.* Boston: Beacon Press.

Berrick, J. D., Barth, R. P., & Needell, B. (1994). A comparison of kinship foster homes and foster family homes: Implications for kinship foster care as family preservation. *Children and Youth Services Review, 16*(1/2), 33–64.

Besharov, D. (1989). The children of crack: Will we protect them? *Public Welfare, 47,* 6–13.

Billingsley, A. (1968). *Black families in white America.* Englewood Cliffs, NJ: Prentice-Hall.

Billingsley, A. (1992). *Climbing Jacob's ladder: The enduring legacy of African-American families.* New York: Simon & Schuster.

Billingsley, A., & Giovanni, J. (1972). *Children of the storm: Black children and American child welfare.* New York: Harcourt, Brace and Jovanovich.

Black, L. (1996). Families of African origin: An overview. In M. McGoldrick, J. Giordana, & J. K. Pearce (Eds.), *Ethnicity and family therapy* (2nd ed., pp. 57–65). New York: Guilford Press.

Boyd-Franklin, N. (1989). *Black families in therapy: A multisystems approach.* New York: Guilford Press.

Brisbane, F. L., & Womble, M. (1992). Working with the strengths of African American families. In *Working with African Americans: The professional's handbook* (pp. 1–20). Chicago: HRDI International Press.

Cappellari, J., Eckenrode, J., & Powers, J. (1993). The epidemiology of child abuse: Findings from the second national incidence and prevalence study of child abuse and neglect. *American Journal of Public Health, 83*(11), 1622–1624.

Carter, B., & McGoldrick, M. (1998). Family life cycle: Individual, family, and social perspectives (3rd ed.). Upper Saddle River, NJ: Pearson Allyn & Bacon.

Chasnoff, I. J., Landress, H. J., & Barrett, M. E. (1990). The prevalence of illicit-drug or alcohol use during pregnancy and discrepancies in mandatory reporting in Pinellas County, Florida. *New England Journal of Medicine, 322*(17), 1202–1206.

Child Welfare League of America. (2004). *Kinship care.* Accessed May 20, 2003, from http://www.cwla.org/programs/kinship/

Close, M. M. (1983). Child welfare and people of color: Denial of equal access. *Social Work Research and Abstracts, 19*(4), 13–20.

Courtney, M. E., Barth, R. P., Berrick, J. D., Brooks, D., Needell, B., & Park, L. (1996). Race and child welfare services: Past research and future directions. *Child Welfare, 75*(2), 99–137.

Cross, T. L., Bazron, B. J., Dennis, K. W., & Isaacs, M. R. (1989). *Towards a culturally competent system of care.* Washington, DC: Georgetown University Child Development Center.

Daniel, J., Hampton, R., & Newberger, E. (1983). Child abuse and accidents in black families. *American Journal of Orthopsychiatry, 53*(4), 645–653.

Deutsch, M., & Brown, B. (1964). Social lnfluences in Negro-white intellectual differences. *Social Issues, 20,* 27–36.

Downs, S. W., Moore, E., McFadden, E. J., & Costin, L. B. (2000). Foster care: A service for children and their families. In *Child welfare and family services: Policies and practices* (6th ed., pp. 307–380). Boston: Allyn & Bacon.

Fanshel, D. (1975). Prenatal failure and consequences for children: The drug-abusing mother whose children are in foster care. *American Journal of Public Health, 65,* 604–612.

Fanshel, D. (1981). Decision-making under uncertainty: Foster care for abused and neglected children? *American Journal of Public Health, 71*(7), 685–686.

Feig, L. (1990). *Drug exposed infants: Service needs and policy questions.* Washington, DC: U.S. Department of Health and Human Services, Office of Assistant Secretary for Policy and Evaluation.

Fluke, J., Yuan, Y., Hedderson, J., & Curtis, P. (2002). Disproportionate representation of race and ethnicity in child maltreatment: Investigation and victimization. *Children and Youth Service Review, 25*(5–6), 359–373.

Frazier, E. F. (1996). *The Negro family in the United States.* Chicago: University of Chicago Press.

Garbarino, J., & Kostelny, K. (1992). Child maltreatment as a community problem. *Child Abuse and Neglect, 19*(4), 455–464.

Garland, A. F., & Besinger, B. A. (1997). Racial/ethnic differences in court referred pathways to mental health services for children in foster care. *Children and Youth Services Review, 19*(8), 651–666.

Garland, A., Landsverk, J., & Lau, A. (2002). Racial/ethnic disparities in mental health service use among children in foster care. *Children and Youth Service Review, 25*(5–6), 491–507.

Gleeson, J. P., & Craig, L. C. (1994). Kinship care in child welfare: An analysis of states' policies. *Children and Youth Services Review, 16*(1/2), 7–31.

Goerge, R., & Lee, B. (2001). *The entry of children from the welfare system into foster care: Differences by race.* (Unpublished paper)

Green, M. (2002, November/December). Minorities as majority: Disproportionality in child welfare and juvenile justice. *CWLA Children's Voice,* 8–13.

Hampton, R. L. (1987). Race, class, and child maltreatment. *Journal of Comparative Family Studies, 18*(1), 113–126.

Hampton, R. L., & Newberger, E. (1985). Child abuse incidence and reporting by hospitals: Significance of severity, class and race. *American Journal of Public Health, 75*(1), 56–60.

Harris, M. S. (1997). *Factors that affect family reunification of African American birth mothers and their children placed in kinship care.* Unpublished doctoral dissertation, Smith College, School for Social Work, Northampton, MA.

Harris, M. S. (1999). Comparing mothers of children in kinship foster care: Reunification vs. remaining in care. In J. P. Gleeson & C. F. Hairston (Eds.), *Kinship care: Improving practice through research* (pp. 145–166). Washington, DC: Child Welfare League of America, Inc.

Harris, M. S. (in press). Kinship care: Best practices for African American mothers and their children. In J. E. Everett, S. S. Chipungu, & B. R. Leashore (Eds.), *Child welfare revisited: An Africentric perspective.* New Brunswick, NJ: Rutgers University Press.

Hartman, A., & Laird, J. (1983). In *Family-centered social work practice* (pp. 29–31). New York: Free Press.

Hill, R. (1972). *The strengths of black families.* New York: Emerson Hall.

Hill, R. (1997). Solutions framework. In *The strengths of African American families: Twenty-five years later* (pp. 1–54). Washington, DC: R & B Publishers.

Hill, R. B. (2003). *Disproportionality of minorities in child welfare: Synthesis of research findings.* Working paper for the Race Matters Consortium.

Hines, P. M., & Boyd-Franklin, N. (1982). Black families. In M. McGoldrick, J. Pearce, & J. Giordana (Eds.), *Ethnicity and family therapy* (pp. 84–107). New York: Guilford Press.

Hines, P. M., & Boyd-Franklin, N. (1996). African American families. In M. McGoldrick, J. Giordana, & J. K. Pearce (Eds.), *Ethnicity and family therapy* (2nd ed., pp. 66–84). New York: Guilford Press.

Hines, P., Garcia-Preto, N., McGoldrick, M., Almeida, R., & Weltman, S. (1992). Intergenerational relationships across cultures. *Families in Society, 73*(6), 323–338.

Hogan-Garcia, M. (1999). Understanding culture as it operates on different social levels. In *The four skills of cultural diversity competence* (pp. 11–42). Belmont, CA: Brooks/Cole.

Jeter, H. (1963). *Children, problems and services in child welfare programs.* Washington, DC: U.S. Department of Health, Education and Welfare.

Johnson, I. L. (1994). Kinship care. In D. J. Besharov (Ed.), *When drug addicts have children: Reorienting child welfare's response* (pp. 221–228). Washington, DC: Child Welfare League of America, Inc.

Jonson-Reid, M., & Barth, R. (2000). From placement to prison: The path to adolescent incarceration from child welfare supervised foster or group care. *Children and Youth Services Review, 22*(7), 493–516.

Korbin, J., Coulton, C., Chard, S., Platt-Houston, C., & Su, M. (1998). Impoverishment and child maltreatment in African-American and European-American neighborhoods. *Development and Psychopathology, 10,* 215–233.

Kusserow, R. P. (1992). *Using relatives for foster care* (OEI-06-90-02390). Washington, DC: U.S. Department of Health and Human Services, Office of the Inspector General.

Locke, D. C. (1992). African Americans. In *Increasing multicultural understanding: A comprehensive model* (pp. 15–29). Newbury Park, CA: Sage Publications.

Maluccio, A., & Fein, E. (1989). An examination of long-term family foster care for children and youth. In J. Hudson & B. Galaway (Eds.). *The state as parent* (pp. 387–400). Dordrecht, The Netherlands: Kluwer Academic.

Martin, E. P., & Martin, J. M. (1978). Introduction. In *The black extended family* (pp. 1–4). Chicago: University of Chicago Press.

McAdoo, H. P. (1981). *Black families.* Newbury Park, CA: Sage Publications.

McCabe, K., Yeh, M., Hough, R., Landsverk, J., Hurlburt, M., Culver, S., et al. (1999). Racial/ethnic representation across five public sectors of care for youth. *Journal of Emotional and Behavioral Disorders, 7,* 72–82.

McMurtry, S. L., & Lie, G. Y. (1992). Differential exit rates of minority children in foster care. *Social Work Research & Abstracts, 28*(1), 42–48.

Morton, T. (1999). The increasing colorization of America's child welfare system: The overrepresentation of African American children. *Policy and Practice of Public Human Services, 47*(4), 23–30.

Moynihan, D. P. (1965). *The Negro family: The case for national action.* Washington, DC: U.S. Department of Labor.

National Black Child Development Institute. (1989). *Who will care when parents can't: A study of black children in foster care.* Washington, DC: Author.

Needell, B., Brookhart, A., & Lee, S. (2002). Black children and foster care placement in California. *Children and Youth Services Review, 25*(5–6), 393–408.

Olsen, L. (1982). Services for minority children in out-of-home care. *Social Services Review, 56,* 572–585.

Prater, G. (2000). Child welfare and African-American families. In N. A. Cohen (Ed.), *Child welfare: A multicultural focus* (pp. 87–115). Boston: Allyn & Bacon.

Roberts, D. (2002). *Shattered bonds: The color of child welfare.* New York: Civitas.

Rolock, N., & Testa, M. (2001, January). *Indicated child abuse and neglect reports: Is the investigation process racially biased?* Paper presented at the Race Matters Forum sponsored by the University of Illinois at Urbana-Champaign.

Rooney, G. D. (2002). Developing resources, planning, and advocacy as intervention strategies. In D. H. Hepworth, R. H. Rooney, & J. A. Larsen (Eds.), *Direct social work practice: Theory and skills* (6th ed., pp. 437–476). Pacific Grove, CA: Brooks/Cole.

Saunders, E., Nelson, K., & Landsman, M. (1993). Racial inequality and child neglect: Findings in a metropolitan area. *Child Welfare, 72*(4), 341–354.

Sedlak, A., Bruce, C., & Schultz, D. (2001). Sample selection bias is misleading. *Child Abuse and Neglect, 25*(1), 1–5.

Shook, K. (1999). Does the loss of welfare income increase the risk of involvement with the child welfare system? *Child and Youth Services Review, 21*(8/9), 693–724.

Slack, K. S. (2002). Assessing the influence of welfare reform on child welfare systems. *Focus, 22*(1), 98–105.

Stack, C. (1974). *All our kin: Strategies for survival in the black community.* New York: Harper and Row.

Staples, R. (1985). Changes in black family structure: The conflict between family ideology and structural conditions. *Journal of Marriage and the Family, 47,* 1005–1013.

Terling, T. (1999). The efficacy of family reunification practices. *Child Abuse and Neglect, 23*(12), 1359–1370.

Testa, M. F. (1992). Conditions of risk for substitute care. *Children and Youth Services Review, 14,* 27–36.

Testa, M. F. (1993). *Home of relative (HMR) program in Illinois: Interim report* (Revised). Chicago: University of Chicago, School of Social Service Administration.

Testa, M. (2001, January). *The changing significance of race and kinship for achieving permanency for foster children.* Paper presented at the Race Matters Forum sponsored by the University of Illinois at Urbana-Champaign.

U.S. Children's Bureau. (1997). *National study of protective, preventive and reunification services delivered to children and their families.* Washington, DC: U.S. Department of Health and Human Services.

U.S. DHHS. (1999, June 18). How many children entered foster care during the period 10/11/97 through 3/31/98? U.S. DHHS. Retrieved September 11, 1999, from http://www.acf.dhhs.gov/programs/cb/stats/arO199.htm

Walker, C. D., Zangrillo, P., & Smith, J. (1991). *Parental drug abuse and African American children in foster care: Issues and study findings.* Washington, DC: National Black Child Development Institute.

White, J. (1972). Towards a black psychology. In R. Jones (Ed.), *Black psychology* (pp. 43–50). New York: Harper & Row.

Wiebush, R., Freitag, R., & Baird, C. (2001, July). Preventing delinquency through improved child protection services. *OJJDP Juvenile Justice Bulletin.*

Williams, C. C. (1991). Expanding the options in the quest for permanence. In J. E. Everett, S. S. Chipungu, & B. R. Leashore (Eds.), *Child welfare: An Africentric perspective* (pp. 266–289). New Brunswick, NJ: Rutgers University Press.

Wulczyn, F., Brunner, K., & Goerge, R. (1999). *A report from the multistate foster care data archive: Foster care dynamics, 1983–1997.* Chicago: Chapin Hall Center for Children at the University of Chicago.

Wulczyn, F. H., & Goerge, R. M. (1992). Foster care in New York and Illinois: The challenge of rapid change. *Social Service Review, 66*(2), 278–294.

Wulczyn, F. H., Harden, A. W., & Goerge, R. M. (1997). *Foster care dynamics 1983–1994: An update from the multistate foster care data archive.* Chicago: Chapin Hall Center for Children at the University of Chicago.

PART II

ASSESSMENT

8

Guidelines and Suggestions for Conducting Successful Cross-Cultural Evaluations for the Courts

Kimberly Holt Barrett

University of Washington

The clinician who works across cultures in conducting psychological evaluations for the courts faces numerous challenges in the assessment process. These challenges arise as a result of the critical need to consider the dynamics of culture, race, language, and ethnicity as they influence the life of the client; as they influence the client's legal case; and as they influence the evaluator and the evaluation process. This chapter is designed to help provide direction and suggestions to the cross-cultural evaluator in order to facilitate the development of culturally competent psychological evaluations in legal settings. The information that is presented is geared toward conducting a general psychological evaluation, with notations that are specific to particular types of cases and legal questions. The reader is encouraged to review Chapters 1, 2, and 3 for background information that addresses issues of racism and cultural bias and the role of psychologists in the promotion of justice. Other chapters in this book provide information useful for working with specific ethnic and cultural groups, or in addressing particular subjects such as hardship and deportation, pertinent political issues, domestic violence, asylum cases, and the like. I also recommend a course of study that focuses on cultural competence in the practice of psychology (Sue & Sue, 2003).

The Ingredients of a Successful Evaluation

In conducting a successful evaluation, the processes, goals, and objectives in the following two boxes should be met.

Checklist—Components of Culturally Competent Evaluations: Critical Perspective

1. The client understands the purpose of the evaluation and how it will be used in the case.

2. The client understands the basics of the evaluation process including:

   what a psychological evaluation is, how it is to be conducted, and the limits of confidentiality;

   who will be involved, how long it will take, and what is expected of the client during the evaluation;

   what the role of the clinician is during the evaluation, what type of information will be gathered during the evaluation, what type of information is important for the client to communicate and contribute, and who will be informed about the results of the evaluation

3. The client understands the procedural format of the evaluation, including whether or not the evaluator will incorporate the use of short questions and answers, personal stories and narratives, or historical or developmental sequences presented in chronological order, or the use of psychological or intelligence tests (if appropriate), and whether or not collaterals will be interviewed and who they will be. Will the client be asked to give his or her perspective on their case and recall events and situations pertinent to the case?

4. The client understands the end results of the evaluation, including how the information that is communicated during the evaluation will be used to formulate opinions and reports; what the final product of the evaluation will look like (written report); deposition, testimony, and the like; what the possible outcomes of the evaluation are—how it may or may not be used in the client's legal case; and how the information may be of use to the client on a personal level.

5. The client is allowed to represent him- or herself and his or her story in a manner that is consistent with the cultural context and congruent with his or her individual and cultural communication style.

6. The client feels that the clinician is sensitive to the dynamics of race and culture in the evaluation and in the legal case.

7. The client feels that the clinician is working to address barriers that may prevent openness and trust in the context of the evaluation.

8. The client feels that he or she is being understood, respected, and accurately represented, with freedom from stereotype, prejudice, and cultural bias.

9. The client has faith in the competence and integrity of the evaluator.

10. The client understands the final results of the evaluation, believes that he or she may gain some benefit from the evaluation, and is not harmed by the process of the evaluation.

11. Although the client may object to the evaluation, or to its outcome, the client feels as though he or she has been treated with respect by the evaluator.

Components of Successful Evaluations From the Clinician's Perspective

The clinician understands the purpose, goals, and objectives of the evaluation, who it is for, and how it will be used.

1. The clinician develops knowledge and understanding about the cultural background of the client.

2. The clinician is able to establish that the client has a clear and accurate understanding of the purpose and process of the evaluation—why it is being conducted, who has requested it, and how it will be used in the case.

3. The clinician is sensitive to the influence of race and culture in regard to the client's ethnicity, personality, behavior, family and community life, and socioeconomic and political circumstances.

4. The clinician attends to dynamics of sociocultural trust and mistrust on the part of the client as related to the evaluation process (see Sue & Sue, 2003) and feels that the client has faith in his or her professional expertise and integrity.

5. The clinician finds that the client is attempting to communicate the information that is needed for the evaluation and is actively participating in the evaluation process.

6. The clinician is able to present information to the court that as accurately as possible represents the identity, behavior, and personality of the client, in the context of culture, inclusive of pertinent socioeconomic and political dynamics, and free of bias and stereotypes.

7. The clinician completes the *DSM-IV-TR* Outline for Cultural Formulation.

8. The clinician succeeds in addressing the legal questions and goals that are integral to the evaluation's purpose.

9. The clinician explains the results of the evaluation to the client and is able to make appropriate referrals or recommendations to assist the client with social, institutional, mental health, or emotional difficulties.

10. The clinician, if appropriate, can offer suggestions to the attorney that may facilitate his or her work with the client.

Preparing for the Cross-Cultural Evaluation

An evaluation would be termed cross-cultural if there is a difference between the racial, cultural, linguistic, and/or ethnic background of the evaluator and the person being evaluated. In developing an understanding of the ways that diversity impacts practice, the clinician must learn to recognize how sociodemographic variables such as race, culture, gender, religious affiliation, linguistic background, sexual orientation, age, and disability may influence the life of the client and the life and practice of the evaluator, including subsequent interactions in the evaluation process. The recognition of the importance of diversity in professional practice includes understanding how culture has influenced the practice of psychotherapy and psychological assessment as well as the diagnostic standards and concepts of normality that are considered in the evaluation process.

Clinicians who are interested in developing a cross-cultural practice can begin by preparing to become culturally competent practitioners. See the introduction to this book and Chapters 1, 2, and 3 for a review of the components of culturally competent practice. The work of Sue and Sue (2003); the American Psychological Association's "Guidelines for Providers of Psychological Services to Ethnic, Linguistic, and Culturally Diverse Populations" (1993); and the U.S. Department of Health and Human Services Surgeon General's Report (2001) provide an excellent introduction to the field.

When a cross-cultural referral is made, the clinician must consider whether or not he or she is the best person to conduct the evaluation, given the range of differences in background between him- or herself and the client. If there is a lack of availability of professionals that are more qualified by virtue of their professional training and their cultural, racial, or ethnic similarities to the client, the clinician should seek appropriate education and consultation to facilitate work from a multicultural perspective. Clinicians from a European American background are often selected over clinicians from the client's ethnic background on the premise that the same-ethnicity clinician will be biased in favor of the client. This presumption is never made when it comes to white client–white evaluator matches. White clinicians should do their best to recommend clinicians that can provide assessment services that are congruent with the client's ethnic background and language skills, if possible. If questions of ethnic bias arise from referring professionals, we must question and confront the prejudicial reasoning that challenges the competence and ethics of minority clinicians who are quite capable of providing unbiased services to clients of similar background.

Accepting a Referral

When the clinician/evaluator considers a cross-cultural referral, he or she should evaluate his or her level of knowledge, experience, and interpersonal comfort in working with a client of a particular racial, ethnic, or cultural background. This is of course in addition to considering one's competency to address the purpose of the evaluation. If the evaluator determines that his or her level of knowledge and experience with the ethnic and cultural background of the individual is low or that his or her interpersonal comfort level with that group is low, or if the evaluator has negative feelings or associations with the group, it is probably best to refer the case to someone else. The clinician can then proceed to work on interpersonal difficulties and knowledge gaps in order to be able to work with such groups in the future. Unfortunately, there have been evaluators who have accepted cases when these three areas did not receive thorough consideration, for example, in a case in which a white evaluator accepted an assignment to evaluate a group of Mexican American clients, despite having had no personal or professional contact with Latino people, with the exception of having been robbed by a group of Latino youth while on a trip to Los Angeles. This lack of familiarity, combined with the possibility of negative bias toward the group, should have led the clinician to seek another referral source. Ultimately, the evaluations in this case were laden with stereotypes and fraught with problems that could have been avoided by referring the case to another psychologist.

Another example of a referral that became difficult on a personal level for an evaluator is in the case of an East African mother who was evaluated by an African American clinician. The clinician had been trained in models of parental effectiveness that utilized white, middle-class values and norms. The clinician was quite adamant about the appropriateness of these standards, which she used in evaluating the parental fitness of the African mother for Child Protective Services. The mother's child was 18 months old. During a consultation with a cross-cultural expert, the evaluator raised the issue of the complex tasks inherent in interpreting parenting styles from a cross-cultural perspective. She mentioned the need to attend to "cultural norms and differences" while conducting the evaluation. However, in her report, the clinician had judged the young mother quite negatively for holding her child "too much" and not allowing him enough "freedom" to play and explore the playroom where the observation was conducted. She viewed African child-rearing methods as less advanced than those of Western mothers and stated that the mother's affection and attentiveness to the child would stifle his development in regard to individuality and autonomy. It also became clear during the consultation that the evaluating clinician wished to distance herself from any cultural associations with Africa. Although the two women were similar racially, their cultural differences were vast. At one point, the clinician expressed great frustration at her position as evaluator: "They expect me to be able to evaluate this mother just because I am black, but I am not like her!" Such "similarities" in racial or ethnic background may be fraught with identity conflicts for ethnic minority clinicians who have assimilated to mainstream culture, perhaps resulting in negative evaluations of clients who are more traditional in their ethnic identity and cultural practices, as was the situation in this case.

It is recommended that clinicians spend time considering their own racial and cultural identity development and exploring the biases, cultural values, and prejudices that may enter into their practice (Sue and Sue, 2003). The work presented by Berry (1998), Cross (1995, 2003), Helms (1995), LaFramboise, Hardin, and Gerton (1998) Phinney (1998), Root (1992, 1996), and

Tatum (1997) is useful for understanding ethnic, racial, cultural, multiracial, and bicultural identity processes for evaluators and clients. An excellent discussion of the implications of racial and cultural identity in professional practice can be found in Sue and Sue (2003) and Thompson and Carter (1997).

Determining the Scope and Purpose of the Evaluation

The clinician should be careful to determine what his or her role is to be and what type of evaluation is to be conducted. The clinician should note whether or not an evaluation is requested because the referring source is having difficulties with understanding the client for reasons of language or cultural differences. Sometimes supposed indications of low intellectual functioning are signs of communication difficulties. Literacy problems may also create confusion about intelligence levels. A lack of reading and writing skills should not be considered evidence of cognitive impairment or retardation unless appropriate testing determines a low IQ. There are times when the attorney or referral source may not be clear about the type of evaluation that they are looking for due to communication problems. In this case, the cross- cultural evaluator may be asked to be somewhat exploratory in beginning the evaluation, and the specific questions that need to be addressed may not be clear at first. For example, in a case in which a Latino youth was accused of murder, the attorney initially asked for intellectual testing. When it was determined that the youth was very intelligent, the lawyer then wished to investigate his personality and moral character, and a broad-based, comprehensive evaluation was conducted. If an attorney asks for an evaluation of competency to stand trial because he or she suspects intellectual deficits or mental disorders, and the evaluator finds that the difficulties arise from communication or cultural barriers, the evaluator may state that the client is competent to stand trial and then proceed (or recommend another professional) to help the attorney and client overcome the barriers that stand in the way of providing adequate representation of the client in the judicial process.

Attorneys will usually find it useful to learn about the parameters of a cross-cultural evaluation in accordance with the APA diversity guidelines. It is helpful to provide the attorney or referring party with a copy of those guidelines. It is also critical for the clinician to encourage attorneys who work with immigrant and refugee clients to consult with an immigration attorney in order to understand how current immigration law may apply to their client. For example, a plea bargain of guilty may assist the client in a criminal case, but this same guilty plea can later lead to the client's deportation under immigration law. The clinician should assess whether or not the attorney understands the racial or cultural dynamics that might be important to the client's case, and whether or not the attorney is comfortable in discussing racial and cultural issues that may arise in court. If not, the clinician may suggest appropriate readings and prepare the attorney by educating him or her about the issues that apply to the client's case. It is important to have the support of the attorney regarding any controversial racial testimony that may arise.

It is also important to consider the sociopolitical context of the evaluation in regard to the current climate that surrounds the particular ethnic group of the client. For example, post–September 11, the sociopolitical climate for Islamic Americans includes stereotypic suspicions of terrorism, creating situations where this group is more vulnerable to cultural bias and threat of deportation. In this book, Chapter 16, by Cahn and Stansell, presents an excellent account of the historical dynamics of and current political climate for Cambodians who face deportation proceedings. The political position of the evaluator may also influence the outcome of the evaluation. How the evaluation will be used in the broader social and political arenas should be thoughtfully considered by the clinician, including a review of the clinician's political opinions.

Preparing for the Evaluation With the Client

In arranging the appointment, the clinician should briefly explain what will take place at the appointment, specify how much time will be needed, and clarify that the client has an understanding of the purpose of the meeting. The clinician should assess for any obstacles that might get in the way of the client coming to the appointment, making sure that there are clear directions given for getting to the office, alerting the client to any parking fees that would need to be paid, and if necessary, giving directions to another person that might drive or accompany the client to the assessment. On occasion, because my office is on a university campus and difficult to find, I arrange to meet the client at an easily reached landmark. Clarity about the length of the appointment and need for timeliness should be discussed with the client. If an interpreter is used, the interpreter should give the client these directions, following the instructions of the clinician. Allow time in your schedule to accommodate the client being late for the first appointment if coming to your office is going to be an unfamiliar task. If the client does not speak English well, it also may be helpful to alert parking or building staff about the client's arrival, so that they might be of assistance in helping the client find the office.

If you anticipate that the client is reluctant to come to the appointment because of avoidance of the traumatic material to be discussed, because of fear of the evaluation's outcome, or because he or she is resisting the evaluation due to adversarial legal proceedings, it might help to discuss his or her reluctance on the telephone in order to clarify misplaced fears or to offer reassurance or a bit of empathy for the stress inherent in his or her situation. This discussion might decrease the likelihood of a missed appointment.

It is also important to learn from the client or from the referral source whether or not the client has a counselor, victim advocate, or psychotherapist in order to recommend supportive therapy that is adjunctive to the evaluation, especially if you anticipate that the evaluation process will be very stressful or if the evaluation is for the assessment of trauma or torture.

If you anticipate the need to interview collateral contacts, you may request that the client bring in a list of names and numbers of people that you may want to interview.

Preparing for the Evaluation: The Clinician

Cultural Background Information

It is useful to conduct a literature search and/or seek consultation in order to gain background information on the ethnic group of the client that you will evaluate, especially if the client is from an immigrant or refugee group that is new or not common to the United States. It is important to consider that many different ethnic groups may live in one country and that specific ethnic groups have particular cultural values, norms, and traditions. Major publishers and bookstores will offer resources for working with ethnic minority groups that have longer intergenerational standing in the United States. Ethnomed and Psychinfo are useful empirical and clinical databases for a wide range of groups. Cross-cultural interviewing techniques may be identified in various resources for interview planning. Sattler (1998) offers excellent, culturally sensitive interview questions that may be applied to many types of legal cases, especially in the assessment of juveniles and child custody, child abuse, parental fitness, and domestic violence situations. Lexis-Nexis offers information on country conditions, ethnic conflict, and war (articles are taken from newspapers and periodicals). There are many books available that focus on psychotherapy and assessment with the major minority groups in the United States (Castillo, 1997; Dana, 2000; Ponterotto, Casas, Suzuki, & Alexander, 2001; Sue & Sue, 2003). University departments that are ethnically or culturally based (such as Chicano, American Indian, Asian, and African American studies programs) may also be a resource. I have gained valuable information for working with Russian clients from our university's Department of Slavic Languages and Literature. Many community agencies are also willing to offer consultation on basic cultural norms, values, traditions, gender roles, family hierarchy, and communication styles. (However, one must take great care about confidentiality—ethnic and clan conflicts sometimes follow refugees to the United States, and your client might be easily identifiable in the community.) The American Psychological Association maintains a list of members of Division 45, which focuses on ethnic minority psychology, and your local/state psychological association might maintain a list of cross-cultural consultants.

Useful background information for getting started includes a review of the cultural style of communication (such as use of eye contact, the use of negative and affirmative statements—how *yes* and *no* are used, whether or not this is a high- or low-context communication culture, and so on [see Sue & Sue, 2003]). Cultural concepts of mental health; mental illness, disease, and treatment; how emotions are expressed; and whether or not indigenous healing systems are used are all important to explore, if possible. Understanding gender and sex role norms, family organization and hierarchy, child-rearing methods and discipline styles, religious and spiritual traditions, central cultural values, and how individuals are likely to approach authority figures are background points to learn about. Social, economic, and political conditions in the client's home country before immigration lend descriptive information that can help the clinician to understand client stresses, potential traumas, and client reasons for immigration. Knowledge about the particular history of an ethnic group within the United States assists the clinician in better understanding the group's historical contributions to this country, as well as the types of discrimination the client and his or her ancestors may have faced as members of a minority group. Having a degree of familiarity with the client's ethnic and cultural background is likely to enhance the client's confidence in the clinician. The clinician must remember, however, not to assume that clients will fall into a pattern of cultural norms that have been described in readings—exceptions abound. We must continue to be on guard against developing stereotypes.

Considerations Regarding Language Use

(Please see Tribe, Chapter 11, on the use of interpreters.)

The need for conducting the evaluation in the appropriate language is paramount. Evaluators are too often willing and eager to proceed without interpreters. Clients are not often the best people to rate their own language ability, because they may fear that they may be negatively judged for a lack of fluency in English and thus may overrepresent their language skills. Finding an interpreter at the last minute, such as a family member in the waiting room, is also not appropriate. I recently consulted on an evaluation where a psychologist had used another inmate in the prison to translate for the inmate that she was evaluating. This was not appropriate under any circumstances. In another case, an evaluator of a Vietnamese immigrant stated that "the client seemed to have a great deal of difficulty communicating in English." The clinician continued with the evaluation anyway, with the justification that he thought the client was "exaggerating his difficulties in communicating with me."

If language abilities are in question, consult with a professional (such as a person who teaches English as a second language) who can determine the client's language ability. For an immigrant to be considered bilingual in a legal proceeding, the party's language level should be at the 12th grade level in both languages (Moore & Mamiya, 1999) Other useful questions regarding bilingual abilities include: How long has the client been here, and how long has the client studied English? What is the client's level of educational attainment? Did the client take English classes in his or her home country? How long has the client spoken English on a regular basis? Where and how frequently does the client use English daily? Does the client read and write in English? What books has the client read in English? Does the client use English in his or her daily thoughts?

In that a great deal of an assessment involves the discussion of feelings and emotional experiences, it is critical for the evaluator to realize that the description of emotions and feelings usually is done most accurately in the client's first language. The ability to describe or represent culture-bound symptoms and syndromes may only occur in the native tongue. In conducting parenting evaluations, it is critical to know which language the parent uses to speak to the child, with the understanding that certain emotions, expressions of affection, basic parenting tasks, and statements regarding discipline, cautions about danger, and instructions about behavior are also likely to take place in the client's first language, or through a mixture of two languages. If conducting an observation of parent and child, the clinician must allow the parent to interact with the child in the language that they usually use at home, with the use of an interpreter who speaks the language of the family. Parenting evaluators should be aware that clients from many ethnic groups are likely to promote polite and respectful behavior from their child, as well as encourage the child to do well on task performance (in games, puzzles, art, play, etc.) during interviews and observations. This should not be viewed as intrusive or overly directive behavior on the part of the parent. Nonverbal behavior and terms of endearment (such as calling little boys "papi" and little girls "mami" in Mexican families) should be interpreted in a cultural context. A child protective services evaluator who did not understand the affectionate use of the term "mami" disapproved of a Latina mother for calling her 3-year-old daughter "mami" and included a paragraph in her report stating that the use of this term with her daughter would lead the child to an early pregnancy.

When using an interpreter, the interpreter may also be a useful source of cultural information before and after the interview. Although interpreters are not allowed in many states to offer their opinions or ideas while interpreting, it is important to ask your interpreter if he or she is willing to provide you with cultural information. You must give assurance that you are not asking the interpreter to evaluate the client, but rather that you are seeking guidance about cultural customs, norms, and traditions. Evaluators should avoid using interpreters of opposite genders if this is likely to inhibit communication in the interview. Take care to select interpreters that speak the same dialect as the client and be wary of any potential ethnic, clan, political, religious, or class conflicts that may exist between the client and the interpreter. Interpreters who are from a higher class or who are more assimilated than the client may be critical or judgmental of the client. In the evaluation of post-traumatic stress disorder (PTSD) for refugees, interpreters from the same country as the client may also have been traumatized, thus their preparedness to deal with client recollections of trauma should be confirmed before the interview. If the evaluator notes ongoing tension between the interpreter and the client, it most likely will interfere with client disclosure of information. This problem should be noted and another interpreter selected if possible.

Allowing Adequate Time for the Assessment

The clinician must use careful interviewing and establish an atmosphere that promotes clear communication in a cross-cultural assessment, particularly if psychological testing cannot be used. I recommend that the clinician conduct the interview using two or three meetings (6 to 8 hours, especially if using an interpreter). Establishing a sense of trust and setting a tone of respect and integrity in the cross-cultural evaluation is difficult to do in one meeting. Allowing more than one interview affords the clinician opportunities to clarify cultural questions or points of confusion if they arise in the first interview. I also find that clients are more relaxed and familiar with the assessment process during the second and third interview and are thus able to provide an increased amount of valuable information.

Consideration of Psychological Testing

The evaluator should establish the population norms and cross-cultural validity of instruments before administration with clients. Language proficiency should also be established if administering a test in English, when English is not the client's first language. Many clinicians assume that conversational English is sufficient to administer testing. Conversational skills do not translate into reading skills, especially with linguistic and cultural groups that utilize high-context patterns of communication. It is also not advisable to have an interpreter read and interpret instruments such as the Minnesota Multiphasic Personality Inventory (MMPI) to a client if the client is not literate. Translated versions of instruments such as the MMPI-2 are not necessarily valid, and evidence of etic versus emic norming of the instrument must be investigated. Test results reported should be grounded in cultural context and include any pertinent cultural information about profile or validity score tendencies for particular groups (e.g., elevated F scores in Latino groups due to cultural tendencies toward the dramatic [Carbonell, 2000]). It is also not appropriate to use computerized assessment profiles, as they are not designed for cross-cultural use. For a more comprehensive discussion of cross-cultural psychological assessment and intelligence testing, see Chapter 10 by Judd and Beggs in this book; Okazaki, Kallivayalil, and Sue (2002); Dana (2000); Mesquita and Walker (2003); Gopaul-McNicol and Thomas-Presswood (1998); Gopaul-McNicol and Armour-Thomas (2002); Samuda (1998); Samuda et al. (1998); and Sattler (1998). Intensive interviews may be needed to replace the use of testing in many cases.

*The Clinician's Socialization
Regarding the Ethnic Background
of the Person to Be Evaluated*

To help guard against bias and prejudice that may be beyond the clinician's conscious awareness, it is important to review what your learning experiences tell you in regard to the ethnic/cultural group of the client—your family attitudes and teaching, educational and peer experiences, societal stereotypes, and media portrayals that may have influenced your view of this group. What have been your personal or professional experiences with people from this group? Have you had high or low contact with the group? Are there antagonisms or stereotypes about the relationship between your ethnic group/religion and the ethnic group/religion of the client? Do you have any fears, anxieties, or negative associations with this group? Do you have any strong disagreements or conflicts with their cultural values, norms, or religion? Is there a danger of stereotypes or prejudice creeping into the evaluation? Will you feel comfortable discussing your racial/ethnic views, knowledge, or lack of knowledge about the group with the client? Are there ways that you have, personally or professionally, actively rejected the values or norms that are important to this group in your own life or practice? Would you benefit from consultation regarding your socialization experiences about this group? Are there any ethical reasons to remove yourself from the evaluation?

Review of Case Records

The evaluator will usually be asked to review documents related to the client's case, such as arrest records and criminal history; client declarations regarding reasons for seeking asylum; parenting evaluations; depositions of other experts in various types of cases; psychological evaluations conducted by other professionals; police reports that document domestic violence,

sexual assault, child abuse, and other forms of client victimization; client depositions that outline discrimination in the workplace; and so on. The clinician should note inconsistencies that arise between written records and data gathered from the client and collaterals during the evaluation interviews. Contradictory, missing, or inconsistent information should be reviewed with both client and attorney. The clinician may find information in the records that is culturally biased, that shows evidence of prejudice or stereotypes, misdiagnosis, or misuse of psychological testing for language or cultural reasons, or that is incorrect because of cultural errors or miscommunication. The evaluator should present this information to the attorney and, if applicable, note these findings in his or her report, especially regarding other psychological diagnoses or test results that may be incorrect as a result of cultural bias or errors. I have found that it is common for evaluators who do not understand racial issues to label minority clients as paranoid if they report experiences with racism during an evaluation. (Several chapters of this book present useful information about racism and discrimination as experienced by ethnic minority groups, particularly in the context of race and justice.) The expression of emotion and cultural norms and practices must also be considered in cultural context. For example, during a record review that was conducted as part of a cross-cultural parenting evaluation, a young Russian mother was labeled histrionic, inappropriate, and lacking in boundaries by a different evaluating psychologist because she had cried about her divorce and subsequent custody battle at her child's daycare center. A consultation with an expert on Russian culture revealed that in Russia, women are very emotionally demonstrative and open about their personal stresses and distress. Thus her public display of sadness would be considered quite normal in her home country. In another custody contest, an Asian mother was judged negatively because she had requested that her children's visitation schedule be changed in the summer because she needed to travel to China for her father's 80th birthday celebration. An evaluator who did not understand the importance of the cultural mandate for attendance at her father's birthday considered it a trivial reason for the mother to try to rearrange the children's summer schedule.

The Initial Interview

Acknowledging the Stresses Inherent in the Evaluation and Legal Process

The initial interview will set the tone for the evaluation. I suggest that the clinician acknowledge the stressfulness of the evaluation for the client, as well as the stress of the client's legal situation. I find that most evaluators never acknowledge the difficult nature of being involved in legal proceedings as a minority or as an immigrant and that the client will greatly welcome an expression of empathy for his or her predicament. Asking the client what he or she finds to be the most stressful aspect of his or her case provides an opening for the conveyance of empathy and will also elicit a good deal of valuable information to be used in the assessment. Discussing the stressful nature of litigation is an appropriate time to bring up issues of trust and mistrust in terms of the role of the evaluator and why the evaluator is in the position of seeking deeply personal information from the client. This is especially important when the evaluator is white and from the majority culture and the client is from a racial and/or ethnic minority group. The evaluator may simply state to the client that he or she is aware that the racial or cultural dynamics that exist between evaluator and client may add to the stressful or adversarial nature of the evaluation and that the evaluator will strive to understand aspects of the client's cultural or racial background that may be unfamiliar to him or her. This acknowledgment will alert the client that the evaluator is trying to be cognizant of and sensitive to the possibility of racial or cultural mistrust and misunderstanding. However, the evaluator should also take care to alert the client to the potentially adversarial role that he or she will play (Melton, Petrila, Poythress, & Slobogin, 1997).

Clarification of Your Role and the Evaluation Process

Evaluators should explain their professional role and credentials and clarify how they are to be involved in the client's case, including who they have been retained by and whether or not they will be testifying in court. Immigrant clients may not be aware of the adversarial nature of legal proceedings and may bestow their trust on professionals who are not working in their behalf. Establishing professionalism and expertise may be particularly important for women clinicians and younger professionals in working with cultural groups in which women are limited to more traditional roles and in which youth may signal a lack of wisdom. The clinician should ask the client what his or her understanding is about why he or she is being seen for an evaluation. This will create the opportunity for the clinician to assist with fears and misconceptions about the evaluation. The purpose of the client's evaluation, a description of a psychological evaluation, and how the information will be used in the case can then be conveyed to the client. The process or procedures involved in the evaluation should also be outlined for the client, as well as the limitations of confidentiality. The clinician should outline what will take place in the first meeting and in subsequent meetings. Sometimes clients worry about the view that family members have about the evaluation. At times, it may be important to explain the evaluation to spouses, parents, or other family members. The clinician should not assume that the client knows how the evaluation will be structured or knows what information is important to report to the evaluator. A clear orientation to the process will provide a great deal of assistance. The evaluator can instruct the client that it is permissible to volunteer information that he or she thinks is useful or important, as clients often may not feel as though it is appropriate to speak up if they have not been asked to do so. The evaluator should take care to periodically verify with the client his or her understanding of the meaning behind what the client has said in order to confirm that he or she is accurately interpreting the information that the client has given. The clinician should ask the client for correction if he or she has made an error, because in some cultures the client may not wish to correct the clinician, who is seen as an authority figure.

Another important task in the first interview, if this has not already been done, is to determine those who would be valuable to interview as collaterals. We often find that evaluators avoid use of collaterals in cross-cultural evaluations (especially in parenting evaluations), perhaps because of difficulties or discomfort with cultural or racial difference and due to the complexities of additional cross-cultural interviews. However, the clinician can greatly benefit from familiarizing himself or herself with the client's culture through others who know the client in same-culture situations (such as religious figures, relatives, friends), as well as by interviewing those who know the client in community contexts (such as teachers, physicians, employers, etc.). For example, in one case, a mother from Thailand was greatly concerned that her American husband would not support her in raising their daughter as a Buddhist, an important connection to the child's cultural heritage. The father, in turn, accused the mother of not being very religious and undermined her requests for preserving her daughter's links to the Thai side of her heritage. The father, who was not a religious person, did not feel that religion was important in the life of his daughter. The mother countered his accusations in her deposition, saying that she was indeed an active practitioner of Buddhism and that each week she brought food to the temple, in addition to attending regular services. The father's attorney dismissed her claims, stating that "bringing food to a church is not a religious activity." In evaluating the mother, the evaluator visited the temple and spoke with the monk about the mother's involvement and religious beliefs and witnessed the ritual of other temple members "bringing food" to the monks. This ritual involved meditation, prayer, and a talk given by the monk. The mother and daughter's deep involvement with Buddhism was confirmed by the monk. This visit and observation was useful in describing the mother's culture and beliefs to the court, including the importance of Buddhism in the development of ethnic and cultural identity for the young daughter.

Content of the Next Meeting

Every Client Has a Story to Tell

If the evaluator is able to plan two or three interviews, it may be best to leave the more

difficult questions, assessment of symptoms, and discussion of traumatic material for the second meeting, unless it seems as though the client is comfortable and at ease in the first meeting. Beginning a developmental history is usually a good place to start and will help to provide the evaluator with information about the client's cultural background, beliefs, and customs. A developmental history that includes an inventory of risk and protective factors in development builds the contextual framework with which to understand any current symptoms described by the client to be used in formulating a diagnosis and in understanding the client's current status and legal situation. We have found that clients often reveal information that has not been expressed to their attorney. This can occur because the client develops a sense of connection with the evaluator through revealing a great deal of intimate information, perhaps because the client feels as though he or she is understood by the clinician if the clinician is genuine in his or her expression of understanding and empathy, and also because the cross-cultural evaluator is interested in the client's history from a perspective that includes the client's cultural and racial background. It is often the only opportunity that clients have had to tell the details of what has happened to them in a context that includes discussing the rest of their life. For many clients, especially immigrants and refugees, it is usually the first time that anyone has truly listened to their story. Every client has a powerful story to tell. In contrast, if the client feels a sense of disrespect, intimidation, impatience, racism, or disregard for his or her cultural background, it is likely that the evaluation will remain at a superficial level.

Assessment of Symptoms

Structured interviews or questionnaires may or may not be appropriate (such as the Structured Clinical Interview for *DSM-IV* [SCID]), in that they may not utilize language or descriptions of symptoms that fit with the linguistic and cultural framework of the client's worldview or representational system. For example, depressive symptoms may be presented through somatic complaints such as headaches, tiredness, or digestive distress and anxiety through nervousness, jumpiness, and physical unrest. Background information on how mental health symptoms are expressed in the culture is helpful in this regard. The clinician may need to be creative in offering language that may better describe symptoms that fit with diagnostic categories he or she suspects may be present. For example, a Latino youth who had been seriously abused as a child did not respond at first to the SCID inventory regarding PTSD symptoms. When the clinician shifted her language to ask about feelings of jumpiness and nervousness, fear of being watched, of having a frequent sense that something was not right, physical tension such as clenched fists and sweats, the frequent need to look around and check out his surroundings, and so on, the youth responded affirmatively in a way that represented the symptoms in a framework that was closer to his worldview. However, having structured interviews at hand provides a useful reference to help the clinician cover the necessary diagnostic categories and symptom sets. I have found that clinicians sometimes are less thorough in doing a methodical sweep of possible diagnostic categories because of being daunted by cultural or language difficulties or because they are not able to use their customary assessment tools. Sattler (1998) offers many culturally sensitive interview formats.

Debriefing

Near the conclusion of the first meeting, the clinician may wish to conduct a short debriefing, inquiring as to whether or not the client feels as though there is any information that he or she wishes to add. This is also a good time to ask the client if he or she has any questions or feedback about the process or content of the evaluation. Any new or important information gained that is pertinent to the case should be passed along to the attorney at this time (e.g., the client has misconceptions or is confused about the legal process; the client has omitted information that is important to add to his or her declaration). I sometimes find that evaluators have withheld information that might be very useful to the client because they want to remain neutral and objective. For example, in a recent domestic violence evaluation, student evaluators were reluctant to provide a client with information about the risks inherent in not following

through with a long-term restraining order because they did not feel that this was the task of an evaluator. Evaluators may use opportunities for psychoeducation in situations that may help to protect clients from risk of harm or may offer short-term coping mechanisms for emotional distress, in addition to longer term treatment recommendations that appear in reports.

Each meeting should open with a reclarification of the purpose of the assessment, an opportunity for questions and comments, and an orientation to the purpose of the current interview. Each interview should be concluded with the opportunity for client questions and comments. The evaluator should ask if the client has other information to add that was not covered. Clients will benefit from encouragement and learning that they are following the interview procedures in the appropriate manner. The evaluator may request permission to call the client to recheck details or to ask questions about minor details by telephone following the evaluation and during report preparation. Although many attorneys do not think about informing clients of the results of the evaluation, most clients will take the evaluation very seriously and will want to know the results. The results are best reported and explained by the clinical evaluator. Arranging an appointment to review the final results, conclusions, recommendations, report, and testimony that will be presented is very important to the client. It is best to go over the results before the evaluator's court appearance, if possible. If the client will be asked to discuss his or her evaluation in any way, the clinician will need to explain diagnostic conclusions and psychological terminology to the client, so as to better connect the clinician's conclusions to the client's experiences and perceptions of his or her problem.

Questions or Areas to Include in a Comprehensive Cross-Cultural Assessment

The headings that follow may be used to structure the organization of the final report, with summaries of client responses and evaluator commentary appearing in the body of the report under the appropriate heading. The clinician should be careful to incorporate all areas covered in the *DSM-IV-TR* outline for cultural formulation (see especially p. 897 of the *Diagnostic and Statistical Manual of Mental Disorders,* American Psychiatric Association, 2000). Pertinent cultural information and cultural context should also be used where applicable in explaining and substantiating diagnoses, test data, and clinical impressions.

Family and Developmental History

In parenting or family-based evaluations, these questions should be asked of each parent regarding his or her upbringing and family of origin, in addition to the assessment of his or her current family life.

- Place and date of birth (note urban or rural)? (Birthdates are sometimes not important, and/or birth records are not kept in some cultures, thus exact dates may be unknown.)
- Racial, cultural, religious, ethnic, and linguistic background of each parent?
- Parents' educational levels and type of employment, income level?
- Ages and names of siblings?
- Deaths in the family?
- Divorces in the family? Stepparents? Cultural or religious views of divorce?
- Core family values and beliefs, religion, family legends, heroes, stories?
- Languages spoken at home?
- Primary cultural values—was there any conflict between parents regarding cultural values, religious beliefs, or the ethnic affiliations of the family?
- Family organizational style, leadership, hierarchy, gender roles, communication patterns, role of extended family members in child rearing and family social support?
- Was there a high or low level of social support for the parents/family? Isolation?
- Sociopolitical environment—ethnic conflict? War? Racism or discrimination: low to high? Religious persecution? Duration: for how many years were such tensions experienced during childhood? Impact on the family?
- Household or farming responsibilities of children?
- Family values about work and education?
- Family methods of child rearing—methods of discipline? Is affection shown? How is affection

displayed? Rewards or encouragement given? What are examples of unacceptable child behaviors? How do children show respect for parents and adults? Is the child's behavior seen as a reflection on the family? Is child and family activity oriented toward the family collective or more toward the promotion of individuality? Did the client ever feel that discipline in the family was too harsh or abusive? Was the family style of child rearing consistent with other families from a similar cultural or community background?

- Family hopes and goals? Hopes and goals for your children?
- Family customs or beliefs about dating, romance, sexuality, courtship, marriage?
- Domestic violence, substance abuse, child abuse, or family history of mental illness?
- Health problems in family members?
- Did you grow up in a safe community? If not, describe what was unsafe.
- Client's developmental milestones met in a timely manner?
- Prenatal and childhood health problems and availability of health care?
- Number of years of education for client and for their siblings?
- Quality of childhood peer/social relationships (note that in many countries children tend to play at home with siblings and cousins rather than with playmates outside the family)?
- Type of first job, and age at acquiring it?
- Dating and courtship history?
- Any incidents of sexual trauma, early sexual relationships, rape?
- Current marriage of client—date, any previous divorces?
- Marital history, marital satisfaction level?
- Names, ages of children?

Repeat applicable questions from the previous list for assessment of the client's current family life.

Immigration and Acculturation

In exploring the dynamics of acculturation, the clinician will be investigating the client's sense of *belonging* in both his or her culture of origin and mainstream culture; his or her level of *participation* in mainstream culture and his or her culture of origin; his or her ethnic/cultural affiliation(s) and practices; his or her sense of *efficacy* in becoming a member of society; and *acculturative stresses* and conflicts. Some of these questions apply more to recent immigrant groups; others can be asked of ethnic minority groups with a longer intergenerational history in the United States.

- When did you or your family arrive in the United States?
- What were the reasons for coming to the United States?
- Please describe the social, economic, and political conditions in your country before you or your parents left.
- Is there a trauma history related to war, torture, and so forth? Physical evidence such as scars? (See Chapter 12 by Freed in this book.)
- Are family members aware of one another's traumatic experiences? Is there secrecy or permission to discuss traumatic events in the family?
- If the family or client were refugees, were they in a refugee camp or other countries before coming to the United States? Describe conditions.
- Risk of having been a victim of trafficking? (See Chapter 15 by Basu in this book.)
- How did you get to the United States? (If the client reports being "handed over" to older adults or organized groups; if money was exchanged; if a marriage or employment was "arranged" with an American citizen; if there are large age differences between a man and a young bride; or if the client was forced to work, locked into a place of residence, or threatened about running away, trafficking should be considered and discussed with an immigration attorney.)
- Did you or your parents feel a sense of loss or regret about leaving your home country? Please describe. Are there family members left behind?
- Have there been any problems with legal residency status or difficulty with citizenship applications? Are all eligible family members documented? Is a referral to an immigration attorney needed?
- Have there been changes in professional status, type of work, income, social class, and/or traditional gender roles in your family since coming to the United States?
- Which family members are the most active in the mainstream community?
- Where do family members work?
- Have you and your family felt accepted in the community? Why or why not?
- How would you rate the level of respect that you feel for your ethnic group's values and traditions in the mainstream culture (low, moderate, high)?
- Have you or other family members experienced discrimination since coming to the United States?
- What ethnic group do you affiliate with? (How does the client label his or her ethnic affiliation?)
- Have you and your family members found an ethnic, religious, or cultural community that fits with your background?
- What percentage of your friends are from your ethnic group? From the mainstream community?
- Do you (or your parents) feel comfortable visiting your children's (or your) school?
- What languages are spoken in your home?
- Are there any conflicts in your family regarding the observance of traditional cultural norms, traditions, and practices and the acquisition of new cultural practices that have been introduced from the mainstream United States?
- Has there been a decline in children's respect for their elders since coming to the United States?
- Have there been any role changes or marital conflicts that have been a result of children acculturating faster than their parents, or because women have been successful in work outside of the home?
- Have children in the family been rejected or marginalized in their school or peer community?
- Have children sought gang affiliations as a way of belonging in the community?
- Have any family members developed health or mental health problems since moving to the United States? Have any family members become distant or isolated? Have they sought treatment?
- Has the client/family been successful in learning about community agencies and services such as health care, social services, counseling, youth activities, and the like?
- What have been the gains and benefits and losses and disappointments as a result of moving to the United States?
- On a scale of 1 to 7, 7 being high and 1 being low, how would you rate your chances of becoming financially stable or comfortable in

the United States? How would you rate your chances of feeling socially comfortable in the mainstream community? How would you rate your feelings of being socially comfortable within your ethnic group?

Experience With Racism

(We suggest the Schedule of Racist Events by Landrine & Klonoff, 1996)

- At what age did you first experience being teased, criticized, or excluded because of the color of your skin, facial features, accent, or your ethnic background? Please describe this situation.
- Did such events happen occasionally or frequently during childhood? How did this affect you (emotionally, with peers, and in school)? Did anyone help you with coping with racist events? To what extent did parents, friends, and teachers provide help?
- Please describe two or three events that occurred as a result of racial discrimination in your community, your school, or at work during the past 2 years.
- Would you say that racist events or racial discrimination have had a small, moderate, or large impact on your life? Please describe.
- How would you rate the frequency of racist events (being followed in a store, being given poor service, being called a racist name, being told a racist joke) during the past year: infrequently, sometimes, often, or frequently?
- Please describe any events involving racial discrimination that have occurred in your life during the past 2 years (being passed over for a job, not getting a raise that you felt was deserved, being stopped by police or arrested for no reason, being the victim of racial violence or a hate crime)?
- Do you feel that racism or discrimination plays a role in your legal case and, if so, how? Please describe.

Ethnic, Cultural, and Racial Identity

A cultural meaning system defines reality for an individual. Meanings about how the world works, the status of people in it, what emotions to feel, and what behavior is appropriate in certain situations are all structured in cultural schemas. Assessment of mental disorders without reference to the client's cultural identity is therefore inappropriate and may lead to less than optimal care. (Castillo, 1997, p. 64)

The assessment of identity also helps the clinician to determine the individual's (or family's) sense of belonging, participation, and contribution across life tasks (work, school, family, friendship, etc.) and social settings—or, conversely, the sense of isolation, exclusion, or marginalization in particular or multiple settings. From these questions, the clinician can develop an idea about the client's degree of assimilation, traditionality, or bicultural adaptation. The clinician may also find that the individual is marginalized (see Berry, 1998) from both his or her culture of origin and mainstream culture. Ethnic, racial, and cultural identity factors need to be explored and discussed in regard to child custody/ placement decisions in order to ensure the child's access to his or her cultural/ethnic group and heritage. For children of immigrants, access to other immigrants, their first language, and religious practices provide the avenues for ethnic and cultural identity development (as opposed to associations with more acculturated and assimilated English-speaking groups).

- How does the client describe his or her ethnic, religious, and cultural affiliations?
- What languages are spoken at home? Have children learned to speak the language of their parents? (If not, this may be a sign that parents are strongly pushing their children to assimilate American culture.) What language do you prefer to speak?
- What ethnic or religious traditions do you celebrate?
- What values are most important to you at this time in your life? Where do these values come from?
- Are there any particular cultural or ethnic traditions or customs that you practice on a regular basis?
- Do you participate in any community organizations of your ethnic affiliation?
- What are the ethnic backgrounds of your friends?
- Have you ever been criticized for having friends outside of your ethnic group?

- Have your ever been teased or criticized because of your ethnic or racial features, or because of your language, traditions, or cultural practices?
- How did this affect you?
- Have you ever rejected your ethnic group, values, and traditions? Describe.
- Do you feel a high, moderate, or low degree of comfort coming and going in mainstream settings (place of work, shopping, parks, theaters, schools, downtown, etc.)? If low, describe.
- Do you feel accepted at school, at your place of work, in the larger community?
- How would you rate your sense of trust in mainstream institutions, such as schools, police, courts, health care systems, and government? High, moderate, or low? (The clinician can ask for a rating of each institution if time allows.)

Client/Family Health and Mental Health History

- Family and client beliefs and attitudes about health, sources of illness, and mental illness
- Use of indigenous or spiritual healers or methods
- Spiritual explanations for mental illness (angry spirits, spirit voices, possession). It is possible for an individual or family to be bicultural in their belief systems and to use Western medicine as well as incorporating traditional beliefs and healing methods. If the client anticipates criticism of traditional beliefs, he or she may deny them. The clinician must convey open-mindedness in this area and respect beliefs that fall outside of a Western, Judeo-Christian framework.
- Current medical care and name of physicians
- Has the client been to counseling or psychotherapy? Describe.
- Client views and perceptions about medical and mental health treatment
- Health and mental health history
- Substance abuse history

Educational and Employment History

- Level of educational attainment
- Have there been any educational difficulties? Describe.
- Occupational history, current employment

Presenting Concerns, Stresses, Current Status

- What are the client's perceptions of his or her current legal difficulties—his or her crime, child custody case, domestic violence, asylum application, and so on?
- If the client is an immigrant, how would the legal problem be handled by the courts in the country of origin? (See Moore, 1999.)
- Client's ability to understand the legal system and work effectively with counsel
- Current life stresses
- Availability of social support
- Hobbies, sports, leisure activities
- How does the client cope with stress and problems (coping and problem-solving skills)?
- Client goals for the future

REFERENCES

American Psychiatric Association. (2000). *Diagnostic and statistical manual of mental disorders* (4th ed., Text revision). Washington, DC: Author.

American Psychological Association. (1993). Guidelines for providers of psychological services to ethnic, linguistic, and culturally diverse populations. *American Psychologist, 48,* 45–48.

Berry, J. W. (1998). Acculturative stress. In P. O. Organista, K. M. Chun, & G. Marin (Eds.), *Readings in ethnicity psychology* (pp. 117–122). New York: Routledge.

Carbonell, S. I. (2000). An assessment practice with hispanics in Minnesota. In R. Dana (Ed.). *Handbook of cross cultural assessment* (pp. 547–572). Mahwah, NJ: Lawrence Erlbaum Associates.

Castillo, R. J. (1997). *Culture and mental illness: A client centered approach.* Pacific Grove, CA: Brooks/Cole.

Cross, W. E., Jr. (1995). The psychology of nigrescence: Revising the Cross model. In G. Ponterotto, J. M. Casas, L. A. Suzuki, & C. M. Alexander (Eds.), *Handbook of multicultural counseling* (pp. 93–122). Thousand Oaks, CA: Sage Publications.

Cross, W. E., Jr. (2003). Tracing the historical origins of youth delinquency and violence: Myths and realities about black culture. *Journal of Social Issues, 59*(1), 67–82.

Dana, R. (2000). *Handbook of cross cultural assessment*. Mahwah, NJ: Lawrence Erlbaum Associates.

Gopaul-McNicol, S. A., & Armour-Thomas, E. (2002). *Assessment and culture: Psychological tests with minority populations*. San Diego: Academic Press.

Gopaul-McNicol, S. A., & Thomas-Presswood, T. T. (1998). *Working with linguistically and culturally different children*. Needham Heights, MA: Allyn and Bacon.

Helms, J. (1995). An update of Helms's white and people of color racial identity models. In G. Ponterotto, J. M. Casas, L. A. Suzuki, & C. M. Alexander (Eds.), *Handbook of multicultural counseling* (pp. 181–198). Thousand Oaks, CA: Sage Publications.

LaFramboise, T., Hardin, L. K., & Gerton, J. (1998). Psychological impact of biculturalism: Evidence and theory. In P. B. Organista, K. M. Chun, & G. Marin (Eds.), *Readings in ethnic psychology* (pp. 123–156). New York: Routledge.

Landrine, H., & Klonoff, E. A. (1996). The schedule of racist events: A measure of racial discrimination and a study of its negative physical and mental health consequences. *Journal of Black Psychology, 22*(2), 144–168.

Melton, G. B., Petrila, J., Poythress, N. G., & Slobogin, C. (1997). *Psychological evaluations for the courts: A handbook for mental health professionals and lawyers* (2nd ed.). New York: Guilford.

Mesquita, B., & Walker, R. (2003, July). Cultural differences in emotions: A context for interpreting emotional experiences. *Behavior Research and Therapy, 41*(7), 777–793.

Moore, J. I. (Ed.). (1999). *Immigrants in courts*. Seattle: University of Washington Press.

Moore, J. I., & Mamiya, R. A. (1999). Interpreters in court proceedings. In J. I. Moore (Ed.), *Immigrants in courts* (pp. 29–45). Seattle: University of Washington Press.

Okazaki, S., Kallivayalil, D., & Sue, S. (2002). Clinical personality assessment with Asian Americans. In J. Butcher (Ed.), *Clinical personality assessment: Practical approaches* (pp. 135–153). London: Oxford University Press.

Phinney, J. (1998). Ethnic identity in adolescents and adults. In P. B. Organista, K. M. Chun, & G. Marin (Eds.), *Readings in ethnic psychology* (pp. 73–99). New York: Routledge.

Ponterotto, G., Casas, J. M., Suzuki, L. A., & Alexander, C. M. (Eds.). (2001). Handbook of multicultural counseling (2nd ed.). Thousand Oaks, CA: Sage Publications.

Root, M. P. (Ed.). (1992). *Racially mixed people in America*. Thousand Oaks, CA: Sage Publications.

Root, M. P. (Ed.). (1996). *Multiracial experience: Racial experience as the new frontier*. Thousand Oaks, CA: Sage Publications.

Samuda, R. J. (1998). *Psychological testing of American minorities' issues and consequences*. Thousand Oaks, CA: Sage Publications.

Samuda, R. J., Feuerstein, R., Kaufman, A. S., Lewis, J. E., & Sternberg & Associates. (1998). *Advances in cross cultural assessment*. Thousand Oaks, CA: Sage Publications.

Sattler, J. (1998). *Clinical and forensic interviewing of children and families: Guidelines for the mental health, education, pediatric, and child maltreatment fields*. San Diego: Sattler.

Sue, D. W., & Sue, D. (2003). *Counseling the culturally diverse*. New York: John Wiley & Sons.

Tatum, B. D. (1997). *"Why are all the black kids sitting together in the cafeteria?" And other conversations about race*. New York: Basic Books.

Thompson, C. E., & Carter, R. T. (1997). *Racial identity theory*. Mahwah, NY: Lawrence Erlbaum Associates.

U.S. Department of Health and Human Services. (2001). *Mental health: Culture, race, and ethnicity—A supplement to mental health: A report to the surgeon general*. Rockville, MD: U.S. DHHS, Office of the Surgeon General.

9

THE CONSEQUENCES OF RACIAL AND ETHNIC ORIGINS HARASSMENT IN THE WORKPLACE

Conceptualization and Assessment

MARIA P. P. ROOT

Seattle, Washington

Mr. Castellano had worked for an auto parts store for 15 years. In this time, he had married, obtained a college degree, and moved from a clerical sales position to an assistant manager position. His goal was to become manager of his small department and eventually manager of his store. However, assigned a new manager, he found himself criticized at least twice a week and threatened being written up for uncooperative, insubordinate behavior in the form of questioning his manager's decisions. He was repeatedly reminded that his position was at-will employment, which he understood to mean that he could be fired without cause. Mr. Castellano was confused, as his work record had previously been unblemished by any corrective action reports. Within the first year as assistant manager under the new store manager, his responsibilities were stripped. Except for the title of assistant manager, he had no assistant manager responsibilities. He was assigned humiliating tasks, criticized for his

accent, and told that his expectations to make management were unrealistic. His selling technique and management style were criticized. His coworkers gradually became less friendly, and he felt more isolated. Eventually, with a few new hires, some of the coworkers began racist teasing, asking him if it was true that Filipinos ate dogs and questioning "how he ever got a white wife." Normally a patient man, Mr. Castellano started to become irritable at home and in the workplace. He had angry outbursts that were out of proportion to the events. His work suffered, he was making some mistakes, and he was given no reprieve. He did not want to complain to management, as he felt that he should be able to fix the situation by himself. Even though he knew he was being harassed, he felt humiliated and ashamed to bring attention to himself as a target of these behaviors. One day without warning, Mr. Castellano, accompanied by his manager, was called into the superintendent's office. He was given notice of termination for poor work performance and conflict with employees. He filed a complaint with the Equal Employment Opportunity Commission and was granted a right to sue his company, which he did.

Mr. Said, an engineer, had been passed up for promotion repeatedly by his company over a period of years. He had the experience, education, and recommendations to lead him to realistically expect that he could be promoted in his company. He tried several strategies. First he tried to be patient as coworkers with less experience and fewer credentials were promoted ahead of him. In order to further his patience, he told himself that he would just have to work harder than the other employees for his worth to be recognized. After two years of patience, he made an inquiry with upper management in writing, as his verbal inquiries had not been taken seriously. After this inquiry, Mr. Said noted that in his next performance evaluation he was rated less positively than in his last two evaluations of the previous year. Although he was multilingual and fluent in English, it was noted for the first time that he needed to improve his communication. Anticipating assignment to a "plumb" job within the company for which he had performed a needs assessment, he found that the assignment was given to a new colleague just out of college. Mr. Said hesitated to think that he was experiencing discrimination, but eventually he contacted a lawyer, as he had run out of explanations for why younger, less experienced, and less qualified white coworkers had been promoted over him, a dark-skinned man of Somali origin. At this point, he was crying many days, taking sick leave on days he could not get out of bed, and skipping some of his prayers because he was too depressed to get out of bed. Eventually taking medical leave, he withdrew from friends and for a while led friends and family to believe that he was still working.

Ms. Fredericks, a machinist, had notified her manager on several occasions that the men in her workstation were making sexually inappropriate comments about women, and about black women in particular. She felt that they were reserving some of these comments for times during which she would hear them. She told her male manager that she was offended by these comments. However, her manager laughed at the comments, told her not to take them personally—they were just being men—and told her that she should speak to the men if the comments continued to bother her. Ms. Fredericks felt that this was a setup to further isolate her in this primarily male environment. She decided not to talk with the men and to try to ignore the comments. However, a pornographic magazine featuring women of color in bondage was taped to her locker on one occasion. Again, Ms. Fredericks went to her manager and reported that the jokes had not ceased and that the magazine had appeared. At this point, he said he would talk to someone. Whether or not he did was never certain, but the behaviors continued to escalate, and comments were now directed toward her clothes and body. Men jokingly made verbal racist sexual innuendoes toward her. More than one man had tried to physically grab her or find an occasion to brush up against her. Ms. Fredericks began to lose sleep and dread going to work after a couple of days off. Eventually she began to have panic attacks and took medical leave.

Gordon Allport, in his classic text *The Nature of Prejudice* (1954), conceptualized racism as "an antipathy based upon a faulty and inflexible generalization. It may be felt or expressed. It may be directed towards a group as a whole, or towards an individual because he is a member of that group" (p. 9). To this I would add that, 50 years later, we might divide racism into aversive racism, which does not have intent, but nevertheless has consequences (Dovidio, 2001), and malicious racism, which has motive to serve personal benefit. The consequence of either has relational impact, as the workplace is a community of sorts in which people spend hours per day. Many people pledge loyalty to a company and are thus willing to give hours of service that are not necessarily compensated. Many people work to derive a sense of well-being from a job. Surveys have shown that the workplace is one of most frequent contexts for discrimination against African American men and women (Gary, 1995; Sigelman & Welch, 1991). Considering that between 35% and 40% of racial or ethnic minorities in the workplace indicated they had experienced such discrimination, it is obvious that the majority of racial or ethnic origins violence is not reported (Weiss, Ehrlich, &

Larcom, 1991–1992). The majority of literature documenting racial or ethnic origins discrimination pertains to persons of African descent (Forman, Williams, & Jackson, 1997; Mays, Coleman, & Jackson, 1999); however, racial minorities either American born or of other ethnic origins are also subjects of this type of discrimination. This type of racism, when an institution is complicitous, constitutes a form of institutional racism characterized by practices or policies guided by misinformed theories, which hierarchically assign groups of people status from superior to inferior based on race, ethnicity, or ethnic origins (Katz & Taylor, 1988).

Lawsuits in which the prosecution seeks damages for a client who has been subjected to racial or ethnic origins harassment are a fairly recent phenomenon made possible by the civil rights legislation passed in the last half of the 20th century. Although Title VII of the Civil Rights Act of 1964 prohibited discrimination based on protected classes, sex, race, color, national origin, and religion, companies were slow to bring internal policies in line with this legislation. In the last decade, many companies have made earnest efforts to do so. In 1991, the Civil Rights Act was amended to allow persons to seek damages through the legal system for failure to uphold protection from discrimination (Lindermann & Kadue, 1999). Only since then has the public been informed of the continued presence of racism and ethnic origins discrimination through lawsuits described in the news (e.g., Haines, 1996).

The forms that racial or ethnic origins discrimination take are many. The most overt consist of racial or ethnic slurs, emblems, jokes, and accent discrimination. Libel, slander, and mischaracterization may involve these overt behaviors, but they may take more subtle forms, where no racial or ethnic references are used but stereotypes are repeatedly employed. Holding racial minority employees to a different standard than white employees, reprimanding behaviors for which other employees are not reprimanded, giving less favorable shifts or territories—particularly in commission structured compensation—and making accusations or writing corrective action memos for petty or nonexistent behaviors fall between overt and the beginning of more covert forms

of discrimination. The latter may include being watched more carefully than other employees; having responsibilities reduced; finding obstacles to opportunities to be in the company eye in the form of meetings, presentations, or participation on committees. The more subtle forms of discrimination take the form of glass ceilings, lack of promotions, and use of labor or intellectual skills without appropriate compensation.

Root (2003) outlined 13 racially discriminatory and harassing behaviors and strategies in the workplace that I summarize here. They include the more obvious forms of *simple discrimination* such as name-calling, graffiti, epithets, and "jokes." For example, a Chinese American fireman is told by a superior, "There is a good Charlie Chan movie on television tonight." The extreme form, *lethal discrimination,* is also obvious with its death threats and attempts to physically intimidate some. For example, a white coworker tells an African American man that he hopes he will not have to use the rifle that he carries to work in his car on him. *Administrative discrimination* takes the form of blocking advancement. A *colonization strategy* pits people of color against one another by using one person to perform the discriminatory acts. One person is cast as the good minority, and the other is the bad minority. The *low expectation strategy* assigns people simple tasks or dead-end assignments. *Bystander apathy* reflects generalized comments to which people are vicariously subjected or complicity by lack of action. *Modern racism* involves a form of aversive racism (Dovidio, 2001) and involves denial of discriminatory intent, but nevertheless the consequences of the discrimination exist. The *servant strategy* reflects requests to perform menial assignments that are not part of the job description, such as child care or extra work on a day off without compensation. One observes the *double standard* when racial or ethnic minority employees are held to a different standard than their white counterparts. The process is infantilizing. A *lack of training* opportunities results in increased disadvantage compared with coworkers. It creates distance between workers in competence, affects opportunities for advancement, and places a person at risk for being less than competent for lack of knowledge or skills.

Unrealistic expectations are used primarily to test and force out a person by public humiliation because of not being able to meet deadlines or perform work that is too difficult. Common to being labeled a problem person by management, one is informally subjected to *isolation*. Other employees start to avoid this employee. *Mischaracterization* uses stereotypes maliciously and sometimes inadvertently to describe an employee's intent and behavior.

White privilege operates to the degree that it counts on being the majority in most workplaces, holding the positions of power and holding the credibility. Certain acts of discrimination can take place where an individual has not examined his or her own assumptions of white privilege and prejudicial attitudes and feels justified in revealing ignorant attitudes and taking actions based on attitudes. Thus, workplaces may have members of the KKK, swastikas may be carved or drawn in places, nooses may be used as symbols of threat, racist cartoons may be brought in or drawn, and racist jokes may be told. Stereotypes often label African Americans as aggressive, Latino men as lazy, Asian Americans as passive and accommodating, and American Indians as passive or as substance users.

Sometimes companies may pit minorities against one another. In a colonized mentality, minorities may put another minority down in an attempt to gain most favored status. With women of color, managers may wittingly or unwittingly pit two women against one another in a Madonna–whore contrast. One woman is the good woman of color who has no problem with administration; one woman is the bad woman who is whistleblowing, speaking up, complaining, or accusing people or the company of violating policy.

Although most major corporations and many intermediate and small companies have company policies that state that discrimination is not permitted and will not be tolerated, many of the suits that have come to legal action exist not for lack of a policy but because the policy was not enforced. The degree to which upper management understands discrimination and harassment and is willing to reinforce the policy sends a top-down message. The ways in which policies are written also communicate the seriousness of the company toward thwarting and arresting discrimination and harassment in the workplace. For example, a policy that provides no direction as to whom to contact by name or title, no phone numbers, and no outline of the process does not convey as serious an attitude about this behavior as a company that does provide this information and reinforce the confidential nature of certain aspects of the process. The policy needs to anticipate that a manager or person with more power may be the perpetrator of actions. Thus, it needs to spell out more than one option for reporting in the event that the most immediate person to report such an action to is the cause of the problem. A company that provides training conveys a more serious message than one that does not. Training as well as written literature needs to provide examples so employees can be educated on the behaviors that constitute discrimination and harassment.

EMPLOYERS

During employment, a person who has experienced discrimination and is complaining may be identified as a "problem person." In this way, other employees start to publicly shun the employee, isolating him or her in the workplace. As a result, an employee can feel more distressed and ultimately more unstable.

Although a company may have a public reputation of integrity, when sued for discrimination, many unsavory actions may be discovered. Employers may purge an employee file of selective documents such as performance evaluations and commendations. Alternately, employers may insert documents that never existed; individual employees may forge documents and create reports to support the employer's defense. Private detectives may be hired to follow the claimant, waiting to discover some negative behavior that will be used against him or her. Phone lines have been tapped.

During the legal action, the employer may extend the case, which may result in the claimant becoming exhausted and withdrawing the case. The employer may also reenact the discrimination and hostile environment that was problematic in the first place. Thus, employers may use public leverage to obtain positive publicity for the company or for the individual accused of discrimination. Depositions can be harassing and can be experienced by the claimant as intimidating and hostile. Character assassination and redrafting occurs to discredit the claimant's character. Key witnesses for the defense may lie out of loyalty, complicity, or defense to cover their problematic behavior. Often the claimant is at these depositions and becomes more distressed that these lies occur under oath.

EMPLOYEES

Several common themes emerge in therapy or evaluation with clients who experience discriminatory behaviors toward them in the workplace. These themes are important to anticipate in an evaluation as a source of confusion and angst when an individual is sent for a psychological evaluation as part of the litigation process. If a client in therapy contemplates litigation, it would be therapeutic not only to be aware of the following themes but to explore how litigation keeps the stress and trauma alive. The process of discovery and depositions often reenact the dynamics that were hurtful, hostile, and damaging, thus in themselves having the potential to further create damage.

Although claimants sue to ostensibly obtain truth and justice, monetary gain often being secondary, many are naive about how the legal system works. The therapist needs to prepare the client for the possibility that although truths may be revealed, the legal system's protocol and the dance created by evidence and legal rules may not mete out the justice sought by the claimant.

Some clients, whose sense of themselves is as strong people, have overestimated their ability to withstand the damage created by discrimination, thereby becoming debilitated by the chronic negative devaluation process and threatening behavior. Chronic conditions such as diabetes, high blood pressure, high cholesterol, asthma, and arthritis may intensify. Otherwise healthy persons who may only visit their physician for an annual checkup need to visit more frequently for new symptoms such as chest pains, odd swellings, high blood pressure, asthma, insomnia, and hair loss, among other possibilities, somatic symptoms that several

researchers have linked to the correlation between racism and stress (Fang & Myers, 2001; Mays et al., 1999). Ren, Amick, and Williams (1997) have specifically found intercorrelations among stress, minority status, racism, and physical health. On an inventory measuring exposure to racist events, Landrine and Klonoff (1996) found a correlation between exposure to racist events and smoking and increased psychological symptomatology. Many employees try to ignore discriminatory and harassing behavior, believing persons will eventually tire of such behaviors if they offer no reaction. Some employees, often men, feel that they should not complain, as it is unmasculine, and they feel that they should be able to handle the situation themselves. In contrast, some women do not complain because they do not want to be seen as weak or whiny. Prolonged exposure to this type of discrimination and harassment in the workplace has always resulted in more physical symptoms with the persons, both men and women, that I have evaluated or treated.

Employees who are racial minorities by U.S. constructions of race, but who grew up in countries where they were not minorities, may not recognize discrimination as immediately as someone born here. Those persons who have come to the United States as adults often describe being drawn to a land that espouses freedom, justice, and fairness versus the corruption to which they were exposed in their country of origin. They may describe the dynamics of feeling excluded, singled out, underestimated, or undervalued, being hurt by teasing about cultural or language habits or foods eaten, being held to a different standard than white American-born employees, being criticized more quickly, being promoted less quickly due to accents or prejudices attributing less leadership abilities or inferior intelligence, but still not recognize that it is ethnic origins or racial discrimination.

Employee claimants may become fixed on trying to understand "Why me?" or "What could I have done differently?" No rational explanations usually exist. Two common observations are sometimes an answer to "Why me?" First, an employee may be shunned, punished, or sabotaged by other employees because they are raising the standard, which may change the work output expectations of other employees. These behaviors are an attempt to get them to conform to informal norms and standards. Second, employees may have confidence coupled with less need to derive their inner circle of friends from work. Supervisors, leads, or managers who have insecurity issues may target these individuals as employees to be "put in their place." Particularly when these supervisory personnel are white, harbor prejudices and discriminations with virulent attitudes, and feel justified in their thinking, discriminatory behaviors may more easily ensue despite company policy.

Intent versus consequence is also a difficult piece to understand personally and in litigation. Some claimants will struggle with the fact that they knew a certain person did not consciously act against them in malice or was possibly a pawn. Nevertheless, they feel very affected by the actions. Lawyers will often depose the psychological expert with an attempt to separate out intent from consequence. Whereas person-perpetrated acts against another person, if perceived as malicious, often have greater effects (Root, 1992), intent is not necessary for psychological damage to occur. When acts of discrimination have repeatedly occurred in the workplace, despite a claimant reporting them, and no effective action has been taken by management, it is difficult for an individual not to perceive some malice in the lack of action. In this way, there is a natural and reasonable psychological interpretation that at some level the malicious behavior is condoned despite company policy that may state that discrimination is not tolerated.

Some managers or administrators take a naive systems view in applying an "it takes two to tango" philosophy to dysfunctional or hostile acts in the workplace. Thus, a claimant who requests relief or asks management to step in and reprimand a coworker or manager may be told that if there is any further trouble both employees will be fired.

CONDUCTING THE EVALUATION

The referral for a psychological evaluation as part of a litigation strategy should come through an attorney, not the individual suing a company. The attorney should provide all of the documents the psychologist requires for the evaluation. The psychologist's job is to evaluate whether or not there have been damages that are more likely than not caused by the racial or ethnic origins harassment and discrimination. It is not a foregone conclusion that there will be damages that are diagnosable. However, the longer the individual has experienced the discrimination and harassment, the more likely there will be observable and diagnosable psychological damages of greater extent affecting more aspects of the individual's life than if there was a single event. This greater likelihood is related to the effects of prolonged exposure to situations in which a person feels helpless and as a target of an attack that historically or contemporarily may result in a threat to one's personal integrity, reputation, or livelihood. It is a wise rule of thumb that the therapist not serve as the evaluator. The roles are very different. This is not to say that a therapist does not conduct evaluations, but one conducted by a therapist does not have the depth of documentation informing such an evaluation as does one performed for a lawsuit.

The psychological evaluation that an expert performs in an alleged case of racial or ethnic origins discrimination or harassment shares all the aspects of a conventional evaluation. This includes family and personal history, job history, educational history, medical history, past use of counseling, alcohol and drug history, and testing and psychological diagnoses. Forensic evaluations include a review of collateral data including the legal claim; sometimes interrogatories; medical records (which include therapy records, any psychological testing, and reports from the defense); employment records including performance evaluations, commendations, and corrective action memos/reports; EEOC findings when available; and deposition of the claimant as well as depositions of selected key witnesses on both sides of the case. Often, psychologists and psychiatrists will also interview collateral persons. I discourage people from doing this, as collaterals often have their own agendas. My experience in employment cases regarding racial, ethnic origins, and sexual harassment and discrimination is that key collateral witnesses for the defense will lie. Because one does not perform a credibility evaluation on collaterals, the data from these sources is more ambiguous and suspect. Their depositions are often a usual alternative. In addition, the psychologist may start to interview and question a collateral in a way that moves him or her out of the role of psychologist and into an attorney role for which he or she is not trained.

Testing is useful. However, it must be remembered that most testing generates hypotheses, and testing that is used must have norms. Thus, applying the Minnesota Multiphasic Personality Inventory (MMPI [now in its second edition, MMPI-2]) to someone born and raised in Somalia or Nepal or the Philippines does not have the validity and reliability that it does when applied to persons born and raised in the United States. I recommend against utilizing this test and most other tests with foreign-born individuals and encourage multiple interviews. Intelligence tests and cognitive tests are seldom useful in these cases.

Testing is oriented to the question at hand (Vasquez, Baker, & Shullman, 2003). Have there been damages? To what degree are you confident that the damages are caused by the individual's experiences in the workplace? (This typically does not preclude damages exacerbating a preexisting condition.) The MMPI-2 is the "gold standard" of tests, despite some criticisms levied against it. Besides being a general measure of responding in the world, it provides hypothesis generation regarding personality style, diagnoses, defensiveness, and in some cases malingering. The evaluator needs to be adept at interpreting this instrument and not solely by relying on a computer printout, though I advocate always using computer scoring for accuracy and the availability of subscales. Many computer services provide reports that provide statistical information for forensic assessment in the personal injury arena. I am not aware that any exist specifically geared toward racial or ethnic origins cases. When such a specialized report exists, the test does not score any differently, but one may use additional tests. For example, some psychologists like to use the Millon Multiaxial Inventory III. It is derived from the MMPI and provides a guided shortcut to hypotheses about personality styles and disorders. The Traumatic Symptom Index may be useful sometimes as a way to differentiate sources of trauma. Recent validated tests assess malingering.

There are additional pieces to the evaluation and exceptions to culturally, ethnically, and racially sensitive evaluation. For this reason, the evaluation is also longer than a conventional evaluation, which may last 2 hours in addition to testing. I estimate at least 4 hours, but it may go 10 or more hours depending on the extent of the discrimination, the degree to which someone's style is linear or not, and how clearly their story emerges. If the person is decompensating or decompensated as a result of their experiences or the litigation process, breaks may be required more frequently so that their story may remain as intact as possible. The interview takes additional time when an interpreter is used or if English is not a first or preferred language. For multilingual persons, the evaluator must anticipate that upsetting emotional material may reside in the primary language system, which may not be English, or that the person will have more difficulty than normal expressing himself or herself in English. Thus, grammar may fall apart, or the person may find it difficult or impossible to choose the words to accurately convey experience. For someone who is culturally different from the evaluator, there is often a tendency to provide much more context to an answer for fear of being misunderstood. If the evaluator does not understand this, he or she may construe this behavior as uncooperative, present explanations as tangential, and interrupt the interviewee before the answer is given. Impatience or demands to "just answer the question" or to avoid telling stories will shape the interviewee's behavior and more likely than not compromise the data that the psychologist obtains. The psychologist also runs the risk of triggering dynamics of the workplace in which the individual was not given a chance to explain his or her experience so that the individual becomes more agitated and distressed or provides little information.

Although one may state that he or she has been hired by the individual's attorney, distrust and fear of being misconstrued may prevail. This anxiety may result in hostility during the interview or in very short answers. The source of this style must be evaluated as to whether it is an enduring style or a consequence of anxiety, depression, or anger related to events in the workplace and to what extent, with feedback, the interviewee has awareness of this behavior and can control it in the interview.

The interview is also longer because of stressful and traumatic experiences. It has seldom if ever been integrated and processed, such that the individual is often incapable of giving a short answer as a question may trigger a flood of emotions and memories of multiple events that were part of a situation of discrimination or harassment that may have occurred over a period of years.

In addition, the interview is longer because it must also include content that is not part of a conventional evaluation. One must take a history of immigration when appropriate, which also includes citizenship and contact with relatives in the country of origin and presence of relatives in this country. A history of discrimination must be obtained in order to understand the meaning individuals place on their experience, their naïveté, or their sophistication in recognizing discrimination and the ways they have or have not developed to cope with it. It is also necessary to take a history of the events that took place in the workplace and to make a determination of which events were the most stressful and why. Obtaining the meaning that individuals place on events, combined with a knowledge of their life history, helps with the diagnoses. In addition, one must obtain a list of other life and work stressors concurrent with the time frame in which events were alleged to take place.

Common Damages

For many claimants, there is an optimism and naïveté that is crushed when employers do not uphold policies or give consideration to their explanations of actions and the effects on them.

Generalized fear of the source of discrimination can become heightened. All white persons or white men or white persons resembling the perpetrator may become stimuli for anxiety. Although this damage subsides, for persons who held open attitudes toward white persons, there is a permanent change in their vigilance against the potential discrimination they may experience by another white person.

For many men, work and the ability to provide for their families and relatives is an integral piece of their identity as provider. For many women, this is also becoming a significant piece of their identity. Termination from employment or medical leave from a job not only feels humiliating to their sense of themselves as good workers but feels like a failure in their family role. Some men and women have avoided the public admission of "failure" by getting dressed for work and pretending that they still have their job. In this way, their families are unaware of the trauma they have sustained.

For many members of racial and ethnic minorities, the stereotypes invoking images of laziness, taking advantage of the system, and irresponsible attitudes toward work result in devastation as they become a statistic as a result of a debilitating and traumatic process: an unemployed black man, an unemployed American Indian woman, an unemployed Hispanic man, and so on.

Persons who are not raised in this country may regret their formerly prized conversion to U.S. citizenship. They may want to move out of the country, and in an attempt to seek refuge and protect themselves, they may seek to eliminate or minimize their dealing with mainstream America. Some cultural orientations may lead a person to work that much harder to win over the person tormenting him or her or to prove that he or she is not the kind of person that his or her manager or coworker thinks. Thus, spending extra time at work, doing favors, showing a willingness to do menial tasks, and even giving gifts may be part of these attempts. The presence of such behaviors should not be construed as a sign that the psychologically difficult behavior does not distress an individual. Rather, the individual's optimism and resilience is still in place, and he or she believes that it may be possible to constructively change the relationship. Unfortunately, working harder and harder as a solution to prove oneself usually leads to an imbalance between one's work and personal life. If the investment in work does not pan out, the exhaustion and demoralization that ensues from a sense of helplessness to effect change can be significant. For many immigrants, their ability to succeed in the U.S. workplace is a source of pride to themselves and to their families here and abroad. For some cultural minorities, such as Asians of different ethnic backgrounds, to be terminated from employment is a source of great embarrassment and humiliation. There will often be a decrease in communication with family, cover-ups for unemployment, and less humiliating explanations for the "change of job."

For many persons, a common result is that they want to change their line of work as it has become paired with the cause of damage and helplessness and anger. This becomes a difficult piece of damage to work through because often a person has worked for years in this line of work as a skilled laborer, or as a professional or was on a career track. They are not trained or equipped to readily change to another line of work and retain the salary or wages they were earning.

Many of the symptoms overlap with various diagnoses. Several years ago I presented a list of 10 related clusters of symptoms I had found in persons who had either sought therapy or been evaluated by me related to workplace racial and ethnic origins harassment (Root, 2001, 2003).

1. Increased anxiety may manifest in dread of going to work, somatic symptoms (e.g., anxiety attacks, headaches, increased blood pressure, asthma attacks) on the night before work starts up, nightmares, and intensification of chronic physical or mental conditions.

2. Extreme self-consciousness or paranoia may manifest in second-guessing other's intentions, worrying about the attributions people make of you based on your race or ethnicity, acute self-consciousness about one's racial or ethnic minority status, and worry about what misinformation people have about you.

3. Depression and worthlessness may be manifested by withdrawal from friends, family, and pleasurable social activities; difficulty getting out of bed; and difficulty paying bills and keeping up with responsibilities and chores. At its most extreme, one wishes to die.

4. Difficulty sleeping may be manifested by difficulty getting to sleep, difficulty staying asleep, or waking up early. Alternately one may sleep a lot to try to pass time and shut down conscious thinking and replay of events. Nightmares and bad dreams may wake one up from sleep or contribute to less than restful sleep.

5. Involuntary obsessional, intrusive replays and recollections of meaning events persist as an attempt to answer the questions "Why me?" and "What could I have done differently?" These intrusive replays may persist in dreams.

6. Loss of confidence or trust in one's self manifests in doubting one's judgments and perceptions of people.

7. Helplessness and anger about being mischaracterized manifests in fear and anxiety of loss of a positive reputation. This contributes to one's difficulty looking for work for fear of what other people may have heard or know about one.

8. A sense of worthlessness regarding one's value or competence is manifested by doubting the value of one's contribution to the workplace that persists even with evidence to the contrary. This makes looking for work, whether one is employed or not, very difficult.

9. Loss of drive or ambition coexists with a wish to abandon one's career. It also impairs the ability to project competence or confidence during a job interview.

10. A conditioned generalized response to stimuli associated with the source or cause of damage in the workplace results in false positives. Commonly, a person may generalize mistrust or fear from a single or a few white persons in the workplace to white men, women, or people in general in order to avoid being caught by surprise. Individuals may drive different, even inconvenient routes, to avoid seeing the workplace site or stimuli associated with it.

Unemployment related to wrongful termination or inability to return to the workplace because of psychological damage also sustains and perpetuates the damage caused by the initial racial or ethnic origins harassment or discrimination. Being unemployed, without a routine, looking for jobs in the paper, collecting unemployment, turning in evidence of job searches, interviewing, and being turned down for jobs serve as reminders of having to leave a job or having being terminated against one's wishes and because of one's race and ethnicity. With increased self-consciousness attached to one's race or ethnic origins as a result of discrimination or harassment, job interviews are more difficult for these claimants than for people who have not been subjected to these hostile environments.

Common Diagnoses

The four most common diagnoses according to the *Diagnostic and Statistical Manual of Mental Disorders* (American Psychiatric Association, 2000) and that I have found in evaluating clients suggest that the effects of particularly chronic discrimination and harassment have similar effects across different people resulting in major depressive disorder, generalized anxiety disorder, panic attacks, and/or posttraumatic stress disorder (PTSD). Many people I have evaluated have histories that suggest that they have some reaction to stress and that the aftermath of a chronic period of experience in a hostile work environment results in a first-time experience with a diagnosable disorder.

Most people who experience panic attacks do not have panic disorder. However, the panic attacks do contribute to some agoraphobic behavior such as restriction of driving or being out in public. Difficulty being in public is related to being overwhelmed by the expansiveness of the environment one needs to scan to feel safe.

Although PTSD's criterion "A1" requires an event that threatens physical integrity, and most persons have not had a direct threat that someone wishes to kill them or harm them, several experiences convey such a threat and can be heard in comments such as "the company killed me," "they have taken my life," or "I feel that I have died." These are not dramatic comments in the contexts in which some persons have experienced the stress of workplace harassment and discrimination. When one has had white supremacist literature placed in one's workplace, been exposed to nooses in the work environment, been called a "gook" in reference to dehumanizing a target of destruction in the Vietnam War, had cars driven at them, had threatening phone calls playing sounds of explosions or gunfire, had a coworker let it be known that he or she carries a gun in his or her car or has a gun permit, it is reasonable that one feels that one's life or family members' lives may be in danger. The PTSD diagnosis does capture the depressive and anxious symptomatology. However, there are times when the level of depression or anxiety may warrant a separate diagnosis to convey the extent to which someone is affected. For example, although one of the PTSD criteria is a sense of a foreshortened future, this is different than wishing to die, a symptom of major depressive disorder. Similarly, the level of constant worry captured by generalized anxiety disorder is not captured in the same way by the PTSD diagnosis. However, the PTSD diagnosis captures the recurrent intrusive thoughts that are very distressing due to specific traumatic experiences in a way that the generalized anxiety and major depressive disorder diagnoses do not.

Personality disorders are not a common result of discrimination. Some persons who lean toward compulsive tendencies may manifest these tendencies in ways that help their case in excellent record keeping, journaling of events, and memory for details. My experience is that persons with borderline personality features often move on to other jobs when they experience some difficulties as well as make their work relationships difficult so as to create a self-protective barrier that discourages others from targeting them. Persons with narcissistic tendencies may feel injured by work environments that have not recognized their contributions, but this does not provide an explanation of "Why me?" It may provide an explanation of why a person may have worked even harder to obtain recognition for their contributions. Persons who are particularly sensitive may not manifest any personality disorder, but will have less resilience for coping with harassment and trauma in the workplace.

Theoretical Conceptualization

The theoretical conceptualizations I have found that provide an explanation of why racial and ethnic origins discrimination and harassment in the workplace are so damaging are similar to theories that have been advanced in the literature on sexual harassment. Both one's overt sex and race have social constructions and subsequent attributions that are made to them. The attributions that originate in stereotypes persist because they maintain some rationalization for discrimination: for example, women are irrational or emotional, Hispanics are lazy, and so on. In discussing racism at length, Allport (1954) observed that antiwomen attitudes are driven by the same dynamic as racism. Twenty-five years later, the literature on sexual harassment and discrimination outlines dynamics (O'Donohue, 1997) that confirm Allport's observation. Nowhere is this similarity more clearly observed than in women of color being harassed in the workplace. Often in these cases, the women are the recipients of both racist and sexual discrimination and harassment.

In one of the earlier theories of sexual harassment, Till (1980) divided behaviors into five general categories: generalized sexist remarks and behavior, inappropriate and offensive but sanction-free sexual advances, solicitation of sexual activity by promise of reward, coercion of sexual activity by threat of punishment, and sexual crimes and misdemeanors. Although sexual harassment is not a perfect analogy for racial or ethnic origins harassment, some similar categories of behaviors can be noted: generalized racist comments and behavior (e.g., sweeping stereotype comments about a group of people, imitation of accents, making fun of cultural ways of being), inappropriate and offensive but unsanctioned racist comments or behavior toward a specific individual (e.g., similar comments and behaviors to those in the first category that are deemed too petty to invoke company policy; the person is told "to dismiss ignorant behavior," "to be the stronger person," "they don't really mean anything by it," or "you're not like other blacks, Filipinos, etc."), encouragement to deny discrimination or harassment by promise of most favored minority status or promotion (e.g., a minority person is made the supervisor or manager in the department where an employee is complaining of discrimination and is made to enforce the company line or to try to convince the employee that there is no discrimination or that it is not bad enough to be distressed by it), and racial crimes and misdemeanors (e.g., messing up the work site, symbols of harm and death such as nooses and guns, harassing phone calls). There is no racial analogy for the threat of sexual activity. In the more than a dozen years since Till's work, many companies have developed policies against discrimination, which prohibit offensive jokes, racist comments, and other discriminatory behaviors.

In another categorical attempt to understand sexual harassment, Gruber (1992) simply separated out differential effects of verbal comments versus sexual requests and nonverbal sexual requests. Verbal comments can include unsolicited personal remarks (i.e., objectification, which is similar to dehumanization that results from racist comments and terms). They can include sweeping racist stereotypes about a group of people, such as references to being an affirmative action hire or to being not like other persons of their race, or assertions that the planet was meant for white people and everyone else is here until their use has expired. Verbal requests heighten the sense of threat, even though they may be done with humor. The sense of racial threat can be heightened by persons making comments such as "come join us so we won't look like a KKK meeting," or "we need someone to show us how fried chicken is really eaten," or "come with us so we will know how to order the food." Nonverbal displays include racist cartoons; symbols such as swastikas, nooses, and caricatures of persons with features attributed to a racial or ethnic group; leaving racist literature around; and listening to racist music and can range from mildly to extremely threatening.

Similar to Gruber, Fitzgerald (1992) describes three categories: gender harassment (e.g., verbal, personal remarks, sexual categorical remarks, sexual material, and subjective objectification), unwanted sexual attention (e.g., relational advances, nonverbal displays, and physical violations), and sexual coercion (e.g., forced sexual activity such as rape). She notes that the first two categories create a hostile work environment.

In summary, regardless of the categorization system, there is much overlap between racial and ethnic origins harassment and discrimination and gender and sexual harassment and discrimination. The differences might rest in how the threat is played out. For women of color, sexual harassment is often interwoven with racial or ethnic origins harassment. The threat in sexual harassment is ultimate rape and the use of male privilege and physical power to tie promotion and favors to sexual advances or to overpower a woman physically. In contrast, with racial and ethnic origins harassment, the threat is tied to feeling that one can be dismissed on grounds of stereotypes. It is often rooted in male-to-male competition or female-to-female competition for perceived scarce resources, promotion, or retention of jobs in hard economic times. Whereas women have been summarily dismissed from jobs out of gender discrimination, dismissal of minorities from jobs conveys the long-lived societal sanctions and complicity with racial and ethnic origins discrimination and harassment. More so with ethnic minorities than with white women, there is a sense of carrying a community on your back or representing community. Your success and ability to negotiate and succeed in the system is still symbolic encouragement that others may also be able to succeed.

Several social psychological theories are directly helpful in understanding why a person commonly ends up depressed or anxious. Learned helplessness theory (Abramson, Seligman, & Teasdale, 1978; Seligman, 1975), originating in conditioning, suggests that when an attempt to escape or correct a situation is blocked, one eventually stops trying because he or she has learned that he or she is helpless and it is useless to try. Depression may result. In another type of conditioning experience, one starts to pair symbols of the original situation—whether they be people, sounds, smells, or visual experiences—with the traumatic or stressful experiences that create a level of second-order conditioning resulting in seemingly unrelated stimuli acquiring stress value. Thus, for some people who have been harassed by white coworkers or a company run primarily by white people that has failed to enforce policy, white men who look like the primary individual involved may become stimuli for anxiety or panic attacks. Immigrants may generalize unjust behavior to a notion of "America" and want to leave the country. This type of conditioning also generates vigilance for threatening cues that are part of PTSD symptomatology. The more second-order conditioning that takes

place, the greater the threat one will experience in the environment.

Trauma theories that originate in the conjunction of social psychology and clinical psychology also provide explanation for symptoms. Janoff-Bulman's (1992) work on assumptions about fairness suggests that many people hold with the theory that if you work hard enough, just rewards come to you. One might interpret this basic schema as the result of privileged lives, so that optimism and naïveté develop. Few people who have experienced hard life circumstances will subscribe to this schema. By extrapolation, the related beliefs are that good things happen to good people, and bad things don't happen to good people. This theory helps us understand the intrusive ruminating attempts to answer the questions "Why me?" and "What could I have done differently?" when people have encountered repeated hostile if not horrible experiences in the workplace. When this assumption of causality crumbles or shatters before one is able to replace it, anxiety and helplessness increase. The inability to answer "Why me?" perpetuates a vigilance to the environment as well as rumination on events characteristic of depression, anxiety, and the intrusive replays of events. Lerner (1980) similarly noted the central schema of belief in a "just world" for a person's explanations for causality. When bad things happen to bad people, this is more comprehensible than bad things happening to good people. The result of the latter creates anxiety.

Perloff (1983) proposes schemas of unique versus universal vulnerability. These perceptions or schemas link well with the "just world" schema of Janoff-Bulman (1992). Unique vulnerability contends that there is some quality, position, or action about a person that makes him or her uniquely vulnerable to a negative action or consequence. In contrast, universal vulnerability suggests that there is some shared quality that makes a category of people vulnerable. In the case of racial discrimination, many persons' defense against racism is that if they are good workers and pledge a certain loyalty to the company, then they will not be uniquely vulnerable to racism. That is, they can prevent it. Implicit in this assumption is the schema of "bad things don't happen to good people," that is, the Just World hypothesis. When a person has conducted himself or herself in the workplace in a way that should not garner harassment or discrimination, he or she becomes confused about how the world works and why things happen. He or she becomes concerned with the ubiquitous questions "Why me?" and "What could I have done differently (to prevent this from happening to me)?" Again, because racial and ethnic origins discrimination and harassment has a long, historically rooted base of negative prejudice and dehumanization, there is not much people can do to guarantee an absence of this behavior if they are members of a U.S. racial or ethnic minority. In order to come to terms with answers to these questions, one has to transform his or her schema from unique vulnerability to universal vulnerability. Essentially, one has to accept the idea that one can be in the wrong place at the wrong time, and that is the most sense that can be made out of a situation. This transformation can also result in depression and anxiety as one realizes he or she cannot prevent discrimination from happening to him or her. The resulting strategies of social withdrawal and retreat into ethnic communities may represent not only symptoms of depression but solutions to attempt to protect oneself from potential discrimination or harassment pertaining to an aspect of self that is physically visible and unchangeable.

Prognosis

Some attorneys want to know a prognosis for an individual regarding his or her return to a better level of functioning or to pretrauma functioning. They may also want you to sort out permanent from transient damages.

For many persons, working again becomes a milestone from which to gauge the beginning of the recovery of their functioning. At this point, it still takes a significant amount time for depression to lift, anxious feelings to cease, panic attacks to cease, and intrusive recollections to significantly diminish or cease. A period of 1 to 2 years is not unreasonable to estimate. Thus, the diagnosable condition should eventually lift, though psychotherapy, medication, or some form of treatment intervention may be necessary.

Many individuals report that they were permanently changed by the experience. Years later, they do not have the drive they had, and they tend to be more cautious about how much of their energy they give to a company. They are still good employees, but are no longer naive, as they have realized that this is not a just world, and bad things *can* happen to good people. The disillusionment may leave them bitter, cautious, or cynical. For persons who believed that racism only happened to other people, they were permanently changed. They were left with an indelible awareness of racism, a loss of a certain type of optimism, and a belief that good people do not act in discriminatory or harassing ways or bad things do not happen to good people. There is more self-consciousness about one's physical appearance, accent, and customs. They come to believe that, because they are a racial minority or ethnic minority with visible or audible identifying features, they are universally vulnerable.

For some persons, a first prolonged episode of major depression, the onset of panic attacks, or a prolonged period of anxiety makes them subsequently vulnerable to a reoccurrence of this type of debilitating symptomatology in the face of less severe stress. It is as though their psychological stamina or reserve has been diminished or depleted. Difficulties in subsequent jobs, the beginning of discrimination or harassment, unreasonable scrutiny, or unfair criticism may trigger previous symptomatology. Nevertheless, some persons, despite the damage and vulnerability, find positive ways to transform their experiences in ways that benefit others.

SUMMARY

Examining the effects of racial and ethnic origins discrimination and harassment in the workplace leads to a conclusion that these behaviors affect not only the intended targets but everyone—coworkers, managers, and an entire company. Intention is less of an issue than the consequences of ignorance, negative bias, and dehumanization of individuals. Significant resources of people, time, and money are expended to attempt to right a wrong or defend against perceptions of wrongdoing when these cases have gone as far as the legal arena. It is imperative that we continue to educate people about the value that each person contributes to this country. Furthermore, we must continue to support the tasks that some companies and agencies have undertaken to underscore a message of zero tolerance for discrimination and harassment in the workplace. Racism in any form takes a toll on all.

REFERENCES

Abramson, L. Y., Seligman, M. E. P., & Teasdale, J. (1978). Learned helplessness in humans: Critique and reformulation. *Journal of Abnormal Psychology, 87,* 32–48.

Allport, G. W. (1954). *The nature of prejudice.* Reading, MA: Addison-Wesley.

American Psychiatric Association. (2000). *Diagnostic and statistical manual of mental disorders* (4th ed., Text revision). Washington, DC: Author.

Dovidio, J. F. (2001). *Why can't we get along? Interpersonal biases and interracial distrust.* Presented at the National Multicultural Summit II, Santa Barbara, CA.

Fang, C. Y., & Myers, H. F. (2001). The effects of racial stressors and hostility on cardiovascular reactivity in African American and Caucasian men. *Health Psychology, 20*(1), 64–70.

Fitzgerald, L. F. (1992). *Breaking silence: The sexual harassment of women in academia and the workplace.* Washington, DC: Federation of Cognitive, Psychological, and Behavioral Sciences.

Forman, T. A., Williams, D. R., & Jackson, J. S. (1997). Race, place, and discrimination. *Perspectives on Social Problems, 9,* 231–261.

Gary, L. (1995). African American men's perceptions of racial discrimination: A sociocultural analysis. *Social Work Research, 19*(4), 207–216.

Gruber, J. E. (1992). A typology of personal and environmental sexual harassment: Research and policy implications for the 1990s. *Sex Roles, 26,* 447–464.

Haines, T. W. (1996, January 12). J.C. Penney told to pay $1.5 million in race suit. *Seattle Times,* pp. A1, A15.

Janoff-Bulman, R. (1992). *Shattered assumptions: Towards a new psychology of trauma.* New York: Free Press.

Katz, P. A., & Taylor, D. A. (Eds.). (1988). *Eliminating racism.* New York: Plenum Press.

Landrine, H., & Klonoff, E. A. (1996). The schedule of racist events: A measure of racial discrimination and a study of its negative physical and mental health consequences. *Journal of Black Psychology, 22*(2), 144–168.

Lerner, M. J. (1980). *The belief in a just world.* New York: Plenum Press.

Lindermann, B. T., & Kadue, D. D. (1999). *Sexual harassment in employment law: 1999 cumulative supplement.* Washington, DC: Bureau of National Affairs.

Mays, V. M., Coleman, L. M., & Jackson, J. S. (1999). Perceived race-based discrimination, employment status, and job stress in a national sample of black women: Implications for health outcomes. *Journal of Occupational Health Psychology, 1,* 319–329.

O'Donohue, W. (Ed.). (1997). *Sexual harassment: Theory, research, and treatment.* Boston: Allyn and Bacon.

Perloff, L. S. (1983). Perceptions of vulnerability to victimization. *Journal of Social Issues, 39,* 41–62.

Ren, X. S., Amick, B. C., & Williams, D. R. (1997). Racial/ethnic disparities in health: The interplay between discrimination and socioeconomic status. *Ethnicity and Disease, 9,* 151–165.

Root, M. P. P. (1992). Reconstructing the impact of trauma on personality. In L. S. Brown & M. Ballou (Eds.), *Personality and psychopathology: Feminist reappraisals* (pp. 229–265). New York: Guilford Press.

Root, M. P. P. (2001). *Ten common sequelae to exposure to racially or ethnically hostile environments.* Multicultural Summit Conference, Irvine, CA.

Root, M. P. P. (2003). Racial and ethnic origins harassment in the workplace: Evaluation issues and symptomatology. In D. Pope-Davis, H. L. Coleman, W. M. Lui, & R. L. Toprek (Eds.), *Handbook of multicultural competencies in counseling and psychology* (pp. 478–492). Thousand Oaks, CA: Sage Publications.

Seligman, M. E. P. (1975). *Helplessness: On depression, development, and death.* San Francisco: Freeman.

Sigelman, L., & Welch, S. (1991). *Black Americans' views of racial inequality.* New York: Cambridge University Press.

Till, F. J. (1980). *Sexual harassment: A report on the sexual harassment of students.* Washington, DC: National Advisory Council on Women's Educational Programs.

Vasquez, M. J. T., Baker, N. L., & Shullman, S. L. (2003). Assessing employment discrimination and harassment. In A. M. *Goldstein* (Ed.), *Handbook of psychology: Forensic psychology* (Vol. 11, pp. 259–277). New York: John Wiley & Sons.

Weiss, J. C., Ehrlich, H. J., & Larcom, B. E. K. (1991–1992). Ethnoviolence at work. *The Journal of Intergroup Relations, 18,* 21–33.

10

CROSS-CULTURAL FORENSIC NEUROPSYCHOLOGICAL ASSESSMENT

TEDD JUDD

Bellingham, Washington

BREEAN BEGGS

Center for Justice, Spokane, WA

In this chapter we offer an introduction to cross-cultural forensic neuropsychological evaluations for the nonneuropsychologist. We will review the types of forensic questions a neuropsychological evaluation can address, the cross-cultural considerations that need to enter into each type of evaluation, the knowledge and skills needed to carry out such evaluations, and the impact of culture and language on neuropsychological tests. We aim to provide the users of such evaluations with the means to understand what can and cannot be determined and a means for judging the quality of the work on a case-by-case basis.

NEUROPSYCHOLOGICAL EVALUATION

Clinical neuropsychology is a specialization of clinical psychology concerned with people with brain disorders. In neuropsychological evaluation the clinician assesses the changes or impairments in thinking abilities, executive functions, emotions, behavior, and functional abilities of these people. The evaluation typically involves review of records, interviews, and behavioral observations, but the most distinctive feature is the use of neuropsychological tests (Lezak, 1995; Mitrushina, Boone, & D'Elia, 1999; Spreen & Strauss, 1998).

FORENSIC ROLES OF NEUROPSYCHOLOGICAL EVALUATION

Clinical neuropsychology was born in a medical setting, and its primary allegiance is still to psychology and medicine. The science and practice of neuropsychological evaluation is aimed at medical and mental health diagnostic and treatment questions. Nevertheless, neuropsychological evaluation has a growing role in the forensic

---

Case 1. Miguel

It was a clean catch. The prosecutor had a videotape of Miguel, a 27-year-old undocumented Mexican immigrant, handing the cocaine to the undercover agent through the car window and accepting the money. His companion, the driver of the car, had already plea-bargained. The public defender was concerned because Miguel did not really seem to understand what was going on in his case. He did not seem concerned, he did not ask questions, and each time she went to see him he acted almost as if they had never met. All he would say about the crime was that he had gone for a ride with his friend because he had a nice radio in his car. The psychologist she hired to determine his competence to stand trial reported that he had completed the 3rd grade in Mexico, similar to his siblings. On a translated test his Spanish word reading was at the 12th-grade level, with an estimate of average intelligence. On a commercially available Spanish IQ test he was in the low normal range. When interviewed through an interpreter, he was cooperative, and there were no signs of psychopathology. On a translated personality test, however, his profile was invalid because of inconsistent responses and a "fake bad" validity scale. The psychologist concluded that he had normal intelligence, was malingering mental illness, and was competent to stand trial.

Although her colleagues thought she was wasting her time, the public defender hired a cross-cultural forensic neuropsychologist. He spoke with Miguel's younger sister, with whom he had lived at the time of his arrest. She reported that Miguel worked as a dishwasher at a nearby Mexican restaurant owned by friends. He knew his way to and from the restaurant, but she did not allow him to walk around the neighborhood or take a bus because he would get lost. He had never learned to drive or to ride a bike. He did not shop and handed all of his earnings over to her. He spent much of his free time watching cartoons on TV or playing with her young children. She did not trust him to baby-sit, because he did not have enough sense to know how to manage the unexpected. As far as she knew, Miguel had always been this way. The neuropsychologist called Miguel's mother in Mexico. She cried on the phone and begged to have her son sent back to her, promising she would never let him leave home again. She said that she had come home one day 5 years earlier and a neighbor had told her that a friend had come by and asked Miguel to go to the United States with him and he had left. She did not hear from him for 2 months until someone dropped him at his sister's apartment. She said that when Miguel started the 4th grade the teacher sent him home because he was not learning. After that he stayed very childlike and never learned skills like the other children. He could do only the simplest of chores. The other children made fun of him, but he did not seem to notice. He played with children much younger than himself. He always stayed close to home and never developed any romantic interests or attachments. When asked about his health she recalled that he had had fevers and chills the summer after the 3rd grade. He later had to take a bitter medicine when the government workers came through to spray for mosquitoes.

On testing, it was revealed that Miguel had severely impaired memory and executive functions, even when compared with Mexicans with no education. The cross-cultural neuropsychologist concluded that Miguel probably had contracted childhood malarial encephalitis and was left effectively mentally retarded. He explained to the public defender that Spanish is a regularly spelled language and so word reading is not a valid estimate of intelligence as it can be in English. He also noted that the first intelligence test used was normed more than 40 years ago on a questionable population and has since been found to produce IQ scores that are about 25 points too high. On a formal test of competence to stand trial, Miguel had minimal knowledge of any legal system. Attempts to educate him about specific points were unsuccessful. The public defender negotiated with the judge, Miguel, and his family to arrange Miguel's deportation to his mother's home in Mexico in lieu of a trial.

The case of Miguel is an amalgam from several cases of the first author's experience and illustrates many of the challenges of cross-cultural forensic neuropsychological evaluation.

setting, and certain aspects of research and practice have become increasingly directed at those needs (McCaffrey, Williams, Fisher, & Laing, 1997; Murrey, 2000; Sweet, 1999; Valciukas, 1995).

The amount of damage caused by a personal injury is one of the chief forensic issues addressed by neuropsychologists. But neuropsychological evaluation is also used to help determine personal competence to manage one's own affairs, to stand trial, to give testimony, to parent, and to benefit from schooling and rehabilitation. It is used to determine level of disability with respect to disability accommodations, qualification for disability benefits, and specialized education. It is used to determine qualifications on an accused criminal's culpability and appropriate sentencing. These many different types of legal needs require the neuropsychologist to answer a variety of questions at several different standards of proof and require a variety of clinical and investigative skills.

Forensic neuropsychological evaluations are typically much more thorough than medical or mental health neuropsychological evaluations and involve distinct skills and standards of proof. They may also involve distinct tests or uses of tests.

The person with the purported brain disorder may be the defendant, the plaintiff, the victim, the client, or someone in another role. For this reason, in this chapter we will call the person with the purported brain disorder the focus person. Also, this is a book published in the United States with mostly U.S. authors. This chapter will be oriented primarily toward the forensic issues and legal system of the United States, recognizing that applications in other jurisdictions may require modification.

CROSS-CULTURAL EVALUATION

We will define a cross-cultural evaluation as taking place whenever there are cultural differences among the examiner(s), the focus person, and the examination materials and/or concepts. This includes not only majority culture examiners working with immigrants or linguistic, cultural, or subcultural minorities but also immigrant or minority examiners working with members of other cultures, including the majority culture. It also includes minority examiners working with people of their own culture, but using tests and materials from another culture.

In the arena of forensic evaluation, we also need to recognize that there are circumstances when what is at issue is the focus person's ability to conform his or her behavior to the norms (laws, justice system, institutional expectations) of another culture. This means that an evaluation may cross cultures between the focus person and that person's adaptive behavior within the host culture, even if the neuropsychologist, the tests, and the norms are all from the focus person's culture/language. For example, suppose an immigrant has marginal cognitive abilities due to a traumatic brain injury, a stroke, or the early stages of dementia. A neuropsychologist from his or her culture, in their language, could examine that person with tests normed on an appropriate population. The focus person could be competent to parent, manage money, or stand trial in his or her country of origin. In a new culture their cognitive limitations could render them unable to work with an interpreter or to learn, understand, or track procedures competently in the new setting. The focus person might therefore be incompetent in the context of the host culture. The neuropsychologist may need to evaluate these adaptive abilities within the context of the host culture. This too would be a cross-cultural evaluation.

Psychologists and neuropsychologists face an ethical dilemma with cross-cultural work. They are bound by statute and professional ethics not to discriminate in the provision of services on the basis of race, ethnicity, language, or country of origin (American Psychological Association, 1993, 2002). Yet they are also bound by those same professional ethics to provide services that are ethnically, linguistically, and culturally sensitive and to act within the confines of their competence. They cannot possibly provide services of equal quality and cultural competence to all ethnic and linguistic groups because it is not humanly possible to become equally knowledgeable of and competent in all cultures and languages. Even if a psychologist were fully bilingual and bicultural and thereby tried to serve just two cultural groups, it is likely that the service could not be of equal quality because it would not be backed by an equal body of research concerning both groups.

How does a neuropsychologist address this dilemma? In some cases, it is clear that the ethical thing to do is to refer the focus person to a clinician more skilled with that linguistic or cultural group. But at times the choice is not clear. There may be no such clinician available. The available clinician who is culturally appropriate may not have the needed neuropsychological or forensic skills. Unfortunately, ethical guidelines offer little help beyond leaving such decisions to the psychologist's judgment. We cannot offer rules to cover all such situations. But we do hope that this chapter will offer the clinician or attorney struggling with such issues some further guidelines on how to make such choices on a case-by-case basis. We also aim to demystify the forensic neuropsychological evaluation for the nonexpert so that its cultural limitations can be examined.

FORENSIC EVALUATION ISSUES

The Forensic Question

The forensic question being asked has a profound influence on the way the assessment is carried out. It determines the degree to which history is relevant, whether the testing focuses on neuropsychological functions or everyday adaptive abilities, whether or not a diagnosis or a cause of handicap is relevant, the level of proof required, and the degree of cross-cultural competence required of the examiner.

Medical Versus Cultural Determinants

Neuropsychological evaluations typically describe weaknesses and impairments in cognitive abilities, peculiarities and pathologies of emotions and behavior, and limitations in adaptive skills and activities. The source(s) of these various impairments and pathologies may be the result of a brain disorder, they may represent limitations or differences in education or cultural norms of an immigrant population, or they may result from a combination of factors.

For some forensic questions it is important to determine the source of the problem. For example, in order for a child to qualify for public special education services due to learning disability, their academic impairment must be due to a medical condition. They do not qualify as learning disabled if their poor academic achievement is due to cultural factors or poor teaching in the past (Educating Individuals With Disabilities Act, 2003; Individuals With Disabilities Education Act [IDEA] Amendments, 1997). Similarly, disability accommodations and pensions, citizenship English test waivers, and diminished capacity criminal defenses are available only when impaired abilities or behavior are due to a defined medical condition (*State of Washington v. Griffin,* 1983; United States Department of Justice, 2002).

For other forensic questions, the medical or cultural source of an impairment may not matter. For example, many issues of competency, such as competency to stand trial, to testify, to parent, or to manage one's own funds depend only on the person's ability to carry out the required activity correctly (Grisso, 2003). "A determination of incapacity is a legal not a medical decision, based upon a demonstration of management insufficiencies over time" (Revised Code of Washington, 2002). It does not matter if limitations in these competencies are due to cultural and educational background, a medical condition, or a combination of factors. Such distinctions are important, however, in predicting whether or not the person may be capable of acquiring a competence that is lacking, which may then dictate the length or the extent of a guardianship, an attempt to educate a defendant into competence to stand trial, a plan to restore parental rights, and so on.

Diagnosis

In some cases a clinician may be reasonably certain that the focus person has an impairment due to a medical condition, but he or she may not know what medical condition caused the impairment. There may be multiple medical conditions that could have caused the impairment, or no known medical cause but a clear impairment, nevertheless. In many instances statutes require a specific diagnosis, and the clinician may need to resort to a "generic" diagnosis such as 294.9 Cognitive Disorder Not Otherwise Specified (American Psychiatric Association, 1994). In other circumstances the specific diagnosis may not be very relevant. For example, an immigrant applying for a waiver from the English test requirement for U.S. citizenship may have a history of an untreated childhood fever with seizures that could have been encephalitis and two traumatic brain injuries. The relevant medico-legal question is whether or not they have an impairment that prevents the learning of English, not which one of these brain insults caused the impairment.

Causality

In personal injury litigation, injured worker claims, and certain criminal assault cases, it is necessary to demonstrate not only that the focus person has an impairment due to a medical condition but also that that impairment was caused by a specific event. Most usually this involves a trauma to the brain, a toxicity, anoxia, or a medical malpractice event. Determining this cause often requires a reconstruction of the history of an impairment and evidence of preinjury ability levels. In many other forensic settings, however, the specific cause of an impairment is much less important.

Prognosis and Prediction

Looking Ahead

Neuropsychological evaluation is often used to predict future behavior regarding competency, rehabilitation, education, disability accommodation, dangerousness, and compensation. For example, it can be important to know if someone is likely to recover from an incompetency so that a trial might be postponed or a guardianship or disability pension revisited. It is also important to know what the prognosis of a condition is in order to set realistic education and rehabilitation goals.

Looking Backward

Neuropsychological evaluation can also be used as part of a determination of past behavior.

It may play a role in reconstructing someone's past state of mind at the time of a crime or one's previous competence to give testimony, to make a confession, to stand trial, to sign a will or contract, or to let a deadline pass.

Culturally Relative Standards

The Need (or Lack Thereof) for Culturally Relative Standards

For some forensic questions it is critically important that the neuropsychological evaluation use a culturally relative standard (Ferraro, 2002; Fletcher-Janzen, Strickland, & Reynolds, 2000; Nell, 2000). The neuropsychologist must determine if the focus person's abilities and behavior are deviant within his or her cultural context in order to determine if a medical condition is present. Tests used must compare the person with an appropriate population in order to have validity as measures of brain disorder. This is especially true for personal injury liability, disability accommodation, and special education.

For many forensic questions the standard is absolute, and it concerns competence within a specific U.S. cultural and institutional framework rather than culturally relative standards. For example, the question of competence to stand trial is a question of the focus person's ability to understand what is going on in a U.S. court and to collaborate in his or her defense with a U.S. attorney. Although an interpreter is provided, the focus person is not given the option of standing trial under another legal system or of having the system simplified. Similarly, the U.S. citizenship examination involves the absolute standard of the ability to learn English and U.S. civics (United States Department of Justice, 2002). Candidates for citizenship do not have the option of demonstrating their knowledge of another language or of another country's civics. Although cultural understanding and sensitivity are quite useful to the neuropsychologist in evaluating people for these purposes, the standard of behavior for which they are being evaluated is not culturally relative.

Many other forensic questions stand somewhere in between. For example, competence to parent, to work, or to manage funds must take into account cultural values and typical behaviors for these activities, but there are also some expectations with regard to U.S. culture and laws that the focus person is expected or needs to manage, such as not abusing or neglecting children or being able to manage U.S. currency.

Specific Cultural Competence in Neuropsychological Evaluation

The neuropsychologist and his or her psychometrist, intern, and other assistants need to have knowledge of the culture of the focus person in order to perform a competent and ethical evaluation. The degree of knowledge needed may depend on the nature of the question asked, as noted earlier. Some degree of general cultural competence is a prerequisite for specific professional cultural competence. Acquiring cultural competence is treated in other chapters of this book.

The aspects of specific cultures that are most relevant to neuropsychological evaluation are as follows:

- Worldview—This includes how a culture tends to view the locus of control of the individual (whether things happen to you primarily because of your own choice and initiative, because of chance, because of the actions of family or society or God, etc.), how the culture views causality (scientific, magical, religious, chance, balances, etc.), how the culture views the purpose of life, and so on.
- Values—This includes concepts of honor, shame, justice, family expectations, time sense, and the like.
- Religion and beliefs—This includes not only the formal theological belief system but also the rituals, social structures, and functions of the religion in everyday life.
- Family structures—This includes not only how the culture describes kinship but also the expectations for participation in a family and expectations for behavior toward specific family members according to role.
- Social roles—This includes expectations for interactions based on age, gender, social class, position of authority, and so on. This also includes how members of the culture view and interact with members of other cultures and ethnic groups.

- Recent history—This includes wars, famines, epidemics, immigration trends, and so on that may give indications of likely causes of brain illnesses, emotional traumas, or other life-shaping events.
- Epidemiology—This includes local diseases, genetic disorders, toxicities, and the like that may be characteristic of a particular population.
- Responses to psychotropic medications— These have been found to vary by ethnicity (Strickland & Gray, 2000).
- Attitudes and beliefs regarding

    Health

    Illness (causation and relief of disease)

    Healing (including traditional practices, religious influences, and attitudes toward Western medicine)

    Mental health (including causation, treatment, culture-specific mental disorders, and attitudes toward Western mental health practices)

    Disability

- Communication and interpersonal style:

    Language (including features such as tonal languages, nature of the writing system, and use of an alphabet)

    Expectations between individuals of various social roles

    Personal disclosure (what is considered appropriate in what contexts)

    Rapport and how to establish it

    Nonverbal conventions such as interpersonal distance, eye contact, pace of exchange, and meanings of gestures and touch

    Expression of pain

- Educational system—This includes the quality and nature of the educational system and the role of testing within that system.

General Cross-Cultural Competence in Neuropsychological Evaluation

Assessing Acculturation and Bilingualism. The cross-cultural neuropsychologist also needs a working knowledge of the principles of acculturation, bilingualism, and literacy. Acculturation is covered in other chapters of this book.

The major dimensions of bilingualism and multilingualism that have been identified include knowledge of each language, usage (frequency and context of use), degree (preference in particular contexts), and balance (ease and frequency of switching and mixing between languages). As with acculturation, there are different models of bilingualism (Hakuta & Garcia, 1989; Usmani, 1999), including additive (learning a second language while retaining the first), subtractive (learning a second language to replace a first), as well as learning two languages together from childhood. Dormant bilingualism is where a language learned has not been used for a long time. Abilities within and between languages may vary dramatically with respect to speaking, listening, reading, and writing, as well as with respect to phonology, grammar, semantics, and pragmatics. For example, a Mixteco Indian from Mexico who migrated to the United States as a young adult might be most comfortable talking about personal matters in Mixteco, have his best literacy and mathematical skills in Spanish (his language of education), be most comfortable talking about work-related matters using an English technical vocabulary, and speak "Spanglish" (a blend of Spanish and English) with his friends. The degree and nature of bilingualism can be assessed through structured interviews (Paradis, 1987), supplemented with bilingual language achievement tests (e.g., *Bilingual Verbal Abilities Test;* Muñoz-Sandoval, Cummins, Alvarado, & Ruef, 1998).

Bilingualism has many varied influences on cognitive processes and on cognitive test performance. For example, people usually do calculations in the language in which they learned them, regardless of their current dominant language. An immigrant fluent in English given a mental arithmetic problem in English may well mentally interpret the numbers into his or her language of education, perform the calculations, and interpret the result back into English, adding two extra mental steps to the process. This may influence the use of mental calculations as a measure of attention. Immediate verbal memory may rely on language-specific functions, whereas delayed verbal memory may rely more on language-independent semantic memory. Bilingualism appears to produce an advantage on some cognitive tests and a disadvantage on others (Ardila et al., 2000; Rosselli et al., 2002).

Likewise, literacy has many varied influences on cognitive processes and on cognitive test performance. Within the United States, illiteracy is found primarily in the learning disabled, the mentally retarded, and immigrants who did not have educational opportunities. The uneducated illiterate typically do poorly on most neuropsychological tests, and comparisons with populations with even a few years of education are very risky (Ostrosky, Ardila, Rosselli, López-Arango, & Uriel-Mendoza, 1998). Literacy can vary greatly by language in bilinguals depending on their educational history and the type of writing system, and it needs to be individually assessed in each language.

Understanding the focus person's language competencies is a prerequisite to determining if there are impairments in those competencies and to using language to evaluate other functions such as memory, attention, and executive functions. In many cases it may be necessary to do selective testing in both languages (cf. Kohnert, Hernandez, & Bates, 1998).

Using Interpreters. Interpreters deal with spoken language. Translators deal with written language. Using interpreters is the subject of another chapter in this book (Chapter 11, by Tribe) and so will be treated only briefly here, primarily with respect to the special considerations of neuropsychology. Using interpreters properly is a relatively easy skill, but if it is not learned, the evaluation may be useless. Professionals should always use professional interpreters, certified in the language and the specialty for which they are used. Unfortunately, not all states have certification for interpreters. It is always a good idea to inquire about the interpreter's qualifications and experience. It is also worthwhile for the neuropsychologist to appreciate the difference between a medical interpreter and a court interpreter. Neuropsychologists will most often have access to medical interpreters who work with a medical vocabulary. They may sometimes break from strict interpretation in order to facilitate understanding by serving as cultural brokers for the professional, although they are rarely formally trained in anthropology.

Court interpreters are strictly bound by training and professional standards only to interpret what is said and not to attempt to clarify in any way, especially in the courtroom setting. They are typically certified at a higher level of language skill. They are highly trained in legal vocabulary, but are not necessarily familiar with medical vocabulary. For these reasons, the communication achieved in the evaluation may differ significantly from that which occurs in the courtroom.

The neuropsychologist also needs to take time to prepare the interpreter in advance for testing. Some tests can be rendered useless when time is taken up in interpretation, especially timed tests such as verbal fluency. Some interpreters may inadvertently reveal too much information about a test to the focus person. Interpretation or sight-translation of a test also greatly alters its characteristics and the uses to which it can be put, in ways that vary greatly from one test to another. These technical details are too extensive for this chapter, and the interested reader is referred to Ferraro (2002); Fletcher-Janzen et al. (2000); the International Test Commission (2000); and Nell (2000).

Culturally Relative Standards—Testing

The Rationale of Normative Based Testing in Neuropsychology

In order to use tests to determine the degree of cognitive loss resulting from a brain disorder, it would be ideal to have neuropsychological test results from the focus person prior to the development of the brain condition. This is rarely the case (although limited cognitive testing is sometimes available from various sources). Lacking such data, neuropsychologists attempt to estimate what the focus person's test scores would have been by comparing them with a similar population. What constitutes a "similar population" can vary from test to test, as can the quality of the norming project. It is most usual to norm by age, and tests are also sometimes normed by gender, education, ethnicity, and other variables.

Once a test has been normed and has met other technical requirements, it must be validated for specific purposes (Lezak, 1995). Validation is the process of demonstrating that the test in fact measures what it was designed to measure. There are many forms of validity and ways of demonstrating validity, and this is a highly developed component of the science of testing. One validation technique important in neuropsychology is to demonstrate that a test discriminates between people with a certain brain condition and those without that condition. The further one gets from the population on which a test was normed and validated, the more tentative are the conclusions that can be drawn.

Determining the presence of brain dysfunction is only one of the roles of neuropsychological testing. These tests are also used to assist in diagnosing different types of brain dysfunction, to assist in determining various forms of competence, to predict future behavior, and to predict educational and vocational potential and other functions. Each of these functions has forensic applications, distinctive types of validation, and distinctive considerations in how norms are used.

The Myth of Culture-Fair Testing. Some naive psychologists still believe that psychological testing is a universal phenomenon and that it can be made culturally fair. There are even tests that incorporate "culture-fair" in their names. This myth has had an unfortunate role in advancing xenophobic and racist agendas (Fraser, 1995; Gould, 1996; Herrnstein & Murray, 1994). Psychological testing is not a universal phenomenon, and there is a great deal of cultural and individual variability in the knowledge and attitudes that people bring to the evaluation (Lonner & Malpass, 1994; Nell, 2000).

Most readers of this book have probably taken some form of college admissions test and can recall long hours of preparation, practice, worry, and learning of test-taking strategies. The readers can likely also recall a very different type of preparation for their driver's license test. And they can likely also recall preparing to be examined by a physician. Test taking is a highly developed part of our culture. The forensic neuropsychological evaluation bears a resemblance to each of these experiences. People from other cultures may or may not share these cultural experiences of being tested, or they may have very different experiences.

Some traditional cultures without formal educational systems may have no tradition of formal testing whatsoever. Others have markedly different attitudes toward testing. For example, independent thinking and making mistakes have long been regarded as dangerous in a large part of Russian culture, to the point that there is a Russian saying, "Thinking is the privilege of the intelligent" (Michael Zawistowski, personal communication, 2002). For cultural reasons, Russians will often say "I don't know" in response to test items rather than risk an error and may appear to be giving inadequate or even invalid effort. Similarly, although "quick" is (in some contexts) a synonym for "intelligent" in English, in many sub-Saharan African cultures, intelligence is associated with wisdom, thoughtfulness, and even taking time to make decisions (Mpofu, 2002). A common testing experience with people from these and other immigrant populations is that it is difficult to "hurry" the focus person on the tests. This can likewise give an erroneous impression of inadequate effort and malingering.

Because of these considerations, adjusting for culture is not simply a matter of new norms for the relevant cultural group or adjusting the interpretation of test scores. It involves an entire set of testing skills to understand how the focus person views the experience, to assure that the focus person understands what is expected, and to interpret the results in light of that understanding.

Adjusting for culture also involves research to determine that the test is measuring what it is intended to measure. For example, in English, oral reading vocabulary (the ability to read various words aloud) gives a fairly good estimate of IQ level and is often used to estimate IQ level prior to the onset of a brain condition (Law & O'Carroll, 1998; Psychological Corporation, 2001b). This works, in part, because English is irregularly spelled, and one has to learn specifically the pronunciation of many new individual words. In regularly spelled languages such as German, Spanish, Italian, Shona, Japanese kana scripts, and the like, this does not work. Once one has learned the basic phonic systems of these languages, one can read virtually any word aloud accurately, even if the word is unfamiliar. Oral reading vocabulary cannot be used to estimate IQ level in these languages (cf. Case 1).

A number of techniques have been developed for translating, adapting, and renorming tests for cultures and languages other than their initial target populations (Ferraro, 2002; Fletcher-Janzen et al., 2000; Nell, 2000). Ethical guidelines have also been issued (American Psychological Association, 1993; International Test Commission, 2000). Unfortunately, these guidelines are not always followed by practitioners, test developers, and test publishers. When translations of tests are available from publishers, it is common to find that there has been no renorming or revalidating, and appropriate cautions in the test manuals may even be lacking.

Even when a test has been renormed and revalidated (e.g., in the country from which an immigrant has come), problems in the application of that test remain. The neuropsychologist is still faced with making an estimate of acculturation and finding a way to interpolate between country-of-origin norms and U.S. norms.

There is an asymmetry that frequently applies to the cross-cultural application of performance or ability tests (but not personality tests). If a person from another culture performs normally on the U.S. test relative to U.S. norms, it is usually fairly safe to interpret that performance as representing adequate or intact abilities in the area the test was designed to measure. If the person performs poorly, however, we must search for an explanation for that poor performance (cultural or language considerations, education, brain impairment, test-taking attitude, malingering, poor translation or adaptation of a test, etc.). It is incumbent upon the clinician to mobilize evidence in support of specific interpretations of such results. (Notable exceptions to this asymmetry of interpretation include word recognition reading, as noted earlier, and digit span tasks [Lau & Hoosain, 1999].)

Mental Status Examination. All physicians and mental health care providers are trained in administering a mental status examination (although some maintain these skills better than others). The mental status examination is very useful for screening, but it is unstandardized, not quantified, and not normed. Its interpretation is based on clinical judgment. It typically covers descriptions of

General appearance (grooming, dress, psychomotor agitation or retardation)

Attitude and general behavior (attentiveness, cooperation, malingering)

Mood and affect (depression, anxiety, suspiciousness)

Content of thought (hallucinations, delusions, suicidal and homicidal ideas)

Stream of mental activity (speech, tangentiality, circumstantiality)

In addition, there is direct testing of

Orientation (to person, place, time, and situation)

Memory (remote memory for events of the past; recent memory, such as the ability to remember three out of three words after 1 minute; immediate memory such as repeating digits)

Fund of knowledge (current events; knowledge of geography, history, science, and the arts)

Concentration (mental arithmetic such as counting by 7s backward from 100 or spelling *world* forward and backward correctly, and following a three-step command)

Abstract thinking (often measured by interpreting proverbs)

Insight, judgment (often measured by a question of practical judgment such as "What would you do if you found a wallet in the street?" or "What would you do if you were stranded in the Denver airport with $1 in your pocket?")

Psychiatrists and other mental health professionals are often quite good at detailing specific qualitative aspects of the focus person's thought processes, such as the nature of his or her delusions, hallucinations, paranoia, and anxieties. They may supplement their examinations with personality tests. Behavioral neurologists are particularly skilled at teasing out mental status changes resulting from focal lesions to specific parts of the brain.

Mental status examinations are heavily dependent on the skills and interpretation of the individual clinician. This can be quite variable, and the research literature indicates that the mental status examination is, in general, not very reliable across clinicians (Rodenhauser & Fornal, 1991; Tancredi, 1987).

Cultural considerations are also up to the individual clinician. These can be quite astute, but horror stories also abound. To give one small example, a psychiatrist was conducting a competence-to-stand-trial evaluation of a Spanish speaker and asked him to interpret the proverb, "People who live in glass houses shouldn't throw stones." The medical interpreter, in an aside, explained to the examiner that this was not a known proverb in Spanish. The examiner insisted that the focus person ought to be able to interpret it regardless. The interpreter afterward made her point by asking the examiner to interpret the Spanish proverb, "A horse with a sore back will always flinch" (Sara Koopman, personal communication, 2003). (It should be noted, however, that not all professional interpreters can be counted on to be cultural brokers in this manner and are often professionally proscribed from doing so.) Similarly, many English speakers may be baffled by the Russian expression "to discover America" and the Spanish expression "to discover warm water," while having no problem with the corresponding English expression "to reinvent the wheel."

The Mini Mental State Exam is a brief exam widely used by physicians primarily to screen for level of delirium or dementia. It consists of items regarding orientation, memory, attention, drawing, reading, writing, repetition, naming, and following directions. It is scored on a 30-point scale and is normed by age and education. Many translations and cross-cultural adaptations and norms are now available (cf. Ostrosky-Solis, Lopez-Arango, & Ardila, 2000; Tang et al., 1999) but are not always known or used. It plays a useful role in the evaluation of mental status, but can rarely stand alone as the basis of a medico-legal opinion.

Cultural differences in judgments of insanity are also well-known. One need only read the headlines to find world leaders hurling accusations of paranoia, delusions, and irrationality at one another. Other chapters in this book treat this theme in more detail.

Cognitive Tests. Cognitive tests, such as IQ tests, are designed to measure thinking abilities in a general population. They are usually designed to measure various components of thinking abilities in a general way as these relate to theories of cognition or to academic or life skills. The tests are not designed to measure specific brain functions. The tests are usually designed to give a "normal" distribution of scores, with most people's scores clustering around the average score (e.g., IQ of 100), with fewer and fewer people scoring farther and farther away from average. Many of the most common cognitive tests used in the United States, such as most intelligence tests and memory tests, are normed on a population representative of the U.S. general population by census matching. Typically only English speakers are used in the norming sample, and sometimes people are excluded because of various disabilities or limited education. Norms are available for the Wechsler Adult Intelligence Scale–III and the Wechsler Memory Scale–III for subtests and indexes that have been adjusted for age, education, sex, and ethnicity (African American, Latino, and white only) for individuals educated primarily in the United States (Taylor & Heaton, 2001). These norms are used for specific inferences, but not for IQs.

The most widely used cognitive tests, the Wechsler Intelligence Scales and others, have been widely translated and adapted and often renormed in other countries. It is less common for these tests to be revalidated. The translated and renormed versions are often relatively difficult to obtain in the United States because they are most typically published in the country where they were adapted (or not published at all) and may not be distributed in the United States. Even their existence may be noted only in regional journals published in the relevant language.

Whether or not it is "fair" or appropriate to use a U.S. IQ test or other cognitive test with someone from another culture depends in large part on the use to be made of that test and even on the results obtained. Certainly there is potential for an egregious error to label a child as mentally retarded based on a test administered in a second language the child has not yet mastered or based on a culture that is still foreign to the child. Similarly, it can be unfair to the defense in a personal injury case to conclude that a plaintiff has brain damage on the basis of poor test results if those poor test results are actually due to cultural considerations. On the other hand, normal test results and strong performances in certain areas might be helpful in qualifying someone for educational and vocational opportunities, for establishing his or her competence, or for inferring good recovery from injury when other information is insufficient to allow for such conclusions. Such results may also add confidence to a conclusion to meet the standards of a certain legal level of proof. Furthermore, impaired test performances may be used to contribute to a conclusion of brain damage, particularly when those impaired performances are congruent in their specifics with converging evidence from other sources (nature and location of the injury, adaptive behavior before and after the injury, etc.).

The question of culturally appropriate norms can, in the extreme, be a life-and-death issue. The U.S. Supreme Court has recently ruled that the execution of mentally retarded individuals is unconstitutional (*Atkins v. Virginia,* 2002). The Supreme Court did not address the specifics of how mental retardation is to be determined. As noted in the case at the beginning of this chapter, IQ results can vary widely depending on the test and norms used. There are no established rules with respect to immigration and acculturation that specify *which* norms to use *when.* Similar problems apply to the interpretation of adaptive behavior, as noted in the following section. Because the fundamental issue in this regard concerns one's ability to conform one's behavior to U.S. laws within a U.S. social and cultural context, we suggest that there should be a preference toward the use of U.S. norms for cognitive ability and adaptive behavior.

Neuropsychological Tests. Neuropsychological tests are most often designed to measure impairments in specific brain functions such as attention, memory, executive functions (abstraction, reasoning, problem solving, decision making, self-control), language, visual-spatial abilities, perceptual abilities, motor skills, and so on.

Many of these tests have a "low ceiling." Most people with intact brains will have few or no errors on such tests, but the tests will not discriminate well among normal people with strong or weak abilities in that area. However, people with specific brain impairments will usually fail the test. Some neuropsychological tests compare the focus person to himself or herself by comparing sensory or motor abilities on one side of the body with the other side. For this reason, norms may be less critical for some of these tests.

Some more cognitively oriented neuropsychological tests have high ceilings and are normed by age and education so as to be able to predict more closely the expected performance of the focus person (Heaton, Grant, & Matthews, 1992; Ivnik, Malec, Smith, Tangalos, & Peterson, 1996).

Most neuropsychological tests in common use in the United States are normed on populations with at least 8 years of education. Research on groups with little or no education has suggested that the first 2 years of education have the greatest impact on neuropsychological test performance (Ostrosky et al., 1998). U.S. neuropsychologists must be especially careful in their interpretations when working with low education populations.

Tests of attention are particularly problematic in cross-cultural application, especially those that measure speed of performance. Attitudes toward speed in test taking are notoriously variable. Culturally appropriate norms are particularly important, but often unavailable, for these types of tests. To some extent, this can be managed with tests that have "control" conditions that measure simpler forms of performance speed and compare them with those that place a greater demand on attention (e.g., the Trail Making Test and Color-Word Interference Test from Delis-Kaplan Executive Function System, Delis, Kaplan, & Kramer, 2001; WAIS-3 Coding and Copy, Wechsler, 1997).

There is a growing literature of attempts to adapt neuropsychological tests, renorm them, and revalidate them for diverse populations (Ferraro, 2002; Fletcher-Janzen et al., 2000; Nell, 2000). One of the most notable efforts is the World Health Organization's Neuropsychological Test Battery (Anger et al., 2000). Important as these efforts are, they are only one part of what is needed. Populations are in constant change and transition. For example, in the United States the IQ of the general population increases by about one point every 3 years (Flynn, 1999; Neisser, 1998; tests are periodically renormed to maintain the defined average score at 100). Choosing the appropriate tests and norms for a given individual and interpreting those results, particularly for someone in cultural transition, still requires clinical judgment.

Functional Abilities Tests. Some tests are designed to measure functional abilities in specific skill areas. These tests are typically used to determine if the focus person is competent to exercise those skills. Such tests attempt to look as directly as possible at the area of competency. For example, the Independent Living Scales (Loeb, 1996) are designed to measure competence for community living primarily in the elderly. The focus person is actually tested on his or her ability to look up a number in the phone book and dial it, read a bill and write a check to pay it, read a clock, and so on. Measures of the competency to stand trial (Everington & Luckasson, 1992; Grisso, 2003) ask a series of questions about the functions of a criminal court and about the person's knowledge of the alleged crime. Tests of academic achievement (e.g., *Wechsler Individual Achievement Test—2nd Ed.,* Psychological Corporation, 2001a; *Wide Range Achievement Test 3,* Wilkinson, 1993; *Woodcock-Johnson III Tests of Achievement,* Woodcock, McGrew, & Mather, 2001) measure reading, writing, math, and other academic abilities. Vocational aptitude tests measure clerical skills, motor dexterity, and other general job skills. Competency tests may have nationally representative norms, or they may be normed or validated on populations with known competency in the areas evaluated.

Adaptive Behavior Rating Scales. Adaptive behavior rating scales are not tests of abilities. The focus person and/or an informant who knows that person well rate the person on the ability to carry out various everyday activities. These scales are particularly important in the diagnosis of mental retardation because the accepted definitions of mental retardation (American Association on Mental Retardation, 2002; American Psychiatric Association, 1994) require impairment not only on IQ testing but also in adaptive behavior. Such scales are typically normed by age on a nationally representative sample (*Scales of Independent Behavior—Revised,* Bruininks, Woodcock, Weatherman, & Hill, 1996; *Adaptive Behavior Assessment System,* Harrison & Oakland, 2000; *AAMR Adaptive Behavior Scale,* Nihira, Leland, & Lambert, 1993; *Vineland Adaptive Behavior Scale,* Sparrow, Balla, & Cicchetti, 1985). These scales typically do not have validity scales to determine if there is response bias on the part of the rater. The cultural competence to complete the rating scales and potential biases of the informant must be taken into account.

Adaptive behavior is clearly culturally relative, and this is evident in the rating scales. For example, the referenced scales contain items referring to the use of telephones, microwaves, small electrical appliances, clothes washers and dryers, repair services, cars, seatbelts, air conditioners, thermometers, handkerchiefs, televisions, menus, dictionaries, alphabetizing, phone books, zip codes, bathroom cleaning supplies, electricity, scales, rulers, schedules, Christmas, Hanukah, forks, reading materials, ticket reservations, shoelaces, clocks, classified ads, and checkbooks. Access to these items is not universal and is related to culture, urbanization, and social class. There are no items referring to clotheslines, chopsticks, domestic animals, Ramadan, and so on.

Other items depend on cultural norms of behavior or values that are not universal (looking at others' faces when talking, ending conversations, not interrupting, carrying identification, traveling independently in the community, stores with hours of operation, obeying street signs, needing time alone, choosing to join group activities, haircuts, daily bathing, punctuality, hospitality, controlling temper, "pleasant breath," saying "thank you," conversational distance, dating, etc.). Although several of these scales have been translated into Spanish (and possibly other languages), there has been minimal cultural adaptation of the items, and there are minimal instructions in the manuals concerning cross-cultural applications.

Some items imply that it is more functional to be compliant than to stand up for oneself. These items include controlling anger when someone else breaks the rules, when an activity is cancelled, when disagreeing with friends, or when not getting one's way; not telling a lie to escape punishment; saying "thank you" for gifts (something that is not a part of many Native American cultures); moving out of another person's way; offering assistance and sympathy; selecting "good" friends; avoiding embarrassing others; doing extra work willingly; and following supervisor's suggestions. There are no items giving credit for knowing when and how to direct one's anger, when it is wise to lie, when to offer assistance and sympathy and when not to, when to use one's own judgment and when to follow others' in selecting friends, when it is appropriate to embarrass others, when it makes sense to do extra work or follow the supervisor and when to object or go on strike, and so on. There are no items reading "Asserts one's rights" or "Stands up for others who are treated unjustly." It is sobering to realize that people might be declared legally stupid for having bad breath, not telling jokes, not making their beds, or not buying tickets in advance.

Adaptive behavior scales can play an important role in cross-cultural neuropsychology. At times they may help document that an individual who does not "test well" on standardized cognitive tests, perhaps for cultural reasons, nevertheless is able to function adequately and competently in this society. Adaptive behavior scales in brain injury cases can document the changes in a way that cognitive tests cannot. However, interpretation of low scores is problematic because the scales are culture bound. In some instances the adaptive behavior scale may function more as a measure of acculturation than of ability. At present such interpretations may require an item-by-item analysis of low-scored items, perhaps including a discussion of those items with the rater and/or other cultural informant. In spite of their cultural limitations, however, these standardized scales have advantages over the evaluation of adaptive behavior exclusively by interview. They are more thorough than typical interviews, they allow for objective comparisons to known populations, and they allow for greater clarity regarding the database for opinions and decisions. They do not, however, replace the evaluation of adaptive behavior via interview, because interviews are likely to bring out the most pertinent impairments in adaptive behavior and may cover areas not found in the scales.

Symptom Validity Tests. In the last 15 years there has been a rapid increase in the number and sophistication of forensic neuropsychology testing instruments and techniques. This is particularly true in personal injury cases where the answers to forensic questions have significant consequences for injured people and the insurance companies that pay their claims. Measures of memory and attention have become increasingly sophisticated so as to detect more and more subtle impairments resulting from mild injuries in plaintiffs. At the same time, techniques to detect inadequate effort or malingering during neuropsychological testing have also become increasingly sophisticated and have been used to undermine plaintiffs' claims (Reynolds, 1998).

The first generation of these forensic techniques to measure test-taking effort consisted of measures of inconsistency of scores across a test battery. The second generation consisted of tests specifically designed to measure inadequate effort (called symptom validity tests). Most of these are memory tests (Vanderploeg & Curtiss, 2001) that exploit the fact that recognition memory is usually relatively preserved even with severe brain impairment. The strongest proof of inadequate effort comes when there is a below-chance performance, that is, a performance in which it was statistically highly likely that the malingerer most often recognized the right answer and intentionally chose the wrong answer. The logic of this approach is difficult to refute and can be applied across cultures with fair confidence. The weaker level of inference of inadequate efforts on these tests depends on comparisons to norms derived primarily from a majority population. Inadequate effort, and sometimes malingering, is inferred if the test taker performs well below the level of people with histories of severe brain disabilities.

Techniques for detecting inadequate effort on nonmemory cognitive tests are less well developed. Validity scales are also found on many personality tests, as noted in the following section. However, validity of cognitive and personality tests cannot be cross-inferred. For example, the test taker may be motivated to appear emotionally stable but cognitively impaired, or emotionally distressed but cognitively normal.

The valid application of symptom validity tests and indexes across cultures is, for the most part, unproven. Considerations of cultural variations in test-taking experience and attitudes as described earlier give reason to suspect that the validity of symptom validity tests will vary across cultures.

Personality Tests. Most "personality tests" used by neuropsychologists are actually psychopathology inventories. They are designed to detect psychopathology according to psychiatric classifications, but they are less sensitive to variations in normal personality. The most common tests (Minnesota Multiphasic Personality Inventory–2 [MMPI-2], Butcher, Dahlstrom, Graham, Tellegen, & Kaemmer, 1989; Millon Clinical Multiaxial Inventory–III [MCMI-III], Millon, 1994; Personality Assessment Inventory [PAI], Morey, 1991) were not designed with brain disorders or the changes in personality resulting from those disorders in mind. Unlike cognitive tests, on personality tests a higher score usually means more psychopathology. Some of these tests (e.g., the MMPI-2) are normed by gender, but most are not normed by age or education within the adult range. Most contain validity scales to determine the test taker's attitude or approach to the test. These validity scales are helpful in determining if the person was being fairly straightforward and honest, if there was defensiveness and denial of emotional problems, or if there was exaggeration of emotional problems.

A new generation of neuropsychological personality tests is emerging. These are specifically designed to measure the changes in personality resulting from brain disorders (for reviews, see Judd, 1999; Judd & Fordyce, 1996). These may be normed by gender, age, and education. Their cross-cultural application is not yet validated.

Decision Making From Test Scores. Historically, there have been many attempts to determine how best to make neuropsychological decisions based on test scores. Most of these attempts have come from clinical (rather than forensic) neuropsychology. Typically, this has involved the determination of either cutoff scores (a score below a certain number on a test is taken as evidence of brain dysfunction, while a score above that number is taken as evidence of an intact brain) or discrepancy scores (when the score on one test is a certain number or proportion below a score on another test, brain dysfunction is inferred). Such procedures have rarely taken into account the base rate of brain dysfunction in the population, the relative consequences of a right or wrong decision, or the standard of proof required in the legal context. These failures make many of these efforts inadequate even for the purposes of clinical neuropsychology. Because of these deficits, those procedures should not be the sole basis for a forensic opinion.

Furthermore, cutoff scores do not address the issue of level of confidence for scores that are remote from the cutoff. For example, the cutoff score for a diagnosis of mental retardation is an IQ of about 70 (American Association on Mental Retardation, 2002; American Psychiatric Association, 1994). The error of measurement for many IQ tests is about five points. It is therefore common for clinicians to use clinical judgment in establishing this diagnosis for individuals with IQ scores between 65 and 75. Within this range there can be said to be reasonable doubt about such a diagnosis (whether the diagnosis has been made or not). One could still make such a diagnosis in this range on a more-probable-than-not basis. On either side of this range the confidence in the diagnosis typically increases, and it would be very difficult to argue that someone with a validly measured IQ of 50 is not mentally retarded or that someone with a validly measured IQ of 100 is mentally retarded. Such classifications are beyond reasonable doubt. Similar principles apply to other types of tests.

The current legal standards for neuropsychological tests used in court are those established by the U.S. Supreme Court in the case of *Daubert v. Merrell Dow Pharmaceuticals, Inc.* (1993). According to these rules of evidence, the admissibility of expert testimony depends on (a) whether the expert's analysis derives from a scientific method that can or has been tested, (b) whether the expert's method has been subject to peer review and testing, (c) the

actual or potential rate of error in the expert's methodology, and (d) whether the relevant scientific community accepts the expert's methodology. The current neuropsychological literature clearly indicates that neuropsychological tests need to be adapted, renormed, and revalidated when applied to distinct culture and language groups. The literature is less clear regarding how to define culture groups and how to apply tests to those in cultural transition. It is especially important for the cross-cultural neuropsychologist to give a careful accounting of the determination of acculturation and the choice of tests and norms.

Standards of Proof

The "standard of proof" is the set of rules that allocates the risk of an erroneous decision between the parties in a court proceeding. In disputes between private parties over money, the standard of proof is usually defined as "more probable than not," or 51% of the evidence. The party advocating a change in the status quo has the burden of proof, but the risk of error is born almost equally between the parties. At the other extreme, the U.S. Constitution requires the government to prove criminal guilt beyond a reasonable doubt (BRD) before a person can be jailed (see *In re Winship*, 1970).

There is no percentage definition for BRD. Instead, juries are directed to free the defendant if they can articulate a reason for a doubt that the defendant did not satisfy even one of the elements of the crime. This was designed to place the entire risk of an erroneous decision on the government. By design, the system expects numerous people who have committed crimes to go free rather than risk convicting and jailing innocent citizens. (Whether the system works as designed is a question beyond the scope of this chapter.)

The clearest example of the differences between these two standards of proof is the O. J. Simpson murder trial. In the criminal trial, Mr. Simpson's lawyers were able to convince the jury that tainted blood samples, contradictions in the police testimony, and a glove that did not fit created reasonable doubts. The criminal jury quickly reached a finding of "not guilty." In the civil trial for money damages, the lawyers for the families only had to convince the jury that it was more probable than not that Mr. Simpson had killed his ex-wife. The jury reached an equally quick decision, but with what appeared to be the opposite result. The evidence did not change, but the questions asked of the jury did. The first jury was asked if there was even one reason to doubt Mr. Simpson's guilt, whereas the second jury was asked if Mr. Simpson was the most likely suspect in the murder. The verdicts were not inconsistent if one considers the differing standards of proof used in cases where a person's life is on the line versus only their money.

The U.S. Supreme Court has also recognized an intermediate burden of proof in court proceedings where the government tries to restrict core personal liberties. In *Addington v. Texas* (1979), the Court held that the state must prove by clear, cogent, and convincing (CCC) evidence that a person is sufficiently dangerous to himself or herself or others before he or she can be restrained in a mental hospital for an indefinite period of time. There is no percentage definition for CCC evidence. Instead it is used in contrast to more probable than not and BRD. The *Addington* decision acknowledged that juries do not always apply these standards logically but stressed that the symbolism of linking the language of these three standards to the liberty interest at stake in the court proceeding was constitutionally required. In addition to long-term civil commitment, the CCC standard is often applied to guardianship and parental termination cases where the government attempts to limit the rights of a person to make important life decisions for himself or herself or his or her children.

Table 10.1 provides a general correlation between the neuropsychological questions that must be answered and the applicable standard of proof. Although there are constitutional minimums for some of these questions, individual states may impose stricter standards than required by the U.S. Supreme Court.

SPECIFIC FORENSIC QUESTIONS

Personal Injury

When personal injury liability work is cross-cultural, it generally requires one of the highest levels of cross-cultural competence of the neuropsychologist. Although the level of proof required is only more probable than not, the neuropsychologist often has to determine whether or not there is brain injury present in cases of subtle injury. The neuropsychologist is also asked to determine if that injury is due to a specific event. This usually requires considerable investigation beyond the testing and interview. It may require interviews of family members or others from the same cultural group as the focus person. The neuropsychologist must be very well versed in cross-cultural knowledge and skills in general as well as in the specific culture of the focus person. The neuropsychologist also needs to be familiar with any available neuropsychological knowledge specific to that culture. The neuropsychologist should also be able to describe the impact of the injury on the focus person's life and family, and this will include cultural considerations. In the case of severe injuries where there is clear impairment, the neuropsychologist's job may be to simply characterize that impairment. In such situations, the need for cross-cultural competence is still present but is not as acute.

Competencies

Issues of the focus person's competence (to stand trial, to testify, to make a will, to consent to medical treatment, to manage funds, to drive, to sign a contract, to parent, etc.) require less cross-cultural skill on the part of the neuropsychologist than personal injury liability. This is because diagnosis and causality are less at issue and also because competence is in part a question of functioning within U.S. culture. Nevertheless, the neuropsychologist should be sensitive to culturally typical ways of functioning around the issue at hand. For example, U.S. mainstream culture places a much greater premium on personal independence than many other cultures. These other cultures use a more interdependent mode of functioning, especially within families. For example, the focus person may rely on family assistance with transportation, the mechanics of money management, dealing with institutions, and child rearing, much more so than is typical for mainstream

Table 10.1   Legal neuropsychological and cross-cultural opinions required relative to specific forensic issues

This table summarizes the pertinent issues that most typically need to be addressed for various forensic cross-cultural neuropsychological assessments. The practitioner can use this information to help determine if the neuropsychologist has the skills to address the issue at hand and if the pertinent issues can be addressed and have been addressed. See text for details.

Forensic Issue	Medical vs. Cultural Determination Needed?	Diagnosis Needed?	Causality Needed?	Culturally Relative Standard Needed?	Standard of Proof
Personal injury liability	Yes	Yes	Yes	Yes	51%
Competence to manage funds, person	No	No	No	Yes/no	CCC
Citizenship test waiver	Yes	Yes	No	No	51%
Competence to parent	No	No	No	Yes/no	CCC
Child custody	No	No	No	Yes/no	51%
Civil psychiatric commitment	Yes	Yes	No	Yes/no	CCC
Competence to stand trial	No	No	No	No	51%
Competence to testify	No	No	No	Yes/no	51%
Special education	Yes	Yes	No	Yes	51%
Disability accommodation	Yes	Yes	No	Yes	51%
Employment disability (Social Security and private disability)	Yes	Yes	No	Yes/no	51%
Injured worker	Yes	Yes	Yes	Yes	51%
Vocational rehabilitation	Yes	Yes	No	Yes/no	51%
Diminished capacity	Yes	No	No	Yes/no	BRD
Mitigation and aggravation	Yes	No	No	Yes/no	51%
Insanity defense	Yes	Yes	No	Yes	51%
Capital punishment	Yes	Yes	No	Undetermined	BRD

Note: CCC = Clear, cogent, and convincing evidence; BRD = Beyond a reasonable doubt

Yes/no—in some respects a culturally relative standard is needed, and in some respects the criterion involves an absolute standard of functioning within the U.S. culture and system.

U.S. culture, and yet that person may be competent in his or her context. Many immigrants deal only in cash and do not use bank accounts, credit cards, or money orders, which some may interpret unfairly as suggesting marginal financial competence.

Many forensic competence issues require a judgment of prognosis, that is, whether the person can become competent. These questions may require more cultural sensitivity, especially when culture is a contributing component to incompetence. The neuropsychologist must be able to take into account the focus person's ability to learn in the context of brain dysfunction and usual patterns of acculturation.

Vocational, Educational, and Disability Issues

Disability accommodations in education, vocational rehabilitation, social services, and other domains require that it be established that the focus person more probably than not has a disability due to a medical condition. Unlike personal injury liability, the disability need not be attributed to one specific cause or medical condition (except in the case of worker's compensation). The disability might be the result of multiple or unknown medical conditions. To this end, the neuropsychologist must have cross-cultural skills to be able to determine the presence or absence of brain dysfunction as in personal injury liability.

When disability is already established, the neuropsychological evaluation may be confined to questions of reasonable accommodations. This type of evaluation has a component that concerns adaptation to the U.S. context, for which cross-cultural considerations are less important. However, the neuropsychologist must be able to understand the goals and expectations of the focus person and family in their cultural context. For example, someone whose inability to learn English and cognitive impairments might render him or her unemployable in the open market might nevertheless play a significant helpful role in a business run by his or her family.

Questions of education and vocational retraining require considerable cross-cultural knowledge, particularly concerning second-language learning and patterns of acculturation (see Case 2). The neuropsychologist also needs knowledge of the processes of the acquisition of literacy in different languages and in bilingual contexts. In addition, the neuropsychologist will need some knowledge of available educational resources and applicable laws (e.g., IDEA, 1997).

CRIMINAL DEFENSES

Neuropsychology can play a role in criminal defense with regard to competence to stand trial (discussed earlier), the insanity defense, the accused's state of mind at the time of the crime, and the mitigating and aggravating circumstances

---

Case 2. Tuyet Tran

Tuyet Tran came to the United State as a baby with her refugee parents, attended preschool, and then entered kindergarten. Her parents spoke only Vietnamese to her at home, but she began learning English at school. Tuyet was so quiet and shy that she did not speak much, and it was difficult to determine just what she knew. Her first- and second-grade teachers worried about her slow progress but attributed it to the fact that she was learning two languages. In fact, she read single words in English well above her grade level.

By the third grade it was clear that Tuyet was not progressing. She had difficulty following what the class was doing and often needed to be shown what was expected. She could do math calculations but had trouble understanding story problems. Her progress in English as a Second Language was slow; she could learn new vocabulary but had difficulty using these words in sentences. When reading, she often got lost and seldom was able to answer questions about what she had read. She could not tell a story back after reading it. She was referred to the school's multidisciplinary team for evaluation. Tuyet's father was reluctant to approve the evaluation as he saw his daughter functioning well in school: "But she can read many words to me!"

Although the IDEA requires that such an evaluation be carried out in the "student's primary language or mode of communication," bilingual children such as Tuyet really speak some of both languages, and an evaluation solely in one of these does not adequately assess their knowledge and skills. The multidisciplinary team worked with a Vietnamese interpreter to explain the evaluation to the father, to gain his permission and gather history, and to test Tuyet's cognitive, academic, and language abilities in both languages. Although the father had stated that her Vietnamese was good, in fact she had language processing difficulties in both languages such that she was significantly delayed in both, beyond what could be expected for a child learning two languages. Her American "grandma" had taught her to read by rote recognition of sight words, a factor that had disguised her learning difficulties. The neuropsychologist successfully argued that she needed to receive both special education and continuing instruction in English as a Second Language because she would not make adequate progress in either without the support of the other.

that might contribute to sentencing considerations. Neuropsychological testing may contribute to establishing a diagnosis and a pattern of cognitive abilities and disabilities that, in many instances, can be reasonably inferred to have been present at the time of the crime. This aspect of evaluation is subject to all of the cross-cultural cautions regarding testing that have already been mentioned.

Frequently, however, what is at issue is a neurobehavioral syndrome—a change in emotions, personality, and self-regulation resulting from a brain condition. Many of these syndromes—especially those associated with damage to the frontal lobes—have few manifestations on most cognitive tests. Those cognitive tests that are somewhat sensitive to these changes are tests of executive functions (Cripe, 1996). However, these tests are among the most problematic in cross-cultural application and are among the least cross-culturally researched (Sbordone, Strickland, & Purisch, 2000). For these reasons, the cross-cultural neuropsychologist who works on these criminal issues must be particularly skilled in understanding and evaluating behavior that is incongruent for the culture, subculture, and individual. This type of evaluation will typically involve extensive interviewing of multiple sources and review of records. It may involve little or no testing (Artiola i Fortuny & Mullaney, 1998), or the testing may turn out not to be very relevant to the case. Rather, the neuropsychologist will be attempting to construct a plausible explanation of the behavior in question based on the accused's perception of the situation and behavioral tendencies. These tendencies must be seen as congruent with other behavior at other times and with what is known about any brain insults or dysfunctions that are present. For these reasons, this type of evaluation is particularly demanding of clinical neuropsychological and cross-cultural skills.

PUTTING IT ALL TOGETHER: COMPETENT FORENSIC CROSS-CULTURAL NEUROPSYCHOLOGICAL ASSESSMENT

To perform a competent forensic cross-cultural neuropsychological evaluation, the neuropsychologist should have

- knowledge and skills concerning cross-cultural evaluation in general (how to work with an interpreter, principles of acculturation, dimensions of cultural impact on behavior, principles of test translation and adaptation, etc.);
- knowledge concerning the specific culture/language of the focus person;
- knowledge of neuropsychological literature regarding the culture/language of the focus person;
- access to appropriate test materials and norms;
- knowledge concerning the specific forensic question(s); and
- knowledge concerning the professional ethical principles applicable to the situation.

When the neuropsychologist is not fully prepared in all of these areas, it may be possible to make up some deficiencies through research and consultation. The neuropsychological report should reflect this background through description of

- the focus person's cultural, linguistic, and acculturation status;
- any use of interpreters;
- tests and their appropriateness and any translations and adaptations made; and
- norms used and their appropriateness.

The evaluation should include information from as wide a variety of sources as is practical and necessary to answer the questions at hand to the standard of proof needed. This diversity of data can include

- review of medical, mental health, educational, employment, criminal, and other records;
- interviews with multiple informants;
- behavioral observations; and
- tests and scales of cognition, neuropsychological functions, personality, functional abilities, adaptive behavior, symptom validity, and personality.

These data should be integrated into one coherent and consistent account. Doubts and limitations of knowledge should be clearly stated. Where competing explanations are plausible, a competent neuropsychological report will weigh the evidence for each. Under the U.S. legal system, the ultimate standard is the ability of the neuropsychologist to convince the jury and judge of the line of reasoning that led to the conclusions. The competent cross-cultural forensic neuropsychologist, in addition to having the above-mentioned knowledge, skills, and qualifications, must be able to communicate that information convincingly to both a lay and a legal audience.

The U.S. legal system itself and the science and art of neuropsychology are cultural artifacts. They produce neither universal justice nor universal truth. U.S. justice may not be the same as Somalian or Mayan or Thai justice. "Disability" as defined by U.S. law and neuropsychology may be quite different from disability as perceived by the Hmong or Inuit. Causality as defined by U.S. law and neuropsychology may be perceived quite differently by the Navajo or Samoan. In many instances those from other cultures may be unaware of their rights or be reluctant to pursue them. Even when cross-cultural law and neuropsychology are done "correctly" by their own standards, the result may not feel appropriate or just to those of other cultures.

The roles of professionals are many in these cases, and it is not always their job to reconcile these differences. But to the degree that they can at least recognize, understand, and respect the distinctive perspectives of those from other cultures, they can all do their jobs better. More than just that, they can work to build better systems of justice and knowledge to better serve a broader segment of human diversity.

REFERENCES

Addington v. Texas, 441 U.S. 418 (1979).

American Association on Mental Retardation. (2002). *The AAMR definition of mental retardation.* Retrieved June 1, 2003, from www.aamr.org/Policies/faq_mental_retardation.shtml

American Psychiatric Association. (1994). *Diagnostic and statistical manual of mental disorders* (4th ed.). Washington, DC: Author.

American Psychological Association. (1993). Guidelines for providers of psychological services to ethnic, linguistic, and culturally diverse populations. *American Psychologist, 48,* 45–48.

American Psychological Association. (2002). *Ethical principles of psychologists and code of conduct.* Washington, DC: Author.

Anger, W. K., Liang, Y. X., Nell, V., Kang, S. K., Cole, D., Bazylewicz-Walczak, B., Rohlman, D. S., & Sizemore, O. J. (2000). Lessons learned—15 years of the WHO-NCTB: A review. *Neurotoxicology, 21,* 837–846.

Ardila, A., Rosselli, M., Ostrosky-Solis, F., Marcos, J., Granda, G., & Soto, M. (2000). Syntactic comprehension, verbal memory, and calculation abilities in Spanish-English bilinguals. *Applied Neuropsychology, 7,* 3–16.

Artiola i Fortuny, L., & Mullaney, H. A. (1998). Assessing patients whose language you do not know: Can the absurd be ethical? *The Clinical Neuropsychologist, 12,* 113–126.

Atkins v. Virginia, 536 U.S. 304 (2002).

Bruininks, R. H., Woodcock, R. W., Weatherman, R. F., & Hill, B. K. (1996). *Scales of independent behavior* (Rev. ed.). Itasca, IL: Riverside Publishing.

Butcher, J. N., Dahlstrom, W. G., Graham, J. R., Tellegen, A., & Kaemmer, B. (1989). *Minnesota multiphasic personality inventory–2: Manual for administration and scoring.* Minneapolis: University of Minnesota Press.

Cripe, L. I. (1996). The ecological validity of executive function testing. In R. J. Sbordone & C. J. Long (Eds.), *Ecological validity of neuropsychological testing* (pp. 171–202). Delray Beach, FL: GR Press/St. Lucie Press.

Daubert v. Merrell Dow Pharmaceuticals, Inc., 509 U.S. 579 (1993).

Delis, D., Kaplan, E., & Kramer, J. (2001). *Delis-Kaplan executive function system.* San Antonio, TX: Psychological Corporation.

Educating Individuals With Disabilities Act, 20 United States Code 1401(26)(C) (West 2003).

Everington, C., & Luckasson, R. (1992). *Competence assessment for standing trial for defendants with mental retardation test manual.* Worthington, OH: IDS Publishing.

Ferraro, R. (Ed.). (2002). *Minority and cross-cultural aspects of neuropsychological assessment.* Royersford, PA: Swets & Zeitlinger.

Fletcher-Janzen, E., Strickland, T. L., & Reynolds, C. R. (Eds.). (2000). *Handbook of cross-cultural neuropsychology.* New York: Kluwer/Plenum.

Flynn, J. R. (1999). Searching for justice: The discovery of IQ gains over time. *American Psychologist, 54*(1), 5–20.

Fraser, S. (Ed.). (1995). *The bell curve wars: Race, intelligence, and the future of America.* New York: Basic Books.

Gould, S. J. (1996). *The mismeasure of man* (Rev. and expanded ed.). New York: Norton.

Grisso, T. (2003). *Evaluating competencies: Forensic assessments and instruments* (2nd ed.). New York: Kluwer/Plenum.

Hakuta, K., & Garcia, E. (1989). Bilingualism and education. *American Psychologist, 44,* 374–379.

Harrison, P. L., & Oakland, T. (2000). *Adaptive behavior assessment system.* San Antonio, TX: Psychological Corporation.

Heaton, R. K., Grant, I., & Matthews, C. G. (1992). *Comprehensive norms for an expanded Halstead-Reitan battery: Demographic corrections, research findings, and clinical application with a supplement for the WAIS-R.* Odessa, FL: Psychological Assessment Resources.

Herrnstein, R. J., & Murray, C. A. (1994). *The bell curve: Intelligence and class structure in American life.* New York: Free Press.

Individuals With Disabilities Education Act Amendments of 1997, 20 United States Code 1400 et seq. (Fed. Reg. 64, 1999).

In re Winship, 397 U.S. (1970).

International Test Commission. (2000). *ITC test adaptation guidelines.* Retrieved June 1, 2003, from http://www.intestcom.org

Ivnik, R. J., Malec, J. F., Smith, G. E., Tangalos, E. G., & Peterson, R. C. (1996). Neuropsychological tests' norms above age 55: COWAT, BNT, MAE Token, WRAT-R Reading, AMNART, STROOP, TMT, and JLO. *Clinical Neuropsychologist, 10,* 262–278.

Judd, T. (1999). *Neuropsychotherapy and community integration: Brain illness, emotions, and behavior.* New York: Kluwer Academic/Plenum Publishers.

Judd, T., & Fordyce, D. (1996). Personality tests. In R. Sbordone & D. Long (Eds.), *Ecological validity of neuropsychological tests.* Winter Park, FL: GP Press.

Kohnert, K. J., Hernandez, A. E., & Bates, E. (1998). Bilingual performance on the Boston naming test: Preliminary norms in Spanish and English. *Brain & Language, 65,* 422–440.

Lau, C. W., & Hoosain, R. (1999). Working memory and language difference in sound duration: A comparison of mental arithmetic in Chinese, Japanese, and English. *Psychologia: An International Journal of Psychology in the Orient, 42,* 139–144.

Law, R., & O'Carroll, R. E. (1998). A comparison of three measures of estimating premorbid intellectual level in dementia of the Alzheimer type. *International Journal of Geriatric Psychiatry, 13,* 727–730.

Lezak, M. (1995). *Neuropsychological assessment* (3rd ed.). New York: Oxford University Press.

Loeb, P. A. (1996). *Independent living scales.* Itasca, IL: Riverside Publishing.

Lonner, W., & Malpass, R. (1994). *Psychology and culture.* Boston: Allyn and Bacon.

McCaffrey, R. J., Williams, A. D., Fisher, J. M., & Laing, L. C. (Eds.). (1997). *The practice of forensic neuropsychology: Meeting challenges in the courtroom.* New York: Plenum Press.

Millon, T. (1994). *Millon clinical multiaxial inventory–III manual.* Minneapolis: National Computer Systems.

Mitrushina, M. N., Boone, K. B., & D'Elia, L. F. (1999). *Handbook of normative data for neuropsychological assessment.* New York: Oxford University Press.

Morey, L. C. (1991). *The personality assessment inventory professional manual.* Odessa, FL: Psychological Assessment Resources.

Mpofu, E. (2002). Indigenization of the psychology of human intelligence in sub-Saharan Africa. In W. J. Lonner, D. L. Dinnel, S. A. Hayes, & D. N. Sattler (Eds.), *Online readings in psychology and culture* (Unit 5, Chapter 2; http://www.wwu.edu/~culture). Bellingham, WA: Center for Cross-Cultural Research, Western Washington University.

Muñoz-Sandoval, A. F., Cummins, J., Alvarado, C. G., & Ruef, M. L. (1998). *Bilingual verbal abilities tests.* Itasca, IL: Riverside Publishing.

Murrey, G. J. (Ed.). (2000). *The forensic evaluation of traumatic brain injury: A handbook for clinicians and attorneys.* Boca Raton, FL: CRC Press.

Neisser, U. (Ed.). (1998). *The rising curve: Long-term gains in IQ and related measures.* Washington, DC: American Psychological Association.

Nell, V. (2000). *Cross-cultural neuropsychological assessment: Theory and practice.* Mahwah, NJ: Lawrence Erlbaum Associates.

Nihira, K., Leland, H., & Lambert, N. (1993). *AAMR adaptive behavior scale residential and community* (2nd ed.). Austin, TX: Pro-Ed.

Ostrosky, F., Ardila, A., Rosselli, M., López-Arango, G., & Uriel-Mendoza, V. (1998). Neuropsychological test performance in illiterates. *Archives of Clinical Neuropsychology, 13,* 645–660.

Ostrosky-Solis, F., Lopez-Arango, G., & Ardila, A. (2000). Sensitivity and specificity of the minimental state examination in a Spanish-speaking population. *Applied Neuropsychology, 7,* 25–31.

Paradis, M. (1987). *The assessment of bilingual aphasia.* Hillsdale, NJ: Lawrence Erlbaum.

Psychological Corporation. (2001a). *Wechsler individual achievement test* (2nd ed.). San Antonio, TX: Author.

Psychological Corporation. (2001b). *Wechsler test of adult reading.* San Antonio, TX: Author.

Revised Code of Washington 11.88.010 (West 2002).

Reynolds, C. R. (Ed.). (1998). *Detection of malingering during head injury litigation.* New York: Kluwer/Plenum.

Rodenhauser, P., & Fornal, R. E. (1991). How important is the mental status examination? *Psychiatric Hospital, 22,* 21–24.

Rosselli, M., Ardila, A., Santisi, M. N., Arecco, M. del R., Salvatierra, J., Conde, A., & Lenis, B. (2002). Stroop effect in Spanish-English bilinguals. *Journal of the International Neuropsychological Society, 8,* 819–827.

Sbordone, R. J., Strickland, T. L., & Purisch, A. D. (2000). Neuropsychological assessment of the criminal defendant: The significance of cultural factors. In E. Fletcher-Janzen, T. L. Strickland, & C. R. Reynolds (Eds.), *Handbook of cross-cultural neuropsychology* (pp. 335–344). New York: Kluwer/Plenum.

Sparrow, S. S., Balla, D. A., & Cicchetti, D. V. (1985). *Vineland adaptive behavior scale.* Circle Pines, MN: AGS Publishing.

Spreen, O., & Strauss, E. (1998). *A compendium of neuropsychological tests* (2nd ed.). New York: Oxford.

State of Washington v. Griffin, 670 P.2d 265 (Washington 1983).

Strickland, T. L., & Gray, G. (2000). Neurobehavioral disorders and pharmacologic intervention: The significance of ethnobiological variation in drug responsivity. In E. Fletcher-Janzen, T. L. Strickland, & C. R. Reynolds (Eds.), *Handbook of cross-cultural neuropsychology* (pp. 361–369). New York: Kluwer/Plenum.

Sweet, J. (Ed.). (1999). *Forensic neuropsychology: Fundamentals and practice.* Royersford, PA: Swets & Zeitlinger.

Tancredi, L. R. (1987). The mental status examination. *Generations: Journal of the American Society on Aging, 11,* 24–31.

Tang, M., Zou, X., Han, H., Wang, Y., Zhang, L., Tang, M., et. al. (1999). Application of the Chinese version of the mini-mental state exam (MMSE) in 55-year-olds and above from districts of Chengdu City, China. *Chinese Mental Health Journal, 13,* 200–202.

Taylor, M. J., & Heaton, R. K. (2001). Sensitivity and specificity of WAIS-III/WMS-III demographically corrected factor scores in neuropsychological assessment. *Journal of the International Neuropsychological Society, 7,* 867–874.

United States Department of Justice, Immigration and Naturalization Service. (2002). Form N-648: Medical Certification for Disability Exceptions. Washington, DC: Author.

Usmani, K. (1999). The influence of racism and cultural bias in the assessment of bilingual children. *Educational & Child Psychology, 16,* 44–54.

Valciukas, Jose A. (1995). *Forensic neuropsychology: Conceptual foundations and clinical practice.* New York: Haworth Press.

Vanderploeg, R. D., & Curtiss, G. (2001). Malingering assessment: Evaluation of validity of performance. *NeuroRehabilitation, 16,* 245–251.

Wechsler, D. (1997). *Wechsler adult intelligence scale* (3rd ed.). San Antonio, TX: Psychological Corporation.

Wilkinson, G. S. (1993). *Wide range achievement test 3.* San Antonio, TX: Psychological Corporation.

Woodcock, R. W., McGrew, K. S., & Mather, N. (2001). *Woodcock-Johnson III tests of achievement.* Itasca, IL: Riverside Publishing.

11

WORKING WITH INTERPRETERS

RACHEL TRIBE

University of East London

And in my situation especially, I know that language will be a crucial instrument, that I can overcome the stigma of my marginality, the weight of presumption against me, only if the reassuringly right sounds come out of my mouth.

—*Lost in Translation*, Eva Hoffman (1989, p. 123)

This chapter reviews issues for participants in the legal/forensic process who do not speak the dominant language of English. Taking it as axiomatic that everyone is entitled to a fair trial, suggestions are made about how the legal process may deal with this by drawing on the skills of interpreters and bicultural workers. A brief review of the relevant research on working with interpreters is given with the aim of assisting organizations in developing guidelines for good practice. Various models of interpretation are reviewed and related issues considered, such as whether interpreters should merely interpret the spoken word or play a role in interpreting important cultural meanings and variables that may bear upon the legal-psychological issues in question. The chapter also considers issues relating to employing interpreters, as well as the roles, rights, and responsibilities

of interpreters, legal representatives, and clinicians who may work alongside them. Some suggestions are offered about how these professionals can better work together and be better integrated into the legal system; these are followed by some general guidelines about working with interpreters.

LANGUAGE AND INTERPRETATION—A COMPLEX TASK

As language forms one of the cornerstones of human communication and interaction, without a common language people may struggle to understand one another and to interact fully with society. It is a multifaceted, rich, and complex phenomenon. This first section looks briefly at what we know about how language

Author's Note: For the ease of the reader throughout this chapter psychiatrists, psychologists, and others working as mental health specialists will be referred to generically as clinicians, and lawyers, barristers, legal advisers, police, detention staff, and others working within a legal context will be referred to as representatives.

shapes or models experience or vice versa and the complexities of the task that face interpreters who interpret spoken language "live." There are a range of views about the exact relationship between language and "lived" experience or meaning. That there is an interplay between the two is certain. The range of views will not be replicated here, but the interested reader is referred to Bartlett (1932), McNamee and Gergen (1992), and Anderson and Goolishian (1992) for further discussion of this issue.

It is often assumed by people who speak only one language that an interpreter simply replaces one word for another. This is often not the case; different languages are not directly interchangeable in the way that is often supposed (Mudarikiri, 2003). Language not only transmits meaning but may also construct and shape it. Language is not a transparent medium but may act as a defining structure in itself (Anderson & Goolishian, 1992; Burr, 1995). As McNamee and Gergen (1992) write, "We not only bear languages that furnish the rationale for our looking, but also vocabularies of description and explanation for what is observed" (p. 1).

It has been argued that it is through language that we create and maintain meanings and beliefs about the world and that the language available to us (through having been passed on to us) contains an implicit set of values/beliefs from previous generations and the prevailing dominant culture. Language has also been used at various times in history to restrict access to due legal process; for example, in South Africa under apartheid all legal proceedings were conducted in English or Afrikaans. This effectively excluded more than half the population (Sacks, 2000). Language may also contain racist and sexist assumptions reflecting the wider society. The words *Negro* and *black* have very different connotations, as do a range of other words associated with race, culture, gender, and age.

A simple example of how language may interact with cultural values in English is the title given to a woman. In more sexist times women were viewed as possessions of men and had limited legal rights of their own. A title was ascribed on the basis of a woman's marital relationship to a man, and she was expected to take on his name. Although men automatically became Mr. on reaching adulthood if not before, women were always known as Miss until they married. Use of the more recent title Ms. gives a woman a title of her own and a choice that is not predicated on a marital relationship with a man, thus reflecting changing times and the legal position and rights of women within most English-speaking cultures.

Language is a dynamic medium, and there is an interactive relationship between the language and its cultural context; hence we find dialects, slang, and other variations. Language is constantly changing, with new words becoming integrated and reflecting the world and culture we currently live in. People who speak more than one language often find that after not using one for some years, they "lose touch with it," and their language skills become rather outdated. Bilingual clinicians who train in one language often report finding it difficult to practice in the other language, particularly at the beginning of their careers. Each language has its own grammatical constructions and codes, and words in one language may not exist in another or may have a slightly different meaning. Language is multifaceted. The same word etymologically may not be the same word semantically. For example, *sympathetique* in French has a meaning that is qualitatively different from the English *sympathetic*. In German there is no word that can be translated exactly as the *mind*, but several words can be used, for example, *Gewissen, Gehirn,* and *Bewusstsein,* which mean "conscience," "brain," and "awareness" respectively. An example of new words being developed that reflect the changing culture of our world might be the plethora of words recently generated in relation to information technology. Certain words that are used frequently and without question by English-speaking clinicians and representatives may not exist in other languages and vice versa, as the words are predicated on a way of viewing the world that may not be shared across cultures.

An example of this may be found in the following scenario. In Sri Lanka, Sinhala and Tamil are spoken, although English is also represented. In Sinhala the words *Manmo, vidhya maadhihathweema* correspond to psychological intervention, the words translating respectively as "mind, science and *maadhath*," meaning neutral or containing elements of mediation, with the full word translating as "mediation" or "interpersonal process." In Tamil *trauma* is not an easy word to translate; attempts to do so led to much discussion. The words most commonly used are *Mannar neru-keedu,* which roughly translates as "the pressure is from many ways, not only from one place," or *mannar aluthaththum,* which means "will feel numbness," "will not get any feelings," or *thakkam,* which has a meaning similar to the previous words but incorporates a notion of withdrawnness and lack of affect. Other possible words might be *kustam,* which means "living in a very difficult situation and one that is not time bound." However, there was concern from other Sri Lankans that these words were derived or made up by mental health professionals and probably would not have percolated into the mainstream language or be widely understood by "the person on the street."

Interpreters, therefore, frequently cannot interpret directly from one word to another, and this needs to be considered when working alongside them. Clinicians sometimes report feeling uneasy when they say one sentence and the interpreter then uses several sentences to interpret to the client (Tribe, 1999). This is sometimes inevitable and may be essential if the interpreter is to pass on the essence of the message.

The following narrative illustrates some of these issues:

> Simon was sitting right behind him in the dock, laughing in the face of death, but in many respects he wasn't there at all. He could not speak for himself and was not expected to. He spoke through an interpreter, in images, poetry, and metaphors that did not translate easily, and would have meant nothing to whites, nothing at all. The interpreter simply rendered them into serviceable English, into words and ideas white men could understand. (Malan, 1990, p. 182)

Another example of the dilemmas and complexities of the task facing interpreters that may have relevance to legal and mental health settings relates to language differences in the treatment and construction of time frames. This is illustrated in the following case example:

When interviewing a client from Ethiopia with the help of an interpreter I asked for her date of birth. This caused a lengthy discussion between the client and the interpreter. It transpired that a birthday does not have the same importance in Ethiopian culture as it does in Western culture and that the client was trying to relate her possible birth date to national events she had been told had been happening at the time of her birth. This is in addition to the fact that in the West we use the Gregorian calendar, and in Ethiopia they use the Julian calendar, which consists of 12 months of 30 days each and a 13th month of 5 days, with 6 days in a leap year. This calendar is therefore about 8 years behind the Western (Gregorian) calendar. Those using the Gregorian calendar might view a birth date based on the Julian calendar as being wrong. Thus a piece of bio-data regarded as important in the West may be positioned differently in other cultures. It is possible that a client who expressed difficulty in giving an accurate birth date might find this piece of information being interpreted by mental health or legal professionals as meaning more than just a cultural difference.

Sequences of tenses may not map well across certain languages, and many languages do not always distinguish clearly between present, perfect, and pluperfect tenses. The dilemmas faced when trying to interpret from one language into another are perhaps recognized in the following expressions which are used in English: *"The translator is the traitor"* and the expression *"The map is not the territory."* Conversation conducted using interpreters is sometimes referred to as mediated communication, as it is mediated through an interpreter or through a second language (Holder, 2002). Meanings can frequently not simply be translated across cultures; they may need to be located in their context for their full meaning to be apparent. Eva Hoffman in *Lost in Translation* writes of her experiences of moving from one country to another and of the difficulties she encountered moving and interpreting between languages and cultures. The following quote is given to illustrate this point.

> "You're welcome" for example, strikes me as gaucherie, and I can hardly bring myself to say

it—I suppose because it implies that there's something to be thanked for, which in Polish would be impolite. Even the simplest adjectives sow confusion in my mind: English kindliness has a whole system of morality behind it, a system that makes "kindness" an entirely positive virtue. (Hoffman, 1989, p.106)

The complexity of language and the fact that languages are not interchangeable entities makes the role of the interpreter a complex and demanding one. The same complexity and difference in attribution of meaning may be true of some cultural views of the legal system and process itself. One aspect of cultural perceptions of law and the legal process may be illustrated by the following case example:

> While conducting a clinical assessment and legal report for a Somalian man in London prior to appearing as an expert witness, I noticed that as the date for the case approached he expressed ambivalence about me appearing in court. He went as far as to suggest that a male colleague of mine (whom he had seen in our waiting room) appear instead. I was confused by this. It transpired that his memory of the legal process and courts in Somalia was that a woman's word was accorded half the status of a man's word, and he had assumed the same was true in courts and the legal system throughout the world.

Issues of racism, culturally insensitive or inappropriate behavior, and sexism in mental health or legal practice require constant consideration and review by all parties. In addition to recommending good interpreting provision, the employment of bilingual clinicians and representatives requires attention to ensure that all clients are able to receive appropriate service provision in legal and mental health contexts. In summary, the substance of interpreting needs to advance meaning in the fullest linguistic and cultural senses (Raval, 2003).

What are the important issues to consider when using interpreters in the area of forensic practice and the law? The legal process can be an intimidating and frightening process for anyone coming into the system. A legal representative is likely to be familiar with the professional culture, rituals, and procedures of the

legal process, whereas a layperson is not. If a person is unable to speak the host language, he or she may face additional dilemmas. The whole rigmarole of a court, police, and detention procedures may differ across countries and to some degree across states in the United States. The processes of a different country may be alien to an individual who requires the services of an interpreter, and legal advocates or health practitioners may initially feel daunted by working with clients with whom they do not share a language.

INTERPRETING FOR THE DEAF AND HARD-OF-HEARING

Interpreting sign language for deaf and hard-of-hearing people is an important area with its own literature and practice. This chapter will not debate this issue at length, but the reader may note the recent findings of the Deaf Studies Research Unit at the University of Durham in England, which conducted a three-year research project titled Access to Justice for Deaf People, concluding that "many people are being denied full and equal access to justice. . . . Deaf people's access to justice cannot be regarded as equal to that of hearing people."

One of the recommendations of the research was that all British Sign Language/English Interpreters working in legal settings should receive specialized training as well as the video-taping of all police and court proceedings where sign language is used. They made 45 detailed recommendations concerning interpreters, their employers, court procedures and officials, police, legal professionals, and deaf prisoners. For further information the reader is referred to Brennan and Brown (1997) and Roe and Roe (1991).

WORKING WITH INTERPRETERS

Finding an interpreter can be done through professional interpreting bodies such as the American Association of Translators, Institute of Linguistics (IOL), National Association of Judiciary Interpreters and Translators (NAJIT), a private or statutory interpreting agency, your local authority, or your organization's team of interpreters or through professional contacts. Telephone interpreting is also available and may sometimes suit requirements.

Some professionals with little experience of working with interpreters assume that it is not possible to work effectively. This is not the case. It is important not to feel overwhelmed by the idea of working with an interpreter but to see it as an opportunity to learn a new skill, as well as potentially gaining information about different languages, cultures, and explanatory health beliefs and worldviews (Fernando, 1991; Patel, 2003; Tribe & Raval, 2003). It may present a number of challenges and will usually require more time than a traditional meeting, as the number of words that are spoken will at least double. Certainly, within a mental health setting, there can be a number of benefits of working with interpreters or bicultural workers. Working transculturally can enrich practice through leading practitioners to question previously held assumptions and to widen their field of focus to incorporate other cultural constructions of behavior. Hoffman (1989) writes of her own experience of the cultural constructions of meanings:

> All immigrants and exiles know the peculiar restlessness of an imagination that can never again have faith in its absoluteness. . . . Because I have learned the relativity of cultural meanings on my skin, I can never take one set of meanings as final. (p. 221)

For example, notions of the self, views of family structure, and ideas of mental health and individualism, to mention but a few, may be positioned variously by different cultures. Much of psychology and psychiatry has been built around a set of assumptions that are located in a Western view of the world and may not be as generalizable as was originally envisaged (Fernando, 1991; Mezzich et al., 1999; Owusu-Bempah & Howitt, 2000; Richards, 1997; Summerfield, 2002).

As previously mentioned, working with interpreters can present some challenges. It demands some skill acquisition and calls for some reflection on the part of the medical/legal practitioner. There is a growing literature on

ways of working effectively with interpreters in many areas including mental health and therapeutic interventions (Tribe & Raval, 2003), which it might be assumed would be the most difficult arena for this work. In using interpreters, the role of nonverbal behavior may be given more prominence than is warranted. As there are strong cultural variations in this behavior, it is important to be aware of this before attributing meaning or psychological state using your own cultural codes (Brislin & Yoshida, 1994; Furnham & Bochner, 1986).

These dilemmas are compounded by differences in cultural views and beliefs about mental health and the legal process, as detailed elsewhere in this book. This chapter will touch these issues only as they relate to working with interpreters and bicultural workers. The importance of cross-cultural understanding and competence in the provision of services and in individual practice is increasingly being recognized (Fernando, 1991; Mezzich et al., 1999; Owusu-Bempah & Howitt, 2000; Patel et al., 2000; Richards, 1997; Summerfield, 2002).

RELEVANT GUIDELINES AND LEGISLATION

The American Psychological Association (APA), British Psychological Society (BPS), American Medical Association (AMA), British Medical Association (BMA), National Bar Association (NBA), American Bar Association (ABA), and British Law Society all have guidelines relating to equal opportunities that consider the issue of diversity in all forms. The American Department of Justice (DOJ) in January 2001 published policy guidance on Title VI prohibition against national origin discrimination as it affects those with limited proficiency in English (Title VI relates to the Civil Rights Act of 1964). The conclusions of the APA National Multicultural Conference and Summit held in January 1999 led to resolutions calling for cultural competence in all psychological endeavors (Sue, Bingham, Porché-Burke, & Vasquez, 1999). The guidelines require all members to consider the needs of ethnically, linguistically, and culturally diverse populations in all aspects of their practice.

PARTICIPATION IN THE LEGAL PROCESS AND THE RIGHT TO A FAIR TRIAL

Ensuring the fairness of trials enshrined in various legal conventions and professional codes around the world will frequently require good practice in the use of interpreters as well as cultural variables. Equal opportunities conventions and legislation also maintain rights that may include the use of interpreters/bicultural workers, as do the codes of practice of medical and legal professionals.

In addition to moral and legal obligations, it may be important to consider that clients may feel vulnerable and exposed, having "lost their voice" by needing to rely on another person to represent their words and concerns. These anxieties can be exacerbated in a mental heath or legal context where the outcomes of the various meetings may be extremely significant for the client.

> We want to be able to give voice accurately and fully to ourselves and our sense of the world . . . linguistic dispossession is a sufficient motive . . . for it is close to the dispossession of one's self . . . and one is perpetually without words, if one exists in the entropy of inarticulateness, that condition itself is bound to be an enraging frustration. (Hoffman, 1989, p. 124)

Because interpreters must also process the material with which they must deal through their own subjective experiences, the very act of interpreting may inadvertently shape the material in some way. This is a highly complex issue, and researchers have understandably encountered difficulties in trying to understand it. The interested reader is referred to Haenal (1997), Marshall, Koenig, Grifhorst, and van Ewjik (1998), and Van der Veer (1998).

EMPLOYING INTERPRETERS

Different countries and American states have different rules about employing interpreters. There appear to be two major issues. The first is ensuring that the interpreter's contribution is recognized and respected. The interpreter has a crucial role in the process, often working in

difficult circumstances. The second is that the interpreters and medical/legal professionals are qualified and experienced for the job and situation. Working with interpreters requires training on the part of both parties (the interpreter and the health/legal professional) if their contributions are to be maximized. Reliable nationwide training and accreditation for interpreters in a wide range of languages is important if interpreters are to be given the professional status and recognition they deserve. A number of organizations and educational establishments currently offer qualifications, though these may be of varying quality recognition and esteem. The U.S. District Courts have federal certification for interpreters, but this is currently available only in Haitian Creole, Navajo, and Spanish. Some states use language testing, others do not. The American Translators Association offers accreditation programs, as do the Institute of Linguists and NAJIT. The latter now offers a nationwide qualification, the National Certified Interpreter and Translator (NCIT) qualification, to interpreters. It is currently available only in Spanish, although there are plans to extend it. NAJIT describes the qualification as being

> awarded to those individuals who pass a rigorous examination of overall language skills and the common body of knowledge relevant to the judiciary and related areas, and who have shown an understanding of and willingness to comply with a professional code of ethics and professional responsibilities. (http://www.najit.org, 2004)

In the United Kingdom, discussions are under way to try and develop a range of qualifications for interpreters that are integrated into the National Vocational Qualifications (NVQ) framework.

A number of recent researchers (Pochhacker, 2000; Vasquez & Javier, 1991) have reported that friends and family are sometimes used to interpret, despite the inappropriateness of this practice, whereas Sande (1998) claims that cleaning staff in hospital settings may be used. The NAJIT, based in Washington, D.C., claims that interpreters are not always used and

> many entities receiving federal funding, especially those in law enforcement, have not done enough

to organise their administration of language services and ensure that the language service they receive is competent. The largest stumbling block has been the fact that the path to qualification is different for different settings (state and federal court; non-court venues; a language other than Spanish). . . . [W]e believe that law enforcement will continue to operate inefficiently in providing language services. (http://www.najit.org, 2004)

Brief Summary of the Research on Working With Interpreters

Very little has been written on the topic of working with interpreters, despite the fact that people are increasingly moving across national boundaries throughout their lives.

Most of the published research is limited to the use of interpreters in health care settings. However, it appears that much can be gleaned from these findings and be cautiously extended to legal or forensic settings. Granger and Baker (2003), in a study that looked at interpreters in a range of settings, found that only 50% of them felt valued by other professionals. This finding must give cause for concern if we are committed to ensuring effective access to legal and mental health services for all.

Interestingly, Raval (1996) reported that practitioners stated that using an interpreter gave them an increased respect for trained interpreters and a positive reaction to the use of interpreting services. Hillier, Huq, Loshak, Marks, and Rahman (1994), Kline, Acosta, Austin, and Johnson (1980), and Mudarikiri (2003) reported that employing interpreters led to clients reporting feeling better understood and heard. On the other hand, Kline et al. (1980) noted that many practitioners reported feelings of being scrutinized. Roe and Roe (1991) noted that clinicians felt they had lost direct contact with the patient, and this led to feelings of lack of control, although Raval (1996) reported that some practitioners said that using an interpreter enabled them to be more reflective in their work and viewed this positively. Working with an interpreter is a qualitatively different experience from working without one, and recognition of this fact may go some way toward making the experience easier. Moving from a dyadic to a

triadic consultation is discussed in a later section of this chapter.

Researchers have reported that practitioners have felt hostile if they believed that the interpreter went beyond the limit of their task to interpret (Kaufert & Koolage, 1984). However, Drennan and Swartz (1999) have noted the many positive accomplishments of interpreters and cite several studies that emphasize interpreter initiative. In addition, Granger and Baker (2003), Kaufert and Koolage (1984), and Raval (1996) all noted that interpreters may find it difficult to render an accurate translation or may feel ill at ease when addressing certain issues, for example, marital strife, sexual issues, child abuse, or psychological issues. Thus, working with interpreters can be challenging, and prior preparation for the task, including undertaking some training, can reap benefits for all concerned. The more you work with interpreters, the easier it will become.

Working With Interpreters/ Bicultural Workers

Although we may accept the need for interpreters, we need to consider the implications of using them. Moving to a triadic interview from the more traditional dyadic interview can be a challenging and an empowering process for the legal/medical professional as well as for the client. It is important to realize that the interpreter is central to your meeting, because without the interpreter you would be unable to undertake your job. They are experts and should be treated with professional respect. Unfortunately, many interpreters report that frequently this is not the case (Razban, 2003; Tribe, 1998). It is important to make interpreters feel at ease and offer them the best opportunity to use their language skills and cultural understandings. Some simple guidelines are presented at the end of this chapter, which it is hoped will assist in developing your practice when working with interpreters.

It is important to work in collaboration with the interpreter and to be aware that he or she is frequently under considerable pressure from clients to assist them beyond what they have been paid for or to "hold" information that they do not want passed on (Nijad, 2003; Tribe and Sanders, 2003). Any power differential or gap between the legal professional, interpreter, and client can be further exacerbated when language and culture are not shared (Mudarikiri, 2003; Patel, 2003; Tribe, 1998). Issues of control, power, triangulation, and accountability may arise. It is worth asking to whom the interpreter is actually accountable. (There is unfortunately a scarcity of literature written from the perspective of the interpreters themselves.) Are interpreters employed by the client, the lawyer, the court, or another part of the judicial process? Do they believe that they have a psychological or moral contract with the client? These issues need addressing before the meeting begins and any professional codes or guidelines on working with interpreters are referred to.

VARIOUS MODES OF INTERPRETING

There are various modes of interpretation, and it is important that the mode to be employed is agreed on by the various participants before the session starts. All parties need to be aware of the mode selected and its fitness for the requirements of the situation. Different modes of interpreting will suit different occasions. For example, in adversarial court settings, it has been argued that word-for-word interpretation with the interpreter retaining a neutral and uninvolved stance (frequently called the linguistic mode) is the most appropriate (Cushing, 2003), whereas in a mental health context the aim is to ensure mutual understanding between the service user and clinician, so that it may be more important to concentrate on the overall meaning rather than interpreting each individual word (Cushing, 2003; Tribe, 1998; Raval, 2003). This is often called the psychotherapeutic or constructionist mode. Kaufert and Koolage (1984) claim that objective neutrality by the interpreter may actually reduce the value of interpreters to service user and clinicians, arguing that interpreters can usefully assist in establishing rapport and negotiating complex terminology and different explanatory models of health. A similar argument could usefully be made for parts of the legal arena.

Another area to consider is whether the interpreter should use first- or third-person interpretation. This is an issue much debated

among interpreters and those working alongside them. Seating arrangements may also need to be considered; some theorists argue that the three participants should sit in a circular formation, others that the interpreter should sit behind the client (this is usually combined with first-person interpretation, where they "become" the client's voice), and yet others argue for a triangular seating arrangement (Tribe & Sanders, 2003).

Methods of Interpreting

The two major methods of interpreting follow with brief descriptions:

- Simultaneous interpretation (where the words spoken are interpreted immediately, either through someone interpreting and the interpretation being passed through the use of headphones or through someone whispering the interpretation to the individual)
- Consecutive interpretation (where what one person says is interpreted before another person speaks and the process is repeated)

Interestingly, Hornberger et al. (1996) noted that patients and clinicians preferred simultaneous interpretation, whereas interpreters showed a preference for the consecutive method.

Modes of Interpreting

For further discussion of the following differences, the reader is referred to Raval (2003), Roy (1992), Tribe (1998), Kaufert, O'Neil, and Koolage (1985), Wadensjo (1998), and Roberts (1997). The different modes are sometimes ascribed different labels by different authors, but in general they may be described as follows:

1. The psychotherapeutic or constructionist mode, where the meaning/feeling of the words is most important, and the interpreter is most concerned with the meaning being conveyed rather than word-for-word interpretation (Raval, 2003; Tribe, 1998, 1999).

2. The linguistic mode, where the interpreter tries to interpret (as far as is possible) word-for-word and adopts a neutral and distanced position (Marcos, 1979).

3. The advocate or adversarial/community interpreter, where the interpreter takes the role of advocate for the client, either at the individual or wider group or community level, and represents the client's or group's interests beyond interpreting language (Baylav, 2003; Drennan & Swartz, 1999; Razban, 2003).

4. Cultural broker/advocate/bicultural worker, where the interpreter interprets not only the spoken word but also relevant cultural and contextual variables (Drennan & Swartz, 1999; Kaufert & Koolage, 1984; Messent, 2003; Tribe, 1998).

As noted in number 4, there will be occasions when an interpreter may be required to interpret more than just the spoken word and to interpret the cultural context or meanings and beliefs to a third party, in this case a legal representative or health practitioner. This may have significant bearing on the case in question as detailed throughout this book. Different cultures may view different behavior/feelings as problematic or may interpret the behavior in different ways. For further discussion of these issues, the reader is referred to Fernando (1991), MacLachlan (1997), Patel et al. (2000), and Summerfield (2002). The latter writes,

DSM IV (American Psychiatric Association, 1994) and ICD 10 (World Health Organization, 1992) are not as some imagine atheoretical and purely descriptive nosologies. They are Western cultural documents, carrying particular ontological notions of what constitutes a real disorder; epistemological ideas about what counts as a scientific evidence; all of psychiatry is culture-bound; even presentations by patients with organic mental disorders are shaped by local points of view and lifeworlds. (Summerfield, 2002, p. 248)

WRITTEN TRANSLATIONS

Ideally, written translations should be back-translated (i.e., documents should be translated from one language into another by one translator and then translated back to the original language by a different translator, the two versions then being compared). This can be a costly and time-consuming business but may be essential to an individual's case. If psychometric instruments are being considered for use, it is absolutely essential that they have been properly back-translated, validated, and standardized for use; otherwise any scores may prove meaningless.

GOOD PRACTICE GUIDELINES

These are some general guidelines that do not attempt to be definitive and that it is hoped will assist you in developing your own specific guidelines for the context and requirements of your own work. (Various references have been inserted into the text to enable the interested reader to follow up specific areas.) You may find it helpful to look at the guidelines and codes of practice for interpreters and for working with interpreters used by other agencies to start with. Local interpreting services and national organizations may also be able to assist.

Working in partnership with an interpreter can be assisted by

- the provision of trained, qualified, and experienced interpreters with ongoing support from either an organization or individual (Pochhacker, 2000).
- the provision of effective guidelines and appropriate training for representatives/clinicians and interpreters—all parties may benefit from this (Tribe, 1998). Granger and Baker (2003) noted that more experienced interpreters are more likely to see the need for training for both themselves and the person they are interpreting. Difficulties seem to arise as a result of inadequate training for both parties. Stolk et al. (1998) found that training health professionals in working with interpreters increased their readiness to work alongside interpreters. The same may be true with legal professionals.
- trying to spend some time considering all the implications of working with a third person (the interpreter/bicultural worker). It can be useful to discuss this with an experienced interpreter or with colleagues who have experience working with interpreters. Working with an interpreter as a conduit makes you

dependent on another person, and this can change the dynamic of the meeting. You may well find that you need to be extremely clear about the objectives of the meeting and the strategy you use to ensure that this is adhered to (Mudarikiri, 2003; Patel, 2003).

- finding out the client's first language and trying to book an interpreter who speaks this language, ideally from the same country, and when necessary the same dialect that the client speaks. Do not assume that someone who speaks a language can speak/understand it in all the dialects (Marshall et al., 1998; Tribe & Sanders, 2003).

- matching for gender, age, and religion, particularly if this is relevant to the legal issue in question, for example, sexual assault or domestic violence (Nijad, 2003; Patel, 2003).

- remembering that it is not appropriate to ask family members or other professionals to help out because they appear to speak the same language as the client (Pochhacker, 2000; Sande, 1998; Vasquez & Javier, 1991).

- trying to use the same interpreter throughout, to make the whole process easier for all the participants, if you are going to see the client for a number of meetings. This is particularly important when undertaking mental health work (Raval, 1996; Tribe & Raval, 2003). In some legal settings, interpreters may require security vetting or clearance to work.

- choosing an interpreter who is not only fluent in two languages but has some understanding of the two different cultural contexts (Razban, 2003; Tribe & Raval, 2003). Ideally, interpreters should have undergone recognized language testing to ensure that they are fluent. The the American DOJ offers some general guidance on this issue. The setting up of statewide registries and a nationwide database based on standard qualification procedures has been recommended by NAJIT, as has the establishment of one person or a foreign language desk to oversee language access issues in each entity. For further information, please contact the American Translators Association, NAJIT, or your local interpreting service in the United States. In Britain, the Institute of Linguists, the National Language Standards, and the Register of Public Service Interpreters would be the organizations to contact.

- remembering that the interpreter is a fellow professional and colleague and should be treated with respect as a member of the team. It is not good practice to ask an interpreter to wait with the client, as interpreters are often put under immense pressure to take on tasks that may go beyond their payment (Mudarikiri, 2003; Tribe & Sanders, 2003).

- telling your client, if you find that he or she is initially uncomfortable with an interpreter being present, perhaps because of concerns about confidentiality and information reaching other members of the community or simply embarrassment, that the interpreter is a professional doing a job, has no decision-making powers, and is bound by the confidentiality policy of the agency and a professional body (Tribe & Sanders, 2003).

- ensuring that your interpreter signs the contract of the organization or their professional body, which should cover such aspects as confidentiality, roles, responsibilities, ethics, and boundaries. For example, it is important that the client or service user maintain self-determination in the same way as any other client, and this is not compromised by an interpreter being involved.

- spending 10 or 15 minutes or so with the interpreter before meeting with the client to decide how you will work together, to explain the objectives of the meeting, and to share any relevant background information. This may save you hours in the long run. This may also be an opportunity to clarify technical concepts, vocabulary, or jargon that is likely to be used, as well as to check whether there are any cultural issues likely to bear on the situation. It is important that you create an environment where the interpreter feels able to ask for clarification if the issues are not understood (Abdallah-Steinkopff, 1999; Gong-Guy, Cravens, & Patterson, 1991; Van der Veer, 1998). If your interpreter is proficient in two languages, it is likely to be an invaluable source of relevant cultural information.

- spending a few minutes with your interpreter after the session reviewing how you worked together and any other pertinent aspects.

- remembering that the meeting is likely to take longer when working with an interpreter and allocating additional time in advance of the meeting (Cushing, 2003; Tribe & Morrissey, 2003).

- adjusting the pace of delivery and breaking your speech into shorter segments, because the interpreter has to remember what you have said and then translate it. You should quickly develop a comfortable rhythm (Razban, 2003).

- including any interpreters in induction courses that your agency runs. As well as having an integrating function, this would provide them with useful insights into the organizational culture and aims of the organization (Tribe & Sanders, 2003).

- trying to avoid using complicated technical language. Every discipline has its own abbreviations and language, so remember that the interpreter is unlikely to have received legal or clinical training in either of the languages he or she is working in. Some medical and legal agencies have found it useful to have a specialized medical or legal dictionary available (Tribe & Morrissey, 2003).

- trying to avoid using proverbs and sayings. If something does not make literal sense, it is best avoided.

- trying to avoid discussing issues with the interpreter that do not require interpretation. This can make the client feel uncomfortable and excluded. If such issues do require discussion, get the interpreter to explain this to the client, or discuss these issues with the interpreter once the client has left (Baylav, 2003; Razban, 2003).

- considering how interpreters are to be supported within your organization. Interpreters frequently hear very traumatic information in sessions, for example, that a client is to be detained in a psychiatric hospital, has not been awarded custody of his or her children, is to be refused refugee status, or other information that may have life-changing implications for the client. An interpreter is entitled to support in the same way as any other professional (Holder, 2002; Patel, 2003).

- remembering that words do not always have precise equivalents and that a short sentence in English may take several sentences to explain in another language or vice versa. So do not become impatient if the interpreter takes longer to interpret than you would have expected (Tribe & Sanders, 2003).

As mentioned earlier, these guidelines do not attempt to be comprehensive or to cover every aspect of working with interpreters. They are intended merely as a guide to enable you to develop your own guidelines for the specific requirements of your workplace.

RECOMMENDATIONS FOR THE FUTURE

The lack of recognition of the work of interpreters by other professionals is a theme throughout the literature (Crawford, 1994; Kaufert & Koolage, 1984; Raval, 2003; Tribe, 1999). There is a need for a proper career structure and training. Lack of regulated training courses and qualifications on a national basis has had an adverse effect on the status and professional identity of interpreters, with employing organizations unable to verify the level of expertise and training that an interpreter holds, restricting the career prospects of interpreters and withholding a vital service to clients who are not proficient in the English language. Formal accreditation procedures for interpreters have been slow in becoming established in a variety of countries (Coresellis, 1997; Tribe & Sanders, 2003). Many interpreters are forced to work on a freelance or ad hoc basis, which offers little security and may decrease the likelihood of experienced practitioners remaining in this profession (Granger & Baker, 2003; Nijad, 2003). Comprehensive nationwide accreditation procedures will lead to more professional status and a clearer career structure for interpreters. It may also give them a broader role and louder voice in advising on the best ways of working with them, and most importantly of all it will ensure that people who are not proficient in the English language will not be at a disadvantage. The importance of the work conducted by interpreters requires adequate recognition, as does the complexity of the work they do. I would suggest that this needs recognizing at the micro level through respecting each individual interpreter as a fellow professional at every encounter and at the macro level through the development of nationwide accreditation and training procedures for interpreters and those working alongside them. As a final point, it may be useful to remember that an interpreter is the one who makes your meeting possible. As well as speaking two languages, he or she may well be an expert on cultural matters that may have relevance to the legal/psychological issues under consideration and may greatly assist in understanding your client's position. This theme will be discussed at more length in other chapters in this book.

REFERENCES

Abdallah-Steinkopff, B. (1999). Psychotherapy of PTSD in co-operation with interpreters. *Verrhalensterapie, 9,* 211–220.

American Psychiatric Association. (1994). *Diagnostic and statistical manual of mental disorders* (4th ed.). Washington, DC: Author.

Anderson, H., & Goolishian, H. (1992). Client as expert. In S. McNamee & K. Gergen (Eds.), *Therapy as social construction* (pp. 25–39). London: Sage Ltd.

Bartlett, F. (1932). *Remembering.* Cambridge: Cambridge University Press.

Baylav, A. (2003). Issues of language provision in health care services. In R. Tribe & H. Raval (Eds.), *Working with interpreters in mental health* (pp. 69–77). London & New York: Routledge.

Brennan, M., & Brown, R. (1997). *Equality before the law: Deaf people's access to justice,* by Deaf Studies Research Unit, University of Durham. Accessed April 12, 2004, from http://www.lrb.co.uk/v20n07/sed12007.htm

Brislin, R., & Yoshida, T. (1994). *Intercultural communication training: An introduction.* London: Sage Ltd.

Burr, V. (1995). *An introduction to social constructionism.* London: Routledge.

Coresellis, A. (1997). Training needs of public personnel working with interpreters. In S. E. Carr, R. Roberts, A. Dufour, & D. Steyn (Eds.), *The critical link: Interpreters in the community* (pp. 77–89). Philadelphia: John Benjamins.

Crawford, A. (1994, July). *Black patients/white doctors: Stories lost in translation.* Paper presented at National Language Project, 1st First World Congress of African Linguistics, Kwaluseni, Swaziland.

Cushing, A. (2003). Interpreters in medical consultations. In *Working with interpreters in mental health.* London & New York: Routledge.

Drennan, G., & Swartz, L. (1999). A concept overburdened: Institutional roles for psychiatric interpreters in post-apartheid South Africa. *Interpreting, 4*(2), 169–198.

Fernando, S. (1991). *Mental health, race and culture.* London: Mind Publications.

Furnham, A., & Bochner, S. (1986). *Culture shock: Psychological reactions to unfamiliar environments.* London: Routledge.

Gong-Guy, E., Cravens, R. B., & Patterson, T. E. (1991). Clinical issues in mental health service delivery to refugees. *American Psychologist, 46*(6), 642–646.

Granger, E., & Baker, M. (2003). The role and experience of interpreters. In R. Tribe & H. Raval (Eds.), *Working with interpreters in mental health* (pp. 99–121). London & New York: Routledge.

Haenal, F. (1997). Aspects and problems associated with the use of interpreters in psychotherapy with victims of torture. *Torture, 7*(3), 68–71.

Hillier, S., Huq, A., Loshak, R., Marks, F., & Rahman, S. (1994). An evaluation of child psychiatric services for Bangladeshi parents. *Journal of Mental Health, 3,* 332–337.

Hoffman, E. (1989). *Lost in translation.* London: Random House.

Holder, R. (2002). *The impact of mediated communication on psychological therapy with refugees and asylum seekers: Practitioners' experiences.* Unpublished master's dissertation, City University, London.

Hornberger, J. C., Gibson, C. D., Jr., Wood, W., Dequeldre, C., Corso, L., Palla, B., et al. (1996). Eliminating language barriers for non-English speaking service users. *Medical Care, 34*(8), 845–856.

Kaufert, J. M., & Koolage, W. W. (1984). Role conflict among cultural brokers: The experience of native Canadian medical interpreters. *Social Science Medicine, 18,* 283–286.

Kaufert, J. M., O'Neil, J. D., & Koolage, W. W. (1985). Culture brokerage and advocacy in urban hospitals: The impact of native language interpreters. *Sante Culture Health, 7,* 3–9.

Kline, F., Acosta, F., Austin, W., & Johnson, R. G. (1980). The misunderstood Spanish-speaking patient. *American Journal of Psychiatry, 137,* 1530–1533.

Lowering the language barrier in an acute psychiatric setting. *Australian and New Zealand Journal of Psychiatry, 32,* 434–440.

MacLachlan, M. (1997). *Culture and health.* Chichester, UK: John Wiley.

Malan, R. (1990). *My traitor's heart.* London: Vintage.

Marcos, L. (1979). Effects of interpreters on the psychopathology in non-English speaking patients. *American Journal of Psychiatry, 136,* 171–174.

Marshall, P. A., Koenig, B. A., Grifhorst, P., & van Ewjik, M. (1998). Ethical issues in immigrant health care and clinical research. In S. Loue (Ed.), *Handbook of immigrant health* (pp. 203–226). New York: Plenum Press.

McNamee, S., & Gergen, K. (Eds.). (1992). *Therapy as social construction.* London: Sage Ltd.

Messent, P. (2003). From postmen to makers of meaning: A model for collaborative work between clinicians and interpreters. In R. Tribe & H. Raval (Eds.), *Working with interpreters in mental health* (pp. 135–150). London & New York: Routledge.

Mezzich, J., Kirmayer, L., Kleinman, A., Fabrega, H., Jr., Parron, D. L., Good, B. J., et al. (1999). The place of culture in DSM-IV. *Journal of Nervous and Mental Disease, 187,* 457–464.

Mudarikiri, M. M. (2003). Working with interpreters in adult mental health. In R. Tribe & H. Raval (Eds.), *Working with interpreters in mental health* (pp. 182–197). London & New York: Routledge.

National Association of Judiciary Interpreters and Translators Web site. Comments on Title VI Guidance. Accessed April 12, 2004, from http://www.najit.org/title_6_committee.pl

Nijad, F. (2003). A day in the life of an interpreting service. In R. Tribe & H. Raval (Eds.), *Working with interpreters in mental health* (pp. 77–91). London & New York: Routledge.

Owusu-Bempah, K., & Howitt, D. (2000). *Psychology beyond western perspectives.* London: BPS Books.

Patel, N. (2003). Speaking with silent: Addressing issues of disempowerment when working with refugee people. In R. Tribe & H. Raval (Eds.), *Working with interpreters in mental health* (pp. 219–237). London & New York: Routledge.

Patel, N., Bennett, E., Dennis, M., Dosanjh, N., Mahtani, A., Miller, A., et al. (2000). *Clinical psychology, "race" and culture: A training manual.* Leicester: BPS Books.

Pochhacker, F. (2000). Language barriers in Vienna hospitals. *Ethnicity & Health, 5*(2), 113–119.

Raval, H. (1996). A systemic perspective on working with interpreters. *Clinical Child Psychology & Psychiatry, 1,* 29–43.

Raval, H. (2003). An overview of the issues in the work with interpreters. In R. Tribe & H. Raval (Eds.), *Working with interpreters in mental health* (pp. 8–29). London & New York: Routledge.

Razban, M. (2003). An interpreter's perspective. In R. Tribe & H. Raval (Eds.), *Working with interpreters in mental health* (pp. 92–98). London: Routledge.

Richards, G. (1997). *"Race," racism and psychology: Towards a reflexive history.* London: Routledge.

Roberts, R. P. (1997). Community interpreting today and tomorrow. In S. E. Carr, R. Roberts, A. Dufour, & D. Steyn (Eds.), *The critical link: Interpreters in the community* (pp. 7–26). Philadelphia: John Benjamins.

Roe, D., & Roe, C. (1991). The third party: Using interpreters for the deaf in counselling situations. *Journal of Mental Health Counselling, 13,* 91–105.

Roy, C. B. (1992). A socio-linguistic analysis of the interpreter's role in simultaneous talk in face to face interpreted dialogue. *Sign Language Studies, 5,* 21–26.

Sacks, V. (2000). Can law protect language? Law, language and human rights in the South African constitution. *International Journal of Discrimination and the Law, 4,* 343–368.

Sande, H. (1998). Supervision of refugee interpreters: 5 Years of experience from Northern Norway. *Nord Journal Psychiatry, 52,* 403–409.

Stolk, Y., Ziguras, S., Saunders, T., Garlick, R., Stuart, G., & Coffey, G. (1998). Lowering the language barrier in an acute psychiatric setting. *Australian and New Zealand Journal of Psychiatry, 32,* 434–440.

Sue, D. W., Bingham, R. P., Porché-Burke, L., & Vasquez, M. (1999). The diversification of psychology: A multicultural revolution. *American Psychologist, 54,* 1061–1069.

Summerfield, D. (2002). Commentary. *Advances in Psychiatric Treatment, 8,* 247–248.

Tribe, R. (1998). If two is company is three a crowd/group? A longitudinal account of a support and clinical supervision group for interpreters. *Group Work Journal, 11*(3), 139–152.

Tribe, R. (1999). Bridging the gap or damming the flow? Using interpreters/bicultural workers when working with refugee clients, many of whom have been tortured. *British Journal of Medical Psychology, 72,* 567–576.

Tribe, R., & Morrissey, J. (2003). The refugee context and the role of interpreters: Perspective. In R. Tribe & H. Raval (Eds.), *Working with interpreters in mental health* (pp. 198–218). London & New York: Routledge.

Tribe, R., & Raval, H. (2003). *Working with interpreters in mental health*. London & New York: Routledge.

Tribe, R., & Sanders, M. (2003). Training issues for interpreters. In R. Tribe & H. Raval (Eds.), *Working with interpreters in mental health* (pp. 54–68). London & New York: Routledge.

Van der Veer, G. (1998). *Counselling and therapy with refugees: Psychological problems of war, torture and repression.* Chichester: Wiley.

Vasquez, C., & Javier, R. A. (1991). The problem with interpreters: Communicating with Spanish-speaking patients. *Hospital and Community Psychiatry, 42*(2), 163–165.

Wadensjo, C. (1998). *Interpreting as interaction.* New York: Longman.

World Health Organization. (1992). *The ICD-10 classification of mental and behavioural disorders.* Geneva: WHO.

12

ASSESSMENT OF ASYLUM SEEKERS

DEBORAH FREED

Doctors of the World

The United Nations High Commissioner for Refugees (UNHCR) currently cares for an estimated 12 million refugees as well as an additional 7.7 million persons of concern.[1] Fleeing persecution, sometimes including physical and/or mental torture, refugees and refugee-like populations have become an international issue concerning many countries of the world. Individuals and communities are being devastated and uprooted, often due to military dictatorships, civil wars, failed or inadequate development policies, and/or conflicts arising from economic, ethnic, racial, religious, and/or political tensions. Already in a fragile state from what may be years of persecution, a refugee may continue to endure further trauma in the country that he or she hoped would grant safety and comfort. Many do not speak the language of the host country and struggle to adjust to a foreign culture. They may be without travel documents because of the way they were forced to escape and may lack evidence of what they have endured except for their physical and/or psychological scars. For those who failed to secure status in advance, obtaining a legal status in their new home countries becomes the most immediate of the many hurdles to be overcome.

This chapter will describe the value and process of psychological assessment of asylum applicants in the United States. These are the people who allege that they have been persecuted because of their irrefutable identities and are thus fleeing their home countries to seek protection in the United States, the country many perceive as the land of liberty, equality, and freedom. The chapter begins with a brief description of immigration law as it relates to this population, followed by a description of the types of trauma that asylum seekers often claim to have endured and its sequelae. In addition, the chapter will describe a clinician's role in the immigration process, as well as the purpose and the process of the evaluation, common challenges encountered during the evaluation, and follow-up services for asylum applicants. The chapter includes a discussion of the importance for an evaluator to be aware of countertransference reactions with asylum applicants, the possibility of vicarious traumatization, and the importance of self-care. A section on the writing of clinical affidavits is followed by a discussion

Author's Note: I would like to acknowledge the valuable assistance of the following: Ms. Maki Katoh for her editing and knowledge of asylum procedures, Dr. Ghislaine Boulanger and Dr. Nina Thomas for their experience in working with traumatized populations, and Dr. Selwyn Freed for his editorial assistance.

2

2

of testifying in court. Each section is described with detailed examples from actual cases.

IMMIGRATION LAW BACKGROUND

The United States provides opportunities for survivors of torture and persecution who did not obtain refugee status before coming to the United States. This process has become increasingly difficult, complex, and hard to navigate. In 1996, Congress passed the Illegal Immigration Reform and Immigrant Responsibility Act (IIRIRA). According to these laws, aliens who arrive in the United States without valid documents, as many who are forced to flee in haste do, are placed on an expedited removal proceeding. An alien may be immediately deported back to his or her home country without an opportunity to receive a hearing. If the alien indicates a fear of persecution before being deported, he or she is entitled to a "credible fear" interview with an Immigration and Naturalization Service (INS) officer and is placed in detention. Those who are found to have a credible fear of persecution remain in removal proceedings and are often held in detention while completing their application process to remain in the United States. During this process, the alien may spend months or even years in detention, which often ends only when he or she is granted protection or is denied it and deported. Those who arrive in the United States legally may also request asylum, and they may do so without being sent to a detention center.

In order to obtain asylum in the United States, an alien must prove that he or she is unwilling to return to his or her home country or the place of last habitual residence because of a well-founded fear of persecution on account of his or her race, religion, nationality, or membership in a particular social group or political opinion. Failure to file an application within 1 year of the date of arrival in the United States, denial of a previous application, history of criminal convictions, participation in the persecution of others, and/or being considered a danger in this country are among the factors that may disqualify an alien from obtaining protection in the United States. If asylum is granted, an individual may remain in this country and receive benefits available for recognized refugees, which include cash assistance, Medicaid, an opportunity to bring in certain family members from the home country, and the right to apply for legal permanent residency (LPR) status and eventual citizenship. Other types of relief available for aliens who are victims of torture and/or persecution include withholding of removal and deferral of removal, which provide limited protections for those who do not qualify for asylum. Gender-based violence is increasingly recognized as persecution on account of a membership in a particular social group. The relief under the Violence Against Women Act (VAWA) allows alien victims of abusive legal permanent residents or United States citizens to leave the relationship without jeopardizing their status.[2] Although any of these individuals may need a clinical evaluation, for the purposes of this chapter they will be referred to as asylum applicants or simply as applicants.

TORTURE AND TRAUMA

Many asylum applicants claim that they have been severely persecuted and/or tortured. The United Nations Convention Against Torture and Other Cruel, Inhuman or Degrading Treatment or Punishment (CAT, 1987) defined torture as "any act by which severe pain or suffering, whether physical or mental, is intentionally inflicted on a person for such purposes as obtaining from him or a third person information or a confession, punishing him for an act he or a third person has committed or is suspected of having committed, or intimidating or coercing him or a third person, or for any reason based on discrimination of any kind, when such pain or suffering is inflicted by or at the instigation of or with the consent or acquiescence of a public official or other person acting in an official capacity. It does not include pain or suffering arising only from, inherent in or incidental to lawful sanctions."[3] The Istanbul Protocol, a publication of the United Nations High Commissioner for Human Rights, describes torture as intending to reduce the individual to a state of helplessness both physically and mentally; victims are dehumanized, personalities are shattered, and social structures are damaged.[4] Although aliens do not have to have been "tortured" to obtain asylum or other protections, the abuses, persecution, and violence many applicants claim to have suffered often amounts to torture.

Herman describes traumatic events as generally involving threats to life, bodily integrity, exposure to violence, or death. She goes on to describe responses to this degree of danger, or trauma, as causing a complex chain of reactions, both physiological and psychological. Traumatic reactions occur when a person's customary defenses are overwhelmed and thus become ineffective; a person's usual ability to integrate the event(s) may be damaged. Traumatic memories are encoded on a somatosensory level as vivid images and bodily sensations lacking a verbal narrative and a context. A person may feel overwhelmed and helpless; there may be alterations in consciousness and a detachment from the event(s) as the only escape from the unbearable reality. These fragmented memories may continue to intrude into a person's consciousness after the trauma(s) has stopped. Physiological arousal in anticipation of ongoing danger may remain. Attempts at avoidance of triggers of trauma may severely restrict the person's life. A feeling of profound loss is common for victims of trauma. These losses include a sense of safety, trust, bodily integrity, connection with self and others, beliefs, faith, and sense of meaning as previously known and understood. Victims may experience feelings of helplessness, humiliation, guilt, and intense alterations in affective states and in relations with others.[5]

The degree of intensity of a trauma, a victim's proximity to the trauma, and whether there has been a single or ongoing trauma(s) will invariably affect the consequences to the individual. Many asylum seekers have experienced some form of trauma. Some have lived for long periods of time in politically unstable environments or in societies where they endured years of discrimination, persecution, and/or torture, with increasing danger until the only alternative was to flee. An asylum applicant may have been the victim of or a witness to the persecution or torture of others including friends, family members, and entire communities; a witness to others' torture may endure feelings of guilt for being unable to prevent the others' torture as well as for being spared oneself. He or she may have endured family members witnessing his or her

trauma such as a rape, exposing the individual to increased feelings of shame and the possibility of being ostracized by others. An individual can be traumatized even if not subjected to or a witness to persecution. He or she may have been notified of a trauma such as the death of a loved one. Another may have received no information, still hoping the loved one will return despite other objective evidence that there is little reason for hope. A victim may have been forced to choose to help persecutors in order to save family members or himself or herself, exposing the person to tormenting feelings of guilt that he or she has betrayed others.

The aftermath of trauma has a major impact on the consequences for an individual. Social support from family, friends, and/or community or lack of it following the trauma(s) will contribute to short- and long-term symptoms and how they are integrated into one's personality. For many of these individuals, in addition to enduring torture, they have been displaced from home, community, loved ones, and all of their social supports. They may have been children at the time, separated from parents, their whole world shattered; parents may be wrenched from their children, no longer able to protect them. Many survived further trauma during life-threatening escapes, traveling on dangerous routes without proper clothing, food, or shelter. Ability to trust may become further eroded if those who are trusted and paid to help in the escape betray the victim(s). Upon arrival in the United States, many are locked in detention centers without understanding what is happening to them without or a means to communicate with others. They continue to undergo hardships and uncertainty about their own lives and safety and that of their families.

CLINICIAN'S ROLE AS AN EVALUATOR

Many aliens seeking political asylum or other types of immigration relief in the United States are represented by attorneys who request psychological evaluations. An affidavit from a clinician may provide support and strengthen an application, particularly when evidence of persecution is lacking. The mental health professional's role in this situation is to evaluate the applicant's psychological state and to determine the consistency of the applicant's history and his or her reported and observed symptoms. This involves interviewing the applicant, obtaining detailed information about the alleged persecution and traumatic events, eliciting information on and observing symptoms of trauma, along with information on his or her premorbid personality and current mental health status.

The role of a clinician in the immigration process is being continually expanded as the application process becomes increasingly complicated. Clinical evaluations are now sought to determine if the persecution and/or torture an applicant alleges to have suffered interfered with his or her ability to file an asylum application within the 1-year deadline, to assess the current mental health status of an applicant in order to assist in the reevaluation of his or her application when there is a claim that the prospect of forced deportation is severely affecting the mental health of the applicant, or to assess whether mandatory detention is affecting the applicant's ability to appear and function in court.

In any of the previously mentioned evaluation processes, it is extremely important for the clinician to remain an independent and objective expert. Clinicians should never presume that the applicant's statements are true. It is only when the clinician objectively and professionally determines the consistency of the applicant's statements with the clinical evidence that the clinical affidavit can be useful in supporting the applicant's claim for asylum. The following section describes how such an evaluation can be achieved, drawing examples from evaluations that the author and her colleagues have conducted.

EVALUATION PROCESS

Preparation for Evaluation

A clinical evaluation may be performed in a variety of settings, including a psychotherapy office, a hospital exam room, or a room provided in a detention center; the clinician/evaluator may ensure that tissues are available and there is access to a bathroom. The evaluator should review in advance available documents provided by the applicant's lawyer, including the applicant's statement, the claim the applicant is making to the INS. This provides some information about what to expect, but the determination of credibility is made based on the material gathered during the evaluation.

It may be beneficial to review symptoms commonly seen following trauma. In addition, it is helpful to familiarize oneself as much as possible with the culture and politics of the applicant's country of origin so that the applicant's statements can be understood within this context. However, the evaluator should know that the applicant is the expert and should defer to the applicant whenever possible to provide information about his or her cultural or political background. The applicant should be encouraged to help educate the evaluator about the applicant's culture and the meanings of certain customs, gestures, comments, or whatever information is presented. It is the evaluator's responsibility to be aware that there are vast differences in the way an individual may respond to trauma. The interpretation of events the applicant may derive as an individual and as part of a culture may differ from the evaluator's, whose understanding of symptoms and psychopathology as part of his or her culture may be inadequate to explain this applicant's experiences. Through this collaborative effort the evaluator can hope to arrive at an understanding of this applicant that will be meaningful and constructive.

It is useful for the evaluator to have an understanding of the preparation for an evaluation. Interdisciplinary work, in this case between the psychologist and the applicant's lawyer, can be enriching for those involved but may require increased efforts to ensure clear communication. A psychologist should not assume that the applicant's lawyer is familiar with how a psychologist's skills and knowledge may be useful. It may be helpful to discuss this with the lawyer as the evaluation process unfolds. In addition, the psychologist should clarify what he or she needs and expects. For example, lawyers representing applicants are expected to make clear the purpose of the referral for the evaluator; referral questions may be defined and expanded through discussion between the evaluator and the lawyer. Lawyers are responsible for preparing the applicants by explaining the purpose, as well as helping them keep their appointments at the scheduled time. It may be necessary to provide the address and time of the appointment in writing, call to remind the applicant, and/or provide an escort for the applicant to come to the evaluation. Nevertheless, it is common for an applicant to be late. It will be the first time meeting with the evaluator, and the applicant may not have understood the time of the appointment, may be unfamiliar with getting around the city, and may get lost. The applicant may be unable to speak English, making it more difficult to find the location or ask for directions. To address some of these difficulties, a contact person needs to be identified and made available for the day of the evaluation in case of an emergency so that both the evaluator and the applicant have the same phone number to call and communicate with each other.

On some occasions an applicant may not come at all because of fears, conscious or not, of having to retell/relive his or her experiences. The applicant may expect that the evaluation will be stressful and thus feel scared, anxious, or depressed. The applicant may be distrustful of doctors, depending on past experiences, particularly if a doctor was an accomplice to the applicant's persecution. A doctor, especially of mental health, may take a different form in this applicant's culture and may have different meanings for him or her. Some applicants may be more comfortable with a religious or community leader or a shaman. For some, psychological problems remain within the family, and for others, psychological symptoms may be expressed as somatic symptoms. Any of the previously mentioned factors may contribute to making the applicant feel wary about coming to the evaluation.

Cross-Cultural Communication

Cross-cultural communication challenges are to be expected when people come from different cultures. This may be the case for the evaluator and applicant. The applicant's use of language, including level of politeness, may differ from the evaluator's. Body language and manner of dress may have meanings for the applicant that the evaluator will not understand, and the evaluator will not know how he or she is perceived. The evaluator may be perceived as an authority figure, more powerful than the applicant, and remind

him or her of a persecutor. The gender and age of the evaluator may affect how comfortable the applicant feels. Attention to the moment-to-moment psychological state of the applicant will enable the evaluator to learn about his or her perceptions and reactions to the evaluation process and to the evaluator. The preparation previously referred to along with training as a clinician, further training in trauma, and empathic observing and listening are tools at the evaluator's disposal.

Structure and Process

The structure of the evaluation process is in part dependent on the style of the evaluator. An evaluator must appreciate that flexibility is necessary because the psychological state of the applicant is unknown until he or she enters the room and may change repeatedly during the evaluation process. Therefore, it is useful to have an idea of what information is needed to complete the evaluation and how to approach gathering the necessary information while being open to change as needed.

Beginning an Evaluation

The evaluation process begins when the applicant enters the room. The evaluator introduces himself or herself and invites the applicant into the office. The evaluator may begin an informal mental status exam, aware that everything must be viewed in the context of evaluating someone from a different culture. An applicant's appearance and style of dress may give information about culture, casualness, and self-care. The evaluator may note the applicant's mood and monitor affective changes throughout the interview. An applicant's language, thoughts, perceptual disturbances, insights, and judgments will all be considered throughout, with an awareness of cultural differences.

It is useful for the evaluator to spend some time preparing the applicant for the evaluation interview. Ask the applicant what he or she understands about the purpose of the evaluation. Depending on the response, the evaluator should clarify any misconceptions. Explain that the applicant's lawyer requested the evaluation and if an affidavit is written it will be submitted along with the asylum seeker's application for asylum.

The evaluator should explain the limits of confidentiality; the information gathered in the evaluation will be shared with the applicant's lawyer, and the affidavit may be submitted to immigration authorities. It is not uncommon for an applicant to share information with the evaluator not yet told to the lawyer. An evaluator should inquire about the applicant's reason(s) for not discussing something with the lawyer and generally the reasons for doing so. The lawyer is in a position to determine whether the information is critical to the applicant's case. For example, an applicant may perceive the lawyer as busy and judgmental about feelings symptomatic of trauma, such as intrusive recollections of the trauma(s) or not remembering the details of the trauma. It is the job of the evaluator to help the applicant understand the meaning of these symptoms and to obtain permission to be a bridge between lawyer and applicant. By educating both, the applicant may feel more comfortable speaking with the lawyer, and the lawyer may be more empathic and in turn obtain useful information related to the content of the applicant's story as well as understanding better how to work with this applicant. An applicant may reveal that he or she had previously seen another lawyer but had not completed the process because of misunderstandings or lack of follow-through on the part of one or the other. For example, he or she may have misunderstood the process because of language barriers and immobilizing symptoms of trauma. He or she may have met someone who presented himself or herself as a lawyer, took the applicant's money, and vanished. The applicant may have missed the 1-year deadline for applying for asylum, in part as a result of one of these circumstances, compounding feelings of helplessness, hopelessness, and confusion. The information the applicant shares can alert the evaluator to issues of trust, already so fragile for many individuals who have been persecuted and lost their belief in themselves and in others.[6] The evaluator may be perceived as another in a series of people who will betray, confuse, or otherwise disappoint the applicant. Understanding and documenting such circumstances and symptoms may be relevant and helpful in reexamining the applicant's claim and in working with the applicant.

As part of the introduction, the evaluator should state clearly what to expect during the interview in order to help put the applicant at ease as much as possible. For many applicants who have been held or imprisoned with the unpredictability of not knowing what would happen next, this may be reassuring. Even though the evaluator will have reviewed the applicant's claim, it is useful to hear the story in the applicant's own words. It may be explained that the more details and understanding the evaluator has, the better he or she can convey the applicant's story accurately. The evaluator may state that he or she will take notes as the applicant speaks.

Some applicants begin speaking following this introduction, whereas others may need more help. If the applicant is reticent, the evaluator may state that he or she wants to know why the applicant is here and what happened in his or her country of origin. Some evaluators may feel more comfortable asking the applicant to start at the beginning. Although it is easier if an applicant tells his or her story sequentially, useful information is obtained from where an applicant begins, what he or she initiates, and what is not reported. Affective changes continue to be monitored. If there is intense affect such as tears and difficulty speaking, it may indicate that the experiences being described were particularly traumatic events and add credibility to the story. On the other hand, if there is little affect, inappropriate to the content of what is being stated, this may also indicate trauma, as the applicant may be attempting to avoid reliving these memories, as for example, an applicant whose range of affect is constricted when recalling being tortured or the loss of a loved one. Either way, the evaluator must make sense of the affect in the context of the person's story and assess the applicant's psychological state at the moment based on the reported and observed content and process.

Trauma and Memory

Memory difficulties related to specific details such as time sequence and dates are a common consequence of trauma. One applicant spoke of feeling embarrassed that he forgot his evaluation appointment time. Another could not remember his wedding date or his child's birthday, acknowledging this with sadness as he thought of the damage to his mind and the loss of his wife and child so far away. One applicant spoke of being raped but did not remember the number of times, number of people present, or exactly when it happened. Triggers can cause powerful traumatic memories to intrude into an applicant's life. The smell of cigarettes reminded one applicant of the men who smelled of tobacco when they raped her. As applicants reveal fragments of their story, the evaluator may ask questions, piecing the story together, recognizing that not all of the information may be available—a consequence of trauma.

Due to their overwhelming nature, traumatic memories may be processed and remembered as fragmented images and bodily sensations without details and words. High stress levels interfere with the role of the hippocampus, the part of the brain that has an integrative function to evaluate and categorize information spatially and temporally.[7] One applicant described feeling numb and detached from her body while being raped. This alerts the evaluator to consider dissociation. It may be helpful to explain to the applicant that she may have been attempting to isolate this overwhelming experience, to dissociate it to protect herself from the full awareness of the experience. Dissociation may become a means of coping with trauma during the event and expose the person to recurrent intrusive memories after the trauma, and it is a predictor for developing posttraumatic stress disorder (PTSD).[8] Another possible cause of memory difficulties is head injury resulting in brain damage, which must be explored by the evaluator. The evaluator should allow time to inquire about inconsistencies and to place the story in sequence, filling in the gaps and documenting symptoms before the trauma(s), premorbid personality, symptoms experienced during the trauma, immediately following the trauma, and up to the present.

Premorbid Personality

People are individuals, unique before and after becoming victims of persecution, torture, or displacement. The circumstances of the traumas differ for each person, and individuals differ in how they cope with trauma and its consequences. Premorbid personality is a baseline for comparison of how an applicant's personality

and symptoms may have changed as a result of the alleged trauma(s). In addition, it alerts the evaluator to an applicant's resources and capacity for making sense of and integrating the traumatic experiences. An individual with psychological difficulties before the alleged traumatic experience(s) may have more intense and enduring symptoms than one who did not. The age of a victim at the time of trauma will affect how the experience is perceived and understood. A young child's experience and how he or she will handle its effects will be affected to a great extent by the reactions and degree of support from caregivers.

In addition, a discussion of an applicant's childhood often brings up emotional and revealing material perhaps not readily shared. For example, one applicant spent most of the evaluation speaking of profound distress. When asked about her childhood before the war, during which she experienced many traumatic events, this applicant's expression changed as though for a moment returning to another time, a happier, more carefree time. The applicant spoke of when family members were alive and thanked the evaluator for bringing her back to a memory of herself as a happy child laughing, playing, and feeling loved. Another applicant recalled dreams and ambitions that were lost to him and family members; another spoke of her happy childhood that was taken from her. As these applicants reported feelings of loss (for which they must grieve) and sadness, they provided information about their earlier resources, existing (or former) social supports and resiliency, which they might be able to make use of in the future. All of these examples inform the evaluator about the applicant before the trauma(s) and are helpful in formulating a diagnosis and, if appropriate, referral for treatment.

Respecting an Applicant's Defenses

The process of obtaining information about an applicant's psychological state includes gathering information from an applicant's subjective report and observations on what the applicant says and when and how he or she says it. Respecting an applicant's defenses is important in working with traumatized individuals. The evaluator may explain that some events may be hard to talk about, and if so to tell the evaluator when it is hard. The evaluator should not force an applicant to speak about something if he or she does not wish to do so. If the applicant feels that the evaluator is empathic, he or she may feel more comfortable explaining these feelings or the reason(s) for choosing not to discuss something.

An applicant may leave out information and, later in the process, feel more comfortable to report it. For example, an applicant spoke softly and told the evaluator after approximately 1.5 hours that he should have mentioned something earlier but felt ashamed. He spoke of being treated badly (he had been repeatedly raped), his sense of helplessness, and how little he thought of himself now; he felt he was no longer a man. He felt that what he did (to be treated in this way) was unforgivable and speaking of it made him feel as though he was losing control.

A female applicant explained how she was able to get on a train to escape from an area where she was being persecuted. She spoke about this only briefly, in contrast to the details she volunteered in other areas. When the evaluator asked for more details, she stated that it was hard to speak of what happened. The evaluator inquired what made it hard, and she paused and spoke quietly. She explained that she had no money to pay for a train ticket and had to sleep with the conductor to be allowed on the train in order to escape; she paused and cried.

Feelings of humiliation may result from the experience of helplessness and violations of one's body.[9] An individual who has been raped, regardless of gender, often carries feelings of shame; he or she may feel a loss of self-esteem and believe that he or she has disgraced himself or herself, his or her family, and the community. Feelings of shame, loss of trust, and loss of sense of self are common sequelae of trauma and part of many evaluations. Consequences for an applicant often include no longer being able to have sexual relations with a spouse, feeling dirty, and/or lacking joy. One woman spoke of feeling as though she had sinned. She believed that if others knew of her rapes they would think less of her, and she therefore tried to avoid seeing people. Others may speak of feeling estranged from children. When applicants share information and feelings in these ways it is important to

be empathic to these feelings. The evaluator may discuss these feelings and the applicant's symptoms as related to the trauma(s) he or she has endured and try to understand this in the context of the applicant's culture. The evaluator needs to be sensitive to the possibility of the applicant's fragility in speaking of these events and feelings and not cause further trauma. It is useful to allow sufficient time to be with the applicant at these moments and not feel pressure that can then be passed on to the applicant.

Therapeutic Evaluations

Evaluations are for the purpose of gathering information for an affidavit, but should also be performed therapeutically. The evaluation may be the first or only time the applicant meets with someone in a therapeutic setting and therefore perhaps the only opportunity to help the applicant understand how his or her feelings are a result of the trauma(s) that occurred. For example, an evaluator spoke to an applicant who had been repeatedly raped about his being a child and unable to protect himself, and that it was the people who did this to him who should feel ashamed. The applicant then stated how helpful this was to him to hear someone tell him that. It may also be helpful to explain to the applicant that his fear of losing control is possibly a reaction to perceived danger triggered by his thinking and speaking of these memories. Providing information sensitively can be therapeutic and can possibly give hope to the applicant who had given up. Furthermore, it may motivate an applicant to pursue treatment if recommended by the evaluator. Although the provision of treatment or treatment plans is not part of the evaluation process, identification of this need may lead to making a recommendation to the applicant, which is generally discussed at the end of the evaluation.

Sometimes applicants are hesitant to speak of symptoms because of fear. For example, an applicant may ask if he or she is going crazy, if these feelings will ever stop, or if he or she will ever feel better. The applicant may report hearing persecutory voices or experiencing vivid, unpredictable, and uncontrollable flashbacks of the traumatic events. An evaluator may be able to speak about and possibly reassure an applicant that symptoms are related to trauma and that the applicant is not going crazy. The evaluator cannot promise that the applicant will feel better. The evaluator may explain that despite what the applicant feels at this moment, with time, support, and possibly with treatment, it is possible for people who have endured traumas such as this to feel better. Powerful emotions and memories can become less overwhelming and frightening and become integrated as part of one's past.

Presenting a Threat to Self or Others

Presenting a threat to self or others is not uncommon as a result of trauma. One applicant described wishing to die to be relieved of life, another wishing for God to take her; others struggle with the loss of their God and others with feelings of rage. An evaluator must make an assessment about the seriousness of an applicant's danger to self or others and know the laws about reporting threats and when hospitalization is warranted. A suicidal threat or threat to another must be explored to determine if it is related to the trauma and if further action is necessary. A trauma-related explanation described by Herman relates to the humiliation of one who is held captive, struggling to survive and unable to express rage toward the captors. This victim may continue to struggle with these feelings even when no longer imprisoned. This rage may be expressed in uncontrolled outbursts directed toward others, including those perceived as not helping the victim, and/or withdrawal from relationships and threats of suicide.[10]

Coping

It is important for an evaluator to assess an applicant's coping mechanisms. An evaluator may inquire about what an applicant does if he or she feels the trauma(s) being relived or if he or she is scared, lost, despairing, hopeless, or suicidal. An applicant may describe how helpful his or her faith was during the trauma(s) and into the present. Another may report finding strength and hope through caring for children, another feeling hope in his or her wish to return to school, and another receiving comfort and guidance through the community. Following the September 11 attacks on the World Trade Center, a study found coping strategies, second only to prior mental health disorders, to be strong predictors of whether or not individuals experienced ongoing difficulties. Actively coping such as "planning and support seeking" were found to protect people, whereas "immediately disengaging from coping efforts" increased the likelihood of "posttraumatic stress symptoms."[11] It is useful to restate and reinforce an applicant's resources and ways of coping; it is also useful to have an understanding of the loss of cultural ways of coping, so common for asylum seekers. While keeping in mind his or her own limitations of knowledge about different cultural ways of coping with stress, an evaluator may be able to elicit this information from the applicant. In this way, an applicant could be helped to utilize resources and rituals he or she might have forgotten.

Individual styles, social support, and current living conditions are important considerations when evaluating how well an applicant is coping with some of these symptoms. This information may also provide useful clues about an applicant's credibility, diagnostic criteria, and any follow-ups as indicated. An evaluator may inquire about how an applicant spends days and nights and with whom; one may ask if the applicant works, goes out, and has a social life. One applicant reported not going out; further discussion revealed fear of going out and wishing to avoid crowds and seeing people in uniforms, which triggered flashbacks of being arrested by the military during a demonstration. Another applicant reported sitting alone and brooding, unable to get a job and feeling dependent on family and friends, who were perceived as becoming tired of this applicant living with them. This exacerbated the applicant's feelings of shame and low self-worth. An applicant may speak of searching for distractions to avoid thinking and remembering; watching television but wishing to avoid specific programs with violent themes that trigger memories of his or her trauma(s). Others may self-medicate with drugs or alcohol to cope with feelings.

Future Persecution

In addition to evaluating the effects of past persecution, it is important to assess the applicant's fear of future persecution because his or her asylum application may be based on such fear. An evaluator should inquire about and document what an applicant believes would happen if he or she were forced to return to his or her country of origin. For many, the idea of being forced to return to where the trauma(s) took place keeps the trauma(s) current and alive. An actual return to the place where further trauma could occur may exacerbate symptoms that had begun to decrease. For many victims of trauma, despite reports that situations have changed and they would no longer be in danger, their experience of threat is real and can be documented as related to past trauma that they have endured.

An applicant may express his or her fears about the safety of family still in the home country. The evaluator should find out if there is communication and if so the frequency and how it is accomplished. The applicant may be afraid to speak freely on the phone, fearing for family who may have been interrogated by people looking for the applicant. He or she may reveal feelings of guilt and feelings of responsibility for his or her family being in danger. Not knowing what happened to family members is another source of distress and continuing trauma for some applicants. Applicants may speak of literally and psychologically feeling the losses of their and their family's dreams and ambitions. Others may speak of hopes and dreams for the future, and a frequent wish is to unite with family. For some, the ultimate hope is to return to their home country to rejoin their family and community when there is peace.

Diagnosis

PTSD has become an accepted way of understanding psychological symptoms following trauma in Western cultures. However, cross-cultural research is lacking; other cultures hold different views of trauma and the meaning it has for individuals and communities. For example, DeVries explains that in some Eastern cultures, people believe that their life is determined by fate, which is in the hands of God, whereas in Western cultures, greater control is attributed to the individual. Cultures have unique ways to understand, support, and provide meaning for individuals affected by trauma. Therefore clinicians who evaluate and treat victims of persecution, torture, and displacement must use care and caution and always view the individual in the context of his or her culture.[12]

The Istanbul Protocol states that phenomenological or descriptive methods can be useful in evaluating the psychological symptoms resulting from trauma as long as they are viewed within the cultural context of the individual. People from different cultures may manifest symptoms that appear similar to PTSD and depression but will carry different meanings.[13] Evaluators must be aware of cultural differences as much as possible; what may be perceived, explained, and treated as a psychological disorder in one culture may be quite differently understood in another. This awareness, along with the knowledge of symptoms of trauma and the prevalence of these symptoms in a given population, can help an evaluator put these symptoms in a context for this individual, providing a more helpful explanation of symptoms and future treatment if indicated.

The fourth edition of the *Diagnostic and Statistical Manual of Mental Disorders* (DSM-IV), published by the American Psychiatric Association, provides descriptions of various symptoms and disorders. People who have been traumatized may suffer from the anxiety disorders, acute stress disorder, and, if not resolved within one month, PTSD.[14] Mood disorders, and frequently major depressive disorder, are seen in addition to PTSD. Chronic trauma often results in long-term depressive symptoms as a consequence of profound psychological losses.[15] Herman describes the complexity of PTSD and broadens our understanding of symptoms of ongoing trauma and the consequences and changes to a victim's personality. Complex PTSD includes alterations in affect regulation, consciousness, self-perception, perception of the perpetrator, and alterations in one's systems of meaning in relation to that of others.[16] A study by van der Kolk, Pelcovitz, Roth, Mandel, McFarlane, and Herman provides further evidence to support the limitations of the diagnosis of PTSD. They conclude that the majority of people with PTSD present with dissociation, somatization, and difficulties with affect regulation.[17] Somatic symptoms as a result of stress include headaches, gastrointestinal difficulties, pain, high blood pressure, sexual dysfunction, difficulty breathing, and so on. Head injuries may also result in headaches, cognitive difficulties, and memory problems among other difficulties. These and other physical symptoms as well as obvious scars and injuries from torture or persecution may require a referral to a medical doctor or a mental health provider for further tests or treatment.

For the majority of asylum applicants who are evaluated months and years after coming to the United States, symptoms will have progressed and changed. Their cultural supports and rituals have been lost long ago. It is more common to see PTSD than acute stress disorder at the time of evaluation. Usually more than one month will have passed since the trauma; at this time, if criteria are met for PTSD, the diagnosis changes accordingly. Symptoms may persist, or there may be complete or partial recovery. Major depression may be in partial or full remission. It is useful to obtain information about symptoms during the trauma(s), immediately following the trauma(s), and in the present. Understanding and documenting this process can aid in obtaining a clearer picture of the progression of symptoms, credibility, and prognosis. It also may be useful in evaluating the possibility of exacerbation of symptoms if the applicant perceives that there will be further trauma or if the applicant is actually exposed to further trauma.

Standardized Tests

Some evaluators may use structured interviews, standardized tests, and symptom checklists as part of the evaluation process. Here also there must be awareness and knowledge of culturally sensitive tests. Hollifield and colleagues' review of instruments measuring trauma and health status in refugee populations describes limitations of current instruments and the need for research in this area.[18] A history of head trauma along with symptoms of brain damage may be reason to consider a referral to a neurologist and/or a neuropsychologist; neuropsychological tests should also be used with caution because of their limitations across cultures. Observed and reported impairments of attention,

concentration, and memory may be due to brain damage and/or PTSD. The Istanbul Protocol points out that when these symptoms are chronic rather than varying in intensity, along with symptoms of anxiety or depression, the possibility of organic brain impairment should be considered.[19]

Credibility

As an objective evaluator, one should always remain alert to the possibility of malingering. Malingering is defined in the DSM-IV as "intentional production of false or grossly exaggerated physical or psychological symptoms, motivated by external incentives."[20] An evaluator may question an applicant's credibility; there may be inconsistencies between an applicant's presentation of symptoms and the trauma(s) he or she alleges to have occurred. In this situation the evaluator must determine if this is a result of the trauma(s) or if the applicant is malingering and document it as such. For example, an applicant may have withheld information or appear evasive because of fear, including fear of deportation; when these inconsistencies are discussed, the applicant may reveal the reasons for not being forthcoming, which can be explained as a consequence of the applicant's symptoms. The applicant may express relief at being able to speak to the evaluator about these fears and confusions. Some cases do not have as much merit as others; a weaker claim may still have some legitimacy even if the clinical findings are not as strong. Lacking obvious symptoms does not necessarily mean that an applicant has not suffered trauma. Symptoms may be milder depending on the duration of time since the trauma(s). Culture, personality, prior mental health disorders, coping strategies, and support systems are among the previously described factors that influence symptoms and how they are expressed. It is also possible that an applicant may not be truthful, and the evaluator must do the best he or she can to determine if this is the case and the reason the applicant is seeking asylum. Substantial evidence should support the claim, and findings should be discussed with the applicant's lawyer. It may be useful to have a second evaluation, sometimes with another clinician, before making this decision. However, when an evaluator does not feel the applicant is credible, the evaluator must discuss this with the lawyer, document his or her opinion of the applicant's credibility, and decline to write an affidavit.

Additional Challenges

In addition to the issues described so far, the use of interpreters and performing evaluations in detention centers may present additional challenges for the evaluator. Besides the logistical difficulties of finding an interpreter or taking time to visit detention centers, which are often located far from city centers or residential areas, the following two issues influence how a clinical interview is conducted.

Use of an Interpreter

If an applicant does not speak English well enough, or any other language(s) that the evaluator speaks fluently, it is best to obtain an interpreter to be present at the clinical interview. Rudimentary English is often not sufficient to express details of traumatic experiences and complex emotions. Interpreters, if used, ideally should be professionals who are familiar with trauma issues. If the interpreter is not a professional, it is important to ask if he or she has had any experience interpreting clinical evaluations for asylum applicants. The evaluator must assess the interpreter's competency and anticipate his or her reactions to hearing an applicant speak of trauma experiences, including torture. If the interpreter has never worked in this area, the evaluator must be more cognizant of his or her mental state during the interview and check on him or her at the end of it.

Interpreters should not be members of the applicant's family. An applicant may feel less comfortable sharing information in the presence of family or friends. The gender of the interpreter may also be a factor in the comfort level of the applicant. For example, a woman who has been raped may feel less comfortable speaking of this in the presence of a daughter or male friend. Some applicants may wish to protect friends or family members from the horror of their experience; some may feel ashamed of what happened and find it easier to share these feelings with a professional.

An evaluator must be aware that the applicant may be more or less comfortable with an interpreter if he or she is from the applicant's own country or familiar with the country's culture and politics. For example, an interpreter who is familiar with an applicant's culture may help the applicant feel at ease. On the other hand, an applicant may have been enslaved and forced to work for a group that raided and killed people; the interpreter may be from a community raided by these groups. It may also be the case that the applicant and the interpreter come from rival political or ethnic groups. Upon learning this, an applicant may feel less trusting, less comfortable with the interpreter, and less open about events. The interpreter too may have feelings that must be clarified. For example, an applicant who is feeling threatened or is struggling with feelings of guilt or shame may feel unable to share information. If the interpreter feels hostile toward the applicant, it will interfere with accurate interpretation. The evaluator must assess the situation and determine if it is possible to proceed. If the decision is made to terminate the interview and reschedule with another interpreter, a clear explanation should be given to both.

Evaluation in Detention Centers

Aliens in deportation proceedings are routinely placed in detention regardless of whether or not they have committed crimes. The asylum applicants arriving in the United States without valid documents are among those who are automatically placed in detention centers. In detention, applicants may have restricted access to an interpreter and may spend months, sometimes years being locked up while waiting for the adjudication of their applications. Often they are taken straight from airports to detention facilities in shackles, forced to wear prison uniforms, and sometimes housed among convicted criminals. Securing legal representation in such conditions can be extremely difficult, because facilities often exist in remote locations. Access to medical and mental health care is limited; facilities usually have clinical staff in-house who provide primary care.

Applicants in detention speak of escaping from traumatic situations and prisons in their own country only to be placed in a prison in the country where they thought they would receive help. One applicant spoke of his disappointment in his treatment, as he thought America would be supportive and help him. Being locked up again, receiving orders from guards, and wearing a uniform reminded him of being locked up in his home country. Detainees speak of having nothing to do but sit and think. Traumatic symptoms are thus exacerbated because of intrusive memories. Applicants in detention frequently present as fragile, with more severe symptoms than those who are not incarcerated. Separation from family and friends and all social supports intensifies symptoms for people in these facilities. For example, an applicant became suicidal while in detention and was heavily medicated. The applicant's lawyer requested an evaluation urgently to help with a parole process so the applicant could leave detention while applying for asylum. The evaluator may be asked to perform one evaluation to assess the applicant's current state in order to request parole and, if granted, another to assess the applicant once out of detention and to gather additional information for the asylum claim.

Sometimes an applicant may choose to return to the country from which he or she claims to have fled because of fear of persecution, torture, and possible death. One applicant whose asylum claim was denied could not tolerate waiting for an appeal process, choosing to risk returning home rather than remain in detention. In this situation, the evaluator may be called back by the lawyer to help the applicant cope with the disappointment. An applicant in such a fragile and hopeless state should be helped to understand his or her legal options before having to make such a decision.

Time is also a factor for the evaluator in performing evaluations in detention centers. The evaluator may be forced to wait before being admitted into a detention center to meet with the applicant, and the facility may limit the time permitted for the evaluation process. The evaluator may not be able to contact this applicant again before the upcoming hearing date. Therefore the evaluation process may be shortened, and the evaluator may have to adjust, quickly gathering the necessary information while still carrying out a therapeutic and sensitive evaluation.

However, if the evaluator feels that there has not been sufficient time to gather the necessary information for a thorough evaluation, he or she must raise this issue with the applicant's lawyer. Sometimes arrangements can be made for another meeting; if not, the evaluator will have to decide if what he or she has is sufficient and document it accordingly.

Ending an Evaluation

Before ending an evaluation, it is important to allow time to answer questions and anything else that an applicant feels it is important to discuss. Concluding the interview in a positive manner is important both to ensure the well-being of the applicant and, if indicated, to motivate him or her to seek follow-up treatment. An applicant may experience a combination of feelings during a lengthy and often stressful evaluation. It may be painful to speak of and relive memories that he or she has been trying to forget. The applicant may feel drained and more fragile than he or she has felt in a long time. The evaluator should have found out during the interview the existing support system and may inquire where the applicant will go after the interview and who will be there. It may be helpful to remind the applicant of his or her resources if he or she should have a return of symptoms after leaving the interview. Identifying and putting into words an applicant's coping behaviors may give new meaning to someone whose esteem has been so damaged. Emphasizing an applicant's resources such as being willing to come to the interview and speak of painful feelings may be helpful.

Despite all of the emotional difficulties applicants may experience during the interview process, some applicants feel relief. People often state at the end of the evaluation process how relieved they feel when opening up to an empathic evaluator, sensing that there is now a witness to some of what they have endured.

The length of an evaluation varies according to an applicant's circumstances, the time it takes to gather the necessary information, the psychological state of the applicant, and a psychologist's style of working. The evaluator has to obtain the information needed to write the affidavit, to assess the mental state of the applicant, and to provide information about follow-up to the applicant.

In some cases it may be useful to meet with the applicant again to obtain the necessary information. Although this is not always possible, it should be considered as an option when time and circumstances permit. It is common to realize after the evaluation, particularly when there are intense emotions, that there are issues the evaluator or the applicant would like to have addressed. This provides an opportunity to fill in these gaps. As previously stated, traumatized individuals frequently present with symptoms that may interfere with sharing their stories with an evaluator. Additional meetings provide an opportunity to observe the applicant on other occasions and to observe consistency of symptoms. An applicant may feel less anxious knowing better what to expect from the evaluator and himself or herself, and thus may share information that would not have been considered during the first meeting.

Follow-Up

An evaluation is not complete without follow-up considerations for the applicant. Considerations and referrals will vary, in part according to the availability of services for trauma survivors in the local area. In some areas there are comprehensive programs that perform many services for victims of persecution and torture, including clinical and medical evaluations, ongoing treatment as needed, and social services. If the evaluator is working within such a comprehensive program, a referral for follow-up treatment may be made before the applicant leaves the evaluation, and the evaluator may follow up with the doctor/service provider to whom the applicant was referred.

It is more common to find networks of organizations that work in conjunction with each other, providing a variety of services. When an applicant is referred to different organizations for various services, it is easier for the applicant to get lost in the system. Such circumstances may demand increased responsibility on the part of the evaluator to ensure that the applicant receives the needed services. The evaluator's involvement in this process may be particularly important if the applicant lacks the support of his or her community, family, and friends. The

loss of trust and feelings of helplessness, fear, and confusion arising from past traumatic experiences may put the applicant in great need of treatment while presenting increased challenges for follow-up care. A positive experience with the evaluator along with clear information on how to proceed may contribute to an applicant's motivation to pursue recommendations for further treatment and care.

PSYCHOLOGICAL EFFECTS ON THE EVALUATOR

Clinicians today are generally aware of countertransference, and many understand that if attended to and understood, their own emotions may provide useful information about an applicant. It is when they are not recognized and understood that they may cause problems for the evaluator and thus the applicant. The more a clinician works at understanding his or her reactions, the more he or she may be able to make use of the material presented during the evaluation.

During and after the interview, the evaluator may feel variations of many of the symptoms that he or she has just heard from the applicant. The evaluator should pay attention to the effect the interview has on his or her psychological state, with the awareness that sitting with and listening to someone describing an experience of trauma/torture may activate similar feelings in the listener. "Vicarious traumatization" may be experienced by evaluators as feelings of helplessness and hopelessness, similar to what the applicant feels. They may experience symptoms of depression, anxiety, and nightmares,[21] as well as other symptoms. Evaluators may experience changes in their clinical boundaries and feel and behave uncharacteristically with the applicant; some may experience effects on their personal relationships, and some may experience burnout. Vicarious traumatization can affect individuals differently, and evaluators have different ways of reflecting on their feelings and managing them.

If an evaluator does not attend to his or her own feelings and manage symptoms of vicarious traumatization, the evaluation process itself may be affected. For example, while an applicant speaks and relives details of his or her traumatic experiences, an evaluator may try to distance himself or herself because it is too painful to have to listen to and take in this horror. The applicant may sense this distance and be further traumatized by the perceived lack of empathy. The experience may remind the applicant of the torturers or those who were unable to hear and tolerate the horror of the applicant's experiences and thus compounds the applicant's fears. On the other hand, an evaluator who is unable to maintain some objectivity may be perceived as being too closely identified with the applicant and may cause the applicant to feel that the evaluator cannot provide a safe environment. Either extreme may limit the applicant's ability to speak of what happened as well as the evaluator's ability to hear what happened. This experience may cause further trauma and damage to the applicant's capacity to trust.

In order to cope with vicarious traumatization, some evaluators may need to take time alone, whereas others choose to seek support. Support group meetings and buddy systems with others who conduct similar activities can be helpful. Whichever way an evaluator chooses, the evaluation process is not complete without addressing this issue.

WRITING AN AFFIDAVIT

Upon completion of the evaluation, the evaluator must decide if the reported and observed clinical findings are consistent with the applicant's statements as related to the asylum claim. If the evaluator concludes that they are, he or she should proceed to document these findings in an affidavit format. The time in between the evaluation and writing the affidavit will vary depending on the urgency of hearing dates and the evaluator's time availability. Some evaluators may choose to have a few days away from the material, particularly when the evaluator feels vicariously traumatized by the experience; others may choose to proceed immediately so as not to lose the details of the event. Either way, clear note taking during the evaluation and at least a review of notes soon after the interview is helpful.

Although evaluators and attorneys will differ in their preference of how to structure an affidavit, including structure and content, some

general guidelines may be useful. An affidavit is a legal document with a legal heading that includes the evaluator's name and a variation of the following: "I hereby swear and affirm the following." An introduction should include the evaluator's qualifications. If an interpreter was used, this should be documented. There should be a clear history of the events, clinical findings, summary (analysis), and conclusion. An evaluator's conclusions should be supported by information gathered during the evaluation. Affidavits should be written as clearly as possible, with clinically relevant details, to provide a clearer picture of the applicant and the events. The evaluator must sign the affidavit and have it notarized.

The evaluator's qualifications should include profession, degree(s), license(s), certification(s), educational institutions attended, and dates of graduation. Current employment along with any relevant background and training working with survivors of trauma or refugee populations should also be included. Attendance at conferences, publications, and research related to these populations should also be stated.

In presenting the narrative of the traumatic events, it must be clearly stated that the material reported is a true representation of the applicant's account. A history of the events should include detailed information on the alleged persecution and traumatic events that are clinically relevant to the applicant's current mental state. The evaluator should also include details of the applicant's life as relevant to the claim before, during, and after the trauma as well as up to the present. It is extremely important for the evaluator to work with the applicant's lawyer when completing this section. Inconsistencies in the details of the history such as the number of people involved in a particular beating episode or the spelling of the applicant's hometown can often harm the applicant's credibility.

Criteria for diagnosis should be specific and clearly presented. The consistency of the applicant's claim with clinical findings, based on reported and observed symptoms, should be demonstrated. The basis for the applicant's credibility should be documented. The conclusion should be brief, summarizing clinical conclusions, assessment of future mental health risks, and, if indicated, treatment recommendations.

TESTIFYING AFTER THE EVALUATION

The lawyer and evaluator may discuss the possibility of the evaluator testifying at a later date as to his or her clinical findings. An evaluator may be asked to testify by phone, in person, or not at all if there are no questions about the evaluator's credibility or affidavit from the government lawyers or immigration judges. There are varying degrees of preparation for testifying, depending on the complexity of individual cases, styles, and comfort levels of lawyers and evaluators. It is advisable that the evaluators speak with the applicant's lawyers in order to prepare for testimony and go over questions the applicant's lawyers will ask as well as possible questions from the government lawyers. The evaluator may provide useful information to the applicant's lawyer, who may then have a better understanding of the applicant's psychological state and possible reactions under stress; it may also help to prepare the applicant for testifying.

The evaluator's testimony may assist immigration authorities to understand not only how the applicant's claim is clinically consistent with the clinical evidence but also why an applicant may behave in a certain manner. For example, an applicant who showed few emotions during the evaluation process explained that he tried not to think and speak of what happened because when he did he felt as though he was losing control of himself. The evaluator explained that the applicant wanted to avoid thoughts, feelings, and conversations associated with the trauma—such symptoms are common consequences of trauma. This added support to this applicant's credibility. If not explained, this applicant's paucity of emotions when testifying could have made him appear less credible. Educating the immigration authorities about the effect of trauma on memory can also be helpful for them to understand the difficulties that applicants may experience remembering dates and other details while maintaining vivid memories of fragments of traumatic events.

It is also important to educate the applicant's lawyers about the symptoms from which the applicant may be suffering. Hearing dates frequently increase the applicant's stress and exacerbate symptoms. An applicant with a hearing date that is within weeks of the evaluation may reexperience symptoms that had subsided, which should be documented. Sometimes applicants miss hearing dates because of fears or memory difficulties. Preparing the lawyer to understand and prepare the applicant, possibly escorting the applicant to the hearing, can ensure that the applicant has every opportunity to have his or her case heard.

CONCLUSION

Working as an evaluator with traumatized individuals who are seeking political asylum is, at times, difficult and yet enormously rewarding work. It offers the evaluator the possibility for an expanded awareness of worldwide cultures and conflicts, human behavior, and the depths of people's pain and resilience.

NOTES

1. Persons of concern include internally displaced persons (IDPs), returned refugees, and asylum applicants. IDPs are refugees who have not yet crossed national borders and thus cannot be classified as refugees according to the definition of the 1951 United Nations Convention relating to the Status of Refugees and its 1967 protocol. Most up-to-date statistics are available at the United Nations High Commissioner for Refugees Web site: www.unhcr.ch

2. See www.ins.usdoj.gov

3. CAT; see http://www.refugees.org/world/articles/asylum-rr99-3.htm

4. Istanbul Protocol, Psychological Evidence of Torture, p. 2; See http://www.phrusa.org/research/istanbul-protocol/isintro.html

5. J. Herman, *Trauma and Recovery* (New York: Basic Books, 1992), 51–52.

6. Herman, *Trauma and Recovery,* 33–73.

7. Bessel A. van der Kolk, "The Body Keeps the Score: Approaches to the Psychobiology of Posttraumatic Stress Disorder," in *Traumatic Stress: The Effects of Overwhelming Experience on Mind, Body and Society,* ed. Bessel A. van der Kolk, Alexander C. McFarlane, and Lars Weisaeth, Lars, 214–241 (New York: Guilford Press, 1991).

8. Bessel A. van der Kolk, Onno van der Hart, and Charles, R. Marmar, "Dissociation and Information Processing in Posttraumatic Stress

Disorder," in *Traumatic Stress: The Effects of Overwhelming Experience on Mind, Body and Society,* ed. Bessel A. van der Kolk, Alexander C. McFarlane, and Lars Weisaeth, 306–314 (New York: Guilford Press, 1991).

9. Herman, *Trauma and Recovery,* 52–53.

10. J. L. Herman, "Complex PTSD: A Syndrome in Survivors of Prolonged Repeated Trauma," *Journal of Traumatic Stress* 5, no. 3 (1992): 377–391.

11. Roxane C. Silver, Alison E. Holman, Daniel N. McIntosh, M. Poulin, and Virginia Gil-Rivas, "Nationwide Longitudinal Study of Psychological Responses to September 11," *Journal of the American Medical Association* 22, no. 10 (2002): 1235–1244.

12. Martin W. DeVries, "Trauma in Cultural Perspective," in *Traumatic Stress: The Effects of Overwhelming Experience on Mind, Body and Society,* ed. Bessel A. van der Kolk, Alexander C. McFarlane, and Lars Weisaeth, 398–413 (New York: Guilford Press, 1991).

13. Istanbul Protocol, Psychological Evidence of Torture, p. 2. See http://www.phrusa.org/research/istanbul-protocol/isintro.html

14. American Psychiatric Association, *Diagnostic and Statistical Manual of Mental Disorders,* 4th ed. (Washington, DC: American Psychiatric Association, 1994).

15. Herman, "Complex PTSD," 377–391.

16. Herman, *Trauma and Recovery,* 121.

17. B. A. van der Kolk, D. Pelcovitz, S. Roth, F. Mandel, A. McFarlane, and J. L. Herman, "Dissociation, Somatization and Affect Regulation: The Complexity of Adaptation to Trauma," *American Journal of Psychiatry* 153 (1996): 7.

18. M. Hollifield, T. Warner, N. Lian, B. Krakow, J. Jenkins, J. Kesler, J. Stevenson, and J. Westermeyer, "Measuring Trauma and Health Status in Refugees: A Critical Review," *Journal of the American Medical Association* 288, no. 5 (2002): 611–621.

19. Istanbul Protocol, Psychological Evidence of Torture, p. 23. See http://www.phrusa.org/research/istanbul-protocol/isintro.html

20. American Psychiatric Association, DSM-IV, 675.

21. Istanbul Protocol, Psychological Evidence of Torture, p. 13. See http://www.phrusa.org/research/istanbul-protocol/isintro.html

13

EVALUATING CHILD ABUSE IN CHILDREN WHO SEEK ASYLUM

Four Cases Studies

ELLEN G. KELMAN

Doctors of the World

T he term *child abuse* has become all too familiar over the past few decades for those of us living in developed countries such as the United States. We see it in the news on a daily basis and have set up elaborate agencies and reporting systems to detect or prevent it when possible. In addition, we tend to have a universal definition for it that basically equates it with dysfunction and evil. Anyone committing such an act is seen as unfit to be around children and perverse. In a sense, it has become a cliché that one can't quite define but knows it is a bad thing. Any individual accused of abuse can find his or her reputation and career in ruins. He or she would face a legal system filled with inconsistencies and possibly misconceptions.

What is child abuse? Can it differ from year to year or decade to decade? What defines it in rural Appalachia or metropolitan New York? Is it the same in Pakistan as it is in South Korea or Great Britain? In this chapter, I will explore the concept of child abuse from a cross-cultural perspective. Specifically, the focus will be on

children seeking asylum in the United States due to abuse in their home country.

DEFINITIONS AND TERMINOLOGY

Before deciding if differences exist across cultures, it is important to look at how these terms are defined. To start at a very basic level, *Webster's College Dictionary* defines the word *abuse* as "harmful or injurious treatment" (Random House, 1996). This can be taken a step further to say for the definition of *child abuse:* "harmful or injurious treatment of a child." The definition does not identify who is performing this injurious treatment. Perhaps a child is harmfully treating another child. Maybe it is a 5-year-old abusing a 2-year-old, or a 12-year-old abusing another 12-year-old. That changes the impression a great deal. It is usually assumed that child abuse implies treatment at the hands of an adult, and it might further be assumed that it is at the hands of a parent.

Another definition comes from the *Merck Manual of Medical Information:* it states, "Child abuse is the maltreatment, physical or mental injury, or sexual abuse of a child. Child neglect is the failure to provide adequate food, clothing, shelter, or love to a child" (Berkow, Beers, & Fletcher, 1997). Again this definition does not imply who the abuser might be, nor does it specifically define the nature of what constitutes a physical or mental injury. When the definition of child neglect is examined, the question arises: What about the mother in Somalia who cannot provide food, clothing, or shelter? She must be guilty of child neglect, because the issue of intent is not really mentioned in this definition.

A third definition approaches the topic from more of an emotional and abstract line of thinking. In the book *Trauma in the Lives of Children,* child abuse is defined as "a betrayal of the trust children have a right to expect" (Johnson, 1998). This appears to be a more accurate definition to take into account when discussing cultural differences. It isn't the hard-and-fast definition of harm or injury that can differ for individuals and cultures. It deals with the idea of abuse from the victim's point of view and alludes to expectations and norms for that individual. Perhaps a child working in the fields 10 hours a day might be considered a victim of child abuse in the United States but not in rural Cambodia.

The term *culture* should not be confused with ethnicity. Actually, ethnicity is a subset of culture. For the most part, cultures include diverse ethnicities and can be viewed as the main category with such subsets as language, child-rearing practices, religious beliefs, gender roles, and more. Within any one society, country, or neighborhood, a vast number of cultures may exist. In other words, for this discussion, culture should be taken as implying a group of people "bound by common beliefs, history, and practices" (Aronson Fontes, 1995).

This chapter will look at the topic of child abuse from the perspective of the professional evaluating children who have entered this country illegally and, most often, alone. They have come to the attention of U.S. authorities such as the Immigration and Naturalization Service (INS) and may be placed in juvenile detention facilities. Their families and comfort level are thousands of miles away. Any money they acquired to facilitate their perilous journey is long gone due to thieves and unscrupulous smugglers or guides. They all have one thing in common: the desire to live a better life away from fear and despair, even if that means away from any loved ones or familiarity in culture and language. These children will seek asylum in an effort to legally remain in this country. Some will do so based on the child abuse they claim occurred at the hands of one or both parents.

Therefore professionals working in a legal setting must determine if abuse exists and what the consequence will be if the child is returned to his or her home country. If asylum is denied, then the minor is sent back to his or her homeland. The minor will either live with his or her family again, facing perhaps greater animosity and abuse, or make his or her own way with little or no help from social service agencies in his or her poor home country. If asylum is granted, then the minor is placed with a foster family and enrolled in school. Some children may be lucky enough to have sponsors who will take them into their homes. This is often a relative, such as an uncle or cousin, who has legal status and has volunteered to care for the minor. It is vital for evaluators in these cases to consider all aspects of abuse, placement, and well-being for the child. This is not only a big decision with many confounding twists and turns but one that will literally determine the very essence of an individual's life. This chapter can be relevant to anyone coming into contact with children in such a situation: psychologists, social workers, attorneys, judges, state or federal authorities (police, INS officers, detention workers), churches, schools, and foster families.

BACKGROUND

Child abuse is a serious problem throughout the world, but often worse in countries with extreme poverty. Conditions such as malnutrition, child labor, neglect, violence against children, and lack of sufficient educational systems place children in danger on a daily basis. For many years, the Committee on the Rights of the Child has attempted to curb the trend of child abuse and serve as a watchdog and facilitator to many countries with serious violations.

In the following discussions, four case studies will be reviewed in which children illegally escaped to the United States seeking asylum from the abuse they experienced in their country of origin at the hands of a family member.

CONDITIONS AND POLITICS IN GUATEMALA

Three of these cases involve Guatemala, which came under observation by the Committee on the Rights of the Child in 1996. The country had experienced 36 years of internal armed conflict and was undergoing significant social and political changes during the 1990s. However, the Committee Against Torture still reported deterioration of the human rights situation from 1990 through 2000. On many occasions, police were the ones violating human rights and were reportedly involved in extrajudicial killings. Although legislation had been developed in terms of the "children and adolescent code," it was not yet implemented and not known to the general public. Nongovernmental agencies working to promote and protect the rights of children were often threatened and hampered from pursuing their activities. The report by the Committee on the Rights of the Child contains information that a climate of fear and intimidation exists that interferes with the ability to ensure respect for human rights. Years of conflict have resulted in the acceptance of violence even within the family. Children, especially indigenous children in rural areas, are at the highest risk for poverty and abuse (Committee on the Rights of the Child, 1996).

CONDITIONS AND POLITICS IN CHINA

Another country we will consider is China. Due to China's limit on the number of children born per family, gender preferences for male children may put female children at risk. In urban areas, couples are allowed one child only. In rural China, parents are allowed to have one child if it is a male and a second if the firstborn is female. One may frequently hear of desperate couples who abuse, abandon, or even murder firstborn females in an effort to try one more time for a male child. Orphanages are overwhelmed with

infant girls who have been left on the doorstep due to this policy.

Children in remote rural areas of either country appear to have no recourse for protection. It is reported by numerous refugees that legal authorities haven't the means or ability to protect children. Often the practice is to turn a blind eye and allow families the autonomy to rule their household in any way they choose. There is fear associated with the attempt to report abuse. It tends to initiate more abuse by an angered parent, provides no assistance, and can stigmatize a family, creating further hardship for everyone.

GENERAL FACTORS IN ABUSE

Children have been abused throughout history in most societies and cultural contexts. This has occurred within the family system as well, even though today most societies consider this behavior to be taboo. Definitions of abuse vary culturally, and some methods of discipline and rituals of initiation or entrance into adulthood may not be viewed as abusive in non-Western cultures. Criteria for abuse can be viewed as relative, and thus, many researchers differentiate between traditional, ordered practices and those that may be random and impulsive. Rites of passage that may inflict pain are performed more systematically, and although we may consider this abusive, within other cultures it is considered perfectly acceptable (Derezotes & Snowden, 1990).

Sociocultural risk factors related to child abuse include poverty, family isolation, high levels of family conflict and domestic abuse, substance abuse, cultural sanctioning of family violence and harsh discipline, cultural beliefs that assume that children are unable to understand and respond to nonphysical discipline, high levels of competition for resources and intergroup conflict, political violence and ethnic conflict, lack of social and community support structures for families, exploitation of children in regard to child labor practices and trafficking, and rituals and initiation practices that involve physical pain and mutilation (Derezotes & Snowden, 1990; Sattler, 1998; see also Basu, Chapter 15, this volume).

Internationally, economic hardship, ethnic conflict, the social marginalization of the rural poor, and a lack of social supports and educational efforts to prevent family violence contribute to problems of child abuse.

SEEKING ASYLUM

Children do not leave their homeland and families with the forethought of seeking asylum. They leave for a variety of reasons, such as fear, desperation, the dream of a better life, a sense of obligation to earn money and send it home, but mostly because someone has raised the money to enable them to leave. Often they would rather stay to care for siblings or protect a nonabusive parent from an abusive one.

It takes a large sum of money to pay a smuggler, and the opportunity for freedom is taken quite seriously. These children know that a lot is at stake in their attempt to make it to the United States, to find employment, and, in many cases, to send money home. The notion of being caught and detained for months while awaiting a hearing is not part of their hopes and plans. However, once apprehended and detained, they usually choose to seek a legal means for remaining in this country.

The process of seeking asylum and putting your fate in the hands of the courts is arduous for anyone, let alone for a minor who does not understand the customs and language of a new country. Once caught by the INS, these children are placed in special juvenile detention facilities with other detainees from all over the world. They are schooled and socialized, but only within the facility. An attorney is assigned, and months of waiting for a hearing begin.

This is usually a very difficult period for these children. They miss their families even if they are relieved to be away from the abuse. As time passes slowly and they have too much time to be idle and alone, a sense of failure and depression can set in. Eventually, a psychological evaluation is conducted by a mental health professional to assess their history and current mental status.

THE FOCUS OF A PSYCHOLOGICAL EVALUATION

When the purpose of a psychological evaluation is to assess the claim of abuse to facilitate the court's decision in granting asylum, a complete personal and clinical history is warranted. The professional needs to substantiate the facts in the case and establish consistency in the individual's reported story. The individual's mood, affect, thought process, behavior, and nonverbal communication are also evaluated. In most cases, a translator is present, so one must consider that phrasing and facts are somewhat at the mercy of third-party interpretation. This is also the time when cultural context is extremely important. For example, eye contact or the lack thereof may be a good indicator of telling the truth in our culture, but diverting the eyes may imply respect for others. When I first encountered Guatemalan youths, I was surprised that most could not consistently report their birth date. Had I not researched this further, I may have concluded that this was an attempt to hide something. Instead, it is just that these rural children do not celebrate birthdays, birth records may not be kept, and they may never have been told precisely when they were born.

The evaluation is then compiled into a concise affidavit by the evaluator and includes a summary of family history and personal background, an account of reasons for the youth leaving his or her homeland, departure and travels to the United States, the youth's experiences in detention, clinical diagnosis if applicable, and overall impressions. In juvenile cases, the evaluator is usually asked to testify in United States Immigration Court. The case is presented before a judge with the minor present along with his or her court-appointed attorney and the INS attorney. The judge will decide whether to grant asylum and place the juvenile with a foster family or sponsor or to deny asylum and return the individual to his or her homeland. Overall, this is a lengthy process; from start to finish, a year or more can elapse before the process is finalized.

Although the collaboration between the fields of psychology and law in child abuse cases is seen as beneficial, it comes with numerous drawbacks. Expert evaluation is complex and may result in communicative difficulties between the two fields. Central concepts are not viewed with the same mutual understanding, and the court is usually unable or unwilling to make independent assessments of the expert's reasoning. The process often fails to ensure quality control when an expert is assigned to the case. In some cases, more could be done to oversee the appointment of an evaluator with expertise or cultural awareness (Gumpert & Lindblad, 2001). Azar and Cote (2002) sum this up best:

> Courts assume the main lens through which we see families is a scientific one as expert witnesses. Yet, our discussion questions this assumption. Given the weaknesses of our current frameworks and database, evaluators may be operating like novice decision makers and, therefore, more likely to fall back on heuristics regarding diverse parents which oftentimes are overly narrow and negative in tone. For example, low SES individuals throughout history have been viewed as hopeless, incompetent, or despicable. Our "scientific" schemas/scripts may be culturally biased filters through which information is processed. Without good frameworks, evaluators may present judgments to courts that are at best untested and at worse ethnocentric. (p. 209)

Summary of Cultural Considerations: Steps to Take When Performing an Evaluation

This section is designed to provide a framework on which to base evaluations. It will provide a step-by-step approach enabling evaluators to systematically consider cultural differences when reviewing a case for child abuse.

1. Before beginning an evaluation, become educated about the cultural backgrounds of all those involved. Solicit information from numerous sources. Take the time to know the country or locale of origin, including the historical and political climate. Do not assume that all persons from the same country (such as Guatemala), have the same cultural background. Explore ethnic variation within each nationality.

2. Always begin an evaluation with more attention placed on listening and observing than on drawing conclusions. Ask a lot of questions and allow the individuals to feel comfortable and open in speaking. You can never have too much information in this type of case.

3. Show true empathy and concern for the client's well-being. The insincere and disinterested evaluator will find that information is often withheld or distorted. Therefore the emphasis should be placed on the people and not the case or the report. This can be accomplished with an even and calm tone of voice and appropriate adherence to cultural issues such as eye contact or physical contact, as well as taking the necessary time, not appearing rushed, and coming back to areas of uncertainty later in the interview rather than harping on one line of questioning.

4. Make sure to leave your personal biases out of the evaluation. This can be an even greater problem in culturally diverse cases. Although everyone is prone to being influenced by past events, it is the professional's responsibility to be a nonpartial third party. If this is simply impossible in a given case, then disqualifying oneself may be the best course of action.

5. Because cross-cultural factors add an extra dimension to the evaluation of child abuse, it is vital to keep a clear, operational definition of abuse in mind. Review such topics as rites and rituals and how intent to harm may play a role. Try to also take the perspective of each individual involved in order to understand how he or she views the situation.

6. The specific risk factors for abuse should be reviewed. Sociocultural risk factors are briefly presented in this chapter, but other individual, child, family, and environmental determinants are variables that must be considered. (See Sattler, 1998, for an excellent discussion of risk factors and a comprehensive guide to the procedures and interviewing formats necessary in the assessment of child abuse.) Cross-cultural differences can confound risk factors, as described in the literature in the United States, and must be viewed in light of this. A review of the child's cultural norms, traditions, and country conditions may reveal culturally specific windows that shed contextual light on the abuse. When it is finally time to form conclusions, all facts and pertinent information should be weighed. Conduct a careful personal review of assumptions and biases that relate to the case at hand in order to avoid adding elements of

judgment or prejudice in the formation of opinions and conclusions. Cultural issues should be addressed and mentioned as possible influencing factors.

CASE STUDIES

The following case studies are factual; however, the names are fictitious.

Antonio was 16 years of age when he left Guatemala with a smuggler and a busload of other emigrants. He was one of five children from an indigenous Mayan family from Guatemala. He claimed that both parents worked as field laborers and would be drunk more than 50% of the time. When this occurred, they became extremely abusive and neglectful. The children would be severely beaten and often there was no food. The parents frequently kicked the children out of the house, and they would be forced to seek shelter at a neighbor's home. Antonio reported having no one to turn to, because the government would not help and the police were corrupt. Other family members were either fearful or too poor to intervene. He felt his only recourse was to leave and look for a better environment where he could work and send money to save his siblings. He reported having a tremendous fear of becoming like his father if he remained in his country of origin. Antonio was detained by the INS in southern Arizona. He was granted asylum and placed in foster care to learn English and continue with his schooling. He had only received approximately 3 years of education in Guatemala.

Felipe had just turned 16 years of age when he left Guatemala. He had two younger sisters and five younger brothers, all still living in Guatemala. He reported that his father was physically abusive his entire life, especially at times when he was drinking, which was "most of the time." When his father worked in construction, he could support the family, but he usually spent the money on alcohol. His father reportedly had killed his first wife in quite a brutal way, and thus Felipe's mother feared intervening if he was beating the children. His mother tried to call the police on one occasion. The father was placed in jail for 5 days, but was more violent when he returned. Felipe began working in a nearby town at the age of 9 and attended school for a half day when he could. He feared his father greatly and claimed that he left to save his life. He remained quite sad and worried about his mother and siblings. Felipe was smuggled out of Guatemala and detained by the border patrol. He also won asylum and will be given an opportunity to further his education and create a better life for himself.

Jose was also 16 years of age when he left Guatemala. He recounted experiencing a great deal of prejudice in his country against indigenous peoples. He remembers his parents fighting most of the time. His father often beat his mother and the children, especially when he drank. He recalls his father using a rope or stick to beat him and being unable to move for days. Once he was forced to watch his father hit his mother with a hose fifteen times. When his mother became fearful for her life, she attempted to report this to the police. She did not speak Spanish, and the police told neighbors that they would not help poor, inferior people. His mother was able to obtain money to help him escape. Jose suffered from flashbacks and nightmares, meeting criteria for posttraumatic stress disorder. He was granted asylum and placed with a foster family.

Ming was 16 years of age when her father put her on a plane to escape the abusiveness of her mother. Ming was the second female born to her parents, which brought disgrace to her family. Without reporting her birth, her parents sent her to another village to live with grandparents. Her parents never contacted her or visited, and they proceeded to have a third child, a boy. At the age of 7, her grandparents could no longer care for her and returned her to her parents. This brought great embarrassment to the family, and the government fined them for failure to report her birth. She was now the third child in the family and the second girl. Her mother was abusive from then on, forcing her to do all the housework. She was either neglected or verbally and physically mistreated. Her father was more sympathetic, but worked as a farmer and was not home often. When her father was away, her mother would beat her with sticks, which caused bloody sores and scars. She was only allowed to attend school through sixth grade, and then her mother expected her to work both outside and inside the home. The other two children were not treated this way and would contribute to the abuse by teasing her. She feared that if she were returned to China, she would bring further disgrace to the family and receive even harsher treatment. Ming was detained by the INS and later granted asylum to remain in this country. She was to live with an uncle who would be her sponsor. This case poses some interesting issues from a cross-cultural perspective. China differs from most countries in the fact that it has a birth policy. Issues of family honor; a severe, authoritarian style of parenting; and gender discrimination all come into play. Although cultural norms provide some context for understanding what Ming had endured, the abuse she suffered is clear and not to be clouded by cultural and political issues. Her father recognized the abuse that was taking place, but did not provide adequate protection for his daughter.

We can see from these case studies that in some countries, the treatment of children is left to the discretion of the parents, with little or no social service or government intervention. Although abuse may be sanctioned or unregulated in some countries, once it comes to the attention of the authorities in the United States, the children must be afforded protection and a safe environment where they can recover from the abuse and return to a healthier course of development.

Child abuse is a very complicated issue with many implications. One should not assume that everyone agrees on what is meant by this term. The discussion of child abuse without addressing culture is incomplete and can lead to many false conclusions. Yet we must be careful as professionals not to excuse maltreatment because of cultural norms and practices. We must strive for a balance in understanding cultural influences in family life, including variations in parenting styles; the impact of poverty; the stresses of prolonged economic hardships; ethnic conflicts that lead to fear, danger, and violence; cultural climates that are oppressive to women and girls; and the demands that accompany migration and acculturation processes.

Achieving objectivity is difficult when observing a child's suffering. However, evaluators are not left with the final decision regarding the disposition of the case, and evaluators will do their best work when their personal feelings do not influence their work. In summary, an evaluator must be open-minded, culturally aware and informed, a keen listener and observer, and well versed in what constitutes child abuse.

REFERENCES

Aronson Fontes, L. (1995). *Sexual abuse in nine North American cultures.* Thousand Oaks, CA: Sage Publications.

Azar, S. T., & Cote, L. R. (2002). Sociocultural issues in the evaluation of the needs of children in custody decision making: What do our current frameworks for evaluating parenting practices have to offer? *International Journal of Law and Psychiatry, 25,* 193–217.

Berkow, R., Beers, M. H., & Fletcher, A. J. (1997). *The Merck manual of medical information.* Whitehouse Station, NJ: Merck & Co.

Committee on the Rights of the Child. (1996, June 7). *Twelfth session: Concluding observations on Guatemala.* Retrieved March 31, 2004, from http://www1.umn.edu/humanrts/crc/crc-Guatemala96.htm

Derezotes, D. S., & Snowden, L. R. (1990). Cultural factors in the intervention of child maltreatment. *Child and Adolescent Social Work, 7,* 161–175.

Gumpert, C. H., & Lindblad, F. (2001). Communication between courts and expert witness in legal proceedings concerning child sexual abuse in Sweden: A case review. *Child Abuse and Neglect, 25,* 1497–1516.

Johnson, K. (1998). *Trauma in the lives of children.* Alameda, CA: Hunter House.

Random House. (1996). *Webster's College Dictionary.* New York: Random House.

Sattler, J. (1998). *Clinical and forensic interviewing of children and families.* San Diego: Jerome Sattler.

PART III

IMMIGRATION

14

Enhancing the Psychosocial Well-Being of Asylum Seekers and Refugees

Angela Burnett

Sanctuary Practice, Hackney, UK

Kate Thompson

The North East London Mental Health Trust

Let's talk about psychology when the war is over. When the war is over I am going to dream all the dreams that I cannot afford now. . . . If I would sit down and start to think of my feelings, I could break down. . . . You, the Europeans can enjoy the luxury of analysing your feelings. We simply have to endure.

—A Palestinian mother (quoted in Punamäki, 1992, p. 4)

This chapter, written from a U.K. perspective, is concerned with the role of how both past and present experiences affect the psychological well-being of asylum seekers and refugees. It is broken down into three sections. The first is a brief overview of the numbers, location, and experiences of people in exile, with some examples of key issues such as culture, safety, and multiple loss. Issues affecting specific groups including women, men, older people, children, families, and survivors of torture and organized violence are discussed. The second section describes and provides examples

of how services can be adapted to meet the specific needs of people. It examines the appropriateness of the diagnosis of post-traumatic stress disorder (PTSD) in this context and stresses the need for holistic intervention. The final section discusses the impact of the immigration system on service provision.

Definition of Terms

Throughout the chapter, the term *asylum seeker* is used to describe a person who has submitted an application for protection under the Geneva Convention. In order to be recognized officially as a refugee, an asylum seeker must fulfill the terms of the 1951 Geneva Convention and demonstrate that

> owing to a well founded fear of being persecuted for reasons of race, religion, nationality, membership of a particular social group or political opinion, is outside the country of his nationality and is unable, or owing to such fear, is unwilling to avail himself of the protection of that country. (United Nations, 1951)

The terms *refugee* and *exile* may sometimes be used to include asylum seekers, those whose claim has been successful and those who do not have the opportunity to submit an application. The chapter is predominantly set within a British context, but many of the issues described have wider relevance.

ISSUES

Nearly 21 million people throughout the world are considered to be asylum seekers or refugees (United Nations High Commissioner for Refugees [UNHCR] Web Site), with an estimated additional 21 million internally displaced within their own countries. Numbers of asylum seekers from each country fluctuate, principally according to the local human rights situation. The vast majority remain in neighboring countries, most of which have scarce resources to provide for their needs. Only those with significant resources travel to industrialized countries. Most seeking asylum in industrialized countries are single men under the age of 40, although worldwide most refugees are women. Many families are without one parent, who may be missing or dead, and a significant number of children are unaccompanied.

Those leaving their country experience many losses. In addition to losing family members through death or separation, they lose their home, family, friends, money, job, and identity and may lose dignity and hope. These multiple losses and, perhaps most important, the loss of role, status, and usual support networks may have a profound impact on their psychological well-being.

Some have been detained and tortured in their own countries, and exposure to violence is widespread, which may have important consequences on psychological health. Some people have been persecuted because of their political or religious beliefs and activities, others because they belong to a minority ethnic group or due to their gender or sexual orientation. Some have left because of an environmental disaster, whereas others migrate due to poverty as disparities between rich and poor, both between and within countries, continue to widen.

Those making the often arduous and dangerous journey to exile are courageous, resourceful, and resilient, and these qualities can assist them to rebuild their lives, although individuals will exhibit different degrees of resilience and vulnerability. After the initial relief of arriving, frustration and disillusionment may ensue, as the reality of life becomes apparent. It is important to enable people to develop independence, acquire language, and have access to education and employment. Integration requires support from the local community.

Most refugees understandably hope that one day, when the situation becomes safer, they will be able to return home. During 2002 almost 2.5 million refugees throughout the world returned to their home country (UNHCR Web Site).

Key Issues for This Client Group

A number of key issues are raised when working with refugees. These are outlined in the following sections, but this should not be regarded as an exhaustive list. One of the central factors in this work is the attempt to really hear the concerns of the client. This allows for a proper focus on the individual, who is thus permitted to present the issues of most importance.

Culture and Health

Health-related behavior and expectations of health care are both affected by culture and beliefs. Each culture has its own frameworks for psychological health and for seeking help in a crisis. Behavior that is considered mental illness or emotional distress in Western countries may be interpreted in a very different way by other cultures, viewed as spirit possession, a sign of divine punishment, genetic weakness, or normal behavior. Behavior that is associated with mental illness can carry marked stigma, which may deter people from seeking help. Culture affects interpretation of individual behavior and tolerance of emotional distress, and it may influence diagnosis of mental illness.

Some people may wish to observe certain rituals and customs associated with birth and death. Individuals may interpret values from their culture differently and may not follow assumed norms of culture or religion.

As health or social care workers, we need to be aware of our own assumptions, stereotyping, and interpretations. Interpreters, health advocates, and health workers from a displaced background may be able to assist with details of cultural background.

Safety

Most refugees and asylum seekers have come from politically unstable situations, so issues around safety and danger may be very salient for them and are ongoing in the country of exile, where safety is often not guaranteed.

1. The long process of seeking asylum in Britain creates great anxiety for asylum seekers. It is difficult to feel safe until leave to remain has been assured, and many asylum seekers present with depression and anxiety. Such fear is often treated as groundless by immigration authorities. Yet in 2001–2002 there were reports of at least seven suicides of asylum seekers in the United Kingdom, some of which followed refusal of an asylum application or threat of deportation. (G. Hinshelwood, personal communication, 2002)

2. When reflecting on the place where they feel safest, most people mention "home." Asylum seekers and refugees are "homeless" in the most profound sense of the word. They have been forced to leave established homes and to build a new sense of home elsewhere. Practical issues to do with housing can be of great importance, particularly if the person feels unsafe or lives in an unsafe area. People commonly find they get lost more easily or cannot use their usual orienteering abilities, something

often complicated by symptoms of depression and difficulties with memory. In the United Kingdom, a dispersal policy, where asylum seekers are sent to areas outside London, where it may be difficult to identify local communities of refugees from the same country or speaking the same language, may add to the lack of safety experienced in the new environment.

3. The negative psychological effects of not being believed should not be underestimated. The adversarial nature of the asylum system and media reporting of "bogus" asylum seekers (Refugee Council Web Site) create a hostile environment in which individuals may find it difficult to feel safe. Insecurity may increase if people are telling their most frightening, humiliating, or secret experiences without being heard or believed.

Helplessness

Both the experiences that refugees and asylum seekers have had in their country of origin and the challenge of dealing with unfamiliar systems in the United Kingdom (particularly immigration, housing, and health systems) can encourage feelings of helplessness and despair. Exiles can often become convinced that they have almost no control over their circumstances and few options to improve the situation. This perception is not without substance, particularly in relation to the asylum process (Asylum Aid 1995, 1999).

The British asylum system creates many of the conditions for the development of a sense of helplessness in those seeking asylum. After the claim is lodged, the asylum seeker waits, with no idea how long it will take to process and little control over the outcome. Following a refusal, this sense of uncontrollability can become more acute, particularly if the person is unable to understand the reasons and cannot predict what will happen at appeal. Feelings of helplessness and lack of control are exacerbated, as the asylum seeker is obliged to disclose past experiences of persecution within an atmosphere of suspicion and disbelief.

Although both meaningful understanding and social support have been listed as factors buffering the effects of learned helplessness

(Silver & Wortman, 1980), the system tends to undermine such protective factors. Dispersal may separate individuals from the support offered by a network of refugee community organizations and the exiled diaspora. Denied permission to work, the vast majority become dependent, with no choice as to where they live. Accommodation and services may be inappropriate, particularly for those who are most vulnerable, including those with a disability. In addition, many refugees report that they were able to endure severe hardships in their own countries because they could understand the situation in political, religious, or otherwise meaningful ways. The difficulties encountered in the country of exile, on the other hand, may feel overwhelming precisely because they contradict expectations of a sympathetic and supportive response to the exile's quest for asylum.

Holding Paradox in Tension

The experience of exile is full of seeming paradox. When working with refugees and asylum seekers, one is always confronted with two sides of their experiences. They can be visualized and may see themselves as "victims" of past persecution and of the political systems, both in the country of origin and in exile. However, to focus solely on the victimized aspect is to ignore the other side of the paradox, their very resilience as survivors. These are people who may have known the most challenging experiences possible and who continue to live and function in the world. To focus on either of these aspects to the detriment of the other is to miss a fundamental part of the person's experience. In many cases, a balanced approach tries to help the victimized person recognize that he or she is also a survivor. It may also be necessary to help some survivors give voice to how victimized they continue to feel.

Similarly, there is a need to recognize both the real-world nature of the difficulties that refugees face, contextualizing and normalizing their problems and symptoms, as well as to leave room for the symbolic nature of what may be being expressed. For example, individuals often present with housing difficulties. On one level, these are quite understandable, as exiles may be placed in poor-quality accommodation, and become involved in struggles to change this.

At another level, however, something additional is being expressed by these refugees about the meaning of the loss of home and safety. Workers providing services to refugees need to allow room for both levels of experience, acknowledging the concrete reality of housing difficulties and how to manage them and allowing room for reflection on the meaning of these difficulties and how they relate to asylum seekers' overall sense of themselves and the world. This balance is crucial but can often be neglected when professionals have a sense of themselves as either therapeutic workers or social workers and feel that their area extends only to part of the refugee's distress.

In addition, there can be a tension between perceiving the person as singled out by his or her experience and allowing the person to be ordinary (Jones, 2002). It is important both to recognize the overwhelming and sometimes cataclysmic nature of the experiences that a refugee may have undergone and to allow the refugee to be a human being like any other, who enjoys certain foods, sports, music, and so on. One result of the polarized political debate about asylum seekers in the United Kingdom has been to allow only two roles—suffering and martyred "genuine refugees" or lying and cheating "bogus asylum seekers." This denies the person any other sense of self and the broader sense of his or her humanity. Service providers should remain mindful of allowing some room for ordinariness, while never denying the uniqueness and horror of the refugee's experiences.

Coping With Loss

Exile is by nature an experience of multiple loss—of home, friends, familiar places, culture, profession, meaning, and so on. Once safety is assured, most exiles will begin to feel the grief of the losses experienced, particularly if they are alone in the United Kingdom and have had to leave close family behind. In some cases, exiles will have had extremely traumatic losses involving the murder of friends and family. Such losses, coupled with situations of loneliness and social isolation in this country, can be very difficult to manage. Eisenbruch (1990) has argued that a bereavement reaction seems a fitting way of conceptualizing what refugees experience. He describes exile as a form of "cultural bereavement"——a normal reaction to the abnormal situation of exile rather than a sign of psychiatric disorder. Eisenbruch's work with young Cambodian refugees in Australia demonstrated traditional healing to be more effective than Western models of psychological support.

Rebuilding relationships and finding sources of social support are often of crucial importance at this point. Refugee community organizations can be key contacts in this, although some exiles may distrust others from the same country because of political difference or because of ethnic or religious conflict. Developing a new social network from scratch is challenging— many exiles report feelings of social anxiety and shyness and become very socially withdrawn.

Effects of Past Persecution

Refugees and asylum seekers' experience of persecution in their country of origin may have included being caught up in war or bombings; being harassed, detained, and tortured by security forces; being targeted for rape and torture; and seeing others ill-treated or killed. Such experiences tend to change the way in which individuals feel about themselves, other people, and the world. Many exiles report symptoms commonly associated with past traumatic experiences including nightmares, intrusive thoughts, hypervigilance, and feelings of anxiety. Particular sounds, smells, or colors may remind them of past experiences of violence, which they may find difficult to tolerate.

Although such effects can lessen, particularly when people begin to feel safe in their new environment, they can cause a great deal of distress. Such symptoms are often tolerated until the effects of helplessness or lack of safety become overwhelming, leading the person to seek help. Given the focus of services on providing intervention targeted primarily at the trauma, the type of help offered can focus on the effects of persecution to the exclusion of other, often more difficult, issues. This is discussed further in the section on PTSD.

Rediscovering Meaning and Direction

An important challenge for all exiles is that of deciding in what direction they want their life to develop in the country of exile. Sometimes this challenge is masked by a focus on mourning the past, which prevents the person moving forward, particularly as embracing the challenge of building a new life creates great anxieties and questions. In countries like the United Kingdom, where asylum seekers wait for a decision, sometimes for years, the development of a future focus and planning can be seriously impeded. Again, socially supportive relationships help provide a space in which individuals can decide to engage in the ways they choose with their new environment. This helps transform the experience of exile such that it comes to be seen as a new challenge, one with potential for positive developments.

Issues for Specific Groups

Gender Issues

Displacement is difficult for all refugees, but women are often affected significantly as a result of their less powerful status in society (Ferron, Morgan, & O'Reilly, 2000). As single parents, or due to the difficulties affecting their partner's travel, immigration, employment, and so on, they may have to take on unfamiliar roles and responsibilities as head of household and breadwinner at a time when they lack the support of important family and community networks.

Many women are survivors of violence in the countries they have left, or passed through, which may have been sexual in nature. In addition, women living in institutions in the United Kingdom may experience sexual harassment (Hinton, 2001). The needs of women may not be identified or prioritized, particularly in cultures where men are traditionally the spokespeople. Women refugees tend to have fewer English language skills and may have limited literacy in their own language, further excluding them from the host society. As a result of these factors, family members may expect to interpret for their female relative, but this creates difficulties in truly hearing the women's voices. An independent professional interpreter is more likely to provide the requisite neutrality, and many women offered the choice prefer a female interpreter, particularly if they have a history of sexual violence.

Men can often feel the change in circumstances that comes with exile more acutely, finding their lower status and powerlessness difficult to deal with. Feelings of depression and anxiety are common (Burnett & Fassil, 2002), and there can be an increase in the use of alcohol or drugs and higher rates of smoking as a result of boredom and frustration. For many men, exile brings unemployment and difficulties in maintaining their professional identities, as overseas qualifications are often unrecognized in the United Kingdom. Women may find it easier to gain employment, which can lead to a change in the balance of power within the family and a risk of domestic violence (Burnett & Peel, 2001a). Men may be more reluctant to access health care and may require initiatives and outreach services, for example, health sessions in hostels or education centers targeted specifically at them.

Although many people prefer that the gender of both health worker and interpreter correspond with their own, it is our experience that this is by no means universal, and offering a choice of gender can be important. We do, however, also realize the limitations of services to be able to offer this.

Children and Their Families

As a result of the circumstances that forced them to flee, children may be living in a fragmented family, missing important members. Some children arrive with unfamiliar caregivers, or distant relatives, and some are unaccompanied minors who arrive in exile alone. Children may have experienced violence or torture themselves or may have witnessed members of their family being tortured. Some may have been abducted to become child soldiers and forced to commit violent acts. All of these different situations bring specific pressures on the child, but even if the family is whole, children may be living with parents who, under the pressures of torture, exile, and loss, are experiencing great difficulty in parenting. As a result, children may develop a deep-seated belief that adults are untrustworthy and that their parents are unable to protect them (Dawes, 1992).

Young people experience loss of family, friends, home, culture, and so on and may have difficulty making friends in an unfamiliar environment in which their usual supportive networks are absent. They may show developmental difficulties, appearing more mature when with their parents, perhaps taking a caring or parenting role themselves, while immature in other situations, for example, at school. Although they may experience, for example, anxiety, nightmares, and regressive behavior such as bed-wetting, withdrawal, or hyperactivity, it is important to note that very few need psychiatric treatment. The restabilization of their environment is the key intervention, providing multifaceted support that aims at creating as normal a life as possible, with a sense of security, promoting education and self-esteem and supporting parents (Melzak & Kasabova, 1999). Unaccompanied children are especially isolated and vulnerable and may need additional help and support.

Critically important to a child's health and development is the ability of parents or caregivers to ensure that the child's needs are being responded to, and support should be offered to both parents and children (Richman, 1998). An understanding of how the family usually functions, and how it functions under stress, can be very helpful in identifying what factors may assist parents in carrying out their parenting roles. Of particular importance is the quality and nature of the relationship between a child's parents, how this affects the child, and the quality of relationships between siblings. In addition, it is important to be aware of the diversity of family structures and differences in who is considered to be family and who is important to the child. When assessing family needs, the family's level of social integration and access to community resources should be considered, while bearing in mind that these may be limited for many refugee families and that coordinated multidisciplinary work may be required.

As families become more settled, parents often experience additional stresses caused by their worries about their children taking on the values of the host country and perhaps losing their cultural identity, language, and customs. Young people often describe their difficulties in terms of being "caught between two cultures," that of their parents and that of their peers, a situation that requires sophisticated switching from one culture to another (Dualeh, 2002). Although this creates psychological pressure on individuals, it also represents an adaptation to the difficulties of exile that can be potentially enriching.

Older People

Older people are not represented in large numbers among newly arrived refugees. They may face particular difficulties, and their needs are rarely prioritized in the planning and delivery of services. They have comparatively poor health and are more likely to have chronic health problems. They may be grieving for losses already sustained and may be fearful of death and burial in a foreign place. Isolation and loss of the usual support mechanisms may compound this. Short-term memory loss and so much change, with few familiar patterns and environments, may result in confusion and disorientation, and they may be less able to cope with activities of daily living (HelpAge International, 2000). Although it is true that families often care for dependent older people from refugee communities, the assumption that this will necessarily take place may mean that services are not offered to them, and they are left vulnerable.

Older people are often considered less able to acquire new language and skills, and education programs are rarely targeted toward them. In fact, older people possess a range of coping strategies and contributions, including indigenous knowledge and experience, traditional healing and crafts, preserving and transmitting cultural heritage, stories and activities, and an important role in the resolution of family or community conflict.

Torture and Organized Violence

Torture is "the intentional infliction of severe pain or suffering, whether physical or mental, upon a person in the custody or under the control of the accused" (Article 7.2 [e], [excerpt] of the Rome Statute of the International Criminal Court 1998).

Organized violence, of which torture is one form, is considered to have a political motive. Survivors of organized violence may have been ill treated by government agents such as the army, police, or security forces or rebel groups and local militias whose power allows them to act as quasi-governing bodies. Estimates of the proportion of asylum seekers who have been tortured vary from 5% to 30%, depending on the definition of torture used and their country of origin (Amnesty International, 2000). There is a multitude of different methods of torture (see Burnett & Fassil, 2002). Individuals commonly describe having been beaten, kicked, slapped, insulted, or threatened. Some methods of torture are typical of certain geographical areas: *falaka* in the Middle East and Turkey (beating on the soles of the feet) and in India the *ghotna* (a pole placed across the legs, on which the torturer stands). In other places, survivors report the use of cigarette burns or electric shocks to various parts of the body, while elsewhere the forcible extraction of fingernails or toenails or inflicting fractures are used as methods of torture. People may be forced to witness or hear others being tortured or may be required to torture others. Many survivors also report the use of mock executions, and in the experience of the authors, these can form a particularly harrowing part of their torture experience. The effects of torture are an accumulation of physical violence, the deprivations of detention, and the psychological consequences of both one's own and others' experiences (Burnett & Peel, 2001b), requiring careful assessment of the meaning that torture represents for the individual (Başoğlu & Paker, 1995; Burnett & Peel, 2001b).

Many people hesitate to admit to the experience of torture, which they may still find extremely frightening, shameful, and humiliating. Sensitive questioning should avoid any repetition of the experience of interrogation. Allowing the survivor to go at his or her own pace and disclose only as much information as feels comfortable for him or her is advisable. Sensitive information, such as that relating to sexual violation, may be hard to disclose to anyone, particularly to someone of a different gender. This can create difficulties in the asylum process, as individuals are often expected to disclose full details of their experiences to immigration officials using an adversarial style of questioning. Health workers may be in a better position to build the trust and empathy necessary to ask about experiences of torture or ill treatment.

As a result not only of the atrocities that people have experienced but also of their current situation in the United Kingdom, refugees may show symptoms of anxiety, depression, guilt, and shame (Burnett, 1999). These are common responses and need to be contextualized with regard to the very difficult situations that may have driven individuals into exile and the ongoing difficulties of living as a refugee.

In addition, in some cases, survivors may feel that their bodies have been irreparably damaged by the torture, and they may experience chronic pain. For some people, pain is linked to physical damage, but for others, investigations may not be able to link the pain to any ongoing pathology or lesion. They may be experiencing a dysfunction of the pain-signaling system set off by their original injuries (Wall, 1999). Making a link between pain and their original experience, explaining that exacerbation of pain in this context does not equate with damage to the body, and developing pain management strategies may be helpful (A. Williams, personal communication, 2003).

Although a minority of asylum seekers develop psychological problems or mental illness requiring psychological or psychiatric intervention, it is important not to overly medicalize distress related to injustice and political persecution.

Rape/Sexual Torture

Many female and some male asylum seekers have experienced sexual violence including rape (Burnett & Peel, 2001b), widely used in conflict situations to degrade and humiliate an enemy. Sexual violation may underlie persistent unexplained distress and anxiety but may be so difficult to discuss that the experience remains secret. In many countries, rape is taboo. Women may be shunned by their community and family and considered unfit to marry. Women who are pregnant as a result of rape may need support in coming to a decision about the pregnancy. Although some may subsequently decide to opt for a termination, others may wish to continue with the pregnancy, particularly if the baby is their only remaining family. However, following the birth, some mothers may reject a baby conceived as a result of rape (Kozaric-Kovacic, Folnegovic-Smalc, Skrinjaric, Szajnberg, & Marusic, 1995).

Men may have doubts about their sexuality and experience intense feelings of shame, and they are more likely not to report experiences of rape. Both men and women survivors commonly report sexual difficulties and may need reassurance about sexual function and fertility (Burnett & Fassil, 2002). Sexual health screening should be offered to exclude infection, including HIV. Sensitivity and choice of gender of interpreter and health worker are important (see section on gender issues).

Detention in the Country of Exile

Many countries, including Britain, detain asylum seekers in immigration detention centers. This is perhaps the most challenging experience faced by exiles, as they can be detained for periods of months at a time without knowing for how long they will be held or for what reasons. Pourgourides, Sashidharan, and Bracken (1996) interviewed detainees and found high levels of depression among the individuals they encountered.

For those who have been previously detained in their own country, the experience of subsequent detention can be devastating, evoking powerful memories of past persecution that may persist for a long time after release from detention (Burnett & Peel, 2001b; Summerfield et al., 1991).

ADAPTING SERVICES TO MEET THE SPECIFIC NEEDS OF ASYLUM SEEKERS AND REFUGEES

Addressing Language Needs Within Service Provision

Most people do not speak the language of the country of exile as their first language, and services need to address this issue as part of their integral development. There are a number of possible ways of addressing language needs within mainstream services, but given the limits on resources and on the availability of trained bilingual practitioners, it is likely that any developing service will need to use a combination of different methods to provide maximum access to the populations served.

One option is the use of interpreters and bilingual health advocates. A number of writers have noted ways in which an interpreter can affect therapeutic work in a positive way (Holder, 2002; Tribe, 1991). The presence of an interpreter can act as a form of reassurance for the client, setting him or her at ease, and interpreters can function as bicultural workers informing professionals about aspects of the culture and language of the client that they might otherwise miss. However, most interpreters have no specialist training in mental health work and little supervision or support in doing such interpreting work. Health workers also need training in how to work with interpreters.

An interpreter working in a counseling setting needs to be sensitive to the fact that the exchange of information is not necessarily the key aim, being aware, for example, of the importance of silence and of not intervening in some situations. The therapist may also find that the views of the interpreter may color the therapeutic rapport established if they are not adequately bracketed. In addition, in the case of clients who have left their country of origin following persecution, there is a need to be sensitive to possible fears related to the interpreter on political/ideological grounds (Jaffa, 1993).

A further option in some cases can be the use of bicultural workers who share language and/or culture with refugee clients. However, there is a need to ensure that services are not set up in such a way that workers are required to work beyond their competence in order to meet the needs of clients of the same language or cultural group. Specialist services should aim to empower clients, ensuring equality of service, rather than creating small ghettoized pockets in which undertrained and underresourced practitioners are obliged to meet the complete service needs for a particular population because colleagues in mainstream services are reluctant to do so. This can be addressed by making sure that all practitioners are linked into mainstream provision, with bicultural workers able to share their specific expertise, training, and information with their colleagues to improve provision overall.

Another option creatively used by asylum seekers and the professionals who work with them is the use of second language communication. This allows working direct without an interpreter but has other effects on the way in which language is used therapeutically. In many cases, asylum seekers choose to work in English as their second language, and they can experience this as very empowering (Holder, 2002). Other scenarios involve work in a language that is not the professional's first language or usual language of work. This can create a unique bond between the worker and the refugee as a result of this special shared way of communicating. There is a need to explore further the impact of these forms of mediated communication (Holder, 2002).

Adapting the Process of Assessment

Expressions of distress and the ways in which people cope differ both between and within cultures, making assessment and treatment of the psychological health problems of refugees complex. A longer period of assessment and an understanding of how the client makes sense and responds to psychological distress from within his or her culture may be needed. Risk of suicide, domestic violence, and concerns about child protection may need to be addressed, but cultural and religious taboos may impede discussing such issues.

Among those requiring mental health intervention, some may have had a history of psychological health problems and contact with mental health services prior to becoming refugees (Summerfield, 1996). However, cultural differences and difficulties with language and communication may increase the possibility of a misdiagnosis of mental illness. Questions used to diagnose mental illness may be unreliable when used in translation or cross-culturally, particularly as diagnostic concepts are often impossible to translate. Black and minority ethnic people in the United Kingdom have been shown to be disproportionately diagnosed with schizophrenia, sectioned under the Mental Health Act (Minnis, McMillan, Gillies, & Smith, 2001), and given high doses of antipsychotic drugs rather than talking therapy (Fernando, 1991).

The Use of the Diagnosis "Post-Traumatic Stress Disorder"

There has been a relatively recent growth in specialist trauma services, which focus on work with those diagnosed with PTSD (American Psychiatric Association, 1980). This reflects the opinion that specialist expertise is always necessary to work with effects of trauma. Refugees and asylum seekers, who often describe devastating experiences of persecution, are increasingly referred to such services. At the same time, there is a lively debate as to whether the diagnostic category of PTSD accurately describes the symptoms of refugees and asylum seekers.

PTSD is seen as a universal reaction to traumatic experiences, observable in both children and adults. It is further assumed to be "expressive of conflicts and disturbances happening within individual minds" (Bracken, 1998, p. 39). In this regard, it has variously been seen as a disorder of memory, arising because traumatic memories have been incompletely processed by the brain, or as one of meaning, arising because the trauma cannot be reconciled with the beliefs the individual held about the world prior to the traumatic experience. Thus the relationship envisaged is directly causal and linked to the kind of precipitative overwhelming events often described by asylum seekers as forms of persecution endured prior to flight. The closeness of this cause-and-effect relationship may be the explanation of why the word *trauma* is often used both for the impinging traumatic experience and for the reactions in the "traumatized" person. Understandably this can lead to some confusion and the assumption that anyone who undergoes a "traumatic experience" is necessarily "traumatized" whether they experience any changes in their functioning or not. Conversely, it should not be assumed that the absence of symptoms of distress makes the likelihood of past traumatic experiences less likely: PTSD is not a marker for torture (Summerfield, 1996).

There are a number of criticisms of the use of PTSD for asylum seekers and refugees. First, the PTSD/trauma model reflects a rather limited view of potential provokers. It was developed to relate to one-off shocking events: car crashes, personal attacks, witnessing a single incident of violence, and the like. Its usefulness is questionable where there is a background of ongoing persecution or multiple "traumatic" events. Although it could be seen as a "good fit" in the case of somebody surviving a car accident whose world is stable before the accident and could potentially return to this stability after the accident, the situation for refugees and asylum seekers is very different. Often their position in the United Kingdom could hardly be described as *post*-traumatic, as they face ongoing worries about their safety and a sense of helplessness. In such cases, the concept of stress may be more useful than that of trauma. It includes ongoing difficulties such as unemployment, poverty, homelessness, social inequality, and marginalization, which are often the reasons given by individuals for their despair, sleeplessness, headaches, or nightmares.

Second, the PTSD/trauma model seems to focus on too limited a range of reactions. In fact, there can be a wide range of responses to shocking events not exhausted by the three groupings of "symptoms" described earlier. There is also a wide area of overlap with other diagnostic categories such as depression and anxiety, which makes it difficult to determine the validity of PTSD as a separate entity of psychiatric disorder (Bracken, 1998). Many "symptoms" can be viewed as adaptive reactions to war or violence; for example, an exaggerated startle could be a learned adaptation to living under fire rather than a symptom of illness. Similarly, withdrawal from others and lack of trust may be lifesaving when living in situations of political violence. Although such reactions may need to be unlearned by people who have left such situations and want to live more appropriately in their new environments, they do not necessarily represent "mental illness."

Third, it has been argued that the PTSD/trauma model undermines traditional coping strategies, leading to increased helplessness and a greater dependence on outside aid in refugee communities (Giller, 1998). Despite the noted differences in cultural conceptions about responses to violence, treatment programs often seek to reproduce Western-style therapeutic settings in refugee camps or destroyed cities. This may be harmful in that financial resources are drained into inappropriate forms of intervention, running the risk of alienating survivors or replacing more empowering forms of coping with Western-style psychiatric intervention. The potentially key role played by traditional healers, shamans, and other important figures is considered in the following discussion.

Fourth, and perhaps most important, the PTSD/trauma model seems to ignore the role of the social world and of culture in shaping meaning (Summerfield, 1998). In a similar vein, some writers have argued that the focus on the medical aspects of trauma in PTSD ignores the political implications of traumatic experiences by creating an illness out of a normal reaction to violence. As Summerfield points out, turning recognizable distress following unbearable experiences into "illness" makes it a technical rather than a political problem. Technical (or medical) problems require technical solutions, solutions that can be presented as politically neutral, and avoid difficult questions about protection and justice, which might otherwise demand answers.

There is no apolitical way to work with asylum seekers, and several commentators have stressed the need for workers to accept the politics inherent in their work (Jones, 1998; Swartz & Levitt, 1989). Jones points out that "a tendency to focus on individual psychology while ignoring political and social context may appear to confer neutrality, but will have adverse psychological and political consequences" (Jones, 1998, p. 239). She remarks of clinicians that "one has a duty not just to be psychologically sensitive, but also politically literate and well informed; otherwise one cannot fully understand the problems, nor the most effective remedies for our patients. . . . Attempts to remain neutral in the face of genocide are likely to be construed as tacit collaboration with the aggressor and make any effective therapeutic work impossible" (Jones, 1998, p. 233).

Psychological Therapies and Counseling

Many asylum seekers in distress are referred for psychotherapy and counseling. Although it has been argued that this can represent a very effective form of intervention for refugees (van der Veer, 1998), counseling is often an unfamiliar concept for asylum seekers, who may be more accustomed to discussing problems with family and community than with a stranger. Issues related to confidentiality require careful explanation and monitoring, particularly in small communities.

Psychological meaning is contextual and socially shaped, and interventions for refugees should reflect this. Although psychotherapy and counseling can be appropriate, offering other options including traditional healing and practical social support may also be important. There is also a need to recognize the collective and sociopolitical realm of the experience of asylum seekers, rather than focusing only on the inner world of the person. In some senses, forms of therapy that focus on the use of "testimony" and on constructing preferred narratives may be of most use in work with asylum seekers. A psychologist describes the importance of "being a witness" and of "politicising rather than pathologising anger" (Webster, cited in Burnett & Fassil, 2002).

Cienfeugos and Monelli (1983), working in Chile, have described work involving political testimony with those who have experienced state repression and torture. For these authors, what is required for healing is not an individual "therapeutic" intervention but the collective recognition inherent in the giving of personal testimony before witnesses. Such a sociopolitical intervention is seen as closely linked to questions of collective justice and political protest, acting to counteract the silence often imposed and maintained by repressive authorities. The telling of the story of persecution, then, becomes a way of publicly informing society about the wrongs perpetrated against individuals, where the "illness" is firmly located within the political system of the society rather than the individual client (Martín-Baró, 1990). Such methods have also been employed to work with asylum seekers in countries of exile with some success (Agger & Jensen, 1990; Aron, 1992), suggesting the benefit of interventions that acknowledge people's need for justice, with regard to both past persecution and the political difficulties inherent in seeking asylum.

Some people are reluctant to talk about their experiences and find the focus on trauma counseling both painful and unhelpful. It is important to respect this, particularly when working with asylum seekers who remain in an unsafe situation. Issues of control and helplessness are key, and offering the choice to the individual about when and how he or she wishes to discuss experiences, if at all, is of vital importance. Gentle uncovering work taking place within a relationship of trust and alliance is most helpful, emphasizing the common humanity between the therapist and asylum seeker. Until the client's social situation is relatively stable and he or she is feeling "safe," it may be better to focus on improving the client's social situation and strengthening his or her coping skills to help with the distressing memories. Group work can offer support and reduce social isolation, whether groups focus on therapeutic aspects or have a more social and practical nature (Fischman & Ross, 1990).

Intervention at a More Holistic Level

The experience of exile is one of such enormous change that intervention in many areas may be both relevant and helpful. It is beneficial to take a holistic view of the needs of refugees in distress. Some of the areas that might be involved are outlined in the following sections.

Recognizing the Importance of Rebuilding the Social World

There is perhaps no greater challenge for exiles than mastering the change to their social world. Even for those who have fled with other close family members, the impact of exile is to shrink the social support networks that are available and to oblige the formation of new relationships without the usual security provided by an established set of close ties on which to build. For asylum seekers who arrive alone in the country of exile, the impact can be complete social isolation and a dependence on others randomly encountered with whom the refugee can communicate. Beiser (1993) notes that individual refugees without access to a "like-ethnic" community may develop rates of depression three to four times higher than others who can access such a resource. In fact, it has been argued that putting isolated individuals in contact with relevant refugee community organizations (RCOs) is one of the most important psychological interventions (Duke, 1996).

RCOs often provide advice in vital areas such as immigration, housing, and benefits as well as social support, interpreting, and translation to asylum seekers and refugees. Some work with specific communities (from particular countries or ethnic groups), and others with subsections of the community such as women or those with disabilities. Educational activities may be offered, including mother-tongue classes and cultural activities for children and English or computer classes for adults. Such activities can be key resources in reducing social isolation, combating helplessness, and improving skills.

Further evidence of the importance of social support in exile is provided by research carried out with survivors of torture. Başoğlu, Paker, Ozmen, Tasdemir, & Sahin (1994) studied Turkish activists with a history of torture. Their research revealed that the secondary consequences of their experiences—on family, social, and economic life—were more important predictors of later well-being than was the experience of torture alone. Similarly, Gorst-Unsworth and Goldenberg (1998) focused on Iraqi torture survivors, again finding low social support to be a better predictor of long-term difficulty and symptom prevalence than severity of torture. This suggests that social support can play a crucial mediating role, buffering individuals from the full impact of experiences of persecution and ongoing difficulty. This fits the wealth of research on depression and shows the way in which high-quality social support can protect against depressive onset (Brown & Harris, 1978; Harris, 1992).

Given this situation, interventions that aim to address the isolation often faced by asylum seekers in the country of exile are important. Recent work from Scotland emphasizes the need for both enabling contact with family and coethnic networks and linking with the indigenous population (Ager, Malcolm, Sadollah, & O'May, 2002). Befriending schemes run by the voluntary sector may help to bridge the gap and forge links between refugees and the local community.

Enabling Clients

Given the ways in which the system faced by asylum seekers induces feelings of helplessness, service providers can play a vital role in challenging the situation. It is important not just to avoid compounding feelings of helplessness but to actively challenge beliefs of personal inadequacy when expressed by asylum seekers and to point out their strengths and resources, evidenced by the fact that they have survived the difficulties they have experienced and are continuing to cope in exile. It is unhelpful to treat refugees and asylum seekers as victims or to cast them in a permanent "sick role." Workers need to empower them to do things for themselves and to avoid being drawn into the role of rescuer.

Drawing from the work of Seligman and others (Mikulincer, 1994; Peterson, Maier, & Seligman, 1993; Seligman, 1975), workers might seek to explore with asylum-seeking clients the extent to which events are actually within their power. This may go some way in correcting generalized perceptions of helplessness and begin to reinvigorate a sense of initiative and resourcefulness. Although the decisions of the immigration authorities remain outside their control, they can be encouraged to make choices, engage in activities, and participate as fully as possible in the host society. An emphasis on coping skills is likely to be helpful (Mikulincer, 1994).

Other Forms of Therapy and Healing

Medication

Although some mental health conditions are amenable to medication, prescribing may not help many of the problems that refugees experience. Alternatives to drugs should be considered, such as massage for pain. Antidepressants may be helpful for clinical depression, if used in conjunction with practical and social support. If prescribing, one should ensure that information about the drug and possible side effects are clearly understood.

Arts Therapies, Creative Arts, and Complementary Therapies

Arts therapies (art, dance movement, drama, and music) offer a variety of different channels of communication in which to engage with psychological issues. Therapists who have a professional training may combine one or more psychological frameworks (e.g., psychodynamic, systemic) with the creative dimension of their art form. Creative therapies have been shown to offer benefits to people who have lived through situations of political conflict, in conjunction with practical support and health care.

In addition, other art-related projects, including acting, music, writing, and poetry, may be helpful in combating isolation, communicating meaning, enhancing self-esteem, and strengthening identity and belonging (Dokter, 1998).

Therapies such as massage, physiotherapy, osteopathy, relaxation, and herbal medicine may lessen chronic pain, anxiety, insomnia, stress, and some of the physical and psychological effects of torture.

Spiritual Support

Religion is important for many refugees, providing much sustenance and strength as well as a meaning framework in which to place their experiences: "It's very hard to see your whole life turned upside down without it being your fault. I honestly can say we couldn't cope with the change of life if it wasn't for faith in God, as being a Muslim you are preparing for any difficulty that arises in your life and have to be resilient, accept it and move on" (Hassan Farah & Smith, 1999). Religious groups and communities often provide emotional and practical support, as well as a new social network with a common viewpoint. Spiritual or community leaders may act as coworkers in ways designed to facilitate social support and the rediscovery of meaning in exile.

Traditional Healing

Eisenbruch (1984, 1990) has argued that traditional healing may be the most appropriate way of dealing with the effects of exile. This conclusion is supported by the work of Peltzer (1997), who describes examples of the use of traditional healing and religious practice in a number of different cultures, showing the use made of cultural meanings to address distress. Littlewood (1992) sees the effectiveness of many traditional healing practices as lying in the fact that both healer and healed share the deep beliefs and "myths" of a common culture through which life is experienced and which contain notions of identity, personality, and action. The person visiting the healer finds that the healer defines his or her difficulties in terms of these myths and makes interventions within this belief context.

The situation is complex, however, and within any society there will be differing conceptions of what form of intervention is appropriate after violence. Littlewood (1992) points out that offering traditional healing as it was used in the country of origin may not be helpful to a client in exile, because his cultural view is constantly changing and meanings are being negotiated anew. Eisenbruch also acknowledges this:

> Individual patients are usually unaware of the details of their "great tradition," whereas the well-intentioned Western observer, having read the classic texts and surveys of Eastern medical philosophy, may superimpose his own construction of Eastern beliefs upon his pre-existent Western medical viewpoint. This may well distort, rather than clarify, his view of the patient's condition. I would therefore argue strongly for the value of meticulously exploring what the patient thinks to be the explanation of his/her symptoms. (1983, p. 325)

Once again, this stresses the value of truly hearing refugees and asylum seekers and understanding the meaning of their experiences to them before attempting any intervention.

Service Provision for Refugee Children

As stated earlier, it is important to restabilize the environment of the child in exile, which means that the most therapeutic chain of events for a young refugee, whether living with familiar caregivers or strangers, probably is to become part of the local school community, to learn, and to make friends (Melzak & Kasabova, 1999). Schools need to be aware of their vital role in this and the dangers that bullying and racial abuse at school can pose to the stabilization of the child's environment.

Most refugee children have to live with enormous uncertainty, and this can lead to noticeable behavioral and emotional difficulties and distress. These children may benefit from supportive listening in schools and both individual relationships with staff and guided group relationships with other refugee children. Enabling young people to come together in a group to discuss their situation with peers who understand the impact of war and conflict, multiple loss, and the difficulties of adjusting to life in a new environment with family pressures can be helpful. It is important to take a multidisciplinary, interagency approach, where all those who have responsibility for different aspects of the child's welfare work in partnership, and refugee community organizations can often be usefully included in this. Supplementary mother-tongue schools can also play an important role in encouraging young refugees to connect with the cultural identity of the country they have left.

Interventions need to be geared toward the enhancement of resilience and protective factors, as well as allowing for elements that permit the child to "belong" to both the local and refugee cultural communities. This is often facilitated by a special relationship with an adult caregiver, ideally a parent but not necessarily. Individual children need time and space to think about their feelings and experiences and to play and express feelings in a creative way through art, drama, music, storytelling, and so forth. In addition, involving children in decision making enhances their ability to make active choices.

Service Provision for Survivors of Organized Violence, Torture, and Sexual Torture

For many survivors of torture, focusing on reestablishing a settled life, as far as this is possible, is a key factor in the promotion of mental health. Most people would rather be active, independent citizens than dependent on the receipt of benefits and support, and efforts to encourage independence act against feelings of helplessness and encourage mastery. By definition, torture survivors have *survived,* often against huge odds, and their resilience may be a strength to be tapped into.

In providing services to survivors of torture, there is an essential need for adequate time, trusting relationships, and, if language is not shared, a trained interpreter who is not a family member or friend. It is important to provide consistent and reliable relationships in order to enhance trust, and steps should be taken to ensure the use of the same interpreter from meeting to meeting as well as avoiding unannounced changes in the therapeutic worker. Systems in which health workers change frequently on rotation, for example, require careful explanation to refugee patients as well as adequate time to prepare for the change of worker. As stated earlier, when prescribing medication, it is important to consider whether the medication is really appropriate given the sociopolitical nature of the causes of distress. However, some symptoms may appear to require specialist intervention, such as consistent failure to function properly, frequently expressed suicidal ideas or plans, marked social withdrawal, self-neglect, and behavior or talk that is seen as abnormal or strange within the person's own culture and aggression toward others (Shackman, Gorst-Unsworth, & Summerfield, 1996). Although on the whole medication should be used judiciously, antidepressants may be helpful for those with symptoms of depression. However, it is crucial to keep in mind a wide range of potential interventions including talking therapies, complementary therapies, and community, religious, spiritual, and creative links, as discussed earlier. Supportive listening can be experienced as very helpful (van der Veer, 1998), and the role of social support as a protective factor for survivors of torture is also well documented (Gorst-Unsworth & Goldenberg, 1998).

In some places, services have been established that focus specifically on the needs of survivors of torture. Their work should complement but not replace mainstream services. The latter should not consider that this work is totally outside their remit or responsibility. Specialist services can provide support and training for others to engage in this work.

*Service Provision for Those
Detained in the Country of Exile*

Although providers have often claimed that immigration detainees receive support and treatment for mental health problems in-house at immigration detention centers, there is little to suggest that such support is of high quality. Health services are often nurse led, and although they may have regular input from a general practitioner and the capacity to refer outside to specialist services (Shephard, 2002), reports suggest that many mental health problems may go unaddressed (Pourgourides et al., 1996).

Aspects of the detention system also make it difficult to provide consistent health care, particularly if there is limited access to interpreters and a high turnover of detainees. Shephard (2002) notes the difficulties of providing psychological support within this environment, and it is debatable whether attempting to take a neutral stance and focusing on psychological distress is possible when detainees are in situations of acute insecurity with little sense of when they might be released. It places mental health professionals in a very difficult position, as they may be seen as a tool of the authorities who are detaining the asylum seekers, making it hard for the professionals to focus on the well-being of the detainees with whom they work. It could also be argued that this has broader validity to include those waiting for a decision on their asylum claim.

Retaining Community Focus by Involvement and Evaluation

A final point that is worth stressing when developing services is the need to involve refugees themselves. This may be a question of user involvement but can also be about consultation with RCOs. Several writers have stressed the importance of a thorough needs assessment when working with refugees and asylum seekers (Harris & Maxwell, 2000). The ongoing involvement of RCOs allows them to influence the development of the work and its emphases by involvement in steering groups; frequent coworking, training, and awareness raising; and evaluation.

Projects working with asylum seekers are often overstretched and underresourced, and there can be a tendency to neglect areas such as community linking, needs assessment, and evaluation. This is a serious error, in that projects need to demonstrate the effectiveness of working models with this client group, particularly if they lack funds or resources. Time spent on evaluation or on building links with communities is rarely wasted. Evaluation methods are most effective when they combine elements of both internal evaluation (an examination by workers from within the project of their working practices and limitations) and external evaluation (using a consultant evaluator from outside the organization to look at the effectiveness of methods employed and feedback from referrers, users, communities, and link organizations).

Overall, it is important to focus on improving services, so that both refugees and the host population benefit. This may diminish the misperception that refugees receive superior services, which can result in hostility and resentment. Although there may be a need for some specialist services, particularly in the short term to facilitate access to services, it is important to emphasize integration and the mainstreaming of psychological support services for asylum seekers and refugees.

THE EFFECTS OF THE ASYLUM SYSTEM ON SERVICE PROVISION

The impact of the asylum system in any given host country on what can be offered to asylum seekers should be considered. Throughout this chapter, reference is made to the British system, but providers in other countries need to be aware of the impact of the system in their respective countries and how this limits what can be achieved by mental health workers, social workers, and advocates.

The Limitations of What Can Be Achieved in the Current Climate

Given the difficulties experienced by asylum seekers in having their status recognized and the negative impact of the immigration system and consequent media coverage on psychological well-being, mental health workers need to be prepared for limitations in what they are able to offer to asylum-seeking clients. In many cases, the key mental health intervention that occurs is the granting of leave to stay by the immigration authorities, guaranteeing safety, allowing the person to become active in challenging his or her helplessness and developing a new life, and freeing him or her to work in a targeted way on any symptoms remaining. Although individuals seeking asylum remain inherently insecure, it can be difficult to work on addressing either past difficulties or the future. It is as if the situation leaves the individual trapped in an ongoing present, where the past represents something

still too frightening, difficult, or painful to approach while hopes for the future feel premature and risky.

The Importance of Testimony and the Question of Credibility

Given that so much of the difficulty experienced by asylum seekers is linked to their status and to ongoing legal insecurity, it is perhaps not surprising that testimony can play an important role in therapeutic work. In addition, the use of testimony can assist individuals to represent themselves more effectively, articulating their past experiences in a way that can be heard more clearly by the immigration authorities. This is in many ways a political act, seeking to give the power of self-definition back to individuals who may have been robbed of such power both by the circumstances that sent them into exile and by the treatment received from immigration authorities.

Professionals can intervene usefully by writing in support of asylum applications, helping to present their knowledge of the client's story and symptoms so that the client can be genuinely heard by the authorities (Harris, 2002). It should be noted, however, that when people repeatedly recount their experiences, discrepancies between accounts will occur, and such inconsistencies do not necessarily indicate a lack of credibility (Cohen, 2001; Herlihy, Scragg, & Turner, 2002).

A powerful negative discourse about asylum seekers pervades much current media coverage and colors the political landscape. Professionals working with this client group are likely to experience the effects of this and require help in monitoring its impact. Professionals need to expend great care in questioning their assumptions and the ongoing process of their involvement in order to determine the influence of dominant narratives in their ways of working with and hearing clients (Harris, 2002).

Issues of belief and disbelief may be particularly salient, entering into any helping relationship established with asylum-seeking clients (Harris, 2002). Professionals may find that they are drawn to assessing their clients' material as "genuine" or "bogus" in a way that they would be unlikely to do with members of another client group. This is enhanced by the key role that mental health professionals may have in writing reports for asylum cases, where their status can allow the client to be heard more effectively by the immigration authorities. It should not be the role of the health or mental health worker to determine the credibility of the asylum seeker's story, although we can often be pressured to do so.

Supervision, peer support, political action, and validation for practitioners have all been suggested as protective mechanisms for guarding against the corruption of their values and their therapeutic approaches by the insidious nature of the political discourse. Workers can fulfill a key role with asylum-seeking clients by forming a genuine relationship that leaves room for the whole person, becoming a witness to the effects of injustice, recognizing the need for social support and validation, and helping to empower clients to begin building new lives in exile.

Racism, Discrimination, and Hostility

Agencies responsible for supporting asylum seekers and refugees should be aware of their potential vulnerability to racism and ensure that effective policies are in place to deal with any incidents. Refugees face racist taunts, threats, arson, bullying at school, and physical violence, which has in some instances resulted in death. The prevalence of racist attacks and harassment should be considered when deciding whether particular locations are suitable for the placement of asylum seekers.

People who are suffering racial harassment need support and advocacy in order to report the incident to the police and to access protection. Racist behavior needs to be challenged by those with the power to do so, including those in the medical and legal professions.

Summary

In this chapter, we have aimed to address the important issues affecting the psychological well-being of asylum seekers and refugees and have suggested ways of enhancing this. Caution is advocated in pathologizing what may be natural expressions of grief and distress toward highly abnormal experiences. In saying this, we are not diminishing these feelings, but rather suggesting that practical and psychosocial support may be more effective in both prevention and care than a more medicalized model. In particular we emphasize the importance of treating people as individuals; taking into account their cultural beliefs, views, and practices; and reflecting these in developing support.

References

Ager, A., Malcolm, M., Sadollah, S., & O'May, F. (2002). Community contact and mental health amongst socially isolated refugees in Edinburgh. *Journal of Refugee Studies, 15*(1), 73–80.

Agger, I., & Jensen, S. B. (1990). Testimony as ritual and evidence in psychotherapy for refugees. *Journal of Traumatic Stress, 3*(1), 115–130.

American Psychiatric Association. (1980). *Diagnostic and statistical manual of mental disorders* (3rd ed.). Washington, DC: Author.

Amnesty International. (2000). *Annual report 2000.* London: Author.

Aron, A. (1992). Testimonio, a bridge between psychotherapy and sociotherapy. *Women & Therapy, 13,* 173–189.

Asylum Aid. (1995). *No reason at all: Home office decisions on asylum claims.* London: Author.

Asylum Aid. (1999). *Still no reason at all: Home office decisions on asylum claims.* London: Author.

Başoğlu, M., & Paker, M. (1995). Severity of trauma as predictor of long-term psychological status in survivors of torture. *Journal of Anxiety Disorders, 9,* 339–350.

Başoğlu, M., Paker, M., Ozmen, E., Tasdemir, O., & Sahin, D. (1994). Factors related to long-term traumatic stress in survivors of torture in Turkey. *Journal of the American Medical Association, 272,* 357–363.

Beiser, M. (1993). Mental health of immigrants in Canada. In V. Robinson (Ed.), *The international refugee crisis: British and Canadian responses* (pp. 213–227). London: Macmillan.

Bracken, P. (1998). Hidden agendas: Deconstructing post traumatic stress disorder. In P. J. Bracken & C. Petty (Eds.), *Rethinking the trauma of war* (pp. 38–59). London: Free Association Books.

Brown, G. W., & Harris, T. O. (1978). *Social origins of depression: A study of psychiatric disorder in women.* London: Tavistock Publications.

Burnett, A. (1999). *Guidelines for healthworkers providing care for Kosovan refugees*. London: Medical Foundation for the Care of Victims of Torture/Department of Health.

Burnett, A., & Fassil, Y. (2002). *Meeting the health needs of refugees and asylum seekers in the UK: An information and resource pack for healthworkers*. London: Directorate of Health and Social Care, Department of Health. Retrieved February 4, 2004, from http://www.london.nhs.uk/newsmedia/publications/Asylum_Refugee.pdf

Burnett, A., & Peel, M. (2001a). The health needs of asylum seekers and refugees. *BMJ, 322,* 544–547.

Burnett, A., & Peel, M. (2001b). The health of survivors of torture and organised violence. *BMJ, 322,* 606–609.

Cienfeugos, A. J., & Monelli, C. (1983). The testimony of political repression as a therapeutic instrument. *American Journal of Orthopsychiatry, 53*(1), 43–51.

Cohen, J. (2001). Errors of recall and credibility: Can omissions and discrepancies in successive statements reasonably be said to undermine credibility of testimony? *Medico-Legal Journal, 69*(1), 25–34.

Dawes, A. (1992, January). *Psychological discourse about political violence and its effects on children*. Paper prepared for the meeting on the Mental Health of Refugee Children Exposed to Violent Environments, Refugee Studies Programme, University of Oxford.

Dokter, D. (1998). *Arts therapists, refugees and migrants: Reaching across borders*. London: Jessica Kingsley.

Dualeh, M. (2002, April). *Putting the past behind us, yet living with its after effects*. Paper given at the Working With Somali Families conference, London.

Duke, K. (1996). The resettlement experiences of refugees in the UK: Main findings from an interview study. *New Community, 22*(3), 461–478.

Eisenbruch, M. (1983). "Wind illness" or somatic depression? A case study in psychiatric anthropology. *British Journal of Psychiatry, 143,* 323–326.

Eisenbruch, M. (1984). Cross cultural aspects of bereavement 1: A conceptual framework for comparative analysis. *Culture, Medicine and Psychiatry, 8,* 283–309.

Eisenbruch, M. (1990). From post traumatic stress disorder to cultural bereavement: Diagnosis of Southeast Asian refugees. *Social Science and Medicine, 33,* 673–680.

Fernando, S. (1991). *Mental health, race and culture*. London: Macmillan Press.

Ferron, S., Morgan, J., & O'Reilly, M. (2000). *Hygiene promotion: A practical manual for relief and development*. London: Care International and Intermediate Technology Publications.

Fischman, Y., & Ross, J. (1990). Group treatment of exiled survivors of torture. *American Journal of Orthopsychiatry, 60*(1), 135–142.

Giller, J. (1998). Caring for victims of torture in Uganda: Some personal reflections. In P. J. Bracken & C. Petty (Eds.), *Rethinking the trauma of war* (pp. 128–145). London: Free Association Books.

Gorst-Unsworth, C., & Goldenberg, E. (1998). Psychological sequelae of torture and organised violence suffered by refugees from Iraq, trauma related factors compared with social factors in exile. *British Journal of Psychiatry, 172,* 90–94.

Harris, K. (2002). The importance of developing a "culture of belief" amongst counselling psychologists working with asylum seekers. *Counselling Psychology Review, 17*(1), 4–13.

Harris, K., & Maxwell, C. (2000). A needs assessment in a refugee mental health project in North East London: Extending the counselling model to community support. *Medicine, Conflict and Survival, 16,* 201–215.

Harris, T. (1992). Some reflections of the process of social support and the nature of unsupportive behaviours. In H. O. F. Veiel & U. Baumann (Eds.), *The meaning and measurement of social support* (pp. 171–189). Washington, DC: Hemisphere.

Hassan Farah, L., & Smith, M. (1999). *Somalis in London*. London: Bow Family Centre.

HelpAge International. (2000). *Older people in disaster and humanitarian crises: Guidelines for best practice*. London: Author.

Herlihy, J., Scragg, P., & Turner, S. (2002). Discrepancies in autobiographical memories— Implications for the assessment of asylum seekers: Repeated interview study. *British Medical Journal, 324,* 324–327.

Hinton, T. (2001). *Working with refugees and asylum seekers in Lambeth, Southwark and Lewisham*. London: Health Action for Homeless People and Crisis.

Holder, R. (2002). *The impact of mediated communication on psychological therapy with refugees and asylum seekers: Practitioners' experience.* Unpublished dissertation, submitted in partial fulfillment of the MSc in Counselling Psychology, Department of Psychology, City University, London.

Jaffa, T. (1993). Therapy with families who have experienced torture. In J. P. Wilson & B. Raphael (Eds.), *International handbook of traumatic stress syndromes* (pp. 715–723). New York: Plenum Press.

Jones, L. (1998). The question of political neutrality when doing psychosocial work with survivors of political violence. *International Review of Psychiatry, 10,* 239–247.

Jones, V. (2002, June). *Do services fit people or do people fit services?* Paper presented at Borderline Refugee Mental Health Conference, London.

Kozaric-Kovacic, D., Folnegovic-Smalc, V., Skrinjaric, J., Szajnberg, N. M., & Marusic, A. (1995). Rape, torture, and traumatization of Bosnian and Croatian women: Psychological sequelae. *American Journal of Orthopsychiatry, 65*(3), 428–433.

Littlewood, R. (1992). How universal is something we call therapy? In J. Kareem & R. Littlewood (Eds.), *Intercultural therapy: Themes, interpretations and practice* (pp. 38–56). Oxford, UK: Blackwell Scientific Publications.

Martín-Baró, I. (1990, January 14). The mental wounds of the violence in El Salvador. *The Guardian.* (Reproduced from *The International Journal of Mental Health*)

Melzak, S. & Kasabova, S. (1999). *Working with children and adolescents from Kosovo.* London: Medical Foundation for the Care of Victims of Torture.

Mikulincer, M. (1994). *Human learned helplessness: A coping perspective.* New York: Plenum Press.

Minnis, H., McMillan, A., Gillies, M., & Smith, S. (2001). Racial stereotyping: A survey of psychiatrists in the United Kingdom. *British Medical Journal, 323,* 905–906.

Peltzer, K. (1997). The role of religion in counselling victims of organised violence. *The Journal of Transpersonal Psychology, 29*(1), 13–29.

Peterson, C., Maier, S. F., & Seligman, M. E. P. (1993). *Learned helplessness: A theory for the age of personal control.* Oxford: Oxford University Press.

Pourgourides, C., Sashidharan, S., & Bracken, P. (1996). *A second exile: The mental health implications of detention of asylum seekers in the United Kingdom.* Birmingham, UK: University of Birmingham & North Birmingham Health Authority.

Punamäki, R. L. (1992, January). *"Natural healing processes" and experiences of political violence.* Paper given at the Mental Health of Children Exposed to Violent Environments conference, Refugees Studies Programme, Oxford, UK.

Refugee Council Web Site. (n.d.). Retrieved October 20, 2003, from http://refugeecouncil.org.uk/news/myths/myth001.htm

Richman, N. (1998). *In the midst of the whirlwind: A manual for helping refugee children.* Stoke on Trent: Trentham Books.

Rome Statute of the International Criminal Court 1998, Article 7.2 (e).

Seligman, M. E. P. (1975). *Helplessness: On depression, development and death.* New York: W. H. Freeman and Co.

Shackman, J., Gorst-Unsworth, C., & Summerfield, D. (1996). *Common experiences after trauma.* London: Medical Foundation for the Care of Victims of Torture.

Shephard, A. (2002, September). *Healthcare services in immigration centres.* Paper presented at the Healthcare of Asylum Seekers and Refugees—Accessible and Appropriate Service Provision conference, London.

Silver, R. L., & Wortman, C. B. (1980). Coping with undesirable life events. In J. Garber and M. E. P. Seligman (Eds.), *Human helplessness: Theory and applications* (pp. 279–340). New York: Academic Press.

Summerfield, D. (1996). *The impact of war and atrocity on civilian populations: Basic principles of NGO interventions and a critique of psychosocial trauma projects.* London: Relief and Rehabilitation Network, Overseas Development Institute.

Summerfield, D. (1998). The social experience of war and some issues for the humanitarian field. In P. J. Bracken & C. Petty (Eds.), *Rethinking the trauma of war* (pp. 9–37). London: Free Association Books.

Summerfield, D., Gorst-Unsworth, C., Bracken, P., Tonge, V., Forrest, D., & Hinshelwood, G. (1991). Detention in the UK of tortured refugees. *Lancet, 338,* 58.

Swartz, L., & Levitt, A. (1989). Political repression and the children in South Africa: The social construction of damaging effects. *Social Science and Medicine, 28*(7), 741–750.

Tribe, R. (1991, November). *Bicultural workers, bridging the gap or damming the flow?* Paper presented at the Second International Conference of Centres, Institutions and Individuals Concerned With the Care of Victims of Organised Violence: Health, Political Repression and Human Rights.

United Nations. (1951). *United Nations convention on the status of refugees.* Geneva: Author.

United Nations High Commissioner for Refugees Web Site (n.d.). Retrieved October 10, 2003, from http://www.unhcr.ch/cgi-bin/texis/vtx/

van der Veer, G. (1998). *Counselling and therapy with refugees: Psychological problems of victims of war, torture and repression.* Chichester: John Wiley and Sons.

Wall, P. (1999). *Pain: The science of suffering.* London: Weidenfeld and Nicolson.

15

THE CHALLENGES OF AND POTENTIAL SOLUTIONS TO THE PROBLEM OF THE TRAFFICKING OF WOMEN AND CHILDREN

An Overview

SUTAPA BASU

University of Washington

This chapter will begin with an introduction and background to the trafficking of women and the matchmaking industry, specifically in the United States. Current U.S. trafficking policy and its implementation will also be discussed. In addition, information on how best to assist women survivors of trafficking via policy expansion and coordination of service organizations, authorities, and government will be included.

AN OVERVIEW OF TRAFFICKING

The Trafficking Network

Simply put, human trafficking, or modern slavery, is the international and domestic transport of human beings solely for the purpose of their exploitation. Though trafficking affects both men and women, the vast majority of trafficking victims are women and children under the age of 24.[1] Most often, the countries of origin of trafficking victims, commonly known as sending countries, are economically troubled areas, including Asia, Africa, Eastern Europe, the former Soviet Union, and Latin America. Traffickers of these women and girls exploit them physically for domestic labor or sexual services, while taking advantage of lax laws and corrupt officials surrounding the business of human trafficking. A number of human rights organizations work to raise awareness about the issue of human trafficking. Governments are also beginning to acknowledge that trafficking is a human rights violation and are starting to create laws to protect survivors and raise awareness among potential victims.

As borders become increasingly permeable and cyberspace continually facilitates human availability, the scale of the international trade in people has skyrocketed. Trafficking in women and girls is now the third-largest grossing sector of international organized crime, surpassed only by drugs and arms.[2] According to the United Nations' calculations, the profits of the trafficking industry may have even surpassed the trade in illegal weapons, generating profits of more than 9 billion dollars annually.[3] Worldwide, at least 4 million people are victims of human trafficking each year, or one person every 30 seconds.[4] It is estimated that "every ten minutes another human being is trafficked to the United States for slavery—a total of 45–50,000 women and children each year," not including men.[5]

A common scenario starts with a naive and desperate young woman attempting to escape bleak employment prospects at home. She receives offers for good wages and "legitimate" work abroad as a waitress, dancer, or secretary from traffickers posing as "employment brokers." Instead, she is unknowingly selling herself into virtual slavery. She will end up working as a domestic servant, or in a sweatshop, or in the sex industry. She will be forced to pay off exorbitant travel debts to her traffickers for smuggling her into the country. Like most other trafficked women, she might find herself confined to her place of employment, forced to work almost continually, and denied wages. For example, for years a complex trafficking ring "lured young women from Asia with the promise of a better life in the United States, only to make them virtual sex slaves in brothels in Seattle and Portland."[6] "Brokers" would sell temporary or student visas to young women seeking better economic opportunities. Upon arrival in the United States, the women were forced into prostitution in order to repay their "debt."[7] In September 2002, after a 2-year investigation, the Federal Bureau of Investigation broke up the ring.

Though many women enter the trade voluntarily, too often they are unaware of the nature of the work they will be performing. In a recent study of child prostitutes in Thailand, "several girls who said they knew they would be working as 'prostitutes' thought that the term meant wearing Western clothes and working in a restaurant."[8] Another scenario is women's participation in the flourishing matchmaking industry. This common and socially accepted form of trade in women is not considered by many governments to be trafficking, despite the fact that women are regarded as commodities and that the system is widely abused.

One of the main causes of the current upsurge in trafficked women is global economic liberalization. It has exacerbated the economic and social stability of women worldwide, especially in developing countries. The U.N. Development Fund for Women describes how women are affected by globalization affected:

> By definition, trade liberalization seeks to create a level playing field on which economies at different levels of development can compete by reducing tariff and non-tariff barriers. However, longstanding power imbalances between nations and among men and women have translated into uneven patterns of growth and heightened inequality. Women—especially poor women—have unequal access to resources such as land, credit and education. This in turn makes them the least able to benefit from trade liberalization and the most likely to suffer from the adjustment costs of trade reform and economic restructuring.[9]

The inability of women in their home or sending countries to find economic advancement opportunities with which to support their families is another cause of their complicity in the trafficking industry. The native countries of most of these women are usually those in economic and social transition, suffering from high levels of poverty and unemployment. *Many times this has little to do with educational level, as 36.8% of Philippine women who are involved in reproductive labor or in the "tourist industry" have obtained college degrees.* For example, studies show that between 70% and 80% of the unemployed workers in the Russian Federation, a major source of trafficking victims, are women.[10] Elina Penttinen, in her paper "Globalization, Bio-power and Trafficking in Women," highlighted that women who can no longer support themselves or their family join the global sex trade, "tak[ing] on the opportunity of international prostitution and thus using their bodies as means for exchange, rather than remain in a place where there are few prospects of making a living."[11] Penttinen contends that "this can be seen as a form of structural violence taking place, that in a situation of impoverishment and unemployment women are 'forced to choose' their own sexual exploitation."

The ways in which women and girls fall victim to trafficking vary in relation to many factors, including nationality, educational background, and employment circumstances in their country of origin. Although many women are enticed by misleading or blatantly false advertisements, others are "bonded" or sold into indentured servitude by family members for financial gain. Some families are unaware of the nature of the service, clinging to the potential for riches gained through legitimate employment.

Although it is a commonly held belief that all trafficked women are forced into the sex trade, this is not wholly true: in actuality, domestic servitude is an equally common type of slavery for these women. "Indentured servitude is in part spawned by the high cost of gaining entry into the United States, with trafficked persons from sending countries often paying up to $50,000 to smugglers. Since few workers from developing nations can afford such fees, immigrants will often agree to work off their smuggling debts over a period of years."[12] In a case that exemplifies this trend, Saeieo, a 59-year-old cook from Thailand, was brought into the United States and enslaved for 5 years by Supawan Veerapol, a wealthy Thai restaurant owner in Los Angeles. She was forced to work from 12 to 20 hours a day, 7 days a week, made to sleep on the floor of a closet-size utility room where Veerapol kept her washer and dryer, and denied any medical care. It was not until her employer was tried and convicted on charges of indentured servitude in 1998 that she was finally freed.

Despite increasing global attempts to monitor and curb the trafficking trade, authorities have been largely ineffective in dealing with the problem. According to Human Rights Watch, "Although trafficking in women and girls has become a lucrative and expanding cross-border trade, it routinely escapes effective national and international sanctions."[13] Also, current laws regard trafficking largely as a migration issue and do nothing to help trafficking victims. The legal context of migration cannot give full justice to the nebulous crime of trafficking. Traffickers are not properly punished for their crime.

An alarming example is the case of Lakireddy Bali Reddy from Berkeley, California. One of the Bay Area's wealthiest landlords, with a fortune estimated at $70 million, he was able to abuse the law and helpless immigrants.[14] Between 1986 and 2000, Reddy and his family members smuggled poverty-stricken girls, men, and women from their hometown of Velavadam, Andhra Pradesh, India.[15] Upon arrival, the victims worked virtually as slaves or indentured servants in Reddy's buildings and restaurants. In addition to their domestic work, the teenage girls, some as young as 13 years old, were forced to sexually service Reddy. Reddy was caught in 1999 when authorities discovered two unconscious Indian girls, brought to the United States for labor and sex, in his apartment building suffering from carbon monoxide poisoning.[16] Tragically, 17-year-old Chanti Prattipati, one of the two girls, died. It was later discovered that she was in the early stages of pregnancy with Reddy's child. In 2001, Lakireddy Bali Reddy was sentenced to 8 years in federal prison, forced to pay $2 million in restitution to the victims, and required register in California as a sex offender.[17]

Reddy was able to exploit, degrade, and victimize these girls, women, and men through abuse of laws, social and cultural norms, and power structures. He is a member of India's most powerful caste and "virtually owns" his hometown where he has built schools and invested millions of dollars.[18] Reddy's clout in Velavadam enabled him to easily take advantage of the local people who were desperate to escape the poverty and lack of opportunity in their village.[19] He was able to traffic people using his resources and contacts to produce fraudulent visas.[20] The people that he trafficked were helpless to do anything about their situation once in the United States. Most of them did not speak English and were reluctant to report Reddy because they did not want to reveal their falsified immigration documents.[21] It is also important to note that when the government prosecuted Reddy, his charges consisted of mostly illegal immigration and fraud as opposed to exploitation.[22]

Another example is the experience of Helen Clemente, which demonstrates how legally framing trafficking as solely a migration issue revictimizes the victim. Clemente was brought illegally to Washington State in 1990 from the Philippines by retired police officer Eldon Doty and his wife Sally to work as their servant. The Dotys were able to bring Helen Clemente to the United States by manipulating laws: They arranged a sham marriage between Clemente and Eldon Doty, which enabled her to immigrate here. The Dotys had divorced to allow Eldon to marry Clemente, but Eldon and Sally continued to live as man and wife. When Clemente ran away after nearly 3 years of servitude, the Dotys worked with the Immigration and Naturalization Service (INS) to deport her in exchange for de facto immunity. Clemente, who was granted permission to remain in the United States while her case is pending, has been fighting a difficult, precarious legal battle. She has courageously rebuilt her life, re-marrying and raising two daughters. However, she still faces the possibility of deportation. The Dotys have never been prosecuted for their abuse of the law and exploitation of Helen Clemente.

In addition, there are many instances outside of the United States that reveal the negative consequences of framing trafficking as a migration issue. A recent study of Eastern European women working within Israeli prostitution rings demonstrated this trend: The victims were freed from bondage only when local authorities raided their place of business. The trafficked women were then imprisoned as illegal immigrants and charged with prostitution; bail was then set and paid by their employer, relinquishing them back into the hands of their captors[23]. In too many similar scenarios, the women involved are treated as criminals rather than as victims. Similarly, until the late 1990s, Vietnam did not recognize trafficking as a legislative issue, and a harsh crackdown on prostitution meant that women trafficked into Vietnam's sex trade were considered guilty.[24] In such situations, trafficked women are often reluctant to seek help or approach the authorities.

Despite the fact that the trafficking of women is a worldwide epidemic, legislation to punish traffickers or to protect victims is rare. This is due, in part, to the fact that government officials and law enforcement officers often facilitate the trafficking process, as the recipients of bribes to ignore the crime or to help falsify documents.

Human Rights Watch goes so far as to say that, "without such corruption and complicity on the part of state officials, trafficking could not thrive."[25]

The Matchmaking Industry

There is another kind of trade in women that is not always recognized as trafficking: the matchmaking industry.[26] Catalogues and Internet sites list women and girls advertising for foreign husbands. Women are sorted by national origin and listed with names, photos, and measurements—so men can pick them out by the color and size they desire, as if they were choosing a shirt to buy. For a fee, men can obtain addresses and begin correspondence with the potential brides. Some girls as young as 13 years old have been advertised in such catalogues, and a considerable proportion of them are aged 15 to 18.[27] The majority of these women are from Southeast Asia, although an increasing number come from Eastern Europe and the former Soviet Union. Like other trafficked women and girls, they are motivated by the desire to escape bleak economic conditions, and they view marriage to a Western man as a ticket out of their desperate situation at home.

Women participating in the matchmaking industry are advertised as being more traditional, feminine, and submissive than the majority of Western women. In addition, "the multi-million dollar mail-order bride business . . . frequently uses marketing techniques that reinforce racial stereotypes." The women are also promoted as being willing to marry men much older than they are—the typical woman from the matchmaking industry is 10 to 20 years younger than her Western husband.[28] The men who make use of matchmaking services are white, financially successful, and politically and ideologically conservative.[29] Gary Clark, the author of the book *Your Bride Is in the Mail,* showcases the motivations of these men: "What [we] want is a woman who will be a more traditional kind of wife . . . because of the confrontational chip-on-the-shoulder attitudes held by so many of today's feminism-influenced American . . . women."[30] Apparently, desire for a submissive, dependent wife is what prompts these marriages.

Why are women from the matchmaking industry at risk? Because many of them do not speak English well and do not have a support system in their new country, they find themselves in a vulnerable position where the husband can freely abuse his position of power and dominance. "The women are dependent on their husbands in regard to their immigration status, due to the conditional basis of their resident status and the fact that they must jointly file for the removal of the conditional status."[31] Academics studying the matchmaking industry conclude that there is a disturbing potential for domestic abuse, including rape and battering. The potential for abuse is stronger if the bride does not live up to her husband's expectations, if she refuses to perform sexual services he demands, or if she becomes more independent as she accustoms herself to her new country, no longer conforming to the expected role of docile and submissive wife. "This is compounded by the fact that since the husband has purchased his wife, there is the belief that he owns her."[32] Women from the matchmaking industry also have limited access to health services due to language and cultural barriers.

The Philippines is a major source of women participants in the matchmaking industry. One reason is that structural adjustment programs have resulted in a much lower demand for migrant Filipino men's labor. Therefore, in order to maintain the survival of their family, Filipino women are filling the gap, and one route is through joining the matchmaking industry.[33] According to Aida Santos, "Many Filipino brides have admitted that marrying foreign spouses assures them of a more materially comfortable life overseas, not just for themselves but also for their families of origin. They expect that their husbands would understand the Filipino culture of married children helping out their elderly parents and siblings who are in less fortunate circumstances."[34]

However, media representation of the industry and the women involved often obscures the complexity of the issue. The topic of the mail-order bride industry gained attention in the Canadian press due to a court case involving a 68-year-old man and his 23-year-old wife. His attempt to obtain a "virgin homemaker" failed to provide him with the compliant wife that he desired. After showing no interest in sex, his wife left after 6 months, sued for support, and won 10% of the family assets valued at $186,000.[35]

The article portrayed the man as misguided and the woman as subtly manipulative and dishonest. Recently Hollywood entered the discourse with the production of "Birthday Girl," a film about a lonely English banker who orders a bride from Russia. The woman is a con artist who works in conjunction with her boyfriend and brother to rob unsuspecting men out of their fortunes. With these images being promoted, the real crimes of abuse, imprisonment, and indentured servitude become lost.

In the United States there have been several high-publicity cases of domestic violence and even murder in such marriages. Such a case recently came to light in Seattle. Anastasia King, a young bride through the matchmaking industry from Kyrgyzstan, was a student at the University of Washington. A vibrant 20-year-old who dreamed of earning a degree in business, Anastasia came to the United States by becoming the wife of a man nearly twice her age who had already divorced a previous mail-order bride. In autumn 2000, she was murdered. Her body was wrapped in a dog blanket and buried in a shallow grave near the Tulalip Indian Reservation. According to court documents, Anastasia was taking steps to obtain a divorce because of domestic violence. Her husband, Indle King, who has since been charged with her murder, apparently started looking for a third wife through the matchmaking industry as early as summer 2000.

After the death of Anastasia King, several women married through the matchmaking industry have come forward to me in my capacity as director of the University of Washington Women's Center. Although all of them relayed similar stories of a life filled with abuse and fear, they were reluctant to seek help. This was in large part due to the Russian Mafia's involvement in trafficking. If any of them were to leave their husbands, the mafia would threaten their family. These women felt trapped and hopeless. Stories like Anastasia's and these other women's remind us of the potential costs of this trade, whether it takes the form of illegal debt-bondage trafficking or the legal matchmaking industry.

DANGERS OF THE TRAFFICKING INDUSTRY: RISKS AND HEALTH CONSEQUENCES

Trafficking and Gender-Based Violence as Public Health Issues

Governments and international organizations have begun to acknowledge the human rights abuses caused by trafficking. However, the health consequences of the problem are still not fully recognized. It is necessary to place more of an emphasis on the public health dimension of trafficking for the following reasons. First, a public health focus helps make the costs of this illegal but profitable trade more visible. Also, there is a pressing need for more intervention and services to deal with the health problems of trafficked women and children. Finally, by reconceptualizing trafficking as a public health issue as well as a human rights violation, another platform for action against the trafficking trade would be created.

In the campaign against violence against women worldwide, scholars and activists have increasingly pointed out the health consequences. According to a World Bank Report, "gender-based violence . . . is a profound health problem across the globe . . . although gender violence is a significant cause of female morbidity and mortality, it is almost never seen as a public health issue."[36] The World Health Organization (WHO) calls violence against women "a priority health issue" and points out that on a worldwide basis, violence against women "is as serious a cause of death and incapacity among women of reproductive age as cancer, and a greater cause of ill-health than traffic accidents and malaria combined."[37] Yet relatively little attention has been paid to trafficking in this context. Although WHO includes "trafficking in women [and] forced prostitution" among the forms of gender-based violence, the focus of most of the work on this issue appears to deal with domestic violence, female genital mutilation, and rape. This approach to gender-based violence must also be applied to the specific health consequences that result from the abuse of women in trafficking, especially in the sex trade.

Health Risks of Trafficked Women

Trafficked women and girls, particularly those who work in the sex trade, face damage to their physical and mental health. In addition, the sex trade is a growing sector for the transmission of HIV/AIDS. Trafficked women and girls are probably more at risk for contracting the virus, as well as other sexually transmitted diseases, than other sex workers. Trafficked Nepali women make up about half of the 100,000 brothel workers in Bombay, India. Twenty percent of the brothel population are under 18, and as many as half were estimated to be HIV positive in the mid-1990s. Even when women are aware of how to protect themselves from disease, they have little autonomy over their bodies or work conditions. Beatings, rape, and other forms of physical abuse are endemic in the trafficking trade. According to Human Rights Watch, the physical abuses to which some trafficked women are subjected constitute "torture."[38]

Trafficked women working as domestic laborers are also often subjected to physical abuse, according to a study of Filipino women who worked in a variety of Middle Eastern, European, and African countries as maids.[39] Working conditions for trafficked women are frequently abysmal. In both domestic labor and sex work, excessive hours are often a problem. Confinement and overwork lead to ill health, and access to medical care is usually strictly controlled by traffickers, employers, and brothel owners.

In addition, as demonstrated through Anastasia King's story, women in the matchmaking industry are vulnerable to becoming victims of domestic violence in their own homes. Because their husbands sponsor their visas, which allow them to reside in the United States, they are often forced to stay in abusive relationships. Oftentimes, the inability to leave their husbands and lack of recourse lead to mental and physical trauma in the women and, increasingly, death.

CURRENT U.S. POLICY

In October 2000, President Clinton signed the Victims of Trafficking and Violence Protection

Act (TVPA). The legislation imposes severe penalties on traffickers and exempts victims from criminal liability.[40] The TVPA also provides benefits for survivors, including social assistance, shelter, medical care, and the right to seek residency.[41] Previously, victims were treated as illegal aliens and criminals. Trafficked women were arrested when they sought help or upon discovery by police. They were held in jails or detention centers alongside convicted criminals, where they did not receive proper medical treatment, until they were deported to their home country.[42] The legislation also includes the introduction of a new nonimmigrant T Visa that can be granted to trafficking victims, allowing them to receive benefits comparable to those of refugees, to remain in the United States for 3 years, and to apply for lawful permanent resident status at the end of that time.[43] This measure is meant to ensure that trafficked women are not treated as illegal immigrants or as criminals and that they have a chance to remain legitimately in their new country and recover from their ordeal.

The passage of the legislation was an important step to legitimize the severity of trafficking and the fact that survivors are not criminals. However, little has been done to implement the law. To date, only five T Visas have been issued despite thousands of requests. Also, women still do not receive proper services because of lack of coordination among authorities and service providers and lack of funding. Finally, to be able to receive social services, trafficked persons must first undergo a "certification" process that evaluates their situation and deems them eligible for benefits and services.[44] Oftentimes, the process is long, and survivors cannot receive assistance immediately after authorities apprehend them, the time of their greatest need for assistance.[45]

In regard to the matchmaking industry, there is no federal law to protect these women. They cannot receive assistance under the TVPA. Nationally, the industry is not regulated. However, the State of Washington, as will be discussed, has become a national leader by establishing legislation to protect women entering the matchmaking industry. Still, more needs to be done to ensure their safety and well-being.

Vanessa B. M. Vergara has argued for the application of the Thirteenth Amendment in cases of abusive mail-order bride marriages. Slavery was more than economic exploitation; "the abomination of slavery also included sexual and reproductive services that clearly fell outside the wage-labor system."[46] An examination of the applicability of the amendment to various cases found the courts upheld that the "words involuntary servitude have a larger meaning than slavery."[47] The cases of the mail-order bride industry and trafficking are closely linked and "have been recognized as institutions which subject women to conditions tantamount to slavery."[48] The application of the Thirteenth Amendment provides another means with which to prosecute offenders and protect future victims of these industries.

POSSIBLE SOLUTIONS FOR VICTIM ASSISTANCE

Need for Coordination Among Service Providers

In the United States, once a trafficking victim is freed from his or her traffickers—via escape or intervention of law enforcement—he or she is afflicted with complicated health, psychological, legal, and economic problems. Currently, service providers across the country, including domestic violence shelters, hospitals, clinics, and authorities, are not capable of successfully assisting these women. This is in part due to the nature of the crime; trafficked women are "invisible" and are scattered throughout the country, well hidden in neighborhoods, rural areas, and cities. As demonstrated in examples throughout this chapter, the type of abuse suffered by victims varies tremendously, as well as their immigration status; some come as new brides, others are smuggled illegally with fraudulent visas. A greater understanding is needed of these women and how services and authorities can best use their skills to provide support.

Needs of Trafficked Women

Women who have been trafficked suffer from severe psychological trauma. For the most part, traffickers have brainwashed women to distrust law enforcement, "as the traffickers have played upon their concerns of [corrupt and inept] law enforcement in their own countries."[49] For example, a *Chicago Sun-Times* article about an INS raid in Chicago's China town reported that upon discovery by authorities "the girls would not say anything at all to our officers, . . . these women are extremely afraid of law enforcement."[50] Importantly, trafficking victims almost always fear deportation and resist cooperating with law enforcement. This can impede efforts to apprehend their captors. They also fear that their traffickers will find them and physically hurt them or their family members abroad. In addition, some women become substance abusers because their traffickers introduce them to illegal drugs in order to easily control them. Therefore, their need for mental health services and protection from traffickers is paramount.[51]

Attorneys representing trafficking victims feel that it is better for them to be housed together after their release rather than split among different shelters. "Trafficking victims have often bonded with one another because of their shared traumatic experiences."[52] Keeping them together allows them to retain their support network and reduces emotional separation anxiety. Also, counseling should be offered in the survivor's native language. Women are trafficked to the United States from more than 49 countries around the world, and most do not speak English.

Some women who are trafficked voluntarily return to their home country to an uncertain future, whereas women from the matchmaking industry may be forcibly removed after leaving an abusive husband. Their return interrupts their counseling and treatment, and oftentimes they do not receive repatriation assistance.[53] This leaves them vulnerable to either rejoining the trafficking industry or being shunned by their community because of trafficking's negative reputation. Alternatively, the women who choose to stay in the United States need assistance finding housing and learning job skills.

Steps That Need to Be Taken

Service providers, law enforcement, immigration attorneys, and health care professionals must collaborate to best assist trafficking survivors. Police officers are most often the first point of contact with the women; therefore they should receive cultural sensitivity training and be made aware of the types of trauma trafficking victims are suffering. This will make it easier for them to identify trafficking victims and address their specific requirements. Law enforcement should be able to work with translators to inform victims of their rights and should have translated material informing them of the situation to dispel myths fed to them by traffickers. Authorities should also know which service organizations are equipped to help trafficking victims and ensure that victims receive assistance from them immediately. Isabel Carter Steward, executive director of the Chicago Foundation for Women, aptly sums up the plight of survivors: "Women and girls who are victims of this crime are being denied access to health service and information, economic self-sufficiency and freedom from violence. In short, they are being denied human dignity."[54]

Domestic violence shelters can also identify victims and what their needs are. Therefore, shelters should receive cultural sensitivity training. Shelter staff should be able to refer women to specialized shelters, agencies, and support groups serving women from their respective countries of origin and that understand their cultural backgrounds and language. Shelter staff should be able to easily access multilingual counselors and know which attorneys to contact. Survivors need lawyers who have the knowledge to help them navigate the complex legal battle that will determine their ability to stay in or leave the United States or to prosecute their traffickers.

Victims who need to remain in the United States for legal reasons (e.g., pending trials, awaiting visas) should be provided with assistance to find safe housing and job training combined with their counseling. They also need protection from their traffickers, whether they are their ex-husbands or members of criminal networks. It is extremely important for them to be protected from the individuals who exploited them. Women who return to their home country need assistance in resettling. Service organizations in the United States should be in contact with groups who can help women transition back into life in their home countries. "According to a professor from California State University with an expertise in Southeast Asian and women's studies, some non-profit organizations in Los Angeles are trying to partner up with NGOs abroad so that returnees can be met at the border or airport upon their return and receive repatriation assistance. In her opinion, these networks are easy to create but time consuming."[55]

In order for these steps to be taken, it is imperative that the aforementioned groups receive proper funding. Currently, most agencies across the country are suffering due to economic downturns and funding cuts for social services. Regardless, it is imperative that support organizations become aware of the crime of trafficking and of other agencies that assist victims. This connectedness will allow for different agencies to identify trafficking survivors and for women to receive help as quickly as possible.

WASHINGTON STATE: A MODEL FOR NATIONAL SUCCESS

In 2001, the Washington state legislature overwhelmingly passed legislation to address human trafficking. It became the first state in the country to legislatively address this modern-day form of slavery. The legislation was drafted at a November 2001 conference at the University of Washington, where lawmakers, activists, service providers, education attorneys, and survivors gathered to discuss the challenges of and solutions to trafficking. From the draft legislation, Senator Jeanne Kohl-Welles produced the Mail Order Bride Act, which requires "international matchmaking services to show women in other countries the results of criminal background checks and marital histories, in the woman's native language, of any Washington state men interested in them."[56] The men have to pay for the background checks themselves. This legislation was a response to the growing violence against women from the matchmaking industry, specifically the murders of Anastasia King and a Filipina woman, Susana Blackwell, who was shot to death by her husband. At the time of her murder, she was pregnant with her first child.

State Representative Velma Veloria and Senator Jeri Costa introduced and led the passage of the Trafficking in Persons Act. This legislation created a task force to study human trafficking in Washington and recommended to the governor and state legislature how to best provide assistance to victims.[57] The task force met between July and November 2002 and assembled representatives from law enforcement; social services; academia; city, state, and federal government; members of the legal community; and survivors of trafficking. The group "measure[ed] and evaluate[d] the state's progress in trafficking-related activities; identif[ied] available services to trafficked persons at the local, state and federal levels; and recommend[ed] methods to provide a coordinated system of support for persons who are victims of trafficking."[58] Their recommendations included establishing trafficking as a state crime, regulating the matchmaking industry and providing comprehensive legal services for victims, "including services during the pre-certification stage," increased funding to community agencies, and increased public awareness, education, and training.[59] The legislation was a result of grassroots mobilization, public education conferences, and media support and coverage. Elected officials also mobilized their colleagues in government.

CONCLUSION

The global epidemic of trafficking of women and children is a complex, multifaceted problem that repeatedly victimizes the world's most vulnerable people. The frequency of this crime will increase in the coming years as its profitability rises in the face of corrupt governments and there becomes an unending supply of people desperate to escape poverty and lack of opportunity in their home countries.

Trafficking is fueled by infinite factors, some as abstract and amorphous as the increase of women who are financially responsible for their extended families, the widespread abuse of laws, corrupt government officials cashing in on the illegal trade of humans, and the increasing connectedness of global criminal networks due to better technology (e-mail, cell phones, etc.).

Possible solutions to ending trafficking must account for its complexity and address the problem on multiple levels. Women who are most likely to be trafficked must be made aware of the crime and the huge risks and consequences. In order to reduce the "supply" of trafficking victims, women should have options of legitimate work in their home countries to prevent them from considering the illegal trade. Severe consequences should exist for traffickers to dissuade them from facilitating the trade. Furthermore, law enforcement around the world should work to disband crime rings. As mentioned earlier in this chapter, lawmakers should provide relevant and coordinated services for victims. Law-makers should develop legislation that does not criminalize victims. In addition, trafficking must be treated as much more than just a migration issue. Currently, traffickers are not accountable for violating victims' human rights.

The Sex Industry as a Cause of Trafficking

A major force propelling trafficking is the growing "demand" of prostitution. Women are moved across the world, increasingly from the global South to North, supplying cheap or free labor to sustain the booming sex business. The negative reputation of prostitution stereotypes participating women as "immoral" and as willingly selling their bodies. However, this is far from true. According to Donna Hughes, professor of Women's Studies at the University of Rhode Island, "Survivors of prostitution often report that each act of prostitution feels like a rape. In order to endure the multiple invasions of the body women use drugs and alcohol to numb the assaults to their dignity and bodily integrity. Eventually, the woman's physical and emotional health is destroyed."[60] In the case of trafficked women, most are unaware that they will end up in strip clubs, brothels, or the street. Some countries have legalized the sex industry, leading to an influx of illegally trafficked women and legitimizing the abuse of women and the commodification of their bodies.[61] I learned through my longtime work with women in the red-light district of Kolkata (Calcutta), India, that trafficked women and local prostitutes did not choose to work in the sex industry. They were driven to prostitution because they were desperately poor, with no other means of providing for themselves and their children. All of the women I worked with told me that they

would give up sex work if they were able to find other sources of income.

One of the most important ways to quell the demand for trafficked women is to crack down on the sex industry, without criminalizing the victims. The women, instead, need to be treated with consideration, and provided health care and social services. The legalization of prostitution must end. Although it is widely perceived as a way to protect women, it is only legitimizing their abuse. In addition, a state-sponsored market for women results in suppliers turning to the developing world to meet the demand. As throughout history, it is often imported labor that provides the meanest level of work in the global North's workforce. This situation threatens to designate prostitution as the work of poor women from the developing world. Finally, by framing prostitution as a legitimate industry, governments relinquish the responsibility to stamp out the factors that drive women to prostitution such as poverty, inequality, and lack of job opportunities.

NOTES

1. "Women as Chattel: The Emerging Global Market in Trafficking," *Gender Matters Quarterly 1* (1999). Accessed April 12, 2004, from http://www.usaid.gov/wid/pubs/q1.htm

2. Francis Miko, "Trafficking in Women and Children: The U.S. and International Response," Congressional Research Service Report 98-649 C, May 10, 2000. Accessed December 3, 2002, from http://usinfo.stat.gov/topical/global/traffic/crs0510.htm

3. Freedom network conference literature, "Human Trafficking," Santa Barbara City College Continuing Education. Accessed April 14, 2004, from http://ce.sbcc.edu/Trafficking_news.htm

4. "Global Market in Trafficking," *Gender Matters Quarterly 1* (1999). Accessed April 12, 2004, from http://www.usaid.gov/wid/pubs/q1.htm

5. Freedom Network Conference Literature, "Human Trafficking."

6. Sam Skolnik and D. Parvaz, "5 Seattle Men Charged in Bust of Prostitution Ring," *Seattle Post Intelligencer,* September 19, 2002. Accessed September 19, 2002, from http://seattlepi.nwsource.com/printer2/index.asp?ploc=b&refer=http://seattlepi.nwsource.com/local/87681_fbi19.shtml

7. Ibid.

8. Unifem Bangkok, as quoted in Sutapa Basu, "Gender Issues Fact Sheet 2: Trafficking in Women and Children," *Unifem Bangkok* (2000). Accessed April 12, 2004, from http://www.unifem-eseasia.org/Gendiss/Gendiss2.htm

9. United Nations Development Fund for Women, *Economic Security and Rights: Gender and Trade,* February 17, 2003. Accessed February 17, 2003, from http://www.unifem.org/economic_security/gender_trade.html; Kimberly Chang and L. H. M. Ling, "Globalization and Its Intimate Other," in *Gender and Global Restructuring,* Ed. Marianne Marchand and Anne Sisson Runyan (London and New York: Routledge, 2000).

10. Amy O'Neill Richard, *International Trafficking in Women to the United States: A Contemporary Manifestation of Slavery and Organized Crime* (Washington, DC: Center for the Study of Intelligence, Exceptional Intelligence Analyst Program, 1999).

11. Elina Penttinen, "Globalization, Bio-power and Trafficking in Women," *World Congress of Political Science* (August 1–5, 2000). Accessed November 20, 2002, from http://www.csun.edu/~iggd00/IPSA_Quebec_papers/IPSAPenttinen.doc

12. Erin McCormick and Jim Herron Zamora, "Slave Trade Still Alive in U.S.: Exploited Women, Children Trafficked From Poorest Nations," *San Francisco Examiner,* February 14, 2000, p. A-1.

13. Sarah Lai and Regan Ralph, eds., *The Human Rights Watch Global Report on Women's Human Rights* (New York: Human Rights Watch, 1995), 198.

14. Press Release, June 21, 2001. San Franscico, California: United States Department of Justice. Accessed December 21, 2002, from http://www.oig.dol.gov/public/media/oi/lbreddy.html

15. Lisa Fernandez, "Berkeley Entrepreneur Sentenced for Importing Minors for Sex," *San Jose Mercury News,* June 20, 2001, 1B.

16. J. M. Shenoy and Suleman Din, "Reddy's 'Sex Slaves' May Stay On in US," Rediff Web site, March 15, 2000. Accessed December 1, 2002, from http://www.rediff.com/news/2001/mar/15us2.htm

17. Press Release, June 21, 2001.

18. Leslie Fulbright, "Poverty Linked to Exploitation of Women," *Oakland Tribune,* April 12, 2000. Accessed April 16, 2004, from http://www.prostitutionresearch.com/mills-trafficking.html

19. Ibid.

20. Press Release, June 21, 2001.

21. Fulbright, "Poverty Linked to Exploitation of Women."

22. Fernandez, "Berkeley Entrepreneur," 1B.

23. Ibid; Michael Specter, "Traffickers' New Cargo: Naïve Slavic Women," *New York Times,* July 11, 1998, p. A1.

24. Therese M. Caouette, "Needs Assessment on Cross-Border Trafficking in Women and Children: The Mekong Subregion," United Nations Working Group on Trafficking in Mekong Subregion, February 20, 1998, p. 23.

25. "Trafficking," *Human Rights Watch,* November 2002. Accessed November 23, 2002, from http://www.hrw.org/women/trafficking.html

26. The matchmaking industry is also known as the mail-order bride industry.

27. Chela Blitt (producer, director), *Sisters and Daughters Betrayed: The Trafficking of Women and Girls and the Fight to End It* [video recording]. Berkeley, CA: University of California Extension Center for Media and Independent Learning, 1995.

28. Vanessa Vergara, "Abusive Mail-Order Bride Marriage and the Thirteenth Amendment," *Northwestern University Law Review 94* (2000): 1547–1599; Blitt, *Sisters and Daughters Betrayed.*

29. Blitt, *Sisters and Daughters Betrayed.*

30. Gary Clark, "The Reason So Many Men Seek 'Mail-Order Brides' Is Dissatisfaction With the Local Women." Accessed October 26, 2001, from http://www.planet-love.com/glcark/gclark02

31. Vergara, "Abusive Mail-Order Bride Marriage," 1552.

32. Ibid.,

33. Janice G. Raymond, Jean D'Cunha, Siti Ruhaini Dzuhayatin, H. Patricia Hynes, Zoraida Ramirez Rodriguez, and Aida Santos, *A Comparative Study of Women Trafficked in the Migration Process: Patterns, Profiles and Health Consequences of Sexual Exploitation in Five Countries (Indonesia, the Philippines, Thailand, Venezuela and the United States).* Amherst, MA: Coalition Against Trafficking in Women International, 2002), 11.

34. Ibid, 27.

35. "Mail-Order Love Backfires: 68 Year Old Man Ordered to Pay Support," *Edmonton Sun,* July 11, 1999. Accessed November 22, 2002, from http://www.catwinternational.org

36. Lori Heise, Jacqueline Pitanguy, and Adrienne Germain, "Violence Against Women: The Hidden Health Burden," *World Bank Discussion Paper 255* (Washington, DC: World Bank, 1994), ix.

37. "Violence Against Women: Definition and Scope of the Problem," World Health Organization, July 1997. Accessed November 23, 2002, from http://www.who.int/frh-whd/VAW/infopack/English/PDF/v4.pdf

38. Lai and Ralph, *Human Rights Watch Global Report,* 202.

39. Philippines-Belgium Project.

40. Michele Clark, "Slavery Happens Here," *Washington Post,* October 13, 2002, p. B8.

41. Ibid.

42. Richard, *International Trafficking.*

43. Miko, "Trafficking in Women and Children."

44. State of Washington, Department of Community, Trade and Economic Development, *Washington State Task Force Report on Trafficking in Persons,* November 2002. 30 March 2003 Accessed March 30, 2003, from http://www.ocva.wa.gov/trafficking_final_report.htm

45. Ibid.

46. Vergara, "Abusive Mail-Order Bride Marriage," 1589.

47. *Bailey,* 219 U.S. at 241, in Vergara, "Abusive Mail-Order Bride Marriage," 1573.

48. Hague, quoted in Vergara, "Abusive Mail-Order Bride Marriage," 1589.

49. Richard, *International Trafficking.*

50. Frank Main, "Team Battles Modern Slavery," *Chicago Sun-Times,* February 25, 2002. Accessed November 19, 2002, from http://www.suntimes.com/output/news/cst-nws-slave25.html

51. Ibid.

52. Ibid.

53. Ibid.

54. Ibid.

55. Ibid.

56. "Washington Responds to Trafficking," Office of Crime Victims Advocacy Quarterly Newsletter *10,* no. 1 (Spring 2002): 4.

57. State of Washington, Department of Community, Trade and Economic Development. Washington State Task Force Report on Trafficking in Persons November 2002. Accessed March 30, 2003, from http://www.ocva.wa.gov/trafficking_final_ report.htm

58. State of Washington, Washington State Task Force.

59. Ibid.

60. Donna Hughes, *Legalizing Prostitution Will Not Stop the Harm,* 1999. Accessed November 22, 2002, from http://www.uri.edu/artsci/wms/hughes/mhvlegal.htm

61. Ibid.

16

FROM REFUGEE TO DEPORTEE

How U.S. Immigration Law Failed the Cambodian Community

DORI CAHN

Seattle, Washington

JAY STANSELL

*Office of the Federal Public Defender
for the Western District of Washington–Seattle*

*P*hnom Penh, Cambodia, 1975. The victory of the Khmer Rouge over the ruling Cambodian government ultimately created an unprecedented migration of Cambodian refugees to other parts of the world. For 4 years, the Khmer Rouge brutally corralled the entire population of Cambodia into rural labor camps, emptying all of the cities and attempting to eradicate all traces of education, skill, and culture. Nearly a third of the country's population died during this time. With the Vietnamese invasion in 1979, thousands of Cambodians fled across the border to Thailand. Many spent several years in refugee camps, awaiting legislation and sponsorship in other countries to allow them to emigrate. Most of these families brought young children with them. More than 100,000 Cambodian refugees eventually found their way to the United States.

Washington, D.C., 2002. In a newly signed agreement with the government of Cambodia, the United States began deporting non-U.S.-citizen Cambodians with criminal convictions or immigration violations. Many of the 1,000-plus deportable Cambodians are under the age of 30, having been in the United States for close to two decades after coming here as young children and having grown up as American teenagers. Until this year, Cambodia had refused to repatriate any of its nationals who had been ordered deported from the United States. Now, for the first time, Cambodia began accepting the deportation of former refugees, many of whom are now unfamiliar with the country, customs, and language.

Cambodian Americans were taken by surprise when the repatriation agreement was signed. At community events throughout the

United States during the summer and fall of 2002, people expressed shock, disbelief, and anger that their friends and family, most of whom had been in the United States safely for close to 20 years, could be treated this way by the government that had provided them safe haven in the first place.

Underlying this reaction was the belief that the United States had a responsibility for the role it had played in destabilizing Cambodia during the Vietnam War. In the late 1970s, after years of warfare in Cambodia and neighboring Vietnam and Laos, the United States was too preoccupied with its defeat in Vietnam and simply ignored the atrocities taking place in Cambodia after the Khmer Rouge takeover in 1975 (see Kamm, 1998, for a detailed description of the U.S. role in recent Cambodian history). As one Cambodian youth phrased it, "In 1975 there were satellites in space that could read the headlines off a newspaper. Why didn't anyone know what was happening in Cambodia?" (Hosking, 2001). Only later did the United States agree to take responsibility for the turmoil it helped produce among the populations of Southeast Asia. With the repatriation agreement in 2002, Cambodian refugees then living in the United States believed that it was abandoning its responsibility to them. The road traveled by refugees is a complicated and often isolated experience.

> A refugee, in the usual conception, is among the world's most unfortunate people. Besides being a victim—of persecution, war, or natural disaster— a refugee has also been uprooted, forced to leave familiar territory because of that same oppression or destruction. (Aleinikoff, Martin, & Motomora, 1998)

The Cambodians in particular were faced with overcoming the trauma they left behind along with the challenge of adapting to a very different culture in the United States. In addition, a generational disconnect existed between the parents who carried their children in arms to this country and the children that grew up as Americans, knowing of their home country's hardships only through the stories of their elders.

The challenges faced by the Cambodians, along with the lack of follow-up for incoming refugees, demonstrates how refugee communities can become isolated where families are struggling unsuccessfully to maintain a semblance of the structure they have known in their home countries. At the same time, U.S. immigration law does not take into account the social experiences of refugees in the United States, as well as the traumatic home country circumstances that distinguish them from other groups of immigrants. Instead, the law has historically lumped all immigrants and refugees together as they travel through the immigration process.

But refugees are unlike immigrants who choose to come to the United States—they do not pack bags, save money, or make plans in anticipation of their arrival. As such, their needs upon arrival are greater, and the transition can be more difficult, last longer, and present greater pitfalls. At the same time, refugees have a greater need to remain in the relative safety of the United States than economic immigrants, as the conditions in their home countries often do not markedly improve over time beyond the conditions that they fled.

The particular needs of refugees as a group should be better delineated within domestic immigration law, and support systems for refugees should acknowledge the possible immigration consequences of failure to adequately acculturate. The most dramatic legal and social consequences of failing to do these things range from repatriation to a country with questionable ability to absorb newcomers to the ripping apart of families whose cohesion sometimes remains as their only major asset. The angst and frustration being felt in Cambodian American communities throughout the United States is a clear demonstration of the impact of these policies.

1970s: Escape From War and the Creation of Refugees

As Southeast Asia was imploding during the 1970s, hundreds of thousands of Cambodians, Vietnamese, and Laotians were escaping their countries' borders by any means possible. Walking through fields of land mines, floating on anything resembling a boat, refugees flowed into other parts of Southeast Asia. Refugee camps mushroomed along the Thai borders, while some refugees made their way to Malaysia and Indonesia.

In Cambodia, the demise of the national government in 1975 was followed by four years of unimaginable terror under the Khmer Rouge. Millions of people were displaced, particularly from urban areas, and forced to live in "collective" rural camps, where the displaced experienced the day-to-day possibility of arbitrary brutal death, torture, or starvation. Survivors have attempted to detail the depth of brutality and terror that defined life under the rule of the Khmer Rouge (see especially Him, 2000, and Ung, 2000, for descriptions of children living in Cambodia during these years; see also Ngor, 1987; Pran, 1997). Dr. Haing Ngor dedicates his 1987 memoir to the memories of his parents and wife, who "died in the most miserable, uncivilized, and inhuman ways under the Khmer communist regime." Another survivor describes his childhood experiences:

> I saw my mother's tears glistening in the dim light of a dying bonfire. A farm labor overseer had just ordered fifteen children to kick me. I was seven. Each child was to kick me five times, and my mother could do nothing to stop it. . . . My mother's tears. Endless labor without pay. Hunger. Beatings. Executions. These are the memories I have of my childhood in Cambodia during the holocaust of the Khmer Rouge. (Darith Keo, in Pran, 1997)

The most horrifying aspect to survivors is the fact that other Cambodians were the perpetrators of the atrocities—unlike the holocaust visited upon Jews by the Nazis during World War II or the "ethnic cleansing" in Bosnia or the tribal rivalries between Hutus and Tutsis in Rwanda in the 1990s. In fact, the term "auto-genocide" was coined specifically to refer to the situation of Cambodia under the Khmer Rouge, where atrocities were committed by members of a single social and ethnic group on its own members (Chung, 2000).

By the time the Vietnamese army invaded Cambodia and took over its governing powers in 1979 (a point in time referred to by survivors as the "liberation"), as much as one quarter of the population had died by starvation, illness, or execution as a result of the Khmer Rouge policies and political purges. Thousands of those remaining fled the country in the days and months following the Vietnamese takeover. Most of these came from the northwestern part of the country, closest to the border of Thailand, where escape by foot was possible.

In Thai refugee camps, those who fled Cambodia were generally safer than in their home, but they were still subject to atrocities. In one well-documented incident, Thai soldiers forced close to 45,000 Cambodian refugees down a steep cliff face, back across the border into the Khmer Rouge minefields that they had all managed to avoid on their escape to Thailand (Kamm, 1998). Other refugees speak of harassment, extortion, exploitation, and assault by Thai soldiers (Him, 2000; Kamm, 1998).

As thousands of people jammed camps that Thailand grudgingly allowed within its borders, the international community, and in particular the United States, recognized the need for an organized process that would allow refugees to escape while preventing Thailand from being overwhelmed. The policies applied to Southeast Asian refugees were the product of decades of public policy debate in the United States regarding the treatment of those fleeing war and terror throughout the world.

The United States' experience with massive numbers of war refugees prior to the end of World War II was fairly limited. Even during the war, when many Jews were desperate to flee the pogroms and Nazi roundups throughout Eastern Europe, the United States refused to increase its immigration quotas to accept these refugees (Simon Wiesenthal Center, 1997). After the end of the war, "[m]uch of the impetus for new American and international efforts . . . derived from a recognition that pre-war efforts, especially on behalf of Jewish refugees, were shamefully inadequate" (Aleinikoff et al., 1998).

Following World War II, the international community established two important international treaties, the Convention Relating to the Status of Refugees, in 1951, and, in the face of the worsening situation in Southeast Asia, the Protocol Relating to the Status of Refugees in 1967 (Goodwin-Gill, 1996). Initially, post–World War II refugee policies in the United States allowed entrance of refugees as parolees with no permanent status, but it quickly became apparent that this approach was inadequate, as "refugee problems" did not dissipate in the years following the war. In 1965, the United States institutionalized refugee admissions as one of the several categories of noncitizens to be allowed into the United States on a fluctuating and numerical basis. But this approach too proved inadequate, particularly in the face of the exodus of refugees from Southeast Asia in the 1970s. Congress then passed the Refugee Act of 1980, establishing the legal framework that is largely still in place today (Aleinikoff et al., 1998).

The 1980 act repealed the congressionally controlled numerical limits of the refugee laws of 1965 and replaced them with a provision for the president to establish yearly ceilings on refugee admissions. The act defined a refugee as a person who fears return to his or her home country because of a well-founded fear of persecution on account of race, religion, nationality, membership in a particular social group, or political opinion. Under the act, 50,000 Southeast Asian refugees a year were allowed into the United States during the first few years, a ceiling that could be raised by the president. In the first year alone, President Carter agreed to accept 166,700 Southeast Asians for resettlement in the United States (Smith-Hefner, 1999).

The increase of admissions from Cambodia was particularly dramatic. From 1952 until 1974, there were a recorded 390 nonrefugee immigrant arrivals in the United States from Cambodia. In the 5 years between 1975, the year of the Khmer Rouge takeover, and the passage of the 1980 Refugee Act, about 13,000 Cambodian refugees were admitted to the United States. In the first year alone after the act's passage, refugee arrivals grew to 16,000, followed by a peak of more than 38,000 the following year. Overall, between 1975 and 1999, there were a total of 145,149 Cambodian refugees who arrived in the United States, with an additional 42,000 nonrefugee arrivals recorded in the same period (Southeast Asia Resource Action Center [SEARAC], 2002b; Smith-Hefner, 1999). The 2000 census counts a total of 206,000 people claiming single or combined Cambodian ethnicity.[1]

The earlier refugees from Southeast Asia that came before the Refugee Act of 1980 was

implemented were generally urban and well educated. The Cambodians who came in this period mainly had worked for the U.S. government or had otherwise been involved in the war effort. The later, larger wave, between 1980 and 1987, when the bulk of Cambodians arrived, tended to be rural and less educated, in part because the purges conducted by the Khmer Rouge were targeted at the educated, professional, and urban residents (Smith-Hefner, 1999).

Initially, U.S. domestic resettlement policies were intended to disperse refugees throughout the country so that no one community would be overburdened. Often these placements were based purely on wherever sponsors were available. However, the refugees would frequently move on from their initial placements to join family members or friends, or to move from uncomfortable climates (Smith-Hefner, 1999). Government policy was later changed to concentrate resettlement in locations where housing and jobs were available and where services could be distributed more centrally. These locations were all medium to large urban areas. Many of the people who came from rural settings and had been living in refugee camps for several years found it difficult to adapt to these urban environments (Fadiman, 1997). The Cambodians faced a process of resettlement and establishing new communities that were different from the Vietnamese communities in the United States, many of which were established by better educated and more prosperous refugees fleeing before the end of the war in 1975; these communities were able to absorb the later wave of rural and less skilled refugees into their midst (Elliot, 1999; Nguyen, 1994; Office of the Surgeon General, 1999).

Federal funding was provided to assist refugees upon their arrival in the United States. Refugees were given language classes, job training, and housing and employment assistance. Many then found their way into minimum wage jobs. However, there was generally little to no follow-up. In fact, although the Refugee Act of 1980 authorized reimbursement to states for assistance, the number of months allowed was continually cut in subsequent years (Jung, 1993). Moreover, the length of assistance varied from state to state, with as little as 4 months in states such as New York. Assistance networks were severely strained by the huge influx of refugees throughout the 1980s while sources of funding were decreasing (Bass, 1996).

1980s: PROBLEMS OF RESETTLEMENT AND ITS EFFECTS ON CHILDREN

Unlike earlier generations of immigrants that came to the United States looking for a better life for themselves or their children, most Southeast Asian refugees came because they had little alternative. Their home countries were ravaged physically and politically by years of war, and the community bonds that held the different cultures together had unraveled. Almost all Cambodians are ethnic Khmer (Smith-Hefner, 1999), a culture so dissimilar to the American one that acculturation and assimilation in the United States would be a challenge under the best of circumstances. But the Cambodians came with additional problems. Those who escaped the killing fields of Cambodia were also traumatized by their experiences, exhibiting what was later recognized as a high incidence of post-traumatic stress disorder (PTSD). Most had also experienced extensive periods of starvation, which may have caused cognitive deterioration in some of the refugees.

Although generally young children adapt to a new culture more easily than adults, the ability of Cambodian refugee families to shepherd their young children through adolescence was encumbered by language difficulties, poverty, and the mental health impacts of trauma. The combination of these characteristics made it difficult for refugees not only to effectively transition to living in the United States but also to pave the way socially and legally for their children's future life in the United States.

According to the 1990 census, 95% of Cambodians spoke Khmer at home, and 73.2% did not speak English well. Many children were raised in homes where their parents could not communicate with their teachers at school or with other service providers. It was not uncommon for children to act as the interpreters for their parents, in a role reversal that is especially difficult in a culture such as Khmer where respect and obedience to elders is fundamental. In addition, as children adopted English as their primary language for school and social settings, they also found it increasingly difficult to communicate with their parents about these aspects of their lives (Hyman, Vu, & Beiser, 2000). This disparity in English language ability among different generations has been a major cause of the unraveling of traditional family structures and diminishing elders' ability to enforce rules in the family.

While poverty rates among all Asian Americans were reported in the 1990 census as slightly higher than the national average of 14%, the poverty rate among Cambodians was 43%. In 1990, Cambodian American per capita income was just $5,120, as compared with the national per capita of $14,143 and the overall Asian American/Pacific Islander per capita of $18,709 (Office of the Surgeon General, 1999). That has not improved much, as 37% of Cambodian households were making less than $12,000 a year by the late 1990s (Khmer Health Advocates, 2002). With limited language and job skills, many parents found it necessary to work several jobs, usually at minimum wage and long hours, leaving them little time for their children (Hyman et al., 2000).

Having come to the United States from an environment where they lived in fear and terror at all times, Cambodian refugees were found, not surprisingly, to have an extremely high rate of PTSD. Studies of mental health disorders among Southeast Asian refugees have found high rates of mental illness, with Cambodians showing the highest levels of problems. A random sample of adult Cambodians in Minnesota found that 45% had PTSD, while 81% exhibited five or more symptoms (Office of the Surgeon General, 1999). Among Cambodians in mental health treatment, 70% to 90% have been diagnosed with PTSD (Boehnlein & Kinzie, 1996; Office of the Surgeon General, 1999). These statistics come as no surprise, as many parents lost children and many children watched family, friends, or other loved ones suffer torture or death under the Khmer Rouge. Many survivors had themselves experienced imprisonment and torture.

Dr. Haing Ngor describes this problem in his memoirs:

> It was clear there was a massive mental health problem among Cambodian refugees. I understood

it because I had my share of mental problems too. We had all been traumatized by our experiences. We had all lost parents or brothers or children. Many of us had horrible dreams, night after night. We felt isolated and depressed and unable to trust anyone. What made it worse was that we were in a culture totally unlike our own. . . . In 1975 the communists put an end to our way of life. We lost everything—our families, our monks, our villages, our land, all our possessions. Everything. When we came to the United States, we couldn't put our old lives back together. We didn't even have the pieces. (Ngor, 1987)

Although the extent of mental health problems is generally accepted knowledge now, the main wave of Cambodian refugees to the United States in the 1980s were not greeted by any clear understanding of the psychological consequences of the traumas they had lived through. In addition to the lack of mental health services, another barrier to treating mental health problems was the social stigma associated with acknowledging trauma or depression within the Cambodian culture. Refugees would hide or deny any problems, as well as refuse to talk about their experiences with their children (Frey, 1999; Hyman et al., 2000; see Him, 2000, for discussion of conducting PTSD studies).

The combination of language difficulties, work and financial stresses, and emotional disconnectedness among older Cambodians all contributed to children's sense of isolation from their families. Hyman et al. (2000) report that refugee youth may feel reluctant to burden mothers and fathers with problems that seem unimportant compared with their parent's need to make a living in a strange country and to deal with a past filled with suffering that the children only dimly comprehend.

The challenge of growing up bicultural, where children are expected to achieve the values of the outside culture while maintaining the traditions and values of the home culture, contributed to a feeling of alienation among young Cambodian refugees. Many refugee children were found to have high levels of depression and anxiety, relating to insecurity about their family situation, pressure from school and peers, and trying to fit in to a strange culture. Moreover, many children who spent years in refugee camps

had not had much formal education prior to their arrival in the United States. These students were hampered by a lack of bilingual programs and English as a Second Language (ESL) support in the schools. Adolescent refugees in general report many negative experiences in school and in other social settings, because of appearing and sounding "foreign" (Hyman et al., 2000). Unfortunately, many parents did not understand what was happening to their children outside of the home.

1990s: THE GROWTH OF GANGS

The popularity of gangs among Cambodian teens has been described as a response to feeling isolated from their families as well as from their peers of other backgrounds.

The gangs are mostly a way for us to be with other people who can understand, who have the same kind of background. Our families are pretty strict, so maybe some of the kids go wild when they get old enough to get out of the house. . . . Being in a gang was a way to feel that I wasn't so different from other kids in school. I never fit in at all. I think it was because I was so old when I got here [about 10 years old]. . . . Maybe because we lived in too many different places—Thailand, Chicago, then Boston, then Providence—it didn't feel like home until I found other Cambodian kids and we just stuck together. (Tithra, in St. Pierre, 1995)

Many of the Asian youths was looking for a place of acceptance. A lot was very young, some was in their early teens, they had no understanding of their culture. Many came from poor living conditions and most was undereducated. Gangster life was a chance for them to build status in post modern America. . . . I spoke some English but not good enough, so I would get teased at school. Most of us got mocked for being different, taunted for being poor, and battered for being foreign. . . . We saw the gang as a congregation for strength and unity . . . there was no more intimidation at school. (Kim Ho Ma, personal communication, 2000)

Gang culture also satisfies what might be termed typical teen rebelliousness, but it is especially prevalent among youth who see little hope for themselves of acquiring mainstream success and values and are likely to "resist assimilation into the middle class as expected by their parents. These trends pose a challenge to all parents, but the challenge is especially daunting for immigrant parents with limited educational backgrounds, frequently limited English skills, and few resources" (Zhou, 1997).

Cambodian community members acknowledge the decrease of parental control as well as difficulties addressing children's needs during the years when adults were developing livelihoods and trying to settle into life in the United States. "Most kids join a gang because of the loss of power as a parent," admits Nisay Nuth, program coordinator for the Khmer Community of Seattle–King County (London, 1998).

Children growing up in an environment where guns are the currency of dialogue, such as Cambodian children under the Khmer Rouge and in the Thai refugee camps, absorbed the lesson of how to use violence. For these youth, the violence often associated with gang life may have made total sense as a response to the hostile environment in which they often found themselves (Isett, 1994).

For Cambodian teens who had lived here most of their lives, along with other Southeast Asian gang youth, there was no understanding that a criminal conviction could mean anything other than prison time. The idea that deportation could be a consequence of criminal behavior was not truly understood, especially because no one had been deported back to Southeast Asia since the end of the Vietnam War. The only reason this was an issue for some had to do with whether or not their parents had ever been naturalized as U.S. citizens. But emphasis on citizenship was generally not part of the package of assistance given to refugees.

1990s: CITIZENSHIP AND CRIMINAL CONVICTIONS

The vast majority of the Cambodians came as State Department sponsored refugees, and most adjusted from refugee status to lawful permanent resident (LPR) status—"green card" holders—when they became eligible to do so, a

year after their entrance into the United States. However, though it was never emphasized to the refugee population, the only true safeguard to securing their safe haven in the United States was to become citizens through naturalization 5 years or more after becoming LPRs. Citizenship allows numerous benefits, including the right to vote and to carry a U.S. passport. Rarely discussed, however, was the simple fact that citizenship is the only way for an immigrant or refugee to ensure that he or she will not be deported from the United States in the future.

To complicate matters, under the naturalization laws, minor children are not allowed to apply for citizenship on their own; they can only acquire derivative citizenship through their parents or apply on their own when they turn 18. Dealing with governmental systems and bureaucracies can be confusing for anyone, but for the adults in the Cambodian refugee community, navigating the Immigration and Naturalization Service (INS) bureaucracy and the culturally restrictive naturalization laws all too often proved virtually impossible. Many refugee families did not understand the need to apply for citizenship and failed to even try. Others avoided the process because of the language and testing required or tried and failed due to the often hostile reception within the bureaucracy or just simple language barriers.

Unfortunately, this meant that minor children did not naturalize only because their parents did not do so. Most children in this situation, especially those who came here very young, were not aware of the fact that there was a difference between them and U.S. citizens. An all too frequent sentiment expressed among potential deportees is "I thought I was just like a citizen." And even if they had understood this, there was nothing they could do about it as minors. Consequently, teens who were involved in gangs and potentially criminal activities rarely had any knowledge of the possible consequences of their actions. And parents who avoided the naturalization process had no idea that their children were at risk of being treated differently than anyone else's children, when in fact they were at risk of permanently losing their children through deportation.

Unfortunately, there was little if any institutional support to ensure that, after the refugees arrived in the United States, they would work toward the ultimate goal of naturalization, with a full understanding of both the advantages of citizenship and the consequences of not naturalizing. From a legal perspective, refugees are personally responsible for navigating their way through the immigration and naturalization laws once they have arrived; but from the perspective of refugee support services, this will not happen for many people without help. Many Southeast Asian refugees were consequently left drifting on their own in legal limbo, not understanding what they needed to do or the consequences of not doing it. The consequences turned out to be huge for many families.

In many Cambodian refugee families, the need for citizenship and the potential risk of deportation went unnoticed for a number of reasons. First, some noncitizen teens had already been arrested and convicted of offenses in juvenile court, where the juvenile convictions have no immigration consequences,[2] and the INS never became involved. This may well have contributed to the feeling of being "untouchable" among refugee youth.

Second, for those families whose children were convicted as adults and ordered deported, there was no immediate true consequence, as Cambodia, along with Laos and Vietnam, refused to accept the repatriation of their own nationals ordered deported from the United States. Young people were convicted, served their jail or prison sentences, and, under the law as it existed and was interpreted before 1996, were released by the INS after they had been ordered deported when it became clear that they could not be physically removed to their home country. The absence of an actual consequence, perhaps coupled with feelings of shame regarding a family member who had served time, discouraged families from seeking larger community support or further legal help.

Two events changed this situation. First, in response to gang violence and increasing rates of drug and violent crimes by youth, the 1980s and 1990s saw a dramatic increase in the numbers of children who were charged and convicted in adult court (Sentencing Project, 2004). Regardless of age, youths convicted as adults are subject to adult penalties; they typically serve their sentences in an adult prison and are subject to the full application of the criminal grounds for deportation. Second, throughout the 1990s, and especially in 1996, the law relating to noncitizens ordered deported for a crime dramatically changed, creating a much broader net applicable to those termed "criminal aliens" and providing the government, for the first time, an argument to indefinitely detain those it could not deport.

But because there had been no deportations to any Southeast Asian countries since the Vietnam War, few people in the refugee community took this as a serious problem. Some of those facing deportation hearings were actually advised to not fight their deportation because "no one thought it would ever happen." There was a belief that they could accept an order of deportation (also called a final order of removal), get out of INS detention, and then go on with their lives as if nothing would change.

1990s: Who Is Deportable?

In the 1880s, Congress passed the first significant immigration laws aimed at a particular class of new immigrants: the Chinese. This was a response to poor economic conditions, racism, and general anti-immigrant hysteria of the time. In a series of decisions following the laws' passage, the U.S. Supreme Court created, essentially out of thin air, an implied constitutional power for the federal government to exclude or expel people from the United States. These decisions set the tone for the treatment of noncitizens into the next century and established the doctrine that the political branches—Congress and executive—had virtually unlimited or "plenary power" over all decisions relating to immigration (*Fong Yue Ting v. United States,* 1893; *Wong Wing v. United States,* 1896). This principle has been soundly criticized ever since, but continues to form the modern-day basis for the federal government's power over immigration matters (Salyer, 1995).

Most recently, these principles of plenary power over noncitizens translated to the passage in 1996 of two of the most extreme laws ever passed relating to immigration: the Anti-Terrorism and Effective Death Penalty Act of 1996 (AEDPA); and the Illegal Immigration

Reform and Immigrant Responsibility Act of 1996 (IIRIRA). Together, these two acts dramatically expanded the types of crimes for which one could be ordered deported and largely eliminated waivers or defenses to deportation for those who had been convicted of crimes. The INS also interpreted the law to claim the power to detain noncitizens who had been ordered deported but who could not be returned to their countries of origin.

These changes were applicable to all noncitizens in the United States, whether they came to this country for work, business, tourism, or to join family members who had already established a life here. Significantly for the Cambodians, there were no exceptions made for those who came to the United States as refugees; development of immigration law in the last two decades has not acknowledged any special needs of trauma survivors who find their way here as refugees from war. Unfortunately, the number of people from around the world who fall into this category has grown in that same time period.

In addition, the legal principle with perhaps the harshest impact on noncitizens facing deportation is that "[d]eportation, however severe its consequences, has been consistently classified as a civil rather than a criminal procedure" (*Harisiades v. Shaughnessy*, 1952, p. 593). When faced with permanent deportation, then, the noncitizen is not entitled to any of the rights that are available to the criminal defendant, such as a court-appointed attorney if he is unable to pay for one. As a result, a full 58% of all individuals in deportation proceedings in fiscal year 2001 had no attorney; the remainder either hired counsel or were able to take advantage of the limited availability of pro bono or low-cost legal services (Executive Office of Immigration Reform, 2001). Without counsel, many noncitizens simply agreed to deportation without fully exploring possible defenses.

Before 1996, immigrants and refugees alike were able to ask for and receive a waiver of deportation if they committed crimes but had subsequently been rehabilitated and could otherwise demonstrate sufficient hardship to justify a discretionary second chance. A refugee might have been more likely to show an extreme hardship in returning to his or her home country than

an economic immigrant. And whereas before 1996 many crimes did not constitute grounds for deportation, people were now being deported for less serious crimes, for example, simple domestic arguments that resulted in misdemeanor convictions with no jail time imposed. As a result, the numbers of deportable convicted felons increased, and the government was faced with the question of what to do with increasing numbers of Southeast Asians and others who could not be sent home. Their response was "detention."

1990s: The "Lifer" Litigation

Some children of the killing fields of Cambodia found themselves not only being ordered deported but also being held in indefinite INS detention because of Cambodia's refusal to accept them back. They, and other INS detainees, were the "lifers." They were serving a potential life sentence because they had been ordered deported to a country that would not accept them. "[I]t seem [*sic*] that the government of the United States had charge [*sic*] me with a new crime—being born in a different country and the sentence was life" (Kim Ho Ma, personal communication, 2002).

Those individuals who had been ordered deported after 1996 found themselves detained under a particular provision of the law that requires the INS to deport or "remove" any alien ordered removed within 90 days (referred to as the "removal period") (8 U.S.C. § 1231 (a)(1)(A)). Following the 90-day removal period, the law provides that "an alien ordered removed [under various provisions of the laws, including those related to criminal convictions] *may be detained beyond the removal period*" (8 U.S.C. § 1231(a)(6), 1998, emphasis added). The INS claimed that this language allowed it to indefinitely detain a noncitizen who had been ordered deported and could not be removed to his or her home country, even if it meant for a lifetime.

These men and women came from a wide variety of countries, though the large majority of them came from countries with which the United States had no repatriation agreement for removing nationals to their home countries: Laos,

Cambodia, Vietnam, and Cuba. In addition, there were many petitioners who were essentially stateless, having been born in a country that no longer exists (e.g., individuals who left the former Soviet Union before its demise and the creation of the new nation-states of that region), or having come from strife-torn areas that made it impossible to seek or obtain travel documents from their home country.

Hundreds of INS indefinite detainees throughout the United States challenged the INS interpretation by filing petitions for writs of habeas corpus in federal district courts. "They call it administrative detention but to me it plain old incarceration. Funny how people try to justify injustice" (Kim Ho Ma, personal communication, 2002).

In Seattle, five "lead" petitioners were designated to represent all other detainees challenging the constitutionality of indefinite detention. Among these five was Kim Ho Ma, a young man from Cambodia, who was then 22 years old. Ma and his family had fled Cambodia in 1979 when he was 2 and had come to the United States as refugees when he was 7, after 5 years in Thai refugee camps. Transplanted from rural Southeast Asia to the urban projects of Seattle, Ma, like many other children from the projects, had become involved with gangs and at 17 was arrested and convicted as an adult of a gang-related shooting. He was ordered deported with no defense and had spent 2 years in INS detention when his habeas case was joined with four others for argument and decision before the five federal district court judges in Seattle.

In 1999, the Seattle judges unanimously ruled that the indefinite detention of noncitizens by the INS where the INS could not deport them in the reasonably foreseeable future violated the detainees' constitutional rights. Ma and the four other petitioners were ordered released. The INS appealed the decision as to Kim Ho Ma to the United States Court of Appeals for the 9th Circuit. That court affirmed in 2000 the trial court's decision to release Ma, setting a precedent that would govern all similar detainees throughout the West Coast. More than 100 detainees had been released in Seattle to return to their families and loved ones. Hundreds more in California, Oregon, and Nevada were released after the 9th Circuit ruling.

With other courts of appeal ruling in favor of the INS on similar cases, the stage was set for a watershed ruling on the constitutional rights of noncitizens when the Supreme Court agreed to hear the INS's appeal of Ma's case, consolidating it with a Louisiana case involving Kestutis Zadvydas, an immigrant who was stateless, having been born in a displaced persons' camp following World War II.

On June 28, 2001, the last day of its term, the Supreme Court affirmed the 9th Circuit in its decision in the cases of *Zadvydas* and *Ma,* ruling that the statute, read in light of the Constitution's demands, limits an alien's post-removal-period detention to a period reasonably necessary to bring about that alien's removal from the United States. It does not permit indefinite detention (*Zadvydas v. Davis,* 2001). The court held that "once removal is no longer reasonably foreseeable, continued detention is no longer authorized by statute" (*Zadvydas v. Davis,* 2001, p. 2498). This meant that Kim Ho Ma, and all of the noncitizens freed from indefinite detention on the West Coast, could remain free, and, significantly, many hundreds more would be released nationwide as a result of the *Zadvydas* decision. In addition, anyone entering deportation proceedings could only be detained for 6 months pending removal after issuance of the final order.

The success of the "lifer" litigation and the win on behalf of Kestutis Zadvydas and Kim Ho Ma in the Supreme Court sent dozens if not hundreds of Cambodian refugees back to their homes, their mothers and fathers, and their wives and children. It did nothing, however, to undo the deportation orders that had been entered against these men and women. Although there was hope in the refugee community that U.S. efforts to establish repatriation agreements with Vietnam, Cambodia, and Laos would continue to founder, that hope was short-lived in the Cambodian American community.

2002: GOING "HOME"

Community members first heard over Radio Free Asia that a repatriation agreement between Cambodia and the United States had been signed on March 22, 2002 (Mydans, 2002). The agreement broadly established that the respective countries would fully cooperate in the repatriation of their own nationals from the other country (Cambodian American National Council, 2002). The Cambodian American community, and some 1,400 young men and women who had been ordered deported to Cambodia, for the first time faced the prospect of the forced return of family members to the country that they had fled. Perhaps lulled into too much trust in the U.S. justice system following the victories in the "lifer" litigation and the subsequent freeing of friends and family members from detention, many in the community believed that deportations to a country such as Cambodia where human rights abuses were ongoing, where the rule of law had not yet been established, and where many government officials were formerly part of the ruling Khmer Rouge of the 1970s, must certainly be unconstitutional or violate human rights.

Having largely ignored the darker side of the immigration laws since arriving in the United States, Cambodian refugees were slow to grasp the legal realities of family members facing deportation. Though the circumstances of their arrival were extraordinary, the broad changes to the immigration laws in 1996 had virtually eliminated any opportunity to present those circumstances as equitable evidence supporting a defense to deportation. For the vast majority of those facing deportation, there was no way to stop it as the law currently exists.

The crisis in the Cambodian community came at a time when the U.S. government was particularly leery of all noncitizens, following the tragic terrorist attacks of the previous year. Although there were two proposed bills in Congress during the 2001–2002 session that would have broadly undone some of the more draconian aspects of the 1996 changes, providing many more individuals the opportunity to request discretionary relief from deportation from immigration judges, neither bill reached either the House or the Senate for a vote.

There is no specific information as to how many Cambodians were affected by the agreement or their circumstances. Estimates range from at least 1,000 to close to 1,500. However, there is information available for Cambodians freed from indefinite detention in Seattle, a group that could be assumed to be representative of Cambodian detainees nationwide.

In Seattle, of nearly 300 clients represented by the Federal Public Defender in habeas proceedings over a 3-year time period, there were 57 Cambodian men and women. Out of the 37 whose information was available, 89% were 15 or younger when they came to the United States, and 76% were 10 or younger. All but one came to the United States between 1978 and 1986, that small window of time that saw exponential growth of Cambodian communities around the United States. None arrived after 1986, which means they had all been in the United States for at least 16 years. Anecdotal evidence from community activists around the country suggests that these statistics are descriptive of many of those facing deportation.

Cambodians in the United States are most concerned that the "returnees" may face serious human rights abuses such as imprisonment or torture. At a minimum, most of them have limited knowledge of the country and social norms. They will be going there with little or no family support, and many are leaving behind most if not all of their immediate families. Many of the returnees have limited Khmer language skills, and most are illiterate in written Khmer. In addition, information from the initial groups of deportees indicates that most are being drawn from the Cambodians who were in INS detention at the time the agreement was signed or had been released fairly recently. Having had little or no time to adjust to freedom from incarceration, this group may face a particularly difficult time acclimating to life "on the outside" in Cambodia, a country with which they have little if any connection.

As the deportations began to occur, advocates for those at risk hurriedly patched together an ad hoc group of individuals in Phnom Penh to monitor the returnees and to support them in their efforts to reintegrate into the society that many had not known since they were children. As of fall 2002, this group had coalesced into a formal nongovernmental organization (NGO) called the Returnee Assistance Project (RAP). On June 22, 2002, the first six Cambodian returnees landed in Phnom Penh and, with the assistance of the RAP and following a 12-day period of detention by Cambodian immigration officials, they walked free into the society from which they had fled years earlier. Two other groups followed in the fall. On September 19, 11 returnees landed in Phnom Penh, and then on October 17, 10 more were returned, including Kim Ho Ma, the former INS detainee whose freedom was secured through the 9th Circuit and Supreme Court victories that bore his name.

Once again, these children of refugees will have to adapt to an unfamiliar culture and will reenact their parents' experiences of coming to a place that they have little knowledge of. This is another heartbreak for families who have lost so much in their lifetimes and now face the loss of yet one more loved one. Having traveled the long road from Cambodia to Thailand to U.S. urban poverty, having been processed through the U.S. criminal justice system, and having fought for freedom from indefinite INS detention, they are now faced with one more hurdle to keeping their families whole, one that may not be possible to overcome.

PROPOSALS FOR POLICY AND LEGAL REFORM

The legal consequences for both refugees and immigrants who do not adapt well to the norms and laws of their new environment can be dramatic. But it is also important to acknowledge the difference between these two groups. The additional difficulties that refugees face in acculturating to the United States leave them even more vulnerable to the harsh consequences of immigration law. And immigration law in turn does not acknowledge the different circumstances of refugees. Even though refugee policy for the last several decades has included assistance for making the transition, problems inevitably occur as people have difficulty adapting to a dramatically different culture, as family structure breaks down in that new culture, and as the laws change beyond the ability of newcomers to understand their rights and responsibilities.

The circumstances of Cambodian refugees facing deportation demonstrate the need for extensive review of refugee policy and law, which should focus on minimizing the sorts of legal problems and subsequent social upheaval

that are being experienced in the Cambodian community today. First, improved access to legal services and support could significantly help ensure family unity. Second, it's clear that language problems are fundamental to breakdown in family structure, as well as to the inability to access services and the reluctance to apply for citizenship—all of which contributed to subsequent problems with the criminal justice system and immigration law. The lack of culturally appropriate services, especially for dealing with mental health issues, has also been a stumbling block for assisting families in transition. And finally, changes to immigration law should be made to acknowledge the different circumstances surrounding refugee arrival and transitions in the United States.

Legal Assistance

Although refugees have always had, to some degree, a social service support network, there has traditionally not been an analogous component providing low-income legal assistance and advocacy for immigration and naturalization matters. This lack of services severely affected the Cambodian refugee community, as many families did not learn of the extreme jeopardy of deportation of their family members until it was too late. A systemic approach to educating the community before their children became adults and educating the children about the immigration-related dangers of gang association and other criminal behaviors might have gone a long way toward preventing the deportation of refugee children to the country from which they had fled.

Legal education and advocacy upon arrival and throughout the following years of acclimation could have accomplished several concrete things. First, advocates could have effectively informed the community of the jeopardy they all faced under the strict immigration laws, particularly those relating to deportation. Most Cambodians believed that once in the United States they were entitled to remain here indefinitely. Few grasped that even relatively simple criminal convictions might have the serious consequence of deportation. The need for such education and advocacy became even more acute after 1996, when the changes to the immigration law vastly expanded the range of crimes for which one could be deported and effectively stripped immigrants and refugees alike of almost all defenses to deportation if convicted of a crime.

Had they known the true risk of deportation, many parents of refugee children could have (and probably would have) put more energy and effort into naturalization as a way to protect themselves and their children from deportation. Instead, many of the older generation did not pursue, for example, the level of English proficiency that is crucial for obtaining citizenship. The simple and straightforward task of institutionalized naturalization efforts in the Cambodian community would have spared many families the pain they are experiencing today.

Similarly, there was never a consistent and institutionalized effort to educate youth and their parents about the broader consequences of criminal behavior, particularly for those high-risk youth who became involved with gangs. The risk of being deported was a critical part of the equation that was missed by most Cambodian families struggling with gangs and criminal behavior. The problem was exacerbated by the counterintuitive immigration enforcement scheme, which ignored juvenile criminality but became deadly serious about crime when youth either turned 18 or were tried as adults. And finally, young refugees harbored the same illusions about the commitment of the United States to its refugees as did their parents; Cambodian "lifers" in INS detention all too frequently have told their lawyers, "I never thought they would send me back."

Finally, legal assistance at the deportation hearing stage would also have helped many Cambodian refugees. However, as previously noted, in immigration proceedings there is no constitutional right to a court-appointed attorney for those who cannot hire one. Because much of this refugee group remained very poor, their children, when placed in deportation proceedings, usually were ordered deported without the assistance of counsel to defend them, although competent counsel could have made a difference for a small but significant portion.

The existing legal services agencies for the poor have always been overextended and underfunded, and those engaged in legal work with refugees and immigrants are no exception. For example, in Seattle there is a single non-profit agency for all of Washington State, with few staff members or pro bono volunteer attorneys available to represent noncitizens in deportation proceedings for no fee, while the Seattle INS district saw more than 2,700 individuals ordered deported in 2000 (INS, 2000). The funding for this agency is constantly in flux, as with most nonprofits. On the other hand, legal assistance to this refugee community would likely have had concrete, positive consequences. The historical absence of legal services should not excuse their absence in the future.

There is currently also a serious need for discrete legal assistance for the more than 1,000 Cambodians who have already been ordered deported. A large number of these individuals have long ago served their prison or jail sentences, have been released from INS detention, and have proven themselves to be rehabilitated. Few of these individuals have had the assistance of competent legal advice to determine what, if anything, may be done now to prevent their deportations, though such avenues do exist for many. For example, an individual may have established sufficient rehabilitation and such strong equities that he or she could present a successful petition for a governor's unconditional pardon for an underlying state conviction, which in turn would allow, in many cases, the reopening of the individual's deportation case. There are also a number of Cambodians who appear to be eligible to reopen their deportation cases and ask for a waiver of deportation under the Supreme Court's decision in *INS v. St. Cyr* (2001). In addition, there are an undetermined number of Cambodians with final orders of deportation who have since married U.S. citizens, which may, under some narrow circumstances, allow for an independent avenue of relief from deportation that could allow the conviction ground to be waived. All of these avenues would, however, be difficult or impossible without legal counsel.

Social Assistance

Delivery of social services to immigrants and refugees is generally complicated by both language and cultural barriers. The cultural distance between many Cambodian families and American society hampered access to a wide variety of social and legal services available for low-income people. In particular, the basic inability to communicate in English isolated many older Cambodians from their adopted country and either prevented or limited access to existing social and health services that would otherwise have been available to this low-income group.

The language barrier many Cambodians faced derived in part from limited ESL programs. The focus of such programs for newly arriving refugees and immigrants generally does not go beyond basic skills and job training. Often these programs are provided through community-based organizations, with no more than several months' education available and job placement expected at the end of that time. With limited funding for these organizations, students are not able to spend time learning much more than survival English, and they are rarely able to find jobs at better than minimum wage. With additional funding and more time to acquire English, ESL learners could better function at a variety of levels, alleviating some of the problems that occur in families when children become the interpreters for their parents and parental influence is diminished as a result. Family literacy programs can also assist in this process, allowing parents and children to acquire language skills and cultural literacy together, while helping to lessen the generation gaps that occur in refugee families. Programs that helped parents maintain parental control and family bonds through improved language skills could have diminished the circumstances that led many Cambodian youths to join gangs.

It is equally important to ensure that children are not struggling in school because of their language skills. Lack of language skills not only holds children back in the classroom but makes it more difficult to function in the social environment of school. Numerous former gang members have spoken of their problems with English being a root cause of getting harassed at school. Lack of progress in school also makes many children feel discouraged about their opportunities for the future and spurs them to seek illegal alternatives. Unfortunately, even though studies show that children in bilingual classrooms learn better and faster than their counterparts in English-only classrooms, bilingual education funding is being cut and replaced by English acquisition programs in many states: the federal No Child Left Behind Education Act of 2001 is one of the most recent efforts to do this (Katz & Kohl, 2002).

A related but distinct problem has been the lack of attention to delivering health and social services in a culturally appropriate manner. For example, merely translating an interaction between a social worker and a Cambodian survivor of the terror of the Khmer Rouge does little to break the various cultural taboos or personal discomfort of disclosing information that is necessary to adequately diagnose the symptoms of PTSD. Failure to recognize not only the extent of the trauma but the lack of willingness within the community or the individual to acknowledge it stems from problems much more complex than a language barrier. "Cultural interpreters"—people who are familiar with both the language and the norms and traditions of other cultures—have been used successfully to advocate on behalf of refugees and immigrants with the medical and mental health professions and should be more widely used with people from different cultures (see Fadiman, 1997, for a discussion of the Hmong experience). If service providers had employed cultural interpreters, they might well have discovered the full extent of mental health problems among the Cambodian community earlier on and thereby helped some families avoid the breakdown in structure that undermined their stability.

Policymakers therefore also need to understand the importance of providing for cultural and language "interpreters" at all possible points of interaction between social and health service providers and refugee communities. Refugee and immigrant advocates also suggest increasing the number of bilingual and bicultural staff in city and county agencies, starting culturally specific gang prevention at earlier ages, and offering culturally accessible courses on the juvenile justice system for parents. These types of services can help provide the long-term strategies that families need to adapt and to avoid some of the problems that have arisen with criminal behavior and its immigration consequences.

There have been efforts in some communities to accomplish many of these things. Cambodians in Lowell, Massachusetts, home to the second-largest Cambodian community in the United States, have an effective program of gang prevention using former gang members to reach out to at-risk youth. Cambodian parents in low-income housing in Seattle, home to the third-largest Cambodian community in the United States, have developed a successful youth group that works to give younger generation Cambodian Americans knowledge and appreciation of their parents' home culture and language while working to prevent gangs and other problem behavior among teens.

But these are examples of communities that are successful in these efforts; like most social ventures, continuity of funding is always a problem, and the success of isolated programs needs to be replicated in other communities. In order to ensure that all communities have access to developing familywide programs, federal funding should "follow the refugee" to ensure that the vagaries of individual choice of residence do not disrupt the necessary, particularized support for refugees and their families. When compared with the actual costs to society when refugee families break down—costs incurred by the criminal justice system, incarceration, INS detention, drug and alcohol abuse, and illiteracy—greater expenditures on the front end are easily justified.

But This Would All Cost Too Much

For critics of this approach who argue that additional money should not be spent on legal or social services, one need only look at where monies are currently being spent. According to information from the Federal Public Defender in Seattle, the 57 Cambodians with final orders of removal represented by that office were detained for an average of 1.2 years, with a cumulative total of 67 years in INS detention since 1996. At an estimate of $24,000 per year to house and feed inmates (Center on Juvenile and Criminal Justice, 2002), the cost was $1.61 million solely for Cambodian detainees in Seattle. However, because INS detention was fought so aggressively in Seattle, and the detainees all had legal representation, the

average time in detention is probably lower in Seattle than in other parts of the country, especially places where detainees have had no legal representation at all. (For example, a 2002 SEARAC survey of detainees in the Washington, D.C., area reports an average of closer to 2 years in INS detention.) Nonetheless, using the lower figure from Seattle detainees of 1.2 years' average stay in detention, and using the minimum estimate of 2,000 "lifers" at the time of the *Zadvydas* decision, it appears that the U.S. government may well have spent at least $57.6 million detaining noncitizens who are unlikely to be deported in the near future. And this number ignores INS detainees from the years prior to 1996 or after 2001.

This approach also grossly underestimates the costs to society of U.S. policy toward refugees who are convicted of crimes. Those who have been deported, or will be in the future, are frequently heads of households, and many remaining family members must now turn to public assistance. A survey by SEARAC found that the majority of the detainees they interviewed were currently employed and contributing to their families (SEARAC, 2002a). Further, these figures do not take into account the costs of incarceration of refugee youth in state and federal prisons, whereas well-focused, preventative outreach might well have pulled refugee kids out of gangs in the first place. Finally, immigration enforcement and the deportation process itself involve another large, but difficult to quantify, cost.

The INS's insistence on an aggressive policy of detaining those facing deportation further adds to this cost. Converting any or all of these monies to legal counseling and support to refugees and immigrants would be more productive in achieving the goals of keeping families together and ensuring that refugees would not face the possibility of having to be forcibly returned to the countries they fled in fear.

Refugee Law Reform

While immigrant and refugee advocates alike legitimately work to roll back the most extreme provisions of the 1996 changes to the immigration laws, the circumstances of Cambodian refugees demonstrate the need to change the law to recognize the dramatically different consequences of deportation for refugees. Because the political branches may currently be reluctant to pass legislation broadly reforming the immigration laws, a more pragmatic starting point may be to at least establish a waiver of deportation for those originally admitted to the United States as refugees. The situation of the Cambodian returnees points clearly to the need for such a waiver, a need that would be shared by, for example, Laotian, Hmong, Mien (if Laos signs a repatriation agreement), or Vietnamese refugees, or any other group that was admitted to the United States because they fled terror and persecution in their home country.

Such a waiver could be modeled after waivers of deportation that existed prior to 1996, which allowed the immigration judge to waive the deportation of a noncitizen for a criminal conviction if the noncitizen demonstrated sufficient rehabilitation, family ties, and other equities and/or hardship that would arise from deportation.

Finally, the circumstances of the Cambodians who have actually been returned to their country demonstrate a glaring deficiency in the immigration laws from a moral and international law perspective. So far, all of the returnees have been systematically subjected to intentional illegal detention by Cambodian officials upon their return, ranging thus far from 2 to 4 weeks. However, the U.S. State Department is fully aware of this policy, and the deportations continue. In a world where the rule of international law has become more important than ever, U.S. domestic law should be changed to prohibit the deportation of any individual to a country where there is substantial evidence that his or her human rights will be violated upon return. This is a provision that would apply to other groups as well, for example, Somalis who are currently facing deportation to a home country with no functional government or rule of law.

Although immigration reform may be unlikely in the wake of the September 11 terrorist attacks, even changes to the law enacted years from now could benefit those who have been deported. Most of the Cambodian returnees are leaving family behind in the United States, many of whom have become naturalized citizens. Long-term goals of liberalizing the laws relating to the readmission of these individuals—for example, by eliminating the 10- and 20-year bars on reentering the country or limiting the age of convictions that can serve as grounds for excluding an immigrant—are worthy and obtainable and would allow for the reunification of families in the United States.

THE LAST WORD

The United States has become a much more diverse society in the years following the wars in Southeast Asia. War, political instability, and economic strife have since brought people from Somalia, Ethiopia, Eritrea, Sudan, Afghanistan, Pakistan, El Salvador, Guatemala, Colombia, Chile, Argentina, Haiti, the Dominican Republic, Iran, Iraq, the former Soviet bloc, and other places to the United States. Many of these newcomers, like the Cambodians, come from societies that are much more culturally homogeneous than the United States, where their traditions and beliefs are generally reinforced by the larger society as a whole. Most do not come from European countries, which formerly made up the bulk of immigration to this country. Transition to the United States can therefore be difficult and overwhelming, even as relief at being offered safe haven is tangible among these groups.

If our international policy is to offer safety to those who flee their homelands, then our domestic policy should complement that goal by striving to ensure the stability and safety of refugee families inside the United States. We should extend aid and assistance to those who need it more effectively than in the past, by modifying immigration laws so that people who escape persecution and war will not be forcibly returned to their home countries except under the most extreme cases. Unfortunately, attempts by policymakers to build even thicker and higher walls around the United States in reaction to the September 11 terrorist attacks run the risk of causing irreparable harm to many who have lawfully rebuilt their homes, communities, and families in the United States. Such an approach is short-sighted at best. Now, perhaps more than ever in our history, the United States must champion the cause of compassion, understanding, and the rule of law in an increasingly divided and hostile world.

NOTES

1. The Southeast Asia Resource Action Center (SEARAC) estimates that these numbers are underreported by up to 25% and suggests a revised total number of 257,000 as a more accurate reflection of the U.S. Cambodian community.

2. A juvenile conviction is, strictly speaking, an order of delinquency and not a conviction.

REFERENCES

Aleinikoff, T. Alexander, Martin, David A., & Motomora, Hiroshi. (1998). *Immigration and citizenship process and policy.* St. Paul, MN: West Group.

Bass, Thomas A. (1996). *Vietnamerica: The war comes home.* New York: Soho Press.

Boehnlein, James K., & Kinzie, J. David. (1996, Winter). Psychiatric treatment of Southeast Asian refugees. *NCP Clinical Quarterly 6*(1). Accessed November 1, 2002, from http://www.ncptsd.org/publications/cq/v6/n1/boehnlei.html

Cambodian American National Council. (2002, March 22). *Memorandum Between the Government of the United States and the Royal Government of Cambodia for the Establishment and Operation of a United States–Cambodia Joint Commission on Repatriation.* Accessed November 1, 2002, from http://www.cancweb.org/canc/deportation.html#mou

Center on Juvenile and Criminal Justice. (2002). *From classrooms to cell blocks: A national perspective.* Accessed November 1, 2002, from http://www.cjcj.org/pubs/higher/highernational.html

Chung, Margaret M. (2000). *Intergenerational effects of genocidal disaster among Cambodian youth.* National Association of Social Workers New York City Chapter, Disaster Trauma Working Group. Accessed November 1, 2002, from http://www.naswnyc.org

Elliot, Duong Van Mai. (1999). *The sacred willow: Four generations in the life of a Vietnamese family.* New York: Oxford University Press.

Executive Office of Immigration Reform. (2001). *EOIR statistical yearbook.* Accessed November 1, 2002, from http://www.usdoj.gov/eoir

Fadiman, Anne. (1997). *The spirit catches you and you fall down: A Hmong child, her American doctors, and the collision of two cultures.* New York: Farrar, Straus, and Giroux.

Fong Yue Ting v. United States, 149 U.S. 698 (1893).

Frey, John J. (1999). Too sad. *Journal of the American Medical Association, 281*(2). Accessed November 1, 2002, from http://jama.ama-assn.org/issues/v281n2/ffull/jpo80281-1.html

Goodwin-Gill, Guy S. (1996). *The refugee in international law.* New York: Oxford University Press.

Harisiades v. Shaughnessy, 342 U.S. 580 (1952).

Him, Chanrithy. (2000). *When broken glass floats: Growing up under the Khmer Rouge.* New York: W. W. Norton.

Hosking, Janine. (2001). *My Khmer heart* [Video]. Direct Cinema Limited, Santa Monica, CA.

Hyman, Ilene, Vu, Nhi, & Beiser, Morton. (2000, Spring). Post-migration stresses among Southeast Asian youth in Canada. *Journal of Comparative Family Studies, 31*(2), 281–294.

Immigration and Naturalization Service. (2000). *INS statistical yearbook.* Accessed November 1, 2002, from http://www.ins.usdoj.gov

INS v. St. Cyr, 533 U.S. 289 (2001).

Isett, Stuart H. (1994). From killing fields to mean streets. *World Press Review, 41*(12), 34.

Jung, Helene E. (1993, November 7). Role swaps hurt refugee families: Newcomers' children adapting to U.S faster than their parents. *Seattle Times,* p. B1.

Kamm, Henry. (1998). *Cambodia: Report from a stricken land.* New York: Arcade Publishing.

Katz, Susan, & Kohl, Herbert. (2002). Banishing bilingualism. *The Nation, 275*(20), 7.

Khmer Health Advocates. (2002). Statement. Accessed November 1, 2002, from http://www.hartnet.org/khmer/stmstaff.html

London, Melissa. (1998). A meeting with the chief of police: SE Asian community talks about escalating youth crime. *Northwest Asian Weekly, 17*(31). Accessed April 5, 2004, from http://nwlink.com/~scpnwan/articles/08-01-98/police.html

Mydans, Seth. (2002, August 9). Dead end for Cambodians who grew so American. *New York Times,* p. A3.

Ngor, Haing. (1987). *A Cambodian odyssey.* New York: Macmillan Publishing Company.

Nguyen, Qui Duc. (1994). *Where the ashes are: The odyssey of a Vietnamese family.* Reading, MA: Addison Wesley.

Office of the Surgeon General (1999). *Mental health: Culture, race, and ethnicity—A supplement to Mental health: A report of the surgeon general 1999*. U.S. Department of Health and Human Services, SAMHSA.

Pran, Dith. (Ed.). (1997). *Children of Cambodia's killing fields: Memoirs by survivors*. New Haven, CT: Yale University Press.

Salyer, Lucy E. (1995). *Laws harsh as tigers: Chinese immigrants and the shaping of modern immigration law*. Chapel Hill: University of North Carolina Press.

The Sentencing Project. (2004). Juveniles in Adult Criminal Courts. Accessed April 2004, from http://www.sentencingproject.org/issues_08.cfm

Simon Wiesenthal Center. (1997). *36 Questions about the holocaust*. Accessed November 2002, from http://motlc.wiesenthal.com/resources

Smith-Hefner, Nancy J. (1999). *Khmer American: Identity and moral education in a diasporic community*. Berkeley: University of California Press.

Southeast Asia Resource Action Center (SEARAC). (2002a). *The impact of detention policies under IRIRA on Southeast Asian families* [Draft]. Washington, DC: Author.

Southeast Asia Resource Action Center (SEARAC). (2002b). *Statistics: Americans of Cambodian, Laotian (including Hmong), and Vietnamese descent (citizens and others)*. Washington, DC: Author.

St. Pierre, Stephanie. (1995). *Teenage refugees from Cambodia speak out*. New York: Rosen Publishing Group.

Ung, Luong. (2000). *First they killed my father: A daughter of Cambodia remembers*. New York: HarperCollins.

Wong Wing v. United States, 163 U.S. 228 (1896).

Zadvydas v. Davis, 121 S. Ct. 2491 (2001).

Zhou, Min. (1997). Growing up American: The challenge confronting immigrant children and children of immigrants. *Annual Review of Sociology, 23*, 63.

PART IV

WORKING WITH CHILDREN AND FAMILIES

17

ASIAN AMERICAN/PACIFIC ISLANDER FAMILIES IN CONFLICT

DAVID SUE

Western Washington University

CONFLICT IN ASIAN AMERICAN/PACIFIC ISLANDER FAMILIES

The focus of this chapter will be on the problems faced by many Asian American/Pacific Islander families and the interplay between traditional family values and those of the society at large. The Asian American and Pacific Islanders group (AA/PI) is composed of approximately 28 different Asian and 19 Pacific Islander subgroups ranging from those with similar to those with very different cultural values, religions, and languages (National Women's Health Information Center, 2002). Asian refers to the peoples with origins in the Far East, Southeast Asia, and the Indian subcontinent (Cambodia, China, India, Japan, Korea, Malaysia, Pakistan, the Philippine Islands, Thailand, and Vietnam). According to the U.S. Census Bureau (2001a), Asian Americans numbered 11.9 million, or 4.2% of the U.S. population. Of this number, 10.2 million, or 3.6% of the U.S. population, self-described themselves as only Asian. An additional 1.7 million reported Asian and one or more other races, the most common combination being Asian and white (52%). The largest Asian groups are the Chinese, Filipino, Asian Indian, Vietnamese, and Korean. In terms of

residence, over one half of Asian Americans live in California, New York, and Hawaii.

The Native Hawaiian and other Pacific Islander group refers to people having origins in Hawaii, Guam, Samoa, and other Pacific Islands. Those who reported themselves as Pacific Islander alone numbered 399,000, or .1% of the U.S. population. An additional 476,000 reported Pacific Islander and at least one other race. Of all the races, the Pacific Islanders have the highest proportion of respondents reporting more than one race. More than half of Pacific Islanders live in two states, Hawaii and California (U.S. Census Bureau, 2001b). In this chapter, AA/PI and Asian Americans will be used interchangeably to apply to both Asian Americans and Pacific Islanders.

For many Asian Americans, the family structure, communication patterns, and relationships among members differ from those of Western-style families. These differences have often resulted in increased conflicts among family members within Asian American families. Because Asian Americans are thought to have done well in American society, they are often considered the "model minority." However, the very real issues of prejudice, poverty, family conflicts, and the lack of institutional responsiveness faced by members of this group have received little attention. Indeed, many Asian Americans feel less than fully accepted in American society.

Some recent findings support this suspicion. In a national survey (Committee of 100, 2001) on attitudes toward Asian Americans (a) nearly half of the adults surveyed believed that Asian Americans would pass on secret information to China, (b) about one quarter would be "uncomfortable" having an Asian American as president versus 15% if the individual were African American or 14% if the president were a woman, and (c) 17% would be upset if a number of Asian Americans moved into their neighborhoods. As Henry Tang observed, "What these numbers do is force us into a realization that we're always having to earn our recognition over and over again. . . . No matter how educated we are, or how well we do, it doesn't matter (Richardson & MacGregor, 2001, p. E1). In addition, many Asian Americans are still victims of harassment. The number of hate crimes against them has increased in recent years (Matthee, 1997). These factors lead to a distrust of American society by many Asian Americans.

In this chapter, I will discuss the diversity, values, and demographics of AA/PIs. Within this framework, I will first present barriers to community services faced by this population. Then I will present the family structure, including more in-depth discussion of family problems such as divorce, domestic violence, parenting issues, and adoption. Counseling and legal implications as well as suggestions for appropriate intervention strategies will also be outlined.

Before we begin, it is important to stress that Asian Americans are a very diverse population for whom few national baseline data are available. Because of the relatively small population and lack of interest in this group by mainstream researchers, Asian Americans are often placed in the "other" category in surveys. Even when research includes a category for Asian Americans, the data are often aggregated and therefore include diverse groups of Asian Americans. Thus, there is little national data available on these groups, and generalizations on Asian Americans are often based on specific groups of Asian Americans such as the Chinese or

Japanese or those living in specific cities in the United States. In this chapter, I will present the findings from specific studies. The reader is cautioned that many findings or conclusions based on specific samples may not be generalizable to other groups of Asian Americans.

FAMILY DEMOGRAPHICS

The AA/PI population is relatively young, with 29% under 18 years of age as compared with 24% of non-Latino whites. AA/PI families tend to be large, with 23% consisting of five or more members versus 13% for non-Latino whites. There is a wide diversity among Asian Americans in regard to family size, with Southeast Asians having the largest average number per household. In general, household size is due to the presence of another relative who is not a child or spouse. Thus, the household unit is generally composed exclusively of family members. Of the different subgroups, Japanese Americans have the lowest average household size (McLoyd, Cauce, Takeuchi, & Wilson, 2000). Given the relatively high percentage of Asian American families that are extended, problems can occur in family research and intervention programs when only parents or their children are considered. Other relatives living with the family unit may have an important influence in family decisions and can serve as social and cultural resources.

Asian American families differ from European American families not only in terms of demographics; strong cultural differences also exist. Immigrant AA/PIs or those living in ethnic communities may have a strong collectivistic rather than individualistic orientation. In addition, they may have specific beliefs regarding mental and physical health, legal issues, and perceived discriminatory practices. These beliefs can sometimes serve as impediments to accessing needed services.

BARRIERS TO APPROPRIATE SERVICES

Communication Problems

Unlike ethnic minority groups such as African Americans and Native Americans, about 60% of

Asian Americans are foreign born (immigrants or refugees). In 1992, of the Asian mothers who gave birth in the United States, only 17% had been born in this country (Martin, 1992). More than 100 different languages and dialects are spoken by AA/PIs. Because of the foreign-born status of the majority of this population, most speak an AA/PI language at home. Therefore, a large minority are linguistically isolated, living in households where no one 14 years or older speaks English "very well." Among the AA/PI population, Southeast Asians have the most limited English proficiency (Ro, 2002).

Nearly half of AA/PIs have problems with the utilization of services because of limited English proficiency and the lack of providers who have appropriate language skills. AA/PIs may not understand written materials or other means of communication regarding services from government agencies. The lack of English proficiency also forces many Asians to work at minimum wage jobs or in sweatshops in which they may lack basic worker rights or fair compensation and may be exposed to unhealthy work environments.

Shame and Stigma

In collectivistic societies, problems among individuals are seen to reflect on the entire family and community. There may be privacy concerns and a reluctance to share family histories even when they are necessary to develop treatment plans (Choi & Wynne, 2000). Many AA/PIs may be reluctant to reveal mental health and physical problems when seeking services because of the potential for stigmatizing the family or community. This may account for the finding that AA/PIs have lower rates of mental health utilization compared with whites. Among those who use these services, severity of condition is high, suggesting a delay in obtaining services until problems become very serious (U.S. Department of Health and Human Services, 2001b). In addition, physical illnesses associated with sexuality such as HIV or the need for physical exams may also provoke feelings of embarrassment or shame. Excessive modesty may account for the fact that, on the average, AA/PI women have significantly lower breast and cervical cancer screening rates

(National Women's Health Information Center, 2002). About 21% of AA/PI women have never had a Pap test, compared with 5% of white women. However, large between-group differences exist. The percentage of those never having the Pap test varies from 8% for Japanese American women to 36% for Vietnamese American women (Ro, 2002).

Cultural Perceptions

AA/PIs may have cultural beliefs regarding "appropriate" medical procedures. Some believe that Western medicines are too potent and will attempt to dilute them. They may also discontinue taking medication because they are also using herbal remedies and believe that the two will clash. Because of these beliefs, there may be high levels of noncompliance with prescribed treatment regimens (Chen & Hawks, 1995). The overscheduling of appointments that is prevalent among medical and dental services in the United States is viewed negatively by some AA/PI groups. Among the Vietnamese, having to wait to receive services is considered to be insulting and degrading. They would prefer to pay more to be seen more quickly (Jamin, Yoo, Moldoveanu, & Tran, 1999). In general, AA/PIs are less content with the quality of health care received. As compared with the overall population, they were more likely to believe that their physician did not understand their culture and did not treat them with respect (11% vs. 5%; Hughes, 2002).

Lack of Knowledge Involving Mainstream Service Delivery

AA/PIs often do not understand or are not acquainted with general health care processes, services available, or the legal system in the United States, because these services often differ from those found in their native country. Also problematic is the fact that many providers may not take the time to explain procedures or the preparation of paperwork. The inability to comprehend services is challenging for many families and may result in noncompliance. Being a minority in the service delivery system can also increase a sense of isolation and result in greater hesitancy to utilize services (Choi & Wynne, 2000).

Additional Cultural Barriers

These cultural barriers to appropriate services for AA/PI populations can be compounded by the collectivistic and hierarchical nature of many of the families. Decisions are often not made independently but by the entire family, and the father may abide by traditional authoritarian rule. In addition, gender role distinctions, appropriate interaction patterns, and parenting behaviors are often very different from European American populations. These differences can produce conflict. Because family structure often underlies many of the family problems faced by AA/PI populations, I will discuss this first and then the issues dealing with divorce, domestic violence, parenting, and adoption.

FAMILY STRUCTURE

The traditional family structure found in many AA/PI populations has functioned as a source of strength for members of these ethnic groups, and most families are doing well in American society as evidenced by low divorce rates, high achievement by most of the children, and low reports of family conflict. However, the situation may not be as ideal as it would seem, especially when family structure and expectations run counter to those of mainstream society. I will present some of the elements of the family that may be problematic when viewed through the lens of European America.

Traditional Asian/Pacific Islander families are collectivistic in orientation. That is, appropriate functioning is dependent on the fulfillment of family and group goals rather than individual needs or desires. Because of this orientation, children are expected to strive for family achievement and are taught not to engage in behaviors that would bring shame to the family. Traditional AA/PI families are not egalitarian in nature but instead hierarchical in structure, with the father, other males, and older family members occupying a higher status. Gender roles are also clearly defined. The father is the authority figure and provides for needs while the task of raising the children falls primarily on the mother. Women are socialized

to sacrifice their own personal needs for the well-being of their husbands and children, often denying their own needs so that the family can be properly taken care of (Ro, 2002).

Communication flows from parent to children, and decisions are made with little input from the children. Different models of Asian family structure exist, and many have become more egalitarian. The most egalitarian families are found among Japanese and Filipino Americans, whereas the most authoritarian styles are found among Korean, Chinese, and Southeast Asian Americans (Blair & Qian, 1998). The institution of marriage is strongly supported by religious, social, and cultural influences.

Divorce

Because of the emphasis on the importance of the family, Asian American families generally are intact with both parents present. They are less likely than white families to be widowed (4% vs. 7%) or divorced (5% vs. 10%; Humes & McKinnon, 2000). Eighty-four percent of Asian American adults had been married just once as compared with 74% of Latinos, 70% of whites, and 65% of blacks. The low percentage of remarriage among AA/PIs is due, in part, to lower levels of divorce (Kreider & Fields, 2001). Whereas 40% of ever-married white and Latina women had divorced from their first marriage by 1996, the corresponding rates are 48% for black women and 24% for AA/PI women. In general, the low divorce rate indicates the strength and functioning of the Asian American families.

Divorce is also low because it may be interpreted by the AA/PI community as an expression of individuality rather than a consideration for the welfare of the family. It is considered a transgression against the norm of maintaining harmony. The onus for a divorce generally lies upon the wife because she is socialized from birth to sacrifice her own personal needs for the good of her husband and/or children (Fong, 1994). For many Asian women, maintaining an intact family assumes precedence over their personal problems. The welfare of children is primary and dependent on keeping the family together. Because of this, marital conflicts are often silenced by family and group pressure. The wife may be told to stay in the marriage for the sake of the children. One South Asian woman seeking supportive counseling was even told by a South Asian female psychiatrist to "adjust" to her husband. After filing for divorce, the woman was shunned by some community members for breaking a cultural tradition and thereby depriving her children of their rights to their father's family (Preisser, 1999). Thus, divorce is a difficult move to contemplate because it involves (a) having to make individual decisions regarding the self or children within a collectivistic framework, (b) ignoring socialization to sacrifice one's own needs for the children and husband, and (c) facing family and social pressures to maintain the marriage.

Domestic Violence

Although AA/PI families are thought to function well, and most do, as with any community, domestic violence may be an issue. It is difficult to determine the prevalence of this problem because little research exists on this matter, and much of it is done on specific groups, thereby limiting the ability to generalize to the AA/PI population as a whole. In addition, domestic violence in AA/PI communities may go unnoticed because of the stigma of admitting such information. Outside intervention is strongly discouraged, because attention to family conflicts produces great shame and dishonor to the family (Yoshioka, DiNoia, & Ullah, 2001). Because a strong stigma is attached to divorce and single parenthood, the wife and children may feel trapped in abusive relationships. As one woman suffering from domestic violence stated, "A lot of Asian people, they always think this way, that even though violent, they want to keep the family together. Some people they think if you divorce, they look at you differently. In the beginning, after I got a divorce, I have a friend who told me things like this. She told me she doesn't like her daughter to play with kids of single parents" (Bauer, Rodriguez, Quiroga, & Flores-Ortiz, 2000, p. 39). Because of concerns such as these, few official complaints about domestic violence have been filed through institutional channels, supporting stereotypes of AA/PI communities as trouble-free.

As mentioned earlier, domestic violence statistics are based on small samples and are not generalizable to the Asian American population as a whole. In the following section, we will present some studies performed in localized communities and with specific ethnic samples. Several studies indicate that domestic violence is a problem among AA/PI populations. In one study surveying domestic violence providers and social service agencies in the Washington, D.C., Maryland, and Virginia areas, 484 battered Asian women and children were reported to have been seen in 1996. The cases of domestic violence involved nearly all Asian ethnic groups, with the majority of clients identified as Korean, Vietnamese, South Asian (Indian, Pakistani, Bangladeshi, Sri Lankan, and Nepali), and Chinese (Preisser, 1999). In Massachusetts, although Asian Americans compose only 3% of the population, it is estimated that 10% in 1995 and 1996 and 18% in 1997 of the women killed by domestic violence were Asian women (Malone, 1999).

Factors Associated With Domestic Abuse

Certain factors and characteristics such as language facility, immigration status, social isolation, and attitudes toward spousal abuse were present in reported cases of domestic abuse. In one sample, nearly half of the battered clients spoke little or no English. Korean and Vietnamese clients were identified as two main groups that needed interpreters (Preisser, 1999). Many immigrant women were fearful of reporting domestic violence, especially those who were in the United States under their husbands' visas, because of the fear of deportation (Malone, 1999). In a study of attitudes related to domestic abuse among 507 Chinese, Korean, Vietnamese, and Cambodian Americans (Yoshioka et al., 2001), interethnic differences were found. Among the Vietnamese, 60% agreed with the statement "a man is the ruler of his home," in contrast to only 14% of the Chinese participants. About one fourth of Cambodians and Vietnamese agreed with the statement "a man is entitled to have sex with his wife whenever he wants it," as compared with 10% of the Chinese and 3% of the Korean participants. The two Southeast Asian groups (Cambodians and Vietnamese) were more likely to endorse male privilege, more likely to see violence with their spouse as justified in specific circumstances, and less likely to approve of alternatives to violence such as moving away or divorce.

Loss of status for the male and stressors such as acculturation conflicts, parent–child problems, unemployment, or employment of the wife may upset the hierarchical structure and contribute to domestic violence. Males may feel that they cannot fulfill the traditional role as the head of the family within the larger community and may behave in a more punitive manner toward their spouse and children (Dinh, Sarason, & Sarason, 1994). In a study of domestic violence involving Vietnamese women, Bui & Morash (1999) found areas of difference between the women and their husbands. The women were more open to a bicultural perspective and believed that their husbands strongly held the traditional gender role model of the submission of women to men. Correlates of domestic abuse were related to the husband's patriarchal beliefs and the imbalance in power between the spouses.

In addition, in many Asian cultures, family violence is viewed as a private matter and is less likely to be considered illegal in their country of origin. For example, among Vietnamese women, most believed that the laws in the United States protected women more than the laws in Vietnam. Even here, culture conflicts were apparent. Although the women had a positive view of laws against domestic violence, many were deeply concerned about the intrusion of law into family life (Bui & Morash, 1999). Domestic violence perspectives were also related to age or degree of acculturation. Among a sample of young and older adults in a Chinese American community, attitudes were associated with age differences (Yick & Agbayani-Siewert, 1997). Older Chinese respondents were more likely to feel that domestic violence, in cases of hierarchical or gender role violations in marriage, is justified.

Interventions in Domestic Violence

The following are suggested steps to take in cases of AA/PI family violence (Lum, 1999):

1. Assess the potential for lethality of the situation. If the danger appears to be high, develop a safety plan. Have the victim identify a person to stay with if she needs to leave the home. Locate shelters that are geared to needs of Asian women, if possible. For example, the Asian Shelter and Advocacy Project, an emergency shelter in Boston, allows women to have extended family members staying at the shelter (Malone, 1999). If a culturally sensitive shelter is not available, prepare the women for resources that do exist.

2. If the potential for lethality is moderate or low and does not require immediate intervention, provide psychoeducational information on abusive relationships, the cycle of violence, legal recourse, and the law against family violence. This might be useful because of the cultural respect for law and hierarchy. Many Asian immigrant women know little about law enforcement or their legal rights, nor are they aware of the availability of abused women's shelters, social services, and other resources (Bauer et al., 2000).

3. Provide appropriate translators and other support. Asian languages often involve dialect differences. A Chinese woman who speaks Cantonese would not be understood by a translator who spoke only Mandarin. Identify support groups that provide language and social transition skills and are willing to accompany clients to court and other service agencies (Preisser, 1999).

4. For immigrant women who are concerned about deportation, the provisions of the Battered Immigrant Protection Act of 2000, which furthered the Violence Against Women Act of 1994, should be made known. The act removed immigration status as a barrier that kept battered immigrant women and children locked in abusive relationships. It provides protection from deportation for battered immigrant women and children who are experiencing domestic violence. Under these acts, victims can obtain protection orders against abusers and are freed from the fear of retaliation by the withdrawal or threat of withdrawal of access to an immigration benefit controlled by the abuser.

5. During counseling, it is important to convey an understanding of the obstacles, both cultural and situational, that the client faces. It may be very important to create a therapeutic relationship, especially if there is no support from relatives. For immigrants or those with a highly traditional orientation, the emphasis could be placed on defining the healthy collective self as one that protects and cares for everyone's welfare, and that physical violence violates this collective self. It can be pointed out that to accept the abuse also injures the abuser and that it is healthier for the family if the violence ends.

6. Attempt to expand the support system and try to obtain support from the client's community. Some Asian women support and advocacy groups are now available. A helpful resource is the National Asian Pacific American Women's Forum, which has chapters in Los Angeles, Detroit, Minneapolis, New York, San Francisco, Seattle, and Washington, D.C.

7. Develop community awareness programs on domestic violence directed toward Asian women. In one community, the provision of awareness and services for Asian women has resulted in a drop in the domestic violence homicide rate in this population (Preisser, 1999).

Parent–Child Relationships

A Korean mother was sentenced to 2 years in prison for caning her teenage stepdaughter. During the trial, more than 20 Korean immigrants filled the courtroom to show support for the mother, claiming it was a traditional method of child discipline (Ippolito, 2000). In many countries, corporal punishment in schools was an acceptable process. It was eliminated in South Korea in 1998, in the Fiji Islands in 2002, and in Thailand in 2000. However, because of reported increases in behavioral problems in schools, there has been a move to reinstate caning in Thailand and South Korea (Corpun, 2002). Asian Americans tend to be somewhat more tolerant of the use of physical forms of discipline in child rearing. For example, many believe that it is permissible to strike a disobedient child (Yick & Agbayani-Siewert, 1997). The greater tolerance for physical punishment in AA/PI populations may account for the finding that

undergraduate Asian students are more likely than their European counterparts to report experiencing physical and emotional abuse and neglect (Meston, Heiman, Trapnell, & Carlin, 1999). However, possibly because of the shame and stigma of acknowledging problems to people or agencies outside of the family, cases of abuse reported to government agencies among Asian American children is low.

In general, the parenting style of the AA/PI population differs from that of European Americans, although there are large between- and within-group differences. Japanese and Filipino American families tend to be the most egalitarian, whereas Korean, Chinese, and Southeast Asian families are more authoritarian (Blair & Qian, 1998). The European American parenting style is described as authoritative in that it includes the use of inductive reasoning with children, allowing choices, encouraging independence, and promoting individual problem solving. There are many AA/PI styles, but the traditional one is hierarchical, with the father being the undisputed leader. AA/PI parenting can be described as somewhat more authoritarian or controlling. The emphasis is on obedience and respect for the parents. A strong sense of family obligation is instilled, and the needs of the family are placed over those of the individual (Jambunathan, Burts, & Pierce, 2000). Adapting one's needs to those of the family is the overarching theme (Rothbaum, Morelli, Pott, & Liu-Constant, 2000).

Discipline is considered to be an essential part in shaping the child. The most "abusive" parent is one who "drowns the child with love" (Meston et al., 1999). The methods of guidance or discipline in AA/PI families include the importance of training (*chiao shun*) and providing clear and concrete guidelines (Chao, 1994), the role of model or teacher for the children to emulate, the use of shame or guilt for misbehavior, and physical discipline for more severe violations.

Factors Associated With the Use of Physical Violence

Exposure of Asian American children to European American parenting styles and parent–child relationships through mass media and educational settings can result in family conflict. The cultural and value differences between the parent and child can be exacerbated because of the more rapid acculturation of children. For example, many South Asians are fighting to maintain traditional values in the face of assimilation and fear cultural erasure because of their "Americanized" children (Dasgupta, 1998). Similarly, in interviews with 73 Korean and Vietnamese children of immigrants, it was found that the behaviors of their parents were viewed through an Americanized lens. The children wanted parents who were less strict, gave them more freedom, were more liberal and open-minded, were more communicative and expressive, and were more affectionate (Pyke, 2000). The degree of acculturation differences between children and parents appears to be a factor in the way parent–child behaviors are viewed or evaluated by family members.

In general, exposure to European American parenting styles leads to a more negative evaluation of AA/PI parenting. Thus, the degree of difference in adherence to traditional cultural values between the parents and their children may play a role in intergenerational conflict. This may be especially true in less acculturated families. In one study, Vietnamese-born students reported a lower quality of family relations than American-born Vietnamese students. Vietnamese-born males were particularly at risk for poor relationships with their fathers (Dinh et al., 1994). Within the school setting, Asian American students often attribute adjustment issues to problems in their relationship with their parents. In school they are exposed to the values of independence, whereas at home there is an expectation of conformity to family wishes (Lee, Choe, Kim, & Ngo, 2000). For the parents, hierarchical violations, gender role reversals, and underemployment or unemployment can contribute to domestic stress and lead to child abuse (Yick & Agbayani-Siewert, 1997).

Interventions for Child Abuse

Although reported cases are low, child abuse does also occur in AA/PI families. Although most families dealing with this issue are highly anxious about the issue, it is considered even more shameful and uncomfortable for AA/PI families. The interventions suggested include the necessity of considering cultural factors along with the protections of the child:

- Report cases of suspected child abuse. Request that Child Protective Services consult with an AA/PI specialist if cultural factors may be involved. Some cultural medical practices found among AA/PI populations to treat illnesses or physical symptoms may produce bruising, which may be interpreted as abuse. For example, among the Vietnamese, *Cao Gio* ("coin treatment") and *Giac Hoi* ("pressure massage") can leave bruises on the parts of the body treated.

- Explain the purpose of counseling and discuss the legal system as it applies to child abuse with the family, if the abuse is verified.

- Assess factors associated with child abuse, paying special attention to acculturation conflicts and hierarchical changes. For example, fathers may feel threatened if they cannot fulfill the traditional role as head of the family, and mothers may become more punitive because of their responsibility in raising the children.

- Focus on acculturation conflicts as the "identified patient" whenever possible to reduce feelings of shame or anger. Identify the struggles that the parents and children face due to acculturation pressures. This will allow the formation of a therapeutic alliance.

- Focus on the more positive methods of discipline for AA/PI families. This serves to reduce the feeling that traditional means of discipline are being attacked. Discuss more appropriate cultural forms of discipline and training of children such as modeling, teaching, and guidance. Help parents develop a sense of authority by setting appropriate standards but allowing the children to make choices within these guidelines.

- Choose appropriate psychoeducational materials. Parenting material and classes based on European American standards may be inappropriate for AA/PI families. Cultural adaptations of parenting instructions have been developed for different ethnic groups.

- Employ a strengths model in identifying and increasing positive parenting behaviors by focusing on what works well within the family and reinforcing these behaviors.

Adoptions

In 2000, the greatest numbers of international Asian adoptees, most of whom are females, were from China, followed by South Korea, Vietnam, India, Cambodia, and the Philippines (Asian Nation, 2002). In the United States, less than 1% of children in foster care in 1999 were AA/PIs (U.S. Department of Health and Human Services, 2001c). Thus, issues involving adoption decisions apply primarily to international Asian children. Transracial adoptions involving Asian children have been a concern for several reasons. First, there may be the difficulty involved in achieving a positive racial identity and the fear over the possible loss of a cultural background. The parents (the vast majority of whom are white) may integrate the children so much into white society that they will lose their Asian identity. Second, because of differences in physical appearance from parents, the children may be asked about adoption and their cultural background and may later have to face the issues of prejudice and discrimination. Third, parents from a different ethnic background (white) will not be able to prepare the adopted child with skills necessary to negotiate problems stemming from ethnic identity or prejudice.

Congress has passed the Multiethnic Placement Act (1994) and the Removal of Barriers to Interethnic Adoption Act (1996), which specifically address transracial adoptions. Placement decisions on the adoption of children are not to consider the race, color, or national origin of the children or their prospective parents. Reductions in Title IV-E funds to private and state agencies receiving federal funds for violations have been used to back up this provision. In other words, race or ethnicity cannot be used as a factor to determine the "best interests of the child" when making adoption placement decisions. A possible exception might be an older child or adolescent who strongly expresses a racial or ethnic preference, although parents of a different race who are able to meet the needs of the child should be considered if they are immediately available. The intent is not to allow a delay in the adoption of the child (Kaplan, 2002). Native American children are excluded from the Multiethnic Placement Act because of the recognition by Congress of its unique relationship with tribal governments. The adoption of Native American children is covered by the Indian Child Welfare Act of 1978.

Research on Adjustment of Asian Adoptees

Determining what adoptive practices result in the "best interest of the child" has been fraught with problems. Research findings on the adjustment of Asian adoptees are difficult to interpret because variables such as the age of the child when adopted; parental preparation of the child for discrimination, prejudice, and cultural identity; and the area where the child grew up are often not taken into consideration. Therefore, the findings of the following studies cannot be directly compared. In a study of 406 adopted Korean children, psychosocial development appeared to be good, especially among those who were adopted at a younger age. Problems during adolescence revolved around discomfort with their appearance and a lack of ethnic identity (Kim, 1977).

In another study of internationally adopted Korean children (Friedlander et al., 2000), the following was found: (a) among very young children, awareness of their physical differences such as skin, eye, and hair color occurred early in life; (b) parents encouraged biculturalism by having the children attend a Korean culture camp and participating in Asian cultural events; (c) most of the children had received comments or insults regarding their physical appearance ("slanty eyes" or a "flat face"); and (d) parents attempted to prepare their children to deal with prejudice or discrimination. Again, this group of children appeared to adjust to transracial adoption.

Although research has been limited and methodological issues remain (studies based on limited populations, questionable questionnaires, and the lack of appropriate control groups), in general, it would appear that Asian adoptees do not differ significantly in adjustment or self-esteem from domestically adopted children in same-race families (Friedlander, 1999).

Legal and Counseling Implications of Transracial Adoptions

In general, adoption concerns for Asian children primarily involved international children, because relatively few AA/PI children are in the foster care system. Most of the following are recommendations for dealing with transracial adoptions (Bradley & Hawkins-Leon, 2002):

- With the passage of the Multiethnic Placement Act (1994) and the Removal of Barriers to Interethnic Adoption Act (1996), racial matching or screening for adoption placement decisions are no longer allowed. Parents who wish to adopt a racially different child cannot be discriminated against because of race.
- Failure to comply with these acts is a violation of Title VI of the Civil Rights Act of 1998. A complaint can be filed with the Office of Civil Rights for investigation.
- Private lawsuits can also be filed for violations of the act.
- It is recommended that those seeking to become parents of racially different children be involved with discussions about racial socialization and the importance of ethnic identity development in ethnic minority children.
- It is also important to prepare both the children and family members to deal with possible discrimination and prejudice within the larger society.

Conclusions

AA/PI populations are considered to be model minorities, and because of this perspective, little research has been directed to the problems faced by these communities. Very limited national baseline data exists, and most of the findings are based on small samples of AA/PIs living in specific communities. Thus, we must be cautious in interpreting the results of existing studies. There is evidence that AA/PIs populations may underutilize both mental and physical health services. This may be due to problems in communication, cultural perspectives, shame and stigma, or a distrust of community agencies and resources. Contributing to difficulties encountered with society as a whole is the collectivistic and hierarchical structure of many Asian American families, particularly among recent immigrants and Southeast Asians. When faced with a more egalitarian societal family structure, AA/PI families may develop problems with acculturation conflicts. This may involve role reversals in which women find it easier to obtain employment and men are either unemployed or underemployed, thereby interfering with the man's ability to be the head of the household. Children also acculturate more quickly than the parents and begin to question their parents as being "old-fashioned" and may rebel. Traditional AA/PI parenting models may no longer be adequate in dealing with acculturated children and may need to be modified. There is currently a move toward developing culturally appropriate parenting materials.

As with other groups in the United States, family problems such as divorce and spousal and child abuse can occur in AA/PI families. Indeed, these family problems, which were hidden in the past, are beginning to come to the attention of both the AA/PI communities and the community at large. Intervention strategies for dealing with these family issues need to consider cultural differences in terms of family structure, health and mental health beliefs, and communication barriers.

References

Asian Nation. (2002, June 26). *Multiracial and adopted Asians.* Retrieved June 26, 2002, from http://www.asian-nation.org/issues9.html

Bauer, H. M., Rodriguez, M. A., Quiroga, S. S., & Flores-Ortiz, Y. G. (2000). Barriers to health care for abused Latina and Asian immigrant women. *Journal of Health Care for the Poor and Underserved, 11,* 33–44.

Blair, S. L., & Qian, Z. (1998). Family and Asian students' educational performance. *Journal of Family Issues, 19,* 355–374.

Bradley, C., & Hawkins-Leon, C. G. (2002). The transracial adoption debate: Counseling and legal implications. *Journal of Counseling and Development, 80,* 433–440.

Bui, H. N., & Morash, M. (1999). Domestic violence in the Vietnamese immigrant community. *Violence Against Women, 5,* 769–795.

Chao, R. (1994). Beyond parental control and author-itarian parenting style: Understanding Chinese parenting through the cultural notion of training. *Child Development, 65,* 1111–1119.

Chen, M. S., & Hawks, B. L. (1995). A debunking of the myth of healthy Asian Americans and Pacific Islanders. *American Journal of Health Promotions, 9,* 261–268.

Choi, K.-H., & Wynne, M. E. (2000). Providing services to Asian Americans with developmental disabilities and their families: Mainstream service providers' perspective. *Community Mental Health Journal, 36,* 589–595.

Committee of 100. (2001). *American attitudes toward Chinese Americans and Asian Americans.* New York: Author.

Corpun. (2002). *World corporal punishment research.* Accessed December 22, 2002, from http://www.corpun.com/krs00203.htm

Dasgupta, S. D. (1998). Gender roles and cultural continuity in the Asian Indian immigrant community in the U.S. *Sex Roles, 38,* 953–974.

Dinh, K. T., Sarason, B. R., & Sarason, I. G. (1994). Parent–child relationships in Vietnamese immigrant families. *Journal of Family Psychology, 8,* 471–488.

Fong, R. (1994). Family preservation: Making it work for Asians. *Child Welfare, 78,* 331–341.

Friedlander, M. L. (1999). Ethnic identity development of internationally adopted children and adolescents: Implications for family therapists. *Journal of Marital and Family Therapy, 25,* 43–60.

Friedlander, M. L., Larney, L. C., Skau, M., Hotaling, M., Cutting, M. L., & Schwam, M. (2000). Biracial identification: Experiences of internationally adopted children and their parents. *Journal of Counseling Psychology, 47,* 187–198.

Hughes, D. L. (2002). Quality of health care for Asian Americans. *The Commonwealth Fund* (Pub. 525). New York: Commonwealth Fund.

Humes, K., & McKinnon, J. (2000). *The Asian and Pacific Islander population in the United States: March 1999.* U.S. Census Bureau. Washington, DC: U.S. Government Printing Office.

Ippolito, M. (2000, June 23). Housewife sent to prison in caning. Stunned by verdict: Traditional Korean punishment ruled child abuse in Gwinnett County. *Atlanta Journal and Constitution,* p. B3.

Jambunathan, S., Burts, D. C., & Pierce, S. (2000). Comparison of parenting attitudes among five ethnic groups in the United States. *Journal of Comparative Family Studies, 31,* 395–406.

Jamin, D., Yoo, H.-H., Moldoveanu, M., & Tran, L. (1999). Vietnamese and Armenian health attitudes survey. *Journal of Multicultural Nursing and Health, 5,* 6–13.

Kaplan, C. (2002, December 2). *Interethnic adoption provisions of the Small Business Job Protection Act of 1996: Implications for social work practice.* Retrieved December 22, 2002, from http://www.thepowerofsocialwork.org/practice/children/adopt.asp

Kim, D. S. (1977). How they fared: A follow-up study of adoption. *Children Today, 6,* 36–38.

Kreider, R. M., & Fields, J. M. (2001). Number, timing, and duration of marriages and divorces. In *Current Population Reports.* Washington, DC: U.S. Census Bureau.

Lee, R. M., Choe, J., Kim, G., & Ngo, V. (2000). Construction of the Asian American family conflicts scale. *Journal of Counseling Psychology, 47,* 211–222.

Lum, J. L. (1999). Family violence. In L. C. Lee & N. W. S. Zane (Eds.), *Handbook of Asian American psychology* (pp. 505–526). Thousand Oaks, CA: Sage Publications.

Malone, H. (1999, September 25). Asian task force encouraged by drop in domestic abuse deaths. *Boston Globe,* p. B3.

Martin, J. A. (1992). Birth characteristics of Asian or Pacific Islander subgroups, 1992. *Monthly Vital Statistics Report: Supplement, 43*(10).

Matthee, I. (1997, September 9). Anti-Asian hate crimes on rise in U.S. but state sees decline in such offenses. *Seattle Post-Intelligencer,* p. A3.

McLoyd, V. M., Cauce, A. M., Takeuchi, D., & Wilson, L. (2000). Marital processes and family socialization in families of color: A decade review of research. *Journal of Marriage and the Family, 62,* 1070–1093.

Meston, C. M., Heiman, J. R., Trapnell, P. D., & Carlin, A. S. (1999). Ethnicity, desirable responding, and self-reports of abuse: A comparison of European- and Asian-Ancestry undergraduates. *Journal of Consulting and Clinical Psychology, 67,* 139–144.

National Women's Health Information Center. (2002). Asian American and Pacific Islander women's health. Accessed December 22, 2002, from http://222.4woman.gov/faq/Asian_Pacific.htm

Pyke, K. (2000). "The normal American family" as an interpretive structure of family life among grown children of Korean and Vietnamese immigrants. *Journal of Marriage and the Family, 62,* 240–255.

Preisser, A. B. (1999). Domestic violence in South Asian communities in America: Advocacy and intervention. *Violence Against Women, 5,* 684–699.

Richardson, L., & MacGregor, H. E. (2001, April 30). To be Chinese in America: A poll finds that Chinese Americans are still viewed in a "very negative" light. *Los Angeles Times,* p. E1.

Ro, M. (2002). Moving forward: Addressing the health of Asian American and Pacific Islander women. *American Journal of Public Health, 92,* 516–519.

Rothbaum, F., Morelli, G., Pott, M., & Liu-Constant, Y. (2000). Immigrant-Chinese and Euro-American parents' physical closeness with young children and themes of family relatedness. *Journal of Family Psychology, 14,* 334–348.

U.S. Census Bureau. (2001a). *The Asian population: 2000.* Washington, DC: U.S. Government Printing Office.

U.S. Census Bureau. (2001b). *The Native Hawaiian and other Pacific Islander population: 2000.* Washington, DC: U.S. Government Printing Office.

U.S. Department of Health and Human Services. (2001a). How many children were in foster care on September 30, 1999? In *The AFCARS report.* Retrieved December 11, 2002, from http://www.acf.hhs.gov/programs/cb/publications/afcars/june2001.htm

U.S. Department of Health and Human Services. (2001b). *Mental health: Culture, race, and ethnicity—A supplement to mental health: A report of the surgeon general—Executive summary.* Rockville, MD: Author.

U.S. Department of Health and Human Services (2001c). *The AFCARS Report.* Rockville, MD: Author.

Yick, A. G., & Agbayani-Siewert, P. (1997). Perceptions of domestic violence in a Chinese American community. *Journal of Interpersonal Violence, 12,* 832–846.

Yoshioka, M. R., DiNoia, J., & Ullah, K. (2001). Attitudes towards marital violence: An examination of four Asian communities. *Violence Against Women, 7,* 900–926.

18

THE CHALLENGE OF CULTURAL COMPETENCE

An Introduction to Working With American Muslims and Their Families

BAHIRA SHERIF-TRASK

University of Delaware

The last several years have witnessed an increased interest in Muslims and their families in the United States. Although Muslims in the United States have a long, complex history, they have only come to the foreground of public attention due to recent political events. Despite a certain amount of media notoriety, there has been scant research on American Muslims and their families. This lack of information leads to biases and assumptions that may influence the delivery and the types of services available to American Muslims. Most important, it obscures the fact that this is a highly diverse group, composed of immigrants from many parts of the world, African American converts, and native-born Muslims. American Muslims are distinguished by different levels of education, types of occupations, arrival times in the United States, adherence to religious beliefs, and level of desire to assimilate into mainstream American society. This diversity among Muslim Americans has contributed to a lack of feeling of solidarity or group identity. On the one hand, Muslim Americans face a unique set of challenges due to their heterogeneity. On the other, they also provide a model for understanding and working with other highly diverse groups that characterize American society.

WORKING WITH CULTURALLY DIVERSE CLIENTS

Although Muslim individuals and their families share the same religion, they come from a wide range of backgrounds and cultures. Currently, professionals and laypeople are only starting to understand how to deliver all types of services with respect to issues of diversity. The popular practice of employing typologies of cultures and "characteristics" of individual groups only serves to obscure the heterogeneous nature of the various segments of American society. For professionals working with American Muslims, it is important not to lose sight of the individuality of the persons within the system (Berg & Miller, 1992).

269

It is generally accepted that in order to work with culturally diverse clients, professionals need to be aware of and challenge the stereotyped images they have of clients, be able to interpret a client's behavior within an appropriate cultural context, and use culturally appropriate interventions. This can roughly be understood to mean that professionals who wish to be effective in working with Muslim American clients need to become aware of their own biases and assumptions with respect to Muslim Americans, understand the cultural and sociopolitical factors affecting the worldview of Muslim Americans, and be able to identify strategies that are relevant to their clients' cultures and experiences (Erickson & al-Timimi, 2001). In order to accomplish this goal, a multipronged approach needs to be instituted for the delivery of services. For example, it may be necessary to spend more time with a client in order to understand the uniqueness of his or her particular experience and to become aware of issues of family, cultural background, regionality, and even neighborhood. As Baca-Zinn (1994) points out, when considering an individual's or a family's situation, it is necessary to remain aware of the potential for intersecting sources of oppression stemming from either religion, race, class, gender, or all of these. The situation becomes exacerbated with respect to Muslim Americans because they are not a clearly definable group. Nevertheless, current political events have lead to assumptions on the part of some that it is possible to identify individuals based on their religious beliefs or ethnicity—and that one can draw conclusions about their lives and beliefs based just on this typology. The purpose of this chapter is therefore to provide an overview of some of the issues relevant to Muslim Americans and to assist those involved in working with Muslim Americans with devising culturally relevant strategies. This chapter should serve as a brief introduction to these issues and may be used as an initial resource for those who would like to understand this highly diverse group.

WHO ARE MUSLIM AMERICANS?

The exact number of Muslims in the United States is somewhat unclear because the census does not collect data on religious affiliation or participation as part of its surveys. Estimates for the number of Muslims in the United States range from approximately 3 million (Smith, 2002) to 4 to 6 million (Stone, 1991; *World Almanac,* 1998). Statistics about American Muslims rely on percentages derived from data on national origin, language use, and mosque association and how these are linked to religious affiliation. These are tenuous linkages given the lack of correspondence between national origin and religion, as well as the secular nature of American society (Smith, 2002). Globally, Islam is one of the fastest-growing religions, with approximately 1.3 billion adherents. The same is true for the United States, where immigration and conversion account for the major part of the growth in this segment of the population.

American Muslims can be roughly divided into several groups: those immigrants who came from Asia, Africa, Iran, and the Middle East; African Americans; and converts from other groups found in the United States (Cooper, 1993).

Muslim American Immigrants

From 1924 to 1975, Muslim immigrants from the Middle East and North Africa outnumbered all those from other parts of the world. More recently, Muslim immigrants have come primarily from Asia, specifically Iran, Pakistan, and India (Walbridge, 1999, p. 392). In the last several years, there has also been a very small increase in the number of immigrant Muslims from Eastern Europe (Smith, 2002).

Immigrant Muslims primarily live in major metropolitan areas that have historically drawn new arrivals. These include some of the largest cities in the United States: New York, Los Angeles, and Chicago. The largest number of mosques and prayer halls are found in California, New York, Michigan, Illinois, and Pennsylvania (Nimer, 2002, p. 169). The fewest number of Muslim immigrants are located in the southeast and northwest portions of the country, with the exceptions of southern Florida and the Seattle area.

The majority of immigrant Arab, African, and Asian Muslims subscribe primarily to Sunni (or orthodox) Islam, whereas those from Iran tend to be Shi'ites. Recent immigrants tend to be highly educated professionals, independent businesspeople, or factory workers.

Muslim American immigrants share a commonality of experience with all other immigrants to the United States: They have left their country of origin behind and have relocated to a new, and often quite different, society. This poses its own set of stresses and challenges for individuals and their families. Each individual's immigration experience is influenced by a set of factors, including country of origin, length of time in the United States, reasons for emigration, whether he or she has family still living abroad, ability to return to or visit the home country, and long-term plans to stay in the United States. These factors are compounded by other issues such as the ability to speak English, their own and their family's educational and economic status in their home country, and the degree to which this status has altered since coming to the United States (Erickson & al-Timimi, 2001).

Often neglected in discussions of the immigration experience is the impact of gender. Women experience immigration quite differently from men, depending on their marital status and their ability to work or not to work once arrived in the United States. Recent studies indicate that although some of the issues faced by immigrant Muslim women overlap with those of Muslim men with respect to finding work and adjustment to new communities, other problems arise that are gender specific (Carolan, 1999; Erickson & al-Timimi, 2001). Depending on degree of religiosity, veiling, working outside of the home, and issues with respect to marital relations may be of great consequence for Muslim immigrant women.

African American Muslims

Again, due to the lack of census data with respect to religion, it is somewhat unclear exactly how many American Muslims are African American. Various estimates suggest that somewhere between 40% and 50% of all Muslim Americans are African Americans who have converted to Islam. The other half is composed almost entirely of immigrants, except for a few who are converts to Islam from various other cultural groups (Stone, 1991; Cooper,

1993). The largest concentration of African American Muslims is located in Illinois (Stone, 1991, p. 34). African American Muslims include Sunnis, members of the Nation of Islam, and other smaller denominations.

The Relationship Between Immigrant American Muslims and African American Muslims

Historically, there has been very little interaction between immigrant Muslims and African American Muslims. The difference in their experience forms the largest barrier to their interaction. Language skills, historical factors, racial issues, and vastly different cultural traditions form barriers between these groups that neither side has been able to overcome. Furthermore, unlike immigrants, many African Americans are converts. In order to observe their new religion, they tend to alter every aspect of their life. They usually adopt Muslim names, styles of dress (particularly among women—veiling), and a consciously projected Islamic image. For many converts, their new religious identity may take precedence over their former ethnic/racial identity. In contrast, many Muslim immigrants work harder to maintain their ethnic instead of their religious identity, while trying to assimilate into American culture (Kolars, 1994, p. 477).

Basic Tenets of Islam

In order to understand the lives and beliefs of Muslims, it is important to explicate some of the basic beliefs of the religion. For Muslims, Islam provides a foundation for understanding the religious beliefs and practices of Muslims and their families (Al-Hali & Khan, 1993). Islam is a monotheistic religion based on the belief that there is one God. This god, known in Arabic as Allah, is the same god that Christians and Jews believe in. The word *Islam* is an Arabic word meaning "submission to the will of God." A Muslim is an individual who follows the religion of Islam.

Muslims regard the Old and New Testaments as revelations that came from God (Allah). With respect to morals and human behavior, Islam, Judaism, and Christianity are virtually identical. A primary difference is that Islam does not accept the Christian concept of the Trinity or Jesus Christ as the son of God. Instead, Jesus is regarded as a prophet who was then followed by Muhammad, the last prophet. Furthermore, there are two major strands of Islam: Sunni Islam and Shi'a Islam, their distinction resulting from a crisis of succession after the death of Muhammad.

In comparison to the other monotheistic religions, Islam has a somewhat less formal structure (Cooper, 1993). The imam of a mosque is perceived as a teacher rather than a leader or mediator and every individual is thought to have a direct relationship to God. Another distinctive feature of Islam is the five pillars of faith. In addition to worshipping Allah (God), a practicing Muslim must pray five times a day, practice the yearly fast from sunrise to sunset during the month of Ramadan, contribute to the poor, and make a pilgrimage to Mecca at least once in his or her lifetime. Furthermore, every Muslim is expected to be moderate and may not drink alcohol, eat pork, or gamble. The visible, daily nature of these practices lead many people to perceive Islam as perhaps more ritualized than other religions (El-Amin, 1991).

Family as Primary Social Institution

In a general sense, the fundamental unit of social organization for many Muslims is the family, not the individual. It is the foundation of all social and economic activities and has remained at the center of contemporary Islamic societies. In America, "family" has come to be thought of by many as simply parents and their children or a single parent and his or her children. For many Muslims, the concept of family not only identifies specific kinship relations but also carries with it the culturally recognized patterns of patriarchy, hierarchy (particularly with respect to sex and age), and extended membership (Carolan, Bagherinia, Juhari, Himelright, & Mouton-Sanders, 2000; Rugh, 1984).

As such, the family constitutes the dominant social institution through which persons and groups inherit their religious, social class, and cultural identities. For many Muslims, family constitutes an economic and social unit in the sense that all of its members work together to secure its livelihood and to uphold and improve its standing in the community. In addition, the extended family provides security and emotional support in times of individual stress. In exchange for this support, the individual members are expected to place the group's survival above their personal desires, especially at the time of marriage, and to uphold the reputation of the family by behaving properly and "maintaining the family honor." The success or failure of an individual member becomes that of the family as a whole: Every member of the family is held responsible for the acts of every other member.

In the United States, a predominant trend is to perceive family acting as a unit that socializes and readies the individual for life outside of the family. Among many Muslims, depending in part on country of origin, the individual is socialized to remain part of the group, and he or she is expected to sacrifice his or her own needs for the greater good of the family. The personal status of each member of the family is defined by group membership, rather than by individual achievement. As a consequence of group membership, individual behavior is only evaluated in terms of its public image; personal lapses in behavior, as long as they remain secret, are of little consequence. An individual sense of shame and personal guilt is created only if such lapses are publicly acknowledged and become associated with the lowering of group status. If the family is highly thought of within the greater society, all of the individuals benefit. Conversely, any acts that arouse public dismay will consequently affect all members of the group.

Particularly for women, relations with family members are the strongest links in their lives. In general and within the family context, women are brought up to find their primary ties and ultimate sources of economic security in their relationships to their fathers, brothers, and sons. The importance of family in all arenas can hardly be overestimated. Some version of the extended family remains the ideal among many Muslims, and living in proximity to one another is considered important especially among recent immigrants. Family is perceived as providing a sense of place, a congenial setting, and a social network for financial and personal support (Macleod, 1991). At least in terms of ideology, the concept of family remains crucial for the network of resources and for the sense of identity it continues to provide.

The Importance of the Father Within Muslim Families

In many Muslim families, the father is the primary authority figure, and he is responsible for the economic and social well-being of his family. This responsibility has both a legal and a social dimension. According to religious law, the father is legally charged with the financial maintenance of his wife, their children, and any of his unmarried, divorced, or widowed female relatives. Within the family, the father expects respect and an unquestioning compliance with his wishes and instructions. While the wife is charged with the domestic responsibilities of the home, the father's role is crucial in supporting, protecting, and guiding his family. This delineation of roles is a vital aspect of social systems in which gender roles are clearly defined and supported by strong beliefs about male and female nature and the proper behavior that should be associated with each. Men and women alike view the male–female relationship as one of complementarity, rather than as one of equality. It is believed that men and women have different natures, which lead them to different roles, duties, interests, and positions. The negotiation of particular problems and decisions takes place within this general ideological context.

Honor, Shame, and Family Name

The code of honor and shame is central to understanding how behavior is regulated and conduct controlled in many non-Western societies. Depending on their national origin, many American Muslims adhere to a greater or lesser extent to this code of conduct. According to this ideology, because an individual represents his or her kin group, his or behavior must be honorable so that the group is not disgraced.

Those who bring shame on their kin are dishonorable because losing one's honor can be irreparable, not just for the affected family but also for future generations. The phenomena of honor and shame bear direct relation to internal family ties as well as relationships between families. The values of honor and shame are more than internalized psychological determinants for individual behavior. This value system operates in the social and political arenas to delineate group identity and to conserve social boundaries. In effect, it is this system that ultimately provides the basis for one's identity in terms of personal worth and one's standing within the community.

Islamic Teachings on Family

Both the Qur'an and the hadiths (the collection of sayings and teachings of the Prophet Mohammad) deal with issues relating to the regulation of mate selection, marriage, children, divorce, authority, inheritance, and family rights and responsibilities. Of the legal injunctions contained within the Qur'an, about one third relate to marriage and the family (Nasir, 1990). In order to understand some of the principles underlying Islamic beliefs with respect to family, it is instructive to look at some of the religious teachings on gender, marriage, parent–child relationships, and divorce.

The Issue of Gender Roles. Many Islamic religious injunctions deal specifically with the relationship between men and women in the family and are often turned to by Muslims as the basis for legitimizing gender roles. Islamic teachings stress the equality of all people before God. Nonetheless, there exists considerable variation in interpretations, particularly with respect to women's roles.

A fundamental Islamic belief is the distinct difference between male and female in terms of their personalities, social roles, and functions. References to women and their appropriate behavior are scattered throughout the Qur'an and the hadiths, and their meanings and interpretation have been a source of controversy since the earliest days of Islam. Various Qur'anic passages focus specifically on women's unique nature, place in society, and role within the general congregation of believers. Innate differences between the sexes are not perceived as a dichotomy of superior and inferior but as complementary (Macleod, 1991). However, underlying Islamic ideological formulations with respect to gender is the belief that women must remain in their place in order for political and social harmony to prevail. Practices such as veiling and distinct male and female activities, both in and outside the family, often reinforce this gender dichotomy. If women do not adhere to this moral order, then society runs the risk of degenerating into *fitna* (temptation or, more important, rebellion, social dissension, or disorder). A saying of the Prophet Muhammad is that there is no *fitna* more harmful to men than women. Women are so potentially powerful that they are required to submit to their husbands, segregate themselves from men to whom they are not immediately related, and restrain themselves, lest the pattern of gender relations at the core of a properly ordered society be overturned.

Even though the Qur'an is the central source of Islamic beliefs with respect to gender roles, there is considerable controversy about the meaning of each of these passages and their implications for the status of women (Fernea & Bezirgan, 1977, p. 13). Contemporary scholarship illustrates that, rather than determining attitudes about women, parts of the Qur'an are used at certain times to legitimate particular acts or sets of conditions with respect to women (Marcus, 1992; Mernissi, 1987). This selective use is part of the way in which gender hierarchies and sexuality are negotiated and enforced. It does not explain gender roles; instead, it is part of a constant process of gender role negotiation. Muslim feminist writers have gone to great lengths to illustrate that gender asymmetry and the status of women cannot be attributed to Islam. Instead, beliefs and practices with respect to women's and men's roles are part of a complicated interwoven set of social traditions, religions, and ever-changing political and economic conditions (Chatty & Rabo, 1997, p. 13). Recent research has highlighted the fact that the teachings of the Prophet Muhammad specified protections and rights for women that were radical departures from the existing culture. These included limitations on polygamy; inheritance

and property rights for women, as well as marriage contracts; and maintenance in cases of divorce and child custody (Baron, 1994, p. 5). These studies have highlighted the fact that gender constructions are always embedded in sociohistorical contexts. What it means to be a Muslim male or female is shaped not only by Islamic traditions and beliefs but also by the social environment in which these concepts are negotiated, as well as the personal characteristics of the individual.

The Significance of Marriage. Marriage is a central aspect of the lives of all Muslim men and women. Every Muslim is expected to marry, and marriage is governed by a complex set of legal rules. A Muslim family is established on the concept of a contractual exchange that legally commences with a marriage contract and its consummation. Every school of Islamic law perceives marriage as a contract, the main function of which is to make sexual relations between a man and a woman licit (Nasir, 1990). Several conditions make a Muslim marriage valid: the consent of the bride and of her legal guardian, two legal witnesses, and payment of a dower or *mahr*. The *mahr*, depending on custom, can range from gifts of a coin to large sums of money or valuables. The signing of the contract entitles the bride to the *mahr*, a suitable home, maintenance (food, clothes, and gifts), and a partial inheritance from the husband. According to Islamic law, women are not required to share in the costs and expenditures of their spouse or their male relatives. They are not expected or required to work outside the home. In return for his financial investment, the husband acquires authority as the head of the family as well as access to the sexual and reproductive abilities of his wife (Mir-Hosseini, 1993).

Once an Islamic marriage becomes valid through the signing of the marital contract, it is the duty of the husband to provide for his wife under three conditions: She also signs this contract, she puts herself under her husband's authority and allows him free access to her, and she obeys him for the duration of the marriage. This division of gender roles in the family is often legitimated by the following quote from the Qur'an:

Men are in charge of women, because Allah hath made the one of them to excel the other, and because they spend of their property [for support of women]. So good women are the obedient, guarding in secret that which Allah hath guarded. As for those from whom ye fear rebellion, admonish them and banish them to beds apart, and scourge them. Lo! Allah is ever High Exalted, Great. (Pickthall, 1976, 4:34)

Beyond its legal components, marriage also has a religious dimension and is invested with many ethical injunctions. Any sexual contact outside marriage is considered adultery and is subject to punishment. Islam also condemns and discourages celibacy. Muslim jurists have gone so far as to elevate marriage to the level of a religious duty. The Qur'an supports this notion with the phrase "And marry such of you as are solitary and the pious of your slaves and maid servants" (24:32), which is commonly interpreted as advocating marriage in order to complete the religion. An often quoted hadith states that the prayer of a married man is equal to seventy prayers of a single man.

The significance of the Islamic ideals of marriage inherent in the Qur'an and the *shari'a* (legal interpretations) is that they provide a primary frame of reference for legitimizing the actions of individuals and validating certain power relations within the family. Ideologies are, however, not unchanging. They are forged, negotiated, and reexpressed in connection with other social, economic, and historical factors. These ideals provide one *potential* area from which individuals draw their beliefs, which they negotiate within their social and cultural environment.

Parent–Child Relationships. The Qur'an and the *sunna* (practices) are extremely concerned with motherhood, fatherhood, and the protection of children from the moment of conception until the age of maturity. Besides the Qur'an, many significant Islamic texts indicate the primary importance of children and their well-being within the family unit. This emphasis can be attributed to several factors. Children are believed to strengthen the marital tie, continue the family line by carrying their father's name, and provide for their parents in old age, and they are partial inheritors of their parents' estate.

The legal aspects of Islam deal with the socioeconomic conditions of children, both within the family and in the event of divorce or death of the parents (Schacht, 1964, p. 168). Islamic law states that every Muslim infant is entitled to *hadana,* which loosely translates into the fulfillment of the physical and emotional needs of a child. This includes, besides care and protection, socialization and education. The child is entitled to love, attention, and devotion to all its needs, because it is unable to take care of itself.

According to religious law, the parent–child relationship parallels the rights and obligations established through marriage, notwithstanding its specific social context. The *shari'a* (religious law) has developed specialized topics that reflect the highly protective attitude of the Qur'an toward minors and aged parents. Specifically, the primary legal relationship centers on adequate maintenance of dependent children and needy parents. The economic and social welfare of children is a major parental responsibility enforceable under Islamic law (Fluehr-Lobban, 1987, p. 184). Reciprocally, it is the legal responsibility of children to take care of their aged parents, both financially and socially.

And that ye show kindness to parents. If one of them or both of them attain old age with thee, say not "fie" unto them nor repulse them, but speak unto them a gracious word. (Qur'an, 17:23)

An examination of the Islamic religious and legal ideals of the relationship between children and parents reveals a strong emphasis on the guardianship of the individual throughout the various stages of his or her life. Islamic tenets stress the responsibility of the parents for the child, which begins at conception. In return, children are obligated to care for their aged parents. It is important to note that there is a reciprocal emphasis on the rights and obligations of *both* parents and children.

Divorce. Divorce is treated as a serious matter in both the Qur'an and hadiths (sayings of the Prophet Muhammad) as well as by Islamic law. Several *suras* (2:225–232; 65:1–7) deal in detail with divorce, and an often-recited hadith states, "No permissible thing is more detested by Allah than divorce." Divorce implicates men and women differently in the legal domain. According to Islamic law, a Muslim husband has the unilateral right to divorce his wife without having to justify his actions before any legal body or any witnesses. A wife, however, in order to initiate a divorce, must place her claim before a *shari'a* court and argue her case on the basis of certain legal precepts. Legally, the most concrete factor that prevents divorce is that portion of the *mahr* (the gift or dower) that becomes owed to the wife upon the dissolution of the marriage (Nasir, 1990). Women who stipulate a *mahr* in their marriage contract will use it primarily as a bargaining tool should their husband threaten to divorce them. Thus, the *mahr* acts as a deterrent to divorce, and it may give a woman some financial security and bargaining power.

Besides the *mahr*, the *'idda* also acts as a restraint to divorce. The *'idda* is the period between an actual separation of the couple and the final termination of marriage, and it carries with it certain obligations and rights for both spouses. These include a temporary legal restraint from remarrying, sexual abstinence for a woman, the mutual entitlement to inheritance, and the maintenance and lodging of the wife, who must wait three menstrual cycles before the divorce is final (Qur'an, 2:228). According to Islamic law, a divorce cannot be finalized until the *'idda* requirement is completed. In the case of a pregnant woman, the *'idda* continues until her child is born (Qur'an, 65:6). The reasons for observing the *'idda* are threefold: (1) to ascertain the possibility of a pregnancy and, if necessary, to establish the paternity of the child; (2) to provide the husband with an opportunity to go back to his wife if the divorce is revocable; and (3) to enable a widow to mourn her deceased husband (Nasir, 1990, p. 99). The stress in the Qur'an and Islamic law on the *'idda* illustrates the Islamic emphasis on ensuring the well-being of the unborn child. Again, this points to the religious emphasis on creating a family and ensuring that the woman and her children have a form of social protection.

The Relevance of Qur'anic Ideals

Although not all Muslims and their families adhere to the principles outlined earlier, they do give some basis for understanding that different belief systems may, at least in part, play a role in the lives of individuals. It is crucial to remember, however, that a Muslim living in a non-Muslim country may potentially have very different concerns than a Muslim living in an Islamic society. Belief systems and how they are played out on a day-to-day basis are constantly forged and renegotiated based on context and personal inclinations. Islamic ideals are only one source from which American Muslims may draw their beliefs.

Issues Facing Muslim Americans and Their Families

Stereotyping

Probably the most significant issue currently facing Muslims is their representation in the popular consciousness as potential terrorists. Political developments and a series of terrorist acts committed in the name of Islam combined with little public knowledge about the religion have led to a rash determination by some that Islam is a violent religion, with its adherents prone to using terror to enforce their will. Even though there has been a concerted effort by both the government and the media to educate the public about the basic tenets of Islam, the complexity of the situation combined with inadequate knowledge about the diversity *within* the Muslim world have led to this situation. Although prejudice and discrimination affect, in some form, all minority groups, Muslim Americans are particularly affected due to a general lack of information about them. Furthermore, despite attempts by scholars, the government, and other private groups to warn the public about penalizing communities for the actions of a few during times of crisis, Muslim Americans and their places of worship have been the object of disparate acts of violence and prejudice. The fear of "shadowy" enemies has led to an increased fear of individuals who are perceived as "foreign" in general. Other recent reports indicate that, oftentimes, cases of vandalism against local mosques and Islamic centers are passed over quietly in order not to incite more severe consequences (Nimer, 2002,

p. 176). Many Muslims, due to fear of being misrepresented because of their religion, prefer to deal with such conflictual situations with as little public attention as possible.

As a response to some of these issues, several Muslim public affairs groups have emerged in recent years to defend Muslims against discrimination, to give them a public voice, and to represent their issues before governmental and nongovernmental bodies (Nimer, 2002, p. 169). Due in part to the efforts of these groups, Muslims are increasingly able to raise concerns about issues of employment, schooling, and even family matters in the public arena.

Religion and the Workplace

For practicing Muslims, employment situations can often cause uncomfortable, complicated dilemmas, forcing them to choose between religious practices and the need for work. While the Civil Rights Act of 1964 advocates that employers allow for reasonable accommodation of the religious practices of company employees, the law is often not enforced. The religious practices of employees are often not mentioned in corporate personnel policy manuals, and companies tend to prefer to deal with issues of religious accommodation on a case-by-case basis to prevent incidents of discrimination (Nimer, 2002, p. 173). The conflict between religious accommodation and employment is highlighted by the fact that women who wear the *hijab* (the head covering worn by Muslim women to signify modesty) are often denied employment because of their dress. In order to be nonconfrontational, many Muslims just opt to not highlight their practices while in the workplace.

In rare cases, practicing Muslims have decided to take on the American legal system with respect to the complicated issue of religious freedom versus the rights of the employer. Nimer (2002, p. 173) describes a case where, on October 4, 1999, the Supreme Court rejected an appeal of a lower court ruling that allowed Muslim police officers in Newark, New Jersey, to wear beards, despite the Newark Police Department's no-beard policy. In the earlier ruling issued by the U.S. Court of Appeals for the 3rd Circuit Court in *Fraternal Order of Police*

v. City of Newark, the court opinion was stated as such: "Because the Department makes exemptions from its policy for secular reasons and has not offered any substantial justification for refusing to provide similar treatment for officers who are required to wear beards for religious reasons, we conclude that the Department's policy violates the First Amendment." This ruling gave the American Muslim community its first major legal victory in many years by accommodating an element of Islamic law within America's secular legal tradition (Nimer, 2002, p. 173).

Religion and Schooling

A growing area of concern for Muslim parents is the relationship of their children to the public school system. While there are a number of Islamic schools spread out throughout the United States, most Muslim children are enrolled in public schools. At issue is the fact that public schools do not offer time and space for prayers. Again, school districts exercise discretionary power in enforcing religious accommodation policies (Nimer, 2002, p. 173). In many districts, time restrictions do not allow for the accommodation of prayer times nor do they take into account the period of fasting (Ramadan) that is required of all Muslims annually. Other concerns center on food prohibitions, because Muslims may not eat pork, yet this is included at times in school lunches without any alternatives. Muslim parents and educators are also increasingly perturbed by portrayals of Muslims and Islam in educational materials, which do not necessarily always represent an objective account of the religion and its adherents. Lately, the Council on American-Islamic Relations (CAIR) has begun publishing and distributing educational materials that explain Islamic religious practices to employees, educators, and health care professionals.

Intergenerational Conflicts

Muslims, depending on country of origin, educational level, and time of arrival in the United States may face complicated issues with respect to family relationships. In particular, the issue of marriage provides the basis for complex determinations as to what extent culture and to what extent the legal system may interfere with decisions determined in families. One of the most controversial of these issues came about in 1996 in Nebraska with the case of the child brides. An Iraqi father of two young girls, who were then 13 and 14 years old, was charged with child abuse because he arranged marriages for his daughters. The *New York Times* reported that this case of "forced" marriages was met with public consternation because the girls were married to two Iraqi immigrants "more than twice their age," who then took the brides home and "consummated the marriages" (in Moore, 2002, p. 197). The coverage in the *New York Times* highlighted the legal and cultural complexity of this case, which posed the dilemma about when to prosecute "when religious traditions become criminal offenses." The accused were charged with and convicted of statutory rape and child abuse. At sentencing, the defendants argued that they had conformed to the norms of Islamic "culture" and therefore deserved leniency. Moore points out that although forced marriages definitely highlight the conflict between gender, class, and religious tradition, they also depict a hegemonic representation of a culture that is inherently deficient when compared with mainstream culture. She points out, very correctly, that women across cultural boundaries experience discrepancies and violence based on various gender and class as well as power relations and that this is not just a culturally specific phenomenon. Muslim crimes that victimize women and children are often portrayed as culturally specific. Sexual violence against women and children in the United States, however, are today understood to have social and psychological roots—except when they happen under the umbrella of an "inferior" culture or society and then are perceived as culturally based (Moore, 2002, p. 198). Cases like the one described earlier illustrate the complexity of disentangling beliefs about law, gender, and culture. Before drawing conclusions about the assumed culturally specific nature of an issue, it is crucial to delineate the problem from the context within which it occurs. Thus, crimes need to be understood as such—and not as the necessary product of a specific culture.

CONCLUSION

Muslim Americans provide an interesting example of the problems that arise when trying to classify groups of people based on typologies or lists of characteristics. Currently, it is often not clear who is Muslim (defined by mosque membership, amount of prayer, country of origin, etc.) and what that means in the context of the United States, a country that is built on the ideology of heterogeneity due to immigration. The lack of group identity among Muslims themselves further exacerbates this problem. Although some individuals may wish to politicize their issues, many others, be they self-identified as religious to varying degrees or secular, do not wish to make religion their primary source of identification. It is incumbent on service providers to be extremely aware of the importance of self-identification in this process. The extent to which someone belongs to a group, especially a religious group, is determined by his or her personal perceptions and affiliations. Most Muslim Americans do not have a political or "cultural" identity based solely on religion. Instead, they struggle with the same issues facing all Americans: They are trying to make a living and maintain solid family lives in the face of an increasingly complex world. To assume a strong political consciousness among Muslim Americans based on religious beliefs is a fallacy, due to the extreme heterogeneity of the group. As was mentioned earlier, Muslims who have arrived recently in the United States may face very different issues with respect to assimilation, jobs, language, and the like than Muslims who are African American or whose families have been here for several decades. Language, class, and cultural issues further divide this group. For service providers, the most important aspect of cultural competence is understanding that individuals and their families may have a different belief system from themselves and being aware of the necessity of understanding some of these differences. The changing demographics of U.S. society indicate the importance of awareness when it comes to working with individuals with different cultural values. A strength-based approach that values difference and formulates interventions based on these values may be the most valuable path for service providers, be they involved with law, health care, family support, or other social services.

REFERENCES

Al-Hali, T., & Khan, M. (1993). *Interpretation of the meanings of the noble Quar'an in the English language.* Kingdom of Saudi Arabia: Maktaba Dar-us-Salam.

Baca-Zinn, M. (1994). Feminist rethinking about racial-ethnic families. In M. Baca-Zinn & B. T. Dill (Eds.), *Women of color in U.S. society* (pp. 303–314). Philadelphia: Temple University Press.

Baron, B. (1994). *The women's awakening: Culture, society and the press.* New Haven, CT: Yale University.

Berg, I. K., & Miller, S. D. (1992). Working with Asian American clients: One person at a time. *Families in Society: The Journal of Contemporary Human Services, 17,* 356–363.

Carolan, M. (1999). Contemporary Muslim women and the family. In H. McAdoo (Ed.), *Family ethnicity* (pp. 213–221). Thousand Oaks, CA: Sage Publications.

Carolan, M., Bagherinia, G., Juhari, R., Himelright, J., & Mouton-Sanders, M. (2000). Contemporary Muslim families: Research and practice. *Contemporary Family Therapy, 22,* 67–79.

Chatty, D., & Rabo, A. (1997). *Organizing women: Formal and informal women's groups in the Middle East.* New York: Berg.

Cooper, M. H. (1993). Muslims in America. *The National Law Journal, 17,* 363–367.

El-Amin, M. M. (1991). *Family roots: The Quaranic view of family life.* Chicago: International Ummah Foundation.

Erickson, C., & al-Timimi, N. (2001). Providing mental health services to Arab Americans: Recommendations and considerations. *Cultural Diversity and Ethnic Minority Psychology, 7,* 308–327.

Fernea, E., & Bezirgan, B. (1977). *Middle Eastern Muslim women speak.* Austin: University of Texas Press.

Fluehr-Lobban, C. (1987). *Islamic law and society in the Sudan.* London: Frank Cass.

Hermansen, M. (1994). Two-way acculturation: Muslim women in America between individual choice and community. In Y. Haddad (Ed.), *The Muslims of America* (pp. 188–204). New York: Oxford University Press.

Kolars, C. (1994). Masjid ul-Mutkabir: The portrait of an African American orthodox Muslim community. In Y. Haddad (Ed.), *The Muslims of America* (pp. 475–499). New York: Oxford University Press.

Macleod, A. (1991). *Accommodating protest: Working women, the new veiling and change in Cairo.* New York: Columbia University Press.

Marcus, J. (1992). *A world of difference: Islam and gender hierarchy in Turkey.* London: Zed Press.

Mernissi, F. (1987). *Beyond the veil: Male-female dynamics in modern Muslim society.* Bloomington: Indiana University Press.

Mir-Hosseini, Z. (1993). *Marriage on trial: A study of Islamic family law.* London: I. B. Tauris.

Moore, K. (2002). Representation of Islam in the language of law: Some recent U.S. cases. In Y. Haddad (Ed.), *Muslims in the West: From sojourners to citizens* (pp. 187–204). New York: Oxford University Press.

Nasir, J. (1990). *The Islamic law of personal status.* London: Graham and Trotman.

Nimer, M. (2002). Muslims in American public life. In Y. Haddad (Ed.), *Muslims in the West: From sojourners to citizens* (pp. 169–186). New York: Oxford University Press.

Pickthall, M. (1976). *The glorious Koran: Text and Explanatory Translation.* Albany, NY: State University of New York Press.

Rugh, A. (1984). *Family in contemporary Egypt.* Syracuse, NY: Syracuse University Press.

Schacht, J. (1964). *An introduction to Islamic law.* Oxford, UK: Clarendon.

Smith, T. (2002). The polls—Review; the Muslim population of the United States: The methodology of estimates. *Public Opinion Quarterly, 66,* 404–414.

Stone, C. (1991). Estimate of Muslims in America. In Y. Haddad (Ed.), *The Muslims of America* (pp. 25–36). New York: Oxford University Press.

Walbridge, L. (1999). Middle Easterners and North Africans. In E. Barkan (Ed.), *A nation of peoples: A sourcebook on America's multicultural heritage* (pp. 391–410). Westport, CT: Greenwood Press.

World almanac and book of facts. (1998). Mahwah, NJ: World Almanac Books.

19

UNACCOMPANIED CHILDREN IN THE UNITED STATES

Legal and Psychological Considerations

DANA CHOU

Doctors of the World

A young unaccompanied child falls out of the hands of organized criminals and into the arms of the law when he is arrested and taken to court accused of a crime. He is physically injured, suffering from a fever, and unable to answer the judge's questions. The well-meaning officer escorting the child offers "the usual answers" for him because he is barely conscious, and the judge accepts these into the record. The child is otherwise unassisted and unrepresented. Though even the victim isn't sure that the boy is guilty, and there are no witnesses to testify one way or the other, the judge finds him guilty and sentences him to three months at hard labor.[1]

There are striking similarities between this scene from Dickens's *Oliver Twist* and the circumstances in which many unaccompanied immigrant children find themselves in the U.S. legal system. Although children in today's courtrooms may not be feverish or fainting, their circumstances and experiences often render them as powerless in court as if they were unconscious. From apprehension through adjudication, our

system has been widely criticized for failing to address the special needs of these children. Their circumstances are extraordinary. They are separated from parents or caregivers and geographically displaced, they may not comprehend the proceedings cognitively or linguistically, they may have very limited ability to articulate their experiences and develop legal claims, they often have no legal representation, they are often unable to make informed decisions that reflect a full understanding of attendant consequences, and they may be profoundly traumatized by horrific life experiences. This chapter will provide an overview of unaccompanied children, their legal situation, and the developmental and psychological issues that professionals working with them should bear in mind.

WHO ARE UNACCOMPANIED CHILDREN?

The United Nations High Commissioner for Refugees (UNHCR) estimates that 25 million children around the world are currently uprooted and displaced.[2] UNHCR cares for about 10 million of these children through various programs for refugees displaced internally, temporarily displaced to other countries, or resettled to other countries. The term "refugee" refers to persons so designated by UNHCR who are eligible for various forms of practical assistance and legal protection. The unaccompanied children discussed in this chapter are non-refugees. Many of them migrate to the United States or other countries seeking asylum, but at U.S. borders they have no entitlement to legal status or practical assistance. About 20,000 unaccompanied children file asylum applications annually in Europe, North America, and Oceania.[3] In the United States, the Immigration and Naturalization Service (INS) detains approximately 5,000 unaccompanied children every year.[4] An unknown number of others cross the border without being detected.

The term "unaccompanied child" is generally understood to refer to anyone under the age of 18 who is separated from his or her parents. In recent years, agencies working with refugee and immigrant populations have increasingly adopted the term "separated child" to reflect the possibility of separation from either parents or other caregivers who by law or custom have assumed a guardian role. The UNHCR subsumes both meanings in its definition of "unaccompanied child," as is done in this chapter.[5]

Many children become separated from parents or customary caregivers due to natural or man-made conditions of crisis or disaster. Forms of trauma frequently reported by separated children include "the violent death of a parent, injury/torture towards a family member(s), witness of murder/massacre, terrorist attack(s), child-soldier activity, bombardments and shelling, detention, beatings and/or physical injury, disability inflicted by violence, sexual assault, disappearance of family members/friends, witness of parental fear and panic, famine, forcible eviction, separation and forced migration . . . endurance of political oppression, harassment and deprivation of human rights and education."[6] To this list we might also add physical destruction of one's home and/or community, physical and/or sexual abuse inflicted by family members, neglect or abandonment by one or both parents, physical or economic exploitation by older persons, and perils associated with chronic and extreme poverty, homelessness, and street life.

When Edwin was 4 years old his father died. His mother abandoned him soon afterwards and he ended up living in the home of a cousin. When he turned 7 his cousin sent him to work daily in the streets to earn whatever money he could. If the earnings were too small his cousin beat him with car tools and other objects, leaving many scars. At 13 Edwin determined to leave his cousin's home for the US rather than endure further abuse or risk the dangers of life on the streets. He'd heard that in the US children were treated better. He left Honduras with the equivalent of $15 in hand and made his way through Guatemala and Mexico to the US border. The journey took six months.[7]

As a second-born daughter in China, Z was the object of hostility and discrimination. Her parents hid her at her grandparents' home for 7 years to avoid consequences to the family of violating the "one child" policy. When she returned to live with her parents, her mother often beat her and she was not allowed to attend school beyond the 6th grade. At age 16, Z made her way to the US to escape the stigma surrounding her in China and to pursue further education.[8]

Some children flee or are sent away before an expected crisis erupts or to prevent anticipated trauma.

Satish came to the US from Sri Lanka. He and his family fled their home due to the civil war and became internally displaced refugees. Fearing that Satish would be kidnapped and forced into military service, his parents paid to have him smuggled out of the country when he turned 15.[9]

Aishat was 7 years old when her father put her on a flight from their native Nigeria to the US to protect her from their tribe's customary circumcision of girls at age 8. Though Aishat's mother was at the US airport to meet her, being undocumented she was too afraid of detection to claim her daughter. Aishat spent the next 15 months in INS detention and was starting to forget her native language by the time a cousin finally gained guardianship of her.[10]

For many children, the decision to migrate is economically based. Many report that prospects for overcoming conditions of poverty in their home countries are few or nonexistent, particularly in the wake of large-scale disruptions such as natural disaster or war. Educational opportunities may be limited, unaffordable, or offered in a mainstream language the child does not speak, or they may require too much time away from tending crops or other necessary work activities. Unemployment rates may be very high, forcing children into competition with older children and adults for jobs. Members of ethnic minorities and indigenous groups may be excluded from benefits, opportunities, and civil protections simply as a matter of practice, and also due to lack of fluency in the majority language. Some children may be assigned or may assume responsibility to become U.S.-based breadwinners in response to chronically bleak local economic conditions. And some are charged to raise not only economic status but also the prestige or honor of the family by working abroad and sending money home.[11]

> Duwin came to the US from Guatemala when he was 17. He traveled on foot, hitched rides, and rode boxcars on his way through Mexico. He worked odd jobs to earn traveling money. During an interview given after being apprehended by INS he said, "I came suffering—sometimes without eating. (But) the poor man from the United States is a millionaire next to the poor man from there."[12]

There are also children who migrate for family reunification. One or both parents or older siblings may already be living or working in the United States. Children remaining at home are usually left in the care of the remaining parent, grandparents, or other relatives. If the caregiver becomes infirm or dies, can no longer afford to care for the child, or has strained or hostile relations with the child, or if the child simply wants to be with the absent family member or follow that person's example, then the child may choose or be forced to migrate. The child may have had little contact with an absent parent since infancy and may not have the parent's address or phone number; the parent may be unaware that the child is migrating.

In other cases the parent may invite and encourage the child to migrate.

> A 15-year-old girl en route to Canada to rejoin her mother was arrested at JFK Airport in New York City. Despite her statement of age INS determined through dental x-rays that she was 18 and placed her in an adult detention facility for non-criminal asylum seekers. When interviewed 4 months later in detention by a delegation of religious leaders she continued to report her age as 15 and said, "I just want to get out of here and be with my mother."[13]

In contrast to those who migrate out of necessity or by choice, children victimized by traffickers are often lured away by deception. Traffickers promise good jobs, education, and even marriage for the children, and naive or desperate parents are convinced to part with them. Other children are sold to traffickers, and some are coerced directly or simply abducted. At their destinations they are usually made to work in the sex industry or as forced laborers. They are paid little or nothing for working long hours; charged for meals and other living expenses; controlled with weapons, threats of death or injury to themselves or their families, and threats of deportation; denied health care or charged for it; prevented from communicating with their families or others; and often kept imprisoned in their workplaces. It is estimated that approximately 50,000 women and children are trafficked into the United States annually and that the numbers are increasing.[14] (See Chapter 15 in this volume for a detailed discussion of trafficking.)

> Phanupong was 2 years old when he arrived at Los Angeles International Airport with a trafficker and a woman being trafficked posing as his parents. His real mother, a drug addict and trafficking victim in Thailand, sold him to a trafficker who used him as a prop for smuggling women into the US to work as prostitutes. When "apprehended" Phanupong was feverish with a severe infection and chicken pox. He was later found to be HIV positive.[15]

These categories of migrating children are by no means discrete, and children often fit into more than one category at the same time. For example, a child living in poverty might be displaced by an armed conflict and separated from caregivers and then go alone in search of a parent or other relative who previously went abroad to raise the family's fortunes. Similarly, trafficking victims are most likely to come from areas where conditions of economic and political instability prevail.[16]

Unaccompanied children who are not trafficked into the United States are very likely to arrange at least some portion of their travel through smugglers. Smuggling is defined as a simple fee-for-service arrangement in which the child or his or her family hires someone to sneak him or her out of one country and into another. It differs from trafficking in that the person being smuggled is a willing participant, and no element of coercion, force, kidnapping, deception, fraud, or intent to enslave the person applies. (It should be noted, however, that many who undertake to be smuggled find out too late that the smuggler's true intention is trafficking.) Costs of smuggling vary depending on factors such as distance, means of transportation, and whether or not false travel documents are provided. At this writing, on the low end one can hire a "coyote" for guidance across the U.S.-Mexico border without documents and on foot for an average of about $1,500.[17] On the high end, "snakeheads" charge up to $80,000 for fake papers, a direct flight from China to the United States, a lawyer standing by to defend the migrant if caught and to falsify (if necessary) an asylum application, and fake relatives who will apply to sponsor the migrant and pay to bond him or her out of detention.[18]

The risks and dangers for children migrating alone or in company with smugglers cannot be overstated. They may be robbed, assaulted, or killed by fellow travelers, the smugglers, thieves prowling the migration routes, and even officials of the jurisdictions through which they pass. Those working their way toward the United States risk abuse and exploitation by employers. Smuggled people frequently travel under extremely dangerous conditions such as in crowded airtight vehicles and containers; in overcrowded, unseaworthy vessels; or on foot across shadeless deserts without adequate supplies of water. Crowded, unsanitary, and undersupplied

conditions are typical. Smugglers sometimes drug children to improve stamina and minimize awareness of hunger and other suffering. Multiple-leg journeys involve stops at safe houses or staging areas where migrants may wait for weeks or months and may be held like prisoners until preparations for the next leg of the trip are ready. Smugglers may be relied on to abandon their clients at the first hint of danger to themselves or detection by authorities.

> Daniel illegally entered the US as a teenager and lived underground until eventually becoming a legal resident. "We knew we could get assaulted and robbed along the way—and I don't know what else. It was worth the risk. We had nothing to lose. If you lost your life, that was already a fear we lived with every day in El Salvador."[19]

LEGAL AND CUSTODIAL ISSUES

Up until passage of the Homeland Security Act in November 2002, the INS was responsible for the processing, detention, and release of unaccompanied children. Since passage of the act, a transition is under way to move responsibility for children's affairs to the Office of Refugee Resettlement (ORR), a division of the Department of Health and Human Services. This section describes the INS's practices regarding children and some changes that may be anticipated under ORR. INS practices are expected to proceed as described until ORR begins implementing its own policies.

Unaccompanied children apprehended in the United States are held in INS's detention system unless they can be immediately deported or qualified sponsors are immediately available to assume custody. Children from some countries such as China, where smuggling rings are highly organized and the smugglees are worth tens of thousands of dollars, are ineligible for immediate release. Their sponsoring relatives must first undergo background checks and home studies to verify family relationships, noninvolvement with smugglers, and the suitability of home environments. These investigations are carried out by nongovernmental organizations under contract to the Department of Justice and may take up to 6 months or longer depending on the availability of caseworkers and the cooperation of the child, the sponsor, and other agencies involved.

A child's detention placement may be in or near the place of apprehension or it may be thousands of miles away. Placement determination is dictated by INS operational concerns, not by a detainee's proximity to family members, sponsor candidates, or legal resources. Just like adults, children are subject to sudden transfers without prior notice to the child, relatives, sponsor, or legal representative. Transfers, and even deportations, can occur even though asylum proceedings or case appeals are in progress.[20] Some detained children undergo multiple transfers and suffer repeated disruptions to their fragile support systems as their cases wind through the system.

Before assigning placement, the INS may seek to verify a child's age if there is doubt that he or she is a minor. In this case, the child may be required to submit to X-ray testing of teeth or bones. Forensic dental assessment is based on eruption patterns of teeth, whereas bone assessment examines bone growth and development patterns. These techniques have come under increasing criticism as being unreliable, and numerous examples of misclassification of children as adults have been documented.[21] At this time INS continues to rely on these methods, though it purports to be exploring other alternatives.

The rules and conditions for detention of children are defined by the settlement of a class action lawsuit filed in 1985 on behalf of Jenny Lisette Flores, a child who suffered abuse when misclassified as an adult and placed in adult detention. After a series of rulings and reversals, the suit was finally settled in 1996 with a stipulated agreement among the plaintiffs, INS, and the Department of Justice.[22] The agreement mandates policies for detaining, processing, and releasing children; specifies the settings in which they may be detained and the services they must receive; and delineates how the INS must account for its performance. Provision is made for children's access to health care, education, recreation, religious services, and legal representation.

The settlement adopts general policies in favor of treating children with "dignity, respect and special concern for their vulnerability as minors"[23] and releasing them from detention without unnecessary delay. It provides that children should be housed in the least restrictive setting available such as a licensed shelter or foster home. Secure jail-like settings are used when nonsecure space is filled and for children identified as criminal or delinquent, dangerous to self or others, or flight risks. Children who "wash out" of nonsecure programs for rule breaking or other inappropriate behavior can expect transfer to a jail setting. In many areas, the INS routinely transfers children to jail once they receive an order of deportation because they are then assumed to be flight risks.

Human rights monitors have roundly and repeatedly criticized the INS for frequent violations of the *Flores* settlement. U.S. policies in general have also been widely criticized for violating international laws based on the "best interests of the child" standard prohibiting routine detention of children.[24] One monitor labeled the United States as "one of the harshest countries in the world" for its practices toward unaccompanied children in immigration proceedings.[25]

Owing to the sustained pressure of critics and catalyzed by widespread accusations of INS incompetence following the terrorist attacks of September 11, 2001, major legislative changes were proposed to improve legal and custodial conditions for separated children. The Unaccompanied Alien Child Protection Act of 2001 was introduced in January 2001 and incorporated in part into the Homeland Security Act signed on November 25, 2002. This act transfers responsibility for the care and placement of unaccompanied children from the INS to the ORR and transfers the rest of the INS's functions to two bureaus within the new Department of Homeland Security. It mandates the abolishment of the INS once these transfers are complete. These changes effectively resolve the conflict of interest inherent in the INS having responsibility of both custodian and prosecutor of detained children. Also resolved is the problem of the INS's lack of expertise in child welfare and resettlement issues; ORR has expertise in both areas as well as a foster placement program for unaccompanied refugee children already in place.

Not included in the act are key components of the Children's Bill that would have significantly reformed aspects of immigration law pertaining to children. Children's advocates will vigorously continue efforts to secure the following:

- Provision of guardians ad litem and court-appointed attorneys. This would bring practices of immigration court in line with standard practices of other U.S. juvenile courts. Currently immigrant children have the right to counsel, but not at government expense. The Homeland Security Act charges the ORR to develop a plan to ensure that each child has legal counsel and to submit it to Congress for approval.
- Exemption of children from expedited removal, the 1-year filing deadline for asylum application, and certain other provisions of the Immigration and Nationality Act of 1996 (a law commonly described as draconian in human rights and advocacy circles).
- Granting of power to the attorney general to waive certain grounds of inadmissibility for deserving children and to protect children who age out of eligibility while waiting for approval of immigrant visas.
- Addition of a requirement for the government to follow up on and report outcomes for children who are deported to their countries of origin.
- Adoption by the Executive Office for Immigration Review (EOIR), the body that oversees immigration courts, of INS's 1998 Guidelines for Children's Asylum Claims.[26] The guidelines were created in collaboration with government and nongovernment entities, including UNHCR, to enable INS asylum officers to better understand the unique vulnerabilities of children and more sensitively elicit information and adjudicate cases. The guidelines are the second such set of instructions ever issued by a country operating a refugee determination system. The Canadian Immigration and Refugee Board issued the first set in 1996. EOIR's adoption of the guidelines would add considerably to efforts it has already made to address the special needs of unaccompanied children, such as designating one judge in each area to preside over juvenile cases, updating the court records system to specifically track juvenile cases, and providing regular training to judges on child-friendly courtroom methods and the proper application of law in juvenile cases.[27]

The American Bar Association (ABA) has strongly encouraged the EOIR and individual judges to adopt additional "best practices" for unaccompanied minors, including judicial intervention when impediments to legal access arise, when unnecessary or excessive physical restraints are used in court, and when children in court are found to be sleep-deprived, hungry, or too traumatized to appear; completion of voir dire[28] with children to ensure their understanding of and ability to participate in the proceedings; assessment of each child's "voluntary and knowing" consent to counsel (given that counsel may have been retained by smugglers); and provision of bond-redetermination hearings to ensure that bond amounts are set appropriately not only to protect society but also to uphold the *Flores* policy in favor of releasing children expediently.[29]

As the ORR and the Department of Homeland Security take over the INS's functions, the future utility of the *Flores* settlement is unclear. Though it was originally intended that the INS establish *Flores* provisions as federal regulations, by the agreement's sunset deadline in early 2002 it had failed to do so.[30] At that point the INS agreed to continue operating under *Flores* and extend the sunset deadline until 45 days after finalization of the regulations.[31] Yet as of this writing, the provisions are still not codified. From this point forward, the ORR is responsible for detention (but not release) policies, including identification of qualified housing facilities, oversight of the infrastructure and personnel of the facilities, investigation and inspection of the facilities, formulation and implementation of placement determinations for unaccompanied children, ensuring that the interests of children are considered in decisions relating to their care and custody, implementation of policies regarding their care and placement, maintaining statistical information on the children, coordination with other government entities to ensure that children are protected from smugglers and other dangers, and reunification of children with a parent abroad when appropriate.[32] The Department of

Homeland Security will presumably handle release policies.

WORKING WITH UNACCOMPANIED CHILDREN

Professionals outside of the detention system may come into contact with separated children in several different ways.

- *Legal representatives* are rarely hired by children or their families. Much more commonly they connect with children by way of nonprofit legal service agencies that provide "Know Your Rights" presentations, individual counsel, or full representation.[33] Many legal service agencies recruit local attorneys as pro bono representatives for detained children (and adults). They provide training and mentoring to enable nonimmigration attorneys to also participate as volunteers. Through the efforts of these agencies, some private firms, and bar associations at local, state, and national levels, thousands of hours are donated annually toward representation of unaccompanied children. Despite this, only about 20% of children enjoy legal assistance.[34]
- *Forensic evaluators* such as physicians and mental health professionals assist children to document sequelae of torture, child abuse, or other physical and psychological issues relevant to their immigration cases. The need for pro bono evaluators is great. Child claimants are unlikely ever to seek evaluation unless they have counsel, and they are even more unlikely to have the means to hire an evaluator. A few organizations such as Doctors of the World–USA, based in New York, and Physicians for Human Rights, based in Boston, provide training and support for volunteer evaluators in various locations around the country.
- *Clinical specialists* who provide services not routinely available through the usual health service contractor (the U.S. Public Health Service in most areas) may contract to accept referrals. Children are usually referred out for dental work (including X rays for age determination), obstetric and gynecological care, emergency care, surgery, psychiatric care, orthopedic follow-up, and other specialty concerns.
- *Caseworkers* for refugee resettlement agencies may work with separated children as clients after they gain asylum or other protection entitling them to assistance and benefits and after they are released from detention. At that point, the children will be in the care of sponsors (who may or may not be relatives) or foster parents.

Assessment Considerations

In seeking to psychologically assess an unaccompanied child for immigration court proceedings, the clinician clearly faces a complex task. The issues to be evaluated form multiple and shifting layers that may be difficult to connect within the often limited time frame given for the evaluation. Clinicians are accustomed to the metaphor of peeling an onion as a model for psychological and relationship assessment. This situation, however, is more analogous to weather forecasting. The most accurate forecast for a given area must take into account not only relatively stable factors such as local topography, climate, and historical patterns, but also many fluid factors such as humidity, temperature, barometric pressure, season, winds and air currents at varying altitudes, developing conditions in neighboring and distant areas, and even changing extraterrestrial conditions such as solar flares. For the unaccompanied child, the relatively stable "topography" includes cultural background, developmental level, and psychosocial history. Fluid variables moving across this landscape include the status of family members and caregivers, the child's current living conditions, his or her legal/case status, health status, connections to smugglers or traffickers, and politics/current events developments within the United States and abroad. The clinician, unlike the meteorologist, has also to build trust and rapport with the subject before meaningful assessment can begin.

Relatively Stable Factors

A child's responses during the clinical interview must be considered within the context of his or her culture, developmental level, and psychosocial history. These categories, of course, interact with and influence each other and the more fluid factors to be described in the next section.

Culture. Cultural perceptions and approaches are among the most ingrained and enduring aspects of a person's worldview. Even those with long experience living in an adopted culture and speaking its language do not forget the ways of their native land and people. Clinicians working cross-culturally must educate themselves as much as possible about the cultures of the children they evaluate. Accurate understanding and interpretation of verbal and nonverbal behaviors of clients requires the proper cultural context. The way a child interacts with the evaluator as an adult, an authority figure, a person of education, and a person of the same or opposite gender is most likely to unfold according to the child's cultural norms. Translators can often be very helpful in explaining cultural nuances.

W, a Palestinian boy, came to the United States alone at age 16. His parents both died as a result of ongoing local hostilities when he was a toddler. His aunt cared for him until she was also killed about 7 years later. He remembered their years together being marked by poverty, hunger, and fear. Having no other relatives, W was taken in by his aunt's friend for about 2 years; then he was left on his own. The psychologist who evaluated W in preparation for his asylum hearing included in her affidavit the translator's comments that W's Arabic was unsophisticated and uneducated but used in a manner indicating average intelligence and also that fear seemed to dominate W's way of speaking.

Culture, in forensic assessment, must include consideration of country politics, societal infrastructure, educational systems, and attitudes and beliefs (including those related to gender roles). The way in which a child chooses to or is forced to cope with circumstances that lead to separation from parents or caregivers may seem incredible when viewed through a Western lens, but be perfectly credible when viewed from within the child's culture and society.

A 17-year-old Honduran girl was raised by her grandparents from age 2 when her father died and her mother migrated to the United States to work. In the grandparents' home she suffered physical and sexual abuse from a gang member uncle for several years. At age 14 she fled to the home of another relative, but that family could not afford to keep her. She returned to her hometown and lived with a neighbor, paying most of her wages from a factory job for rent. On the verge of homelessness and terrified by renewed threats from her uncle and his associates, she decided to follow her mother to the United States.

A Westerner might wonder why this girl did not seek assistance from authorities or welfare agencies. In fact experience had taught her that the local authorities could do little to control gangs; police would not even enter her neighborhood. A number of reports on country conditions in Honduras verified that the few relief agencies operating could not begin to cope with the thousands of abandoned, abused, and homeless children living on the streets of major cities and that police officers were actually prime suspects in a number of these children's murders. Within the existing political and social culture of her country, this girl had no realistic resource for protection.

Culturally embedded behavior patterns may be mistaken for evidence of psychiatric diagnosis at worst or socially inappropriate for a setting at best. Clinicians should explore any response or behavior that seems unusual to rule out a cultural explanation before attributing it to pathology.

M was 15 years old and in INS detention when interviewed by a psychologist. He correctly listed materials used in building a house and named several types of fruit but could not name any large cities. He did not know that the sun rises in the east and could not state the number of days in a month, but spontaneously volunteered that the world has nine planets. He was not able to correctly complete simple addition problems. He stated that the happiest time of his life had been his stay at the detention shelter. The fact that M was the oldest son of a large, impoverished, rural Guatemalan family who worked instead of going to school (as many children in Guatemala do) explained his otherwise unusual responses.

Developmental Level. Developmental level is a multifaceted variable that changes slowly and fairly predictably. It encompasses development of the physical body, language, moral reasoning and other cognitive processes, emotions, intelligence, spirituality, gender identity, and socialization skills. Western models typically divide development into chronological stages and describe characteristics associated with each stage. Many characteristics generalize fairly well across cultures, but it is important to be alert to those that do not. For example, children everywhere begin talking between approximately 9 and 12 months of age, but in Western societies, activities such as marriage and employment tend to occur later than in many other cultures.

A psychologist evaluated a 17-year-old indigenous Guatemalan boy from an impoverished rural area relative to his claims of abuse and neglect at the hands of his parents. The psychologist observed in the boy short stature, facial characteristics sometimes associated with fetal alcohol syndrome, slow and flat affect, inability to complete most of a standard mental status exam, and symptoms of anxiety focused on issues of well-being and safety. In her affidavit, she diagnosed generalized anxiety disorder and noted that she could not rule out developmental deficits stemming from his environment as causative to what appeared to be low IQ and learning disabilities.

Although it is completely beyond the scope of this chapter to discuss development and maturation in any comprehensive way, some general points pertinent to children as reporters of experience are offered. An excellent summary of abilities by age-group is given in a Lutheran Immigration and Refugee Services publication on working with immigrant children.[35] The summary divides childhood into three age ranges: birth to 5, 6 to 12, and 13 to 18.

Children in the youngest range usually develop sufficient perceptual and verbal skills to relate experiences by the time they are about 4 years old; however, clarity is limited by the factors that follow:

- They have little ability to separate fact (what is objectively true) from fantasy (what is imagined to be true). Their reports usually reflect their own subjective experience of events and may seem inaccurate if compared with an older person's more objective report.

- They have little ability to understand another person's perspective or to recognize the larger context in which an event occurs. They report from their own perspective and are not usually able to help the listener understand by reframing or rephrasing.

- They make sense of events in a relentlessly logical way that is limited by their knowledge and experience; thus, their conclusions often seem quite illogical to older people. For example, an American child mistakes "vanilla folder" for "manila folder" because "vanilla" is the familiar word and the folder is, after all, the same color as vanilla ice cream.

- They tend to criticize and blame others when something goes wrong. They may tend to view bad events as being the fault of those who suffer for them, though the sufferers may well be innocent victims.

Children in the middle age range show the following characteristics:

- They gradually increase their abilities to differentiate between fact and fantasy and to see things from the other person's point of view. Their reports seem more understandable to adults not because they are necessarily more accurate but because the reporting style becomes more objective.

- They begin to understand the antecedents and consequences of events and intent and motivation in others but do not yet project well to future events. Thus, they may be unable to comment on their risk for future persecution or continued child abuse or neglect.

- They tend to assume that they are the cause of events and blame themselves. This may result in inconsistent or vague reporting of events as they attempt to cover their perceived guilt.

- They have an increasing ability to grasp abstract concepts and to solve problems. Their logic is still relentless, but as it becomes better informed by knowledge and experience, misconceptions occur less frequently.

Children in the older age range can be characterized as follows:

- They remain family centered to varying degrees depending on culture; the influence of the peer group becomes increasingly prominent in the child's activities and decisions. In group detention settings, peers may exert a great deal of influence over each other's choices, including legal decisions.

- Thy enter adulthood at puberty in some cultures and are considered ready to marry, earn a living, and become parents. An unaccompanied teenager who is already a spouse and/or a parent may feel confused and angry when the U.S. system ignores these realities and bases placement and release decisions only on age.
- They may have more maturity physically than socially, emotionally, and so on. Evaluators should not assume that physical maturity or the adoption of adult roles equates with emotional maturity. For example, a hallmark of teenage thinking in a number of cultures is the belief that everyone else shares the teen's knowledge and point of view. American teens evidence this in frequent frustrations with others, especially adults, who seem "dense" and who fail to "get it." Evaluators must take care to explore narratives thoroughly with teenagers to be sure that they have not omitted important details that they thought were obvious.
- They usually begin to understand abstract concepts such as oppression and abuse and become able to project their future risk of encountering or reencountering such ills.

Trauma. Trauma experiences affect development in a number of ways depending on a child's age at the time of the trauma, his or her access to assistance or protection by parents or others, and the frequency and duration of the experience(s). The following generalizations should be considered:

- Children who experience chronic trauma conditions tend to have survival rather than maturation as a developmental focus. For example, they develop trust as a tool for filtering out negatives (which group of street children is less likely to hurt me?) rather than as a foundation on which to build increasingly complex and meaningful relationships.
- Malnutrition may be an overlooked "side effect" of trauma that interferes with intellectual development and functioning as well as with physical development.

- Children may respond to trauma by reverting to earlier developmental levels. For example, verbal children may cease talking; children who were comfortable playing away from home suffer separation anxiety if not in sight of a parent.
- Damaging effects of trauma can be mitigated when children remain with their primary caregivers, and the caregivers continue to function as normally as possible in their roles. It is crucial when a child has been separated from caregivers that evaluators clearly understand the conditions leading to the separation.

Psychosocial History. Psychosocial history, by definition a summary of a person's historical experience, would seem to be a matter of record and not subject to change. But the "facts" of this history are usually self-reported. An unaccompanied child must obviously serve as his or her own reporter; therefore, the report's accuracy is limited by the child's narrative skills and his or her ability to comprehend the relationship of personal experiences to the family and larger social contexts. Children are prone not to have full information about why they are separated from families because adults have shielded them from painful truths, events of crisis swept them apart too quickly or chaotically, or the reasons were abstract and beyond their ability to understand. Events powerful enough to separate family members from each other may even have been beyond the understanding of the adults involved. In addition, memory does not function like a video camera, but is subject to many influences and is malleable. Therefore, psychosocial history can evolve over time as the reporter gains additional knowledge and as he or she matures in ability to understand and interpret events.

The psychosocial history may begin with information gathering about the child's premigration or preseparation history. This helps to establish the overall health status and level of functioning that the child experienced before the onset of traumatic events or other precipitators of separation. Topics to assess may include family roles and relationships, the child's physical health and development, substance use and abuse, educational and occupational experience, religious affiliation and activities, personal interests and favorite activities, and peer relationships. Older children and teenagers may also describe their premigration or preseparation goals and expectations for the future. It is useful to solicit a history of past psychological symptoms, as in most cases this provides the evaluator with at least a rough baseline for comparison of any current symptoms.

Having outlined the child's general history and experience, the evaluator next assesses the child's trauma history. For some children who experience very early separation from nurturing caregivers and/or grow up in chronically conflicted, unstable settings, the general and trauma histories may be inseparable. Abused and neglected children, for example, may escape dangerous home environments only to become street children at high risk for physical and sexual assault, prostitution, substance abuse, malnutrition, and disease. Children raised in the midst of armed conflicts may witness repeated acts of violence and destruction and live in constant fear of death or injury to themselves and their loved ones. The trauma history must also include exploration of trauma experienced during migration, an area that may be overlooked when premigration traumas are considerable.

Though not all children will have experienced chronic trauma conditions, all will have experienced significant losses. Even the child who migrates for simple economic reasons loses his or her familiar culture and language as well as the support of friends and family. Older children often realize that if they remain in the United States they are very unlikely ever to see loved ones in the home country again. The realities of loneliness and isolation for the separated child can be overwhelming, even for the child who originally looked on migration as something of an adventure.

Fluid Variables

The factors most strongly affecting a separated child's current psychological functioning, which is the "core of the evaluation,"[36] are often the immediate issues and pressures related to being unaccompanied and detained. This section specifically addresses the influence of the status of family members and caregivers, the child's current living conditions, legal/case status, health status, connections to smugglers or traffickers, and conditions of politics/current events within the United States and abroad on the child's psychological state.

Status of Family Members. The status of family members or customary caregivers is usually of great concern to separated children. About 40% of unaccompanied children have no relatives in the United States and are truly removed from this primary source of support.[37] It is usually imperative to them to establish a link with their loved ones in order to report both well-being and location. Children find it very disquieting to have their whereabouts unknown to their families. A speedy link may be difficult to establish, however, if the family does not have a telephone or reliable postal service, or if there is no relative in the United States who can facilitate communication. The stress of disconnection from loved ones may be revisited many times as children are transferred to different facilities within the system. Once communication is established, the regularity of contact may still be problematic and a source of stress for the child. Depending on the detention facility, children may be limited to a small number of outgoing letters and phone calls each week, or they may have scheduled times to make calls that do not coincide with the receiver's availability.

Circumstances at home are also of great concern to children. Those who flee abusive situations often worry about the safety of siblings and the nonabusive parent, if any. Children migrating for economic reasons may feel great distress about being detained and unable to earn money to send home, and their families may pressure them to somehow hurry the release process along. Children with smuggling debts to pay are often increasingly distressed the longer detention continues because failure to pay may jeopardize the safety of family members. Children whose family members remain in oppressive or dangerous circumstances or who don't know their family's whereabouts will certainly suffer additional stress. Children whose families encounter relatively commonplace difficulties such as ill health or unemployment tend to experience both worry about the problems and guilt due to the assumption that their immigration problems and detention caused or exacerbated the family's difficulties.

292 • WORKING WITH CHILDREN AND FAMILIES

Many Honduran children were stranded in INS detention following the devastation of Hurricane Mitch in October 1998. As Honduras had no resources for repatriating unaccompanied children following the disaster, those who would normally have been deported remained in detention for many months. Most of the children were frantic to go home despite the disaster because communication lines were badly disrupted and they had no other way to determine if their families were alive or dead.

A 15-year-old Chinese girl's father suffered serious health problems. She was worried about him, but he and the family assured her over several weeks of phone calls that he was improving. Not long after the first call in which he did not come to the phone, the family finally revealed that he was terminally ill. Knowing of her stress being in detention they concealed the truth as long as possible to spare her additional worry. Her father died about 3 months into her 10-month-long detention.

Detention Conditions. Detention conditions heavily influence children's psychological status. Little research exists on the effects of detention on children, but the few studies available agree that "children living in shelters, camps, and processing centres are subjected to increased risk for psychological dysfunction," due in part to "the compounding stress of being supervised and/or communal living with others outside their family/cultural group."[38] Other factors contributing to psychological stress in detention may include lack of privacy, routine daily activities with little variety, limited opportunity to make choices for oneself, unfamiliar foods, lack of peers and/or staff who speak the child's language, limited communications with family or legal advisers, arbitrary transfer between facilities, and restriction or lack of access to customary religious practices. Children in secure facilities may be subjected to body searches including strip searches, the use of shackles or other restraints, and commingling with violent offenders.

The staff focus in detention facilities is usually on behavioral compliance and adherence to program schedules rather than on detainees' emotional needs. Cultural explanations for "misbehavior" are easily overlooked, leading to misapplied punishments and increased tensions among staff and detainees.

In correcting behavior problems with Latino children in a shelter setting, some staff were offended and even frightened when Latino children smiled or laughed through the process. They thought that the children did not take them seriously, were mocking them, or were "crazy." They disciplined the children for misbehaving and for being disrespectful, failing to realize that in many Latin American cultures smiling or laughing during a serious situation is indicative of nervousness or fear.

Two 15-year-old Sri Lankan boys arrived at a shelter care facility where they were the first and only Tamil speakers. Initially, they often found themselves at odds with the staff, none of whom knew that in Sri Lanka the gesture of head-nodding means "no," and head-shaking means "yes."

Detention settings are generally very high-pressure environments due to the acute and chronic stresses affecting individual children, constant turnover in the population, and the mix of cultures. Whether a particular facility's atmosphere is crowded and overstimulating or isolating and tedious, detention is a psychologically arduous place for stressed and traumatized children. Yet, as was noted in a case example earlier in this chapter, a few children experience detention as the most secure and stable environment they have ever known. They may for the first time enjoy regular meals, daily baths and changes of clothes, safety from physical threat and harm, medical care, respite from labor, and the chance to attend school. For such children, the issues surrounding legal status are likely to be a greater stressor than the fact of detention itself.

Legal or Case Status. Legal or case status is the point of greatest stress for many children. It often outranks even family concerns because children tend to believe that if they can just get out of detention then any family or other problem will be more easily solved. The goal for which most children aim immediately is release from detention, even though paroled release through bond payment confers no legal status or privileges. Because the steps needed to attain release vary depending on nationality, children facing longer processes suffer the discouragement of seeing perhaps hundreds of other children released before their own opportunity finally arises.

Another stressful facet of the legal component is that removal proceedings run concurrently with and independent of release and family reunification efforts. Thus a child may receive notice that his or her sponsor is finally approved at the same time that he or she is ordered deported by the immigration judge. In such a case the judge's order would take precedence. Children tend to feel as though they are in a race to obtain release before having to confront either an asylum application or a deportation order, even though release merely postpones the confrontation. Each successive court appearance becomes increasingly stressful if good progress is not being made toward approval of a sponsor.

Children who cannot locate an acceptable sponsor before the 1-year asylum application filing deadline usually move directly to asylum proceedings (or application for other forms of relief[39]) and remain in detention through case completion. Writing the asylum application is extremely stressful for children who are old enough to contribute to its preparation. The pressure of writing a declaration, or personal account of persecution or abuse, is usually quite intense both because the child relives difficult experiences to some degree through the writing and because the document is often the most important piece of evidence that he or she will present.

A 16-year-old Chinese boy started skipping meals as his asylum hearing date approached, and for at least one meal each day he avoided the cafeteria all together. Concerned staff encouraged him to eat but he declined. Though he was reluctant to explain, eventually he revealed that he was fasting, a practice of his Christian denomination, as a plea to God to bless his hearing. After being granted asylum he continued fasting one day per week as an expression of gratitude.

Legal representation, or lack thereof, is another stressful issue for many children. Approximately 80% of children appear in court without an attorney.[40] This is a huge disadvantage considering that immigrants with counsel are four times more likely to gain asylum than those without.[41] Some children have the benefit of pro bono assistance or representation, and some work with attorneys hired by their families or their smugglers. Particularly in the case of smuggler-affiliated attorneys whose only goal is to get the child out into the workforce, falsified asylum claims may be put forward, legitimate claims may not be investigated or developed, and cases may be mishandled or dropped.

A 16-year-old Chinese boy was unable to explain why two different attorneys both claimed to be his legal representative. He had never heard of nor spoken to either attorney, neither had his family been in contact with them. Yet one attorney filed a notice of representation that supposedly bore the boy's signature. He felt quite frightened for himself and his family to realize that two smugglers must be vying for control of him.

A 15-year-old Chinese girl was ordered deported because her attorney, based across the country from her detention location, failed to file her asylum application on time. Her repeated attempts to contact the attorney before the deadline all went unanswered. She spent almost 1 additional year in detention, the last 6 months on antidepressants, before finally being allowed to bond out while a different attorney handled her appeal.

Older teenagers face the additional stress of their approaching 18th birthdays, legal adulthood, and a complete change of standing before the immigration court. As adults, they lose several options for relief that are available only to minors. The prospect of transfer to adult detention is naturally frightening.

A 17-year-old Brazilian boy became increasingly tearful, distracted, and withdrawn as his 18th birthday and transfer to an adult facility approached. He had seen the adult facility a number of times because the Public Health staff there serviced the children's medical needs. The children's clinic was located in a perimeter building so that they never actually entered the compound, but 20-foot-high fences, concertina wire, and uniformed guards were easily viewed from the street. The boy's appetite diminished and he increasingly reported headaches, insomnia, and other somatic complaints until the day of his transfer.

Health Needs. Health needs of unaccompanied children can range from treatment for ordinary mild illnesses and injuries to obstetric procedures and surgeries. Children coming into detention not uncommonly need treatment for head lice, scabies, and exposure to tuberculosis, and they are routinely screened for these conditions. Older girls are also routinely tested for pregnancy. No screening is provided for such concerns as sexually transmitted diseases or intestinal parasites, even though many children are at high risk for exposure.

Children whose diets change drastically often report digestive complaints, and those accustomed to vegetable-rich diets can have difficulty adjusting to starch-heavy American institutional fare. Stress-related complaints are very commonly reported. Children often feel insecure about their health concerns in the absence of customary caregivers and treatments. They wonder if their concerns are taken seriously enough or if health care providers are missing signs of something serious; they wonder if the treatments prescribed are adequate and effective; sometimes they wonder if prescribed treatments are necessary. It is easy for fears about physical health to become exaggerated when a child has little trust in providers or their methods.

Delays in provision of treatment contribute to low confidence in the system. Children in need of eyeglasses, for example, may wait months for prescription lenses to arrive. Children with dental pain also may have to wait weeks or months until dental services are approved. In authorizing specialty services, consideration is given to the child's likely length of stay. Sometimes medical authorizations are delayed because release or removal is expected before treatment might start or conclude. Children can become very frustrated when treatment time is wasted on removal or reunification schedules that may or may not materialize.

Smugglers and Traffickers. The element of smugglers and traffickers adds psychological stress in a variety of ways. Children may be traumatized in transit either directly by their handlers or indirectly due to the means or methods of transportation.

A 15-year-old Honduran girl reported that the smugglers who led her on foot across the Mexico-Arizona border drugged her with a stimulant when she got tired in order to keep her moving with the group, and later raped her while she was still under the influence of the drug.

A shipping container holding several Chinese stowaways arrived at a U.S. port after an ocean crossing of about two weeks. Two of the stowaways were teenage boys who suffered not only the rigors of the crossing, but also the shock of another stowaway's death and confinement with his corpse for several days before reaching port.

For children who have yet to pay off smuggling debts, financial burdens of up to tens of thousands of dollars weigh heavily on them. Every day in detention prolongs the start of repayment and pushes the anticipated day of financial freedom farther into the future. Few children realize how truly ruthless and dangerous their smugglers are until pressure for payment is applied, and then they may begin to fear release from detention. It is often the fear of harm to their families that bolsters them to face release.

A 16-year-old Chinese boy in his eighth month of shelter detention became very distraught after learning of his parents' plan to sell his older sister into marriage with a smuggler. He asked at every opportunity to call his family so that he could encourage his sister to refuse the marriage and threaten to ask for voluntary deportation if his parents forced her to accept. He felt overwhelmed with grief and guilt for his sister's dilemma, realizing that the price of his journey to the United States was the leverage the smuggler now held over her.

In order to force more money from a teenager's family, smugglers intimidated his potential sponsors into withdrawing so that he could not bond out of detention. He was detained for more than 2 years before being granted asylum. Eventually he was released to foster care since his relatives did not dare to take him and to better hide his whereabouts from the smugglers.

Political/Current Events. Political/current events, like solar flares, are distant events that can have surprisingly specific and immediate local effects. For example, as late as 1998, the People's Republic of China would not repatriate its juveniles who were ordered deported from the United States. Having no fear of deportation, these children's wait for approval of sponsors was relatively stress free. They were usually released within two or three months. By the following year, China had changed its policy, and deportation became a worrisome reality. With this measure of leverage against smuggling secured, the United States took aim at other facets of the trade. Seeking to prevent smuggler "relatives" from applying to sponsor children, the INS gradually restricted the applicant list to eliminate most nonrelatives and distant relatives. At the same time, home study requirements were tightened to more carefully screen the remaining applicants. The home-study caseworkers then began encountering resistance from smugglers in the form of applicants who were increasingly difficult to vet and threats to their personal safety. In order to more tightly control their investigations, they requested that detention caseworkers withhold progress updates from children, thus preventing the children from inadvertently or intentionally leaking information back to the smugglers. The results for the children included a twofold increase in average length of detention; increased conflict with staff members, especially their caseworkers; increased display of angry and aggressive behavior; decreased cooperation with and participation in daily activities; and increase in subjective reports of anxiety and depression symptoms.

The INS has since implemented the additional restriction of not releasing children to otherwise qualified sponsors if a parent is present in the United States. If the parent is undocumented, he or she is required to come forward, risking apprehension and placement in removal proceedings, or the child remains in protracted detention. This creates a torturous dilemma for children to realize that reunification with their parents may be the first step toward losing them all over again and that their freedom may only come at the cost of the parent's.

Building Trust and Rapport

Most resources for professionals working with children suggest that trust and rapport are most effectively built by spending relaxed time with a child in a child-friendly environment, for example, a trip to an ice cream parlor, before approaching the professional reason for the contact. Most professionals find, however, that the limits of their own schedules and the restrictions on the children as detainees turn time and access into luxury items. Given that time with the child is often limited and the child's cooperation in his or her own case is crucial, the professional may bear in mind the following points.

1. From the detained child's point of view, there is little reason to trust anyone. Being unfamiliar with the system that holds them, they have no way to tell the "good guys" who might help them from the "bad guys." If the authorities in their home countries are corrupt, unreliable, or dangerous, they may assume that every authority figure is untrustworthy.

2. The newer a child is to the system, the less trusting he or she is likely to be. Children tend to confer trust on whoever is perceived to be helping them. As newcomers, they often continue to view smugglers and other migrants with whom they've traveled as trust figures. These guides have frequently coached the children to give false identity and background information if they are caught. The children usually follow this advice and will stick to false stories until convinced by a new trust figure that the truth will serve them better.

3. Children tend to trust people who show concern for them. If possible, assist the child to solve immediate problems he or she may be experiencing in addition to your work on his or her case. A child whose basic needs for food, rest, activity, medical care, and respectful treatment are not being met will have difficulty trusting a professional who seems oblivious to such deficiencies.

4. Tell the child who you are, what your role is in his or her case, how you will help, and how the child can cooperate with you on his or her own behalf. Just as important, tell the child who you are not, for example, that you do not work for the government, the INS, and so on. Be very clear about the limits of your work so that the child does not expect help that you cannot deliver.

5. Approaching children with warmth, friendliness, honesty, and respect encourages trust and openness. The sharing of appropriate personal information or stories by the professional may encourage the child to share needed personal information.

6. Acknowledge the child's courage in revealing personal information that may be embarrassing, shameful, painful, or traumatic. The retelling of traumatic experience is often very stressful and very hard work.

7. Be honest with the child about how the information he or she shares will be used and who else will see it. Some children have experienced societal or family circumstances in which their own or another's safety depended on keeping personal information secret. Some will be sensitized to the dangers of being an informant or being connected to one. Some may fear negative consequences if their information reaches detention staff or other detainees. They may worry that other detainees will pass information to smugglers or enemies back home, endangering relatives and friends.

If your work for the child will entail multiple visits, be reliable and consistent in keeping appointments. Be prepared to update the child on case progress. Prepare the child adequately for visits of any other professionals you schedule.

Conclusion

Unaccompanied children are a diverse population with a variety of reasons for migrating. Many have endured traumatic experiences before or during migration, and all have suffered the loss of association with family members or other caregivers. Their reception in the United States is harsh by international standards, usually including detention, legal processing without representation, and custodial care provided by the agency in charge of their prosecution. In addition to the psychological difficulties resulting from historical losses and trauma and the stresses of the U.S. immigration system, they face pressures related to age and developmental limitations and the difficulties of understanding and being understood by people of other cultures. They must also cope with the effects of separation from their families, stressful detention environments, confusing legal requirements, and even changing political conditions. Some also face dangerous complications from dealings with smugglers and even significant health concerns. By understanding this complex array of influences, evaluators with expertise in trauma and its sequelae significantly improve their ability to assist these children to fully and clearly present their claims in immigration court.

Although recent changes in the law hold promise for improved detention conditions, lawmakers continue to ignore the irregularities of routinely detaining children in the first place, failing to ensure that they have legal representation, and by these omissions failing to provide for their best interests as required by international law. The vast majority of unaccompanied children at this time are still dependent on luck and the kindness of volunteer professionals to help them through an increasingly unfriendly U.S. immigration system. In addition to advocating for continued improvements to the law, professionals are encouraged to volunteer direct services to children until such time as the law comes into compliance with international standards.

Notes

1. See Charles Dickens, "The Adventures of Oliver Twist," Chapter 11. *Works of Charles Dickens* (New York: Avenel Books, 1978), 337–340.

2. "The World of Children at a Glance," UNHCR Web site, accessed June 17, 2002, from http://www.unhcr.ch/children/glance.html

3. Ibid.

4. "Prison Guard or Parent? INS Treatment of Unaccompanied Refugee Children," *Women's*

Commission for Refugee Women & Children (May 2002).

5. *Refugee Children—Guidelines on Protection and Care,* UNHCR, 1994.

6. Trang Thomas and Winnie Lau, "Psychological Well Being of Child and Adolescent Refugee and Asylum Seekers: Overview of Major Research Findings of the Past Ten Years," literature review submitted to the Human Rights & Equal Opportunity Commission (Australian) National Inquiry Into Children in Immigration Detention, May 24, 2002. Accessed July 26, 2002, from http://www.humanrights .gov.au/human_rights/children_detention/psy_review .html

7. Edwin Larios Munoz, testimony before the Senate Judiciary Subcommittee on Immigration, February 28, 2002. Accessed July 24, 2002, from http://judiciary.senate.gov/testimony.cfm?id=172&w it_id=237

8. Cindy Albracht-Crogan, "My Pro Bono Experience," *La Linea*, The Newsletter of the Florence Immigrant and Refugee Rights Project, June 2002, p. 5.

9. Greg Allen, "Profile: Criticism of INS for Its Handling of Juvenile Illegal Aliens," report aired on National Public Radio's *All Things Considered* program, May 27, 2002. Audio link available at http://www.npr.org/rundowns/rundown.php?prgId=2 &prgDate=27-May-2002

10. Transcript of the (Phil) Donohue program aired September 2, 2002, with guests Wendy Young et al.

11. I know a number of children who accepted homesickness, loneliness, fear, and uncertainty about their futures, and smuggling debts of up to $40,000 or $50,000 rather than shame their families by going home. Had they gone home, they expected to be shunned rather than welcomed.

12. Diane Smith and Marisa Taylor, "Fleeing Poverty and Abuse, Immigrant Children Are Illegally Entering the US in Record Numbers," *Fort Worth Star-Telegram,* May 19, 1999, p. 1.

13. "People Fleeing Persecution Held in 'Worse Than Prison' Conditions in US," National Council of Churches News Service, April 30, 2001. Accessed June 17, 2002, from http://www.ncccusa.org/news/ 01news38.html

14. "Trafficking in Women and Children: A Contemporary Manifestation of Slavery," U.S. Committee for Refugees Report, July 2000. Accessed June 17, 2002, from http://preview.refugees.org/ world/articles/slavery_rr00_5.htm

15. "Boy Used in Smuggling Scheme Can Stay in U.S.," CNN.com/Law Center, July 24, 2001. Accessed September 10, 2002, from http://edition .cnn.com/2001/LAW/07/23/human.trafficking/

16. U.S. Department of State, Office to Monitor and Combat Trafficking in Persons, "Trafficking in Persons Report," June 5, 2002.

17. Tessie Borden, "Loan Sharks Bleeding Families of Mexican Migrants," *Arizona Republic,* June 4, 2002, p. A1.

18. Amon, Elizabeth, "The Snakehead Lawyers," *The National Law Journal,* July 15, 2002. Accessed July 15, 2002, from http://www.law.com/jsp/article .jsp?id=1024078985479

19. Smith and Taylor, "Fleeing Poverty and Abuse," p. 1.

20. William F. Schultz, "Amnesty International USA Testimony on Children in INS Detention," testimony given before the Senate Subcommittee on Immigration, February 2002.

21. "Prison Guard or Parent?" p. 16.

22. Stipulated settlement agreement, *Flores v. Reno,* case No. CV85-4544-RJK (C.D. Cal. 1996).

23. Ibid., paragraph 11.

24. United Nations Convention on the Rights of the Child, General Assembly Resolution 44/25 (November 20, 1989) (enforced September 2, 1990).

25. "Prison Guard or Parent?" p. 9.

26. U.S. Department of Justice, Immigration and Naturalization Service, "Guidelines for Children's Asylum Claims," December 10, 1998.

27. Michael Creppy, testimony before the U.S. Senate Committee on the Judiciary Regarding the Unaccompanied Alien Child Protection Act, February 28, 2002.

28. A process of formal examination, especially to determine qualification (as of a proposed witness).

29. Robert E. Hirshon, "Remarks Before the Immigration Judges Conference," San Juan, Puerto Rico, June 6, 2002.

30. The original proposed regulations are titled "Processing, Detention, and Release of Juveniles," Federal Register, p. 39759 (July 24, 1998). The regulations were later reproposed under the same title, Federal Register, p. 1670 (January 14, 2002).

31. Andrew Morton, testimony before the U.S. Senate Committee on the Judiciary Regarding the Unaccompanied Alien Child Protection Act, February 28, 2002.

32. Homeland Security Act of 2002, Title IV, Subtitle E, section 462, pp. 171–178. Accessed

December 4, 2002, from http://news.findlaw.com/cnn/docs/terrorism/hsa2002.pdf

33. Prominent examples include the Florence Immigrant & Refugee Rights Project in Arizona, Casa Cornelia in southern California, the Midwest Immigrant & Human Rights Center in Chicago, the Rocky Mountain Immigrant Advocacy Network in Denver, and the Florida Immigrant Advocacy Center.

34. Morton, testimony.

35. *Working With Refugee and Immigrant Children, Issues of Culture, Law & Development* (New York: Lutheran Immigration and Refugee Service, 1998), 7–11.

36. Istanbul Protocol, *Manual on the Effective Investigation and Documentation of Torture and Other Cruel, Inhuman or Degrading Treatment or Punishment*, United Nations Publication ISSN 1020-1688, August 9, 1999, p. 50.

37. Wendy Young, testimony before the U.S. Senate Committee on the Judiciary Regarding the Unaccompanied Alien Child Protection Act, February 28, 2002.

38. Thomas and Lau, "Psychological Well Being." Accessed July 26, 2002, from http://www.humanrights.gov.au/human_rights/children_detention/psy_review.html

39. Special Immigrant Juvenile Status, T Visa (for victims of trafficking), and U Visa (for victims of crime) are other possible forms of relief.

40. Morton, testimony.

41. Hirshon, "Remarks."

20

AMERICAN INDIAN FAMILIES

Resilience in the Face of Legal, Economic, and Cultural Assault

WALTER KAWAMOTO

County of Sacramento, California, Department of Human Assistance

TAMARA CHESHIRE

California State University, Sacramento

I n this chapter we will be discussing specific points of reference regarding American Indian history and their significance for interacting with Indian families and individuals in forensic contexts. These points consist of key events, policies, and laws that have been directed at American Indian people. Furthermore, these reference points will be used as a way to illustrate historical trends and contemporary realities in the overall relationship between American Indian families and the United States government. The chronological points of reference we will be using include boarding schools, the Dawes Allotment Act, the Indian Child Welfare Act, the growth of tribal enterprise, and tribal Head Start programs.

There are several historical themes that will recur in this chapter. First there is the distinctly American Indian issue of land and inconsistent federal legal acts and policies that have led to the

taking of land and resources previously used for the survival of indigenous nations. A second issue—distinct yet related—is the era of termination of all tribes and total disregard of treaty obligations. These treaties, regarded by many American Indian nations as their founding documents in the same way that the Constitution is a founding document, have played interesting roles in the lives of families in different American Indian nations. Third, once the federal government decided to honor many of the treaties made with indigenous sovereign nations, it was contractually bound by these land deals to care for these nations in terms of providing them with housing, food, medical care, education, and all essential means for survival and life until the end of time. Honoring these treaties also meant honoring tribal sovereignty and the power that comes from successful tribal businesses. Finally, the previous points culminate in an overarching and durable duality whereby American Indian tribes are paradoxically experienced both as distinct political communities or domestic dependent nations of the United States and as sovereign equals.

In sum, the historical context can be tracked through many different pathways to its direct and indirect impacts on families today. For instance, this chapter will focus on the shame of federal American Indian boarding schools created in an attempt to assimilate American Indian people by kidnapping American Indian children and forcing them to conform. This resulted in generations not knowing their culture or how to parent. Then in an attempt to address this tragedy, the Indian Child Welfare Act was passed to keep American Indian children in the comfort and support of their extended family, or at least their community. Today, the cycle of healing continues with federal reviewers coming to American Indian communities with humility and respect, asking these nations how they define successful services to their children via programs like tribal Head Starts.

BENCHMARKS CONSTITUTING THE HISTORICAL CONTEXT

The arrival of European immigrants in the Americas negatively affected American Indian nations. Not only did the immigrants inflict their social, religious, and economic values on American Indian people, but they also brought and promoted disease in an attempt to annihilate the indigenous population (Colley, personal communication, 1992; Kawamoto & Cheshire, 1997).

Over the past 200 years, federal policy affecting indigenous nations has been inconsistent (Kawamoto & Cheshire, 1999), shifting from "regarding tribes as sovereign equals, to relocating tribes, to attempts to exterminate or assimilate them, and recently, to encouraging tribal self-determination" (Pevar, 1992, p. 2). Despite this inconsistency, there are key events, policies, and laws warranting enumeration and description. These benchmarks include (a) initial federal recognition; (b) broken treaties, stolen land, and relocation; (c) reorganization; (d) termination; and (e) self-determination.

Federal Recognition

This two-sided relationship was also evident during the 1800s. In 1828, Andrew Jackson supported the Indian Removal Act passed by Congress in 1830. The Indian Removal Act "authorized the President to 'negotiate' with eastern tribes for their relocation west of the Mississippi River. Between 1832 and 1843 most of the eastern tribes either had their lands reduced in size or were coerced into moving to the west. Indian Treaties were broken by the government almost as soon as they were made" (Pevar, 1992, p. 4).

However, in 1832, just two years after the Indian Removal Act was passed by Congress, the Supreme Court recognized Congress's desire to obtain allegiance with the Indian nations. "The early journals of Congress exhibit the most anxious desire to conciliate the Indian nations. . . . The most strenuous exertions were made to procure those supplies on which Indian friendships were supposed to depend; and everything which might excite hostility was avoided" (*Worcester v. Georgia,* 1832, pp. 515, 548). Clearly, opinions varied on how to deal with the native inhabitants of North America.

Assimilation

During the mid-nineteenth century, Congress passed laws that increased federal control over American Indians and promoted assimilation into white society (Pevar, 1992). Special emphasis was on "educating and civilizing Indian youth" (pp. 4–5), otherwise known as assimilation. More than 200 federally supervised, Christian-based schools with enrollment of more than 14,000 American Indian students had been established by 1887 (Pevar, 1992; Strickland, 1986; Tyler, 1973). Federal agents were hired to kidnap American Indian children and place them in boarding schools, sometimes hundreds of miles away from their homes. These children were beaten, placed in solitary confinement, and essentially used as slave labor by many of the administrators of the boarding schools. Accounts of rape and child molestation committed by the teachers and administrators of these schools have also been documented. If these children even attempted to speak their native language or practice any of their traditions, they were severely punished. Sometimes children ran away, attempting to find their own way home. Many of their attempts to escape the horrors of the boarding schools were in vain because full-time federal agents were specifically hired to track children who ran away and bring them back to the school.

The scars of this assimilationist policy go deep for many American Indian families, whether they had members in boarding schools or not. This is why integrating into larger mainstream white society is seen by many as a betrayal of their culture and surrender to external oppression. Practitioners interested in helping family members adapt to the expectations of mainstream society need to be mindful that adaptation can be accomplished while still being true to a person's core culture.

Broken Treaties, Stolen Land, and Relocation

Roughly 100 years had passed (1871) since the 1787 Northwest Ordinance was ratified when Congress decided to "eliminate the practice of making treaties with Indian tribes" (16 Stat. 544, 566, codified as 25 U.S.C. Sec. 71, as cited in Pevar, 1992, p. 5). This meant that any treaties made after 1871 were not legal, and many Indians therefore found themselves dispossessed of land and resources.

During this new era, Congress would pass statutes and acts that would negatively affect tribes. One such act was the 1887 Dawes Allotment, which was intended to force the assimilation of American Indians by dividing up reservation land and disbanding tribal governments (*Hodel v. Irving*, 1987; Pevar, 1992; Tyler, 1973). Between 1887 and 1934, 90 million acres of land were taken from native nations (Pevar, 1992). What made this even worse was that much of this land was taken through legal means via levied taxes by federal and state governments.

As part of the effort to assimilate Indian people into white society, Congress decided in 1924 to grant U.S. citizenship to all American Indians. Even though indigenous people now had the right to vote, this new civil and human right did not help with the ramifications of the Dawes Act. American Indian families found themselves without basic resources such as land, housing, and food. Many were forced to leave what was once reservation land to look for jobs in the cities.

In the 1930s, the Great Depression hit the United States. In the government's efforts to deal with this economic downturn, they rethought American Indian policy once again. Pevar (1992) states that "the Great Depression all but eliminated the desire of whites to obtain additional Indian lands . . . [and] it also had become widely recognized that the General Allotment Act was very harmful to Indians, disrupting their reservations, their culture, and their well-being" (p. 6). Truly, President Roosevelt must have also considered not only the public criticism about the inhumane treatment of the indigenous population, casting them essentially into poverty, but that a large influx of indigenous people into urban areas taxed the limited job market and added to the numbers of out-of-work Americans who needed federal and state assistance. Roosevelt's change in American Indian policy was considered to be a positive turnaround from the previous era.

Reorganization

In 1933, President Roosevelt appointed John Collier as Commissioner of Indian Affairs. Collier's first point of office was to declare a policy of noninterference in tribal religion or cultural expression. He stated, "The cultural history of Indians is in all respects to be considered equal to that of any non-Indian group" (as cited in Pevar, 1992). Congress seemed to follow Collier's lead by passing the Indian Reorganization Act (Wheeler-Howard Act) of 1934. This act was specifically intended to "rehabilitate the Indian's economic life and to give him a chance to develop the initiative destroyed by a century of oppression and paternalism" (H.R. Rep. No. 1804, 1934, p. 6). The Indian Reorganization Act stopped the allotment of tribal land and gave power to the Secretary of the Interior to restore land that had not yet been sold to non–American Indians (Pevar, 1992). American Indian nations were now encouraged to assert their inherent powers of local self-governance by adopting their own constitutions and become federally chartered corporations (Pevar, 1992). For nearly 20 years (1935–1953), positive developments came from the Indian Reorganization Act, "Indian land-holdings increased by over two million acres, and federal funds were spent for on-reservation health facilities, irrigation works, roads, homes, and community schools" (Pevar, 1992, p. 7).

Termination

Congress changed its mind again, and in 1953, they adopted House Concurrent Resolution No. 108, which supported the new policy of termination. Termination meant that Congress had decided that all of the hard work and economic improvements made by American Indian nations since the Allotment era were now subject to scrutiny and criticism. Federal tribal recognition, reservations, resources, and benefits originally guaranteed by treaty were now terminated (Tyler, 1973). In the 10 years that followed, 100 tribes were terminated. They were ordered to divide up the reservation land once again and disband their governments. In addition to Resolution No. 108, Congress also passed Public Law 83-280, which "conferred upon certain designated states full criminal and some civil jurisdiction over Indian reservations and consented to the assumption of such jurisdiction by any additional state that chose to accept it. P.L. 280 thus gave power and responsibilities to the states—the traditional enemy of Indian tribes—that previously had been assumed by the federal government" (Pevar, 1992, p. 7).

Self-Determination

In the mid- to late 1960s the federal government once again changed federal policy. In 1968, President Johnson focused on reaffirming "the rights of the first Americans to remain Indians while exercising their rights as Americans. . . . [W]e must affirm their rights to freedom of choice and self determination" (Johnson, 1968, p. 10). Spanning from the late 1960s to today, Congress has passed a number of statutes that helped to encourage self-determination and economic development. Congress even changed the power that states

held over American Indian nations by prohibiting "states from acquiring any authority over Indian reservations without the consent of the affected tribe" (Pevar, 1992, p. 7).

IMPACT OF FEDERAL POLICY ON THE MODERN ERA

This dramatic series of policy changes led the way to the extremely diverse nature of American Indian communities today. Termination and the Dawes Act led to high numbers of urban American Indian families. Many families that still have their land are defiant and live isolated lives. Families in tribes that have been recently reorganized are busy dealing with the trauma of having members in many different locations. In addition to different cultural traditions, practitioners should expect a wide range of American Indian family types due to historical consequences.

The Self-Reliance Emphasis and Economic Complexities

Within the last 30 years, a number of different acts have been created by Congress to help stimulate American Indian business, employment, self-governance, and self-reliance: the Indian Business Development fund, the Indian Financing Act, and the Native American Programs Act, to name just a few. A very important act, passed in 1975, was the Indian Self-Determination and Education Assistance Act. This act "allows Indian tribes to administer the federal government's Indian programs on their reservation, and many tribes have used this opportunity to rid themselves of unnecessary federal domination" (Pevar, 1992, p. 8). Other acts that encourage self-reliance include the Indian Mineral Development Act (1982), the Indian Tribal Government Tax Status Act (1982), and one of the most important acts known to date, the Indian Gaming Regulatory Act of 1988, which "authorizes Indian tribes to engage in gaming, such as bingo, to raise revenue and promote economic development" (Pevar, 1992, p. 8).

Although some have jumped to the conclusion that all American Indians are now getting rich off both government handouts and casino riches, the truth is certainly far more complex. This change in policy has led to an extremely wide range of economic possibilities for American Indian families.

The following points briefly summarize this complex picture of economic possibilities. First, more than half of the people who identify themselves as American Indian live in cities. They are usually cut off from tribal resources and are dealing with massive cutbacks in city services for minorities. Second, of the 500-plus recognized tribes, only a small percentage have successful businesses (most of the successful business are casinos). Of the small percentage of tribal members with a successful business, every tribe chooses to share the wealth differently. Some give payouts to individual members (referred to as "per capita payments"), whereas many others use the resources for community development projects and educational programs. We have yet to encounter a person who gets *both* tribal support and government funding. The truth of the matter is that American Indian families continue to be at the top of most high-risk categories, including poverty, especially in urban areas and rural areas where the general area is economically depressed. Practitioners would do well to be aware of this range of possibilities, while understanding that most are still economically struggling.

Banishment

There are other recent internal self-governance factors that Indian nations must consider. With the newfound self-governance and self-reliance through the development of economically sound businesses such as casinos, fishing, and timber, Indian nations must look at the recent high payoffs that not only lift American Indian people out of poverty and despair but also facilitate internal disputes for these resources. They must be aware of the high rates of banishment occurring across the nation.

Banishment was a policy that was enacted by tribal leaders of the past, who found specific people a threat to the very existence of the tribe. Individuals or entire families who would breech taboos or create unbearable living conditions in the community would be exiled from that community. This would often lead to death because the individual and/or family's survival depended on the community working together as a group. Because of the newfound values of independence and individualism, several tribal councils have reversed the ideology that they must depend on one another to survive, and they now hold the individual or the particular family who holds power in the tribal council as more prominent and important than the entire community. With this newfound value system that has been adopted from white society, many American Indian people are so wrapped up in family feuds that they don't realize that they are contributing to the decline in numbers of American Indian people, in effect fulfilling the federal government's early attempts at assimilation.

One such issue of banishment or dis-enrollment occurred in Las Vegas, with the Paiute Tribal Council dis-enrolling "about a quarter of the membership . . . in June and July 1999" (NiiSka, 2001, p. N51). The reason that was given by the council was the small percentage of Paiute heritage of the former members. The problem is that American Indians can only be federally enrolled in one tribe even though they may be blood related to many tribal nations or ethnic groups. When the Las Vegas Paiute Tribal Council decided to dis-enroll 25% of its membership, this meant that the money the nation was receiving from their smoke shop and their upscale golf resort could now be divided up between fewer people (NiiSka, 2001).

Dis-enrollment or banishment is a complicated issue. In addition to internal prejudices due to heritage, sometimes this action is politically motivated when one family in the tribe has the most power or the most seats on the tribal council. Sometimes, with family holding many seats on the Tribal Council, nepotism occurs where tribal council members give their own family members jobs without consideration of qualifications or any other fair-hiring practices. The system of checks and balances is sometimes disregarded in tribal constitutions, and some tribal councils hold all of the power to make unilateral decisions.

The issue of heritage is also referred to as a person's "blood quantum." The federal government defines minimum blood quantum guidelines to determine who has Indian ancestry for many federal programs. To qualify for benefits provided by the federal government, one must meet the minimum requirements of blood quantum and tribal recognition. Perhaps the most fundamental element of tribal sovereignty is an individual tribe's right to decide what criteria it will use to determine membership. Accordingly, tribal requirements for memberships are almost as varied as the number of tribes in existence. What is very confusing here is that a person can be considered "American Indian" by the federal government and not be recognized by a tribal nation. To further complicate the issue, many urban American Indians can be recognized by their urban intertribal community as American Indian but not necessarily by a federally recognized tribe.

So what does this all mean in relation to federal benefits? Because the tribe now has the power to distribute federal benefits, many people who are recognized by the federal government and not by their own tribal government do not have access to these benefits. This issue becomes very confusing when discussing dis-enrollment or banishment, especially because tribal governments are able to add to minimum qualifications and even require less or much more than the minimum requirements of the federal government. Tribal governments have the power to change enrollment qualifications randomly as the Las Vegas Paiute Tribal Council did.

The Las Vegas Paiute Tribal Council was reconsidering the enrollment of all of its members, some whose families had been enrolled for more than 100 years. The council even attempted to determine that some members should be enrolled with other tribes by pointing out close individual ties with families of neighboring tribes. Arguments have been made on either side about the lack of consideration of the tribal constitution versus the power tribal council elders have to make unilateral decisions that affect the entire nation. Disenrolled members make the argument that "ancestry, heritage, life commitments and cosmology" (NiiSka, 2001, p. N51) and the fact that they only identify themselves as Las Vegas Paiute should count, "whether the current Tribal council acknowledges that fact or not" (p. N51). The disenrolled tribal members have won this specific case in tribal court, but the Las Vegas Paiute Tribal Council is appealing the decision and arguing that their constitution makes no provision for a tribal court to make any type of ruling on the case at all and that the final decision and authority of the tribal council is what stands.

Felix Cohen (1982) stated that "in practice, tribal courts are often subordinate to the political branches of tribal governments." In reality, tribal courts only have power and authority when it is vested in them by the tribal council or constitution. Ultimately at issue here are individual American Indian civil rights guaranteed by the Indian Civil Rights Act versus tribal sovereignty and immunity in dealing with tribal courts. Either way, American Indian people and nations lose unless there is some sort of effort made to remedy this situation.

The lesson from this issue for practitioners is that not only is there no one American Indian voice, there is often no one voice for a particular tribe. Like any community, there are power struggles in American Indian communities. These internal conflicts on many issues, including the issue of membership, become more pronounced when it comes to the distribution of resources. Practitioners should be mindful of the possibility of such conflicts and patient when it comes to barriers they may cause. If one faction is an obstacle today, the next administration may be more supportive.

Children and Families

Maintaining strong American Indian communities was the central motivation behind the introduction of the Indian Child Welfare Act (ICWA). A groundbreaking piece of legislation, the ICWA was passed in 1978 in an effort to keep American Indian children with American Indian people and help to promote American Indian cultural identity (Hazeltine, 2002). This was done as a reaction to the effects of boarding schools and the high rates of adoption placements in non–American Indian homes. In the years before the ICWA, as many as 30% of American Indian children were being placed in non–American Indian environments, primarily due to a national federal program conducted in cooperation with the Child Welfare League of America called the "Indian Adoption Project" (Hazeltine, 2002).

Johnson (1999) and Cross, Earle, and Simmons (2000) provide good historical accounts of events prior to and after the passage of the ICWA, as well as fundamentals about the specific regulations based on the act. Among the interesting characteristics of the ICWA, Cross et al. (2000) report that tribal courts have jurisdiction over children who are tribal members, regardless of location. The key issue is that the "best interests of the child," under the ICWA, refers to the child's healthy cultural identity and place in the tribal community, and this can often be in conflict with a state's interest in expeditious "freeing" of a child from a potentially neglectful or abusive home (Hazeltine, 2002). This conflict is also shared by Matheson (1996), where he details another case where children's "needs" could have been addressed but for political conflicts involving the ICWA.

There have been significant legislative efforts since the ICWA that have also addressed American Indian family health and identity. Cross et al. (2000) noted that there was a companion piece of legislation passed in 1990 titled the Indian Child Protection and Family Violence Prevention Act, which set up new federal guidelines for investigating abuse on tribal lands. ICWA programs are also beneficiaries of the Social Security Act, with its handful of special sections devoted to families: Title IV-E, focusing on Foster Care and Adoption; Title IV-B (subparts 1 & 2), concerned with Child Welfare and Safety; and Title XX, addressing Social Services (Cross et al., 2000). The problem is that the designers of these Social Security programs took little or no interest in the intricacies of American Indian tribal or urban communities.

Although the ICWA has been a key player in the lives of many American Indian children over the years, it has been most evident in the literature concerning two states, California (Barth, Webster, & Lee, 2002) and Alaska (Andrews, 2002). California cases have sometimes involved accusations of violence (Humphrey, 2000; Lacayo, 1988). Madrigal (2001) details how the American Indian community of northern San Diego, California, created the Indian Child and Family Consortium shortly after the ICWA was passed. The community had started the Consortium as an organization that only addressed child safety and placement

issues, but they realized that to honor the spirit of the ICWA they should also provide everything from therapy sessions to cultural events and expand to three counties.

The Alaska activity has revolved around a history of court cases and a new law. The historical issue is that, from the passing of the ICWA, there has been an implication that there is a different standard by which child protective agencies are to approach cases involving American Indian children. This was played out in the Alaska courts: As Andrews (2002) reports, the difference between "active" and "reasonable" efforts on the part of the state, as defined by earlier statements from the Alaska Supreme Court, is that active efforts are characterized by state workers directly taking part in helping to keep a family unified. In addition, Andrews reports that earlier Alaska Supreme Court decisions also held that the ICWA standards for unification efforts are higher than non-ICWA cases and that ICWA cases should involve tribal cultural resources. But this distinction seems to have changed in recent years. Andrews suggests that a 2002 ruling by the Alaska Supreme Court was a decision unifying both standards, effectively stating that there is no different standard for American Indian or non-American Indian child custody cases.

This homogenization of Alaskan policy can also be seen in recent Alaskan law. Hazeltine (2002) and Andrews (2002) discuss Alaska's Child in Need of Aid (CINA) law, passed in 1998. Although Andrews believes that the law merely enhanced non–American Indian case standards to the level of ICWA standards, Hazeltine notes that the law does not take into account protections of the federal ICWA and unduly accelerates termination of parental rights of American Indian parents. Hazeltine reports that state efforts to abide by the federal Adoption and Safe Families Act (ASFA) of 1997 with the passage of the CINA make it even easier to take American Indian children from their parents. States like Alaska sometimes take this position, even when the ASFA explicitly states that the ICWA should still be honored. The problem is that the ICWA is barely mentioned in the ASFA, and no specific guidelines for integrating the two acts are mentioned in the ASFA.

Although the future of the ICWA remains uncertain, and challenges to tribal authority mentioned in the act are chronic (Mitchell, 1996), examinations of its past give cause for hope. A review of the history of the ICWA by McEachron, Gustavsson, Cross, and Lewis (1996) indicates that it seems to be working in its efforts to minimize the numbers of placements of American Indian children outside American Indian families. Plantz, Hubbell, Barrett, and Dobrec (1989) reviewed the status of ICWA programs based on a number of different criteria. Based on assessment of quality and length of time in foster and substitute care, removal standards and procedures, services to American Indian families, and resources for these programs, they noted significant, yet qualified and uneven, progress.

At every turn, the key to a beneficial relationship between governmental laws and American Indian families is the need to be responsive to the needs of indigenous nations and urban intertribal communities. For example, Cross et al. (2000) discuss how coordinating both substance abuse and welfare reform programs with child abuse prevention programs is critical in many American Indian communities.

One of the authors of this chapter, Walter Kawamoto, was pleased in the spring of 2002 to be a part of a federally based endeavor that truly seems to be honoring the principle of respecting the wishes of local American Indian nations. Although national Head Start programs are constantly being reviewed and assessed to meet changing standards, Tribal Head Start programs are administered under a separate "region" and are rarely reviewed. So when endeavoring to remedy this oversight and review tribal Head Starts nationally, the government, with the aid of an outside contractor, moved to act carefully and appropriately. Before doing any specific national assessment, the contractor, ORC Macro, was commissioned to do national "listening sessions" to determine the nature of the research agenda for future reviews. They wanted to find out what exactly a "successful" Head Start program is according to local American Indian communities, and what questions should be asked when working to support tribal Head Start programs. But before going out and listening to local Head Start stakeholders, they gathered a consultant panel of American Indian Head Start leaders and American Indian family research scholars to review the protocols for the initial visits. As a member of the consultant panel, Kawamoto was pleased with the respect for tribal sovereignty and the openness to panel suggestions displayed by both the ORC Macro staff and the federal civil servants at the panel meeting. Although some might find these steps at respecting local tribal communities redundant, Kawamoto looks at such kinds of efforts as long overdue.

CONCLUSION

We can see by the inconsistent treatment of Indian nations that there are many conflicting institutionalized stereotypes of American Indian people supported by the federal government. One end of the stereotype spectrum labels indigenous people savages, considering them a threat to be destroyed. Following this ideology, the federal government has created policies such as the Indian Removal Act. The other end of the stereotype spectrum labels indigenous peoples as childlike dependents, a group of people to be cared for and guided, or else they will be taken advantage of. The ideology that goes along with this stereotype is "it is in their own best interest, and we must do this for them," instead of allowing people to be self-reliant and run their own government and sovereign nation. This dialectic between social stereotypes and legislative policies again highlights the cross-cutting paradox of a dependent-yet-sovereign people.

Moreover, within the spectrum of stereotypes lies "the lazy Indian" or "the drunken Indian" or "the poor Indian" or, more recently, "the dead Indian because they no longer exist" or "the newly rich Indians getting their checks from the casino." This spectrum of stereotypes doesn't allow for any real or accurate look at these sovereign nations or indigenous people. As long as the president of the United States, members of Congress, and the American public continue to have stereotypes about American Indian people, American Indian policy will continue to oscillate. As long as American Indian nations continue to live as domestic dependent nations within the United States, the federal government will continue to affect American Indian self-governance.

Currently, there are more than 500 federally recognized tribes and more than 2 million American Indians in the United States (Benokraitis, 2002). American Indian nations have always considered themselves as sovereign nations with human rights and freedoms. It is time for the federal government and local practitioners to stop relying on stereotypes and look at indigenous people as human beings who deserve the respect of sovereign nations. Efforts have been made by the federal government to establish policies that help American Indian nations maintain their sovereignty and promote self-reliance. Many American Indian nations have created their own constitutions and are currently fighting to be recognized by the federal government to begin establishing their own self-reliance. In this new state of growth, tribal councils need to consider keeping their nation a cohesive unit, because with numbers there is strength to maintain current growth and work for future prosperity.

REFERENCES

Andrews, M. (2002). "Active" versus "reasonable" efforts: The duties to reunify the family under the Indian Child Welfare Act and the Alaska Child in Need of Aid statutes. *Alaska Law Review, 19,* 85–118.

Barth, R. P., Webster, D., & Lee, S. (2002). Adoption of American Indian children: Implications for implementing the Indian Child Welfare and Adoption and Safe Families Acts. *Children and Youth Services Review, 24,* 139–158.

Benokraitis, N.V. (2002). The changing ethnic profile of U.S. families in the twenty-first century. In N. Benokraitis (Ed.), *Contemporary ethnic families in the United States* (pp. 1–14). Upper Saddle River, NJ: Prentice Hall.

Cohen, F. (1982). *Handbook of Federal Indian Law.* Washington, DC: United States Government Printing Office. Accessed April 10, 2004, from http://thorpe.ou.edu/cohen.html

Cross, T. A., Earle, K. A., & Simmons, D. (2000). Child abuse and neglect in Indian country: Policy issues. *Families in Society: The Journal of Contemporary Human Services, 81*(1), 49–58.

Hazeltine, S. L. (2002). Speedy termination of Alaska Native parental rights: The 1998 changes to Alaska's child in need of aid statutes and their inherent conflict with the mandates of the federal Indian Child Welfare Act. *Alaska Law Review, 19,* 57–85.

Hodel v. Irving, 481 U.S. 704 (1987).

H.R. Rep. No. 1804, 73rd Congress, 2nd Session (1934).

Humphrey, K. (2000, December 20). Custody dispute tangled by kidnapping charge: Father charges various agencies fail to follow regulations. *Indian Country Today (Lakota Times),* p. D2.

The Indian Gaming Regulatory Act of 1988 (25 U.S.C. Secs. 2701–21).

The Indian Mineral Development Act of 1982 (25 U.S.C. Secs. 2101–8).

The Indian Self-Determination and Education Assistance Act of 1975, Pub. L. No. 93-638, codified as 25 U.S.C. Secs. 450f et seq. and in scattered sections of 5, 25, 42, and 50 U.S.C.

The Indian Tribal Government Tax Status Act of 1982, Pub. L. No. 97-473, 96 Stat. 2607 codified as amended in scattered sections of 26 U.S.C.

Johnson, L. B. (1968). Weekly compilation of presidential documents. Vol. IV, No. 19. Washington, DC: Government Printing Office.

Johnson, T. J. (1999). The state and the American Indian: Who gets the Indian child? *Wicazo Sa Review, 14,* 197–214.

Kawamoto, W. T., & Cheshire, T. C. (1997). American Indian families. In M. K. DeGenova (Ed.), *Families in a cultural context* (pp. 15–34). Mountain View, CA: Mayfield.

Kawamoto, W. T., & Cheshire, T. C. (1999). Contemporary issues in the urban American Indian family. In H. P. McAdoo (Ed.), *Family ethnicity: Strength in diversity* (pp. 94–104). Thousand Oaks, CA: Sage Publications.

Lacayo, R. (1988, May 2). The battle over Baby K.: Native Americans resist adoption of their children by non-Indians. *Time, 131*(18), 64–65.

Madrigal, L. (2001). Indian Child and Welfare Act: Partnership for preservation. *American Behavioral Scientist, 44,* 1505–1511.

Matheson, L. (1996). The politics of the Indian Child Welfare Act. *Social Work, 41,* 232–235.

McEachron, A. E., Gustavsson, N. S., Cross, S., & Lewis, A. (1996). The effectiveness of the Indian Child Welfare Act of 1978. *Social Service Review, 70,* 451–464.

Mitchell, G. (1996, July). History that repeats is not always good in Indian country. *News From Indian Country,* p. 17a.

NiiSka, C. (2001). St. Paul law professor to hear Las Vegas Paiute appeal. *Ojibwe News, 13,* N51.

Northwest Ordinance, 1 Stat. 50 (August 7, 1787).

Pevar, S. (1992). *The rights of Indians and tribes: The basic ACLU guide to Indian and tribal rights* (2nd ed.). Carbondale: Southern Illinois University Press.

Plantz, M. C., Hubbell, R., Barrett, B. J., & Dobrec, A. (1989). Indian child welfare: A status report. *Children Today, 18,* 24–29.

Strickland, R. (1986). Genocide-at-law: An historic and contemporary view of the Native American experience. 34, *University of Kansas. Law Review, 34,* 7-342 *Rev.* 713, 716.

Tyler, S. L. (1973). *A history of Indian policy.* Washington, DC: Government Printing Office.

Worcester v. Georgia, 31 U.S. (6 Pet.) 515 (1832).

PART V

JUVENILES

21

RACE DISPARITIES IN THE JUVENILE JUSTICE SYSTEM

EILEEN POE-YAMAGATA

National Council on Crime and Delinquency

MADELINE WORDES NOYA

National Council on Crime and Delinquency

The disproportionate representation of youth of color in the U.S. juvenile justice system is undisputed (Bishop & Frazier, 1990; Kempf, Decker, & Bing, 1990; Krisberg et al., 1987; Pope & Feyerherm, 1992). In fact, overrepresentation of minority youth is evident at every stage of system involvement. Reasons given for disparities in the juvenile justice system often suggest that minority youth simply commit more serious and frequent offenses. Indeed, for every 100,000 arrests of youth under age 18 in 2000, 4,654 black youth were arrested compared with 2,650 white youth. However, the degree to which minority youth are overrepresented in the juvenile justice system suggests other reasons. Research on racial disparities indicates that racial bias affects the juvenile justice processing of minority youth. According to Pope and Feyerherm (1990), "there is substantial support for the statement that there are race effects in operation within the juvenile justice system, both direct and indirect in nature."

The juvenile justice system is composed of an array of decision-making points, presenting many opportunities for bias to enter the system. For example, in the earliest stages prior to arrest, the police may differentially patrol an area and arrest more minority than nonminority youth (Sampson, 1986). The police decision to either refer the youth to court or detention or to handle the case informally may also be biased (Wordes & Bynum, 1995). As a result, the pool of youth referred to the court is disproportionately represented by youth of color even before formal court processing begins. The court process also comprises several critical decision-making points that may also be biased and that can ultimately result in a population of incarcerated youth who are mainly youth of color (Krisberg & Austin, 1993). Some have used the term "bias amplification" to indicate that as juveniles are processed further into the system, small biases at each stage can lead to large race differentials at the most severe sanctions (Bridges & Crutchfield, 1988; Farrell & Swigert, 1978).

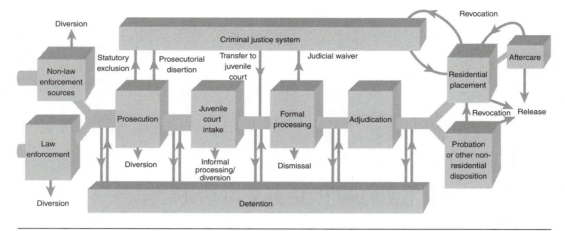

Figure 21.1   Juvenile Justice System Caseflow

SOURCE: Office of Juvenile Justice and Delinquency Prevention (2002).

STUDYING BIAS IN THE JUVENILE JUSTICE SYSTEM

Detection of bias in the juvenile justice system is complicated by several factors. As mentioned earlier, there are many decision-making points involved in processing a case through the juvenile justice system. Depending on local practices and traditions, states and communities may differ in the way that they process juvenile law violators. However, a common set of critical decision points regarding arrest, intake, detention, adjudication, and disposition have become the cornerstone for researchers' examination of minority overrepresentation (Figure 21.1). These critical points include the following:

- *Arrest:* police decide to either refer the case to the juvenile justice system or to divert.
- *Detention:* Juvenile probation and/or detention workers decide whether or not to detain youth initially. A detention hearing—generally held within 24 hours—is required to judicially determine whether continued detention is warranted. Youth may be held in a secure facility through the adjudicatory and dispositional hearings and, if out-of-home placement is ordered, until a residential space becomes available.
- *Transfer to criminal court:* Some cases may be transferred through statutory exclusions or at the discretion of the prosecutor.

- *Juvenile court intake:* Probation workers and/or the prosecutor decide to dismiss, divert, or formally process the case.
- *Formal case processing:* A petition is filed requesting either a juvenile court adjudicatory hearing or a waiver hearing to judicially transfer the case to criminal court.
- *Adjudicatory hearing:* Facts of the case are presented and—in most cases—a judicial determination regarding the youth's responsibility for the offense is made. Judicial adjudication of "delinquency" differs from language used in the criminal court system, where an offender is "convicted."
- *Dispositional hearing:* A judicial decision regarding case disposition is informed by the dispositional recommendations of probation staff and the prosecution.

Another issue that complicates the detection of bias is the need to view the juvenile court system as a process. Although more recent studies discuss the importance of estimating the cumulative effects of earlier decisions on later decisions (Bridges & Crutchfield, 1988; Frazier & Cochran, 1986), earlier studies simply isolated each decision point, viewing each decision as distinct and unrelated to another.

Studying bias in the juvenile justice system is also complicated by the fundamental functions of the system. The Progressive Era reformers who created the modern juvenile justice system designed it as a means of protecting the community as well as providing treatment to youthful offenders (Platt, 1969). According to Bell and Lang (1985), "The juvenile justice system was created in order that special circumstances and problems of youth could be accommodated by a wider variety of formal and informal procedures and 'treatment' alternatives" (p. 309). Accordingly, the reformers created a juvenile court system in the United States that now serves three main functions: (a) to keep social order, (b) to extend due process to juveniles, and (c) to provide "treatment" (Fenwick, 1982). These three fundamental functions may actually add to disproportionate representation.

The first function, to keep social order, can also be interpreted as maintaining the status quo. The Progressive reformers of the early 1900s were generally people with many resources who wanted to "help" others, but not at the sacrifice of their own status in the capitalist system (Rothman, 1980). According to Rothman, the reformers did not want to change the American economic and social system, because they benefited from it. Thus, maintaining the status quo, which meant keeping the "rabble class" in its place, was one implicit function of the juvenile court. Disproportionate representation would arise because the lower economic class contains a disproportionate number of racial minorities and young people (Quinney, 1977).

The second function, to extend due process, may also lead to greater disproportionate representation. Some have stated that due process is more likely to be extended to those with resources (Huizinga & Elliot, 1987). It is possible that extending due process is a function of access to resources. Accordingly, youth who have access to attorneys and resources for private mental health treatment may be disproportionately white, leaving a greater percentage of minority youth to be handled by the juvenile justice system.

The third function, providing treatment or being therapeutic, led to the doctrine of in loco parentis, which allows courts to fulfill the parental role when it deems the parents unfit or unable to do so. Research is then "complicated by the juvenile court philosophy of 'parens patriae,' which, contrary to the rule of law that governs adult criminal cases, not only accepts, but justifies relatively high levels of discretion at all stages of the juvenile justice process" (Johnson & Secret, 1990). Thus, the juvenile justice system was designed to take social factors into account when making dispositional decisions. It should offer no surprises that extralegal factors play a role in decision making. According to Cohen and Kluegel (1979), "In systems such as the juvenile court, where the boundaries and limits of discretionary power regarding the application of rules are not very clear, the possibility of unequal treatment of clients increases" (p. 147).

NATIONAL ARREST STATISTICS

Police are typically the first officials of the justice system that a youth encounters. In 2000, U.S. law enforcement agencies made an estimated 2.4 million arrests of persons under age 18 (Table 21.1; Snyder, 2002). Although the majority (72%) of these arrests involved white youth, white youth were underrepresented and black youth were overrepresented among most offenses in 2000.

Decisions by law enforcement are pivotal in determining the profile of cases formally involved in the juvenile justice system. At arrest, a decision may be made to either send the matter further into the justice system or divert the matter, usually into alternative programs. There are many factors that may be incorporated into the police decision. Observational studies, most notably Pillavin and Briar (1964), have found that demeanor and appearance were associated with police decisions. Black youth were perceived by officers to have a more negative demeanor and be less appropriately dressed. In addition, more recent research has noted the impact of the complainant's desire for formal court involvement on the police decision to further the case. Some complainants may be more likely to request such action for offenses involving youth of color (Black & Reiss, 1970; Smith & Visher, 1981). Complex indirect relationships involving such factors as demeanor and social and family situation may then interact with race/ethnicity to exert an influence on police decisions. Another explanation may be that the police are more likely to

Table 21.1   Arrests of Youth Under Age 18, 2000

Racial Proportions of Youth Under Age 18		79%	16%	1%	4%
			Percentage of total arrests		
Most serious offense charged	*Estimated number of juvneile arrests*	*White*	*Black*	*Native American*	*Asian*
Total	2,369,400	72	25	1	2
Violent crime index	98,900	55	42	1	2
Murder	1,200	47	50	<1	3
Rape	4,500	63	35	1	1
Robbery	26,800	41	56	1	2
Aggravated assault	66,300	61	37	1	2
Property index	518,800	69	27	1	2
Burglary	95,800	73	25	1	1
Larceny-theft	363,500	70	26	1	2
Motor vehicle theft	50,800	55	41	1	2
Arson	8,700	79	18	1	1
Non-index	1,751,800	74	23	1	2
Other assaults	236,800	65	33	1	1
Forgery and counterfeiting	6,400	77	20	1	2
Fraud	10,700	63	34	1	2
Embezzlement	2,000	62	35	<1	3
Stolen property, buying, receiving, possessing	27,700	60	37	1	2
Vandalism	114,100	82	16	1	1
Weapons: carrying, possession, etc.	37,600	67	31	1	2
Prostitution and commercialized vice	1,300	57	39	2	2
Sex offenses (except forcible rape and prostitution)	17,400	71	27	1	1
Drug abuse violations	203,900	70	28	1	1
Gambling	1,500	12	86	<1	2
Offenses against the family and child	9,400	77	20	1	2
Driving under the influence	21,000	93	5	1	1
Liquor laws	159,400	92	5	3	1
Drunkenness	21,700	91	7	1	1
Disorderly conduct	165,700	66	32	1	1
Vagrancy	3,000	74	25	1	1
All other offenses (except traffic)	414,200	75	22	1	2
Suspicion	1,200	72	25	<1	2
Curfew and loitering law violations	154,700	72	25	1	2
Runaways	142,000	76	18	1	4

SOURCE: *Juvenile Arrests* (2000). Office of Juvenile Justice and Delinquency Prevention (2002).

patrol areas with a higher population of black youth (Sampson, 1986).

One way to view whether disproportionate representation at the arrest stage is due to system bias is by comparing data on self-reported delinquency to data in official records. Studies that have compared self-reported delinquent behavior with official records have found little difference among racial groups in self-reported behavior, yet differential representation in official records (Huizinga & Elliot, 1987; Krisberg et al., 1987). Huizinga and Elliot used self-report delinquency data from the National Youth Survey and official data from police records on the same youth.

These authors concluded that "there are few if any substantial and consistent differences between the delinquency involvement of different racial groups" (p. 215). There were no significant differences in the self-reported delinquency for most of the serious offenses either, including felony assaults, felony thefts, and index offenses in general. In examining arrest rates, they found that the overall arrest rate for blacks for serious offenses was about two or three times the rate for whites. According to these authors, the negligent differences in delinquent behavior across racial categories could not account for the differences in arrest or incarceration rates.

JUVENILE COURT PROCESSING

Referral

Although most delinquency cases are referred to juvenile court by law enforcement, others are referred by schools and parents. In 1999, an estimated 1.7 million cases were referred to juvenile court (Stahl, Finnegan, & Kang, 2002). Although the majority (68%) of these cases involved white youth, the proportion of referred cases involving a black youth (28%) was almost twice the proportion of black youth in the U.S. population (15%) in 1999 (Table 21.2).

Table 21.2 Racial Proportions of the Juvenile Population and of Referrals to Juvenile Court, 1999

	Percentage of	
	Population	*Referrals*
White	79	68
Black	15	28
Other	6	3
Total	100	100

SOURCE: *Easy Access to Juvenile Court Statistics: 1990–1999* (data presentation and analysis package). Office of Juvenile Justice and Delinquency Prevention (2002).

NOTE: Details may not add to totals due to rounding.

Detention

Much like the process of holding adults in county jails prior to a preliminary hearing and/or trial date, juveniles may also be detained—with sight and sound separation from adults and generally in a completely separate facility—awaiting the dispositional outcome of their case. An initial decision to detain may be made by a probation officer or detention worker, but a formal court hearing—usually within 24 hours of arrest—is required to detain youth thereafter. A judge may decide to detain a youth out of concern for the youth's or the community's protection and to ensure appearance in court. In 1999, an estimated 336,200 youth were detained by U.S. courts. Across all offense categories, black youth were overrepresented among youth detained, whereas white youth were underrepresented (Figure 21.2). This was most dramatic among drug offenses. Cases involving white youth were 71% of those referred but 53% of those detained. In contrast, drug offense cases involving black youth were 27% of those referred but 45% of those detained.

Detention was also more likely for nonwhite than white youth across all offense categories. In 1999, 25% of black youth and 23% of youth of other races were detained, compared with 18% of white youth (Figure 21.3). Most dramatically, a black youth was more than twice as likely as a white youth to be detained for a drug offense (38% vs. 17%).

The decision to incarcerate a youth in a detention facility is of paramount importance. Frazier and Cochran (1986) studied the effect of detention on subsequent decisions. They found that "detainees are more likely to receive more harsh intake recommendations, more severe action by the State Attorney, and both more formal and more severe final dispositions of their cases" (p. 300). Thus, controlling for other legal factors, they found that detention had an independent effect on disposition.

Case Petitioning

Unlike in adult criminal courts, where prosecutors make decisions regarding the filing of cases, juvenile court probation generally determines the handling of cases. Cases may be either formally processed or petitioned through the juvenile court, handled informally or diverted from formal court processing, or

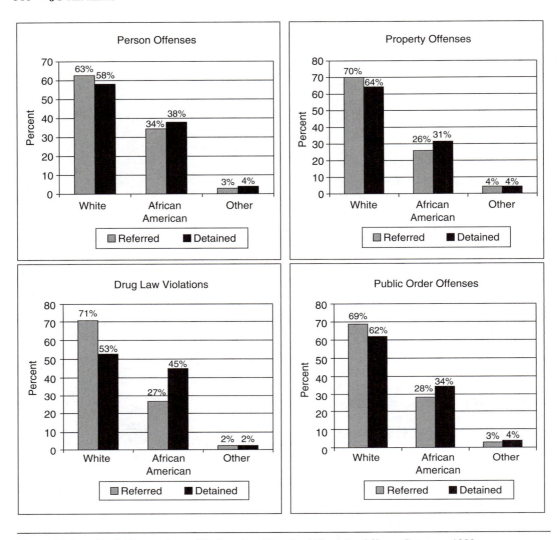

Figure 21.2   Racial Proportions of Referred and Detained Youth by Offense Category, 1999

SOURCE: *Easy Access to Juvenile Court Statistics: 1990–1999* (data presentation and analysis package). Office of Juvenile Justice and Delinquency Prevention (2002).

dismissed altogether. Though probable cause must be established to formally act on both adult and juvenile cases, a greater amount of discretion is involved in the decision to file a petition in juvenile court than in adult court.

While a significant number of juvenile court cases are diverted from formal processing to services operated by the juvenile court or outside, decisions by juvenile court intake may be based on both social and legal factors, whereas a district attorney's decision regarding filing a

case in adult court is based largely on legal facts. In 1999, an estimated 962,000 delinquency cases were formally processed or petitioned by juvenile courts. Black youth represented a somewhat higher percentage of cases petitioned than cases referred to juvenile court (32% vs. 28%), whereas white youth made up a smaller proportion of cases petitioned than referred (65% vs. 68%; Figure 21.4). Youth of other races accounted for about the same proportion of cases petitioned and referred (3%).

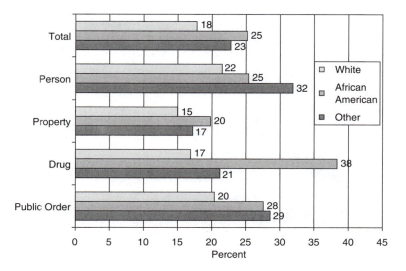

Figure 21.3   Likelihood of Detention by Offense, 1999

SOURCE: *Easy Access to Juvenile Court Statistics: 1990–1999* (data presentation and analysis package). Office of Juvenile Justice and Delinquency Prevention (2002).

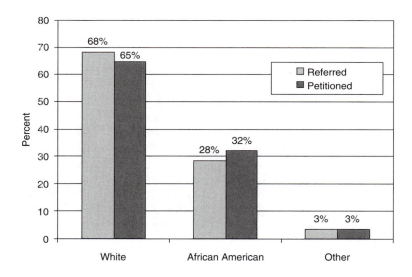

Figure 21.4   Racial Proportions of Referred and Petitioned Youth, 1999

NOTE: Details may not add to totals due to rounding.

SOURCE: *Easy Access to Juvenile Court Statistics: 1990–1999* (data presentation and analysis package). Office of Juvenile Justice and Delinquency Prevention (2002).

Cases involving black youth were also more likely than others to be petitioned or for- mally processed by the courts. This was true among each of the four offense categories as well and was especially apparent among drug offense cases (Figure 21.5). In 1999, 80% of

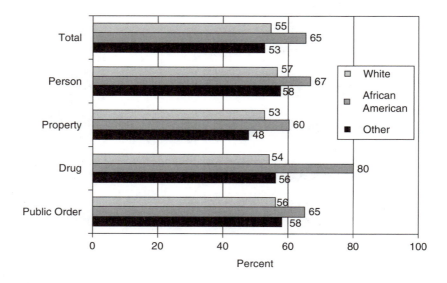

Figure 21.5 Likelihood of Case Petitioning by Race and Offense, 1999

SOURCE: *Easy Access to Juvenile Court Statistics: 1990–1999* (data presentation and analysis package). Office of Juvenile Justice and Delinquency Prevention (2002).

drug offense cases involving a black youth were petitioned compared to 54% among white youth and 56% among youth of other races.

One important observational study found race effects in the decision to petition a case (Fenwick, 1982). The observational methodology used in this study was rare and adds insight into court decision making. Fenwick measured disaffiliation (a composite variable consisting of family member present at hearing, caregiver interested or disinterested in youth's welfare, behavior problems at home, and family structure) and demeanor (coded as negative, positive, or neutral). Fenwick used multiple classification analysis to show that all the independent variables were significantly related to the petition decision. He found that black youth were more likely than others to be petitioned as were youth who were socially disaffiliated and showed a negative demeanor. As such, it may be that decision makers may be more likely to negatively view the demeanor and social situation of a black youth, thereby compounding the direct effect of race.

CRIMINAL COURT PROSECUTION OF JUVENILE OFFENDERS

During the 1980s and 1990s significant changes occurred in terms of treating more juvenile offenders as criminals. An estimated 200,000 youth are prosecuted as adults each year (Amnesty International, 1998). Some offenses previously filed in juvenile court are now excluded from juvenile court jurisdiction. In addition, in a growing number of states, the legislature has given the prosecutor the discretion of filing a defined list of cases in either juvenile or adult court.

For many years, most states have had provisions to "waive" juvenile court jurisdiction and transfer cases to criminal court if the prosecutor or intake officer believes that a case under jurisdiction of the juvenile court would be more appropriately handled in criminal court. A judge's decision in these cases generally centers on the issue of whether the juvenile is amendable to treatment in the juvenile justice system considering the youth's prior criminal history and the seriousness of the crime. In 1999,

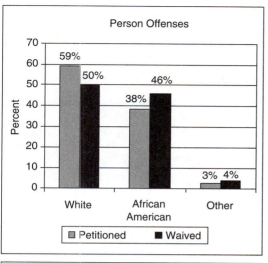

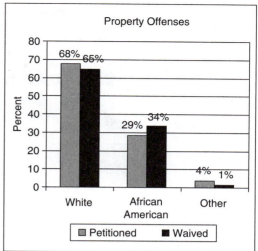

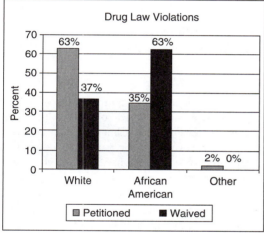

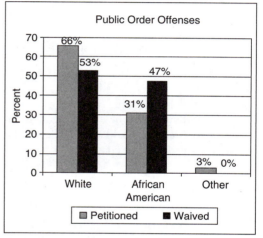

Figure 21.6   Racial Proportions of Petitioned and Judicially Waived Juvenile Court Cases by Offence
Category, 1999

SOURCE: *Easy Access to Juvenile Court Statistics: 1990–1999* (data presentation and analysis package). Office of Juvenile
Justice and Delinquency Prevention (2002).

about 7,500 delinquency cases were waived to
criminal court, representing less than 1% of all
cases referred.

Overall, cases involving white youth represented a smaller proportion of waived cases
than petitioned cases (54% vs. 65%). In contrast,
cases involving black youth represented a larger
proportion of waived cases than petitioned cases
(44% vs. 32%). Youth of other races were about
the same proportion of waived and petitioned

cases (2% vs. 3%) in 1999. This was the pattern
among all offense types as well; however, the
differences were particularly striking among
cases involving drug charges (Figure 21.6).

Black youth were also more likely than white
youth to be judicially waived to criminal court
(Figure 21.7). In 1999, .4% of white youth were
waived compared with .7% of black youth and
.3% of youth of other races. Although this was
generally true for every offense category, it was

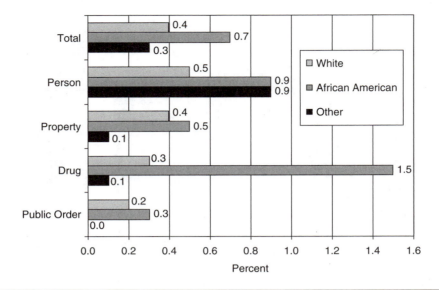

Figure 21.7 Likelihood of Judicial Waiver to Criminal Court by Offense, 1999

SOURCE: *Easy Access to Juvenile Court Statistics: 1990–1999* (data presentation and analysis package). Office of Juvenile Justice and Delinquency Prevention (2002).

again striking among drug offense cases. In 1999, drug offense cases involving black youth were at least five times as likely as others to be judicially waived to adult court.

Disposition

Between the time the youth is adjudicated delinquent and the dispositional hearing, a dispositional plan is developed. This report is generally prepared by probation staff and is based on diagnostic tests, psychological assessments, and evaluations of the youth, his or her support systems, and the availability of programs. In addition to this dispositional recommendation made by probation staff, the prosecutor and the youth may also present dispositional recommendations to the judge.

Though most juvenile dispositions are multifaceted, probation was the most severe disposition in the majority (62%) of adjudicated delinquency cases in 1999. About one in four adjudicated cases (24%) received the more severe disposition of out-of-home placement. The remaining cases were either released (4%) or received some other type of disposition (10%) such as victim/community restitution, drug counseling, and the like.

With respect to the proportion of adjudicated delinquency cases overall, white youth were underrepresented among cases receiving the more severe sanction of residential placement (66% vs. 61%), whereas black youth were overrepresented among these cases (31% vs. 36%). These trends were generally true in all offense categories, but were most notable among drug offenses (Table 21.3).

In addition to the Fenwick study cited earlier, Kurtz, Giddings, and Sutphen (1993) conducted a study of juvenile court decision making using observational data. Their results suggested a complex relationship between race, social class, and disposition. Socioeconomic status had strong indirect and direct effects on disposition. Youth with lower socioeconomic status received more severe dispositions. Race also showed direct and indirect effects. Blacks were more likely to have been charged with more serious offenses and to have shown a more negative demeanor. Through these variables, race had an indirect effect on disposition.

Juvenile Corrections

The juvenile correctional system involves an array of public and private facilities for

Table 21.3   Racial Profile of Adjudicated Delinquency Cases, 1999

	Percentage of Cases		
	Adjudicated Delinquent	Placed on Probation	Residential Placement
Person			
White	61	61	58
African American	36	36	38
Other	3	3	3
Total	100	100	100
Property			
White	69	69	65
African American	28	28	32
Other	4	4	4
Total	100	100	100
Drug			
White	65	69	49
African American	32	28	49
Other	2	3	2
Total	100	100	100
Public Order			
White	67	66	64
African American	30	31	33
Other	3	3	3
Total	100	100	100

NOTE: Details may not add to totals due to rounding.

SOURCE: Easy *Access to Juvenile Court Statistics: 1990-1999* (data presentation and analysis package). Office of Juvenile Justice and Delinquency Prevention (2002).

court-ordered and voluntarily committed and detained youth. The environments of these facilities range from group homes and small, minimum-security residential facilities to wilderness and boot camps and to facilities resembling adult prisons. According to the Office of Juvenile Justice and Delinquency Prevention (Sickmund & Wan, 2001), there were 108,931 youth in juvenile detention facilities prior to adjudication or committed to state juvenile correctional facilities following adjudication during a 1-day count on October 27, 1999. Most of these youth (74%) were committed as part of a court-ordered disposition and one in four (25%) were detained either prior to disposition or while awaiting an appropriate residential placement.

Minority youth were just 39% of the total youth population in the country in 1999, but they were 62% of detained or committed youth in state juvenile correctional facilities (Table 21.4). Minority youth were overrepresented in residential placement for all offense types. In fact, minority youth were at least one half of all youth in residential placement among each of the major delinquency offense categories (Figure 21.8).

Public juvenile facilities are typically locked local detention facilities or locked state correctional institutions. Private juvenile facilities are often less restrictive and less prisonlike. Minorities represented a greater proportion of youth in public (66%) than private (54%) facilities in 1997 (Figure 21.9). In fact, the minority proportion of youth in public facilities was almost twice the white proportion (66% vs. 34%).

Table 21.4   Racial Profile of Youth in Residential Placement by Offense, 1999

Racial Proportion of Youth Under 18, 1999		*61%*	*15%*	*17%*	*1%*	*4%*	*1%*
Most Serious offense	*Total*	*White*	*Black*	*Hispanic*	*Indiam*	*Asian*	*Other*
Total juveniles in residential placement	100%	38%	39%	18%	2%	2%	1%
Delinquency	100%	37	40	19	2	2	1
Person	100%	35	41	19	2	2	1
Violent Crime Index*	100%	32	42	21	2	3	1
Other Person	100%	44	36	15	2	2	1
Property	100%	42	36	18	2	2	1
Property Crime Index**	100%	42	36	18	2	2	0
Other Property	100%	42	36	17	2	2	1
Drug	100%	26	52	19	1	1	0
Public order	100%	37	38	20	2	2	0
Technical violation	100%	39	39	18	2	2	1
Status offense	100%	54	31	10	2	1	1

NOTE: Details may not add to totals due to rounding.

* Includes criminal homicide, sexual assault, robbery, and aggravated assault.
** Includes burglary, theft, auto theft, and arson.

SOURCE: *Easy Access to Juvenile Court Statistics: 1990–1999* (data presentation and analysis package). Office of Juvenile Justice and Delinquency Prevention (2002).

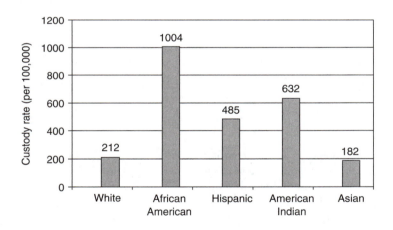

Figure 21.8   Number of Juveniles per 100,000 in Residential Placement by Race, 1999

NOTE: The custody rate is number of youth in residential placement per 100,000 youth ages 10 through upper age of juvenile court jurisdiction in each state. U.S. total includes 2,645 juvenile offenders in private facilities for whom state of offense was not reported and 174 juvenile offenders in tribal facilities.

SOURCE: *Census of Juveniles in Residential Placement Databook.* Office of Juvenile Justice and Delinquency Prevention (2001).

Adult Corrections

Legislative changes have enabled prosecutors and juvenile court judges to send more youth into the criminal justice system or to automatically exclude certain youth charged with certain offenses from the jurisdiction of the juvenile court. As a result, a growing number of

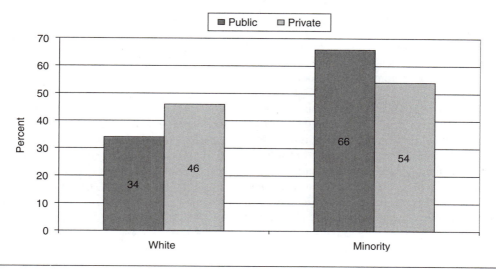

Figure 21.9   White and Minority Proportion of Juveniles in Public and Private Residential Placement on October 29, 1997

SOURCE: *Juvenile Offenders and Victims: 1999 National Report* (p. 195). Office of Juvenile Justice and Delinquency Prevention (1999).

youth are being sentenced to adult corrections such as state and federal prisons and county jails. The number of youth admitted to state prisons more than doubled between 1985 and 1997 (Strom, 2000). Of the estimated 7,400 youth under the age of 18 admitted to the nation's state prisons in 1997, 3 out of 4 were minorities—58% of these youth were black, 15% were Latino, and 2% were youth of other races.

Between 1985 and 1997, violent crimes grew from 34% to 54% of all admissions involving a white male while remaining relatively stable among black males (Table 21.5). In contrast, drug offenses accounted for 15% of admissions involving a black male in 1997, up from 2% in 1985. This proportion changed little among white males. As a result, in 1997, black males under the age of 18 were three times more likely than white males to be in a state prison for a drug offense (15% vs. 5%).

Although the "sight and sound separation" provisions of the Juvenile Justice and Delinquency Prevention Act prohibit youth under juvenile court jurisdiction from being within "sight or sound" of adult inmates, it does not cover youth under the jurisdiction of adult criminal court. Therefore, youth prosecuted as adults

Table 21.5   Offense Profile of Male Prisoners Under Age 18, 1997 (Percentages)

	White		Black	
	1985	*1997*	*1985*	*1997*
Total	100	100	100	100
Violent	34	54	62	63
Property	59	36	32	16
Drug	2	5	2	15
Public Order	4	5	4	5

NOTE: Proportions are based on estimated data. Data were not disaggregated by Hispanic origin. Includes only those with a sentence of more than 1 year.

SOURCE: Adapted from *Profile of State Prisoners under Age 18, 1985-97,* Bureau of Justice Statistics (2000).

can be incarcerated with adult inmates in jails and prisons.

CONCLUSION

These data have strong policy implications for the practices of the juvenile court. These findings suggest that the court does not adequately screen police decisions that may have been racially biased. Thus, black and

Latino youth may have begun their entrance into the juvenile justice system in a racially biased manner, and generally no rectification of that decision is made. Further, this early detention decision gets amplified in the disposition decision.

There are several types of intervention that may aid in reducing disparate treatment by race/ethnicity. The first is instituting strict detention criteria and/or objective risk assessment screening procedures for detention. In this way, only youth who are at risk to public safety or who are likely to fail to appear in court will be detained. In lessening discretion, Multnomah County, Oregon, was able to reduce the rate of disproportionate minority confinement (Hoytt, Schiraldi, Smith, & Ziedenberg, 2001). In the state of Connecticut, disparity in the justice system was greatly reduced through a number of interventions, including strict detention admission criteria, the development of alternatives to detention, and implementation of standardized assessment for placement decisions. They were able to reduce disparity in petitioning, court adjudication, disposition, and placements (Hartstone, 2001).

Other non-justice system interventions may include developing alternative dispute resolution forums. If a youth does not become involved in the juvenile court system, and the case is handled within his or her own community, disparate treatment may be less likely. Another possible intervention would be to develop community commissions who have the power to review patterns of decisions in the juvenile justice systems in their communities. With empowered oversight committees, communities may be able to understand and rectify any directly or indirectly discriminatory practices that may be taking place in law enforcement and the juvenile court.

It is important to remember that changes must be made at the individual, justice system, and societal levels. As Fagan, Slaughter, and Hartstone (1987) stated, "It is important to remember that inequality and disparity are endemic in our society, and that juvenile justice agencies are no less a part of that society than any other institution." The justice system is a critical place to begin changing these endemic societal problems.

REFERENCES

Amnesty International. (1998). *Betraying the Young: Human rights violations against children in the U.S. justice system.* AI Index: AMR 51/60/98.

Bell, D., Jr., & Lang, K. (1985). The intake dispositions of juvenile offenders. *Journal of Research in Crime and Delinquency, 22*(4), 309–328.

Bishop, D. M., & Frazier, C. S. (1990). *A study of race and juvenile justice processing in Florida.* Report. Gainesville: University of Florida.

Black, D. A., & Reiss, A. J. (1970). Police control of juveniles. *American Sociological Review, 35,* 63–77.

Bridges, G. S., & Crutchfield, R. D. (1988). Law, social standing and racial disparities in imprisonment. *Social Forces, 66,* 699–724.

Cohen, L. E., & Kluegel, J. R. (1979). The detention decision: A study of the impact of social characteristics and legal factors in two metropolitan juvenile courts. *Social Forces, 58,* 146–161.

Fagan, J., Slaughter, E., & Hartstone, E. (1987). Blind justice? The impact of race on juvenile justice process. *Crime and Delinquency, 33*(2), 224–258.

Farrell, R., & Swigert, V. (1978). Prior offense record as self-fulfilling prophecy. *Law and Society Review, 12,* 437–453.

Fenwick, C. R. (1982). Juvenile court intake decision making: The importance of family affiliation. *Journal of Criminal Justice, 10*(6), 443–453.

Frazier, C. E., & Cochran, J. C. (1986). Detention of juveniles: Its effects on subsequent juvenile court processing decisions. *Journal of Criminal Law and Criminology, 76*(4), 1132–1152.

Hartstone, E. (2001). *A reassessment of minority overrepresentation in Connecticut's juvenile justice system.* Report. Farmington, CT: Spectrum Associates Market Research.

Hoytt, E., Schiraldi, V., Smith, B., & Ziedenberg, J. (2001). *Reducing disproportionate representation of minority youth* (Pathways #8). Baltimore The Annie E. Casey Foundation.

Huizinga, D., & Elliot, D. S. (1987). Juvenile offenders: Prevalence, offender incidence and arrest rates by race. *Crime and Delinquency, 33,* 206–223.

Johnson, J. B., & Secret, P. E. (1990). Race and juvenile court decision making revisited. *Criminal Justice Policy Review, 4,* 159–187.

Kempf, K., Decker, S., & Bing, R. (1990). *An analysis of apparent disparities in the handling of black youth within Missouri's juvenile justice systems.* Technical Report. St. Louis: University of Missouri–St. Louis.

Krisberg, B., & Austin, J. (1993). *Reinventing juvenile justice.* Newbury Park, CA: Sage Publications.

Krisberg, B., Schwartz, I., Fishman, G., Eisikovits, E., Guttman, E., & Joe, K. (1987). The incarceration of minority youth. *Crime and Delinquency, 33,* 173–205.

Kurtz, P. D., Giddings, M. M., & Sutphen, R. (1993). A prospective investigation of racial disparity in the juvenile justice system. *Juvenile and Family Court Journal, 44,* 43–59.

Office of Juvenile Justice and Delinquency Prevention, U.S. Department of Justice. (2002). Accessed January 27, 2003, from http://www.ojjdp.ncjrs.org/images/flwchrt.bmp

Pillavin, I., & Briar, S. (1964). Police encounters with juveniles. *American Journal of Sociology, 69,* 206–214.

Platt, A. (1969). *The child savers: The invention of delinquency.* Chicago: Chicago University Press.

Pope, C. E., & Feyerherm, W. F. (1990). Minority status and juvenile processing. *Criminal Justice Abstracts, 22*(2), 327–336, and *22*(3), 527–542.

Pope, C. E., & Feyerherm, W. F. (1992). *Minorities and the juvenile justice system.* Report. Washington, DC: U.S. Department of Justice, Office of Juvenile Justice and Delinquency Prevention.

Quinney, R. (1977). *Class, state and crime: On the theory and practice of criminal justice.* New York: David McKay Company.

Rothman, D. J. (1980). *Conscience and convenience: The asylum and its alternatives in progressive America.* New York: HarperCollins.

Sampson, R. (1986). Effects of socioeconomic context of official reaction to juvenile delinquency. *American Sociological Review, 51,* 876–885.

Sickmund, M., and Wan, Y. (2001). *Census of juveniles in residential placement databook.* Accessed January 27, 2003, from http://www.ojjdp.ncjrs.org/ojstatbb/cjrp

Smith, D. A., & Visher, C. A. (1981). Street level justice: Situational determinants of police arrest decisions. *Social Problems, 29*(2), 167–177.

Snyder, H. (2002). *Juvenile arrests 2000.* Washington, DC: Office of Juvenile Justice and Delinquency Prevention.

Stahl, A., Finnegan, T., & Kang, W. (2002). *Easy access to juvenile court statistics: 1990–1999.* Accessed January 27, 2003, from http://ojjdp.ncjrs.org/ojstatbb/ezajcs/

Strom, K. (2000). *Profile of state prisoners under age 18, 1985–97.* Washington, DC: Bureau of Justice Statistics.

Wordes, M., & Bynum, T. S. (1995). Policing juveniles: Is their bias against youth of color? In K. Kempf, C. Pope, & W. Feyerherm (Eds.), *Minorities in juvenile justice* (pp. 47–65). Thousand Oaks, CA: Sage Publications.

22

A CULTURAL APPROACH FOR PROMOTING RESILIENCE AMONG ADJUDICATED MEXICAN AMERICAN YOUTH

FELIPE GONZÁLEZ CASTRO

Arizona State University

CULTURAL CONTEXTS AFFECTING MEXICAN AMERICAN YOUTH

This chapter examines elements of culture that relate to working with adjudicated Mexican American youth. This analysis moves beyond simple *surface structure* to provide a *deep structure* analysis (Resnicow, Soler, Braithwaite, Ahluwalia, & Butler, 2000) of factors affecting the adjustment of Mexican American youth. A major question examined in this chapter is "How can we promote resilience among Mexican American youth, who from early life are at high risk for adjudication based on being born into compromised life circumstances?" Such circumstances include a fragmented home environment; parental conflict; an impoverished *barrio* environment; exposure to drugs, gangs, and criminal activity within the *barrio;* low quality of schools; and a juvenile justice system where national data reveals a disproportionate confinement of Latino youth (Villarruel & Walker, 2002).

The Challenge of Identity Formation for Mexican American Youth

Mexican American and other Latino adolescents face the conventional challenges of adolescent growth, as well as the challenges of adjustment when exposed to two distinct cultures. For most Mexican American youth, identity formation occurs within the context of exposure to cultural conflicts and developmental stressors from which some Mexican American youth emerge stronger and more resilient by developing an integrated bilingual/bicultural identity.

Maturation and growth toward adult maturity can be observed along a youth's "life trajectory" (Newcomb & Bentler, 1988). Youth who exhibit the "Problem Behavior Syndrome" (Jessor & Jessor, 1977) also exhibit an antisocial life trajectory that ultimately leads to legal problems and future incarceration. Youth, including Mexican Americans, who in early childhood exhibit impulsive and aggressive traits, often suffer from co-occurring psychological and medical disorders that place them at higher risk for future involvement within the juvenile justice system. Youth with arrest records, as compared with those without them, have been observed to have a higher prevalence of diagnosed conduct disorder (Rosenblatt, Rosenblatt, & Biggs, 2000), and those youth who exhibit such co-occurring disorders are more likely to receive harsher legal sentences (Stewart & Trupin, 2003). Thus, understanding the complex personal and social barriers to normal youth development within a cultural context as observed among high-risk Mexican American youth will aid in developing culturally informed prevention programs to reduce risks and to promote resilience in youth development.

Conceptualizing Issues of Culture, Race, and Ethnicity

Understanding Culture, Race, and Ethnicity

Culture is a rich yet complex construct, one that gives people a sense of identity, direction, and purpose (Locke, 1998). Thus, when the "culture of protection" within a stable home environment disintegrates, the resulting "culture of risk" deprives youth of identity, direction, and purpose. Culture can be conceptualized as consisting of two major components: (a) environmental culture, the social norms or rules established by family and/or community that define appropriate conduct; and (b) subjective culture, a person's beliefs, attitudes, values, expectations, and introjected social norms, or subjective norms, for self-control of one's own conduct.

Within an ethnic community, adaptive adjustment to the local environment typically prompts the evolution of certain cultural styles. One specific cultural style is conceptualized along a continuum ranging from traditionalism to modernism (Ramirez, 1999). Under a traditional cultural orientation, strong family identification and loyalty are valued, whereas under a modernistic cultural orientation, individualism and independence are valued. This "modernized" Eurocentric cultural orientation emphasizes Protestant ethics that value individual initiative, upward social mobility, consumerism, and freedom of expression and action. Accordingly, Mexican American youths who are "highly acculturated" toward mainstream U.S. culture often emulate these modernistic cultural ideals.

Traditionalism. Among Mexican Americans, traditionalism refers to a system of beliefs, attitudes, and values that reflect conservative and often agrarian life views. Within the Latino/ Spanish-speaking cultures, Catholicism and its system of beliefs and values has served as a foundation for many secular life ways. Thus, strong religiosity; belief in loyalty to family, to the church, and to the community; and specific gender role expectations such as machismo and marianismo (Gil & Vazquez, 1996) constitute core aspects of traditional Mexican culture.

Ramirez (1991, 1999) has described cultural styles along the dimension of traditionalism versus modernism, where traditional value orientations include (a) distinct gender roles, (b) a strong level of identification with the family, (c) a strong sense of community involvement, (d) high family loyalty and family identification, (e) a greater present time orientation, (f) greater reverence for elders, (g) a greater value placed on cultural traditions, and (h) a greater value placed on spirituality and religion. Traditionalism has its roots in agrarian societies, where survival of the group was dependent on mutual cooperation and on maintaining harmony in interpersonal relations. Within this system of sociocultural values, individuals judged as "intelligent" and "socially competent" were those who exhibited exceptional capabilities in relating well with others and in maintaining harmonious social ties, along with leadership in promoting cooperation between members of the group (Gardner, Kornhaber, & Krechevsky, 1993). For the purpose of the assessment of cultural traditionalism, items and scales are presented in Table 22.1. This self-report survey, Community Life Ways, consists of three scales: Family Traditionalism, Rural Lifestyle, and Macho Privilege. These scales were developed from Manuel Ramirez III's theoretical framework and original scales that examined the dimension of traditionalism–modernism.

Within this context, Ramirez (1991) and Buriel, Calzada, and Vasquez (1983) have indicated that the most successful Mexican American children and adolescents, and perhaps those who are most resilient, are those who develop bicultural flexibility, a skill that

Table 22.1 Community Life Ways

Please answer how *you* feel about these questions regarding life values. There are no right or wrong answers. Please answer each question by indicating whether you (1) strongly disagree, (2) disagree, (3) have no opinion, (4) agree, or (5) strongly disagree.

	Strongly Disagree	Disagree	No Opinion	Agree	Strongly Agree
1. You should know your family history so you can pass it along to your children.	1	2	3	4	5
2. The good life is lived by staying home and taking care of the family.	1	2	3	4	5
3. It is OK for a man to get drunk now and then at a family celebration.	1	2	3	4	5
4. Children should be taught to be loyal to their family.	1	2	3	4	5
5. Small town communities offer a closeness to nature (the country) that is lost in the big city.	1	2	3	4	5
6. A family celebration without alcoholic drinks is just no fun.	1	2	3	4	5
7. Mothers who have small children should *not* work outside the home.	1	2	3	4	5
8. The quality of life is better in a rural community, where a person can feel safe and close to nature (the country).	1	2	3	4	5
9. It is OK for a man to smoke cigarettes and cigars as much as he wants.	1	2	3	4	5
10. Traditional celebrations such as baptisms, weddings, or graduation ceremonies add meaning to life.	1	2	3	4	5
11. I prefer to live in a small town where everyone knows each other.	1	2	3	4	5
12. Wives should always obey their husbands, even if they disagree with his wishes.	1	2	3	4	5
13. I dislike city life because it destroys cultural traditions and ruins family unity.	1	2	3	4	5
14. Adult children should visit their parents often as an expression of love and respect.	1	2	3	4	5
15. Men have the right to be the total decision maker within their home.	1	2	3	4	5
16. The good life is lived by spending time with people and doing things at a leisurely pace.	1	2	3	4	5
17. In the country, people usually are more cooperative, friendly, and helpful.	1	2	3	4	5
18. Big cities are better to live in because life in small towns is boring.	1	2	3	4	5
19. Living in a big city is too fast paced and stressful; I prefer the serenity of life in a small town.	1	2	3	4	5
20. Children should always be respectful of their parents and older relatives.	1	2	3	4	5

NOTE: The *Family Traditionalism Scale* consists of items 1, 4, 7, 10, 14, 16, 20 ($\alpha = .71$); The *Rural Lifestyle Scale* consists of items 2, 5, 8, 11, 13, 17, 19 ($\alpha = .87$); The *Macho Privilege Scale* consists of items 3, 6, 9, 12, 15 ($\alpha = .57$).

allows them to move between traditional and modernistic cultural styles. That is, these children develop a hybrid set of cultural styles and related skills described as "cultural flex" (Ramirez, 1999).

Acculturation, Assimilation, and Biculturalism

Acculturation is a process of special importance for people affected by economic, social, or political changes that force social migration and/or adaptation to new social and economic conditions. For persons of Mexican heritage, whether they are immigrants (Mexican nationals) or natives of the Southwest (Mexican Americans/Chicanos), acculturation conflicts often emerge that impose remarkable life challenges. Acculturation refers to changes in values, attitudes, behaviors, and lifestyle induced by the need to adapt to a new social or cultural environment. The process of acculturation is often accompanied by stress and conflict as the person struggles with issues of upward mobility, often at the expense of a loss of family unity, identity formation, and other cultural value conflicts. For some Mexican Americans, discrimination and barriers to upward mobility constitute chronic life strains that can prompt life dissatisfaction, distress, depression, and at times the abuse of alcohol and illicit drugs.

Berry (1980) postulated four varieties of acculturation that reflect differing strategic resolutions to the conflicts that surround the process of cultural adaptation: (a) assimilation, (b) integration, (c) rejection, and (d) deculturation. In the process of cultural adaptation, acculturation conflicts revolve around (a) ways to become successful within mainstream American culture; (b) establishing and maintaining personal and cultural identity, including conflicts over loyalty to one's native cultural heritage; and (c) choice of peer groups (peer clusters)—cultural identification with certain peers who are chosen as close friends (Oetting & Beauvais, 1987). Within this framework, important questions arise for high-risk Mexican American adjudicated youth regarding their cultural identity formation and forms of social connectedness within the context of their antisocial conduct, especially as this involves being

culturally marginalized and thus identifying neither with mainstream American society and its values nor with traditional Mexican society and its values.

Several studies have examined ways to measure acculturation as well as the effects of acculturation among various Latino adolescents. These studies suggest that a degree of assimilation in early childhood to fit in within mainstream society, followed by enculturation—that is, the development of a bicultural identity in adolescence or young adulthood—produces more positive outcomes as indicated by superior psychological adjustment (Castro & Garfinkle, 2003; Cuellar, Arnold, & Maldonado, 1995; Felix-Ortiz & Newcomb, 1995; Gil, Vega, & Dimas, 1994; Marin & Gamboa, 1996; Moyerman & Forman, 1992; Oetting & Beauvais, 1991; Rotheram-Borus, 1990; Szapocznik & Kurtines, 1989).

Hispanic Families and Ethnic Culture

Family as the Source of Protective Culture. Within all cultures, the family broadly conceived is the primary source of cultural transmission, the source that communicates values, beliefs, traditions, and practices that are passed down from elders to children (McGoldrick & Giordano, 1996). Among Mexican American and other Hispanic families, variations exist regarding the level of parental conservative-traditionalism or liberal-modernism used in child-rearing styles and practices (Bernal & Shapiro, 1996; Falicov, 1996). A family's cultural traditions and practices give family members their cultural identity and sense of belonging, based on an abiding sense of *nosotros* (we-ness) that comes from having common values, beliefs, and traditions. Many racial/ethnic groups give strong credence and value to interpersonal relationships, thus being described as "relational cultures." This attention to nuances in family relationships appears to have originated from adaptive behavior among members of *extended family networks*. This remarkable closeness observed within many Mexican and other Latino families is a characteristic described as *familism* (Sabogal, Marin, & Otero-Sabogal, 1987). Familism refers to a "strong identification with and attachment to one's nuclear and extended families, and strong feelings of loyalty, reciprocity, and solidarity among members of the same family" (Marin & Marin, 1991, p. 13).

There exist other cultural elements observed often within traditional Latino families. These include *personalismo,* the value ascribed to interpersonal relationships rather than to completing tasks; *simpática,* the commitment to maintain harmonious social interactions and conflict avoidance; *dignidad,* the value ascribed to personal dignity; *respeto,* the value ascribed to respect, with expectations that a person should show deference and respect to persons of higher stature and authority within the family and in the community; and *confianza,* a sense of trust, comfort, security, and intimacy found within special interpersonal relationships (Keefe, Padilla, & Carlos, 1978).

Disrupted Affective Bonds and Youth Risks. In the mainstream literature, risk factors for alcohol and other drug use among adolescents include three major factors: (a) a disrupted family system, (b) youth difficulties in school, and (c) youth associations with deviant peers (Hawkins, Catalano, & Miller, 1992; Oetting & Beauvais, 1987). Szapocznik and Kurtines (1989) have reported on differential rates of acculturation between Cuban children and their parents, where children acculturate at a faster rate. These differential rates of acculturation are associated with a growing emotional distance and communication conflicts occurring between parents and their children. Consequently, as some of these youth may become alienated culturally from their family, they may then engage in antisocial activities, including illicit drug use (Chavez, Edwards, & Oetting, 1989; Vega, Zimmerman, Warheit, Apospori, & Gil, 1993). Conversely, strong affective bonds to family, school, and church and to other prosocial institutions operate as sources of guidance and social support that are protective against antisocial conduct, including illicit drug use (Jessor, 1993).

Affective Bonds in Protection and Risk. In examining the role of religious involvement, one of several protective factors among African American youth, Johnson and collaborators observed that the relationship of neighborhood

disorder and criminal behavior is mediated and thus attenuated by religious involvement as measured by frequency of attending religious services (Johnson, Jang, Li, & Larson, 2000). Furthermore, in an analysis of the link between domestic violence and youth victimization, Mitchell and Finkelhor (2001) observed that adolescent girls living in households that have an adult victim of domestic violence are themselves at higher risk for crime victimization. In summary, impaired parent–youth relationships, those marked by parental neglect and/or aggressiveness toward their children, impair normal youth development and impede the development of youth resilience.

Issues in Working With Mexican American Adjudicated Youth

Theory-Based Approaches for Promoting Resilience Among Mexican American Adolescents

This section reviews theories and issues relevant to understanding and working with adjudicated Mexican American youth. As noted previously, the challenges to promoting resilience among Mexican American adolescents are compounded by youth conflicts in identity formation that result from exposure to two often conflicting sets of cultural norms. Despite these challenges, a growing body of literature endorses the advantages of developing a bicultural identity and the benefits of developing "cultural flex," which involves skills for responding effectively within two distinct cultural environments (Felix-Ortiz & Newcomb, 1995; LaFromboise, Coleman, & Gerton, 1993; Ramirez, 1999).

Stage Theory Views of Adjustment. Ethnic identity development has been conceptualized as progressing through a series of three distinct developmental stages: (a) diffuse/foreclosed identity, (b) moratorium on identity, and (c) achieved identity (Phinney, 1989, 1990, 1993). Youth who are aware of their ethnic/racial identity but have not resolved their feelings about their ethnicity experience cultural conflicts in a moratorium stage of ethnic identity development. Adolescents at this stage become sensitive to prejudice and discrimination and often feel in the "out-group"; they feel "different" and perhaps "inferior." If an adolescent at this stage introjects these negative attitudes about being in the out-group, then that adolescent can develop self-doubt or self-hatred. Helping youth resolve moratorium stage conflicts and transition to the achieved identity stage is a general strategy for building resilience among Mexican American and other Latino youth.

Peer Clusters and Social Bonding. Peer cluster theory (Oetting & Beauvais, 1987) is a "lifestyle theory" about youths' connections with family, school, and peers, and it postulates that "bonding" with an antisocial group of adolescent peers compromises adaptive adjustment. Gang or peer group involvement is typically governed by a balance of social forces involving the "push–pull" of two processes: a youth's attraction to a certain peer group based on that youth's self-concept and life preferences, and the reference group's acceptance of youths who conform to the group's norms and its rejection of youths who fail to conform to these norms. Thus, a youth's peer involvement is initiated and maintained by that youth's choice of reference group and loyalty to that group and by conformity with the group's unique group norms.

Emotional Intelligence. The concept of emotional intelligence is especially meaningful for youth from relational cultures, such as the Latino cultures, which place a high value on maintaining strong interpersonal relationships (Gardner et al., 1993). Emotional intelligence is a meta-ability involving emotional and social competencies associated with successful social function, and emotional intelligence appears to operate above and beyond the influence of cognitive intelligence as measured by the intelligence quotient (IQ). The major components of emotional intelligence are (a) the capacity for self-control; (b) the capacity to motivate and guide one's own behavior; (c) the ability to defer gratification and to channel one's urges; and (d) the capacity for empathy and skills in listening to others and in taking another person's perspective (Goleman, 1995). These capacities are associated with strong personal character, self-discipline, and the capacity to work

successfully with others, all features also associated with strong resilience.

Among preschool children, key factors identified as components of emotional intelligence are (a) confidence—the child's belief in his or her own abilities, (b) curiosity—a child's interest in discovering new things, (c) intentionality—persistence in working toward a desired outcome, (d) self-control—the child's ability to modulate his or her actions in an age-appropriate manner, (e) relatedness—the child's ability to engage others, (f) sharing—the capacity to communicate and to share information with other children, and (g) cooperativeness—the child's ability to balance his or her own needs with the needs of other children (Goleman, 1995). Especially within relational cultures, exceptional skills at managing one's emotions and in motivating others to work on behalf of a group or community constitute important capabilities necessary for exercising strong community leadership, and these skills suggest the presence of strong resilience for a successful involvement within communal environments.

Sources of Cultural Conflict—Contrasting Two Cultures. As an aid to the analysis of salient cultural conflicts often observed among Mexican American and other Latino youth, Table 22.2 presents contrasting value orientations regarding the idyllic Anglo American and the idyllic Mexican American cultures. This table presents absolute differences while recognizing that any bicultural community will contain elements of both cultures represented among its families. For further elaboration, see Castro, Boyer, and Balcazar (2000). It has been postulated that adolescents who develop strong skills in adaptive coping with the aid of others will also develop a hybrid and resilient bilingual/bicultural identity (Felix-Ortiz & Newcomb, 1995).

As indicated in Table 22.2, the idyllic Anglo American and Mexican American cultures present contrasting *cultural prescripts,* cultural norms or rules of conduct, "life shoulds" in the areas of (a) social orientation, (b) family orientation, (c) interpersonal style, and (d) expressive style (Castro et al., 2000). Table 22.2 simplifies the more complex real-world value orientations and the nuances that exist within the two cultures (Locke, 1998) into a cultural dialectic,

Table 22.2   Sources of Cultural Conflict: Contrasting Value Orientations

Lifestyle Areas	Value Orientations	
	Anglo American	*Mexican American*
Social orientation	Individualism	Collectivism
	Competition	Cooperation
Family orientation	Achievement oriented (doing)	Family oriented (*familism*)—(being)
Interpersonal style	Precision in verbal expression	Focus on the relationship (*personalismo*)
	Confrontation	Social harmony (*simpático*)
	Efficient task completion	Respect (*respeto*)
Expressive style	Rational, restrained	Affective, expressive

SOURCE: Castro, Boyer, and Balcazar (2000, p. 159).

while acknowledging that these idyllic contrasts do not suggest that a value orientation observed in one culture is absent within the opposing culture.

Promoting Resilience and Bicultural Adjustment. The complex influences imposed by the processes of acculturation and ethnic identity formation on the mental health of Mexican American and other Latino youth have been examined previously (Recio Adrados, 1993; Rogler, Cortes, & Malgady, 1991). In a 3-year longitudinal study of 849 middle school youth observed during the seventh, eighth, and ninth grades, Griffin, Scheier, Botvin, and Diaz (2001) found that personal competence skills in the seventh grade as mediated by psychological well-being in the eighth grade were associated with lower substance use in the ninth grade. These investigators indicate that having competence skills promotes a sense of personal satisfaction, mastery, and well-being, which in turn appear to protect against the use of illicit drugs.

Table 22.3 presents a multidimensional framework of skills for healthy adjustment, both conventional and culturally specific (Castro et al., 2000). For each dimension, this table examines criteria that serve as indicators of three distinct levels of function: *abnormal* (maladaptive), *normal* (adaptive), and *exceptional* (proficient) adjustment. These criteria on adjustment at these three levels of function are based on information from several sources (Goleman, 1995; Hawkins et al., 1992; Jessor & Jessor, 1977; Mitchell & Beals, 1997; Phinney, 1992;

Ramirez, 1991, 1999). By implication, Mexican American and other Latino youth who develop strong resilience would be expected to exhibit the traits of exceptional adjustment.

Youth exhibiting abnormal (maladjusted) development often exhibit chronic dysphoric emotions such as chronic anxiety, depression, anger, and the like. They often exhibit a lack of empathic regard for others, impulsivity, a lack of future planning and problem-solving skills, and a lack of creative self-directed behavior, and they often exhibit limited attachments to parents and to school, along with an attachment to deviant peers. These youth would likely also exhibit a lack of spiritual connectedness with a church or other prosocial institution and thus would exhibit weak resilience. Regarding culturally specific aspects of adjustment, Mexican American or other Latino youth with abnormal traits would likely exhibit cultural marginality and thus a disinterest or dislike for their cultural heritage. They would likely exhibit an ethnic identity in the "diffuse stage" of development, while also exhibiting a lack of cultural flex, a disinterest in service to their community, and a lack of leadership skills. Unfortunately, many adjudicated youth are likely to exhibit certain skills deficits and behaviors consistent with abnormality and maladjustment as described here. Thus, aims in prevention and treatment programs for such high-risk adjudicated youth would be to promote adjustment toward normality on the various noted domains, both for the conventional and the culturally specific areas.

Table 22.3   Dimensions of Healthy Adjustment: Some Skills and Capabilities

	Abnormal (Maladaptive)	Normal (Adaptive)	Exceptional (Proficient)
Conventional			
Emotionality	Frequent dysphoria and symptomatology: anxiety, depression, anger, etc.	Occasional dysphoria and symptomatology	Occasional dysphoria and symptomatology
Empathy	Lacking	Some capacity	Strong capacity
Self-control	Impulsive	Some delay of gratification	Delays gratification
Planning	Lacking	Some	Strong skills
Problem solving	Lacking	Some	Strong skills
Creative self-directedness	Disinterest in creative activities	Does some creative activities	Invests time and effort in creative activities
Attachments			
Parents	Neglect or parental rejection	Supportive attachments	Supportive attachments
School	Dislikes school	Likes school	Loves school
Peers	To deviant peers	To prosocial conventional peers	To prosocial conventional peers
Spirituality	Lacking	Some	Strong
Culturally Specific			
Cultural heritage	Dislike or disinterest in heritage	Some interest in heritage	Strong appreciation for heritage
Ethnic identity	*Diffuse* stage of identity formation	*Moratorium* stage of identity formation	*Achieved* stage of identity formation
Cultural flex	No flex	Some flex	Strong flex; bicultural capabilities
Community interest	Disinterest in service to community	Some interest	Strong interest in service to community
Leadership	Lack of leadership or antisocial behavior	Some leadership activity	Strong leadership activity

SOURCE: Castro, Boyer, and Balcazar (2000, p. 159).

SOCIAL AND INSTITUTIONAL BARRIERS TO RESILIENCE

Villarruel and Walker (2002) have documented and described the problem of racial/ethnic disparities observed within the criminal justice system that involve the disproportionate confinement of Latino youth and of other minority youth. These disparities for Latino youth relative to white youth include higher rates of arrests, higher admission rates to detention, and harsher punishments for the same crime. These harsher consequences among Latino and Latina youth are the product of institutional inequities observed within the American criminal justice system, problems that include (a) the overrepresentation of Latinos and Latinas within several correctional facilities nationwide; (b) inadequate data collection that, among other limitations, lacks the standardized and reliable collection of information by ethnicity; (c) lack of adequate bilingual services to Latino youth; (d) lack of cultural competence of correctional staff working with Latino youth; and (e) the use of antigang laws to impose harsher and unfair sentences on adjudicated Latino youth.

These investigators illustrate the disparities using data for Los Angeles County for 1998, where the disproportionalities for Latino youth relative to white youth include arrest rates among Latino youth that are 1.9 times higher for violent offenses, 2.0 times higher for drug offenses, and 1.8 times higher for felony offenses. Similarly, as compared with white youth, Latino youth spend "more time for the same crime," such as a rate of incarceration among Latino youth relative to white youth that is 13 times greater for drug offenses, 5 times greater for violent offenses, and 2 times greater for property offenses (Villarruel & Walker, 2002). Along these lines, despite controlling for other variables, Brownsberger (2000) observed that youth sentencing laws disproportionately affect young adult minority males ages 20 to 39 years of age. The contemporary emphasis on trying some youth offenders as adults and the imposition of harsher criminal sanctions is seen as counterproductive and harmful to these adjudicated youth, while also creating family problems and weakening communities. Thus, policy-related reforms are needed, especially those that can protect minority youth within the juvenile justice system, youth who often receive these harsher sentences. Adjudicated youth constitute a special population affected by multiple life problems and social and institutional barriers, and they face oppressive environments. These complex and challenging conditions prompt the need for prevention and treatment programs that are culturally informed and comprehensive enough to address these multiple areas of need.

Prevention and Treatment With Adjudicated Mexican American Youth

In an analysis of ethnocultural factors that affect substance abuse among racial/ethnic minority persons, Terrell (1993) has identified three substantive areas: (a) the acculturation experience, (b) sources of stress, coping, and social supports, and (c) beliefs and attitudes regarding substance abuse. Terrell also notes that many existing prevention interventions still *do not* take into account the role of cultural factors in drug use initiation and its progression. Thus, in prevention and in treatment, the need

exists for specific culturally relevant program components, especially as organized in the form of a treatment manual that outlines specific cultural activities and their evaluation under a well conceptualized program evaluation protocol (Castro, Barrera, & Martinez, 2004; Castro & Garfinkle, 2003; Schinke, Brounstein, & Gardner, 2002).

Culturally Sensitive Interventions With Mexican Americans

Culturally Responsive Assessment and Treatment Planning. A Mexican American family's history of experiences with the legal system and with illicit drugs may influence that family's preparedness to help a drug-using family member. Among young heroin-addicted Mexican American/Chicana females, Moore (1990) notes that multigenerational drug-using families have developed a system of support that allows the recovering young women to return home and function adaptively. By contrast, young Mexican American women from more conservative "traditional" families who had never before contended with drug problems had families that were less supportive of their daughter's deviant behavior.

Regarding gender issues in treatment, Gutierres and Todd (1997) found that relative to female Mexican American and Anglo American clients, a higher percentage of their American Indian female clients completed their treatment program. These high completion rates were attributed to the *culturally sensitive* residential program that provided the American Indian women with traditional healing practices, a sweat lodge ceremony, a talking circle, and child care, all within a therapeutic community.

In the process of cultural program adaptation, a dynamic tension exists between sensitivity to the unique cultural needs of cultural subgroups, as contrasted with the competing need to promote "acculturative" and "Western" behaviors and skills that promote survival and success within mainstream American society (Castro et al., 2004). Regarding this source of program tension, the treatment program developer must recognize the adaptive challenges of acculturation to U.S. mainstream cultural norms and also recognize and respect the need and desire of many racial/ethnic minority people to retain aspects of their ethnic traditions.

Here, some "universal" or "one-size-fits-all" programs that ignore issues of culture can be described as "culturally blind," programs that are insensitive to cultural needs (Ja & Aoki, 1993). Such needs include (a) feelings of being discriminated against, alienated, or not feeling accepted; (b) identity conflicts in addition to typical youth developmental issues; (c) value conflicts imposed by social processes that force acculturation or conformity with mainstream American life ways; and (d) racial/ethnic family dynamics that can inadvertently interfere with treatment and can promote relapse (Locke, 1998; Ramirez, 1999). The development of such culturally informed programs should be guided by relevant theories that are also culturally sensitive and that are designed as best practice or model programs for Mexican American youth (Castro & Hernandez-Alarcon, 2002; Resnicow et al., 2000; Schinke et al., 2002).

Culturally responsive relapse prevention and recidivism efforts must also address issues of family support of youth within the criminal justice system by offering an integrated program of treatment (LaFromboise, Trimble, & Mohatt, 1990) that for Mexican Americans includes treatment in their native language when relevant and treatment that includes cultural, psychological, and spiritual activities. Thus, clinic administrators must recognize the need for such treatments and may develop a parallel treatment track. Alternately, a less costly approach is to offer a set of treatment components or modules that complement the original treatment program and that address specific and relevant cultural issues. In addition, clinic staff should make a commitment to developing cultural competence in order to be more capable of providing further therapeutic interventions (Castro & Garfinkle, 2003).

Self-Concept, Ethnic Identity, and Machismo. Although machismo is often cited as an explanation for maladaptive male drinking practices, Lex (1987) has pointed out that the original positive concept of machismo has been distorted in a pejorative stereotypical fashion to emphasize male entitlement, sexual exploitation, and toughness, including a man's "right" to drink alcohol. By contrast, the original Mexican concept of machismo was associated with the more positive male traits of personal integrity, autonomy, dignity, strength, honor, respect, and responsibility as a family provider (Gil & Vazquez, 1996), perhaps a cultural form of Latino male fortitude and resilience. Unfortunately, some of the negative aspects of machismo such as male entitlement are observed among certain Mexican American adolescents and adults (see the items for the Macho Privilege Scale). When these negative aspects of machismo are observed among certain adjudicated youth, these negative attitudes and behaviors should be addressed, as these forms of machismo are likely maladaptive and may operate as barriers to the development of resilience. Culturally sensitive prevention interventions for Mexican American and other Latino youth under adjudication may focus on self-concept/self-esteem and values clarification by promoting positive forms of machismo, while also discouraging the negative attitudes and behaviors involved in macho privilege (Cuellar, Arnold, & Gonzalez, 1995; Garfinkle & Castro, 2003). For Mexican American youth, community-oriented prosocial values can also be promoted that emphasize responsible and "giving" behaviors toward the family and the community.

Skill Building and Family Strengthening. A total of 44 prevention programs have been identified that qualify as science-based model programs now incorporated into the Substance Abuse Mental Health Services Administration (SAMHSA) and the Center for Substance Abuse Prevention's (CSAP's) National Registry of Effective Prevention Programs (NREPP) (Schinke, Brounstein, & Gardner, 2002). The Institute of Medicine has classified such prevention programs into one of three types: (a) universal—programs designed for the general population; (b) selective—programs designed for youth at higher-than-average risk; and (c) indicated—programs designed for youth already engaging in high-risk behaviors (Schinke et al., 2003). Currently, of these 44 programs, only 5 are specifically designed as "indicated programs," that is, programs designed explicitly for high-risk youths such as those under adjudication. And of these 5, only 2 are oriented for work with Latino youth: Brief Strategic Family Therapy and Family Effectiveness Training, both developed by Jose Szapocznik and collaborators at the University of Miami.

Brief Strategic Family Therapy (BSFT) is designed for youth ages 8 to 17 and their families. It addresses youth emotional and behavioral problems by improving family function by way of facilitating healthy family interactions. Family Effectiveness Training (FET) is designed for youth ages 6 to 11 and aims to improve school performance, reduce problem behaviors, improve child self-concept, and improve family functioning. Its program activities target intergenerational conflicts to eliminate maladaptive behaviors, and it provides training for healthy family interactions.

The Strengthening Families Program (SFP) has been designed by Karol Kumpfer and colleagues at the University of Utah. This program was designed for youth ages 6 to 11 and their families. This is a "selective type" of prevention program that aims to decrease substance use, improve social/family skills, improve parent–child attachments and family relations, and improve parenting skills. This program has been further developed and adapted to offer cultural sensitivity for work with Hispanic and American Indian populations (Kumpfer, Alvarado, Smith, & Bellamy, 2002). A related family-focused approach is the Multidimensional Family Therapy (MDFT) developed by Howard Liddle and colleagues at the University of Miami. This program is a comprehensive outpatient family-based treatment for adolescent substance-abusing youth that aims to (a) treat the drug-using youth's cognitive and emotional problems, (b) improve parenting practices, and (c) enhance family interaction patterns. This program's treatment goals include improving youth function to reduce or eliminate drug use and to promote prosocial activities as well as growth-enhancing activities and relationships (Liddle et al., & Tejeda, 2001).

To make these programs more culturally relevant for adjudicated Mexican American youth and their families, culturally oriented skills training modules specific for youth under adjudication should be added. Effective skills training that is educationally and culturally relevant for Mexican American youth under adjudication should consider developing (a) critical thinking skills for youth to understand and practice appropriate forms of assertiveness, (b) decision-making and behavioral skills for relating effectively and with *respeto* to elders and to certain authority figures, and (c) communication and interpersonal skills that acknowledge issues of traditionalism–modernism and youth capacity for developing biculturalism and cognitive/cultural flex. Adjudicated youth should be helped to develop these skills. In addition, oppressive and unfair policies and procedures operating within the juvenile justice system must also be changed to reward youth who work diligently to improve themselves, who work toward acquiring prosocial skills and values, and who work toward making constructive contributions to their community.

CONCLUSION

Challenges in Working With Adjudicated Mexican American Youth. Within some Mexican American families, the erosion of a culture of protection based on a deteriorating parent–child relationship, poor parental monitoring, and family instability and oppressive social policies and institutions set the stage for deficient adolescent development. Here, two significant questions are "How much can resilience and other prosocial skills and competencies be developed among Mexican Americans youth who are under adjudication?" and "What specific elements of traditional Mexican culture may be incorporated into prevention and treatment programs to promote normalcy, and ideally, to enhance resilience and thus to move these youth beyond normal to exceptional adjustment?"

Prosocial Goals and Challenges. Working effectively with adolescents and young adults who exhibit antisocial behavior and multiple skills deficits is a major challenge. Such work requires patience and strategic limit setting, as well as mature guidance and adaptive role modeling. The use of culturally responsible contingency management is one behavioral approach that may help structure activities to develop prosocial goals, skills, and behaviors among youth from this special population. However, issues arise regarding the choice of contingencies that should be established and rewarded so that Mexican American youth under adjudication are not forced to conform to culturally destructive assimilationist agendas that would erode or discourage cultural pride and the retention of Mexican cultural beliefs and values. The aim of such behavioral treatments is to build resilience by (a) advancing ethnic identity development toward the achieved stage, (b) fostering affiliations with prosocial peer groups and institutions, (c) increasing emotional intelligence and resilience skills including empathy and self control, and (d) identifying prosocial life goals and fostering a commitment toward pursuing them.

Prevention Program Principles. Recently, a set of principles for effective prevention program development have been proposed in the areas of (a) program characteristics, (b) matching program to target population, and (c) program implementation (Nation et al., 2003). In the area of program characteristics, effective prevention programs should (a) be comprehensive, (b) include varied teaching methods, (c) have a sufficient dosage of program activities to have an effect, (d) be theory driven, and (e) foster positive interpersonal relationships.

Systemic Changes to Reduce Disproportionate Confinement. Beyond a focus on individual youth development, the issue of disproportionate rates of incarceration and punishments observed among Latino and Latina youth relative to white youth calls for several forms of social and community action. According to Villarruel and Walker (2002), these action approaches include (a) mobilizing Latino communities to challenge unfair policies and procedures operating within the criminal justice system, (b) implementing alternatives to detention that include culturally relevant prevention programs for Latino youth, and (c) having Latinos and Latinas appointed to state advisory groups to oversee and hold the criminal justice system accountable. Latino parents can also participate by becoming more informed about this

problem of disproportionality and by developing support groups to address sources of injustice within the criminal justice system.

The law-enforcement system can address this issue by working with community leaders to improve its own policies and procedures, improving data collection procedures, and training its staff in cultural competence. The criminal justice system can improve itself by actively addressing its contributions to the problem of disproportionality, by improving its methods of data collection by way of instituting more standardized procedures that include valid indicators of race and ethnicity, by increasing cultural competence in administering racially unbiased needs assessments, by developing guidelines for greater accountability, and by hiring and training practices that promote cultural competence in their own personnel. Policymakers can help by enacting legislation that aims to reduce disproportionality and by developing initiatives to reduce the juvenile justice system's overreliance on incarceration. Finally, researchers can address this problem of disproportionality by conducting longitudinal studies of Latino and Latina youth within the U.S. justice system by tracking trends in Latino youth incarceration and sentencing, by using qualitative and quantitative methods to study the cases of Latino youth who have been incarcerated, and by conducting studies on the critical factors that lead to this disproportionality by race and ethnicity, as it occurs for Latinos and Latinas within the U.S. juvenile justice system.

REFERENCES

Bernal, G., & Shapiro, E. (1996). Cuban families. In M. McGoldrick, J. Giordano, & J. K. Pearce (Eds.), *Ethnicity and family therapy* (2nd ed., pp. 155–168). New York: Guilford.

Berry, J. W. (1980). Acculturation as varieties of adaptation. In A. M. Padilla (Ed.), *Acculturation: Theory, models and some new findings.* Boulder, CO: Westview Press.

Brownsberger, W. N. (2000). Race matters: Disproportionality of incarceration for drug dealing in Massachusetts. *Journal of Drug Issues, 30,* 345–374.

Buriel, R., Calzada, S., & Vasquez, R. (1983). The relationship of traditional Mexican American culture to adjustment and delinquency among three generations of Mexican American male adolescents. *Hispanic Journal of Behavioral Sciences, 4,* 41–55.

Castro, F. G., Barrera, M., & Martinez, C. R. (2004). Cultural adaptation of prevention interventions: Resolving tensions between fidelity and fit. *Prevention Science, 5,* 41–45.

Castro, F. G., Boyer, G., & Balcazar, H. G. (2000). Healthy adjustment in Mexican American and other Hispanic adolescents. In R. Montemayor, G. R. Adams, & T. P. Gullota (Eds.), *Adolescent diversity in ethnic, economic, and cultural contexts* (pp. 141–178). Thousand Oaks, CA: Sage Publications.

Castro, F. G., & Garfinkle, J. (2003). Critical issues in the development of culturally relevant substance abuse treatments for specific minority groups. *Alcoholism: Clinical and Experimental Research, 27,* 1–8.

Castro, F. G., & Gutierres, S. (1997). Drug and alcohol use among rural Mexican Americans. In E. B. Robertson, Z. Sloboda, G. M. Boyd, L. Beatty, & J. Kozel (Eds.), *Rural substance abuse: State of knowledge and issues.* NIDA Research Monograph Series, No. 168 (pp. 498–533). Rockville, MD: National Institute on Drug Abuse.

Castro, F. G., & Hernandez-Alarcon, E. (2002). Integrating cultural variables into drug abuse prevention and treatment with racial/ethnic minorities. *Journal of Drug Issues, 32,* 783–810.

Chavez, E. L., Edwards, R., & Oetting, E. R. (1989). Mexican American and white American school dropouts' drug use, health status, and involvement in violence. *Public Health Reports, 104,* 594–604.

Cuellar, I., Arnold, B., & Gonzalez, G. (1995). Cognitive referents of acculturation: Assessment of cultural constructs in Mexican Americans. *Journal of Community Psychology, 23,* 339–356.

Cuellar, I., Arnold, B., & Maldonado, R. (1995). Acculturation rating scale for Mexican Americans II: A revision of the original ARSMA scale. *Hispanic Journal of Behavioral Sciences, 17,* 275–304.

Falicov, C. J. (1996). Mexican families. In M. McGoldrick, J. Giordano, & J. K. Pearce (Eds.), *Ethnicity and family therapy* (2nd ed., pp. 169–182). New York: Guilford.

Felix-Ortiz, M., & Newcomb, M. D. (1995). Cultural identity and drug use among Latino and Latina adolescents. In G. J. Botvin, S. Schinke, & M. A. Orlandi (Eds.), *Drug abuse prevention with multiethnic youth* (pp. 147–165). Thousand Oaks, CA: Sage Publications.

Gardner, H., Kornhaber, M., & Krechevsky, M. (1993). Engaging intelligence. In H. Gardner (Ed.), *Multiple intelligences: The theory in practice* (pp. 231–248). New York: Basic Books.

Garfinkle, J., & Castro, F. G. (2003, June). *Gender identity and ethnic identity as predictors of drug use and restraint among Mexican American adults.* Poster session presented at the 11th Annual Meeting of the Society for Prevention Research, Washington, DC.

Gil, A. G., Vega, W. A., & Dimas, J. M. (1994). Acculturative stress and personal adjustment among Hispanic adolescent boys. *Journal of Community Psychology, 22,* 43–54.

Gil, R. M., & Vazquez, C. I. (1996). *The Maria paradox: How Latinas can merge old world traditions with new world self-esteem.* New York: G. P. Putnam's Sons.

Goleman, D. (1995). *Emotional intelligence.* New York: Bantam.

Griffin, K. W., Scheier, L. M., Botvin, G. J., & Diaz, T. (2001). Protective role of personal competence skills in adolescent substance use: Psychological well-being as a mediating factor. *Psychology of Addictive Behaviors, 15,* 194–203.

Gutierres, S. E., & Todd, M. (1997). The impact of childhood abuse on treatment outcomes of substance users. *Professional Psychology: Research and Practice, 28,* 348–354.

Hawkins, J. D., Catalano, R. F., & Miller, J. Y. (1992). Risk and protective factors for alcohol and other drug problems in adolescence and early adulthood: Implications for substance abuse prevention. *Psychological Bulletin, 112,* 64–105.

Ja, D., & Aoki, B. (1993). Substance abuse treatment: Cultural barriers in the Asian American community. *Journal of Psychoactive Drugs, 25,* 61–71.

Jessor, R. (1993). Successful adolescent development among youth in high-risk settings. *American Psychologist, 48,* 117–126.

Jessor, R., & Jessor, S. (1977). *Problem behavior and psychosocial development.* New York: Academic Press.

Johnson, B. R., Jang, S. J., Li, S. D., & Larson, D. (2000). The "invisible institution" and black youth crime: The church as an agency of local social control. *Journal of Youth & Adolescence, 29,* 479–498.

Keefe, S. E., Padilla, A. M., & Carlos, M. L. (1978). The Mexican American extended family as an emotional support system. In J. M. Casas & S. E. Keefe (Eds.), *Family and mental health in the Mexican American community* (pp. 49–67). Los Angeles: University of California.

Kumpfer, K. L., Alvarado, R., Smith, P., & Bellamy, N. (2002). Cultural sensitivity and adaptation in family-based prevention interventions. *Prevention Science, 3,* 241–246.

LaFromboise, T., Coleman, H. L. K., & Gerton, J. (1993). Psychological impact of biculturalism: Evidence and theory. *Psychological Bulletin, 114*(3), 395–412.

LaFromboise, T. D., Trimble, J. E., & Mohatt, G. V. (1990). Counseling intervention and American Indian tradition: An integrative approach. *The Counseling Psychologist, 18,* 628–654.

Lex, B. W. (1987). Review of alcohol problems in ethnic minority groups. *Journal of Consulting and Clinical Psychology, 55,* 293–300.

Liddle, H. A., Dakof, G. A., Parker, K., Diamond, G. S., Barrett, K., & Tejeda, M. (2001). Multidimensional family therapy for adolescent drug abuse: Results of a randomized clinical trial. *American Journal of Drug and Alcohol Abuse, 27,* 651–688.

Locke, D. C. (1998). *Increasing multicultural understanding: A comprehensive model* (2nd ed.). Thousand Oaks, CA: Sage Publications.

Marin, G., & Gamboa, R. J. (1996). A new measurement of acculturation for Hispanics: The bidimensional acculturation scale for Hispanics (BAS). *Hispanic Journal of Behavioral Sciences, 18,* 297–316.

Marin, G., & Marin, B. V. (1991). *Research with Hispanic populations.* Newbury Park, CA: Sage Publications.

McGoldrick, M., & Giordano, J. (1996). Overview: Ethnicity and family therapy. In M. McGoldrick, J. Giordano, & J. K. Pearce (Eds.), *Ethnicity and family therapy* (pp. 1–27). New York: Guilford.

Mitchell, C. M., & Beals, J. (1997). The structure of problem and positive behavior among American Indian adolescents: Gender and community differences. *American Journal of Community Psychology, 25,* 257–288.

Mitchell, K. J., & Finkelhor, D. (2001). Risk of crime victimization among youth exposed to domestic violence. *Journal of Interpersonal Violence, 16,* 944–964.

Moore, J. (1990). Mexican American women addicts: The influence of family background. In R. Glick & J. Moore (Eds.), *Drugs in Hispanic communities* (pp. 127–153). New Brunswick, NJ: Rutgers University Press.

Moyerman, D. R., & Forman, B. D. (1992). Acculturation and adjustment: A meta-analytic study. *Hispanic Journal of Behavioral Sciences, 14,* 163–200.

Nation, M., Crusto, C., Wandersman, A., Kumpfer, K. L., Seybolt, D., Morrissey-Kane, E., et al., (2003). What works in prevention: Principles of effective prevention programs. *American Psychologist, 58,* 449–456.

Newcomb, M. D., & Bentler, P. M. (1988). *Consequences of adolescent drug use: Impact on the lives of young adults.* Newbury Park, CA: Sage Publications.

Oetting, E. R., & Beauvais, F. (1987). Peer cluster theory, socialization characteristics, and adolescent drug use: A path analysis. *Journal of Counseling Psychology, 34,* 205–213.

Oetting, E. R., & Beauvais, F. (1991). Orthogonal cultural identification theory: The cultural identification of minority adolescents. *International Journal of the Addictions, 25,* 655–685.

Phinney, J. S. (1989). Stages of ethnic identity development in minority group adolescents. *Journal of Early Adolescence, 9,* 34–49.

Phinney, J. S. (1990). Ethnic identity in adolescents and adults: Review of research. *Psychological Bulletin, 108,* 499–514.

Phinney, J. S. (1992). Ethnic identity and self-esteem: An exploratory longitudinal study. *Journal of Adolescence, 15,* 271–281.

Phinney, J. S. (1993). A three-stage model of ethnic identity development in adolescence. In M. E. Bernal & G. P. Knight (Eds.), *Ethnic identity: Formation and transmission among Hispanics and other minorities* (pp. 61–79). Albany: State University of New York.

Ramirez, M. (1991). *Psychotherapy and counseling with minorities: A cognitive approach to individual and cultural differences.* New York: Pergamon Press.

Ramirez, M. (1999). *Multicultural psychotherapy: An approach to individual and cultural differences* (2nd ed.). Boston: Allyn & Bacon.

Recio Adrados, J. (1993). Acculturation: The broader view—Theoretical framework of the acculturation scales. In M. R. De la Rosa & J. L. Recio Adrados (Eds.), *Drug abuse among minority youth: Advances in research and methodology.* National Institute on Drug Abuse, Research Monograph No. 130 (pp. 57–78). Rockville, MD: National Institute on Drug Abuse.

Resnicow, K., Soler, R., Braithwaite, R. L., Ahluwalia, J. S., & Butler, J. (2000). Cultural sensitivity in substance use prevention. *Journal of Community Psychology, 28,* 271–290.

Rogler, L. H., Cortes, D. E., & Malgady, R. G. (1991). Acculturation and mental health status among Hispanics: Convergence and new directions for research. *American Psychologist, 46,* 585–597.

Rosenblatt, J. A., Rosenblatt, A., & Biggs, E. E. (2000). Criminal behavior and emotional disorder: Comparing youth served by the mental health and juvenile justice systems. *Journal of Behavioral Health Services & Research, 27,* 227–237.

Rotheram-Borus, M. J. (1990). Adolescents' reference-group choices, self-esteem, and adjustment. *Journal of Personality and Social Psychology, 59,* 1075–1081.

Sabogal, J., Marin, G., & Otero-Sabogal, R. (1987). Hispanic familism and acculturation: What changes and what doesn't? *Hispanic Journal of Behavioral Sciences, 9,* 397–412.

Schinke, S., Brounstein, P., & Gardner, S. (2002). *Science-based prevention programs and principles 2002.* DHHS Pub No. (SMA) 03-3764. Rockville, MD: Center for Substance Abuse Prevention, Substance Abuse and Mental Health Services Administration.

Stewart, D. G., & Trupin, E. W. (2003). Clinical utility and policy implications of a statewide mental health screening process for juvenile offenders. *Psychiatric Services, 54,* 377–382.

Szapocznik, J., & Kurtines, W. M. (1989). *Breakthroughs in family therapy with drug abusing and problem youth.* New York: Springer.

Terrell, M. D. (1993). Ethnocultural factors and substance abuse toward culturally sensitive treatment models. *Psychology of Addictive Behaviors, 7,* 162–167.

Vega, W. A., Zimmerman, R. S., Warheit, G. J, Apospori, E., & Gil, A. G. (1993). Risk factors for early adolescent drug use in four ethnic and racial groups. *American Journal of Public Health, 83,* 185–189.

Villarruel, F. A., & Walker, N. E. (2002). *Donde esta la justicia? A call to action on behalf of Latino and Latina youth in the U.S. juvenile system.* East Lansing: Institute for Children, Youth and Families, Michigan State University.

23

LAW AND SOCIAL IDENTITY AND ITS EFFECTS ON AMERICAN INDIAN AND ALASKA NATIVE YOUTH[1]

JOSEPH E. TRIMBLE

Western Washington University

ROBIN A. LADUE

University of Washington

We must come to recognize that one of the fundamental human rights of individuals and of groups includes the right to self-identification and self-definition, so long as one does not adopt an identity which has the effect of denying the same rights to others.

—Jack D. Forbes (1990, pp. 48–49)

The words of the American Indian historian Jack D. Forbes set the tone and theme of this chapter as he asserts that self-identification and self-declaration are rights—privileges granted by birth, perquisite, prerogative, or law. Whatever form it takes, identity is a complex construct, as it implies a specific set of behavioral or subjective characteristics by which an individual is recognizable; it can be one's individuality or selfhood that may involve the quality or condition of being exactly the same as something else.

Viewed from an ethnocultural perspective, the broad implication of the construct begs several questions. What is social and individual identity from a social and psychological perspective? Who and with what authority is identity formed, altered, embellished, or changed from group declarations or assertions? Is identity the internalization of external messages? Is it an understanding of our place in the world, our connections to others, a naming of our assets and attributes? Is it the work we do in the world or anticipate doing? Is it our culture or ethnocultural group, our nationality, our religion, our politics? Is it a set of images, sometimes if not often controlled by the media, in the past controlled by visual caricatures and stereotypes fostered by the government with the underlying policy of dehumanizing indigenous

343

people and other ethnocultural people? Is it the misunderstanding of society at large, which continues to foster both media images and internalized self-doubt? Is it the press of history and the view of the future, collected in one's psyche? Is it the foundation and the result of decisions one makes? These are not simple academic questions, although many of the questions influence and drive social and psychological research and inquiry on social and individual identity. The distinguished cultural anthropologist Clifford Geertz (2000) reminds us that "there are nearly as many ways in which such identities, fleeting or enduring, sweeping or intimate, cosmopolitan or closed-in, amiable or bloody-minded, are put together as there materials with which to put them together and reasons for doing so. . . . [A]nswers people sometimes give to the question, whether self-asked or asked by others, as to who (or, perhaps, more exactly, what) they are—simply do not form an orderly structure" (p. 225).

Although Geertz claims that self-declarations do not follow an orderly process in truth, for many if not most indigenous or ethnocultural people, identity is deeply rooted in the people they are descended from, the land they lived on, and the obligation they believe they have toward the land and those who come after them; for many of them, identity is orderly and tightly structured. It can be as simple or complicated as how one "looks" or whether stereotypic images are congruent with how others believe they should be.

The fundamental theme of this chapter focuses on presenting the historical, familial, cultural, and personal factors that illustrate the influence of personal and social identity on American Indian and Alaska Native youth and its implications for the legal system. It is based on all of the factors listed earlier and more. But it is also grounded in the ideation of the clinical psychologist Maria P. P. Root in her "Bill of Rights for Racially Mixed People" (Root, 1996). Although these rights are intended for people of mixed ancestral heritage and Indian or Native background, they do provide a basis for building a sense of social and personal identity regardless of one's ethnic affiliation, national origin, and ethnocultural background. Root's propositions emphasize the right of people to choose their identity, a right often denied to Indian and Native youth in their sovereign lands. These rights encourage people to take all aspects of their life and define themselves in terms of factors that most closely connect with their souls.

Root (1996) maintains that: "I HAVE THE RIGHT . . . Not to justify my existence in this world; Not to keep the races separate within me; Not to be responsible for people's discomfort with my physical ambiguity; Not to justify my ethnic legitimacy. I HAVE THE RIGHT. . . to identify myself differently than strangers expect me to identify; To identify myself differently from how my parents identify me; To identify myself differently from my brothers and sisters; and To identify myself differently in different situations. I HAVE THE RIGHT . . . To create a vocabulary to communicate about being multiracial; To change my identity over my lifetime—and more than once; To have loyalties and identification with more than one group of people; and To freely choose whom I befriend and love" (p. 7).

SOCIAL AND PERSONAL IDENTITY

The psychoanalyst Erik Erikson undoubtedly has contributed to the ongoing debate in psychology and psychiatry about social identity and its development and formation (Erikson, 1968). According to Erikson, identity is located in the self or core of the individual and one's communal culture; self-esteem and one's sense of affiliation and belongingness are deeply affected by the process. For Erikson, identity is inextricably linked to self-understanding and therefore can be posited "as the academic metaphor for self-in-context" (Fitzgerald, 1993, p. ix). Moreover, Erikson maintained that the transformations from childhood through adolescence presented role clarification challenges that often created identity confusion. The confusion often emerged from interactions with peers and the context and situations youth face on a daily basis. Without a context, identity formation and self-development couldn't occur. Identity is a part of one's sense of self, and it enables if not permits one to respond to "the question, whether self-asked or asked by others, as to who (or, perhaps, more exactly, what) they are" (Geertz, 2000, p. 225).

The late U.S. Senator and sociologist D. Patrick Moynihan (1993) points out that identity is "a process located in the core of the individual and yet, also, in the case of his communal culture" (p. 64). It's a powerful phenomenon that strongly influences personality, one's sense of belonging, one's sense of sameness, and one's quality of life. To further an understanding of identity, most social and psychological theorists must contend with the concept of self. And to approach an understanding of self-concept, one is obliged to provide plausible if not substantial explanations for the following domains: physical traits and characteristics, personal experiences and their memory, personal behaviors, "what belongs to me and what I belong to," "the person I believe myself to be," and "who and what others tell me I am" (Cirese, 1985). Explanations for these domains consume volumes with little agreement between differing theories.

As psychosocial constructs, ethnic identity and ethnic self-identification are not without controversy as there are varied views on their salience, relevance, stability, characteristics, and influences. Add to the discussion and debate that identity, whatever form it takes, is rarely static and immutable. To emphasize this point, Fitzgerald (1993) maintains that it is a mistake to think of identity as an unchanging entity as "it is the illusion of unity that is still quite real with most people" (p. 32). Social categories of people change.

Ethnic identification, declarations, and transformations are not solely private acts "but are usually if not predominantly public concerns, problematic situations, and issues of public contention as well as private debate" (Strauss, 1959, p. 26). Often ethnic and racial identity declarations, especially those of mixed-ethnic background, require external validation, and thus the judgments of others play a key role in the transaction (Root, 2000; Trimble, Helms, & Root, 2003). People typically construct their identities within the context of their biological background and the sociopolitical context in which they are socialized. Moreover, people often construct autobiographies to place themselves in the social order and seek out settings and situations for confirmation (Harré, 1989).

Hence, we find people constructing their identity and self-image to fit preferred sociocultural contexts and constructing the situations and contexts to fit the preferred image (Fitzgerald, 1993). Identity and all its derivatives are not static—people change, and their identities and sense of self change accordingly.

Social and psychological interest in ethnicity and identity has generated a prolific increase in journal articles and books on the subject. Few doubt that ethnicity is a benign topic; some refer to it as the "new ethnicity" because it is viewed as divisive, inegalitarian, and racist (Morgan, 1981). On occasion, the mention of ethnicity and identity, especially in academic circles, sparks discussion about segregation and that without it ethnicity would not survive. Sometimes the discussion can and often does turn to the possibility that Americans tend to overemphasize and exaggerate the existence and beneficence of ethnicity (Yinger, 1986). Phrases such as "imagined ethnicity" and "pseudo-ethnicity" are used interchangeably to refer to those who foist some ethnic factor to justify an action. In a related vein, when it comes to conducting research on ethnic factors, Gordon (1978) maintains that "students of ethnicity run the risk of finding ethnic practices where they are not, of ascribing an ethnic social and cultural order where they do not in fact influence the person" (p. 151). Consequently, critics will argue about some fanciful line that somehow separates ethnocultural influences from nonethnocultural ones. The argument begs the questions "When can behavior, personality, values, attitudes, and the like be attributed to ethnic and racial factors?" and "If an ethnic or racial attribution is not possible or discernible, then what sociocultural and psychological influence can account for the phenomenon?"

Greeley (1974) also asks an important and related question: "Why . . . is ethnic identity important and useful for some Americans?" (p. 298). One plausible answer is that ethnicity serves as a convenient form of differentiation and categorization—ethnic minorities can be differentiated from the dominant society and from one another (American Indians from African Americans, Puerto Ricans from Cuban Americans, Japanese Americans from Chinese Americans, etc.), neighborhoods and communities can be differentiated from one another

(Navajo Nation reservation, Chinatown, Japantown, Little Italy, etc.), and it can serve to differentiate among and between individuals who do not appear to subscribe to a generalized normative behavioral diet that often occurs in stereotypic imagery, ethnic labeling, and the pejorative nomenclature of intergroup relations.

Identity is a complex concept that is not easily quantifiable. It often consists of intangibles such as self-esteem, connection to others in one's family and community, one's religious and spiritual beliefs, and one's view of oneself in the world. Social identity can be thought of as the core on which the foundation of oneself and one's sense of place in the world rests, for example, an American Indian nurse, a teacher who is a mix of African American and Native blood, a cannery worker from Alaska who is an Alaska Native and Filipino, and a Navajo (Dine) councilman. How the world, family, work environment, and friends view and identify the youth can all be significant factors of the youth's view of his or her social identity. A healthy identity, particularly for Indian and Native youth, many if not most of whom are of mixed blood, will thus incorporate the factors and notions listed in the previously mentioned "Bill of Rights" by Root. The question is how can Indian and Native youth reach the level of comfort with their social identity even in the face of disapproval. This question will be addressed in the latter sections of this chapter.

Social development cannot be separated from chronological, psychosocial, emotional, and moral development. It is thought that all adolescents progress through typical stages of moral development, albeit at different rates (Erikson, 1968; Piaget, 1980). In precontact or pre–European American contact days among America's indigenous people, the moral and social progression of the person from childhood through adolescence into adulthood was generally clearly directed by the elders in the kinship and tribal group. After contact with European Americans, with the loss of life, land, language, traditions, and the traditional structure of families, the normal progression was frequently disrupted with devastating consequences. American Indian and Alaska Native youth, particularly those raised in federal-government-sponsored and -directed boarding schools or those

of mixed blood not accepted in either their traditional culture or the European American culture, often were given the social identity of shame, rejection, and subsequent mental health issues (Boyce & Boyce, 1983; Chrisjohn & Young, 1997; Weaver & Brave Heart, 1999). It is believed that it was the loss of family and a positive social and self-identity that led to so many of the issues now present among many Indian and Native youth.

In the 1980s, R. Dale Walker and Patricia Silk Walker focused on the notion of American Indian and Alaska Native cultural identification (LaDue, 1983; Walker & LaDue, 1986; Walker et al., 1996). They developed a scale that examined the participation of Indian and Native people in their languages, traditional spiritual activities, and how they identified themselves in terms of tribal and/or traditional practices. They also found that the greater the distance from one's "home base," the more psychosocial difficulties a person might experience, for example, alcohol use, depression, and loss of identity. Walker and LaDue found that the more closely to their traditional culture the person identified, the more protected from such problems they were and the more able they were to handle stress and pressure. One of the useful aspects of the Walkers' earlier work was the clarification of items that might contribute to social identity. They found that it was not simply what activities they participated in, but also their spiritual beliefs, and that these beliefs might differ from other members of their families (LaDue, 1983).

Using a variation of the cultural identification scale developed by Oetting and Beauvais (1991), Trimble (2000) tested a statistical model of the American Indian version of the scale and generated seven factor dimensions. The factor model was constructed from items to conform to three domains of a four-part ethnic measurement model, specifically natality, behavioral orientations, and subjective perceptions advocated by Trimble (1991, 1995). The 14-item scale was administered to 846 self-identified American Indian youth in eight communities located in both reservation and nonreservation settings in the central southwestern region of the United States. Results show that 71% "all" or "nearly all" identified with the American Indian group. The results also indicate that some of the

Indian self-identified youth identified to some degree with other groups (e.g., about 9% indicated that they "mostly" or "nearly all" identified as Anglo-white and that 7% did so for the Spanish-Mexican American group). However, 11% indicated that they identified "little" or "not at all" as American Indian, yet these resspondents self-identified nominally as American Indian. In addition, perceived ethnic self- identification of one's parents influences levels and degrees of identification among offspring. Results from Trimble's analysis show that the ethnic background of one or both parents varied but had an influence on the identity declarations of the respondents. One's parental ethnic background along with one's self-claimed affiliation with and attachment to an ethnic group can influence the degree to which one affiliates with his or her ethnic declaration to the extent that he or she may declare an affiliation with other ethnic groups, as Oetting and Beauvais's model and theory predict. These findings are supportive of Maria P. P. Root's "Bill of Rights," which supports that people make their own identity, even in the face of differing input from society and family (Root, 1996). They also suggest positive adaptation and integration of tradition and contemporary society in a way that allows comfort, flexibility, and positive change.

In her seminal work on bicultural identity, Root discusses the rights of multiracial people and their rights to identify themselves (Root, 2000). For many Indian and Native youth, this has been a struggle for decades if not generations, not just for those of mixed Native descent but also for those of full blood: the sense of identity has been something often defined by outside pressures. Root's "Bill of Rights" also addresses people's acceptance or rejection of stereotyping that can lead to internalized social roles. It is the internalization of positive self-image and an understanding of where one comes from—familial, cultural, historical, and societal background—that allows for the positive development of self-image. This chapter is intended to explore (a) the effect of historical and cultural factors on social identity, (b) the impact of laws and legislation on social identity, (c) the role of social stereotyping in establishing social identity, and (d) the synthesis of these elements into current social identity.

To understand the present, one must have at least a working knowledge of the past. One must also understand the complexities of applicable laws, no small feat when addressing the very existence of tribal and indigenous people today; there are reportedly more than 5,000 federal laws that apply directly to American Indians and Alaska Natives in the United States. For example, there are federally recognized tribes, terminated tribes, state-recognized tribes, and, most recently, tribes such as the Duwamish and Chinook in the Pacific Northwest who have been declared extinct by the misguided politics of yet one more U.S. government hostile to American Indians (Eskenazi, 2002; Shukovsky, 2002). Imagine the cultural, social, and personal trauma of being told you that you and your tribe or community are now extinct: a unilateral federal decision that provides you with little hope for reversal and consequently has made your extended family and your tribe extinct. It is in this—one of hundreds of examples—that a start of understanding can begin of the social implications of the laws of this land on American Indian and Alaska Native youth. But, for the moment, let us return to the time after contact, specifically the 1700s.

The word *law* has many connotations: the laws we are supposed to live by, the laws that govern us, when we run afoul of the law, the law of the land. Typically, when the word *law* is connected with American Indian and Alaska Native youth, it is assumed that the youth in question are in trouble with the law. Law and laws, however, have a deeper social, cultural, and historical meaning for Indian and Native youth than for mainstream American youth. Indian and Native youth are defined, determined, and validated through a series of laws dating back from before the existence of the United States. Part of this chapter will present an overview of some of the laws defining and governing Native people as well as the implications for social identity that such laws have had and still have on native youth.

LEGAL DEFINITIONS OF AMERICAN INDIANS AND ALASKA NATIVES

A Massachusetts Native asked the missionary John Eliot in the seventeenth century, "Why do you call us Indian?" The query undoubtedly was sincere and born out of bewilderment (Berkhofer, 1978). The term had no meaning for the Massachusetts Native, yet for Eliot the term was one that not only was inclusive of the Western Hemisphere's indigenous population but was rife with imagery and stereotypy fueled by a then short history of European American contact. "In short, character and culture were united into one summary," remarks historian Robert Berkhofer (1978, p. 25). He continues by pointing out that the practice persevered, where European Americans are "(1) generalizing from one tribe's society and culture to all Indians, (2) conceiving of Indians in terms of their deficiencies according to white ideals rather than in terms of their own various cultures, and (3) using moral evaluation as description of Indians" (pp. 25–26).

At most, scholars know the term *American Indian* is an imposed, invented ethnic category— an "ethnic gloss" (Trimble, 1991)—that was originally foisted on a now extinct Caribbean basin tribe. The label continues to be used to the extent that almost all indigenous native peoples of the Western Hemisphere are referred to as Indians. Along with the label, many historical stereotypical images persist and in some instances influence people's decision to identify as an American Indian or Alaska Native (Trimble, 1988). The persistence of the category, however, has led many contemporary Indians to express a common identity on the basis of having a common mythlike "charter." Speaking to this point, Trosper (1981) cogently argues that "American Indians have transformed themselves from a diverse people with little common identity into an ethnic group" and "have done so by mobilizing, with respect to a charter, the shared history of broken treaties" (p. 247). By forging a common ethnic category, America's indigenous population has created a social and political force that has far greater strength and influence than individual tribal governments—the emergence of the pan-Indian category has created a conventional label with which one can identify (see Hartzberg, 1971). Yet attached to the seemingly persuasive category is an array of definitions that vary appreciably.

Tribal-Specific Definitions

Tribal groups had names for themselves and language-specific names for other tribal groups. Tribes with such names as Lakota, Cheyenne, Navajo (Dine), and Hopi referred to themselves as "human beings" or "the people." Within tribes, bands such as "those with burned thighs" or "those who plant near the water" and moieties such as "Eagle" or "Raven" were given more specific names to refer to some unique characteristic. In addition, tribes such as the Lakota referred to other tribes according to their physical features and characteristics—the Cheyenne were referred to as Sihiyena (people with a shrill voice), the Winnebago as Hotanke (loud voice people), and the Navajo as Sna-hde-hde-ha (those with striped blankets). Such distinctions were typically ignored by American colonialists, historians, and novelists, leaving the world with the erroneous impression that American Indians were a distinctive but singular lot. It appears that it is more convenient to gloss a group than to deal with the discrete entities within it.

Within the past decade or so, efforts to replace the term *American Indian* with *Native American* were initiated by Indian activist groups, aided by conscientious liberal sympathizers and by universities and colleges in their affirmative action policies and considerations. The effort died rather suddenly when Indian political groups such as the National Congress of American Indians (NCAI) and the National Tribal Chairman's Association (NTCA) recognized that many descendants of early colonialists could indeed consider themselves natives, as their ancestors have been in America for about 400 years. Despite the stance taken by the NCAI and NTCA, many non–American Indians insist on using the term *Native American*. In the state of Alaska, indigenous peoples are referred to as Alaska Natives and nonindigenous folks are native Alaskans—the distinction is clear, and most abide by the encompassing categories.

Federal Government Attempts at a Definition

For logistic and political reasons, the federal government, through the Bureau of Indian Affairs (BIA), found it necessary to provide a *legal definition* of an American Indian, the only ethnic group in the United States that is afforded this distinction. The definition has undergone numerous revisions in the past 100 years or so, but currently the BIA defines an American Indian as a person whose American Indian blood quantum is at least one fourth and who is a registered or enrolled member of one of the 600 or more federally recognized tribes. The hard-and-fast criteria eliminated many people of American Indian background who affiliated in one form or another with one of some 60 federally nonrecognized tribes, ones that in many cases never signed formal treaties with the government or were part of scattered small groups in the northeast, northwest, and southwest parts of the United States (see Snipp, 1989).

Some recognized or "treaty" tribes do not agree with the BIA criteria and have developed their own specifications. Some have lowered the blood quantum criterion to one eighth and even one sixteenth and a few have eliminated it all together; however, the burden of proof for the claimant lies with his or her ability to prove ancestral lineage. One tribe in Oklahoma in the late 1960s opened its rolls to anyone who could prove ancestral ties; the specificity of blood quantum was not viewed as an important criterion in that occasion.

For some American Indians, the BIA's restricted definition is not representative of the range of Indian and Native lifestyles and levels of identification. The U.S. Bureau of the Census and the U.S. Department of Education (DOE) each developed their own criteria. The census bureau allows each citizen to declare his or her ethnic origin on the basis of the group with which he or she most identifies; in a word, the criterion is self-enumerative. The criteria developed by the DOE are probably more pragmatic and perhaps closer to reality. After conducting an extensive survey among Indian people throughout the United States in the early 1980s, DOE staff generated some 70 distinct definitions. After a careful review of the results, the DOE decided on a definition that closely resembles BIA criteria but provides more latitude for tribal-specific criteria, regardless of federal status (U.S. Department of Education, 1982).

Government definitions have been developed to determine who is eligible for services provided by treaty arrangements and congressionally mandated programs. The definitions do not include the extent to which an individual follows tribal custom and tradition or the degree to which he or she professes an ethnic identification. Francis Svennson (1973), a political scientist of American Indian background, recognized this when she stated that being Indian "is a state of being, a cast of mind, a relationship to the Universe. It is undefinable" (p. 9). Yet this definition may cause difficulties with those concerned with emerging "New Age" philosophies and the search for an indigenous identity.

The identity question is most salient and relevant for those "who report their race as Indian but include non-Indian ancestry in their ethnic background" and those "who cite a non-Indian race yet claim Indian ancestry for their ethnic background" (Snipp, 1989, p. 51). Because of their mixed-ethnic backgrounds, such individuals presumably have a choice of groups with which to identify. Many, indeed, may be enrolled or registered members of a tribe or village corporation, making the choice straightforward. Others are not. Yet many choose to identify more with their Indian background than some other part of their ethnic ancestry. Then there are those who do not have any American Indian or Alaska Native ancestors but nonetheless choose to identify themselves as American Indians. Perhaps the most illustrious of these individuals is Grey Owl, or Archie Belaney, who claimed that he was a descendant of the Jicarilla Apache band on his mother's side. Biographical evidence indicates that he was not, yet he was accepted by some Canadian Indians and non-Indians as an Indian, in part because of his wilderness lifestyle, knowledge of Ojibwa traditions, and deep, abiding concern about wildlife preservation (Dickson, 1973). Finally, there are countless Americans who could legitimately claim Indian ancestry but choose not to do so; their motives and reasons are as varied as droplets of rain on a mountain lake. Many choose to pass as European American because of the perceived opportunities available to them. Others prefer to identify with some other salient aspect of their ethnic heritage. Because they do not identify themselves as Indian, we may never know the reasons for their choice.

Americans are keenly interested in their genealogy, their ancestral heritage, and the meaning attributed to locating a long-forgotten ancestor. With this attention to ethnicity, a revival in celebrating and pronouncing traditions has occurred such that many Americans believe that they must declare an ethnic background or identity so that they may join in the celebration. Self-pride and a sense of belonging may be among the motives for declaring American Indian and Alaska Native roots. There is another side to the movement, represented by individuals who believe they can receive awards and attention for their ethnic declaration. Clifton (1989) calls it the "Indian windfall syndrome," in which individuals and "reconstituted Indian communities" stand to gain substantial economic benefits as witnessed by the alleged growing profits of reservation-based Indian casinos. It's likely that some Americans declare their Indian identity in hopes of receiving economic dividends generated by the gaming profits. To lend credence to their declaration, some appeal to the "Cherokee grandmother" effect (Thornton, 1990) and identify as descendants of the widely distributed Cherokee Nation. The 2000 U.S. Census data show that Cherokee is the most frequently mentioned tribe (U.S. Bureau of the Census, 2001).

Rewards and incentives have driven many Americans to self-identify as Indian to enhance their likelihood for securing jobs, receiving preference for admission to academic institutions and corresponding grants and scholarships, and placing them in a unique position to receive entitlements that otherwise would not be available. Out of this momentum has emerged the "academic Indian" (Clifton, 1989, p. 20), who claims his or her Indian ancestry to gain a foothold in entering and climbing up the rigorous steps of the academy's promotion and tenure ladder. Apart from the economic and self-serving motives, many Americans of Indian ancestry choose to identify because it creates a new identity for them that brings with it pride along with the desire to learn about tribal customs, traditions, and language. In addition, there are many who, regardless of the degree of their blood quantum, are obligated by family tradition to continue their identities as Indian. Invariably they are descended through matrilineal or patrilineal lines that are part of a highly complex clan or moiety system in which identity and participation serve to preserve and sustain a deeply shared belief system; to sever the tie often brings about banishment from the clan and hence the tribe.

PRE-EUROPEAN AMERICAN CONTACT AND IDENTITY INFLUENCES

One of the most common errors people make when thinking about or discussing American Indian and Alaska Native people is the assumption that all have the same historical and cultural backgrounds. In fact, there are more than 600 identifiable American Indian and Alaska Native groups, each with its own unique language, culture, laws, and social structures. The social rules and structures were passed from generation to generation, based on an unbreakable link with the earth and available resources. These rules and expectations were passed on through an oral tradition that included legends, stories, and personal as well as family histories.

Social identity for youth came through the social structures of each individual kinship group or village. Expectations of young women and men were clear and often based on their families' social standing within the kinship group or village. Families were extended in the true sense of the word, with other adults in the village acting as aunts, uncles, and grandparents. Discipline, corrections, and teachings were provided, in many situations, through any adult in the village (Bataille & Sands, 1987; Erdoes & Ortiz, 1998; Walker & LaDue, 1986). Such highly developed structure made clear what expectations and social roles were for the individual youth. At the same time, many if not most tribal groups also allowed for inclusion of group members with disabilities or other characteristics that, in today's society, might have set them apart from the group.

Contact

As displacement, removal, and new laws came into play, American Indian and Alaska Native people were no longer self-defined but became legal entities. Government officials with little sense of kinship groups or tribal identities often wrote treaties that were signed by people who were not representative of Indian and Native groups. The ramifications of these signings led to the placement of portions of tribal and kinship groups onto separate reservations, or the loss of land completely. In other situations, some members of the tribe were recognized; others were not. In some families, even today, one sibling will be enrolled and one will not be, simply because of a change in tribal government or who sits on the enrollment committee.

The signings of yesterday have often led to intratribal conflict in the modern era. For example, blood quantum requirements vary from group to group and enrollment requirements may change over time, leaving some family members enrolled and others not. For example, because of intermarriage, one can be a mixture of several different tribal backgrounds—one sixteenth from two different tribes, one eight from another tribe, a thirty-second degree from yet another tribe, and a sixty-fourth blood quantum degree from an unrelated tribe—and thus not have sufficient blood quantum to be enrolled or registered with any one of them because of the tribal specific standards for enrollment set by each of the tribes represented in one's genealogy. This circumstance and others has led to family conflict, a sense of confusion among siblings, and animosity among individual tribal members. For young people, "choosing" an identity can be stressful and can lead to anxiety and a lack of a clear sense of self in the context of their preferred Indian identity. Maria P. P. Root has written eloquently on the rights of people to choose their own identities, even if such an identity clashes with those of other family members. It is through validation of self-identity, such as through Root's "Bill of Rights," that can help lead from a sense of despair to pride and confidence in the life of a young person.

After the time of contact and with the implementation of the doctrine of Manifest Destiny, the federal government began to develop reservations and require "proof" of tribal membership. In addition, in 1887, the Dawes or allotment act was passed, moving much of traditional lands out of tribal hands and into those of speculators and settlers. The loss of a land base, along with forced placement of children into government and religious boarding schools and with laws passed forbidding the speaking of traditional language and practicing traditional religions, led to depression, loss of identity, and many, if not most, of the social problems seen today in many Indian and Native youth.

The Twentieth Century and Legal Influences

Legislation that forbade the speaking of American Indian and Alaska Native languages and the practice of religious beliefs were, of course, in violation of the First Amendment rights guaranteed by the U.S. Constitution. However, Indian and Native people were not allowed voting rights in the United States until 1924, and in 1948 in New Mexico and Arizona, Indians were not allowed any equal protection under the law.

Essentially, what legislation of this type did, in addition to relegating American Indian and Alaska Native people to aliens in their own lands, was to give the clear psychological message of not existing or being removed as obstacles or nuisances in the way of progress. Such messages led to cultural, community, familial, and individual trauma, leaving many Native people without traditions to call on or a sense of who they were, had been, or could be. Many Indian and Native communities continue to experience various degrees of individual and community trauma as a consequence of European contact, a "wound to the soul of Native American people that is felt in agonizing proportions to this day" (Duran & Duran, 1995, p. 27). Moreover, Brave Heart and DeBruyn (1998), LaDue (1994), and Duran and Duran (1995) all maintain that postcolonial "historical and intergenerational trauma" has left a long trail of unresolved grief and a "soul wound" in Indian and Native communities that contributes to high levels of social and individual problems such as alcoholism, suicide, homicide, domestic violence, child abuse, and negative career ideation. The cumulative trauma has been fueled by centuries of incurable diseases, massacres, forced relocation, unemployment, economic despair, poverty, forced removal of children to boarding schools, abuse, racism, loss of traditional lands, unscrupulous land mongering, betrayal, broken treaties—the list goes on. Metcalf (1976), for example, emphasizes the changes in identity among Navajo (Dine) schoolgirls who were relocated off the reservation and the consequences of such relocation.

Not allowing American Indian and Alaska Native parents to raise their own children, being taken far away from one's family, being in the often abusive environment of the boarding school—all of these contributed to poor self-image, depression, grief, and, ultimately, the loss of a sense of family and self in many people so affected. The results of the legislation and its implementation have been documented in countless studies. Similar legislation, which indicated that Indian and Native parents were not "able to raise their children," contributed to mass adoptions off the reservations and out of Native communities. Again, the message to families: and individual children is that they are not "qualified" to even have the basic right of being a family. Over the past 25 years, considerable research has documented the devastating effects of children being raised away from their families: for example, increased depression, alcoholism, poor parenting skills, and increased dropout and unemployment rates (Beals et al., 1997; Beauvais & Trimble, 1997; Howard, Walker, Walker, Cottler, & Compton, 1999; Howard, Walker, Walker, & Suchinsky, 1997; Manson, Ackerson, Dick, Baron, & Fleming, 1990; Manson, Beals, Dick, & Duclos, 1989; Manson, Walker, & Kivlahan, 1987; Trimble & Bagwell, 1995; Walker & LaDue, 1986; Walker et al., 1996).

Among youth, Oetting and Beauvais (1990), Beauvais (1996), and Welty (2002) document that over 60% of all American Indian and Alaska Native youth are at risk for substance use and abuse, tied directly to the cultural and emotional devastation of past legislation, laws, and attitudes implemented by the United States and individual state actions against Native peoples (see Mail, Heurtin-Roberts, Martin, & Howard, 2002).

The origins of many present laws were the treaties drawn up between certain American Indian and Alaksa Native entities and the colonial and then newly formed U.S. government. They were originally intended to establish territories and trading agreements (DeLoria, 1995). As the westward push for expansion grew, the treaties changed to establish specific tribal entities as well as reservations. Other laws came into existence, including the outlawing of Indian and Native religious practices, disenfranchisement, the establishment of the boarding schools, and, ultimately, up through 2002, termination of tribal groups (Gidley, 1979). Although the treaties and many laws were based on a government-to-government basis, in actuality, the sole purpose of many of the enacted laws was to ensure the eventual cultural and physical destruction of America's indigenous people.

In the 1900s, several laws were changed that began to allow a resurgence of American Indian and Alaksa Native independence and changes in social structure and, ultimately, social identity. In 1924, as noted earlier, Indian and Native people, with the exception of those in two states, were finally given the right to vote. A disenfranchised people are essentially a powerless people, having no input in laws and legislation that may well determine the direction of their lives. With the right to vote, Indian and Native people, although small in number in most areas of the country, with the exception of the Southwest, did not necessarily have a significant impact on all voting outcomes, but it provided some voice in the political process.

Greater changes came in 1934 with the Howard-Wheeler Act, or the Indian Reorganization Act. This legislation established the rights of American Indian and Alaska Native tribes to establish their own governments, the precursors to today's tribal councils. Theoretically, these tribal councils allowed for tribes to establish their own laws, determine who could belong to the tribe, and determine what types of laws could be enacted on the reservation. In some cases, tribes were allowed to have jurisdiction over custody issues and to ensure that the children of the tribe were given the chance to remain within the confines of the tribal group.

There was a shift from the Indian Reorganization movement in the 1930s to the termination and relocation practices of the 1950s to 1960s. In this time period, American

Indian and Alaska Native children were still being sent to boarding schools or adopted off the reservations, being punished for speaking their own languages, and having their home-lands and reservations "terminated" by govern-ment order and the land sold off to non-Native people. This was a continuation of the loss of land from warfare and the disastrous policy of the Dawes Act of 1887 (see Trimble, 1987).

Along with termination came the massive push to move American Indian and Alaska Native people into urban areas, away from their homes, lands, and families. The push was yet another insidious attempt to absolve the govern-ment of responsibility for treaty obligations and to once again push assimilation. In 1956, the BIA under directives from the Eisenhower administration (known as the Employment Relocation Program and later the Employ-ment Assistance Program), essentially gave the promise of permanent jobs in urban areas for reservation Indians. The BIA provided appli-cants with "one-way bus tickets," the promise of temporary housing, job orientation training, and a job suited to their skills. To lure people away from their reservation homes, the BIA often couched their recruitment messages in the lan-guage of the tribes. For example, in the Dakotas, urban areas such as Chicago, Denver, and Los Angeles were referred to as "waste"—"waste Chicago," "waste Denver" (literally "beautiful or good Chicago" in Lakota); the term was used to heighten the attractiveness of a city. The ploy was a ruse, as many "relocatees" quickly dis-covered that city life was filled with prejudice, discrimination, crime, and high unemployment—in a word, the city was not "waste." During the height of the relocation program, approximately one in four families eventually returned to their reservation homes or villages. The fact that promised jobs often were slow in materializing coupled with the pace and pressure of urban life contributed heavily to the "reverse relocation" phenomenon.

With these moves, many families were fur-ther disrupted, which led to an increase in alco-holism, depression, identity confusion, and a host of other psychosocial ills that American Indian and Alaska Native people are still trying to overcome (Johnson, Nagel, & Champagne, 1997; Manson, 1983). These effects have included depression, loss of culture, and attempts to "integrate" into urban lives with resulting higher rates of psychosocial problems. This has been the typical pattern of a long march from pre-European American contact tribal life and expectations to contemporary changes and resurgence of pride and hope.

The termination and relocation era partially ended in 1975 with the passing of the Indian Self Determination Act. This act affirmed the right of Native people to direct the courses of their lives and the rights of tribal councils to set laws and standards for their own people. It led to the formation of many tribal courts, which, in conjunction with the 1978 Indian Child Welfare Act (ICWA), asserted that tribal people had the right to raise their own children and ensure that guidelines were followed before removing a Native child from his or her family, community, and tribal group (Wilkinson, 1987). In 1976, the Indian Health Care Improvement Act was passed, which led to tribal-specific health plans and the passing of responsibility for such programs to the tribe.

Just as important as the previously men-tioned Indian legislation was the 1978 passing of the Indian Religious Freedom Act that, more than 200 years after the adoption of the U.S. Constitution, finally allowed Native people to practice, without fear of legal and other reprisals, their own traditional beliefs. Since that time, there has been a resurgence and return to traditional activities. Participation by youth in pow-wows, sweat lodges, and other subsistence activities has become more acceptable. All of this has led to Native youth having a greater basis on which to build a positive self-identity.

Some readers may have a difficult time understanding how such laws could lead to low self-esteem and a confused identity. In actual-ity, in any environment where people are not allowed to participate in the most basic of activities—raising children, practicing reli-gions, and speaking their own language—depression, anxiety, and increased psychosocial problems occur. A comparable set of laws that were clearly demonstrated to have horrible emo-tional and psychological implications for those affected were the "Jim Crow" laws of the South, overturned by the civil rights legislation of the 1960s. What is different for Native people, however, is that many of the laws that legally define or disallow the existence of a tribal group and individual members remain.

Shortly before the end of President Clinton's second term, federal tribal recognition was awarded to the Duwamish people of the Seattle area, Chief Seattle's own people. Within months of being named Secretary of the Interior for the United States, Gale Norton, acting for President George W. Bush, saw fit to terminate and wipe out the existence of the Duwamish people. The implications for a proud people, such as the Duwamish, to be wiped out of existence by the mean-spiritedness and shortsightedness of one person are devastating. How can youth develop any sense of stability and positive identity if the world is so unstable as to ignore both history and contemporary facts?

SOCIAL IMAGES, STEREOTYPES, AND IDENTITY INFLUENCES

The previously described situation did not happen in the last century or before. The Duwamish are the first tribe to be terminated in the 21st century. Can others be far behind? Are today's American Indian and Alaska Native youth facing a return to termination and relocation and all of the attendant psychosocial problems? The contempt and denigration of Native people has been present in many arenas ranging from termination to school mascots and the name of the football team in the nation's capital, the Washington Redskins, being a caricature of Native people (see Trimble, 1988). No other group would be demeaned with such a name, for example, the Seattle "Whiteskins" or the Atlanta "Blackskins." In high schools and colleges across the United States, mascots have been called the Chiefs, the Fighting Sioux, the Fighting Illini, and the Florida Seminoles. Here we have non-Indian and non-Native students and possibly Indian and Native students from other tribes grouped under an honorable and traditional name with it being discounted to a caricature to be run across a football field (Nichols, 2003). What is the message of such actions to Indian and Native youth? That they are subhuman, no more important than a character or cartoon?

The question is, in the face of social and legal racism, how can American Indian and Alaska Native youth move from high risk to high self-esteem and connection? The next section will outline some methods that are being used and legislative changes that have aided in youth achieving positive self-esteem.

Social Identity in the 21st Century

Given the factors listed earlier, what is the status of social identity for today's American Indian and Alaksa Native youth? There is no simple answer to that question. Differences exist between tribal groups, urban versus rural youth, and geographic factors. The remainder of this chapter will focus on the effects of family, community, and society, along with laws, on the social identity of Indian and Native youth. One of the more positive changes that have occurred in the past few years is the refusal of Indian and Native students to allow school mascots to be named after Native peoples. In the Seattle, Washington, area, in spite of a group of alumni objecting to such a change, the school board upheld the notion that there will be no further use of Indian characters as mascots.

Owners of professional sports teams, such as the Cleveland Indians and the Atlanta Braves, along with the Washington Redskins, have come under fire for their blatantly racist use of such nicknames. Although none of these entities have chosen to act in a socially responsible way and change their names, the objection to such terms is coming from American Indian and Alaska Native youth as well as older Indian and Native people (Jensen, 2003; Nichols, 2003). Taking a stand at one's school to not participate in a demeaning practice is a huge step forward for young people to boost their social identity, even in the face of people who "do not get it!" as one Indian youth so eloquently stated.

Other changes that are occurring in American Indian and Alaska Native communities that are leading to more positive self-esteem for Indian youth are the increasing numbers seeking to learn their native languages. Immersion schools are opening in Indian and Native communities. Young American Indian authors, such as Sherman Alexie, are writing about their experiences and making films that show Indian and Native youth in both the struggle for identity and the triumph over problems (see http://fallsapart.com/).

Although there are many who criticize the development of gambling casinos in numerous American Indian and Alaska Native communities, such endeavors have allowed, in many cases, more chances for economic development and employment. The casinos have allowed more Indian communities to educate their citizens and make plans for the future. They have also allowed for greater financial freedom and greater tribal control over lands and resources. In some communities, the influx of casino monies has allowed for the development of tribal courts and law enforcement. This has, in turn, provided for positive implementation of the ICWA by tribes.

Not all, however, are in favor of tribal casinos. In a recent series of articles by Bartlett and Steele (2002) in *Time* magazine, a primary focus was, once again, on the negative stereotypes of American Indian and Alaska Native people as poverty-stricken, too foolish to take care of their own business, having their resources stolen by outsiders, and being at the mercy of corrupt tribal officials. It is such images as this, across the ages, that have made it highly difficult for Indian youth to find positive media and public images or things about their lives and communities to feel positive about.

Is it possible for an American Indian or Alaska Native youth to be born, enrolled in a tribe with full privileges as such, be enrolled in an immersion school, be multilingual, be able to participate in traditional activities without the fear of reprisal or arrest, and be educated with resources provided by the tribe? Can Native youth attend college and sit on their tribal councils, and become an integral part of the future of their people? In reality, this scenario is true for only a small portion of Native youth.

According to the 2000 census, the number of people identifying themselves as American Indian, Alaska Native, or of mixed race has dramatically increased. Based on the 2000 Census, the U.S. Bureau of the Census (2001) declared that 2,475,956 citizens are American Indians and Alaska Natives—a 26.4% difference from the 1990 Census, when the figure was 1,959,234.

The 2000 count represents less than one tenth of 1% of the total U.S. population of 281 million (U.S. Bureau of the Census, 2001). In the 2000 U.S. Census, individuals had the option of marking more than one "race" category and so were able to declare identification with more than one group. Whereas less than 3% of the total U.S. population chose to do so, more than 4,119,000 individuals who chose to mark multiple categories marked "American Indian and Alaska Native" along with one or more others. The "race alone or in combination" count is much higher than the "race alone" count of 2,475,956. The discrepancy raises the question about which count is more accurate or representative of the "true" Indian population. It is quite possible that many who chose the "race in combination" category may be enrolled members of federally recognized tribes. In addition, many who chose that category may not be enrolled in any tribe; thus it is safe to conclude that the "true" count is somewhere between the two counts.

The current American Indian population is relatively young, with a median age of 28; close to one third (840,312) of the total Indian population is under the age of 18. More than 50% of Indians and Natives reside in urban areas, and that may mean they have less access to traditional activities and family connections. With an influx of Native people into urban areas, there may be less chance to explore one's identity in the context of one's family, yet more opportunity to understand the significance of pan–American Indian movements and the need for unity. What are the laws, now, that promote or inhibit Native youth from developing self-identity? What are the consequences of yet one more aggressive, invasive action on a nonwhite people by the American government, particularly for those young Native people who are fighting for the U.S. government in the military?

Although life is not, by any stretch of the imagination, perfect for Native youth, there have been positive changes. The implementation of the ICWA, particularly when monitored and guided by tribal governments, is a chance for Native people to claim their children from birth, to give a beginning where the beginning is known, and there is at least a chance for learning of one's ancestors and relations. With the recognition of several tribes, there is a chance for the restoration of positive identity, hope, and possible healthy connections.

As has historically been true, there continues to be a wide diversity of culture, language, and experience among American Indian and Alaska Native youth in the United States. More now than in the past 500 or so years, Native youth have choices and chances to fulfill their potential and bring honor and respect to their ancestors, families, communities, and themselves. Educational programs, casino monies, positive role models, and rescinding of racist laws all have led to Native youth facing their futures with more hope.

Yet, even as this is true, it is also true that many of the challenges of the past have come to haunt us in the present. Laws that led to internalized self-loathing may be changed, but the emotional legacy of such laws may take generations to remove. The curse of alcohol, now seen in children struggling to overcome the damage from being prenatally exposed to alcohol as well as living in communities drenched in liquor, continues to fray the fabric of Native life, urban and rural. A racist government that condemns entire tribes to extinction promotes a pattern of disenfranchisement of Native people begun 500 years ago.

American Indian and Alaska Native youth, wherever they are, should be encouraged to practice the principles and choices Root writes about so eloquently (Root, 1996). Legislators and politicians should be educated to recognize and take responsibility for the social impact of their decisions, often bought and paid for rather than based in the spirit of empowering people. Native youth should be supported at all levels in sobriety, healthy living, and the knowledge that their history is not full of shame and stereotypes. It was young Indian and Native people that fought to get the use of Indian mascots out of their schools. It was a court that affirmed this choice. Which came first, the feeling of power to change the law or a changed law that led to a greater sense of power?

It is difficult to say. What matters is that, with the changing of laws that gave Native people the right to vote, the right to organize their tribal governments, the right to practice their spirituality, the right to raise their own children, and the right to exist came as beacons of hope for Native youth to choose who, how, and what it means to be Native. Although it may be convenient to say that "you cannot legislate morality," in fact, laws can shape attitudes and behavior. Good laws can and do lead to healthier people. A cycle into the positive began with some of the legal changes listed earlier. Educate American Indian and Alaska Native youth, give them the right to choose and value their choices, and they will be able to live in both worlds.

SUMMARY AND CONCLUSIONS

We come to the end of our inquiry into the theme of this chapter—the influence and effect of the legal system on the social identity of American Indian and Alaska Native youth. The inquiry began with Jack D. Forbes's assertion that the "rights of individuals and of groups includes the right to self-identification and self-definition." Although his keen observation is not the central theme of this chapter, it sets a tone that personal and social identity is complicated and filled with many problems when viewed within the context of the history of America's indigenous people. The tone is consistent with Maria P. P. Root's contention that people can choose their identity but that it may be a right that is denied to Indian and Native youth in their sovereign lands.

To extend the inquiry, this section is devoted to a summary of the thoughts and theoretical perspectives on social and personal identity. Although there are several compelling definitions of the construct, it is not without controversy. Most scholars agree that the construct is a social construction. Some view it as an invention, a synonym for identity—symbolic, political, fictional, imagined, and pseudo or contrived. Ethnicity and race are linked to identity; however, the linkage is not straightforward, as there are varying opinions on what is more salient and in need of emphasis to understand identity formation and development. Several scholars insist that the concept of the self must be factored into the discussions. Many have been influenced by the seminal work on social identity initiated by psychoanalyst Erik Erikson, who viewed the self as the core of the identity process.

With the summary background in hand, the inquiry turns to a review of several historical influences that helped shape the lives of American Indian and Alaska Native people. The inquiry starts off with a review of nominal approaches to self-identification such as those used recently by the U.S. Bureau of the Census and the U.S. DOE—here again, use of nominal approaches to capturing Indian and Native identity is not without controversy.

Several important conclusions emerge from the section: most notable is the undeniable fact that various forms of federal laws and legislation have disrupted and continue to disrupt the lives of American Indians and Alaska Natives in untoward and insidious ways to the extent that a form of "historical trauma" continues to have deleterious effects on lives and communities. Some of the laws led to the termination of once federally recognized tribes that subsequently eliminated tribal identities along with their rights and privileges. Along with this "formal" loss of tribal identities comes grief and struggles to remain connected to one's ancestors, lands, language, and traditions. It is the continuing disenfranchisement of Native people that poses the greatest risk for the long-term problems inflicted on Native people since the occupation of Native lands began more than 500 years ago.

Also, what emerges from the inquiry is uncertainty and ambiguity—uncertainty about the meanings of Indian identity; uncertainty about their usefulness in describing the census of the U.S. population; uncertainty about a person's appraisal of the social world and its significance as an expression of self-identity; uncertainty about one's marginal status and its accompanying psychosocial dynamics, components, and processes; and an uncertainty as to why identity can be subjected to law and legislation when it is a personal right and privilege. Apart from accounting for demographic distributions, there are uncertainties about the causal relationship between identity and outcomes, such as its influence on drug and alcohol use, depression, adolescent delinquency, grieving, eating disorders, and suicide, among many others.

The inconsistencies, incongruities, and confusion in our inquiry should not deter or dissuade the scholar and scientist from conducting further inquiry into this daunting topic. Quite the contrary, the field is not whimsical, patchy, or unsteady—it is in desperate need of structure and order. To accomplish orderliness and structure, scholars are challenged and encouraged to engage further and deeper into the topic to sort out and smooth over the discrepancies and incongruities. A good starting point for a probing inquiry is the emergence of a multiracial or multiethnic classification category. In the cultural and ethnic comparative research realm, researchers typically rely on mono-ethnic or mono-racial categories to test hypotheses about the contribution of one's cultural life ways and thought ways to some outcome variable or variable domain. What deep or surface cultural attributes will a multiethnic category permit? If a researcher is interested in discovering deep cultural or ethnic contributions to a cognitive learning style, for example, how will the contributions be disentangled from one's multiethnic worldview or orientation?

In summation, although many events in Native history have been devastating and debilitating, there have also been challenges overcome, victories won, and a resurgence of hope. In spite of the present administration's blatant anti-Native policies and intent to gain control over Indian energy and timber resources, Native people, particularly Native youth, are speaking up, claiming their heritage, and fighting back against past abuses. It is in these small and not-so-small battles that the possibility of positive self-identity and empowerment rests. In spite of past and present challenges, on all fronts, Native people have survived and looked to the future. With the inherent strengths that Native people have demonstrated and the light that the next seven generations shine on today, hope exists even in this dark hour. As past generations looked to the white buffalo calf, so can today's Native youth take heart from the words of Maria P. P. Root: "I have the right . . ."

NOTE

1. Throughout this chapter, we use different terms to refer to the indigenous peoples of North America;

these terms include *American Indians, Alaska Natives, First Nations peoples, Native American Indians, Native Americans, Indians,* and *Natives.* We use the briefest of these terms frequently for ease of reading and to make the best use of our limited space. Although all these terms have historical and socio-political value, in fact the indigenous peoples of the Americas generally prefer to be referred to by the names of their tribes or village affiliations.

REFERENCES

Bartlett, D., & Steele, J. (2002, December 16). Wheel of misfortune. *Time, 44.*

Bataille, G. M., & Sands, K. M. (1987). *American Indian women: Telling their lives.* Lincoln: University of Nebraska.

Beals, J., Piasecki, J., Nelson, S., Jones, M., Keane, E., Dauphinais, P., Red Shirt, R., Sack, W., & Manson, S. M. (1997). Psychiatric disorder in a sample of American Indian adolescents. *Journal of the American Academy of Child and Adolescent Psychiatry, 36*(9), 1252–1259.

Beauvais, F. (1996). Trends in drug use among American Indian students and dropouts, 1975–1994. *American Journal of Public Health, 86,* 1594–1598.

Beauvais, F., & Trimble, J. E. (Eds.). (1997). *Sociocultural perspectives on volatile solvent use.* New York: Harrington Park.

Berkhofer, R. (1978). *The white man's Indian: Images of the American Indian from Columbus to present.* New York: Random House.

Boyce, W. T., & Boyce J. C. (1983). Acculturation and changes in health among Navajo school students. *Social Sciences and Medicine, 17,* 219–226.

Brave Heart, M. Y. H., & DeBruyn, L. (1998). The American Indian holocaust: Healing unresolved grief. *American Indian and Alaska Native Mental Health Research, 8*(2), 56–78.

Chrisjohn, R., & Young, S. (1997). *The circle game: Shadows and substance in the Indian residential school experience in Canada.* Penticton, BC: Theytus.

Cirese, S. (1985). *Quest: A search for self.* New York: Holt, Rinehart, & Winston.

Clifton, J. (Ed.). (1989). *Being and becoming Indian: Biographical studies of North American frontiers.* Chicago: Dorsey.

DeLoria, V. (1995). *Red earth, White lies.* New York: Scribner.

Dickson, L. (1973). *Wilderness man: The strange story of Grey Owl.* New York: Atheneum.

Duran, E., & Duran, B. (1995). *Native American postcolonial psychology.* Albany: State University of New York.

Erdoes, R., & Ortiz, A. (Eds.). (1998). *American Indian trickster tales.* New York: Viking Penguin.

Erikson, E. (1968). *Identity, youth, and crisis.* New York: Norton.

Eskenazi, S. (2002, January 11). Reversal of tribe's status blasted: Man behind Duwamish recognition says ruling was "final." *Seattle Times,* p. B1.

Fitzgerald, T. K. (1993). *Metaphors of identity: A culture-communication dialogue.* Albany: State University of New York Press.

Forbes, J. D. (1990). The manipulation of race, caste, and identity: Classifying Afroamericans, Native Americans and red-black people. *Journal of Ethnic Studies, 17*(4), 1–51.

Geertz, C. (2000). *Available light: Anthropological reflections on philosophical topics.* Princeton, NJ: Princeton University Press.

Gidley, M. (1979). *With one sky above us: Life on an Indian reservation at the turn of the century.* Seattle: University of Washington Press.

Gordon, M. M. (1978). *Human nature, class, and ethnicity.* Oxford: Oxford University Press.

Greeley, A. M. (1974). *Ethnicity in the United States.* New York: John Wiley & Sons.

Harré, R. (1989). Language games and the texts of identity. In J. Shotter & J. J. Gergen (Eds.), *Texts of identity* (pp. 20–35). Newbury Park, CA: Sage Publications.

Hartzberg, H. (1971). *The search for an American Indian identity: Modern pan-Indian movements.* Syracuse, NY: Syracuse University Press.

Howard, M. O., Walker, R. D., Walker, P. S., Cottler, L. B., & Compton, W. M. (1999). Inhalant use among urban American Indian youth. *Addiction, 94*(1), 83–95.

Howard, M. O., Walker, R. D., Walker, P. S., & Suchinsky, R. T. (1997). Alcohol and drug education in schools of nursing. *Journal of Alcohol and Drug Education, 42*(3), 54–80.

Jensen, J. J. (2003, March 11). Judge says Seattle schools can expel "Indians" nickname. *Seattle Times,* p. B1.

Johnson, T., Nagel, J., & Champagne, D. (1997). *American Indian activism: Alcatraz to longest walk*. Champaign: University of Illinois Press.

LaDue, R. A. (1983). *Standardization of the MMPI for the Colville Indian reservation*. Unpublished doctoral dissertation, Washington State University.

LaDue, R. (1994). Coyote returns: Twenty sweats does not an Indian expert make. *Women and Therapy, 5*(1), 93–111.

Mail, P. D., Heurtin-Roberts, S., Martin, S. E., & Howard, J. (Eds.). (2002). *Alcohol use among American Indians and Alaska Natives: Multiple perspectives on a complex problem* (pp. 49–70). National Institute on Alcohol Abuse and Alcoholism Research Monograph No. 37.

Manson, S. M. (Ed.). (1983). *Issues and topics in American Indian mental health prevention*. Portland: Oregon Health Sciences University Press.

Manson, S. M., Ackerson, L. M., Dick, R. W., Baron, A. E., & Fleming, C. M. (1990). Depressive symptoms among American Indian adolescents: Psychometric characteristics of the Center for Epidemiologic Studies Depression Scales (CES-D). *Psychological Assessment, 2*(3), 231–237.

Manson, S. M., Beals, J., Dick, R. W., & Duclos, C. W. (1989). Risk factors for suicide among Indian adolescents at a boarding school. *Public Health Reports, 104*(6), 609–614.

Manson, S. M., Walker, R. D., & Kivlahan, D. R. (1987). Psychiatric assessment and treatment of American Indians and Alaska Natives. *Hospital & Community Psychiatry, 38*(2), 165–173.

Metcalf, A. (1976). From schoolgirl to mother: The effects of education on Navajo women. *Social Problems, 23*, 534–544.

Morgan, H. W. (1981). *Drugs in America*. Syracuse, NY: Syracuse University Press.

Moynihan, D. P. (1993). *Pandaemonium: Ethnicity in international politics*. New York: Oxford University Press.

Nichols, L. (2003, March 16). Making sport of Indians. *Seattle Times*, p. C4.

Oetting, E. R., & Beauvais, F. (1990). Adolescent drug use: Findings of national and local surveys. *Journal of Consulting and Clinical Psychology, 58*(4), 385–394.

Oetting, E. R., & Beauvais, F. (1991). Orthogonal cultural identification theory: The cultural identification of minority adolescents. *International Journal of Addictions, 25*(5A & 6A), 655–685.

Piaget, J. (1980). Intellectual evolution from adolescence to adulthood. In P. H. Mussen (Ed.), *Carmichael's manual on child psychology*. (Vol. 1, 3rd ed.). New York: Basic Books.

Root, M. P. P. (1996). *The multiracial experience: Racial borders as the new frontier*. Thousand Oaks, CA: Sage Publications.

Root, M. P. (2000). Rethinking racial identity development. In P. Spickard & W. J. Burroughs (Eds.), *Narrative and multiplicity in constructing ethnic identity* (pp. 205–220). Philadelphia: Temple University Press.

Shukovsky, P. (2002, July 9). Duwamish will take their case for recognition to Congress; Tribe decides to sidestep White House in its effort to gain recognition; Chinook also rejected. *Seattle Post-Intelligencer*, p. B2.

Snipp, C. M. (1989). *American Indians: The first of this land*. New York: Russell Sage Foundation.

Strauss, A. L. (1959). *Mirrors and masks: The search for identity*. Glencoe, IL: Free Press.

Svensson, F. (1973). *The ethnics in American politics: American Indians*. Minneapolis, MN: Burgess.

Thornton, R. (1990). *The Cherokees: A population history*. Lincoln: University of Nebraska Press.

Trimble, J. E. (1987). American Indians and interethnic conflict: A theoretical and historical overview. In J. Boucher, D. Landis, & K. Arnold (Eds.), *Ethnic conflict: International perspectives* (pp. 208–229). Newbury Park, CA: Sage Publications.

Trimble, J. E. (1988). Stereotypical images, American Indians, and prejudice. In P. Katz & D. Taylor (Eds.), *Eliminating racism: Profiles in controversy* (pp. 181–202). New York: Plenum Press.

Trimble, J. E. (1991). Ethnic specification, validation prospects, and the future of drug use research. *International Journal of the Addictions, 25*(2A), 149–170.

Trimble, J. E. (1995). Toward an understanding of ethnicity and ethnic identity, and their relationship with drug use research. In G. Botvin, S. Schinke, & M. Orlandi (Eds.), *Drug abuse prevention with multiethnic youth* (pp. 3–27). Thousand Oaks, CA: Sage Publications.

Trimble, J. E. (2000). Social psychological perspectives on changing self-identification among American Indians and Alaska natives. In R. H. Dana (Ed.), *Handbook of cross-cultural and multicultural personality assessment* (pp. 197–222). Mahwah, NJ: Lawrence Erlbaum Associates.

Trimble, J., & Bagwell, W. (Eds.). (1995). *North American Indians and Alaska Natives: Abstracts of psychological and behavioral literature, 1967–1995* (No. 15), *Bibliographies in Psychology*. Washington, DC: American Psychological Association.

Trimble, J., Helms, J., & Root, M. (2003). Social and psychological perspectives on ethnic and racial identity. In G. Bernal, J. Trimble, K. Burlew, & F. Leong (Eds.), *Handbook of racial and ethnic minority psychology* (pp. 239–275). Thousand Oaks, CA: Sage Publications.

Trosper, R. L. (1981). American Indian nationalism and frontier expansion. In C. Keyes (Ed.), *Ethnic change* (pp. 247–270). Seattle: University of Washington Press.

U.S. Bureau of the Census. (2001). *Census of the population: General population characteristics, American Indians and Alaska Natives areas, 2000.* Washington, DC: Government Printing Office.

U.S. Department of Education. (1982). *A study of alternative definitions and measures relating to eligibility and service under Part A of the Indian Education Act.* Unpublished report, United States Department of Education, Washington, DC.

Walker, R. D., Howard, M. O., Walker, P. S., Lambert, M. D., Maloy, F., & Suchinsky, R. T. (1996). Essential and reactive alcoholism: A review. *Journal of Clinical Psychology, 52*(1), 80–95.

Walker, R. D., & LaDue, R. A. (1986). An integrative approach to American Indian mental health. In C. B. Wilkinson (Ed.), *Ethnic Psychiatry* (pp. 143–193). New York: Plenum Press.

Walker, R. D., Lambert, M. D., Walker, P. S., Kivlahan, D. R., Donovan, D. M., & Howard, M. O. (1996). Alcohol abuse in urban Indian adolescents and women: A longitudinal study for assessment and risk evaluation. *American Indian & Alaska Native Mental Health Research, 7,* 1–47.

Weaver, H. N., & Brave Heart, M. Y. H. (1999). Examining two facets of American Indian identity: Exposure to other cultures and the influence of historical trauma. In H. N. Weaver (Ed.), *Voices of first nations people: Human services considerations.* New York: Haworth. (Reprinted from *Journal of Human Behavior in the Social Environment, 2*(1–2), 19–33, 1999.)

Welty, T. (2002). The epidemiology of alcohol use and alcohol-related health problems among American Indians. In P. D. Mail, S. Heurtin-Roberts, S. E. Martin, & J. Howard (Eds.), *Alcohol use among American Indians and Alaska Natives: Multiple perspectives on a complex problem* (pp. 49–70). National Institute on Alcohol Abuse and Alcoholism Research Monograph No. 37. Bethesda, MD: National Institute on Alcohol Abuse and Alcoholism.

Wilkinson, C. F. (1987). *American Indians, time, and the law: Native societies in a modern constitutional democracy.* New Haven, CT: Yale.

Yinger, J. M. (1986). Intersecting strands in the theorization of race and ethnic relations. In J. Rex & D. Mason (Eds.), *Theories of race and ethnic relations* (pp. 20–41). Cambridge, UK: Cambridge University Press.

24

THE IMPACT OF THE
JUVENILE PRISON ON FATHERS

ANNE NURSE

The College of Wooster

In the last 20 years, the incarceration rate of young men has risen dramatically. The period from 1983 to 1995, for example, saw an increase in juvenile incarceration of almost 50%. By 1995, there were more than 86,000 young men in public and private correctional institutions, camps, and treatment centers nationwide (Sickmund, Snyder, & Poe-Yamagata, 1997). Although juvenile arrests for both violent and property crimes have dropped in the last 5 years, there will not be an immediate impact on prison population statistics. In 1997, the U.S. House of Representatives passed a bill authorizing the distribution of 1.6 billion dollars to states that toughen penalties for juvenile offenders. These changes to the juvenile laws are resulting in the incarceration of a greater number of young people for longer periods of time.

Although it is rarely discussed, fathers are disproportionately represented in the juvenile prison population. Few states keep accurate count of the number of fathers in prison, but in California, for example, the Youth Authority has data suggesting that well over 25% of its juvenile wards are fathers (California Youth Authority, 1995). In Ohio, the statistics are similar; a study conducted by the Department of Youth Services estimates that 22.4% of their inmates are fathers (Abeyratne, Sowards, & Brewer, 1995). There are several reasons for the large number of fathers in juvenile prisons. First, rates of both incarceration and young out-of-wedlock childbearing are disproportionately high in impoverished areas and in African American and Latino communities. In addition, it appears that fathers, regardless of their backgrounds, are more likely than their nonfather counterparts to engage in delinquent behaviors and to go to prison (Christmon & Lucky, 1994; Elster, Lamb, & Tavare, 1987; Lerman, 1993; Stouthamer-Loeber & Wei, 1998).

The overlap of risk factors for incarceration and young parenthood means that time in prison has, in effect, become a part of life for many young fathers. This chapter explores the ways in which the structure of the prison shapes the attitudes and relationships of incarcerated fathers.

METHODS

The data for this chapter were drawn from three sources: a survey administered to 258 paroled fathers under the jurisdiction of the California Youth Authority (CYA) in Northern California, in-depth interviews conducted with a subset of 20 of the original survey respondents, and observations at three CYA prisons. The CYA is one of the largest juvenile correctional systems in the United States, and it is the "last stop" for serious juvenile offenders in the state. The northern region extends from Bakersfield north to the Oregon border.

To compile a list of fathers on parole, I requested names from the caseloads of individual parole agents. These agents spend time with the young men and with their families and girlfriends. For this reason, they are in a unique position to identify fathers. I supplemented the agent lists with Youth Authority records of prison-intake interviews. These interviews were done when the young men first arrived at prison. One of the questions they were asked concerned their fatherhood status. I obtained records of the answers to this question for all men who were on parole during the period of the study (October 1996 until October 1997). Using the parole-agent lists combined with the intake records, I identified 380 young fathers. I believe this was a fairly complete list of all those who were willing to divulge their fatherhood status to authorities at the CYA. To locate men who were not willing to admit to being fathers, I spent time in the waiting rooms of parole offices talking with parolees. Most parolees are required to report to their agents at least once a month, so I was able to explain the study to a large number of men. In this way, I added 20 young fathers who were not on any list.

In total, I identified 400 young fathers on parole in Northern California during the period of the study. Out of these men, a group of interviewers and I ultimately contacted 275; of the 275, we interviewed 258. There were 125 men we were unable to contact, about half of whom were absent without leave (AWOL) and could not be located by the parole office. About as many had been returned to prison before we could interview them. There were also 17 young men whom we contacted but who did not participate in the study: 5 refused; the other 12 agreed to be interviewed, but logistical problems made contact impossible. It should be noted that for the purposes of this chapter I only analyze responses from 181 of the 258 surveys. I exclude 77 respondents because their children were born after they were released from prison, and consequently they never had the experience of being an incarcerated father.

After doing preliminary analysis of the survey data, I constructed an in-depth interview schedule. The purpose of the in-depth interviews was to explore areas of interest revealed during the survey stage of the project and to do further probing of the young men's construction of fatherhood. Because fathering behavior and attitudes are complex and emotionally charged, the in-depth interviews were especially important. They allowed me to explore attitudes, feelings, and reasons for behavior with a depth and sensitivity that are not available to an observer or to a survey interviewer. I analyzed the in-depth interviews by looking for themes that consistently emerged from the men's responses. To select candidates for the in-depth interviews, I stratified the survey respondents by race/ethnicity and then randomly sampled. I then made some minor adjustments so that the sample was geographically representative and contained a representative number of involved and noninvolved fathers.

The final phase of data collection was observation during visiting hours at three different Youth Authority prisons. The purpose of these trips was to observe the conditions under which inmates receive visits from children. I made the prison selection on the basis of the size of the facilities (choosing three of the largest) and because two of the three are intended for older wards (over the age of 18). I focused on this population because older wards tend to have more children than do younger ones, and visiting these institutions maximized my chances of witnessing father-child contact. I also chose the institutions I visited based on the percentage of my survey respondents who had spent time at each location.

PRISON'S IMPACT ON FATHER-CHILD RELATIONS

All correctional facilities in the United States have strict rules governing the contact inmates have with the outside world. These limitations are intended as a security measure and as part of an inmate's punishment. Interestingly, the rules that govern the outside contacts of juvenile inmates are sometimes more restrictive than the corresponding policies in adult correctional facilities (Bortner & Williams, 1997). These institutional rules have profound implications for the relationships that incarcerated fathers are able to build or maintain with their children.

Juvenile facilities in the United States generally allow incarcerated fathers to have three kinds of contact with their children: letters, phone calls, and visitation. The data from my paroled-father project suggest that incarcerated fathers do take advantage of their ability to make calls and to write to their children. About 80% of the survey respondents said that while they were incarcerated they spoke with their children on the phone. In addition to talking with their kids, most men also talked to their children's caretakers to find out how the children were doing. Over 85% of the respondents said that they had talked with the child's mother or other member of her family about how the child was doing. Excluding those men with infants, about 75% of the respondents reported sending their child a letter, and about 70% received a picture their child had drawn.

Of all the types of contact inmates are allowed with their children, visitation is the most direct. It is also the area in which correctional institutions exert the most control. From the beginning of a young man's stay at the Youth Authority, policies limit his access to his child. New inmates are generally denied visiting privileges during their first few weeks at the institution. This policy is intended as a security measure, but it also acts to distance inmates from significant aspects of their previous lives, notably their children. Prisons are not the only institutions to engage in such practices. Erving Goffman, in his work on the "total institution," points out that distancing policies are common; they are a way of "ensuring a deep initial break with past roles and appreciation of role dispossession" (Goffman, 1959, p. 114).

After the first few weeks in the institution, most Youth Authority inmates are allowed a normal visiting schedule. At least every 2 weeks, they are permitted to spend several hours with a maximum of four visitors. Among the fathers in my study, however, this privilege was not always used as an opportunity to see children. About 22% reported seeing their child weekly; 17% reported two or three visits a month; and 6% said they saw their children monthly. At the other end of the spectrum, 22% saw their children infrequently, meaning that they saw their children only once or twice during their entire stay in the Youth Authority. A full 33% of the respondents did not see their children at all.

There are many reasons that young incarcerated fathers fail to use all the time allowable to see their children. Setting aside those that originated before their incarceration, the men reported three policies that played a significant role in limiting the number of times they saw their children. These include inmate placement policy, visiting-list restrictions, and entrance requirements.

The policy most influencing the number of visits is the one regulating the placement of inmates. Youth Authority institutions and camps are scattered throughout the state of California, and inmates can be assigned to any of these facilities. Sometimes men are placed hundreds of miles from their home, and their families find it difficult, if not impossible, to visit. Even when inmates are placed closer to home, many families find it hard to visit because they do not have cars or gas money, or they have to work on the designated visiting day. On average, juveniles nationally are confined 58 miles from their homes (Parent et al., 1994).

Many of the young men, in the survey and their in-depth interviews, talked about the serious problems their families had finding transportation to the institution. About a third reported that these transportation problems sometimes prevented them from seeing their child. One respondent, for example, told me that he was not able to see his son very much because his grandmother was the only person in his family with access to a vehicle. About a year into his 2-year sentence, his grandmother died, and the young man did not see his child until his release. Although there are nonprofit groups that provide transportation to some of the institutions, the services are simply not sufficient to help all the families needing assistance.

The second policy that prevents men from seeing their children involves the visiting list. Each inmate is asked to submit a list of the people they would like to be allowed to visit. Institutional staff then determine which of the people are eligible and establish the inmate's official "visiting list." People on the visiting list must be members of the inmate's immediate family—parents, siblings, wives, grandparents, or biological children. At most institutions (although not at all), an inmate can also see his girlfriend. These visiting-list rules were created in order to ensure institutional security and to prevent overcrowding at visiting hours. Their unintended result, however, is to keep some men from seeing their children.

The fact that only immediate family and one girlfriend are allowed on the visiting list causes problems for men who have children by multiple women. Because they are allowed to list only one woman in the "girlfriend" or "wife" category, they cannot include both, or all, mothers at the same time. Because mothers are the primary people bringing children to the prison, inmates in this situation must make a choice about which of their children they want to see. This dilemma is fairly common—about 20% of the survey respondents had children with multiple women. In the in-depth interviews, I asked one young man what he had done when faced with this choice. He told me he decided which mother to choose based on who was the angriest at him. On the rare occasion that he was allowed to make changes to his list, he would switch the women. This strategy was obviously not ideal, and ultimately managed to alienate both women. As a result, he ended up missing substantial periods in the lives of his children.

The one-girlfriend rule is also a problem for those men whose girlfriend is not the mother of their children. In these cases men are forced to choose between their girlfriend and the mother of their children. Few can resist seeing their girlfriends, even when it means they cannot see their children. Some inmates solve one-girlfriend dilemmas by arranging for their own mothers or another member of their family to bring the children, but this strategy is contingent on the willingness of the mother to send her child to the institution without her. As will be discussed later, the relationship between incarcerated men and the mother of their children is often extremely tenuous, and some mothers are unwilling to allow their children to go to the institution with the inmate's family.

The third set of policies affecting men's contact with their children involves entrance requirements. Visitors can be denied entry to the institution for a variety of reasons. First, visitors need proper identification, and girlfriends and wives under the age of 18 must have a notarized letter from one of their parents giving them permission to visit. In addition, all visitors must comply with the dress code. Over 20% of the survey sample reported that family members had been turned away from the institution at least once for violation of one of these visiting-hour rules.

When families are refused entry, children miss an opportunity to see their fathers. Furthermore, families may become less willing to make the long trip to the institution because they fear they will be refused admittance again. Their fear is not unfounded, especially because there are days when no one is allowed into the institution. This situation is referred to as a lockdown, and it occurs when there has been fighting, a riot, or the threat of a riot. Individual inmates, whole groups, or entire institutions can be put on lockdown and not allowed visitors. About 36% of the survey respondents reported that a lockdown had prevented at least one visit with their child. Usually when a lockdown occurs, inmates are able to call their families and tell them not to come, but sometimes the lockdown occurs the night before visiting day. In these cases, families arrive at the institution and are denied entry.

All of these policies—inmate placement, visiting lists, and entrance requirements—have a reason for their existence. For example, inmates are placed in age-graded institutions for their own safety. The number of visitors is limited so that visiting hours do not become overcrowded. Inmates are only allowed to receive visits from immediate family members both as a form of punishment and as an effort to limit their contact with former gang associates. The reality, however, is that these policies often stand in the way of the men's ability to build a relationship with their children.

Nothing to Do:
Children at Visiting Hours

Visiting hours are an important way for men to build a relationship with their children from prison; consequently, they are the focus of high expectations and great excitement. Many of the inmates have not seen their children in months and eagerly anticipate their arrival. Alberto, a Latino father of a 1½-year-old son, was back in the institution at the time of his interview. He told me,

> It feels good, just to know that I'm getting a visit this Sunday—my mom's coming, my son's going to come—cause I miss my son a whole lot and it's like—it feels different. I can't explain the feeling but it's like—it feels good 'cause you want to see him and it's been a while and you finally see him—oh, that's my son and you start telling your son how much you love him.

When I observed institutional visiting hours, I watched the obvious happiness with which many of the inmates greeted their children. It was clear that they were excited to see the children and to spend time with them. After the initial excitement wore off, however, visiting hours turned out to be a disappointment for many of the men. This disappointment can often be explained by the way the structure of visiting hours interferes with positive father-child interaction.

At Youth Authority facilities, visiting hours take place in two locations: a large room filled with tables and an adjoining outdoor patio area. The outside areas have trees and picnic tables and, at some facilities, there are barbecues available. Eating is the central activity during visiting hours. At some prisons, families can bring food from the outside, and many arrive with bags of chicken or hamburgers. At other institutions, families are limited to purchasing food from the vending machines in the institution. When they are not eating, inmates and their visitors sit at the tables or walk around in the yard. On rainy days, everything must take place inside, and the visiting hours become quite loud and chaotic.

The Youth Authority strives to "normalize" visiting hours so that the facility feels friendly and noninstitutional. Prisons that allow barbecuing and outside food are especially good at creating a welcoming atmosphere. None of the efforts, however, can hide the extensive security precautions, the barbed wire, and the guards. As a result, older children are quite aware that they are in prison. For many inmates, their children's awareness causes shame and embarrassment. About half of those survey respondents who received prison visits from their children reported feeling this way. Tony, an 18-year-old man who was back in prison at the time of his in-depth interview, talked about his embarrassment when his son became old enough to start asking him questions:

> Actually, the last time he came and saw me, it was 2 weeks ago. . . . The visit was almost going to end . . . and he's like are you coming home with us? And it shocked me, I just sat there for a moment, and I told him no. And he say, why. . . . I was shocked, a 3-year-old baby, where are these questions coming from? I was hurt, I felt low actually, I felt like I was the lowest man on the planet.

Sometimes young fathers are so ashamed of being seen by their children that they limit their visitation time, or refuse visits altogether. Among survey respondents who did not see their child while incarcerated, about 20% told me that shame was one of the reasons, and about 10% said that shame was the single most important reason.

Shame causes visiting hours to be awkward and embarrassing for some men. Further increasing this awkwardness is the fact that there are few opportunities for "normal" interaction between fathers and their children. Outside prison, men generally relate to children through play or other social activities (Bailey, 1994). This simply is not possible in the institution because, at most facilities, there are no toys. This makes it difficult to interact with the children or to keep them entertained. About 20% of the survey respondents said that their children sometimes did not like coming to visit at the institution because "there was nothing for them to do there." A staff member at one of the institutions told me that they do allow families to bring in a limited number of toys, but none of the families

I saw had any. Several staff members told me that the limitations on toys were a necessary security measure because drugs could easily be placed inside of them.

Not having toys or games is a particular problem for the juvenile-inmate population because so few have experience with their children. Most have been in prison for the majority of their children's lives, and even those who were involved with their children before they were incarcerated must adjust to each new developmental stage. Toys or games could provide an excellent way for the men to interact with their children. With current regulations in place, however, visiting hours can be extremely tense and uncomfortable. I watched one young child, clearly bored, who kept wandering away from the table where her parents were visiting. The inmate kept ordering her back, and both he and the child ended up looking frustrated and exhausted. Marco, a 19-year-old Latino father from a small town in the Central Valley, talked about visiting with his daughter while he was incarcerated:

> You don't pay attention to your kid when they come visit you there. Some people do, but other times, you know, I noticed I wasn't. . . . My mind was other places, my eyeballs and everything you know. You're always like, you know, looking around over here and over there, and seeing people you know and whoop-de-whoop, and the kids are just there running around, you've got to chase 'em. There ain't nowhere for them to play or nothing. You know, you miss 'em and everything, you hug 'em, they might sit on your lap and everything, but you know, after 15–20 minutes any kid would get bored just seeing a bunch of people, a bunch of chairs and tables. You know. What's the use of them being there?

From my observations and the reports from the young men, it appears that eating is the primary activity the fathers engage in with their children. Once the food is gone, many of the fathers simply hand the children over to the mothers.

A final aspect of visiting hours that interferes with "normal" father-child interaction is that the men usually receive several visitors at once. Visiting hours occur only weekly, or biweekly,

and inmates often want to see several family members and their girlfriend. At the institution, I noticed that many of the young men tried to engage in serious conversations with their adult visitors, but they were so distracted by their children that they could not communicate well. The young men, torn between their desire to talk with their adult visitors and their desire to pay attention to their children, are not able to do a good job of either.

THE PRISON ENVIRONMENT: FATHERS' RESPONSES

The structure of the prison encourages fathers to develop particular attitudes and coping mechanisms. These attitudes and mechanisms, in turn, affect the relationship they have with their children.

Hard Timing

As previously noted, juvenile correctional facilities across the nation have become increasingly crowded and violent in the last 20 years. Living in such stressful and crowded conditions encourages inmates to develop various coping techniques. Although many of the techniques are extremely adaptive for prison life, some have a harmful impact on the inmates' relationships with their children. The first technique commonly employed is called hard timing.

Hard timing, according to the in-depth interview respondents, happens when inmates feel so overwhelmed by life in the institution that they cut off all ties to the outside world. They do this because it is simply too difficult for them to deal with problems inside and outside of the institution simultaneously. To illustrate the phenomenon of hard timing, I include two lengthy but illustrative quotes from the in-depth interviews. In response to a question asking what advice he would give to a father being sentenced to a few years in the CYA, Charles began to talk about the intense stress inmates feel:

> Some people get in there and it will be like a lot of problems from the outside coming in, they're constantly telling you about this problem and Mom's telling you about this problem . . . so you got all

these problems coming at you at one time, you get so stressed out. So the first thing you do is you block your stress out from the outside. . . . You try to concentrate on your living, it's just like survival skills, you know. If you're in the forest with a bear, the bear's attacking you but . . . you're trying to get back to Sacramento because somebody's in the hospital, you've got to deal with the bear first. So that's why people get caught up and cut off all the outside, and then they just call it hard time. They just forget everything, they don't work on any mail, no phone calls, they're just hard timing.

Hard timing, as the young men describe it, is their response to the stresses of incarceration. It is a reaction to the prison environment combined with guilt about an inability to support those they care for on the outside. Because most inmates are from the lowest economic classes, their families face the many hardships associated with poverty. Not only do problems such as being evicted from homes and losing welfare benefits continue while a young man is in prison, they sometimes increase in his absence. Incarcerated men hear about these problems and often feel guilty and powerless. As a result, some simply decide that it is easier not to know about the problems at all.

The structure of the prison encourages the hard-timing response because it provides few opportunities for inmates to help or support their families during times of crisis. I was told by staff that in the 1970s and 1980s there was much more flexibility in the rules applied to inmates whose families were undergoing difficult times. For example, inmates were sometimes allowed to attend funerals, albeit in handcuffs and accompanied by prison staff. Today, rules strictly forbid inmates from attending funerals or other important family events. The official rules also prohibit extra phone time or visiting hours during family crises. A sense of guilt about their families, and feelings of powerlessness, often cause young inmates to rely on hard timing as a coping strategy. Men who resort to hard timing restrict contact with their children as well as with the rest of their family. As a result, they miss out on key moments in their children's lives, which may harm any bond they might have had. In addition, it is likely that hard timing causes resentment among family members, which may hinder men's successful reintegration into family life after incarceration.

Everybody's a Pimp: Misogyny and the Gendered Nature of the Prison

One of the most obvious, and least discussed, characteristics of the juvenile justice system is that almost all prison facilities are single gender. The fact that males and females are housed separately has important consequences that affect inmates' interaction with their children. In prison, the father-child relationship depends, to a large extent, on the relationship he has with his child's mother. The mothers are the primary people to bring children to the institution, and they have the power to withhold visitation. If the relationship with the father is poor, the mother can refuse to allow any father-child contact. Poor father-mother relationships can often be traced to attitudes prevalent within the prison environment.

Inmate attitudes reflect negative feelings about women that are profoundly influenced by the gendered nature of the prison. Research with all-male adolescent groups has shown how misogynistic attitudes are fostered as men use negative talk about women to affirm their masculinity and to bolster their own standing in the group. For example, Gary Allen Fine, in his study of Little League baseball (1987), demonstrates that when preadolescent males spend time together they engage in talk that is "consistent with male domination and female submission" (p. 110). Elijah Anderson (1990) documents how the denigration of women serves to unite groups of adolescent males. He shows that young men use tales of their sexual exploits with women as a way to elevate their status within the group.

The fact that a prison is single gender exacerbates the misogynistic tendencies of all-male groups in several ways. First, the grouping of rival gang members in a prison means that the need to demonstrate one's toughness and masculinity can be even more essential than it is on the streets. The structure of the institution, however, closes many of the avenues adolescents generally use to assert their masculinity. Inmates obviously do not have the opportunity to engage in the heterosexual sexual exploits used to gain status outside the institution. As a result, talk becomes the primary way to demonstrate masculinity: talk about past sexual liaisons and negative talk about women. Because the inmates spend 24 hours a day with their peer group, there are plenty of opportunities for conversation, and there are virtually no counterbalancing influences to the young-male culture.

The in-depth interview respondents talked at length about how life in the institution encouraged misogyny. For example, Tony said,

> When a bunch of guys who really have nothing to do sit around . . . sometimes we have good conversations but then most again we have conversations about the worse ones [women]. We hardly ever talk about the good ones because it makes you seem like you're not the stud, you're not the big time playboy that you want the appearance, you know what I'm saying.

Marco had a somewhat more balanced view. He felt that, although there was negative talk about women, not everyone participated in it:

> Um, from different guys you hear different things. It matters what kind of guy it is, what kind of person he is, if he has respect for his girlfriends, or whatever, and he has respect for his mom and everything, you don't talk bad about women or girls, but some guys do. Whores, sluts you know, I did this to 'em, I did that, whoop-de-whoop, just telling stories, make yourself look good or something, you know.

The talk that goes on in the institution is not significantly different from the talk among young males on the streets. What is different is the intensity of the talk and the fact that inmates have little contact with women (other than prison staff) who might have a counterbalancing influence.

The Summer Shake: Fostering Distrust of Women

Misogyny in the institution is not simply a result of men's need to assert their masculinity in an all-male environment. Imprisonment changes the power balance between men and their wives or girlfriends, and this is deeply upsetting to the men. In the outside world, men are fairly

independent of women and pride themselves on being able to come and go as they please (Anderson, 1990). They are able to monitor the behavior of their girlfriends and make sure that they are being faithful and are acting in what they consider to be an appropriate manner. The institution turns this power relationship upside down. Men suddenly become completely dependent on their wives or girlfriends. Women chose when and if they visit, and they have the power to withhold money, packages, and access to children. At the same time, the men are no longer in a position to monitor or control the women's behavior.

Inmates' inability to control the behavior of their wives and girlfriends causes stress and worry that they are seeing other men. Their concern is fueled by rumors they hear through the mail and during visiting hours. Friends and siblings tell them gossip about their girlfriends' behavior. One young man told me that this happened frequently when he was in the institution. He said, "You might get a letter from your brother or your family member or friend or something, telling you they seen her do something here and there, and that they seen her with this different person or whatever. And it's like, you know it's true."

Fueling the distrust of women caused by insecurity and gossip, many stories of girlfriend infidelity circulate within the institution. Although some of the stories are untrue, significant numbers of women do choose to end their relationships with incarcerated men. The survey and in-depth respondents told me that many of their girlfriends tried to wait for them to be released from prison but, after a period of time, began to date other people. This was so common that the young men in the institution called it "the summer shake." I asked Tyrell what this meant and he told me:

> Like in the summertime, you know all the girls get dressed up and go out and have fun—it's cool out. You know, it's summertime and they shake their boyfriends off. The summer shake . . . we all used to make fun of each other. Like somebody's girlfriend stop writing them or whatever and we'd say "Ah, she gave you the summer shake!"

The large number of breakups in the already negatively charged prison environment further reinforces a deep distrust and anger toward women. Vance, a 20-year-old father of two children, whose relationship with the mother of his first child ended while he was incarcerated, told me what he learned in prison:

> Just that all women are not any good and if you have a girlfriend out there, you know she's cheating on you no matter what you think or what she tells you, she is no matter what. We get that a lot. That they're all the same. You know, a lot of people—if you tell them you had a wife out there and you know she's faithful—they would laugh at you, and diss you for believing that.

The constantly reinforced message is that women are not to be trusted. One in-depth interview respondent revealed this attitude when I asked him what advice he would give to someone sentenced to a few years in the CYA. He said, "Well, I'd give him advice. Don't trust the baby's mom."

MITIGATING FACTORS

For the most part, the prison environment and system structure encourage young men to withdraw from their children and from their children's mothers. There are, however, countervailing tendencies in the institutional culture. Two important factors help men be more responsible fathers: group support for active fathering and parenting instruction.

Group Support for Active Fathering

Goffman, in his work on institutional life, discusses the possibility of solidarity and support among the inmates of a total institution. He finds that friendships are possible but are limited by the institutional structure and by staff fears that friendships lead to disruptive activities (Goffman, 1959). Although my in-depth interview data confirm that inmate solidarity is difficult to maintain, they also indicate that inmates can provide a great deal of support for one another. Such support is particularly prevalent among fathers. They often seem able to form a support system in the prison and to encourage each other to be active participants in their children's lives. There are clearly

exceptions, but among the in-depth interview respondents, many felt free to talk about their children with other inmates and to discuss problems they might be having. When asked if he talked with other men in the institution about his daughter, Charles responded,

> Always. . . . When you get a picture everybody rushes to show each other a picture. They're always saying, talking about, you know, "she's got your nose, she's got your eyes," you know just talking about it like that. And we'd be talking about what they're doing, talking about them to different parties and stuff.

A significant number of the in-depth interview respondents told me that other inmates had encouraged them to be actively involved with their children. Vance commented,

> Uh, you see a lot of like if someone has two or three kids out there, and a lot of their friends or stuff in there will tell 'em, you should go out and be with your kids, you need to be there for them instead of being in here. It's rare you'd hear someone say something negative about someone else's kids or anything. Mostly people they know, kind of like everybody'll preach to everybody else, they need to know they don't do it themselves so they tell everybody else what they should be doing, they should be out there doing the right things for their family.

The support for being a father stands in striking contrast to the lack of support for maintaining relationships with women. Unfortunately, the two are intimately connected; men who destroy their relationships with the mothers of their children are unlikely to see their children. In the survey, I asked respondents about the factors influencing how often they saw their children in prison. The one selected as most important was the relationship with the children's mother. A support system for fathers is of little use without one to support the parents' relationship.

Parenting Classes

The "Young Men as Fathers" Parenting Program was begun in 1993 as a pilot program at four CYA institutions, two in Northern California and two in Southern California. In 1995, Governor Pete Wilson became interested in the program and directed that it be extended to all Youth Authority institutions and camps. Its main goal is to promote active fathering by teaching young men parenting skills. Another goal is to decrease violence against children and to encourage young men to spend more time with their children.

Participation in the parenting classes is required of selected inmates. The selection is made by a caseworker at the reception center, the parole board, or an intake worker at the institution. Fathers are given first priority for these classes, and young men who are father figures, or who are considered to be at "high risk" for becoming fathers, are given second priority. Approximately 75% of the young men in the survey sample were required to take one or more parenting class while in prison.

I asked the survey respondents to rate the helpfulness of the classes on a scale of 0 to 5, with 0 being "not at all helpful" and 5 being "extremely helpful." Over 45% of the sample reported that they found their classes to be extremely helpful. The average response was a 3.63 out of 5, and only 11% of the men who took a parenting class rated it a 0.

Perhaps the most compelling evidence for the positive effect of the classes comes from the comments made by many of the in-depth interview respondents. I did not ask them specifically about the classes, but frequently the young men brought up the topic themselves. Tony told me how the parenting class he had taken in the institution helped him:

> It helped me understand more what I was supposed to do. . . . You know . . . before I went to CYA, I didn't know nothing about the baby shaking syndrome or whatever. And I used to . . . like a little rough horseplay. I figure he was laughing, there wasn't nothing wrong with it. After going through that class, that's how a lot of babies are injured. Also, I know a lot of people who before I went to YA, I used to do it too, give babies alcohol to put them to sleep, and blowing marijuana smoke in their face and I thought it was cool, I thought it was funny until I realized what could actually happen to the baby.

The in-depth interviews suggest that young men benefit from this comprehensive parenting instruction. They gain general background knowledge, master specific techniques, and learn new behavior patterns.

IMPLICATIONS AND POLICY RECOMMENDATIONS

This chapter describes the various ways in which the juvenile-prison experience shapes an inmate's relationship with his children. The impact of incarceration on this relationship, especially the negative impact, is not intentional. The prison environment is structured with little concern for inmates who are fathers. Instead, the structure is largely determined by public opinion about the purpose of prison and the nature of young people. Currently, we find ourselves in a cycle of public opinion that emphasizes the prison as a site to punish inmates for their crimes. Increasingly restrictive policies have been implemented at the juvenile level—restrictions that are equal to, or sometimes more severe than, those at adult facilities (Bortner & Williams, 1997). I have argued that this punitive and high-stress environment contributes to young fathers' disengagement from their children and from the mothers of those children.

Given the effects of prison on fathers and children, I believe that one of the primary goals of public policy should be to reduce the number of incarcerated young fathers. One way to do this is to provide educational and employment opportunities for teenagers, particularly impoverished teenagers—outside of prison. There is evidence to suggest that juvenile criminal behavior can, in some cases, be reduced by the creation of strong ties to employment and school (Sampson & Laub, 1993). Another strategy for reducing the number of fathers in prison is to reconsider the current guidelines increasing the length of juvenile sentences. We need to assess carefully our sentencing policies in order to protect the public but still limit the amount of time served by juveniles.

I believe that policies intended to decrease the number of young incarcerated fathers, such as those I have just described, make sense in light of the prohibitive costs of their imprisonment. Unfortunately, current public opinion regarding criminals indicates that such policies will be difficult to implement. As a result, large numbers of young fathers will continue to enter our correctional system. This project suggests some policies that may mitigate the harmful effect of incarceration on father-child relationships. The first is that parenting classes should be offered to all fathers. Such classes may be able to help men develop a strong relationship with their children. Although classes can cover a wide range of topics, practical skills relating to basic child care should be emphasized. These skills are particularly critical for young men who have little or no experience with children. Prison parenting classes also have the potential to help inmates develop realistic expectations for how their children will react to their homecoming.

In addition to parenting classes, juvenile prisons should develop policies that encourage inmates to spend time with their children. The data from this project suggest that most inmates are interested in contact with their children and plan to resume seeing their children upon their release. Given this, it is in the interest of both fathers and children that men are helped to develop and maintain healthy relationships. Prison provides a unique opportunity for fathers to spend time with children in a supervised setting. It may also ease the trauma associated with parent-child separation. Denise Johnston's work (1995) shows that children who have an incarcerated parent are more likely to experience depression, anger, guilt, and academic problems. She also finds, however, that prison visits allow both parents and children to work out feelings of grief and loss that frequently accompany separation. Her work suggests that children who visit with their incarcerated parents are also better able to develop realistic images of them.

Given the positive findings regarding parent-child visitation in prison and men's desire to interact with their children, it makes sense to implement policies that facilitate contact. One of the primary ways this can be done is to make visitation more child friendly by providing toys and activities. Although it may be expensive, the prison system should become more flexible

in its policies toward child visitation. Every effort should be made to ensure that children who come to the prison are admitted and allowed to see their fathers. Nonprofit groups who provide transportation services for the families of inmates should be encouraged. Finally, it should be recognized that visitation is not the only way that fathers spend time with children. Phone calls are also very important. Fathers should be allowed to call their children on a regular basis, even if this means that they are allowed to make more calls than other inmates.

Each year, an increasing number of young fathers spend time in our nation's correctional facilities. Public and academic ignorance about these men hinders the development of public policy and research. Learning about the experiences and attitudes of young incarcerated fathers can help us to find ways to mitigate the damage done to families and communities by their incarceration. The fathers introduced in this chapter are only a small part of a much larger national population of criminal fathers. A failure to recognize the impact of prison structure and policies on their relationships with their children may have serious and troubling social consequences.

REFERENCES

Abeyratne, S., Sowards, B., & Brewer, L. (1995). *Youths incarcerated in ODYS institutions who have children and youths incarcerated in ODYS institutions who are children of teenage parents.* Columbus: Ohio Department of Youth Services, Office of Research.

Anderson, E. (1990). *Streetwise: Race, class, and change in an urban community.* Chicago: University of Chicago Press.

Bailey, W. T. (1994). A longitudinal study of fathers' involvement with young children: Infancy to age 5 years. *The Journal of Genetic Psychology, 155,* 331–339.

Bortner, M. A., & Williams, M. L. (1997). *Youth in prison.* New York: Routledge.

California Youth Authority. (1995). *Office of criminal justice planning juvenile-justice and delinquency prevention program project summary.* Sacramento, CA: CYA.

Christmon, K., & Lucky, I. (1994). Is early fatherhood associated with alcohol and other drug use? *Journal of Substance Abuse, 6,* 337–343.

Elster, A. B., Lamb, M. E., & Tavare, J. (1987). Association between behavioral and school problems and fatherhood in a national sample of adolescent youths. *Journal of Pediatrics, 111,* 932–936.

Fine, G. A. (1987). *With the boys: Little League baseball and preadolescent culture.* Chicago: University of Chicago Press.

Goffman, E. (1959). *Asylums: Essays on the social situation of mental patients and other inmates.* New York: Doubleday.

Johnston, D. (1995). Jailed mothers. In D. Johnston & K. Gabel (Eds.), *Children of incarcerated parents* (pp. 3–20). New York: Lexington Books.

Lerman, R. I. (1993). A national profile of young unwed fathers. In R. I. Lerman & T. Ooms (Eds.), *Young unwed fathers: Changing roles and emerging policies* (pp. 27–51). Philadelphia: Temple University Press.

Parent, D. G., Leiter, V., Kennedy, S., Livens, L., Wentworth, D., & Wilcox, S. (1994). *Conditions of confinement: Juvenile detention and corrections facilities: Research summary.* Washington, DC: Office of Juvenile Justice and Delinquency Prevention.

Sampson, R., & Laub, J. (1993). *Crime in the making: Pathways and turning points through life.* Cambridge, MA: Harvard University Press.

Sickmund, M., Snyder, H. N., & Poe-Yamagata, E. (1997). *Juvenile offenders and victims: 1997 Update on violence.* Washington, DC: Office of Juvenile Justice and Delinquency Prevention.

Stouthamer-Loeber, M., & Wei, E. (1998). The precursors of young fatherhood and its effect on delinquency of teenage males. *Journal of Adolescent Health, 22,* 56–65.

PART VI

VIOLENCE

25

IMMIGRANT WOMEN AND DOMESTIC VIOLENCE

JEANETTE ZANIPATIN

Attorney, Private Practice, Oakland, California

STACY SHAW WELCH

University of Washington

JEAN YI

University of Washington

PATTY BARDINA

University of Washington

This chapter will discuss the relationship between immigrants, domestic violence, and immigration law. Battered immigrants often face unique obstacles in escaping domestic violence due to their unlawful or unstable legal status in the United States. The Commission on Domestic Violence (1997) reported that immigrant women in the United States experience higher rates of battering than citizens do because their cultural backgrounds often tolerate domestic violence and because they believe that they cannot be protected by the U.S. legal system. This chapter will describe legal remedies that are available for battered immigrants. We will then turn to the psychological issues related to domestic violence and the specific challenges faced by certain immigrant populations.

PART 1. IMMIGRATION RELIEF FOR BATTERED IMMIGRANTS—THE LAW

The relationship between immigration law and domestic violence was formalized in 1994, with the introduction of the Violence Against Women Act (VAWA; U.S. Congress, 1994). Under the VAWA, Congress recognized that domestic violence plays a unique and disabling role in the lives of battered immigrants. Domestic violence creates a barrier for battered immigrants because batterers are able to deny immigrants the right to obtain legal status in the United States. This act addressed the role of domestic violence in immigration to the United States and provided battered immigrants with forms of legal relief. The first part of this chapter will review immigration law in general terms. The forms of relief available under immigration law are described to provide a general understanding of the legal requirements necessary to obtain these forms of relief. This review is not meant to serve as a substitute for individual legal counseling, which can only be obtained from a licensed immigration attorney.

Basic Overview of Immigration Law and Definitions

It is important to start this review by defining a few immigration terms in order to understand the basics of immigration law. Immigration law divides most individuals into the following three categories: United States citizen (USC), legal permanent resident (LPR), and undocumented immigrant. A USC is an individual who was born in the United States and who derived his or her U.S. citizenship through a USC parent (Immigration and Naturalization Service, 2002). In addition, certain LPRs are eligible to apply for U.S. citizenship provided they pass a U.S. civics and history exam and can demonstrate basic English reading and writing skills.[1]

A LPR, on the other hand, is an individual who has applied for lawful immigration status and can demonstrate that he or she is admissible into the United States.[2] A LPR is granted a "green card,"[3] which allows LPRs to live and work permanently in the United States so long as they do not violate the terms of their immigration status.

An undocumented immigrant is an individual who does not have any legal status and is not authorized to live or work in the United States. Although legally this is a civil violation, 8.5 million undocumented immigrants live and work in the United States and often make the United States their home for many years (Passel, 2002).

The process of immigrating to the United States primarily involves two distinct areas of immigration law. Most individuals immigrate to the United States through either a business visa or a family-based immigrant visa. Although many immigrants enter the United States with a business visa, obtaining a permanent green card for family members typically occurs through the family-based visa process. Within immigration law, this process most frequently intersects with domestic violence. Thus, our focus in this chapter will be on the family-based visa process, as well as other immigration processes available to individuals experiencing violence.

The Family-Based Visa Process

The family-based visa process involves two steps and necessitates that a family member, either a USC or a LPR, apply for the immigrant visa (Immigration and Naturalization Service, 2002). The USC or LPR must first establish that a family or marital relationship exists and that the relationship is one that is recognized by law. This requirement is usually fulfilled by presenting copies of a birth certificate or marriage certificate to establish a bona fide familial or marital relationship.

The USC or LPR must then file a visa petition, form I-130, for his or her relative to obtain a visa to immigrate to the United States. By filing a visa petition, a USC can request an immigrant visa for his or her spouse, children, parents, and siblings. A LPR, on the other hand, can only petition for his or her spouse, children under 21 years of age, and adult children who are single.

Thus, the family-based visa process is initiated and controlled by the USC or LPR, often called "the petitioner." The petitioner is the individual who begins the process and can withdraw the petition at any time by simply notifying the Immigration and Naturalization Service (INS) of his or her intent to have the petition withdrawn. The role of the petitioner in this process has proven to be problematic when the petitioner is the perpetrator of domestic violence, because it provides the batterer with legal power and control in the familial or marital relationship. In these cases, many battered immigrants are forced to rely on their abusive spouse or parent to obtain legal status in the United States. Batterers who have USC or LPR status often use the constant threat of deportation to control the battered immigrant and his or her children. This dependence on the batterer creates a group of immigrants who are qualified to legalize their immigration status but remain undocumented because the batterer has control of the process.

The Violence Against Women Act

In 1994, the VAWA (U.S. Congress, 1994) was enacted to include provisions that allow battered immigrants to file a visa petition on their own behalf. Thus, battered immigrants who formerly were forced to rely on the batterer to legalize their status could now self-petition if their LPR or USC spouse or parents abused them or their children. This process permits them to obtain lawful permanent residency for themselves and their children. The VAWA of 1994 also created VAWA cancellation, a form of immigration relief for battered immigrants who are involved in deportation or removal proceedings.

In 2000, Congress enacted the Violence Against Women Act of 2000 (U.S. Congress, 2000). VAWA II, as it is commonly known, was enacted as a technical cleanup bill for VAWA and created forms of immigration relief for battered immigrants who did not qualify for immigration relief under the self-petitioning process. In VAWA II, Congress created two additional forms of immigration relief for crime victims and victims of human trafficking under the U visa and the T visa, respectively.

The following sections will describe three forms of relief for battered immigrants: the self-petitioning process, VAWA cancellation, and the U visa. Each section will include a case study that exemplifies a typical situation for which each form of relief is relevant.

Self-Petitioning Process for Battered Immigrants

Under the self-petitioning process, battered immigrants can file a self-petition to obtain LPR status in the United States. To be eligible to self-petition, the battered spouse or intended spouse of a USC or LPR must demonstrate that he or she (a) is a person of good moral character,[4] (b) is or was married to a USC or LPR, (c) is or was subjected to battery or extreme mental cruelty, and (d) is or shared a joint residence with the USC/LPR spouse.[5] Battered children must establish all the previously mentioned requirements as well as establish a parent–child relationship, which can also include a child–stepparent relationship.[6]

In addition to meeting the basic eligibility requirements listed previously, the battered immigrant must file the self-petition while married to the USC/LPR or prior to the second anniversary of divorce from the USC/LPR batterer. In cases where the batterer is a LPR and the batterer was previously deported due to domestic violence or some other immigration violation, the self-petitioner must file before the second anniversary of the batterer's deportation.

In order to file a self-petition, a battered immigrant must complete Form I-360 and document all of the requirements listed earlier. This includes submitting documentary evidence such as a marriage or birth certificate, proof of joint residency, a police clearance letter or criminal background check, evidence of a bona fide/valid marriage, and evidence of battery or extreme mental cruelty. For many battered immigrants, this process can be very difficult because the USC or LPR batterer is often the one in control of such items as the marriage certificate, identity documents, passports, wedding photos, rent or mortgage receipts, and proof of battery or extreme mental cruelty.

Under the self-petitioning process, the INS is aware of the complexities involved in domestic violence cases and will accept any credible evidence to establish the requirements for a self-petition. Thus, battered immigrants can submit affidavits with their self-petition to demonstrate proof of battery or extreme mental cruelty, despite the fact that the battered immigrant does not have hard evidence of abuse such as a police report, restraining order, medical report, witnesses, or photos documenting the abuse.

Case Study—Cecelia[7]

Cecelia fled from El Salvador in 1990 when she was 22 years old. She left behind a 1-year-old son in the care of her mother. She met Rodrigo, a naturalized U.S. citizen from Panama, in 1992, and dated him for more than 1 year before marrying him in 1993.

Rodrigo began abusing Cecelia in 1994, 1 year after they were married, when he discovered that she was sending money home to her mother and son. At first Rodrigo verbally abused Cecelia, telling her that she was worthless because she had a child with another man. Rodrigo threatened Cecelia several times, saying that he would forbid her from working if he caught her sending money home. Rodrigo then began to beat her physically by kicking Cecelia on her back and punching her in the stomach so that no one would see her bruises. He told Cecelia that if she ever called the police or told anyone about the beatings, he would send INS agents to her work and have her deported. Does Cecelia qualify for a self-petition?

VAWA Cancellation

The VAWA of 1994 also created a remedy for battered immigrants who are in removal proceedings and face deportation from the United States (U.S. Congress, 1994). Cancellation of removal is a form of relief that immigrants may use to cancel the deportation and obtain LPR status. By obtaining LPR status, a battered immigrant can live and work in the United States and obtain services that can help them end the cycle of abuse.

To be eligible for VAWA cancellation, a battered immigrant must prove the following statutory requirements: (a) three years of continuous physical presence in the United States, (b) battery or extreme mental cruelty, (c) a bona fide marriage or parental relationship, (d) good moral character, and (e) extreme hardship. In addition, VAWA allows a battered immigrant who has a child in common with a USC or LPR to apply for VAWA cancellation without having to be married to the batterer. A child in common refers to a biological child with a USC/LPR batterer.

The main difference between VAWA cancellation and the self-petitioning process is that VAWA cancellation requires the battered immigrant to establish his or her eligibility before an immigration court in front of an immigration judge and a trial attorney representing the INS. In addition, the battered immigrant is subject to cross-examination by the INS trial attorney whose purpose is to discredit the witness's testimony and convince the judge to deny the immigrant's case.

Case Study—Svetlana

Svetlana is a 33-three-year old female from Russia. She met her husband, Randy, through the Internet and exchanged various e-mails with him for 2 years. In May of 1997, Randy flew out to St. Petersburg, Russia, for 2 weeks to meet Svetlana for the first time. Randy started abusing Svetlana during this visit when he found out that she had a boyfriend who lived nearby. Svetlana believed Randy abused her due to the stress of meeting her family. During his stay, Randy asked Svetlana to marry him. In June of 1999, he returned to St. Petersburg to marry Svetlana among her family and friends. Randy and Svetlana moved to the United States in February of 2000, after Svetlana completed her studies at the university.

After they arrived in the United States, Randy continued to beat Svetlana. On one occasion, Randy threw her out of their home in the middle of the night when she was 8 months pregnant. Svetlana roamed the streets all night because she did not know anyone in the United States. When she returned home the next day, she found that Randy had changed all the locks and had left Svetlana's clothes scattered all over their front yard. Svetlana called a family friend who lived in the area to pick her up.

Svetlana divorced Randy in 1999 and was placed in deportation proceedings. What factors in her case make Svetlana eligible for VAWA cancellation?

U Visa—Humanitarian/Material Witness Visa

Another form of relief, created under the VAWA II, is the U visa (U.S. Congress, 2000). This visa allows immigrants who are victims of certain crimes[8] to obtain a nonimmigrant visa for 3 years. At the end of the 3 years, the immigrant may apply for LPR status. This visa allows battered immigrants who are subjected to domestic violence to be eligible for a form of relief without having to be married to the abuser or requiring that the abuser have legal status in the United States.

Although the INS has not drafted or published final regulations on the U visa, the regulations will be codified in the Immigration and Nationality Act at sections 101(a)(15)(U), 214(o), and 245(1)(1). Because the regulatory process gives wide discretion to the agency interpreting the statutory provisions, some changes in the final regulations are likely to expand or narrow the scope of eligibility to qualify for a U visa. As currently drafted,

however, the statute would allow a nonimmigrant visa to be given to an immigrant whom the Attorney General considers to be a material witness in the detection, investigation, or prosecution of a crime (Immigration and Naturalization Service, 2002). A U visa may also be granted to family members such as the spouse, child,[9] or parent of the immigrant in order to avoid extreme hardship.

To qualify for a U visa, the immigrant must demonstrate that (a) the immigrant is or was the victim of a crime;[10] (b) the immigrant has suffered substantial physical or mental abuse as a result of the crime; (c) the immigrant possesses information concerning the criminal activity; (d) the immigrant has been helpful, is being helpful, or is likely to be helpful in the investigation or prosecution of the criminal activity; (e) the criminal activity violated the laws of the United States or occurred in the United States or its territories; and (f) the immigrant obtained a certification from a federal, state, or local law enforcement official, prosecutor, judge, or other authority investigating the criminal activity.

Case Study—Iselda

Iselda is a 14-year-old female from Bolivia. She entered the United States when she was 2 years old and is currently undocumented. Iselda's mother, Lilia, threw Iselda out of the house when she claimed that her mother's boyfriend, Ilario, had been sexually molesting her since she was 12. Iselda called the police one night when Ilario tried to force himself onto her while her mother was at work.

After Iselda filed the police report, Lilia was initially supportive of Iselda. However, soon after Ilario was arrested, Lilia began to blame Iselda for all her troubles. She threw Iselda out of her home because she no longer believed that Ilario had molested her daughter.

Iselda has been involved with the prosecution of Ilario and will be testifying at his trial in the next few months. Does Iselda qualify for a U visa?

PART 2. DOMESTIC VIOLENCE AND IMMIGRANTS—PSYCHOLOGICAL ISSUES

Although it is essential that battered immigrants become familiar with the three forms of relief described earlier, it would be difficult to break the cycle of domestic violence without understanding the psychological factors that maintain the cycle. This section will discuss the psychological issues surrounding domestic violence in order to provide a more thorough understanding of the experiences of battered immigrants.

The psychological issues involved in domestic violence have been addressed from multiple standpoints. Why do men batter?[11] Why do some women stay? When do women leave? Though many notable contributions addressing these questions have come to the table, there has been an empty chair; the cultural context of domestic violence has been largely ignored (see Yoshihama, 2001). As clarified by the previous section, immigrant women are especially vulnerable to domestic violence. We will focus first on the difficulties they face as a group and then discuss specific issues related to particular cultures.

Theories of Domestic Violence

Multiple models have been suggested to explain domestic violence; these are often divided into three categories based on their primary emphasis. They include *intrapersonal* theories, which focus on characteristics that increase the risk of aggression, *interpersonal* theories, which focus on the patterns of interaction between a couple, and *sociocultural* theories, which propose that domestic violence is linked to the way society condones the use of violence as a means of subjugating women.

The first ideas about domestic violence came from an *intrapersonal* perspective. This perspective viewed abused women as masochistic, mentally ill, suffering from learned helplessness, or experiencing serious intimacy-dependency conflicts. This classic "blame the victim" approach perceived women as responsible for staying in an abusive situation and perceived their partners as ill, alcoholics, violent personalities, or unable to tolerate intimacy (see Rounsaville, 1978). Another example of an intrapersonal perspective is Bandura's social learning theory of aggression, which applies to male batterers (e.g., Dutton, 1995). This theory suggests that aggressive behavior is acquired via learning, through either modeling or direct experience, and that particular stimuli serve as cues for aggressive behavior when they are associated with reinforcers for the behavior.

One of the most influential of the interpersonal theories of domestic violence is family systems theory, which argues that the relationship between two people functions as a system. Thus, patterns of behavior between the couple define the relationship. Couple violence is viewed as a product of dysfunctional patterns where both partners contribute to the escalation of these dysfunctional interactions and to eventual violence.

Feminist scholars have criticized such approaches for implying that the woman contributes to her own battering. Sociocultural theories, heavily influenced by feminist scholars, propose that violence against women is caused by a patriarchal social system, where men benefit from both greater power and privilege and the social ideology that supports this privilege. Male violence is assumed to be perpetuated by peer support and a lack of societal controls regulating male violence (e.g., lack of police response to domestic violence, lack of consequences in the legal system). Other sociocultural theories have suggested that family violence is linked to frustration resulting from a lack of social/economic power outside the family; a man in this position might be more likely to use violence to exert control in at least one area of his life. Other theorists suggest that cultural norms about violence and gender might contribute to the problem (for a review, see Bersani & Chen, 1988; Gelles & Straus, 1979; Holtzworth-Munroe, Meehan, Rehman, & Marshall, 2002).

Recent writers have suggested an ecological model, which attempts to provide a more comprehensive, complex view of violence and seeks to emphasize the contextual framework of the individuals/populations being studied. Here, it is assumed that violence within a couple cannot be understood without taking into account the complex context of their situation or the characteristics of the individuals, couple, culture, and society (see Pence & Paymar, 1993;

Perilla, 1999; Perilla, Bakeman, & Norris, 1994). This approach may prove especially useful in the understanding and development of effective interventions for immigrant populations. However, immigrant groups are unfortunately largely absent from current research.

Culture and Domestic Violence

Because few studies have examined immigrants to the United States and their experiences with domestic violence, it is impossible to make any conclusive statements about the subject from a solid empirical base. A host of problems likely contributes to this vacuum (see Yoshihama, 2001). Domestic violence, by its nature, is very difficult to research. Trying to understand domestic violence among immigrant populations is even harder, as many immigrants who do not speak English fluently are excluded from research studies. Furthermore, they may not have access to studies, may not be recruited by researchers, or may be mistrustful and hesitant to participate.

When immigrant/minority groups are included in research studies, they are often amalgamated into one group. For instance, the category "Hispanic" or "Latino" typically incorporates any number of individuals from different cultural traditions, with distinct histories and economic, religious, and social norms. Different levels of acculturation can also profoundly influence individual and community norms. Early indications show that both country of origin and acculturation level are associated with different patterns of risk for domestic violence (Kaufman-Kantor, Jasinski, & Aldarondo, 1994; Sorenson & Telles, 1991). Despite these limitations, this section will summarize the existing research in this area.

Research on domestic violence has primarily concentrated on African American and white samples. Most studies have found that there is more violence in African American groups. However, many of the studies find that these results no longer hold after considering socioeconomic status. For instance, African Americans from higher economic groups have lower rates of domestic violence than whites. These findings suggest that a complex relationship between cultural factors such as ethnicity and socioeconomic status affects the prevalence of domestic violence (Cazenave & Straus, 1990; for a review, see Holtzworth-Munroe, Smutzler, & Bates, 1997).

The handful of other research studies on domestic violence has focused primarily on Latinos. In their comparison of violence rates among Cuban, Mexican, Puerto Rican, and white couples, Kaufman-Kantor and colleagues (1994) found that acculturation level also plays a major role in domestic violence. This finding was supported by Sorenson and Telles (1991), who also demonstrated a significant relationship between acculturation and domestic violence among Latino groups. Both studies showed that being born in the United States (whether Latino or white) was a significant risk factor for increased violence. In addition, Sorenson and Telles found that participants who chose to take the interview in Spanish, as opposed to English, had lower rates of violence. These studies suggest that Latinos who retain closer connections with their native culture have a decreased risk of violence than those who are more acculturated to the United States. However, further research is needed to clarify the role of acculturation in domestic violence.

Special Problems Immigrant Women Face

Although the previously mentioned studies found that some protective factors in recent immigrant populations mitigate the effects of domestic violence, there are also a number of conditions that make immigrant women especially vulnerable to domestic violence. Although further research is needed to understand these relationships more fully, the following factors put immigrant women at risk for domestic violence.

Isolation and Fear

Any woman in an abusive situation faces an overwhelming, frightening set of circumstances should she decide to leave the situation or get help. For an immigrant, especially an immigrant without documentation, this situation is likely to be more extreme (see Abraham, 2000; Ayyub, 2000; Bauer, Rodriguez, Quiroga, & Flores-Ortiz, 2000; Dasgupta, 2000).

Two major obstacles for battered immigrants include limited access to information and social isolation. For instance, immigrants often have no knowledge of support systems such as shelters and nonprofit legal organizations. Lack of fluency in English contributes to their limited access to resources, as well as making it difficult to come forward even when they do know about legal rights and services (Bauer et al., 2000). Furthermore, immigrant women are often forced into further isolation by abusive partners who purposely discourage communication with family and new friends to increase the woman's dependence on the batterer (Abraham, 2000; Jacobson & Gottman, 1998). When the woman is an immigrant without family nearby or people who could offer her support, the abusive situation is likely to be even graver.

Isolation among batterers is a risk factor for domestic violence as well. The batterer, if he is an immigrant, is also likely to experience social isolation, which has been related to violence in men (Magdol, Moffitt, Caspi, & Newman, 1997). Consistent with this finding, Cazenave and Straus (1990) found that social connection was associated with decreased violence in African American couples. Interestingly, social involvement (the number of groups to which an individual belongs) is not predictive of violence. On the other hand, individuals involved with peers who support the use of aggression or who are involved in delinquent behavior show increased violence (Holtzworth-Munroe et al., 2002).

Related to the limited access to information and social isolation they experience, many undocumented immigrants are extremely afraid of being deported and may not seek help for fear of discovery by the authorities. They often also fear for their children; in many situations, the woman may lose custody of her children if she leaves the batterer (see Bauer et al., 2000; Goldman, 1999). These factors are likely to make the use of services even lower among immigrants than among other minority groups, who also show reluctance in their use of mental health services (Sue & Sue, 2003).

Finally, it should not be forgotten that the social climate in the United States interacts with the political climate, in which scathing discussions about immigrants frequently occur. Racist, scapegoating messages only increase the fear, hesitancy, and isolation of the immigrant community. As a result, many immigrant women list racism as a barrier to seeking help for domestic violence (Bauer et al., 2000).

Dependence on the Batterer

Many immigrant women depend on their partners for both economic support and legitimization of their status in this country (Immigration and Naturalization Service, 2002; Thomas, 2000). Often the fear, social isolation, and limited access to information that these women experience contribute to an increased dependency on their partners (Walker, 1980). This dependence places them at risk for domestic violence (Edelson, 2000). In particular, isolated women whose status in their families is lower than that of their male partners are more likely to be abused.

Economic dependence on a partner also limits women's ability to leave abusive situations by limiting their resources outside of the home (Wetzel & Ross, 1983). One survey conducted in Australia found that 42% of battered women reported staying with their partners for economic reasons (see Women's Issues and Social Empowerment, 2003). Not only does economic dependence often prevent women from leaving abusive situations; it also causes them to return to the violence. In fact, a U.S. survey of more than 1,000 battered women revealed that abused women who depended on their spouses economically almost always returned to the batterers after leaving the abusive situation (Aguirre, 1985). These findings highlight the significance of dependence as it relates to domestic violence. Although they do not address immigrant women in particular, they demonstrate the risk immigrant women face if they move to a new environment depending both legally and economically on their spouses.

Traditional Values

Many recent immigrants to the United States value traditional cultural practices such as the maintenance of rigid sex roles that encourage women's dependence on their spouses. These values are often thought to contribute to both the occurrence of violence and the woman's acceptance of it (Schecter, 1982; Wetzel & Ross, 1983). However, the research on this topic is contradictory. In one review of literature that examined the link between women's traditional sex role beliefs and abuse, only about half of the studies found a relationship (Hotaling & Sugarman, 1986). A stronger finding emerging in the literature shows that certain attitudes in men are related to violence against their female partners. These attitudes include support of violence, approval of force against women, and hostile, adversarial views toward women (see Holtzworth-Munroe et al., 2002; Sugarman & Frankel, 1996). Thus, separating traditional values from the approval of violence toward women is an important distinction when investigating risk factors for domestic violence among immigrant populations. This approval of violence in combination with women's social isolation and dependence on their male partners places immigrant women at significantly greater risk for domestic violence.

The Immigration Process

The social isolation, limited access to information, and dependence on their partners that many immigrant women experience make the immigration process described in Part 1 of this chapter extremely difficult. First of all, many immigrants come from areas that have significantly different legal systems. For instance, they may have difficulty understanding and participating in the U.S. common-law system, which emphasizes oral testimony (see Goldman, 1999). They also may distrust the legal system based on experiences from their countries of origin or from stories about the INS.

Second, women's social isolation and economic dependence on their partners form barriers to seeking legal assistance. Legal assistance is typically necessary to assess and implement the appropriate immigration process. Immigrants who lack fluency in English and social support often have difficulty finding legal organizations that can assist them in this process.

Finally, when battered immigrants find legal assistance and proceed with the appropriate immigration process, they often endure psychological trauma that interferes with this process. For instance, as described in Part 1, VAWA

cancellation requires that battered immigrants testify in front of a judge and an INS trial attorney. Battered immigrants often feel too embarrassed or ashamed to publicly discuss the level of abuse they endured. Also, some immigration judges and trial attorneys do not fully understand the dynamics of domestic violence and often ask inappropriate questions of the battered immigrants testifying before them. For example, women are often asked why they stayed with their batterers or why they decided to marry their batterers, which sounds as though the victim is to blame for the abuse.

Furthermore, battered immigrants may suffer from post-traumatic stress disorder (PTSD). Common symptoms of PTSD include memory loss, physiological reactivity to reminders of the abuse, and intense psychological distress, which are exacerbated by stress or recalling stressful events (American Psychiatric Association, 1994). These symptoms impair the immigrant's ability to testify under cross-examination, which can further exacerbate the disorder.

PART 3. DOMESTIC VIOLENCE WITHIN SPECIFIC ETHNIC GROUPS

Thus far, domestic violence with immigrant women has been discussed in general terms. In particular, immigrant groups can be vulnerable to domestic violence due to immigration stresses, language difficulties, economic concerns, and social isolation. As culture can influence some of the factors that put immigrant women at risk for domestic violence, this section will examine the role of domestic violence within specific ethnic groups. Because little research exists in this area, we will focus on those ethnic groups most often studied: Asian American and Latino groups.

Asian Americans

The model minority myth presumes that Asian Americans experience very few problems. This stereotype also prevails within the domestic violence literature (Masaki & Wong, 1997; Preisser, 1999; Yick, 2001). However, Asian Americans do experience domestic violence. The problem may be masked by the aggregation of different Asian groups (Yoshihama, 2001).

The term "Asian" encompasses 30 different ethnic groups. Thus, the differences between the Asian groups can be lost, which also occurs with the term "Latina" (Yoshihama, 2001). It is essential to consider these differences when reading the following research findings.

Several factors have been shown to contribute to the cycle of domestic violence among Asian Americans. Asian American batterers report that their reasons for abuse include immigration stresses, racism, and the change in status they experience after immigrating to the United States (Masaki & Wong, 1997). In addition, Asian culture can prevent battered women from seeking assistance, as domestic violence is seen as a family issue (Abraham, 2000). The Asian American immigrant family would "lose face," which means losing status and respect in the community, if the woman ever told anyone about the abuse (Bauer et al., 2000; Tran & des Jardins, 2000). If Asian American women overcome this expectation and seek help, they perceive many social services for women as culturally insensitive, which can further deter them from using these services.

When considering domestic violence among immigrant women, it is also important to note the legal status of the batterers, as USC/LPR batterers will use their status in the United States to control immigrant women (Masaki & Wong, 1997). Abusers will use threats of deportation and/or separation from the children to keep women in the relationship (Sharma, 2001). In these cases, female immigrants believe they are dependent on their American husbands for visa sponsorship, even though the VAWA stipulates that if an immigrant is being abused by her husband, she can petition on her own behalf (Perilla, 1999).

Korean Immigrants

Korean immigrants form one Asian immigrant group that has received some research attention. Korean culture, like that of some other Asian cultures, is patriarchal, collectivistic, and influenced by Confucian values (Yick, 2001). These characteristics promote the belief that women are submissive and may be subjected to degrading treatment from their husbands. Korean immigrant women are thought to be at increased risk for domestic violence because of their husbands' strong adherence to traditional attitudes, which promote this subservience to their husbands (Yoshioka, DiNoia, & Ullah, 2001). If a woman is beaten, she is forbidden from telling anyone, as it would bring shame to the family and to the wife because it is presumed that she did something to deserve the beating. As the head of the household, the husband controls the dissemination of information, which also serves to conceal the domestic violence (Yick, 2001).

If a woman wanted to leave an abusive situation, she would feel societal pressure against leaving, as Asian culture frowns on divorce or separation. This expectation is consistent with Confucianism, which stresses harmony and interdependence. This value contrasts with U.S. culture, which stresses individuality (Sharma, 2001). The value of interdependence discourages women from Asian cultures from leaving abusive situations, as they would also be considered "bad mothers" for leaving the family (Yick, 2001).

In addition to the effects of cultural values, economic hardship has been shown to contribute to abuse within the Korean community. Song (1996) conducted a study of 150 Korean immigrant women in Chicago, Illinois. Fifty-eight percent of the abused women reported that their husbands had experienced downward economic mobility. Furthermore, during the 3rd to 5th years postimmigration, three times as many Korean women experienced abuse. Other studies have found similar time frames, supporting the economic stress of immigration as a factor in domestic violence for Korean immigrants (Song, 1996).

Vietnamese Immigrants

Vietnamese immigrants have also been studied in regard to domestic violence. Like Korean families, Vietnamese families view domestic violence as a private family matter (Bui & Morash, 1999). They also perceive the police and courts as sources of oppression. These perceptions potentially influence help-seeking behaviors.

Interestingly, in a study of 10 Vietnamese immigrant women, the women rejected their gender roles and expressed positive views of divorce, though they also did not think of divorced women as good role models (Bui & Morash, 1999). However, this finding is contradicted by Yoshioka et al. (2001), who found that Vietnamese immigrants were more likely than other Asian groups to endorse male privilege and less likely to endorse leaving their husbands. Vietnamese immigrants also reported witnessing more marital violence than did Korean and Chinese immigrants. Thus, it seems that although some Vietnamese immigrant women reject traditional gender roles, Vietnamese immigrants experience more domestic violence and are less likely to leave their husbands relative to other Asian groups.

Indian Immigrants

Asian Indian culture is very restrictive regarding the role of women. The culture's denial of domestic violence combined with having an immigrant status complicates abusive situations for Indian immigrant women (Dasgupta & Warrier, 1996). Research examining domestic violence among Indian immigrants has focused on case studies. In particular, cases of wife-burning have received some attention (Singh & Unnithan, 1999).

Two cases of wife-burning took place in the Dallas-Fort Worth, Texas, area (Singh & Unnithan, 1999). In one case, Mr. Varghese was charged with killing his wife by pouring gasoline on her and lighting a match. He claimed that his wife had done this to herself in a suicide attempt. The jury found him guilty of first-degree murder and sentenced him to life in prison. In another case of wife-burning, Mr. Aziz was convicted of voluntary manslaughter for killing his wife. He also poured gasoline on her and lit a match. Mr. Aziz claimed not to remember setting his wife on fire. Both of these cases occurred within traditional Indian marriages in which women are discouraged from leaving their marriages (Singh & Unnithan, 1999). Caution should be taken in reviewing these two cases, as they are not indicative of all Indian immigrant families.

In addition to spousal abuse, Indian women also may experience abuse from their in-laws, particularly from the mother-in-law. Families from India not only recognize a gender hierarchy,

but also a generational hierarchy (Fernandez, 1997; Preisser, 1999). In other words, older women are given the same authority as men and may be asked to supervise their daughters-in-law. This hierarchy places younger Indian women at risk for physical abuse by their mothers-in-law as well as their husbands.

Physical abuse is not the only concern for immigrant women. Marital rape is seen as a "right" in Asian Indian culture (Abraham, 1999; Raj & Silverman, 2002). Although physical abuse is perceived as violence, Asian Indian communities are reluctant to acknowledge sexual coercion as violence (Dasgupta, 2000). Male aggression is perceived as normal, and the woman's silence during the rape is construed by the man as "shyness" (Abraham, 1999; Raj & Silverman, 2002). However, women who experience marital rape are often too shocked to say anything, and they know that their silence is necessary to maintain the marriage (Abraham, 1999).

Even though the situation seems bleak for Indian immigrants who have been abused, they seem to be resisting the abuse. Indian immigrants were asked about their responses to abuse (Mehrota, 1999). The women reported fighting back in ways that felt comfortable to them. The most common method was refusing to cook (Mehrota, 1999). Some women refused to have sexual relations with their husbands. Other women had no source of income and would take small amounts of money from their husbands' wallets. Women whose husbands refused to allow them to contact their families in India would call their families from public phones (Mehrota, 1999). Though these forms of resistance may not be typical for an average American woman, these women are clearly not passively accepting the abuse (Mehrota, 1999).

The Asian Women's Self-Help Association (ASHA) in Washington, D.C., is an agency that is helping to serve South Asian Indian immigrants (Preisser, 1999). ASHA was founded with the idea that South Asian women would be more comfortable disclosing domestic violence to women of similar ethnic backgrounds (Preisser, 1999). The agency provides a range of services: peer counseling, legal information, emergency medical and shelter information, and loans (Preisser, 1999). Evaluations of the effects of the services offered by this agency could serve to promote the disclosure and treatment of domestic violence for Indian and other immigrant groups.

Latinas

As with Asian Americans, Latino immigrants represent a vast number of diverse ethnic groups. A few studies have examined domestic violence within these groups. Aldarondo, Kantor, and Jasinski (2002) compared risk factors for more than 1,000 Mexican, Mexican American, Puerto Rican, and white families. Mexican American and Puerto Rican families reported experiencing greater rates of domestic violence than the Mexican and white families. Interestingly, Mexican and Mexican American women were less likely than their husbands to report violence, possibly due to greater personal vulnerability for immigrant women (Aldarondo et al., 2002). Consistent with this study, Sorenson and Telles (1991) found that the rates of domestic violence were higher for Mexican Americans born in the United States than for Mexican and white women. Thus, Mexican American families seem to be at greater risk for domestic violence than Mexican families.

When domestic violence occurs among Latino families, some beliefs and experiences with Latino cultures prevent Latina immigrant women from seeking help. For instance, similarly to the values of some Asian cultures, the value of *familismo* stresses family unity and deters women from leaving their families. Some of these women also emigrated from countries where the police typically do not respond to domestic disputes, so many battered Latina women feel as though the police or medical professionals would not assist them (Bauer et al., 2000). Thus, some of the women develop a sense of fatalism regarding the domestic violence, as if the violence were inevitable and a "cross to bear" (Bauer et al., 2000; Perilla, 1999).

Finally, as with other immigrant groups, factors related to living in the United States also prevent Latina women from leaving abusive situations. For instance, one qualitative study found that most Latina immigrants reported feeling isolated after the immigration (Bauer et al., 2000). Furthermore, limited fluency in English and the need for interpreters create distance between women and service providers (Bauer et al., 2000). Latina immigrants also felt that their interactions with health care professionals had undertones of racism and prejudice (Bauer et al., 2000). These experiences in the United States make it exceedingly difficult for immigrant women to find the support they need to leave an abusive partner.

CONCLUSION

This chapter has reviewed the major factors that contribute to domestic violence among immigrant women. In particular, immigrant women are especially vulnerable to abuse because of the social isolation, limited access to information, legal and economic dependency on spouses, and traditional attitudes toward women that they often experience. Although these experiences place them at risk for domestic violence and form great obstacles to leaving abusive situations, several legal remedies exist to aid battered immigrants. In addition to the use of social service organizations and legal services, battered immigrants can gain independence from their batterers by obtaining legal status in the United States. This chapter discussed three means of obtaining legal status: the self-petitioning process, VAWA cancellation, and the U visa.

Though this chapter describes the legal and psychological aspects of domestic violence among immigrant women, research in this area is relatively new. Thus, future research is needed to understand which aspects of culture lead to domestic violence and which ones protect against it. For instance, examining families who immigrate to the United States but do not experience domestic violence might shed some light on protective factors. Also, prospective studies focusing on the course of immigration could better address the characteristics of domestic violence among different groups of immigrant families. Finally, research examining the effectiveness of community agencies that serve battered immigrants would assist in the development of better treatment programs. At the community level, it is also important to raise consciousness about domestic violence in immigrant communities so that people become aware of the problem and the services available to women (Perilla, 1999). These efforts can help eliminate domestic violence for immigrants in the United States.

NOTES

1. An applicant for citizenship must demonstrate that he or she is a person of good moral character and prove that he or she has had his or her status for 5 or 3 years depending on how lawful status was obtained.

2. To be admissible into the United States, an immigrant must provide a medical exam, not be convicted of certain crimes, and demonstrate that he or she will not be a public charge to the U.S. government.

3. For years, the Immigration and Naturalization Service issued lawful permanent residents an alien registration card that was green. Now the lawful permanent resident card is pink; however, individuals still refer to this identity document as a green card.

4. Good moral character in immigration law has a technical meaning and is determined by honesty and criminal records. "The INS may decide that a person lacks good moral character if he should have, but has not filed income tax returns; if he should have, but did not register for Selective Service; if he is an alcoholic; if he has had children out of wedlock or committed adultery; if he has failed to pay child support; if he has gotten any public benefits that he wasn't entitled to get; or if he is found to have lied in his answers to any of the questions on the naturalization application, among the more common reasons" (Immigrant Legal Advocacy Project, 2002).

5. If the battered spouse or child live abroad, the batterer must be an employee of the U.S. government or a member of the uniformed forces or the battered spouse or child must have been subjected to battery or extreme cruelty in the United States.

6. Some children can apply as principal applicants or as derivatives/beneficiaries of the principal applicant's petition.

7. The names and details of each case study have been altered to protect the confidentiality of the individuals described.

8. The criminal activity referred to for the U visa involves the following or any similar activity in violation of federal, state, or local criminal law: rape, torture, trafficking, incest, domestic violence, sexual assault, abusive sexual contact, prostitution, sexual exploitation, female genital mutilation (FGM), being held hostage, peonage, involuntary servitude, slave trade, kidnapping, abduction, unlawful criminal restraint, false imprisonment, blackmail, extortion, manslaughter, murder, felonious assault, witness tampering, obstruction of justice, perjury or attempt, conspiracy, or solicitation to commit any of the above-mentioned crimes.

9. A child who is not a principal applicant must be under the age of 16 to qualify for a U visa.

10. For list of qualifying crimes, see footnote 8.

11. Some authors have raised the point that women also batter men. Although this is admittedly the case, we considered this discussion to be outside the scope of this chapter. Because men battering women is the most common and destructive scenario (Tjaden & Thoennes, 1998), we have used this language here. Of course, it is also the case that battering occurs in same-sex relationships.

REFERENCES

Abraham, M. (1999). Sexual abuse in South Asian immigrant marriages. *Violence Against Women, 5,* 591–618.

Abraham, M. (2000). Isolation as a form of marital violence: The South Asian immigrant experience. *Journal of Social Distress and the Homeless, 9,* 221–236.

Aguirre, B. E. (1985). Why do they return? Abused wives in shelters. *Social Work, 30,* 350–354.

Aldarondo, E., Kantor, G. K., & Jasinski, J. L. (2002). A risk marker analysis of wife assault in Latino families. *Violence Against Women, 8,* 429–454.

American Psychiatric Association. (1994). *Diagnostic and statistical manual of mental disorders* (4th ed.). Washington, DC: American Psychiatric Association.

Ayyub, R. (2000). Domestic violence in the South Asian Muslim immigrant population in the United States. *Journal of Social Distress and the Homeless, 9,* 237–248.

Bauer, H. M., Rodriguez, M. A., Quiroga, S. S., & Flores-Ortiz, Y. G. (2000). Barriers to health care for abused Latina and Asian immigrant women. *Journal of Health Care for the Poor and Underserved, 11,* 33–44.

Bersani, C. A., & Chen, H. (1988). Sociological perspectives on family violence. In V. B. Hasselt, R. L. Morrison, A. S. Bellack, & M. Hersen (Eds.), *Handbook of family violence* (pp. 57–86). New York: Plenum.

Bui, H. N., & Morash, M. (1999). Domestic violence in the Vietnamese immigrant community: An exploratory study. *Violence Against Women, 5,* 769–795.

Cazenave, N. A., & Straus, M. A. (1990). Race, class, network embeddedness, and family violence: A search for potent support systems. In M. A. Straus & R. J. Gelles (Eds.), *Physical violence in American families* (pp. 321–339). New Brunswick, NJ: Transaction.

The Commission on Domestic Violence. (1997). *Statistics.* Accessed August 10, 2003, from http://www.abanet.org/domviol/stats.html

Dasgupta, S. D. (2000). Charting the course: An overview of domestic violence in the South Asian community in the United States. *Journal of Distress and the Homeless, 9,* 173–185.

Dasgupta, S. D., & Warrier, S. (1996). In the footsteps of "Arundhati": Asian Indian women's experience of domestic violence in the United States. *Violence Against Women, 2,* 238–259.

Dutton, D. G. (1995). *The batterer.* New York: Basic Books.

Edelson, J. L. (2000, February). *Primary prevention and adult domestic violence.* Paper presented at the meeting of the Collaborative Violence Prevention Initiative, San Francisco, CA.

Fernandez, M. (1997). Domestic violence by extended family members in India: Interplay of gender and generation. *Journal of Interpersonal Violence, 12,* 433–455.

Gelles, R. J., & Straus, M. A. (1979). Determinants of violence in the family: Toward a theoretical integration. In W. R. Burr, F. I. Nye, S. K. Steinmetz, & M. Wilkinson (Eds.), *Contemporary theories about the family* (pp. 549–581). New York: Free Press.

Goldman, M. (1999). The Violence Against Women Act: Meeting its goals in protecting battered immigrant women? *Family and Conciliation Courts Review, 37,* 375–392.

Holtzworth-Munroe, A., Meehan, J. C., Rehman, U., & Marshall, A. D. (2002). Intimate partner violence: An introduction for couple therapists. In A. S. Gurman & N. S. Jacobson (Eds.), *Clinical handbook of couple therapy* (3rd ed., pp. 441–463). New York: Guilford Press.

Holtzworth-Munroe, A., Smutzler, N., & Bates, L. (1997). A brief review of the research on husband violence: Part III. Sociodemographic factors, relationship factors, and differing consequences of husband and wife violence. *Aggression & Violent Behavior, 2,* 285–307.

Hotaling, G., & Sugarman, D. (1986). An analysis of risk markers in husband to wife violence: The current state of knowledge. *Violence and Victims, 1,* 101–124.

Immigrant Legal Advocacy Project. (2002). *US Citizenship.* Accessed August 10, 2003, from http:// immigrantlegaladvocacy.org/citizenship .html

Immigration and Naturalization Service. (2002). *Immigration and nationality act (Public Law 107-234).* Accessed August 10, 2003, from http://www.ins.usdoj.gov/lpBin/lpext.dll/inserts/slb/slb-1/slb-21?f=templates&fn=document-frame.htm#slb-act

Jacobson, N. S., & Gottman, J. M. (1998). *When men batter women.* New York: Simon & Schuster.

Kaufman-Kantor, G., Jasinski, J. L., & Aldarondo, E. (1994). Sociocultural status and incidence of marital violence in Hispanic families. *Violence and Victims, 9,* 207–222.

Magdol, L., Moffitt, T. E., Caspi, A., & Newman, D. L. (1997). Gender differences in partner violence in a birth cohort of 21-year-olds: Bridging the gap between clinical and epidemiological approaches. *Journal of Consulting and Clinical Psychology, 65,* 68–78.

Masaki, B., & Wong, L. (1997). Domestic violence in the Asian community. In E. Lee (Ed.), *Working with Asian Americans: A guide for clinicians* (pp. 439–451). New York: Guildford Press.

Mehrota, M. (1999). The social construction of wife abuse: Experiences of Asian Indian women in the United States. *Violence Against Women, 5,* 619–640.

Passel, J. (2002). *New estimate of the undocumented population in the United States.* In Migration Information Source. Accessed August 10, 2003, from http://www.migrationinformation.org/Feature/display.cfm?ID=19

Pence, E., & Paymar, M. (1993). *Education groups for men who batter: The Duluth model.* New York: Springer.

Perilla, J. L. (1999). Domestic violence as a human rights issue: The case of immigrant Latinos. *Hispanic Journal of Behavioral Sciences, 21,* 107–133.

Perilla, J. L., Bakeman, R., & Norris, F. H. (1994). Culture and domestic violence: The ecology of abused Latinas. *Violence and Victims, 9,* 325–339.

Preisser, A. B. (1999). Domestic violence in South Asian communities in America: Advocacy and intervention. *Violence Against Women, 5,* 684–699.

Raj, A., & Silverman, J. (2002). Violence against immigrant women: The roles of culture, context, and legal immigrant status on intimate partner violence. *Violence Against Women, 8,* 367–398.

Rounsaville, B. J. (1978). Theories of marital violence: Evidence from a study of battered women. *Victimology: An International Journal, 3,* 11–31.

Schecter, S. (1982). *Women and male violence: The visions and struggles of the battered women's movement.* London: Pluto Press.

Sharma, A. (2001). Healing the wounds of domestic violence: Improving the effectiveness of feminist therapeutic interventions with immigrant and racially visible women who have been abused. *Violence Against Women, 7,* 1405–1428.

Singh, R. N., & Unnithan, N. P. (1999). Wife burning: Cultural cues for lethal violence against women among Asian Indians in the United States. *Violence Against Women, 5,* 641–653.

Song, Y. I. (1996). *Battered women in Korean immigrant families: The silent scream.* New York: Garland.

Sorenson, S. B., & Telles, C. A. (1991). Self-reports of spousal violence in a Mexican-American and non-Hispanic white population. *Violence and Victims, 6,* 3–15.

Sue, D. W., & Sue, D. (2003). *Counseling the culturally diverse.* New York: John Wiley & Sons.

Sugarman, D. B., & Frankel, S. L. (1996). Patriarchal ideology and wife-assault: A meta-analytic review. *Journal of Family Violence, 11,* 13–40.

Thomas, E. K. (2000). Domestic violence in the African-American communities: A comparative analysis of two racial/ethnic minority cultures and implications for mental health service provision for women of color. *Psychology: A Journal of Human Behavior, 37,* 32–43.

Tjaden, P., & Thoennes, N. (1998). *Prevalence, incidence, and consequences of violence against women: Findings from the National Violence Against Women Survey.* Accessed August 10, 2003, from http://www.ncjrs.org/pdffiles/172 837.pdf

Tran, C. G., & des Jardins, K. (2000). Domestic violence in Vietnamese refugee and Korean immigrant communities. In J. L. Chin (Ed.), *Relationships among Asian American women* (pp. 71–96). Washington, DC: American Psychological Association.

U.S. Congress. (1994). *Violence Against Women Act of 1994 (Pub. L. 103–322/H.R. 3355 Title IV).* Washington, DC: U.S. Government Printing Office.

U.S. Congress. (2000). *Violence Against Women Act of 2000 (Pub. L. 106-386/H.R. 3244 Division B).* Washington, DC: U.S. Government Printing Office.

Walker, L. E. (1980). *The battered woman.* New York: Harper Perennial.

Wetzel, L., & Ross, M. A. (1983). Psychological and social ramifications of battering: Observations leading to a counseling methodology for victims of domestic violence. *Personnel and Guidance Journal, 61,* 423–428.

Women's Issues and Social Empowerment. (2003). *Domestic violence information manual.* Accessed August 10, 2003, from http://www.wise.infoxchange.net.au/DVIM/DVMyths.htm

Yick, A. (2001). Feminist theory and status inconsistency theory: Application to domestic violence in Chinese immigrant families. *Violence Against Women, 7,* 545–562.

Yoshihama, M. (2001). Immigrants-in-context framework: Understanding the interactive influence of socio-cultural contexts. *Evaluation and Program Planning, 24,* 307–318.

Yoshioka, M. R., DiNoia, J., & Ullah, K. (2001). Attitudes towards marital violence: An examination of four Asian communities. *Violence Against Women, 7,* 900–926.

26

RACE AND SEXUAL OFFENDING

An Overview

JENNIFER WHEELER

Sex Offender Treatment Program
Monroe Correctional Complex—Twin Rivers Unit, Monroe, WA

WILLIAM H. GEORGE

University of Washington

The white women of the South are in a state of siege. . . . Some lurking Demon who has watched for the opportunity to seize her; she is choked or beaten into insensibility and ravished, her body prostituted, her purity destroyed, her chastity taken from her. . . . Shall men . . . demand for the right to have a fair trial and be punished in the regular course of justice? So far as I am concerned he has put himself outside the pale of the law, human and divine.

> South Carolina Senator Ben Tillman, in his 1907
> speech before Congress arguing for the abandonment
> of due process for blacks accused of sex crimes
> against white women (as cited in Wiegman, 1993)

The stereotype of the African American male as a rapist, with the white female as "the flower of civilization he intends to violently pluck, and the white male as the heroic interceptor" (Wiegman, 1993), emerged with ferocity in the antebellum South. Racist sentiments associated with this stereotype were manifested by discriminatory legal sanctions against alleged black male rapists, and "justice" often took the form of violence—including the castration and execution of black men who were accused of sexually assaulting white women (Getman, 1984; Warner, 1980; Wiegman, 1993; Wyatt, 1992).

Data have since emerged to refute the stereotype of the black male as a "lurking Demon" waiting to sexually assault white female victims. Although perpetrators and victims of sex offenses[1] exist in every race and ethnic group, research has clearly demonstrated that perpetrators

391

and victims of sexual offenses are far more likely to be of the *same* race (known as *intraracial* offenses) than of *different* races (known as *interracial* offenses; Koch, 1995; O'Brian, 1987; U.S. Department of Justice, 1997). Research on potential racial differences in characteristics of sexual offenses (e.g., Kirk, 1975; LaFree, 1982) and in rates of victim reporting (e.g., Wyatt, 1992) has further elucidated the relationship between race and sexual offending.

Despite data that refute the stereotype of the black rapist/white victim, some lingering effects of this outdated myth may still persist (Giacopassi & Dull, 1986; Mann & Selva, 1979; Wriggins, 1983).[2] Specifically, people's attitudes and responses to sex offenses continue to be influenced by the race of both perpetrators and victims (e.g., Giacopassi & Dull, 1986; Hymes, Leinart, Rowe, & Rogers, 1993; Ugwuegbu, 1978). Such a selective focus on black sex offenders who perpetrate against white victims may result in harmful social consequences. For example, sex offenses perpetrated against non-white victims are less likely to be perceived as criminal acts (e.g., Cahoon, Edmonds, Spaulding, & Dickens, 1995; Williams & Holmes, 1981; Wyatt, 1992), and more severe legal sanctions are applied to black sex offenders than to white offenders (LaFree, 1980).

Given that people's attitudes and responses continue to be influenced by the race of sex offenders and their victims, it is crucial that our society's collective consciousness accurately reflect what is *known* about race and sex crimes. Toward this end, this chapter reviews relevant literature published in the last approximately 30 years on the subject of race and sexual offending. We begin with a review of the literature on the incidence of interracial and intraracial sex crimes, including historical efforts at collecting and explaining data on interracial versus intraracial rape and current rates of these offenses (including racial differences in perpetrator-victim dyads, characteristics of the offense, and rates of victim reporting). We then review research on the influence of race on people's attitudes toward and responses to sex offenses. This review includes data from college and community samples, data based on rape vignette experiments, data based on "mock jury" studies, and

data from the criminal justice system. We conclude with a discussion of the trends and implications of these data.

HISTORICAL DATA AND EXPLANATORY THEORIES

Amir (1971) was the first researcher to dispel the myth of the black male rapist "preying upon" white female victims. In his study of 646 rape incidents in Philadelphia, Amir found that 93% of rapes were intraracial; specifically, 77% were black offender-black victim (B/B), 16% were white offender-white victim (W/W), 4% were white offender-black victim (W/B), and 3% were black offender-white victim (B/W). Although these data would ultimately be shown to be unusual for their high rate of B/B rapes and comparatively low rate of W/W rapes, these data were the first to support the fact that rape is largely an intraracial phenomenon.

In the years following Amir's report, however, undue emphasis continued to be placed on the incidence of and explanatory theories for B/W rape. LaFree (1982) examined data collected between 1958 and 1977 to compare the relative rates of interracial (B/W and W/B) rapes. Interracial rapes represented the minority (25%) of the total number of rapes during that time (but because the author's focus was the comparison of B/W to W/B rapes, the lower base rate of interracial rapes received no comment). Of the 25% of rapes that were interracial, the incidence of B/W rapes was higher than that of W/B rapes. According to LaFree, these differences were *not* a result of differences in reporting rates for B/W versus W/B rapes, but rather a result of the fact that the "white dominated sexual stratification system has enshrined the white female as a symbol of sexual attractiveness, freedom, and power." Thus, LaFree's theory ascribes the motivation for B/W rape as black males' reverence for white females' symbolic attractiveness.

In addition to LaFree's explanatory theory for B/W rape, other explanations for the phenomenon of B/W rape emerged in the 1970s. For example, Curtis (1975, 1976) described the "normative model" of interracial rape, which suggested that rates of B/W rape could be expected to increase as a result of "legitimate social interaction" between black males and white females. Curtis (1975) also postulated the "conflict model" of interracial rape, which suggested that B/W rape was "the penultimate way for a black male to serve up revenge on his white male oppressor." Compared with other racial dyads, B/W rape received particular attention in the rape literature—despite earlier data demonstrating that this was the *least* representative rapist/victim racial dyad (Amir, 1971).

While early literature on interracial versus intraracial rape focused on the incidence rates of various racial dyads, a subsequent approach examined perpetrators' choice of victims to demonstrate the "predominance of inter-racial crime for black offenders" (Wilbanks, 1985). Using data from the 1981 National Crime Victimization Survey (NCVS), Wilbanks reported that although the majority (78%) of rapes were intraracial, 59% of black offenders chose white victims (compared with 95% of white offenders who chose white victims). Thus, Wilbanks suggests that black rapists "tend to choose white victims." The author hypothesizes that "black rapists are expressing hostility towards whites *and* women through rape, while whites are simply expressing hostility towards women" (Wilbanks, 1985). Thus, Wilbanks argues that it is misleading to merely examine overall rates of intraracial versus interracial rape and that the "choice of victim" approach highlights the "previously unexamined fact" of interracial (specifically B/W) rape.

In an effort to distill more up-to-date and accurate data about interracial versus intraracial rape, O'Brian (1987) conducted a structural analysis of U.S. Department of Justice statistics. O'Brien compared the *observed* proportions of victim-offender dyads (W/W, B/B, B/W, and W/B) with the *expected* proportions of each dyad based on the actual population of blacks and whites in the United States. Using this method, O'Brian found that intraracial rapes (W/W, B/B) occur 20% *more* often than is statistically expected and that observed rates of interracial rapes (B/W, W/B) are all much *lower* than would be statistically expected based on population rates (38% less for B/W rape, and 79% less for W/B rape). In other words, not only are base rates of intraracial rape much higher than those of interracial rape, the rates of intraracial rape are higher (and rates of interracial rapes much lower) than the rates we would expect to see based on the population distributions of black and white males and females in the United States. This type of analysis paved the way for subsequent analyses based on U.S. Department of Justice statistics.

CURRENT DATA ON INTRARACIAL AND INTERRACIAL SEX OFFENSES

Perpetrators

According to 1997 U.S. Department of Justice statistics, on an average day in the United States, about 234,000 convicted sex offenders are under the control of corrections agencies. Rape and sexual assault offenders represent slightly less than 5% of the total correctional population, and the majority of convicted sex offenders are not in prison but are under conditional supervision in the community.

Of those individuals who were arrested for rape in 1995, the racial distribution was similar to that for all arrests in the FBI's Uniform Crime Report (UCR): 56% were white, 42% were black, and 2% were of other races. Of those who were arrested for other sex offenses, the majority were white (75%; U.S. Department of Justice, 1997).

The racial distribution of incarcerated offenders is similar to the racial distribution of arrest rates. Among incarcerated rapists, 52% are white, 44% are black, and 4% are of other races. And among those incarcerated for sexual assault, 74% are white, 23% are black, and 3% are of other races (U.S. Department of Justice, 1997).

Compare these rates with those for individuals incarcerated for any violent crime: 48% are white, 48% are black, and 4% are of other races (U.S. Department of Justice, 1997). It is notable that there is a higher percentage of white sex offenders than would be expected based on the proportion of white males incarcerated for all violent crimes. West and Templer (1994) found that of black and white inmates, a disproportionate number of the white inmates were child molesters, rapists, and sex offenders. In fact, the combined information gathered from the FBI's arrest data, victim reports from the NCVS, court convictions data, and prison admissions data characterize the "typical" sex offender as more likely to be white than nonwhite (U.S. Department of Justice, 1997).

Victims

The NCVS (U.S. Department of Justice, 1997), which gathers information from victims that may not have been reported to law enforcement agencies, found no significant differences in rates of rape/sexual assault among racial groups. However, reports from incarcerated perpetrators indicate that victims of sexual offenses are more likely to have been white than is the case for victims of other violent crimes. This discrepancy may reflect racial differences in rates of reporting sex offenses and/or racial differences in rates of incarceration (both will be discussed later in this chapter). Among perpetrators who were incarcerated for raping or sexually assaulting a single victim, 68% to 76% report that their victim was white, whereas 20% to 28% report that their victim was black (U.S. Department of Justice, 1997). Data from the National Incident-Based Reporting System (NIBRS) indicate that 88% of rapes are intraracial (U.S. Department of Justice, 1997). Thus, the conclusion to be drawn from these data is that most rapes and sexual assaults involve a white offender–white victim dyad.

According to the U.S. Department of Justice statistics (1997), the W/W dyad also predominates among rates of a rare but sensationalistic crime—the sexual assault murder. These are murders that involve rape or other sex offenses, and they represent only 1.5% of all murders (of those with known circumstances). Although rare, sexual assault murders are particularly heinous crimes and often receive a disproportionate amount of media attention relative to other murders and sex crimes. Among known perpetrators of sexual assault murders committed between 1976 and 1994, 58% are white, 40% are black, and 2% are of other races. Individuals incarcerated for all types of murder are 48% white, 50% black, and 2% of another race. Compared with all murder victims, victims of sexual assault murders are substantially more likely to be white females (U.S. Department of Justice, 1997). Of these sexual assault murders,

80% were intraracial (55% were W/W, 24% were B/B), while 17% were interracial (15% were B/W, 2% were W/B).

In summary, all of these current data demonstrate the following: (a) the greater percentage of offenders incarcerated for sex crimes (including rape, sexual assault, and sexual assault murder) are white, (b) adjudicated sexual offenders report perpetrating against white victims more often than they perpetrated against victims of other races, and (c) rates of intraracial sex offenses are much higher than rates of interracial sex offenses.

Offense Type

Many authors have reported differential rates of interracial rape based on geographic region, year of study, age of victim, and other circumstances of the sexual assault (see Katz & Mazur, 1989, for review). For example, LaFree (1982) found that compared with W/W and B/B rapes, B/W rapes were more likely to involve strangers and to be public assaults (i.e., they do not occur in a private residence) and were less likely to occur at night.[3] Compared with W/W and B/W rapes (i.e., white-victim rapes), B/B rapes were less likely to involve college-educated victims and married women (which Lafree notes is confounded by differential rates of education and marriage for white vs. black women) and more likely to involve use of weapons (which Lafree suggests may reflect an expectation that black women are more likely to be armed than white women are).

Other research has found racial differences in the nature of the offender-victim relationship and the use of force or weapons during sexual assault. Heilbrun and Cross (1979) found that white rapists were increasingly likely to use force with increased familiarity with the victim, whereas for black rapists the likelihood of using force decreased with familiarity with the victim. Heilbrun and Cross note that it is not clear whether these data reflect differences in perpetrator aggression or differences in victim resistance.

With regard to the nature of the sexual offense (e.g., type of sexual acts perpetrated, adult vs. child victim), Kirk (1975) found that black offenders appeared have a significantly greater tendency to engage in penile-vaginal penetration as compared with white offenders, and black offenders also showed a nonsignificant trend to use physical violence during the event. Kirk notes that this data may reflect the fact that black offenders were more likely to perpetrate against adult females than were white offenders (34% and 11%, respectively).

West and Templer (1994) also found that in their sample of incarcerated sex offenders, a disproportionate number of rapists (i.e., who perpetrated against adult victims) were black and a disproportionate number of child molesters were white. However, overall in this sample, a disproportionate number of both rapists and child molesters were white.

Victim Reporting

In 1994 and 1995, the rate of rapes and sexual assaults reported to a law enforcement agency represented 32% of those reported in the NCVS (U.S. Department of Justice, 1997). Of the one third of rapes that are reported to law enforcement agencies, about one half are cleared by arrest, and about two thirds of those convicted of rape get a prison sentence (U.S. Department of Justice, 1997). Thus, incarcerated offenders represent, at the most, about 10% of the total number of perpetrators of sex offenses reported by victims in the NCVS. Although data based on victim report (i.e., NCVS) revealed no significant differences in rates of rape/sexual assault among racial groups, the assumption of this finding is that there are no racial differences in rates of reporting rape and sexual assault on the NCVS. This assumption may be invalid, given research that indicates that white women may report incidents of rape and sexual assault at higher rates than do black women (Howard, 1988; Wyatt, 1992), particularly as compared with black victims who were attacked by white perpetrators (Howard, 1988; Katz & Mazur, 1989).

In a study that investigated actual reporting rates among 55 women reporting 146 incidents of rape, Wyatt (1992) found no significant ethnic differences in the prevalence of rape, controlling for marital status and socioeconomic status (SES). However, African American women were significantly less likely to disclose incidents of sexual assault. The author suggests that this

discrepancy may be related to the victim's awareness of (a) the fact that the credibility of black rape victims has never been as well established as that of white rape victims (see Estrich, 1987), (b) racial discrimination in cases that get selected for prosecution, (c) racial discrimination in how rape cases are sanctioned (see LaFree, 1980), and/or (d) past racial incidents where ethnicity mediated police responses.

In a study of 100 women representing four ethnic groups (African American, Asian, Latina, and white), researchers asked subjects to indicate the likelihood that they would report a rape (Feldmann-Summers & Ashworth, 1981). White women indicated a greater likelihood to report rape than did minority women, and particularly a greater likelihood to report to a public agency (including the police) than did the minority women. Although these data do not report actual rates of reporting behavior among women of different ethnic groups, they do suggest that white women are more likely to report a sexual assault to law enforcement agencies than are women of other races. Thus, when evaluating data on rates of intraracial versus interracial sex offenses, it is important to consider that racial differences in these rates may not reflect actual incidence of rape/sexual assault but rather differences in the reporting of white versus black victims.

RACIAL INFLUENCES ON PEOPLE'S ATTITUDES ABOUT, PERCEPTIONS OF, AND RESPONSES TO SEX OFFENSES

Race—because of commonplace stereotypes and myths about blacks and rape—is likely to affect attitudes, perceptions, judgments, and reactions concerning rape. Researchers using a variety of methodologies and samples have investigated this possibility.

Race and Attitudes About Rape

Attitudes about rape constitute an important factor, which may affect racial differences in reporting rates of rape and sexual assault. An ample body of research conducted on adolescents and college students supports the fact that there are indeed gender and race differences in rape-supportive attitudes: specifically, to support the fact that African American women see themselves as unlikely to be believed as rape victims (Williams & Holmes, 1981).

In her sample of 932 adolescents, Howard (1988) found no racial differences in attitudes toward rape; however, there were racial differences in females' beliefs about the aftermath of the rape. White females were more likely than other groups to think that the police would try to catch the rapist, whereas black females were more likely than other groups to expect the police to question why they were walking alone. Overall, compared with white adolescents, black adolescents were more likely to endorse distrust of the police and less likely to turn to legal agencies after the assault. Obviously, such distrust may significantly reduce the probability of a black female reporting a sexual assault to law enforcement agencies.

In a 1993 study of three ethnic groups (101 African American, Hispanic, and non-Hispanic white rape victims, and 89 matched non-victims), Lefley, Scott, Llabre, and Hicks (1993) examined women's responses to rape. Findings indicated significant ethnic differences in women's responses to rape, including the following: (a) Hispanic women were most punitive toward the victim, whereas white women were the least punitive; (b) African American women were most likely to perceive the community as victim blaming; and (c) white victims of rape had lowest symptomatology severity scores compared with Hispanic and African American victims of rape. These findings suggest that following a rape, nonwhite females are more likely to blame themselves and more likely to perceive their community as blaming them, and they are likely to have more severe symptomatology. Each of these findings supports the possibility that nonwhite victims of rape may report rape less often than do white victims.

In a study of 449 college students, Giacopassi and Dull (1986) examined differences between black and white males' and females' acceptance of rape myths. Consistent with the findings of Field (1978) and Edmonds and Cahoon (1993), black students were generally more accepting of rape myths than were white students. Specifically, these authors found that black males were more accepting of rape

myths than any other race-sex grouping. The authors hypothesized that black males may respond more defensively when questioned about rape as a result of the historic stereotype of the black male as the "typical" offender in our society. Regarding interracial rape, white males were the group that was most accepting of the statement that one of the most common types of rape is a black offender attacking a white victim. Black females were more likely than white females to disagree with this statement, although, as the authors note, is it unclear which aspect of this statement black females disagree with (i.e., that black men commonly rape, that white women are commonly victims of rape, or that black men commonly rape white women). Nonetheless, these findings support racial differences in the acceptance of this myth regarding interracial rape.

In their sample of 109 college students, Cahoon et al. (1995) found that white females were more likely than black females to view sexual coercion in marriage as rape. These findings suggest that white women may be more likely than black women to define forced sex in a relationship as rape, and therefore perhaps white females would be more likely to report such an event to authorities.

It is possible that racial differences in perceptions of rape victims and acceptance of rape myths are changing as a result of increased consciousness regarding race and gender. For example, Carmody and Washington (2001) surveyed 623 undergraduate women and found no differences between whites and blacks in their acceptance of rape myths. In their sample of 383 college students, Kalof and Wade (1995) found no significant differences between white and black men in their attitudes about sex-role stereotyping, acceptance of interpersonal violence, acceptance of rape myths, or adversarial sexual beliefs. However, white females were significantly more likely than black females to endorse traditional, rape-supportive attitudes. These findings are different from earlier research that noted more traditional beliefs among black students. The authors attribute this finding to a nontraditional, feminist consciousness held by contemporary black women (specifically, black college women) and encourage further research on the evolving social differences between black and white males and females, which might influence sexual attitudes and behavior.

Contemporary white female college students may also be more aware of the greater likelihood of intraracial versus interracial rape. In a recent study of 145 black and white female college students, Smith, Edmonds, Cahoon, and Sappington (1997) asked subjects to indicate their belief that rape had occurred in eight hypothesized scenarios. Subjects were then asked to estimate the likelihood that males from each of four references groups (a black/white male from their college and a "typical" black/white male) would behave similarly in the described situation. Unlike earlier research, there were no significant differences between white and black females in deciding whether or not rape had occurred in each of the eight scenarios, suggesting that racial differences in acceptance of traditional rape myths may be dissipating. In addition, both black and white females rated white males as most likely to behave as described in each of the eight scenarios. Black college males were viewed least negatively, followed by "typical" black males, while "typical" white males were viewed most negatively. Among white females, college males were rated more positively than typical males. Although the authors suggest that these findings may reflect a desire among white females not to appear racist, these findings may also reflect that contemporary white females have a more accurate perception of rape and race; specifically, that white males are more likely to commit rape than black males and that intraracial rape is more common than interracial rape.

Race and Victim Blaming: Rape Vignette Experiments

Investigators have also examined racial influences in sexual assault through experimentation on perceptions of victim blame. In such experiments, participants are presented with a vignette describing a hypothetical rape in which the races of victim and perpetrator have been systematically varied; participants are subsequently queried about the incident.

Willis (1992) studied 83 female and 81 male white undergraduates. She found that participants perceived black victims as more responsible for date rape than stranger rape, but they did not so distinguish white victims. Also, participants attributed more blame toward black than white victims and toward victims who had dated a black defendant than victims who had not done so.

Foley, Evancic, Karnik, King, and Parks (1995) administered "forced sex encounter" vignettes to 53 female and 17 male mostly (83%) white students. The investigators found that date rape was perceived as less serious for a black victim than a white victim. In a subsequent study involving 126 students (76% white), Varelas and Foley (1998) found some support, though limited, for the black rapist and white victim myth about rape. Specifically, white respondents—but not black respondents—attributed less blame to the victim of a B/W rape than the victim of a B/B rape.

In a study of 335 predominantly white and Asian college students, George and Martinez (2002) varied victim and perpetrator race in a vignette depicting a stranger or acquaintance rape. These investigators found that victims of interracial rapes were generally seen as more blameworthy than were victims of intraracial rapes. Specifically, interracial rapes were less likely judged as "definitely rape" than were intraracial rapes. Victims of interracial rapes were rated as more culpable and less credible than victims of intraracial rapes. Conversely, perpetrators of interracial rapes were rated as less culpable than perpetrators of intraracial rapes.

In a study of 336 white and Latino college students, Jiminez and Abreu (2003) administered four different rape vignettes varying whether the victim and perpetrator were depicted as white or Latino(a). They found that white women exhibited more positive attitudes toward rape victims than Latina women, but only when the victim was white. The investigators attributed this finding to the possibility that white participants were susceptible to commonplace stereotypes about Latina women being more sexually "hot-blooded" and may have accordingly perceived the Latina victims as more blameworthy.

These experiments demonstrate that race continues to influence social perceptions about rape. Attributions of blame were determined by victim race and/or by dyad race. Thus, to varying degrees, these judgments suggest that long-standing stereotypes about race and rape remain active. Such findings attest to the durability of stereotypes despite countervailing epidemiological evidence about the infrequency of interracial rapes and unsoundness of race-based theories of rape.

Hypothetical Adjudication Outcomes: Mock Jury Studies

Hypotheses regarding the differential treatment of black and white offender-victim dyads in the criminal justice system have also been tested using "mock juries": that is, samples of people asked to act as if they were a jury, read case vignettes, and assign charges, verdicts, and sentencing. These studies are uniquely informative because the hypothetical "jury set" presumably fosters findings indicative of the mediating processes and resultant outcomes that would characterize adjudication of actual cases.

In a study of on 256 African American and white college students, Ugwuegbu (1978) examined the effect of offender/victim race on subjects' evaluations of the rape. Subjects read transcripts of a rape case, in which offender and victim race was manipulated, and were then asked to evaluate various aspects of the case. Ugwuegbu found that black defendants were rated as more culpable than white defendants were (especially when the evidence against the defendant was marginal as opposed to minimal or strong). A black offender who committed interracial rape was rated as most culpable when compared with a white offender committing interracial rape or black and white perpetrators of intraracial rape. In addition, victims were rated more negatively when they were racially dissimilar to the subject. These data all indicate that the dissimilarity of offender-victim race and subject-victim race influence the opinions of those asked to evaluate the culpability of victims and offenders of sexual assault.

Hymes et al. (1993) asked 96 white college students to read a legal brief about a rape in which the racial composition of the offender-victim dyad was manipulated. Subjects were then asked to assign a verdict to the case. The authors found that sentence recommendations made by male subjects did not significantly differ by racial composition of the offender-victim dyad. However, female subjects demonstrated several significant differences in their assignment of verdicts. Women recommended longer sentences for perpetrators of interracial rape (W/B and B/W) than for intraracial rape. The defendant's race had no impact on verdict or sentence recommendation in either interracial or intraracial cases. Thus, this study found that among female subjects, both black and white defendants were likely to be convicted if their victim was of a different race.

In a study that manipulated only the race of the victim, Miller and Hewitt (1978) also found that racial similarity of subject and victim appeared to be influential in "jurors" decisions. Subjects were shown a video of an interview of a black male defendant accused of assaulting a 13-year-old female. Consistent with other research, the authors found that subjects were significantly more likely to convict the defendant when they believed the victim was of their own race. Among black subjects, 80% convicted when the victim was black, versus 48% when the victim was white. Among white subjects, 65% convicted when the victim was white, while only 32% convicted when the victim was black. These data provide further evidence for racial bias in jurors' decision making.

Further data support the idea that racial similarity/dissimilarity regarding rape may influence "jurors'" decision making among African American subjects. Ugwuegbu (1976) studied the effects of racial dissimilarity of offender-victim dyads on the evaluations of 186 African American college students. Subjects read transcripts of a rape case, in which offender and victim race were manipulated, and were then asked to evaluate the defendant and victim. The author found that racial dissimilarity negatively affected subjects' evaluations of both defendants and victims. Specifically, subjects attributed more negative traits to a white defendant than to a black defendant; black defendants were rated as more intelligent than a white defendant; a black defendant was rated as less intelligent if he had raped a black women than if had raped a white woman; defendants in a W/W rape and a B/B rape were rated as equally intelligent, but a defendant in a W/B rape was rated as less intelligent; and black victims were seen as more sexually attractive than white victims. Thus, as the author concludes, the "prejudicial social evaluation of the out-group member is a two-sided, perhaps a universal phenomenon" (p. 199).

One study, which examined the effect of both race and attractiveness, failed to find an effect for race on subjects' assignment of sentences. In a study of 120 subjects randomly selected from the community, Barnett and Field (1978) asked subjects to read a legal case involving either a rape or a burglary, each of which varied the race and attractiveness of the defendant. In each case, subjects gave the unattractive defendant a significantly longer prison term than the attractive defendant, regardless of race. The data suggest the possibility that it is attractiveness, not race (although the two may be related in some cases), that differentially affects jurors' decision making.

Landwehr et al. (2002) presented 384 white undergraduates with a videotaped testimony of a white or black rape victim who described having been raped by a man she met at a bar. The investigator then presented students with videotape of a silent white or black defendant. The investigators found an interaction effect between race of victim and race of defendant such that respondents were more likely to believe a victim who claimed that a racially dissimilar defendant assaulted her. However, this was only true for respondents who also scored high on a "Right-Wing Authoritarianism Scale."

Wuensch, Campbell, Kesler, and Moore (2002) investigated racial bias in decisions made by mock jurors (161 white and 152 black undergraduates) evaluating a case of sexual harassment. Jurors were more favorable to litigants who were similar to them on race and gender. Racial bias polarized most among white jurors—highest for men, lowest for women. The investigators described this finding in terms of a cultural stereotype of black men as a sexual threat to white women and in differences in stereotyping of black and white women.

Generally, the previously mentioned studies yield evidence of juror bias and are consistent with the results of a meta-analytic review of mock jury studies. Sweeney and Haney (1992) found that perpetrator race biased sentencing decisions of jurors. This bias against the black rapist varies depending on the ambiguity of jury

instructions (Hill & Pfeifer, 1992; Rector, Bagby, & Nicholson, 1993), race of victim (Field, 1978), race of juror (Rector & Bagby, 1997), and racial match of victim and defendant (Hymes et al., 1993; Varelas & Foley, 1998; Willis, 1992).

Actual Adjudication Outcomes: Arrests, Convictions, and Sanctions

In an extensive study of 881 suspects charged with "forcible sexual offenses" between 1970 and 1975, LaFree (1980) analyzed the effect of the racial composition of the offender-victim dyad on the criminal selection process, from case report to final disposition. Overall, LaFree found that from case report to sentencing (a) the percentage of B/B assaults declined, (b) the percentage of W/W assaults remained constant, and (c) the percentage of B/W assaults steadily increased.

Although black suspects who were accused of assaulting white victims were no more likely to be arrested or found guilty as compared with other suspects, LaFree found significant racial differences in the sanctions assigned for these offenses. Specifically, compared with other suspects, black men who assaulted white women received more serious charges and longer sentences, they were more likely to have their cases classified as felonies, and they were more likely to be incarcerated in the state penitentiary for their crime. Among all of the cases, less than 32% of suspects who were arrested were eventually convicted, and less than 10% of these convictions resulted in a sentence of incarceration. Although B/B rape made up 45% of all of the reported rapes, B/B rapes accounted for only 26% of the men sentenced to prison and 17% of the men who received sentences of 6 years or more. In contrast, B/W rapes made up only 23% of the reported rapes, but accounted for 45% of the men sent to prison and 50% of the men who received sentences of 6 years or more. Finally, W/W rapes made up 36% of the arrests but only 29% of the men sent to prison and 33% of those men sentenced to 6 years or more. Lafree demonstrated that the racial composition of offender-victim dyad had a greater effect on decisions that measured the seriousness of the sex offense than on decisions regarding the suspect's guilt or innocence.

Bradmiller and Walters (1985) examined 89 cases of sexual assault and found that the most important predictor of the seriousness of the defendant's charge was the use of a weapon and whether or not the offender penetrated his victim. However, race of offender was also a significant predictor, such that black defendants were given more serious charges than were white defendants. This variable was a more significant predictor than the age of the victim (adult vs. child).

Discussion

Contemporary data indicate that the majority of sex offenders are white, the majority of victims of sex crimes are white, and the most common offender-victim racial dyad is W/W. This predominance of W/W rape may reflect differences in reporting rates between white and African American victims and/or differences in the response of the criminal justice system to white versus African American males. In turn, these differences in reporting rates and punitive sanctions may be due to differences in the attitudes of black and white males and females regarding interracial rape, intraracial rape, and defendant culpability. Ironically, these attitudes and responses may be base on misconceptions about base rates of interracial versus intraracial rape and by the persistence of the myth of the black male as a "lurking demon" waiting to attack white females.

That people's attitudes and responses to sex crimes are influenced by race remains problematic judicially. The deliberations that shape the criminal justice sequelae to rape can be construed as a cascading sequence of opportunities for racially prejudicial influences and discriminatory outcomes: a victim's decision to report rape, confidantes' willingness to support her decision, witnesses' willingness to testify, authorities' commitment and vigor in pursuing cases and trying perpetrators, a jury's decision to convict, a prosecutor's decision to recommend incarceration, and a judge's decision to impose incarceration penalties. At each of these opportunities, racial stereotypes and racism are likely to operate subtly, thereby potentially escaping detection. But collectively, these opportunities conduce toward patently discriminatory outcomes: Black women are discriminated against when their victimization experiences are minimized relative to white victims, and black men are discriminated against when they are more vigorously pursued and receive harsher sanctions for their crimes than white men.

Although data suggest that contemporary black and white males and females may have a more realistic appraisal of the relationship between race and sexual offending (Kalof & Wade, 1995; Smith et al., 1997), it is important to continue to raise our collective awareness with regard to the intraracial nature of sexual offending. This is especially true in legal settings. Only in this way can we hope to dispel the myth of the "lurking Demon" black rapist who waits to attack his white victim—a stereotype that has persisted throughout our nation's history and the sequelae of which continue to affect all of us at individual and institutional levels.

Notes

1. In this chapter, the terms "rape," "sexual assault," and "sex offender" are applied according to the definitions in the Bureau of Justice Statistics's *Sex Offenses and Offenders: An Analysis of Data on Rape and Sexual Assault* (U.S. Department of Justice, 1997). Rape refers to forced sexual intercourse; sexual assault refers to attacks in which unwanted sexual contact occurs, and may include statutory rape, forcible sodomy, lewd acts with children, fondling, molestation, and indecent liberties; sex offender refers to those offenders convicted of rape or sexual assault.

2. Such as the suggestion that African American males may have a genetic "proneness" to commit rape (Ellis, 1989).

3. W/B rapes were excluded from all of these analyses because their base rate was too low (2.2%).

References

Amir, M. (1971). *Patterns in forcible rape*. Chicago: University of Chicago Press.

Barnett, N. J., & Field, H. S. (1978). Character of the defendant and length of sentence on rape and burglary crimes. *The Journal of Social Psychology, 104,* 271–277.

Bradmiller, L. L., & Walters, W. S. (1985). Seriousness of sexual assault charges: Influencing factors. *Criminal Justice and Behavior, 12,* 463–484.

Cahoon, D. D., Edmonds, E. M., Spaulding, R. M., & Dickens, J. C. (1995). A comparison of the opinions of black and white males and females concerning the occurrence of rape. *Journal of Social Behavior & Personality, 10,* 91–100.

Carmody, D. C., & Washington, L. M. (2001). Rape myth acceptance among college women: The impact of race and prior victimization. *Journal of Interpersonal Violence, 16,* 424–436.

Curtis, L. A. (1975). *Violence, rape, and culture.* Lexington, MA: Lexington Books.

Curtis, L. A. (1976). Rape, race, and culture: Some speculations in search of a theory. In M. J. Walker & S. L. Brodsky (Eds.), *Sexual assault.* Lexington, MA: Lexington Books.

Edmonds, E. M., & Cahoon, D. D. (1993). The "new" sexism: Females' negativism toward males. *Journal of Social Behavior & Personality, 8,* 481–487.

Ellis, L. (1989). *Theories of rape: Inquiries into the causes of sexual aggression.* New York: Hemisphere Publishing.

Estrich, S. (1987). *Real rape.* Cambridge, MA: Harvard University Press.

Feldmann-Summers, S., & Ashworth, C. D. (1981). Factors related to intentions to report a rape. *Journal of Social Issues, 37,* 53–70.

Field, H. (1978). Attitudes towards rape: A comparative analysis of police, rapists, crisis counselors, and citizens. *Journal of Personality and Social Psychology, 36,* 156–179.

Foley, L. A., Evancic, C., Karnik, K., King, J., & Parks, A. (1995). Date rape: Effects of race of assailant and victim and gender of subjects on perceptions. *Journal of Black Psychology, 21,* 6–18.

George, W. H., & Martinez, L. (2002). Victim blaming in rape: Effects of victim and perpetrator race, type of rape, and participant racism. *Psychology of Women Quarterly, 26,* 110–119.

Getman, K. (1984). Sexual control in the slaveholding South: The implementation and maintenance of a racial caste system. *Harvard Women's Law Review, 7,* 115–153.

Giacopassi, D. J., & Dull, R. T. (1986). Gender and racial differences in the acceptance of rape myths within a college population. *Sex Roles, 15,* 63–75.

Heilbrun, A. B., & Cross, J. M. (1979). An analysis of rape patterns in white and black rapists. *The Journal of Social Psychology, 108,* 83–87.

Hill, E. L., & Pfeifer, J. E. (1992). Nullification instructions and juror guilt ratings: An examination of modern racism. *Contemporary Social Psychology, 16,* 6–10.

Howard, J. (1988). A structural approach to sexual attitudes: Inter-racial patterns in adolescents' judgments about sexual intimacy. *Sociological Perspectives, 31*(1), 88–121.

Hymes, R. W., Leinart, M., Rowe, S., & Rogers, W. (1993). Acquaintance rape: The effect of race of defendant and race of victim on white juror decisions. *The Journal of Social Psychology, 133,* 627–634.

Jiminez, J. A., & Abreu, J. M. (2003). Race and sex effects on attitudinal perceptions of acquaintance rape. *Journal of Counseling Psychology, 50,* 252–256.

Kalof, L., & Wade, B. H. (1995). Sexual attitudes and experiences with sexual coercion: Exploring the influence of race and gender. *Journal of Black Psychology, 21,* 224–238.

Katz, S., & Mazur, M. A. (1989) *Understanding the rape victim: A synthesis of research findings.* New York: John Wiley & Sons.

Kirk, S. A. (1975). The sex offenses of blacks and whites. *Archives of Sexual Behavior, 4,* 295–302.

Koch, L. W. (1995). Inter-racial rape: Examining the increasing frequency argument. *American Sociologist, 26,* 76–86.

LaFree, G. D. (1980). The effect of sexual stratification by race on official reactions to rape. *American Sociological Review, 45,* 842–854.

LaFree, G. (1982). Male power and female victimization: Toward a theory of inter-racial rape. *American Journal of Sociology, 88,* 311–328.

Landwehr, P. H., Bothwell, R. K., Jeanmard, M., Luque, L. R., Brown, R. L., & Breaux, M. (2002). Racism in rape trials. *Journal of Social Psychology, 142*(5), 667–669.

Lefley, H. P., Scott, C. S., Llabre, M., & Hicks, D. (1993). Cultural beliefs about rape and victims' response in three ethnic groups. *American Journal of Orthopsychiatry, 63,* 623–632.

Mann, O. R., & Selva, L. H. (1979). The sexualization of racism: The black as rapist and white justice. *Western Journal of Black Studies, 3,* 168.

Miller, M., & Hewitt, J. (1978). Conviction of a defendant as a function of juror-victim racial similarity. *The Journal of Social Psychology, 105,* 161–162.

O'Brian, R. (1987). The inter-racial nature of violent crimes: A reexamination. *American Journal of Sociology, 92,* 817–835.

Rector, N. A., & Bagby, R. M. (1997). Minority juridic decision making. *British Journal of Social Psychology, 36,* 69–81.

Rector, N. A., Bagby, R. M., & Nicholson, R. (1993). The effect of prejudice and judicial ambiguity on defendant guilt ratings. *Journal of Social Psychology, 133,* 651–659.

Smith, E. P., Edmonds, E. M., Cahoon, D. D., & Sappington, J. T. (1997). Black and white females' judgements of rape related to black and white males. *Psychology: A Journal of Human Behavior, 34,* 26–31.

Sweeney, L. T., & Haney, C. (1992). The influence of race on sentencing: A metaanalytic review of experimental studies. *Behavioral Sciences and the Law, 10,* 179–195.

Ugwuegbu, D. C. E. (1976). Black jurors' personality trait attribution to a rape case defendant. *Social Behavior and Personality, 4,* 193–201.

Ugwuegbu, D. C. E. (1978). Racial and evidential factors in juror attribution of legal responsibility. *Journal of Experimental Psychology, 15,* 133–146.

U.S. Department of Justice, Bureau of Justice Statistics. (1997). *Sex offenses and offenders: An analysis of data on rape and sexual assault.* U.S. Government Publications, Document No. NCJ-163392.

Varelas, N., & Foley, L. A. (1998). Blacks' and whites' perceptions of interracial and intraracial date rape. *Journal of Social Psychology, 138,* 392–400.

Warner, C. G. (1980). Rape and rape laws in historical perspective. In C. G. Warner (Ed.), *Rape and sexual assault: Management and intervention* (pp. 1–7). London: Aspen Publications.

West, J., & Templer, D. I. (1994). Child molestation, rape, and ethnicity. *Psychological Reports, 75,* 1326.

Wiegman, R. (1993). The anatomy of a lynching. In J. C. Fout & M. S. Tantillo (Eds.), *American sexual politics: Sex, gender, and race since the Civil War* (pp. 223–245). Chicago: University of Chicago Press.

Wilbanks, W. (1985). Is violent crime intra-racial? *Crime and Delinquency, 31,* 117–128.

Williams, J. E., & Holmes, K. A. (1981). *The second assault: Rape and public attitudes.* Westport, CT: Greenwood.

Willis, C. E. (1992). The effect of sex role stereotype, victim and defendant race, and prior relationship on rape culpability attributions. *Sex Roles, 26,* 213–226.

Wriggins, J. (1983). Rape, racism, and the law. *Harvard Women's Law Review, 6,* 103–122, 140–141.

Wuensch, K. L., Campbell, M. W., Kesler, F. C., & Moore, C. H. (2002). Racial bias in decisions made by mock jurors evaluating a case of sexual harassment. *Journal of Social Psychology, 142,* 587–600.

Wyatt, G. E. (1992). The sociocultural context of African American and white American women's rape. *Journal of Social Issues, 48,* 77–91.

27

CULTURAL ASPECTS OF SEXUAL AGGRESSION

RACHEL E. GOLDSMITH
University of Oregon

GORDON N. HALL
University of Oregon

CHRISTINA GARCIA
University of Oregon

JENNIFER WHEELER
Sex Offender Treatment Program, Monroe
Correctional Complex—Twin Rivers Unit, Monroe, WA

WILLIAM H. GEORGE
University of Washington

Sex offenders in the United States compose a heterogeneous group in terms of cultural and individual variables. However, research regarding sexual assault and abuse has all too often neglected cultural aspects (Futa, Hsu, & Hansen, 2001; Gahir & Garrett, 1999; Hackett, 2000; Romero, Wyatt, Loeb, Carmona, & Solis, 1999). Hall, Teten, and Sue (2002) explain that most theoretical models have not been adequately investigated using samples other than European Americans. Incorporating cultural considerations advances current theoretical models of sexual assault and abuse and informs treatment, intervention, and prevention (Hall et al., 2002).

In general, the field of psychology has been slow to recognize the influence of culture on

Authors' Note: The authors thank Anne Mannering.

people's thoughts, attitudes, and behaviors. Many psychologists consider cultural research to be a specialty field and marginalize cultural contributions in curricula and discourse, rather than incorporating them into the canon of introductory psychology and mainstream approaches (Hays, 1995). Despite these limitations, recent work elucidates important connections between culture, cognition, and behavior, including the relevance of these connections for sexual assault and abuse. Although most research on sexual abuse and assault among ethnic minorities concentrates on victims, that research provides insight into cultural risk and protective factors, culturally sensitive treatment, and appropriate avenues for intervention and prevention. Research that concentrates specifically on ethnic minority sex offenders, however, is a necessary complement to understanding sexual offending among populations and in developing effective treatment and prevention strategies. Ethical treatment of ethnic minority individuals requires appreciation for and knowledge of diverse backgrounds, ongoing consultation with ethnic minority community members, and the integration of culturally sensitive methods into assessment, treatment, prevention strategies, and research.

Current research aids in understanding how sexual assault and abuse among ethnic minorities may be affected in many and diverse ways by cultural issues. For instance, cultural values and related cognitions may influence etiological pathways to sexual aggression (Hall, Sue, Narang, & Lilly, 2000). These culture-specific pathways may also stem from painful experiences with the dominant culture (Comas-Diaz, 1995; Duran, 2002). Aspects of ethnic minority life such as poverty and isolation, although not primarily related to culture, may place individuals at greater risk for being sexually aggressive (e.g., Okamura, Heras, & Wong-Kerberg, 1995). Racism, discrimination, and colonialization are other important influences on sexual aggression (e.g., Comas-Diaz, 1995).

Service providers who lack appreciation or knowledge of complex interactions between culture and sexual abuse and assault are at risk of conflating variables and perpetuating stereotyping and prejudice. Although providers should cultivate cultural knowledge and sensitivity, they must remember that individuals vary more than groups (e.g., Rider, 2000) and respect their clients' individual experiences rather than relying wholly on stereotypic assumptions or even research aggregated across individuals. When we speak of Asian Americans, American Indians, or African Americans, we must be certain to remember that these are broad categories and further remember the cultural diversity within each group. Remembering that ethnic minority individuals' experiences contain unique combinations of influences of the dominant culture, specific ethnic and cultural groups, peer groups, family background, spiritual beliefs and religious affiliations, and individual differences, as well as interactions among these variables will inform assessment and treatment. Providers serving ethnic minority populations who fail to consider such factors may form faulty attributions about their clients.

This chapter offers an overview of current perspectives and research concerning ethnocultural elements relevant to the assessment, treatment, and prevention of sexual abuse. This research is in its beginning stages and has been influenced by the insufficiency of traditional, European American psychological models and treatment approaches to satisfy the needs of a multicultural population. Several common themes are emphasized in the perspectives and research discussed. There is a need for culturally competent assessment and treatment practices. We highlight the need for culture-specific theoretical and research endeavors that examine models of sexual aggression and evaluate treatment and prevention effectiveness. All ethnic minority individuals have experienced some degree of discrimination and marginalization and may be greatly affected by intergenerational trauma and associated coping mechanisms. Because many sex offenders are themselves victims, addressing relationships between those experiences and current behaviors may be an important treatment component. Understanding culture-specific risk and protective factors pertaining to sexual assault and abuse appears key in providing ethical and effective services; inattention to cultural issues could increase the possibility of relapse, have legal consequences, or contribute to other detrimental outcomes. Though psychologists often conceptualize assessment and treatment as individually based, and most current models of sexual coercion rely on intra-individual factors (Hall et al., 2002), those working with ethnic minority sex offenders and victims have stressed a need for community-based interventions. Increasing ethnic minority membership among treatment providers and researchers will enhance this work.

RISK AND PROTECTIVE FACTORS

Racism, Discrimination, Oppression, and Colonialization

The United States' transgressions against ethnic minority populations, such as the capture and enslavement of Africans, the American Indian holocaust, and the internment of Japanese Americans during World War II are not circumscribed events but complex, systemic traumas whose transgressions and effects endure through racism and discrimination among individuals and institutions. Cross (1998) articulates the ways that viewing a legacy such as African American slavery, an institution lasting hundreds of years with enduring social and economic injustices, defies traditional models of trauma and recovery. American Indians describe the "soul wound" left after centuries of murder, forced migration, involuntary placement of children in boarding schools, and other forms of colonialization (Duran, Duran, Brave Heart, & Yellow Horse-Davis, 1998; Ertz, 1998). The intergenerational impact of these experiences, combined with current situations of poverty and marginalization, can interact in social problems such as alcoholism and sexual abuse (Lewis, 2001). Sexual assault and abuse may also be one outcome of internalized oppression and colonialism, in which sexual violence is the reenactment of power and domination or an active self-defeating mechanism (Comas-Diaz, 1995; Duran, 2002).

Racist stereotypes may also influence sexually aggressive behavior. Perceptions of African American or Latino men may become self-fulfilling prophecies for sex offenders. Hall (2002) contends that emasculating stereotypes of Asian men may provoke individuals to assert masculinity through violent means. Though many cultures value the ability to endure suffering (e.g., Okamura et al., 1995), stereotypes

regarding resiliency may prevent ethnic minorities from receiving effective services. Examples of this include the myth that "black women can handle it" (Abney & Priest, 1995, p. 15).

Individuals may also have encountered trauma experiences in countries other than the United States. For instance, people living under oppressive Latin American regimes may have experienced or witnessed torture, rape, or other atrocities (e.g., Moro, 1998). Among the atrocities of the Cambodian holocaust was the use of rape as torture and sexual abuse as exploitation both in Cambodia and in the refugee camps in Thailand (Scully, Kuoch, & Miller, 1995). Contributions of cultural oppression are central in the "displacement model" of sexual coercion (Comas-Diaz, 1995), also called "horizontal violence" (Ertz, 1998). When ethnic minority males are unable to directly express anger about oppression with those in power, this anger may instead be directed at those seen as less powerful, such as women or children (Comas-Diaz, 1995). Finally, discrimination experiences with social service providers and justice system personnel may inhibit ethnic minorities from reporting abuse or assault or from utilizing social services or treatment facilities for fear of incurring more hostility toward their ethnic group.

Oppressive experiences necessitate coping strategies that provide some degree of relief from pain but that may ultimately exacerbate it. Denial and dissociation can facilitate the spread of abuse across generations (Duran, 2002; Egeland & Susman-Stillman, 1996). Scully et al. (1995) note that denial has been an important defense mechanism for Cambodians and Cambodian Americans. They also explain that under the Pol Pot regime, maintaining consistent lies was a skill integral for survival. In order to receive help in escaping the terrible conditions of refugee camps in Thailand, Cambodians often had to alter their accounts of trauma and its effects. Ethnic minority individuals in America have had to relegate painful experiences to the background in order to succeed in white environments (Guthrie, 1995). For those treating ethnic minority sex offenders, assessing current and intergenerational trauma and adaptive skills will inform therapeutic processes. When sex offenders work through denial regarding past painful experiences, they may be more emotionally available to understand the ways their behavior hurts others.

Although the United States' violent treatment of ethnic minority individuals has had devastating, enduring consequences, most models of psychology have paid little attention to these effects (Hays, 1995). Mainstream psychological diagnostic nosology, codified in the *Diagnostic and Statistical Manual of Mental Disorders,* 4th edition (*DSM-IV;* American Psychiatric Association, 1994), centers on the experiences and sample of European Americans. Such a limited, majority-culture perspective of mental health and disorder is unacceptable. Specific instances in which this is problematic include an emphasis on "genetic" or other biological factors in disorders and the lack of consideration for the effects of discrimination and oppression on individual cognition and behavior (Dana, 2001). The effect of such social influences (e.g., suspiciousness of authority), which in fact be normative in a minority culture, may be pathologized according to the majority-culture diagnostic nomenclature (e.g., as paranoid or antisocial thinking). A secondary result of pathologizing these effects is perpetuating an oppressive cycle that serves to exacerbate these "symptoms." In an effort to prevent diagnosticians from pathologizing normative responses to abuse and oppression, Brown (1992) has suggested the inclusion of "Abuse and Oppression Artifact Disorders."

Cultural Risk and Protective Factors

Cultural Identity

Cultural identity can protect against or exacerbate sexually aggressive behavior (Hall, Windover, & Maramba, 1998; Hall et al., 2002). Members of any cultural or ethnic background will vary in their level of identification with that culture (e.g., Ertz, 1998). Individuals of mixed ethnocultural backgrounds may face additional challenges. Although bicultural individuals may have greater accessibility of culture-specific behaviors and contexts (Hall et al., 2002), they may feel especially marginalized. Chao (1995) refers to her experience as a bicultural person as being "a minority of minorities" (p. 37). Another example of "double minority status" is being a gay or lesbian person with an ethnic minority background.

Acculturation

Ethnic minority individuals will vary in the extent to which they identify with the dominant culture and their family's culture of origin. Aspects of acculturation can include languages spoken and read; choices in food, friends, and dating partners; participation in cultural events; and religious observations. Elements of choice regarding acculturation may vary. Lewis (2001) stresses that those working with American Indian/Alaska Native persons should understand that there is a range of acculturation and should understand that the historical policies related to forced acculturation are important. In communities where there are many others who share one's cultural background, acculturation may not be related to psychosocial functioning. Social or geographical isolation, however, places families at greater risk for sexual abuse (Ross & Stauss, 1990, as cited in Lewis, 2001; Okamura et al., 1995).

Peer Groups

Community and group ties are especially important for individuals who are deemed "other" by mainstream society (Cross, 1998). Hall and Barongan (1997) describe ways that people's reference groups can increase or decrease the likelihood of sexual aggression. Peer groups may promote misogynous thinking, thereby making sexually coercive behavior more acceptable, or may protect individuals against discrimination resulting from minority status, a factor that influences sexual aggression in ethnic minority men (Nunez, Hall, & Sue 2002).

Interdependence

Writers and psychologists have identified differences among cultures regarding individualist and collectivist orientations. Complexities within these variables require appreciation for those values that surpass an individualist/collectivist dichotomy. Despite stereotypes of the westerner as the paragon of individualism, Oyserman, Coon, and Kemmelmeier (2002) conducted a meta-analysis of individualism and collectivism among ethnic groups that indicated

African Americans were most individualistic, followed by European Americans and Latino Americans, with no significant differences, and finally by Asian Americans. There were differences, however, among Asian countries: collectivism was not higher in Japanese or Koreans than in European Americans, but was higher in Chinese persons. The authors explain that individualism and collectivistic orientations may represent diverse value systems. For instance, individualistic values may include a sense of independence, uniqueness, and self-knowledge; collectivistic values can include relatedness, duty, hierarchy, and harmony (Oyserman et al., 2002). Lewis (2001) notes that many American Indian/Alaska Natives adhere to notions of personal integrity that rely on distinct concepts of an individual, but that part of that notion of integrity involves care for one's community.

Persons who are more individualistic are more likely to be influenced by intrapersonal factors, whereas more collectivistic individuals' behavior is more likely to be influenced by interpersonal motivations. Although, in general, isolated individuals fare worse than those affiliated with a community, if community values promote sexism and violence, then they place individuals at greater risk. Comas-Diaz (1995) describes *familismo* (familism) among Puerto Ricans as a system in which the needs of the family transcend the needs of the individual. A cultural value of maintaining family relationships can be beneficial but can promote denial and abuse continuation when family members are not confronted (Comas-Diaz, 1995; Scully et al., 1995). However, treatment providers can incorporate collectivism and *familismo* into treatment techniques by affirming the role of family members in protecting all members, including those who have been victimized. They may also validate the importance of a cultural value, such as collectivism, while addressing the impact that such a value may have in responses to sexual abuse.

Loss of Face

Loss of face, a value of maintaining one's own honor and dignity as well as that of one's family, may vary among Asian and Asian American populations (Hall, 2002). Latin American families also often place great importance on family honor and may be reluctant to share information that they perceive as damaging to the family (Moro, 1998). Hall et al. (2000) found that for Asian American men who endorsed misogynous beliefs, worry about loss of face predicted sexual aggression. Cultural values of maintaining honor may also affect reporting behaviors. The value of machismo, the concept of both male virility and responsibility, may prevent men from acknowledging sexual abuse or assault (Comas-Diaz, 1995). Hall (2002) notes that fear of losing face may prevent reporting and seeking treatment for sexual assault or abuse. Scully et al. (1995) explain that the need to save face has meant that Cambodian women have had to employ mechanisms of denial that may facilitate cycles of sexual abuse and assault.

Respect for Elders

Respect for one's elders is an important value for many ethnic minority cultures; several authors, however, identify this value as one that may contribute to the occurrence and continuation of violent behavior. Among American Indian/Alaska Native populations, cultural values extolling respect for elders may prevent the identification and disclosure that an elder has done something wrong (Ross & Stauss, 1990, as cited in Lewis, 2001). Comas-Diaz (1995) describes *respeto* (respect) for elders among Puerto Ricans as a cultural factor that could contribute to the lack of reporting of sexual abuse. Similarly, Hall (2002) describes patriarchy as both a risk and a protective factor around sexual aggression. Hall and Barongan (1997) note that patriarchal elements of many ethnic minority cultures can encourage male aggression and acceptance of victimization. Aspects of patriarchal structures that may be helpful in treatment include an emphasis on caring for one's family.

CULTURAL PATTERNS OF SEXUAL AGGRESSION

Etiological Pathways and Theory

Recent work has demonstrated that pathways to sexual aggression differ among ethnic groups. Although violence against women is pervasive worldwide, and often legitimized within the dominant culture of the United States (e.g., Rozee, 2000), people's attitudes and behaviors regarding sexually coercive behavior depend on their unique cultural background. Etiologic components of sexual aggression may include affective, cognitive, physiological, and developmental motivational variables (Hall & Hirchman, 1991). Intrapersonal variables are most strongly implicated in European American men, whereas ethnic minority males' sexual aggression stems from both intrapersonal and interpersonal factors (Nunez et al., 2002). Hall et al. (2002) found that misogynous beliefs chiefly influence sexual aggression in European American men, whereas both misogynous beliefs and cultural elements contribute to Asian American men's sexual aggression. In a model accounting for sexual aggression among European American males, Hall et al. (2000) noted a path from rape myth acceptance to hostility toward women to sexual aggression. However, for Asian American men, three paths were identified. In the first path, loss of face was correlated with hostility toward women, which was related to alcohol consumption before or during sex. In the second path, the number of consenting partners was related to alcohol consumption before or during sex, which was correlated with sexual aggression. The third path revealed that perceived negative effects of sexual aggression diminished the likelihood of sexual coercion. Nunez et al. (2002) discovered that minority status, most likely reflecting discrimination, contributes to sexual aggression for Latino and Asian American men.

Additional research will uncover mechanisms behind cultural differences in sexual offending. Lewis (2001) found a that American Indian/Alaska Native sex offenders used alcohol at greater rates than black or white sex offenders and that they were more likely to have been under the influence of alcohol during the offense. Exploring connections between alcohol use and sexual aggression will provide increased insight into these ethnic differences. Culture may also influence the type of sexual offense that individuals commit. For instance, West and Templer (1994) found that of 206 felons convicted of sexual offenses at Southern

Desert Correctional Center, more white men were incarcerated for child molestation than rape, and more black men were incarcerated for rape than for child molestation. Future work could include the development and application of theoretical models to account for cultural variables, as well as variables related to culture such as socioeconomic status.

Treatment Environment

Many professionals working with ethnic minority clients describe the importance of having an environment, including posters and décor, that reflects positive aspects of clients' cultural backgrounds (e.g., Jones, Winkler, Kacin, Salloway, & Weissman, 1998; Larsen, Robertson, Hillman, & Hudson, 1998). The treatment setting plays an important role in assuring comfort, convenience, and care for clients. Treatment settings range from prisons and other high-security facilities to outpatient hospital settings or community centers. It is paramount that the treatment environment be safe and supportive (Ertz, 1998). In addition, several treatment providers discuss the importance of having treatment centers located within clients' communities. Jones et al. (1998) share their experiences that reimbursement for public transportation, flexible hours, and offering food and drink increases treatment centers' accessibility for clients. Because many sex offenders have other biopsychosocial issues, both related and unrelated to their offending, treatment within a broader context, such as a hospital, cultural center, or general community help center, may assist with accessibility and assuage stigma associated with program participation.

CULTURALLY SENSITIVE ASSESSMENT

Assessment for sex offenders can include psychometric tests, risk assessment, clinical interviews, family and community assessments, and psychophysiological measures of arousal (Moro, 1998; Sciarra, 1999). Treatment providers must consider whether assessment techniques are culturally appropriate. Many assessment instruments have questionable reliability and validity across cultures, as psychologists have most commonly created test constructs, materials, methods, and norms using European American populations (Padilla, 2001). Assessment techniques for ethnic minority individuals are scarce (Futa et al., 2001; Moro, 1998). Both language barriers and cultural differences challenge the accuracy of assessors' interpretations. Translating and back-translating measures do not ensure their relevance; furthermore, important cultural constructs are unlikely to be reflected in many psychometric tests (Hall et al., 2002). Perhaps this is the reason that traditional psychometric tests find few differences between sex offenders of different cultures (e.g., Velasquez, Callahan, & Carrillo, 1989). Moro (1998) notes that "Hispanic" or "Latino" sex offenders more commonly identified as "El Salvadoran" or "Peruvian" and had diverse backgrounds, beliefs, and dialects; for them, the Spanish translation of the Minnesota Multiphasic Personality Inventory (MMPI) is insufficient because it uses the Spanish spoken in Spain. Pencil-and-paper tests may have little face validity for some populations and may be vulnerable to educational levels and experiences. Culturally insensitive methods often lead to the misdiagnosis of ethnic minority individuals; for example, American Indians have been labeled "avoidant" or "schizoid" because of culturally influenced behaviors such as evading eye contact (Braveheart-Jordan & DeBruyn, 1995). Assessors must carefully consider cultural factors that could bias outcomes in their assessment planning, execution, and interpretation.

Those persons determining offenders' placements must assess clients' unique cultural identity. While some ethnic minority clients will describe a strong ethnic identity, others may not consider their ethnicity to be an important personal feature. In smaller communities, interconnectedness may be especially important, and maintaining a reputation perceived as positive can be central to one's identity. Care must also be taken to not place offenders in a community where they feel culturally marginalized; attendant stressors could edge the offender toward relapse.

Those conducting assessments might consider some of the following questions: How identified is this client with his or her group and subgroup systems? How connected is this client to his or her ethnic or cultural community? Have experiences of racism, discrimination, oppression, or colonialism contributed to a sense of learned helplessness or external locus of control? Do the client's cultural values include maintaining a strict hierarchical structure within the family, and if so, has this structure been disrupted through power violations such as sexual abuse or acculturative differences across generations? How do socioeconomic factors influence this person? What forms of social support (including religious groups, churches, or elders) are available? What are the risk and protective factors within these groups? For instance, some religious communities may provide individuals with social support but encourage misogynist values.

Many sex offenders were themselves the victims of sexual abuse or assault; for others, intergenerational transmission does not play a part in their offending. Depending on clients' age and family situation, family treatment may be an integral component of rehabilitation. For instance, Sciarra (1999) maintains family treatment's central role in serving adolescent sex offenders. Jones et al. (1998) describe an ecological approach in assessing youth offenders' environments, including visits to clients' homes, neighborhoods, and schools.

The co-occurrence of sexual offending with other psychosocial challenges necessitates flexible and inclusive treatment. For instance, alcohol use can play a role in sexuality generally (George & Stoner, 2000) and in sexual aggression (Seto & Barbaree, 1995; Testa, 2002). Ertz (1998) describes relationships between substance use and abuse, sexual offenses, depression, and anxiety as important treatment considerations in American Indian sex offenders, and Hall et al. (2000) identify alcohol's role in sexual aggression among Asian American men. Treatment centers that offer comprehensive care are generally more effective than those focusing on a single issue, especially when those issues are interrelated (Kimerling & Goldsmith, 2000). Moro (1998) describes many sex offenders affected by trauma, especially physical abuse, sexual abuse, and neglect. Assessments should include important comorbidity elements such as trauma history, substance use, and overall mental health, as well as the ways these factors relate to sexual offending and to each other.

Providers should pay special attention to ways in which culture influences attitudes toward sexuality in both the assessment and therapeutic processes (Cullen & Travin, 1990). Many ethnic minority cultures in the United States feel that sexuality is not something to be discussed, especially with a stranger (Futa et al., 2001). For instance, Comas-Diaz (1995) discusses a taboo against discussing sexuality among Puerto Ricans as a potential barrier in psychotherapy. Ethnic minority individuals may also be influenced by cultural stereotypes regarding sexuality (Abney & Priest, 1995). Ertz (1998) points out that many American Indian individuals are unaware of traditional values surrounding sexuality because of forced acculturation. Peripheral correlates of culture can also influence sexual aggression. Moro (1998) describes clients who have grown up living in close quarters as more likely to witness sex early in life and writes that, in some families affected by incest, adolescents reported that they would attempt sexual acts with younger siblings or cousins.

Attitudes toward authority, especially within the fields of psychology, medicine, and law, constitute another important assessment topic. Many cultures promote respect for authority, and clients may be hesitant to question staff or express dissatisfaction if they view treatment providers as authorities. Moro (1998) describes *respeto* as a major value in Latin American culture and explains that clients and families may be cooperative and agreeable because of this value, yet may not actually agree or plan to "follow through" (p. 453). Because treatment is legally mandated for most sex offenders, treatment may be seen as punitive, and genuine engagement most often takes some time and effort (Cullen & Travin, 1990; Sciarra, 1999). Those providing assessment and treatment should also be aware of clients' attitudes toward psychology and the legal system (Jones et al., 1998). Those who have had negative prior experiences with psychologists, legal workers, or law enforcement personnel may be rightfully suspicious of people working in these professions. Members of many cultures view psychological services as necessary only for the severely mentally ill or may feel that emotional and behavioral problems are best addressed in a family or church setting (Moro, 1998). Assessing clients' needs and attitudes, as well as those of the family and community, can assist those providing services in planning an approach that effectively combines psychoeducation, treatment, and rapport building.

CULTURALLY COMPETENT TREATMENT

We use the word *competent* to signify a basic appreciation for the role of culture in people's lives, a respect for differences among individuals and groups, and an ongoing commitment to increase awareness and understanding of cultural issues. Psychologists must employ specific, conscious attention in order to develop and provide actively antiracist treatment (Hackett, 2000). Because most interventions are less successful with minority clients (Jones et al., 1998), providers and researchers are obligated to investigate reasons for these discrepancies and attempt to ameliorate them.

It is essential that a provider working with an offender of a different culture be knowledgeable about that culture. Both intellectual and experiential knowledge with cultures dissimilar to one's own are integral to the development of cultural awareness (Christensen, 1995). Ethnic minority clients describe the need for treatment providers to approach them with cultural comprehension. For instance, Scully et al. (1995) state that Cambodian clients identify an understanding of events in Cambodia and Thailand as the most important quality in a treatment provider.

White identity considerations are routinely ignored. Although ethnic minority individuals have often had to develop racial identity at an early age, many European Americans have not approached or completed this process (Tatum, 1997), which includes recognizing one's participation in the perpetuation of racism (Gerrard, 1995). It is essential that professionals working in this field have completed some amount of racial and cultural identity formation before beginning work with minority clients. Otherwise, it is more likely that the therapist's behavior toward his or her client could reflect cultural stereotypes and racism that will exacerbate the client's difficulties (Christensen, 1995). Persons working in the field of sexual assault and abuse also need to address their own issues and responses to trauma, oppression, and abuse (Comas-Diaz, 1995). For instance, a psychologist who was once robbed by an African American bandit later experienced an African American client as "intimidating." Though it is important that therapist reactions be genuine, countertransference stemming from the therapist's past is unhelpful to the client. In their description of the Project for Rape and Abuse Prevention (Project RAP), a community treatment center for adolescent sex offenders almost entirely composed of Latino and African American clients, Jones et al. (1998) advocate ongoing cultural training for all agency staff, supervision that treats cultural components as central, and culturally representative, bilingual treatment teams.

Multicultural treatment teams constitute a great asset in working with ethnic minority populations. When this is not possible, therapists working with clients whose background differs substantially from their own should engage in consultation with colleagues and others who share the client's background, read literature concerning the client's cultural group, and prepare for and repair inevitable misconceptions. Some contend that therapy is most effective when the client and the therapist are matched, while others believe that cultural disparities between treatment providers and clients are inconsequential (Fontes, 1995). Some clients may prefer a therapist from a different ethnocultural background. For instance, Wasserman (1995) writes that some American Indians prefer a non-Indian therapist for reasons including confidentiality and internalized views of Anglos as more competent than Indians; Comas-Diaz (1995) describes similar concerns among Puerto Ricans. A "matched" therapist may also remind clients of their families (Fontes, 1995). Fontes advocates matching according to clients' wishes. Providers should also ascertain client preferences pertaining to language. Moro (1998) describes difficulties that arose when therapists assumed Latino clients would want to go in the same group. Clients who were bicultural and had been in the United States for some time felt that they expressed themselves better

in English, whereas recent immigrants wanted and needed a Spanish-speaking group. Fontes also describes clients who resented assumptions that they would prefer treatment in Spanish rather than English. Making sure clients have options in terms of language and cultural groups allows for optimal treatment outcomes. Professionals committed to serving ethnic minority populations should also encourage recruitment and career development of ethnic minority individuals, provide education incentives, and consider ethnic minority clients' needs during hiring decisions (Fontes, 1995; Jones et al., 1998).

Most therapeutic treatment for sex offenders follows a cognitive-behavioral paradigm (e.g., Cullen & Travin, 1990; Jones et al., 1998; Moro, 1998; Sciarra, 1999). Relapse prevention has been an especially popular cognitive-behavioral approach, and it has proven useful in treating sex offenders (Laws, Hudson, & Ward, 2000). However, these techniques have been developed largely by and for European Americans. Understanding which cognitive-behavioral techniques work best with different ethnic groups will inform successful treatment. Hays (1995) describes cognitive-behavioral therapy's emphases on individual uniqueness, empowerment, ongoing assessment, and attention to specific behaviors, thoughts, and emotions as strengths in its use with multicultural populations, and its inattention to client histories, reliance on rational thinking and the scientific method, and support of the status quo as possible barriers for its use with those populations. Aspects of cognitive-behavioral models that emphasize personal responsibility are congruent with cultural beliefs of American Indians (Ertz, 1998) and have been helpful with African American and Latino youth (Jones et al., 1998). Another strength of cognitive-behavioral therapy with this population involves eliciting and incorporating client feedback into treatment. Jones et al. (1998) describe successful therapy groups for ethnic minority sex offenders in which group members are themselves responsible for determining rules and procedures.

Cultural values influence the efficacy of specific therapeutic techniques. Cultural attitudes such as fatalistic thinking, common in Asian cultures influenced by Confucianism, may inhibit models emphasizing behavioral and cognitive changes (Hall, 2002). The best care for ethnic minority sex offenders emphasizes relevant cultural strengths and combines current treatment practices with culturally traditional ones (Duran et al., 1998). For American Indian clients, Ertz (1998) and Ellerby and Stonechild (1998) describe including a council of elders in the planning and treatment of sex offenders as a valuable program component; Lewis (2001) also stresses the importance of integrating conventional treatment and traditional healing practices. Psychoeducational materials also should be culturally representative and relevant (Patel & Lord, 2001).

Group treatment is often helpful in that group members can challenge each other's denial, identify attitudes related to sexually coercive behavior, and provide empathy and support from a culturally similar standpoint (Sciarra, 1999). Moro (1998) describes Latin American clients as more cohesive and willing to challenge each other in a group therapy environment than clients from other backgrounds. Jones et al. (1998) describe sex offender participation in peer education as a technique that has codified clients' learning, provided an opportunity for positive peer interaction, and heightened clients' self-esteem. Peer education may be especially helpful in preventing others' sexually aggressive behavior. Sciarra (1999) notes the paucity of social skills in many adolescent sex offenders, particularly in child molesters. Treatment programs that include social skills training may most effectively prevent further offenses. Similarly, Jones et al. (1998) describe the ways ethnic minority sex offenders benefit from a life skills group that offers job preparation and planning, help with literacy and communication, and development of personal interests.

Because many sex offenders have personal histories of victimization, examining residual pain from these experiences and forming empathic connections between oneself and one's victims can be a powerful transformative process (Sciarra, 1999). Denying past trauma, together with defense mechanisms of denial, dissociation, and numbing, may make it difficult for sex offenders to empathize with the pain of their victims, if they do not emotionally experience their own pain (Scully et al., 1995).

Community outreach programs targeting both victims and perpetrators of sexual victimization seem warranted, especially as these groups often overlap. Such an approach concentrates on the problem of sexual victimization, thus lessening victim blaming, a phenomenon likely to perpetuate sexual assault and abuse.

RECONNECTION WITH COMMUNITY

Peer groups and community involvement can be risk or protective factors. Those planning treatment need to assess whether clients' sexually aggressive behavior stems from community or peer group and if these affiliations increase or decrease the likelihood of future offenses. For some offenders, a return to the community can provoke feelings of isolation if the clients' former group holds values challenged by offenders who have completed treatment. There may be maladaptive elements in clients' families that threaten positive changes made in treatment. Other considerations in returning clients to their communities include community perceptions of sexual offending and rehabilitation. For instance, Lewis (2001) warns that American Indian/ Alaska Native victims and communities may not perceive treatment as sufficient compensation for offenders' actions, a perception likely shared by those with diverse backgrounds.

Many ethnic minority communities value extended family relationships. In many cases, individuals other than biological parents are responsible for children's caretaking. It is often helpful to identify someone such as an aunt, uncle, cousin, or grandparent who can serve as a resource for an offender returning to his or her community. In cases in which sex offenders are returning to a home they have shared with their victims, treatment providers need to exercise extreme care to ensure that former victims are kept safe.

LEGAL CONSIDERATIONS

Legal representation and outcomes for ethnic minority sex offenders may be worsened by a lack of familiarity with the legal system, a learned lack of trust for the legal system, or a combination of these. There may also be language barriers that prevent these offenders from receiving appropriate advocacy. When offenders, their families, or community members are immigrants, legal processes are especially confusing (Moro, 1998). Also, concerns about immigration violations and deportation can severely influence the decision-making processes for these individuals. When treatment is legally mandated, decision makers should attempt to place clients in a setting that appreciates the culture and context of the offender's behavior. Collaborations between justice systems and treatment providers will advance care for sex offenders, victims, and their communities.

PREVENTION

The incidence and prevalence of sexual assault and abuse is likely to decrease through community risk assessments and primary prevention. Although there is a shortage of research examining cultural elements in abuse and assault, sex offender treatment outcome, and prevention, professionals working with ethnic minority sex offenders and victims are united in their call for community outreach and education. Lewis (2001) asserts that social problems among American Indians/Alaska Natives may only be assuaged if community interventions become the mode. Comas-Diaz (1995) notes schools, churches, neighborhoods, social clubs, and mass media as forums for psychoeducation and prevention; Hall (2002) adds community centers and professional organizations as possible intervention environments.

Psychoeducation and community outreach will help dismantle barriers to reporting sexual abuse and assault. Rape is largely underreported in the general population (Kenny & McEachern, 2000; Rozee, 2000) and especially underreported among ethnic minority women. For example, research indicates that Asian Americans may be less likely to report child sexual abuse than other ethnic groups (Rao, DiClemente, & Ponton, 1992). Ethnic minority victims may be more reluctant to report sexual assault perpetrated by members of their ethnic group for several reasons. They may fear incurring additional negative stereotypes for their ethnocultural

group, may be influenced by previous negative experiences with the legal system (Rozee, 2000), or may fear that children will be removed from the family (Fontes, 1995; Okamura et al., 1995). In cultures in which family units are important, victims or witnesses may be especially unwilling to disrupt the family unit (Kenny & McEachern, 2000). Plans for community outreach should address cultural and circumstantial values that impede reporting. For example, Okamura et al. (1995) describe reluctance in Asian American families to report abuse as stemming from fear of loss of face, lack of education about abuse, and lack of trust in outsiders. Romero et al. (1999) note that many Latinas are hesitant to report abuse, fearing deportation or harassment from immigration officials and consequences that could include moving children from a safer environment to one that is less safe. Abney and Priest (1995) describe several factors preventing African American women from reporting child sexual abuse, including a lack of awareness of services, previous negative interactions with authorities, feelings of betraying African American men whom they perceive as having enough challenges already, and fear of not being believed due to stereotypes about African American sexuality.

Psychoeducation can help prevent the occurrence of sexual violence and reduce victim blame (Okamura et al., 1995). Community attention to sexual assault and abuse may assuage the shame that is pervasive in victims (Futa et al., 2001) as well as people's reluctance to discuss sexuality, which can prevent the disclosure and treatment of child sexual abuse (e.g., Okamura et al., 1995). Comas-Diaz (1995) describes Puerto Rican parents who fear that sexually abused boys will become homosexuals. Psychological research can inform community members of existing stereotypes and beliefs relevant to sexual violence. For instance, White and Kurpius (2002) reported that after reading a rape scenario, undergraduate participants tended to blame male rape victims more strongly than female victims, and homosexuals more strongly than heterosexuals. These beliefs are also reflected in legal decisions. Using analyses that controlled for offense gravity and prior charges in 255 male sexual offenders, Walsh (1994) noted that homosexual sex offenders were more than six times more likely than were heterosexual offenders to receive prison sentences for their crimes. Awareness of existing attitudes, values, and stereotypes regarding sex offenders and victims will help reduce stigma as well as the incidence of sexual violence.

Dismantling rape myths, an important component of treatment with sex offenders, may change rape's normative status. Community outreach can incorporate awareness of rape myths, especially as they affect ethnic minorities. White, Strube, and Fisher (1998) describe ways that racism and rape myth acceptance interact to produce racist rape myths. Research among undergraduates demonstrates that racism influences victim blaming, especially among male subjects (George & Martinez, 2002). It is especially important to note that sexual victimization of ethnic minority persons is frequently not investigated as seriously or punished as severely as complaints from white victims (Rozee, 2000). Judges, attorneys, and jurors should be aware of the prevalence of racist biases in sentencing, in which cases where the victims are white are punished more harshly, particularly when the perpetrator is an ethnic minority (White et al., 1998).

Feminist models of sexual victimization describe dominant cultural influences on sexual abuse and assault. However, many feminist models have been criticized as monocultural. Hall and Barongan (1997) assert that multicultural and feminist education across the lifespan may reduce sexually coercive behavior. Combining feminist thought with increased levels of cultural knowledge, including interactions among cultures, will best serve sex offenders, victims, and society.

Healing trauma and loss in ethnic minority community environments may be a fundamental step in preventing further victimization. Dialogue and awareness about the ways in which past and current cultural oppression affect ethnic minority individuals constitute important preventive factors (Duran et al., 1998). Community mental health services can play a vital role in this regard. However, several researchers note that Asian Americans underutilize health services (e.g., Futa et al., 2001) and that African Americans do not use mental health services at the same rate as European Americans (Abney &

Priest, 1995). Community mental health services should maximize their visibility and accessibility and promote services that feature bilingual and bicultural providers. In addition, health services to minority populations need advocacy to ensure funding and prevent inequalities (Duran et al., 1998). Abney and Priest (1995) advocate comprehensive services that promote community awareness. Outreach should address acculturation without inhibiting cultural strengths (Okamura et al., 1995).

FUTURE DIRECTIONS

One key development regarding sex offenders is the emergence of "risk assessment" as a dominant conceptual framework for managing sex offenders in correctional, treatment, and community settings. For sex offenders, their evaluators, and treatment providers, risk assessment has assumed a particularly important role, as these types of assessments are being used to guide critical decisions involving sentencing, civil commitment, conditional release, family reunification, community tracking, and treatment eligibility. Thus far, cultural factors generally have not been considered in generating actuarial risk assessment for minority offenders. It is clear from this chapter that cultural factors are exceedingly important to consider in all aspects of sexual aggression. Risk assessment should include the identification of protective cultural factors as well as cultural factors that place people at risk. Consequently, future work should aim to incorporate cultural factors in risk assessments for sexual offenders. For offenders from minority communities, community risk assessment constitutes an important tool in planning and delivering services.

Research that addresses cultural factors in sexual violence and recovery is critical for developing appropriate intervention and treatment strategies. Hall (2002) notes that anonymous research may be helpful in assessing rates of violence in Asian Americans. Anonymous methodology is especially appropriate for gaining insight into rates of sexual abuse and assault among cultures that place importance on honor and loss of face, especially because these populations may be more unlikely to seek mental health treatment or to disclose these experiences to a counselor. Hall (2002) describes several of the field's research needs. These include investigations of violence among specific ethnic groups, cultural contexts, protective factors, and sound theoretical models. We must be vigilant to ensure that research encompasses diverse groups. Researchers must clearly articulate their methods and incorporate participant and community needs and voices into their work (Fine, 1992). Currently, there is a dearth of research in general concerning ethnic minorities; research attention and funding must not perpetuate further discrimination. Fontes (1995) advocates public policy and funding priorities of culture-specific research on sexual violence that attends to identification, treatment, and intervention. Finally, Hall and Barongan (1997) contend that increasing the numbers of ethnic minority individuals conducting psychological research and treatment and requiring multicultural components of graduate education, rather than marginalizing this focus, are essential to giving this topic the focus it deserves.

CONCLUSIONS

Sexual aggression among ethnic minorities requires attention to complex contextual factors. Health professionals, legal workers, community advocates, and policymakers must incorporate cultural elements into plans for community outreach, prevention, treatment, and research. Additional research is necessary to determine which cultural factors influence the prevalence of sexual aggression, assessment procedures, treatment modalities, and prevention strategies. Research suggests that culture-specific models for sexual aggression may be most useful. Current contributions emphasize the importance of cultural assessment for ethnic minority clients, culturally competent treatment, identification of cultural risk and protective factors, and the need for community-based intervention and prevention strategies.

The interface of culture, the legal system, and sexual offending/abuse is complex. Each element of this interface necessitates consideration of critical variables and parameters. Until recently, culture has been largely ignored in

these interchanges. It is evident from our coverage in this chapter that this is no longer acceptable. For ethical and effective services to be delivered justly, cultural factors must increasingly be emphasized in this complex interface. Hopefully, although we are still in the beginning stage, the material presented in this chapter will provide interim guidance in this mission.

REFERENCES

Abney, V. D., & Priest, R. (1995). African Americans and sexual child abuse. In L. A. Fontes (Ed.), *Sexual abuse in nine North American cultures: Treatment and prevention* (pp. 11–30). Thousand Oaks, CA: Sage.

American Psychiatric Association. (1994). *Diagnostic and statistical manual of mental disorders* (4th ed.). Washington, DC: Author.

Braveheart-Jordan, M., & DeBruyn, L. (1995). So she may walk in balance: Integrating the impact of historical trauma in the treatment of Native American Indian women. In J. Adleman & G. M. Enguidanos (Eds.), *Racism in the lives of women: Testimony, theory, and guides to antiracist practice* (Haworth Innovations in Feminist Studies) (pp. 345–368). New York: Harrington Park Press/Haworth Press.

Brown, L. S. (1992). A feminist critique of the personality disorders. In L. S. Brown & M. Ballou (Eds.), *Personality and psychopathology: Feminist reappraisals* (pp. 206–228). New York: Guilford Press.

Chao, C. M. (1995). A bridge over troubled waters: Being Eurasian in the U.S. of A. In J. Adleman & G. M. Enguidanos (Eds.), *Racism in the lives of women: Testimony, theory, and guides to antiracist practice* (Haworth Innovations in Feminist Studies) (pp. 33–43). New York: Harrington Park Press/Haworth Press.

Christensen, C. P. (1995). Cross-cultural awareness development: An aid to the creation of anti-racist feminist therapy. In J. Adleman & G. M. Enguidanos (Eds.), *Racism in the lives of women: Testimony, theory, and guides to antiracist practice* (Haworth Innovations in Feminist Studies) (pp. 209–227). New York: Harrington Park Press/Haworth Press.

Comas-Diaz, L. (1995). Puerto Ricans and sexual child abuse. In L. A. Fontes (Ed.), *Sexual abuse* in nine North American cultures: Treatment and prevention (pp. 31–66). Thousand Oaks, CA: Sage Publications.

Cross, W. E. (1998). Black psychological functioning and the legacy of slavery: Myths and realities. In Y. Danieli (Ed.), International handbook of multigenerational legacies of trauma (The Plenum Series on Stress and Coping, pp. 387–400). New York: Plenum Press.

Cullen, K., & Travin, S. (1990). Assessment and treatment of Spanish-speaking sex offenders: Special considerations. Psychiatric Quarterly, 61(4), 223–236.

Dana, R. H. (2001). Clinical diagnosis of multicultural populations in the United States. In L. A. Suzuki & J. G. Ponterotto (Eds.), Handbook of multicultural assessment: Clinical, psychological, and educational applications (2nd ed., pp. 101–131). San Francisco: Jossey-Bass.

Duran, E. (2002, May). Wounding seeking wounding: The psychology of internalized oppression. Paper presented at the conference Healing Our Wounded Spirits, Warm Springs, OR.

Duran, E., Duran, B., Brave Heart, M. Y. H., & Yellow Horse-Davis, S. (1998). Healing the American Indian soul wound. In Y. Danieli (Ed.), International handbook of multigenerational legacies of trauma (The Plenum Series on Stress and Coping, pp. 341–354). New York: Plenum Press.

Egeland, B., & Susman-Stillman, A. (1996). Dissociation as a mediator of child abuse across generations. Child Abuse and Neglect, 20(11), 1123–1132.

Ellerby, L., & Stonechild, J. (1998). Blending the traditional with the contemporary in the treatment of aboriginal sexual offenders: A Canadian experience. In W. L. Marshall & Y. M. Fernandez (Eds.), Sourcebook of treatment programs for sexual offenders: Applied clinical psychology (pp. 399–415). New York: Plenum Press.

Ertz, D. J. (1998). Treatment of United States American Indians. In W. L. Marshall, Y. M. Fernandez, S. M. Hudson, & T. Ward (Eds.), Sourcebook of treatment programs for sexual offenders: Applied clinical psychology (pp. 417–430). New York: Plenum Press.

Fine, M. (1992). Disruptive voices: The possibilities of feminist research. Ann Arbor: University of Michigan Press.

Fontes, L. A. (1995). Culturally informed interventions for sexual child abuse. In L. A. Fontes (Ed.), Sexual abuse in nine North American cultures: Treatment and prevention (pp. 259–266). Thousand Oaks, CA: Sage Publications.

Futa, K. T., Hsu, E., & Hansen, D. J. (2001). Child sexual abuse in Asian American families: An examination of cultural factors that influence prevalence, identification, and treatment. Clinical Psychology—Science and Practice, 8(2), 189–209.

Gahir, M., & Garrett, T. (1999). Issues in the treatment of Asian sexual offenders. Journal of Sexual Aggression, 4(2), 94–104.

George, W. H., & Martinez, L. J. (2002). Victim blaming in rape: Effects of victim and perpetrator race, type of rape, and participant racism. Psychology of Women Quarterly, 26(2), 110–119.

George, W. H., & Stoner, S. A. (2000). Understanding alcohol and sexual behavior. Annual Review of Sex Research, 11, 125–157.

Gerrard, N. (1995). Some painful experiences of a white feminist therapist doing research with women of color. In J. Adleman & G. M. Enguidanos (Eds.), Racism in the lives of women: Testimony, theory, and guides to antiracist practice (Haworth Innovations in Feminist Studies, pp. 55–63). New York: Harrington Park Press/Haworth Press.

Guthrie, P. (1995). Racism in academia: A case study. In J. Adleman & G. M. Enguidanos (Eds.), Racism in the lives of women: Testimony, theory, and guides to antiracist practice (Haworth Innovations in Feminist Studies, pp. 45–63). New York: Harrington Park Press/Haworth Press.

Hackett, Simon. (2000). Sexual aggression, diversity and the challenge of anti-oppressive practice. Journal of Sexual Aggression, 5(1), 4–20.

Hall, G. C. N. (2002). Culture-specific ecological models of Asian American violence. In G. C. N. Hall & S. Okazaki (Eds.), Asian American psychology: The science of lives in context (pp. 153–170). Washington, DC: American Psychological Association.

Hall, G. C. N., & Barongan, C. (1997). Prevention of sexual aggression: Sociocultural risk and protective factors. American Psychologist, 52(1), 5–14.

Hall, G. C. N., & Hirchman, R. (1991). Toward a theory of sexual aggression: A quadripartite mode. Journal of Consulting and Clinical Psychology, 59, 662–669.

Hall, G. C. N., Sue, S., Narang, D. S., & Lilly, R. S. (2000). Culture-specific models of men's sexual aggression: Intra- and interpersonal determinants. *Cultural Diversity and Ethnic Minority Psychology, 6*(3), 252–268.

Hall, G. C. N., Teten, A. L., & Sue, S. (2002, June). *The cultural context of sexual coercion.* Paper presented at the conference of the New York Academy of Sciences, Washington, DC.

Hall, G. C. N., Windover, A. K., & Maramba, G. G. (1998). Sexual aggression among Asian Americans: Risk and protective factors. *Cultural Diversity and Ethnic Minority Psychology, 4*(4), 305–318.

Hays, P. A. (1995). Multicultural applications of cognitive-behavioral therapy. *Professional Psychology: Research and Practice, 26*(3), 309–315.

Jones, R. L., Winkler, M. X., Kacin, E., Salloway, W. N., & Weissman, M. (1998). Community-based sexual offender treatment for inner-city African-American and Latino youth. In W. L. Marshall, Y. M. Fernandez, S. M. Hudson, & T. Ward (Eds.), *Sourcebook of treatment programs for sexual offenders: Applied clinical psychology* (pp. 457–476). New York: Plenum Press.

Kenny, M. C., & McEachern, A. G. (2000). Racial, ethnic, and cultural factors of childhood sexual abuse: A selected review of the literature. *Clinical Psychology Review, 20*(7), 905–922.

Kimerling, R., & Goldsmith, R. (2000). Links between exposure to violence and HIV-infection: Implications for substance abuse treatment with women. *Alcoholism Treatment Quarterly, 18*(3), 61–69.

Larsen, J., Robertson, P., Hillman, D., & Hudson, S. M. (1998). Te Piriti: A bicultural model for treating child molesters in Aotearoa/New Zealand. In W. L. Marshall, Y. M. Fernandez, S. M. Hudson, & T. Ward (Eds.), *Sourcebook of treatment programs for sexual offenders: Applied clinical psychology* (pp. 385–398). New York: Plenum Press.

Laws, D. R., Hudson, S. M., & Ward, T. (2000). Remaking relapse prevention with sex offenders. Thousand Oaks, CA: Sage Publications.

Lewis, L. G. (2001). American Indian/Alaska Native sexual abuse perpetrators: A quantitative study in two parts. *Dissertation Abstracts International: A (Humanities and Social Sciences), 62*(3-A), 1211.

Moro, P. E. (1998). Treatment for Hispanic sexual offenders. In W. L. Marshall, Y. M. Fernandez, S. M. Hudson, & T. Ward (Eds.), *Sourcebook of treatment programs for sexual offenders: Applied clinical psychology* (pp. 445–456). New York: Plenum Press.

Nunez, J., Hall, G. C. N., & Sue, S. (2002). *Culture, ethnic minority status, and sexual aggression: A comparison of Latino American, Asian American, and European American men.* Manuscript submitted for publication.

Okamura, A., Heras, P., & Wong-Kerberg, L. (1995). Asian, Pacific Island, and Filipino Americans and sexual child abuse. In L. A. Fontes (Ed.), *Sexual abuse in nine North American cultures: Treatment and prevention* (pp. 67–96). Thousand Oaks, CA: Sage Publications.

Oyserman, D., Coon, H. M., & Kemmelmeier, M. (2002). Rethinking individualism and collectivism: Evaluation of theoretical assumptions and meta-analyses. *Psychological Bulletin, 128*(1), 3–72.

Padilla, A. M. (2001). Issues in culturally appropriate assessment. In L. A. Suzuki & J. G. Ponterotto (Eds.), *Handbook of multicultural assessment: Clinical, psychological, and educational applications* (2nd ed., pp. 5–27). San Francisco: Jossey-Bass.

Patel, K., & Lord, A. (2001). Ethnic minority sex offenders' experiences of treatment. *Journal of Sexual Aggression, 7*(1), 40–50.

Rao, K., DiClemente, R. J., & Ponton, L. E. (1992). Child sexual abuse of Asians compared with other populations. *Journal of the American Academy of Child and Adolescent Psychiatry, 31*(5), 880–886.

Rider, E. A. (2000). *Our voices: Psychology of women.* Belmont, CA: Wadsworth/Thomson Learning.

Romero, G. J., Wyatt, G. E., Loeb, T. B., Carmona, J. V., & Solis, B. M. (1999). The prevalence and circumstances of child sexual abuse among Latina women. *Hispanic Journal of Behavior Sciences, 21*(3), 351–365.

Ross, H. W., & Stauss, J. (1990, November). *Child abuse and neglect among the American Indian: Are we still blaming the victim?* Paper presented at the annual meeting of the National Council on Family Relations, Seattle, WA.

Rozee, P. D. (2000). Sexual victimization: Harassment and rape. In Maryka Biaggio & Michel Hersen (Eds.), *Issues in the psychology of women* (pp. 93–113). New York: Kluwer Academic/Plenum Publishers.

Sciarra, D. T. (1999). Assessment and treatment of adolescent sex offenders: A review from a cross-cultural perspective. *Journal of Offender Rehabilitation, 28*(3/4), 103–118.

Scully, M., Kuoch, T., & Miller, R. A. (1995). Cambodians and sexual child abuse. In L. A. Fontes (Ed.), *Sexual abuse in nine North American cultures: Treatment and prevention* (pp. 97–127). Thousand Oaks, CA: Sage Publications.

Seto, M. C., & Barbaree, H. E. (1995). The role of alcohol in sexual aggression. *Clinical Psychology Review, 15,* 545–566.

Tatum, B. D. (1997). *"Why are all the black kids sitting together in the cafeteria?" and other conversations about race.* New York: Basic Books.

Testa, M. (2002). The impact of men's alcohol consumption on perpetration of sexual aggression. *Clinical Psychology Review, 22,* 1239–1263.

Velasquez, R. J., Callahan, W. J., & Carrillo, R. (1989). MMPI profiles of Hispanic-American inpatient and outpatient sex offenders. *Psychological Reports, 65,* 1055–1058.

Walsh, A. (1994). Homosexual and heterosexual child molestation: Case characteristics and sentencing differentials. *International Journal of Offender Therapy and Comparative Criminology, 38*(4), 339–353.

Wasserman, E. B. (1995). Personal reflections of an Anglo therapist in Indian country. In J. Adleman & G. M. Enguidanos (Eds.), *Racism in the lives of women: Testimony, theory, and guides to anti-racist practice* (Haworth Innovations in Feminist Studies, pp. 23–32). New York: Harrington Park Press/Haworth Press.

West, J., & Templer, D. I. (1994). Child molestation, rape, and ethnicity. *Psychological Reports, 75,* 1326.

White, A. M., Strube, M. J., & Fisher, S. (1998). A black feminist model of rape myth acceptance: Implications for research and antirape advocacy in black communities. *Psychology of Women Quarterly, 22*(2), 157–175.

White, B. H., & Kurpius, S. E. R. (2002). Effects of victim sex and sexual orientation on perceptions of rape. *Sex Roles, 46*(5–6), 191–200.

28

ADVOCACY IN THE LEGAL SYSTEM

Cultural Complexities

KARI A. STEPHENS
University of Washington

SANDRA IBARRA
Seattle, Washington

KIM MOORE
University of Washington

Many people involved in the legal system have experienced abuse, racism, sexism, classism, or other forms of oppression. This chapter will address these issues as they relate to persons from diverse populations. Although every individual has a unique set of cultural influences and beliefs, we specifically highlight a definition of diversity that includes race, gender, sexual orientation, disability, nationality, indigenous status, age, and social class. These designations of diversity can lead to barriers and obstacles that result in unfair and disparate treatment. To cover all issues of diversity as they relate to advocacy would entail a very lengthy discussion. In order to create a realistic scope and offer a reasonable discussion, we have focused this chapter on advocacy as it relates to ethnic minority status. Legal cases for culturally diverse people are often complicated by economic marginalization and undiagnosed or untreated psychological issues (i.e., depression, anxiety, post-traumatic stress disorder, drug and alcohol abuse). The crimes they are accused of or victimized by often reflect their marginalization in our society and are often intimately tied to being poor, people of color, or both.

Advocacy is essential to the ethical assessment, treatment, and movement of individuals through the legal system. According to Merriam-Webster (1993), to advocate means to plead in favor of; an advocate is one who pleads the cause of another. In this chapter, we define *advocacy* as "providing immediate emotional and physical support to an individual in crisis;

educating about legal rights; helping identify problems and developing problem-solving skills, examining alternatives, setting realistic goals, and supporting him or her in meeting them; empowering the individual in reestablishing self-confidence and self-esteem; ensuring that the individual is receiving appropriate services through courts and agencies; helping the individual navigate the legal system; and working to change the legal system for the better." Advocacy is not therapy, legal advice or practice, or medical advice or practice.

Advocacy is essential to lifting the cloak of invisibility surrounding cultural issues. Advocacy can bring understanding and justice for culturally diverse persons entangled within the legal system. This chapter has four goals aimed at conveying the essential nature of advocacy in the legal system: (a) to increase knowledge about the roles and benefits of legal advocates (LAs), (b) to discuss the ways advocates address racial injustices and disparities, (c) to stress the importance of and offer guidance for expanding cross-cultural competency throughout the legal system, and (d) to discuss how forensic psychological evaluators can ethically incorporate advocacy into their practice.

Who Are Legal Advocates, and What Do They Do?

The state, with community organizations, has developed legal advocacy programs employing LAs, whose sole responsibility is to advocate within the legal system. A LA is either an employee or a volunteer who provides information and support to his or her clients throughout their legal process. The LA's mission is to advocate for, protect, and advance the legal, human, and service rights of people. Some LAs have become organized around the principle of visibility and support for culturally diverse populations.

Ethnic minorities and culturally diverse populations have unique needs and experiences within the legal system. Court employees may not have the time or requisite knowledge to handle these individual needs. LAs provide the unique support needed by these clients. Legal advocacy is now a career for some activists. LAs have become part of many prosecutors' offices,

and many have come from grassroots social work organizations. These activists are motivated to address oppression within the legal system.

LAs critique the priorities of the legal system that give a higher priority to building more jails and prisons than to cultural competency education for legal staff, social services, and welfare. They urge a fundamental redirection and reexamination of these resources and help remedy the inadequate provisions given to legal staff that serves diverse populations. LAs have become the humanitarian watch guards for many victims and defendants of different cultures interacting with the legal system.

The role of the LA has typically focused on the victim's needs; however, this primary focus on victims limits the LA's scope of influence. As a result, legal advocacy efforts via LAs only begin to meet the needs of those involved in the legal system. The main goals of legal advocacy are minimally to help victims navigate the criminal justice system and ensure the client's safety. Some of the services provided by LAs to victims include crisis intervention, emotional support, education, counseling, assistance with referrals, information and detailed explanations of current case activity, and assistance with court orders and crime victims' compensation. A large part of a LA's job is to provide emotional support to the victim. For some victims, having another person working on their behalf shows the victims that they do not have to cope with the violence alone and that someone is concerned with their safety and well-being (Bell & Goodman, 2001). LAs provide emotional support by accompanying victims to court hearings, being in the courtroom when the victim has to testify, and being present during other case-related stressful situations.

Although LAs are not mental health counselors, they partake in some of the same activities as counselors. LAs listen to their clients' stories and treat them seriously, thus reflecting understanding, respect, and concern (Gottlieb, 1978). They help their clients determine their needs and link them to vital services. LAs provide empathy as they try to understand their clients' pain.

LAs are also a source of legal information. This legal advice can improve the thoroughness of the protective order and give the victim ways to maximize the enforcement of his or her court order. With regard to tangible support, LAs provide access to community resources that can help their clients obtain transportation, housing, welfare money, police protection, sole possession of the residence, or child or spousal support (Finn & Colson, 1990).

However, many barriers exist that limit the effectiveness of LAs. Barriers include a possible distrust of the criminal justice system by clients, differing definitions of crime and victims, location of victim service programs, language, prejudice, and different cultural responses to trauma (Anand & Shipler, 1998). Also, unfortunately, many victims are unaware of the services that LAs provide, and defendants and families involved in the legal system are generally excluded from these services. Service limitations imposed on LAs lead to most ethnic minorities not receiving the benefits of a LA.

Furthermore, LAs themselves are often marginalized due to their demographics. LAs are typically young (in their 20s through 40s) women, who may or may not be college educated, and very few are ethnic minorities. For ethnic minority LAs, pressures are high due to agencies putting them in the role of "resident expert" on cultural issues and expecting them to educate their peers about ethnic minority issues. LAs' roles are not well understood, particularly by the legal personnel or those enforcing the law. They can experience ridicule as young women when they try to press questions for their clients and at times are accused of impeding a case's progress. The professional community can misunderstand or deem a LA's questions and/or comments as ignorant or inappropriate.

Despite these barriers, LAs provide invaluable advocacy to those they serve. LAs deter the revictimization of their clients by the legal process. Increasing understanding of the LA's role among the legal community and those affected by crime will aid LAs in performing their jobs more effectively.

Efficacy of LAs

A dearth of research exists demonstrating the effectiveness of legal advocacy. However, the few studies that do exist exemplify the power legal advocacy can have in helping victims throughout the legal system. LAs serve as a source of legal information and advice that can improve the quality of the protective order and the tangible support embedded within it (Finn & Colson, 1990). LAs also decrease a victim's sense of isolation, improve the victim's emotional well-being, and increase the victim's physical safety (Bell & Goodman, 2001).

Many women who petition the court for a restraining order or a protection order are of color and lower economic status. These women are more likely to experience patronizing attitudes of court personnel (Wan, 2000). Protective orders and other legal actions are more effective for women who can afford legal representation. Legal representation helps these women maneuver through the complex legal proceedings. This means women of higher economic status are often better served by the legal system. Race, class, and gender can all have an effect on the interactions between court personnel and the victims, so it is important to have accessible and effective advocacy services for victims during legal processes (Wan, 2000). Legal advocacy is a growing service area providing great benefit. However, more research is needed to legitimate the benefits and hone the utilization of legal advocacy.

WHO PARTICIPATES IN THE LEGAL SYSTEM: THROUGH A CULTURAL LENS

Ethnic minorities have a particular disadvantage due to their cultural backgrounds being juxtaposed with the Eurocentric legal system. Advocacy is key in combating these disadvantages and promoting change that will foster cross-cultural competency throughout the system. The ethnic composition of the legal system plays a critical role in perpetuating the insensitive treatment that many ethnic minorities experience within the system.

Although ethnic minorities are slowly increasing in number and in positions of power in the United States, the people who have shaped the U.S. legal system have predominantly been white. According to the U.S. Census Bureau's 2000 census, ethnic minorities constitute 25% of the U.S. population and are on the rise. Yet, on examination of people in power within the legal system, ethnic minorities are extremely underrepresented. In 2000, only 10% of the 535 members of the 106th Congress were ethnic minorities. Judges appointed to the U.S. District Court have been predominantly white since the court's instantiation. President Clinton made an attempt to diversify his appointees with the lowest percentage of white judges ever (75.1%) in 2000 (U.S. Department of Justice Statistics, 2000a). At this time, ethnic minority appointees for U.S. District Court were 17.4% black, 5.9% Latino, 1.3% Asian, and .3% Native American (U.S. Department of Justice Statistics, 2000a). For the first time in U.S. history, there were appointees of Native American descent. Despite these moderate gains in ethnic minority representation, the vast majority of court officials continue to be white.

According to a National Institute of Justice survey (National Institute of Justice, 1995), of the 319 full-service victim assistance programs within law enforcement agencies and prosecutors' offices, approximately 65% of the victims served were white, 22% were African American, 8% were Latino, and 5% were Asian, Native American, or of another ethnic group. Despite the fact that ethnic minorities are excessively affected by crime compared with whites, the majority of victims served by formal agencies are white. These statistics are evidence of the lack of services received by victims of color.

ADVOCATES EDUCATING WITHIN THE LEGAL SYSTEM

Advocacy is needed to educate legal staff about the racial disparities and societal factors that lead to the overrepresentation of ethnic minorities in prison and jail. These factors include, but are not limited to, racism fostered by society, institutions, and systems; high poverty levels; inadequate education; lack of jobs; and a lack of cross-cultural competency training for those in the legal system. Steffensmeier (2001) notes that the cultural emphasis on loyalty and honor among Hispanic males might prevent them from informing on criminal associates or reducing their sentence through plea-bargaining.

Therefore, Hispanic males are often more vulnerable to longer sentencing and often labeled as uncooperative by authorities. This is just one example of how a positive cultural influence may be used against persons of color in the legal system.

Many ethnic minorities, but especially immigrants, are viewed as a tax and welfare burden and as competitors for jobs. They struggle against these biased perceptions and disparities to hold jobs and obtain education. All these factors can hinder legal staffs' ability to view ethnic minorities within an appropriate cultural context.

Racism

Advocates mitigate the negative impact of the racism their clients experience. We live in a context of racism; however, clients are entitled to be treated fairly and justly by the system regardless of their racial status. Advocates can lend support to those experiencing racism in the criminal justice system and society. Advocates also work to eradicate racial disparities in the legal system by bringing attention to racism and demanding social change within the legal system.

Arrest Rates and Perceptions of Victims

Racism affects arrest rates and victim perceptions. Arrest rates often vary based on ethnicity. Police officers may be ignoring mandatory arrest rules due to a biased exercise of discretion. Avakame and Fyfe (2001) found that police were more likely to make an arrest of the perpetrator if the victim was white, if the defendant was African American, and if the victim was a wealthy, white, older, suburban person. On the other hand, police were less likely to make an arrest if the victim was young, black, poor, and residing in an inner-city area (Avakame & Fyfe, 2001).

Prosecution

Evidence of racism exists at the prosecutors' level and within juries as well. In 2001, Hirschel and Hutchison conducted a study to investigate which characteristics most influenced a prosecutor's decision to prosecute. They found that

African American defendants were significantly more likely to have their cases prosecuted than white offenders. Furthermore, in theory, defendants are tried by a jury of their peers. Unfortunately, this is not always the case. Juries are often not reflective of the community from which defendants originate. This can increase the chance that stereotyping and racism will negatively influence verdicts. However, general advocacy can promote knowledge regarding what to expect at trial and can make victims stronger witnesses and help them feel empowered when participating in the complex legal process (Hartley, 2001).

Sentencing

The issue of racial influences on legal and criminal justice outcomes is an issue that is highly debated. A newly identified issue in judicial sentencing disparities among different ethnicities is the effect that the ethnicity of the judge has on the sentencing of ethnic minority defendants. Steffensmeier and Britt (2001) reported several findings that shed light on this issue. Black judges were on average 1.66 times more likely than white judges to send the defendant to jail. However, black judges' sentences were typically one month shorter than white judges' sentences. Whites, females, and older defendants received shorter prison sentences among both black and white judges. Steffensmeier and Britt also found that black judges were younger, had served less time on the bench, and were less likely to have prosecutorial experience than white judges. Black judges were harsher in their decision to send an inmate to jail, but length of incarceration was comparable to that given by white judges. Black judges were influenced more strongly by offense conduct than white judges in making sentencing decisions, and black judges were more punitive toward offenders convicted of more serious crimes and/or drug violations. Black judges ruling more harshly in their sentencing decisions was consistent with the "speculation that black judges may behave more like conservative elites and as 'tokens' than as underdog sympathizers" (Steffensmeier & Britt, 2001, p. 761).

A study by Welch, Combs, and Gruhl (1988) found that black judges treated black and white defendants the same, but white judges were somewhat more likely to incarcerate black defendants. On the other hand, Spohn (1990a, 1990b) found few differences by race and concluded that judge's race is not a factor in sentencing. Despite the need for more studies regarding the interaction between race and judgment, it is evident that racism affects ethnic minorities at the judge's level as well.

Although judges, juries, prosecutors, and police officers are affected by racism, this is also true for defense lawyers, LAs, psychological evaluators, and any professional in the legal system. Cultural competency training at all levels is needed to combat this systemic racism. The lack of cultural competency training at all levels in the legal system is evidence of the denial of the problem of racism and contributes to its perpetuation in the system. Although racism complicates advocacy, it is also one of the major drivers for advocacy. Advocates attempt to curtail the impact of racism experienced by those they serve.

Cultural Overgeneralization

Another cultural barrier is the tendency of some people to overgeneralize prior knowledge of an ethnic/cultural group or to rely on stereotypes without emphasizing individuality. This presents a problem for ethnic minorities and others because it discounts the heterogeneity within groups. Educating legal staff about intragroup and intergroup differences, as well as the importance of individual histories and circumstances, is crucial.

Overgeneralization by legal personnel occurs when they assume that all cultural/ethnic groups understand and comprehend the customs of the predominantly white dominant culture. Legal personnel make the assumption that everyone shares "normal" patterns of behavior. Although advocacy can help shed light on these assumptions, this self-reference is ingrained and complex, and an extensive cross-cultural competency program is needed to combat self-referencing and stereotyping tendencies.

Cultural customs in the United States are not universal. Therefore, U.S. cultural demeanors or gestures should not be generalized to other cultural/ethnic groups. For example, in many cultures, it is customary for listeners to nod to let the speaker know that they are paying attention (Tapestri, 2000). This does not necessarily mean that the people understand or agree with what is being said. In order to be polite, clients may nod or indicate an understanding even if that is not the case (Abugideiri, 2000). In many cases, victims or defendants will not make eye contact with the police or other persons in an authority role. In many countries, especially Asian countries, it is a sign of disrespect and defiance to look an authority figure, such as a police officer, in the eye (Tapestri, 2000). Some of these customs may be deemed inappropriate by a judge. The judge may feel as though the person is in contempt if he or she does not make eye contact. The jury may perceive the lack of eye contact as a sign of deceit or shame and may attribute a lack of trustworthiness to the one testifying. The judge may consider nodding or a statement of "I understand" by the witness to mean that all terms and conditions in a particular hearing were comprehended. Advocacy can help educate judges and witnesses about the cultural discrepancies that may lead to misinterpretations.

Not only does assumed similarity and stereotyping impede the provider's ability to discern a victim's needs, but it also serves to break down the trust and mutual respect that are essential to effective service delivery (Anand & Shipler, 1998).

Interpreter Issues

Language barriers that keep a person from understanding the complex procedures of the legal system and understanding his or her own LA are also issues for many ethnic minorities. Language is a serious problem for legal staff, particularly when dealing with immigrants and refugees, because many do not speak English or have limited English skills. Language barriers can severely hinder clients' ability to express questions and concerns regarding their case. Therefore, when working with clients with limited English skills, advocates must determine whether the client needs an advocate who speaks his or her language or gauge the client's eagerness and capacity to communicate through an interpreter and his or her comfort level in doing so. This twofold assessment is a good model for any professional in the legal system to follow. However, once this assessment has been made, barriers may still exist.

It is not uncommon for the client to reject the services of an interpreter. The client may reject the service because the interpreter may live within his or her own community, and the client may not want the community to learn of his or her current situation within the courts. This service rejection can cause further problems. For example, the judge may refuse the victim/defendant a continuance on a hearing if the client rejected the interpreter. In such instances, this problem could force the client to (a) accept the service of the interpreter, which could lead to the client's resistance in reporting information for fear of losing anonymity; (b) reject the interpreter, which may lead to an unwanted legal agreement; (c) use family members for interpretation; or (d) be left without necessary interpreter services. When dealing with clients with these issues, it is important to understand why the client is reluctant to use the interpreter. The presenting problem should be assessed and used as a consideration toward making a decision while incorporating the victim/defendant's language barriers, cultural heritage, and values.

The need for interpreters is increasing. Advocates can educate clients, interpreters, and colleagues about interpreter issues, as well as call for an increase in resources and training for interpreter services.

Complexity of the Legal System

Legal procedures, jargon, hierarchies, and rights are generally not public knowledge. One of the most confusing obstacles for victims/defendants, especially immigrants unfamiliar with the U.S. legal system and Native Americans who contend with complicated interactions between tribal and federal/state law, is the complexity of the legal system. There are three different types of domestic sovereign governments recognized by the laws of the United States: federal, tribal, and state. A victim/defendant could potentially have a case in each system. The LA is responsible for monitoring the case and informing the client of how each system functions. Any advocate, however, can offer information and explanations about legal proceeding and help promote a client's understanding of the complexities of the legal system.

Many victims of crime do not know that the state provides an attorney who works on their behalf by prosecuting the perpetrator in court. One of the most common questions asked is how much the attorney will charge for these services. While reporting a crime, the victim is rarely told that, as a citizen or not, the state is obligated to defend them and may prosecute the perpetrator. The victim is also rarely informed that he or she must be willing to participate and provide witness testimony in trial. Police officers should utilize LA services before taking victims' statements to prevent any confusion on the part of the victim in understanding the complete process.

Every procedure following the police report should be made known to the victim/defendant involved. Unfortunately, when the victim/defendant cannot speak English or is not knowledgeable about whom to call, he or she misses out on obtaining information to which he or she is entitled. An advocate can monitor the case and inform the victim/defendant of the next hearing, the details involving the hearing, and the victim/defendant's participation within that hearing.

It can be very frustrating to a client when procedures and/or the terminology of those procedures are unknown. Technical legal jargon such as *arraignment, omnibus hearing, adjudication,* and *advocate* can be hard to understand. Although many of these terms do not directly translate into other languages, they can be described and labeled in a way that closely resembles the actual meaning. Advocates can help by asking the legal staff to explain in great detail the procedures and jargon while communicating with clients. LAs give their clients the option of taking a succinct recess to clarify certain jargon or procedures separate from legal staff during a meeting/interview. This way, the clients can freely express what they do not understand and take a break from the meeting if they feel overwhelmed with the legal jargon and their personal/emotional stress. Any legal professional can offer this type of sensitivity and advocacy around the stress of the process as well.

In addition to the legal jargon and procedures, the hierarchy of the legal personnel

adds another layer of complexity. Judges, commissioners, deputy prosecuting attorneys, defense attorneys, filing deputies, police officers, and detectives are just some of the legal personnel involved in the federal, criminal, tribal, and civil systems. These positions are all very different from one another, and they all provide different services. An advocate can help reduce the confusion between the roles of the various legal staff by providing information about legal personnel. But legal personnel can also clarify their own roles. This can aid in better cooperation on the part of the victim or defendant as well as eliminate confusion.

The cultural barriers in navigating the legal system are complex. Ethnic minorities and immigrants with limited knowledge of laws and procedures may become particularly frustrated with the process. Advocates and legal personnel must attempt to clarify the stipulations surrounding laws, and advocates must be aware of and present options to ensure that the community and clients understand their options and rights within each sovereign government, whether federal, state, or tribal.

Tribal Law

Tribal law adds another layer to the already complex legal system. The Civil Rights Act limits tribal court criminal jurisdiction to misdemeanors (U.S. Code, 2002). This limited jurisdiction is confusing to many people involved in the tribal courts. Some would argue that tribal courts should not have that much power or even exist within the U.S. legal system, and others would argue that tribal courts are not given that power because they continue to be oppressed by the white dominant culture. In either case, it complicates the legal system, causing many criminal cases further complexities. These add to the turmoil that many Native Americans experience in the legal system.

Statutes and Supreme Court decisions have made the determination of Indian country criminal jurisdiction even more confusing. The Indian Country Crimes Act (U.S. Code, 1948) creates federal court jurisdiction for certain types of offenses committed by Indians against non-Indian victims and for all offenses committed by non-Indians against Indian victims. The paramount complexity lies in the determination of where the crime occurred and who has jurisdiction to deal with the crime. For example, if there is a dispute about where the crime occurred, the various systems may have difficulty holding the perpetrator accountable. In some cases, this has resulted in the inability to charge the perpetrator properly. No action can be taken until there is determination of the jurisdiction and "Indian" status. These determinations can be insulting because determining whether or not a person is part of a tribe depends on blood quantum, membership in a federally recognized tribe, and/or his or her ancestors appearing on a list of tribal members.

Native Americans have a history of persecution in the United States. The complexity of the legal system around tribal land and tribal law negatively affect many Native American people. It is important to consider the historical context of Native Americans as well as the complex legal system they encounter when advocating. Consulting with local social work agencies that deal with particular tribal groups can be an important asset to advocacy.

Lack of Trust

Perception of the legal system plays a key role in determining advocacy. All advocates must be aware that their clients may inherently distrust them and/or the legal system, and this may be particularly true for ethnic minorities who have experienced racism by the system. For example, in Muslim and Middle Eastern communities, the victim or defendant may distrust the legal system and believe judges and lawyers generally do not understand Muslims or Islam and may delight in tearing apart Muslim families (Alkhateeb, 2002). They may also believe that the justice system is full of bribery and that those with money will prevail (Alkhateeb, 2002). Anand and Shipler (1998) point out that police relations with racial, ethnic, and other minorities have historically been controversial, often rising to national attention as a result of specific incidents (e.g., the videotaped beating of Rodney King by Los Angeles police and the subsequent trial and resulting riots; the Liberty City riots following the acquittal of police officers who were accused of beating to

death an African American man in Miami; and the case against Brooklyn police officers accused of beating and torturing Abner Louima, a 33-year-old Haitian man).

Also, victims or defendants that are undocumented immigrants may have a real fear of deportation. Since September 11, 2001, laws have made cultural/ethnic groups extremely fearful that the police are enforcing immigration laws. Many constitutional rights have been stripped from immigrants since September 11. Undocumented immigrants, especially Muslim immigrants, are hesitant to contact an authority of any type for fear of being held indefinitely by the Immigration and Naturalization Service (INS), now part of the Department of Homeland Security, or the police due to racial profiling. It is also true that before September 11, many of these communities believed that law enforcement was the INS and did not understand the difference between the various law enforcement agencies. Communities would benefit by being educated about their rights as immigrants and as victims or defendants.

Furthermore, lack of trust in the mental health field by ethnic minorities is common. This is partly due to the accurate perception that modern psychotherapy has developed out of the dominant Eurocentric culture (Sue & Sue, 1999). As a result, counseling and intervention services are based on a select population of people culturally different from many ethnic minorities. Immigrant and ethnic minority communities often negatively perceive therapy approaches that do not take their culture and faith into consideration. Their accessibility to and satisfaction with available resources are linked to the resource's ability to fulfill cultural and linguistic needs. Using cross-cultural psychotherapy techniques as well as providing counseling services by ethnically similar clinicians can alleviate feelings of mistrust (Sue & Sue, 2003).

Advocates can help repair these trust issues by being sensitive to them and offering education and resources. Rather than having cultural difference be a hindrance to a legal proceeding, advocates can clarify experiences in a cultural context and lay out the relevant issues. Also, all legal professionals are in a position, regardless of how peripheral their positions may be, to educate clients about the legal process. This can help build trust immediately between the legal professional and the client, and ultimately between the client and the legal system.

Lack of Services

Advocacy can alleviate problems caused by a lack of both culturally competent services and coordination between services. Emigrating from foreign countries can involve fleeing from political turmoil, hardship, or economic hardship. Regardless of the cause of the relocation to a different country, immigrants leave their established support systems and way of life and often become financially and emotionally unstable while in the United States. Some of this instability can be due to culture shock. Pederson (1988) describes culture shock as the anxiety resulting from losing one's sense of when to do what and how. When familiar practices are removed and strange and culturally insensitive practices of the U.S. social services are used to alleviate financial hardship or provide health care for immigrants, immigrants can have a range of responses. These responses include trying to improve the situation without the social service, accepting the help that is not culturally appropriate, or settling with instability, all of which can be psychologically damaging to the individual.

Cultural and linguistic isolation are barriers that greatly compromise the ability of refugee and immigrant people to access services and information regarding community resources and to navigate the different government systems. The lack of multicultural and multilingual resources prevents refugee or immigrant people from taking advantage of all options available for health care, mental health care, welfare, housing, and various social services such as parenting classes. Gaps in social services also discourage cultural/ethnic groups from seeking help. Social service organizations serving refugee and immigrant people need advocates and lawyers who are up-to-date in their understanding of cultural sensitivity and immigration laws. Bilingual/bicultural staff should be used whenever possible (Abugideiri, 2000). Advocates within these organizations can create resource guides that include therapists, doctors, social workers,

counselors, parent educators, and organizations that are culturally aware and sensitive. This type of resource guide needs to be created and available for each immigrant community. Guides can help alleviate some of the instability caused by culture shock by promoting services for immigrants within their cultural context.

Frequently in a given urban or rural community there are very few multicultural and multilingual treatment/counseling centers. Judges and other legal professionals can only refer clients to so many multicultural treatment centers. As a result, the victim and the defendant may be forced to seek treatment at the same treatment facility. It is difficult for an advocate to intercede with a solution because there is a lack of multicultural and multilingual treatment centers. Advocates can coordinate a time with the counselors so that the related members seeking treatment are not in contact. However, having the same treatment provider may complicate the provider's ability to develop appropriate trust to carry out treatment. Advocates can also help pinpoint services that are lacking and promote their instantiation.

ACHIEVING CROSS-CULTURAL COMPETENCY

Advocacy can take many shapes and forms, but regardless of how it is dispensed, advocacy to culturally diverse populations requires appropriate cross-cultural competency training by the individual attempting to advocate. Sue and Sue (1999) state, "In order to be culturally competent, mental health professionals must be able to free themselves from the cultural conditioning of their personal and professional training, to understand and accept the legitimacy of alternative worldviews, and to begin the process of developing culturally appropriate intervention strategies in working with a diverse clientele" (p. ix). Cultural competency is a concept that can benefit more than the mental health community and one that needs to be spread throughout the legal system.

To effectively help people of color in the U.S. legal system, it is vital that the social and human service organizations along with the legal system be culturally competent. Culture is a set of behaviors and beliefs that also include an individual's communication style, actions, social customs, religious beliefs, and values. For an agency to be culturally competent as a whole, it must integrate its clients' beliefs, values, and practices into the missions and goals of the organization. Cultural competency encompasses a set of congruent behaviors, practices, attitudes, and policies related to embracing cultural differences and integrates them into the agency's culture (Mays, De Leon Siants, & Viehweg, 2002). Being culturally competent requires the ability to function effectively within the sociocultural context and behaviors as defined by the racial/ethnic group (Mays et al., 2002). Cultural competency allows the agency to respond to the unique needs of diverse populations, including those outside the "dominant" culture.

Current Status of Cross-Cultural Competency in the Legal System

Cross-cultural competency training is in its infancy. Many of the organizations involved in the legal system have yet to adopt any formal training around cultural issues. Cross-cultural competency training manuals are available to any legal personnel including law enforcement. However, currently no culturally sensitive training is mandated for police officers, prosecutors, defense attorneys, or judges. Unfortunately, these legal professionals are not trained to be cross-culturally competent unless they take the initiative to acquire the training voluntarily. Although there is much effort on the part of victim assistance programs around the country to launch targeted outreach efforts, to translate materials into a variety of languages, and to recruit a diversity of staff members and volunteers, there is less of an attempt to examine the structure of assistance programs and what those structures assume about the nature of victims' needs (Anand & Shipler, 1998). It is the assessment of the larger structure that is needed to achieve cross-cultural competency.

Key issues an agency can assess to determine its cultural competence are "(a) appraising the cultural competence of group members; (b) determining standards of cultural inclusion; (c) evaluating organizational process used to develop and implement mission, goals, and initiatives; (d) identifying agency projects that support cultural inclusion; and (e) evaluating the agency's compliance with civil rights legislation" (Mays et al., 2002, p. 139). The most effective assessment methods include individual interviews, questionnaires, focus group interviews, and a review of the agency's written documents and policies.

In order for an agency to improve its cultural competency, it must educate and promote the understanding of valuing cultural diversity, cultural self-awareness, cultural interactions, and cultural knowledge. Valuing cultural diversity includes respecting cultural differences and valuing our differences. This includes integrating cultural diversity themes into policies, programs, and services that are being developed. Cultural self-awareness is assessing your own sense of self, developing a sense of one's own culture, and understanding how one's culture's way of doing things interacts with other cultures in the community. Providing services to victims in a manner that minimizes cross-cultural barriers should also be utilized. With an increased understanding of cross-cultural dynamics and interactions, misunderstandings and misjudgments will occur less often, resulting in greater cross-cultural communication between service providers and clients and vice versa.

Effective culturally competent family service agencies should include crisis counseling and emotional support services, advocates, long-term counseling, support groups, interpretation services for non-English-speaking clients, and a bilingual/bicultural staff. Culturally competent victim services should include provisions for financial assistance; job training; help in making the transition to a new country; information about immigration laws, maternal rights, and securing custody of children; help dealing with past trauma; and culturally sensitive social support. They should also incorporate a focus that promotes the empowerment of those they serve.

These goals can be achieved through a solid multicultural training program that is continued throughout the employment of the legal personnel. Cultural competency is a continued process of learning. Any advocate should pursue this type of training, and all legal personnel should be required to participate. Furthermore, interactive activities facilitate a lasting absorption of the new material (Anand & Shipler, 1998); therefore programs should be made as interactive as possible. The facilitators should be persons who are skilled and experienced in cultural awareness training. Community-based, cultural, and nonmainstream organization leaders within the community should be included in training legal personnel.

To educate nonmainstream communities about U.S. law, government services, and immigration services, the mainstream agencies should develop multiple strategic plans for outreach in these communities. This could include cultivating networks to do word-of-mouth outreach and advertisement in community newspapers, on buses, and through community institutions (Senturia, Sullivan, Ciske, & Shiu-Thornton, 2000). In addition, in several communities, ads on language-specific radio stations are critical for reaching communities who are unable to read (Senturia et al., 2000). Beyond government efforts, all legal personnel can promote and advocate for cross-cultural competency training by insisting that it be added to their work environments and seeking out individual training.

ADVOCACY AND FORENSIC PSYCHOLOGICAL EVALUATION: HOW THEY INTERACT

Psychological issues are often a complicating factor in many legal cases. Many courts employ the services of forensic psychological evaluators to assist in determining appropriate mental health evidence. Forensic psychological evaluators have unique opportunities to provide advocacy to clients. However, advocacy has become a controversial issue due to the potential dangers it may pose in creating dual relationships and decreasing scientific objectivity. This controversy and racism fostered within the field of psychology contribute to mental health professionals' reluctance to advocate.

According to Wrightsman (2001), substituting advocacy for scientific objectivity is a temptation for forensic psychologists. It is implied that this "temptation" to advocate obviates scientific objectivity. We argue that this is not the case. Psychologists can advocate for psychological issues in forensic settings without sacrificing scientific objectivity. Directives to forensic

evaluators that call for a stance of pure neutrality and objectivity are dangerous and harmful because they do not allow for the appropriate consideration of complex cultural issues tied to an evaluation. Forensic evaluators have an obligation to consider the sociopolitical environment involved in all legal cases, particularly those involving ethnic minorities. Ethical guidelines (APA, 1993) govern this obligation. The practice of delivering mental health services, whether in a forensic setting or not, includes a social obligation to fight oppression.

Statements made by Greenberg and Shuman (1997) and Wrightsman (2001) cautioning mental health practitioners to avoid getting involved in cases beyond a factual assessment of the client are dangerous and misleading. They promote an environment of fear among mental health professionals that helps excuse their lack of involvement. Mental health professionals have become excessively concerned with overstepping their professional boundaries and getting sued for acting inappropriately, when in fact, they are acting unethically when they do not advocate for clients and consider the importance of cultural context in every case they participate in.

Sue and Sue (1999) included two points in their call to the profession of psychology that relate to promoting advocacy for ethnic minorities in the legal system. The first point involves confronting the potential political nature of counseling, in this case forensic psychological evaluation. Sue and Sue (1999) claim that assuming that the field of psychology is built on a database based on moral, ethical, and politically neutral data is false and has led to several detrimental conclusions: "(a) subjugation of the culturally different, (b) perpetuation of the view that minorities are inherently pathological, (c) perpetuation of racist practices in treatment, and (d) provision of an excuse to the profession for not taking social action to rectify inequities in the system" (p. 24). Forensic psychological evaluation must take into consideration the biased data from which the field of psychological research has grown when evaluating ethnic minorities. Sue and Sue's second point was that "therapists must realize that many so-called pathological socio-emotional characteristics of ethnic minorities can be directly attributed to unfair practices in society" (p. 25). It is important that forensic evaluators not overdiagnose or psychopathologize clients who may experience racism and cultural stigmas that affect their ability to function and to legitimize the negative psychological impacts that may result from marginalization.

Forensic evaluators can educate courts about the influence that cultural issues have on mental health and are well positioned to tease out the difference between marginalization and psychopathology. Mental health practitioners have the opportunity to explain to courts the potential origins of clients' mental illness. The impact of a racist society not only should be a consideration in the evaluation but should be a point of education for the courts as they consider the mental illness issues of ethnic minority clients. Forensic evaluators must take advantage of opportunities to educate those in the legal system about such impacts. This education can directly benefit the welfare of ethnic minorities by contextualizing the clients' evaluations both within the political nature of psychology and within the sociopolitical realms of their environment.

Ethical Guidelines for Forensic Psychologists: In Support of Advocacy

The American Psychological Association's *Guidelines on Multicultural Education, Training, Research, Practice, and Organizational Change for Psychologists* (2002) describe cross-cultural guidelines that should be used when evaluating culturally diverse populations. These guidelines not only call for cross-cultural understanding and training but also advocate for proliferation of education by psychologists about multiculturalism and encourage psychologists to use organizational change processes to change policy in favor of culturally sensitive practices. Furthermore, ethical guidelines targeted specifically at governing forensic psychology practices (APA, 1992; Committee on Ethical Guidelines for Forensic Psychologists, 1991) state that psychologists must comply with all other provisions of the ethics codes mentioned earlier. Cross-cultural competency is essential to the ethical practice of forensic psychology, yet many mental health practitioners lack this competency. This may be in part because most

psychological training programs do not have sufficient culturally sensitive material taught in the curricula (Sue & Sue, 2003).

It is important to recognize that it is precarious to call out racism and issues of culture professionally, particularly if the evaluator is of color herself. However, it is a cause that psychologists are ethically guided to support, and one that can be done successfully with proper training and consultation. Accusations of unethical behavior by colleagues when advocating for ethnic minorities may be driven by society's and the field of mental health's need to maintain a status quo rather than by a legitimate evaluation of the evaluator's performance. In the current climate, cross-culturally competent forensic evaluators are pioneers in the area of cultural considerations and may be barraged by criticism from ignorant legal professionals who would benefit from education about cross-cultural issues.

How a Forensic Mental Health Practitioner Can Ethically Advocate

Forensic psychological evaluations are principally heterogeneous depending on the type of legal case and the variations in the individuals being evaluated. Psychologists, psychiatrists, and other mental health professionals conduct these evaluations often at the request of either the judge or an attorney involved in litigation. The clients being evaluated are involved in a myriad of legal issues involving the civil, criminal, or immigration courts. These legal issues can include divorce, custody, personal injury, DUIs, assault, robbery, rape, homicide, competency to stand trial, and deportation, to name just a few. Despite this heterogeneity, at each level of the evaluation there are opportunities to advocate and issues to consider when doing so.

Taking a Case

Deciding to do forensic evaluations is a professional and personal choice for a mental health practitioner. Mental health professionals typically do these evaluations through a private practice and therefore have great freedom of choice about what cases they decide to take or turn down. The decision to take a case is influenced by many factors, including one's range of competency and experience and one's comfort level with various populations. Demographics reveal that most clients involved in the legal system are ethnic minorities. Although making a living is a real concern, allowing room for pro bono work or consciously choosing to provide evaluations to marginalized clients who can benefit most from an evaluation should be a priority. Choosing predominantly affluent groups to work with can exclude the cases most in need of forensic evaluation and advocacy. Therefore, simply choosing to work with certain populations in a forensic setting can be a way to advocate for marginalized clients.

Beyond choosing a case and developing a consultation network for cultural issues, forensic evaluators can also work to develop a positive reputation with lawyers and judges who hire them. This reputation can be a great strength to advocacy by not only increasing caseloads but also promoting an environment that positively portrays the importance of advocacy. Providing evaluations with consistent consideration toward psychological issues in a cultural context will work toward promoting awareness and understanding of how psychological issues and culture impact the legal community.

Conducting the Evaluation

Several avenues of advocacy exist for a mental health professional conducting a forensic psychological evaluation. Sharing information about mental illness findings (or lack thereof) and explaining cultural circumstances related to psychological functioning can be a powerful way to advocate. An evaluator can promote understanding of psychological issues with all parties involved in a case.

For example, an evaluator may collaborate with other service providers involved in the client's case as part of the routine evaluation. Forensic evaluators and service providers can share information about mental illness and cultural issues. Cultural circumstances and impacts motivating the client can vary (e.g., a mother or father violating court orders to see his or her children, drug or alcohol addiction exacerbated by cultural isolation, seemingly erratic or

unreliable behavior based on misunderstandings driven by cultural barriers). Advocating for the consideration of these types of issues promotes their inclusion when delivering services to the client. As a result, service providers can become more effective in treating these clients, as well as become more sensitive to the complexity of culture and mental illness interactions, and forensic evaluators can determine a more accurate evaluation.

Educating clients directly about the realities of the power differentials they face in court and the cultural biases of the system can help clients better cope with legal proceedings. This type of advocacy can be done during the one-on-one sessions often involved in forensic evaluations. By validating client's cultural experiences, offering clear explanations of court repercussions of their behavior, and offering differing perspectives, cultural gaps may be bridged for the client.

Clients can also be educated about various treatment options available to them during an evaluation. For many clients, their forensic evaluation may be the first time they have interacted with a mental health professional. Mental health professionals can offer clinical impressions to the client in an empathic and constructive way. Forensic evaluators can also take advantage of the opportunity to educate clients about mental health treatment. These types of advocacy for ethnic minorities will help combat the dearth of information available them.

Directly arranging follow-up services for a client can be one of the most powerful ways to advocate. As a mental health professional, a forensic evaluator can articulate the client's situation to service agencies quickly and efficiently and with great credibility. A phone call to one service may arrange follow-up treatment for a client that he or she may not have had access to otherwise. Although it is not the forensic evaluator's responsibility to arrange follow-up mental health services, it is a way to advocate and help bridge the chasm between available services and clients who are mentally ill.

An evaluation is a very brief period of time, but great gains can be made through sensitivity and actions that promote understanding from the client's perspective as well as the legal perspective. Operating from a frame of reference of advocacy will promote taking advantage of opportunities to advocate and positively influence the legal system.

Writing the Report

The report produced from a forensic evaluation is the most direct way to convey to the court the relevance of psychological issues and cultural influences. Written reports are a powerful vehicle for documenting and conveying to the courts the negative and positive impact culture has on the client. These reports should include detailed information about the relevance of the client's cultural experiences as they relate to his or her mental health. Including this type of assessment in the report will advocate for cultural complexities as they relate to the client's mental status by adding a legitimate cultural context.

As part of the court's records, these reports become legal documents and are therefore permanently tied to the client. Being conscientious about how a client's cultural background is documented in writing advocates for sensitivity around issues of culture. This is particularly true for U.S. non–citizens who are concerned about their legal status in the United States and the repercussions caused by what they divulge about their native countries.

Although the report produces a written document that can be used to advocate, the process of writing the report also provides advocacy opportunities. A forensic evaluator can advocate for her client by openly discussing with the client what will and will not go into the written report. This discussion conveys respect and candidness, which can promote self-efficacy for the client around his or her legal issues. It also allows the client to give feedback to the evaluator about how he or she wants his or her cultural background discussed, it increases awareness for the client about these issues, and it gives the evaluator a chance to consider the perspective of the client.

Once a draft of the report is written, lawyers may request changes in an attempt to influence the content of the report. It is important to remain objective as well as conscientious about how these requests may promote marginalization of the client. This interaction between the lawyer and the evaluator is an opportunity to advocate. The evaluator can verbally communicate the client's cultural issues to the lawyer in a productive and educational exchange. This exchange can also be used to gather legal information from the lawyer that may help the evaluator better understand the legal procedures.

Court Testimony

Testifying in court as a forensic evaluator is an opportunity to explain to the court from a psychological perspective the client's circumstances. By offering consistent and relevant testimony in culturally diverse cases, a forensic evaluator can convey the importance of cultural sensitivity to the courts.

As a forensic evaluator prepares to give testimony, it is common for the lawyer calling the forensic evaluator as a witness to brief her on her testimony. This briefing is an opportunity to advocate. The forensic evaluator can advise the lawyer on how to best elicit relevant expert mental health testimony, particularly as it relates to culture, as well as further clarify the mental health issues for the client to the lawyer.

The forensic evaluator can also brief the client on her testimony. Although it may not always be appropriate for the forensic evaluator to discuss her potential testimony with the client directly, if it can be discussed ahead of time, it should be. This discussion with the client can help further clarify the forensic evaluator's role and the legal process in which the evaluation was done. It can also provide an opportunity for the client to ask questions of the forensic evaluator.

It is also important to consider that a forensic evaluator's testimony can be traumatic for and have a negative emotional impact on some clients. An evaluator can advocate for the client by debriefing the testimony with the client. This can provide connectedness to clients who are more community and collectivist oriented compared with clients who are individually oriented and more compatible with the mainstream culture. It can also provide an opportunity to validate the client's experience within the court setting.

Following Up With the Client and Legal Staff

Building professional relationships with legal staff is an important part of forensic psychological work. A forensic evaluator can become a better advocate through strong professional relationships with legal staff. It is important to follow up on cases with legal staff after the service of the evaluation and testimony has been completed. Following up with legal staff after an evaluation has concluded can be a symbiotic process. It can be educational for the evaluator to learn of the legal outcome for the client. It can also be beneficial for the legal staff to debrief issues around the psychological evaluation.

Following up with the client after the evaluation is also an important component to advocacy. The client has often shared intimate details of his or her life with the evaluator, and the evaluator, as a trained mental health provider, can provide feedback and perspective for the overall process, as well as be a resource for referrals to appropriate services. This type of follow-up is obviously not necessary to complete the forensic evaluation; however, it can provide invaluable advocacy to the client.

CONCLUSION

Advocacy in the legal system is integral to the U.S. legal process. Knowledge, awareness, and consideration of cultural contexts are crucial components to legal cases. Advocacy provides a service and caring that culturally diverse people are in desperate need of. Racism, complex cultural issues, and complexities of the U.S. legal system create a hostile environment for marginalized populations. Advocacy is a tool that can be used to curtail this hostile environment and push the legal system ultimately toward change for the better.

All legal professionals can advocate. LAs formally advocate by offering support to their clients and offering education and resources/referrals for other services. Beyond LAs, professionals within the legal system can perform advocacy on a daily basis and have opportunities to expand advocacy throughout the system. Culturally diverse populations will benefit immensely from a coordinated effort of advocacy throughout the legal system.

Advocacy for culturally diverse populations requires cross-cultural competency from the individuals performing the advocacy. From the police officers to the parole officers, from the lawyers to the judges, from the LAs to the psychological forensic evaluators, all these individuals must be cross-culturally competent to advocate for culturally diverse people. Ethnic minorities are grossly overrepresented in our legal system. The demographics of the legal system demand attention and growth of cross-cultural competency throughout the legal system. Without cross-cultural competency, advocacy efforts will have minimal impact. Ultimately, changing the legal system as a whole to one that guarantees the ethical and just treatment of all people will take years. However, immediate advocacy and action can propel this change. As the United States becomes progressively culturally diverse and society continues to battle racism and the complications of living in a diverse environment, the need for advocacy continues to grow.

REFERENCES

Abugideiri, S. (Ed.). (2000, April). *Strategies for working with immigrant women in abusive relationships*. Available from Center for Multicultural Human Services, 701 West Broad Street, Suite 305, Falls Church, VA 22046.

Alkhateeb, S. (2002 October). *Understanding Muslim and Middle Eastern women in domestic violence work*. Information presented at the Understanding Muslim and Middle Eastern Women in Domestic Violence Work workshop, Seattle, WA.

American Psychological Association. (1992). Ethical principles of psychologists and code of conduct. *American Psychologist, 47,* 1597–1611.

American Psychological Association. (1993). Guidelines for providers of psychological services to ethnic, linguistic, and culturally diverse populations. *American Psychologist, 48,* 45–48.

American Psychological Association. (2002). *Guidelines on multicultural education, training, research, practice, and organizational change for psychologists.* Accessed November 1, 2002, from http://www.apa.org/pi/multiculturalguidelines.pdf

Anand, S., & Shipler, S. (1998). *Cultural considerations for victims of crime.* Washington, DC: National MultiCultural Institute.

Avakame, E. F., & Fyfe, J. J. (2001). Differential police treatment of male-on-female spousal violence. *Violence Against Women, 7,* 22–45.

Bell, M. E., & Goodman, L. A. (2001). Supporting battered women involved with the court system. *Violence Against Women, 7,* 1377–1404.

Committee on Ethical Guidelines for Forensic Psychologists. (1991). Specialty guidelines for forensic psychologists. *Law and Human Behavior, 15,* 655–665.

Finn, P., & Colson, S. (1990). *Civil protection orders: Legislation, current court practice, and enforcement.* Washington, DC: U.S. Department of Justice.

Gottlieb, B. H. (1978). The development and application of a classification scheme of informal helping behaviors. *Canadian Journal of Behavioral Sciences, 10,* 105–115.

Greenberg, S. A., & Shuman, D. W. (1997). Irreconcilable conflict between therapeutic and forensic roles. *Professional Psychology: Research and Practice, 28,* 50–57.

Hartley, C. C. (2001). He said, she said. *Violence Against Women, 7,* 510–544.

Hirschel, D., & Hutchison, I. W. (2001). The relative effects of offense, offender, and victim variables on the decision to prosecute domestic violence cases. *Violence Against Women, 7,* 46–59.

Mays, R. M., De Leon Siants, M. L., & Viehweg, S. A. (2002). Assessing cultural competence of policy organizations. *Journal of Transcultural Nursing, 13,* 139–144.

Merriam-Webster, Inc. (1993). *Merriam-Webster's collegiate dictionary.* Springfield, MA: Author.

National Institute of Justice. (1995). *Criminal victimization in the United States, 1995.* Accessed November 1, 2002, from http://www.ojp.usdoj.gov/bjs/pub/pdf/cvus95.pdf

Pederson, P. (1988). *A handbook for developing multicultural awareness.* Alexandria, VA: American Association for Counseling and Development.

Senturia, K., Sullivan, M., Ciske, S., & Shiu-Thornton, S. (2000). *Cultural issues affecting domestic violence service utilization in ethnic and hard to reach populations* (Award numbers 98-WT-VX-0025 and 98-WE-VX-0028). Seattle, WA: U.S. Department of Justice, Office of Justice Programs.

Spohn, C. (1990a). Decision making in sexual assault cases: Do black and female judges make a difference? *Women & Criminal Justice, 2,* 83–105.

Spohn, C. (1990b). The sentencing decisions of black and white judges: Expected and unexpected similarities. *Law & Society Review, 24,* 1197–1216.

Steffensmeier, D. (2001). *Hispanics penalized more by criminal justice system than whites and blacks.* University Park: Pennsylvania State, Population Research.

Steffensmeier, D., & Britt, C. L. (2001). Judges' race and judicial decision making: Do black judges sentence differently? *Social Science Quarterly, 82,* 749–764.

Sue, D. W., & Sue, D. (1999). *Counseling the culturally different.* New York: John Wiley & Sons.

Sue, D. W., & Sue, D. (2003). *Counseling the culturally diverse.* New York: John Wiley & Sons.

Tapestri, Inc., Refugee and Immigrant Coalition Against Domestic Violence. (2000, April). *Police response to domestic violence in ethnic communities.* Chart presented at the Understanding Muslim and Middle Eastern Women in Domestic Violence Work Workshop, Seattle, WA.

U.S. Code. (1948). *Title 18—Crimes and criminal procedure.* Accessed November 1, 2002, from http://uscode.house.gov/title_18.htm

U.S. Code. (2002). *Title 25, Indians.* Accessed November 1, 2002, from http://uscode.house.gov/title_25.htm

U.S. Department of Justice Statistics. (2000a). *Characteristics of presidential appointees to U.S. district court judgeships.* Washington, DC: U.S. Department of Justice.

U.S. Department of Justice Statistics. (2000b). *Probation and Parole in the United States.* Washington, DC: U.S. Department of Justice.

Wan, A. M. (2000). Battered women in the restraining order process: Observations on a court advocacy program. *Violence Against Women, 6,* 606–632.

Welch, S., Combs, M., & Gruhl, J. (1988). Do black judges make a difference? *American Journal of Political Science, 32,* 126–136.

Wrightsman, L. (2001). *Forensic psychology.* Belmont, CA: Wadsworth.

29

IMMIGRATION AND HARDSHIP

Living With Fear

SONIA CARBONELL

California School of Professional Psychology

> They grew from thousands to several millions
> They are voiceless people living with us
> Working in the fields
> Doing the jobs that we don't want
> Their stories are living with us
> Their pain and fear need a social voice
> And a place in our heart
>
> —S. Carbonell

In order to write this chapter, I had to first acknowledge my goal: to bring into the open the sensitive and painful descriptions of a reality shared by several millions of voiceless people living in the United States. As a group, they are voiceless because they are financially poor and without power. In addition, they are in violation of the United States' immigration laws, and so they live in fear of deportation. Illegal or unauthorized immigrants enter the United States by avoiding official inspection, pass through inspection with fraudulent documents, enter legally but overstay the terms of their temporary visas, or somehow violate other terms of their visas.

Two central questions guide this chapter: How does illegal immigration status shape the psychology of these individuals and their families? How do they describe their experience? Most attempts to speak, meet, or explore the needs of undocumented immigrants and their children encounter social resistance and little empathy. A common objection is "But they broke the immigration laws, and they are paying the consequences." This chapter postulates that we, as individuals working in helping professions, should be aware of and understand the pain of living with the fear of deportation, and that, as providers of social, mental, and legal services, we need to help to give voice to the suffering of this population. Just as our professional ethics dictate a responsibility to heal humans regardless of race, ethnicity, religion, or political and other affiliations, humanitarian ethics also include serving individuals who have broken the immigration laws of this country. Illegal migratory status affects the quality of life and the psychological and social functioning of this population. In treating them, regardless of our personal ideologies, the protection of human rights is a value that must be embedded in our professional practices.

The narrative of this chapter focuses on examples from clinical work with one of the largest group of immigrants, Latinos. They now constitute the largest ethnic minority group in the United States, at 12.5% (U.S. Census Bureau, 2000).

SUMMARY OF OFFICIAL DESCRIPTIONS AND DEFINITIONS OF LEGAL TERMS

The following information and definition of terms provides an overview of the legal language used in this chapter and serves as a reference for narratives; mostly, it comes from the Immigration and Naturalization Service's (INS) publications. An immigrant is a person who leaves his or her country of origin to seek residence in another country. An alien is any person not a citizen or national of the United States. Noncitizens entering the United States are divided into three groups: lawful permanent residents (LPRs), nonimmigrants, and undocumented migrants. According to immigration law, a LPR is any person who is not a citizen of the United States but who resides in the United States under legally recognized and lawfully recorded permanent residence. Lawfully admitted persons are also known as permanent resident aliens, resident alien permit holders, or green card holders. Such immigrants may enter the United States through family-sponsored immigration, employment-based immigration, or refugee and asylum admissions. Immigrants whose immediate relatives are U.S. citizens are exempt from the numerical limitations imposed on immigration.

In INS legal terms, immediate relatives are spouses of citizens, children (under 21 years of age and unmarried) of citizens, and parents of citizens 21 years of age or older. Family-sponsored immigration accounts for three quarters of all regular immigration into the United States. Generally, U.S. citizens and LPRs file an immigrant visa petition with the INS on behalf of a spouse or child, so that these family members may emigrate to or remain in the United States. The person who files is the petitioner and the family member is the beneficiary.

Permanent residents may also enter through the "diversity visa lottery program." This program allots additional immigration visas to strongly underrepresented countries in the U.S. immigration streams. In addition, individuals can enter the United States with a nonimmigrant status; however, they need to request a visa (e.g., a tourist visa). There are dozens of nonimmigrant visa classifications, including the F-1 category for students in academic or language programs and the J visa for those entering for cultural exchange purposes.

There are two basic administrative paths open to aliens wishing to become LPRs, depending on their residence at the time of application. Aliens living abroad apply for an immigrant visa at a consular office of the Department of State. Once issued a visa, they may enter the United States. However, their legal permanent residence is in effect only when they pass through the port of entry. Aliens already living in the United States, including certain undocumented immigrants, temporary workers, foreign students, and refugees, become legal immigrants by filing an application with the INS for adjustment of status to legal permanent residence.[1] The status of legal resident occurs after the application's approval.

By using the adjustment to immigrant status, aliens admitted to the United States in a nonimmigrant, refugee, or parolee category may have their status changed to that of LPR if they are eligible to receive an immigrant visa, and if one is immediately available. In such cases, the alien is counted as an immigrant as of the date of adjustment, even though the alien may have been in the United States for an extended period. A parolee is an alien who appears, to the inspecting officer, to be inadmissible, but who may enter the United States if there is an urgent humanitarian reason or when that alien's entry is determined to be for significant public benefit. Parole does not constitute a formal admission to the United States and confers temporary status only, requiring parolees to leave when the conditions supporting their parole cease to exist.

New legal immigrants obtain authorization to work immediately. They should receive alien registration cards (green cards) within several weeks of becoming LPRs: But in recent years, this process has become more prolonged. Work-entitled nonimmigrants may also obtain green cards.

Although there are millions of undocumented workers in the United States, they do not meet the requirements for labor certification. This certification is a requirement for U.S. employers seeking to employ certain persons whose immigration to the United States is based on the job skills of nonimmigrant temporary workers. They are coming to perform services for which qualified authorized workers are unavailable in the United States. Labor certification is issued by the Secretary of Labor and contains attestations by U.S. employers as to the numbers of U.S. workers available to undertake the employment sought by an applicant and the effect that the alien's employment will have on the wages and working conditions of U.S. workers similarly employed. Determinations of labor availability in the United States occur at the time of a visa application and at the location where the applicant wishes to work.

STATISTICS FROM A HISTORICAL PERSPECTIVE

Since the 1860s, the United States has regulated immigration, strongly favoring immigrants from Europe over other regions. A historical review suggests that the 1924 National Origins Act and the Immigration and Nationality Act of 1952 sought to implement an overall limit on immigration; however, the forces shaping current immigration patterns to the United States emerged in 1965 with the Immigration and Nationality Act Amendments. Moreover, beginning in 1965, the United States began to witness the transformation from predominantly European immigration to Latin American and Asian flows, and this flow still characterizes immigration patterns today (Passel, 2000). The 1965 amendments abolished the national origins quota system. A seven-category preference system for the allocation of immigrant visas replaced the quota, and numerical limits

increased (from 154,000 to 290,000). In this increase, 120,000 were reserved for immigrants from the Western Hemisphere. The 290,000-person limit did not include "immediate family members" of U.S. citizens. Furthermore, the Immigration and Nationality Act, as amended by the Refugee Act of 1980, expanded the number of persons considered refugees. Previously, the definition of refugee had centered on those affected by World War II. However, the new framework took into account other global conflicts contributing to the refugee population (Passel, 2002).

Any country can have illegal and clandestine immigration due to religious, political, and economic reasons; however, the uneven economic development of world societies is the predominant reason for illegal immigration to the United States. Although most undocumented populations are economic refugees, poverty, hunger, and lack of opportunities for prosperity do not meet the requirements for asylum. According to the INS, an asylee is an alien who is found to be unable or unwilling to return to his or her country of nationality and is unable to seek the protection of that country because of persecution or a well-founded fear of persecution. This persecution or the fear thereof must be based on the alien's race, religion, nationality, membership in a particular social group, or political opinion. In the United States, an asylee is eligible to adjust to LPR status after 1 year of continuous presence in the country. Unfortunately, this type of immigrant adjustment is limited to 10,000 per fiscal year and, in addition, a large percentage of political asylum applications are denied (Passel, 2002). In the 1980s and 1990s, Eastern Europeans were successful in gaining asylum in the United States, whereas Salvadorans, Guatemalans, and Haitians were not.

According to the INS official Web site, the number of persons granted legal permanent residence in the United States increased to 849,807 in fiscal year 2000, from 646,568 in fiscal year 1999. The increase concentrated on adjustments of migratory status and reflected efforts to address the application backlog at the INS. A client's statements illustrate the meaning of the backlogs. "My father worked in the fields for many years and he obtained legal residence.

In 1992, he filed a petition on my behalf; I am still waiting for a visa. I can work, but I cannot leave the U.S. If I do, I have to star [*sic*] the process again." At the end of fiscal year 2000, there were 1 million adjustments of status cases pending a decision.

In 2000, as in 1999, the leading countries of origin for legal immigrants were Mexico, the People's Republic of China, the Philippines, India, and Vietnam. These five countries represented 39% of all immigrants in 2000. The primary destination states for legal immigrants in 2000, as in every year since 1971, were California, New York, Florida, Texas, New Jersey, and Illinois. These six states accounted for 66% of all legal immigrants in 2000. According to the 2001 Census Bureau Current Population Survey, immigrants comprise 13.5% of the population age 16 and over and account for nearly the same percentage of the labor force. During the latter half of the 1990s, immigrants of all legal statuses contributed a net 35% to total growth in numbers, while the number of foreign-born workers increased by nearly 25%, compared with just 5% for all native-born workers.

A Narrative of Immigrant Psychological Issues and a Discussion of Reality and Myths

Jeffrey S. Passel, principal research associate in the Immigration Studies program at the Urban Institute in Washington, D.C., has studied methods of measuring undocumented immigration since the late 1970s. Passel (2002) estimated that about 8.5 million undocumented immigrants lived in the United States in 2000 (this estimate combined data from Census 2000, the INS, the March 2000 Current Population Survey, the Census 2000 Supplementary Survey, and previous estimates). This figure represents an increase of about 5 million above the estimates for 1990. Therefore, on average during the 1990s, the undocumented population increased by about a half-million every year (Passel, 2002). Undocumented immigrants of Latino origin represent about three fourths of the total. Mexicans alone represent about 4.7 million, or 55%, of the total undocumented

population. The rest of Latin America accounts for another 22%, or 2 million, approximately. El Salvador, Guatemala, Peru, Colombia, and the Dominican Republic follow Mexico as the largest sources of undocumented Latino immigrants. Slightly more than 1 million undocumented immigrants are from Continental Asia: India, China, Korea, and the Philippines. These four regions also send the largest numbers of legal immigrants to the United States. Finally, Passel (2002) indicated that there do not appear to be significant numbers of undocumented immigrants from the Middle East.

While practicing in Minnesota, I observed that approximately 40% of the individuals accessing private psychological services were illegal immigrants; in public social services agencies, the percentage was 30%. In California, I also observed that the undocumented population range increased from 40% to 80%. Many of those individuals use the benefits provided by their workplace medical insurance; however, the instability that illegal status brings into their lives often affects the continuity and consistency of access and treatment. According to statements made to me by illegal immigrants, in 1996, in Minnesota, some factories may have employed up to 80% of their workers illegally. These workers had "fake green cards." "Give me my next appointment in four weeks," a client told me. "I am going to Mexico because I have problems with immigration, and I will have to cross the border again." In California, given the proximity of the border, the length of the process (deportation and illegal reentry) may be short: 2 weeks on average. However, the financial cost alone has an impact on social and psychological functioning. "I can't continue treatment. Now I have to work two full-time jobs to pay the coyote."

"Coyote" is a popular term used to describe the individual who guides the illegal entry or reentry into the United States. The cost varies according to how the illegal smuggling happens. It may include services such as hotel, documents, and transportation. Just crossing "the line" (the term used for the Mexican-U.S. border) may cost from $1,500 to $3,000 per person. Crossing through the mountains, deserts, or rivers is more dangerous, but cheaper. This cost clearly affects the lives of immigrants and the choices they must make once they arrive. For example, a 25-year-old woman from Guatemala explained why she could not report her husband for domestic violence: "I do not have a way to pay the money we borrowed, and my four children and parents are back in my country. They need the money we send." For Central Americans, the journey to enter the United States may take 2 to 4 months. Given the distance, Latinos from other countries tend to immigrate with tourist visas to Mexico, and from there, they cross the U.S. border. "You are the first person I know who traveled to [the] United States in an airplane," stated a client from Guatemala.

Economic resources and social class and status may facilitate the process of entering the United States legally. However, going to an immigration office or to a U.S. consulate is a stressful and unpredictable process. In general, proof of material wealth and financial stability are requirements for the acquisition of a visa. Financial considerations are also involved when a legal resident or a U.S. citizen files a residency petition on behalf of a relative. The individual must meet income guidelines ($24,000 to $28,000 per year) and sign an affidavit of support for sponsored immigrants, which is an enforceable contract. Sponsors become financially liable for any public assistance that the immigrant receives.

After many years of illegal residency, some individuals may have the possibility of legalizing their status. "My father has been in this country for 25 years, we all were born here, but *no quiere arreglar* [he does not want to apply]."

Illegal individuals can have steady jobs, working for years with the same employer. Often, they earn less than minimum wage and tend to describe layoffs as "*se acabo el trabajo* [there is not more work]." Although it is still a popular myth that undocumented workers are a burden to U.S. society, the facts show otherwise. Proof of citizenship is now necessary to receive most public benefits, and verification of immigration status is required to receive Social Security benefits and financial aid for college. Many unlawful workers pay taxes, but do not receive returns or benefits. Although undocumented workers make a valuable economic and social contribution to society, currently labor

laws do not protect them. This population is reluctant to seek legal protection in civil and family court matters. Undocumented workers often speak about the stress of unsafe working conditions and housing discrimination, yet they rarely assert their rights. Adequate housing is a common problem. Two or three families habitually live in a two-bedroom apartment (an average of four to six adults and six to eight children).

Separation from loved ones is a constant pain, and the uncertainty surrounding the fate of family members often results in depression. A client explained, "For 5 years, I was saving to go to my country to visit my family; now with this pregnancy, I cannot do it. I was going to leave my children here. I will risk my life, but I cannot risk the life of a newborn." Another client stated, "My brothers and sisters are here; we have not seen my mother for 12 years. Three times, she attempted to cross the border. It is dangerous, when it is not the *migra,* it is the coyotes who bring you to remote places; then they steal your money and abandon you. We are a large family; I have seven brothers and two sisters. She has not seen my children or my nephews and nieces. I am depressed because immigration denied her passport [she was referring to a tourist visa]." The *migra* is a popular term used to identify the officers of the INS.

Directly or indirectly, clients share information about their legal status, and their behaviors and narratives leave a trail. As a trusting relationship develops, the information unfolds spontaneously. "My name is Maria but if you call my home, please ask for Carmen. I work with the social security number of my cousin, who lives in Puerto Rico."

Among undocumented individuals, anxiety and mood disorders are common. "I am afraid to leave my room to do my laundry or to go grocery shopping. Immigration officers are now going to those places. Every time I leave home, I do not know if I am coming back. My husband says that I should not come to my appointment walking."

Single working mothers who leave their children in daycare live in constant fear. "Every day I wonder what will happen to them if the *migra* stop me going to or coming from work." Immigration raids are common. Since 1996, there has been an increase. They target places of employment, recreation areas, shopping centers, and bus stops. In general, immigration officers seem to know where illegal immigrants work and live. A client explained, "We do not have papers to open a checking account, but there is a place, in which for a fee, my husband cashes his paycheck. However, yesterday the *migra* was there."

During the process of entering the United States illegally, many individuals are sexually assaulted or robbed, and often they have traumatic experiences. Many suffer from insomnia, recurrent nightmares, and symptoms of post-traumatic stress disorder. Paranoia is the psychological price paid by illegal immigrants who seek a better life in the United States.

When working with undocumented individuals, how does a service provider distinguish between symptoms of mental illness and immigration stress? Impairments in psychological functioning and overall severity of symptoms are indicators. In addition, the identification of family-of-origin issues, dynamics, and personal history provide clues. However, the long exposure to the stress generated by illegal immigration is enough to alter the individual's behavior, thoughts, emotions, interpersonal relationships, and reality testing. A client explained, "Since I found out that my children have crossed the border and they are safe, I stopped crying. I am not afraid of dying, and I do not have that impulse to harm myself."

The psychological literature on acculturation issues often covers identity problems; however, research about the identity of individuals living in the United States illegally is limited. Identity crises are common. "I have two jobs; in one I am Pedro, in the other I am Juan. My name is Julio and I don't know anymore who I am." In California, Latinos report the importance of behaving and speaking as Mexicans. A client explained, "Because, if I am deported to Tijuana, then I can cross the border faster."

The daily possibility of encountering an INS officer affects the individual's modes of relating to others and social functioning. Fear mediates the individual's coping and conflict resolution skills. "We have to move because the landlord wants to increase the rent again, and he will call immigration if we do not do it." During a session, a client asked, "Will you report me to immigration if I do not come to see you anymore?"

The migratory status affects the undocumented individual's interactions with service providers (i.e., in social welfare and mental health and legal systems), but it also colors and shapes the interpersonal relationships at work and home. A client narrated, "I cannot leave my husband and request child support, because he will leave and go to Mexico." Another said, "One of my coworkers wants my supervisor position, and to get it he might call immigration."

Undocumented individuals are vulnerable socially, and crimes and different forms of aggression against them often go unreported. "I cannot talk to the police because they will find out that I am here illegally."

Information about illegal status is also often used to retain control and power in family matters. "My mother-in-law said that if I divorce my husband, she will call immigration." U.S. citizens and LPRs control when or if the petition is filed, and they may misuse their power to abuse their family members, including threatening to report them to the INS. As a result, most battered immigrants are afraid to report domestic abuse to the police or other authorities.[2]

Latino children born in the United States often learn to undermine their parents' authority. This is more predominant among teenagers challenging their families cultural values.

Many undocumented individuals have fewer opportunities to learn English, because in addition to everyday responsibilities, and a history of educational deprivation, they often have two jobs. Because they speak English, children become mediators between the family and social systems. Forced by circumstances, parents rely on the judgment, decisions, and choices of their children. This type of role reversal undermines children's psychological (social) development. "We do not know if there is a problem in the school, because in meetings our daughter translates for us."

The individual's capacity to recover and cope with life phase problems (i.e., marriages, divorces, work-related problems, relocations) is also compromised, especially when they confront the illness and death of loved ones. When the death occurs in the United States, they often want to take their loved one to a burial ground in their country of origin. The danger of returning safely to the United States is an added burden to their mourning, as much as the uncertainty of how they will return to their lives in the United States. Complicated bereavement is also common when there is a death in the family and they cannot travel.

ASSESSMENT OF HARDSHIP

I began to work with immigration cases in 1990. The following descriptions are born of experience and limited to working with Latinos. They are not exhaustive or intended for generalization. Prior to 1995, the predominant requested service was psychological evaluations for political asylum of Central Americans. Changes in immigration law in 1994 and 1996 generated psychological assessment focused on describing the hardship of removal. This type of evaluation is almost unknown to mainstream providers of psychological and social services and explicit academic training is mostly nonexistent.

A description of the assessment of hardship requires remembering that the INS is an administrative agency and that changes in immigration law included adding and reviewing procedures (i.e., deportation, exclusion, and removal). In general, immigration hearings are less formal than proceedings in juvenile, criminal, and civil court. Immigration judges are federal administrative law judges who exclusively hear immigration cases. They tend to take a more active and inquisitive role in proceedings than do their counterparts in civil or criminal court. For example, more frequently, they may interrupt witness testimony to ask their own questions.

In the language of the INS, deportation is the formal removal of an alien from the United States. The Illegal Immigration Reform and Immigrant Responsibility Act of 1996 included a comprehensive revision of the procedures for removal of aliens. Exclusion and deportation proceedings were consolidated into one removal proceeding, and these new provisions became effective on April 1, 1997. Prior to that date, deportation and exclusion were separate removal procedures, or a two-step process. Exclusion was the formal term for denial of an alien's entry into the United States. First, the immigration judge made a determination about whether the person was unlawfully in the United States,

and therefore subject to exclusion or deportation. After an exclusion hearing, the judge then made the decision to exclude the alien. Since April 1, 1997, aliens living in and admitted to the United States may be subject to removal based on deportability. The process of adjudicating inadmissibility may take place either in an expedited removal process, or in removal proceedings before an immigration judge.

The Illegal Immigration Reform and Immigrant Responsibility Act of 1996 authorized the INS to remove quickly certain inadmissible aliens from the United States. In other words, the law authorizes an *expedited* removal, and INS officers now have authority to order the removal of aliens who are inadmissible without first referring them to an immigration judge. Aliens are inadmissible when they have no entry documents. They are also inadmissible when they have used counterfeit, altered, or otherwise fraudulent or improper documents. The authority of the INS also covers the removal of aliens who arrive in, attempt to enter, or have entered the United States without having been admitted or paroled by an immigration officer at a port of entry. Except under certain circumstances, the INS refers aliens to an immigration judge (i.e., when an alien makes a claim that she or he has legal status in the United States, or when he or she demonstrates a credible risk if deported).

When referred to an immigration judge, the alien has an opportunity to secure legal representation, but with the expense not paid by the government. During the hearing, an immigration judge reads the charging document. The individual will either admit or deny the factual allegations and charges contained in the document, after which the immigration judge makes a finding on those charges. After finding that the alien is removable for violating immigration law, the judge orders the deportation, without imposing any other type of punishment. If any relief is available, the judge will adjudicate the application in a proceeding at which both sides are present (i.e., the alien and his or her lawyer and the lawyer representing the INS). Either party may appeal the judge's decision to the Board of Immigration Appeals (BIA). Aliens may seek cancellation of removal through two new provisions. These new forms of relief are available to both inadmissible and deportable aliens. Aliens lawfully admitted for permanent residence for not less than 5 years, and who have resided continuously in the United States for 7 years after having been admitted in any status, may request cancellation of removal provided they have not been convicted of an aggravated felony.

An alien who has been physically present in the United States for a continuous period of at least 10 years may also seek cancellation of removal and adjustment of migratory status. However, there are several requirements, including the requirement that the alien is deemed to be a person of good moral character. Second, the individual must not have been convicted of a criminal offense that could result in his or her removal. Finally, the alien must have a spouse, parent, or child who is a U.S. citizen or LPR. However, cancellation may only be granted if aliens demonstrate that their removal from the United States would result in exceptional and extremely unusual hardship to a spouse, parent, or child who is a LPR or U.S. citizen. According to the law, in any fiscal year, only 4,000 aliens can have an adjustment of status.

A hardship assessment is a psychological evaluation of the alien and his or her family unit. The assessment focuses on documenting the psychological evidence, which may prove or disprove the exceptional and extremely unusual hardship that the alien's deportation may have on an immediate relative. The attorneys use the information to prove or disprove the claim of hardship. It is a mistake to argue the case in a psychological report. To argue is the job of the attorney; to explore and document the hardship to a U.S. citizen or legal resident and the moral character of the alien are the jobs of the provider (i.e., a psychiatrist, psychologist, or social worker). In addition, to have relevance, the findings of the psychological evaluation must be reliable. The basis of the conclusions should be able to withstand the scrutiny of cross-examination.

Psychological evaluations to determine exceptional and extremely unusual hardship include a description of the alien's current psychological functioning. Documentation of clinical findings and mental status are essential. A clinical finding occurs when the individual reports relevant symptoms, or the evaluator observes and concludes that the information meets criteria for a diagnostic classification.

Testing may be useful and necessary to assess the individual's coping mechanisms and intellectual resources. Personality appraisal provides evidence of the individual's capacity to deal with the stress. The good character of the alien and his or her relationship to a U.S. citizen or a LPR are the focus of the evaluation. The evaluator needs to consider psychosocial history, acculturation level, employment history, ties to the community, and overall social functioning. In a sense, the evaluation focuses on an appraisal and description of the individual's strengths and weaknesses. The referring lawyer must provide useful background information. The evaluator of psychological hardship should become familiar with the facts of the case and have access to affidavits that the lawyer plans to submit.

The alien's counsel may have a preliminary draft of the report. The purpose is not to change the information or receive feedback but to brief counsel about the salient findings. Counsel must be made aware of factual conflicts arising in the information. Psychological evaluations do not always provide evidence to support the alien's claim of exceptional and extremely unusual hardship. Both the client and his or her counsel should be aware of this fact. An informal consultation with the alien before making the decision about whether or not to accept the case is helpful. If the conclusion is that the results of a complete psychological evaluation will not support the claims, counsel has the opportunity to withdraw his or her request of services. The results of a psychological assessment might not always help clients in their claims of hardship, and it is the counsel who makes the decision to use the report of the evaluation and the expert testimony. Hardship evaluations are time-consuming and expensive. It is unethical to proceed without a warning in those cases when one already knows that the results will not be helpful in court. For example, a preliminary contact with an alien may suggest the presence of an antisocial personality disorder, and a criminal record will disqualify an alien for this type of relief. A history of mental illness is a relevant finding but may not be enough for the alien to receive legal protection. The illness is relevant when removal becomes a serious threat to the condition, and when it may lead to a deterioration of psychological and social functioning that will affect the life of a U.S. citizen or a legal resident.

In hardship cases, psychological testing is an appraisal of the emotional, social, and intellectual resources that the individual possesses to deal with the stress of deportation and relocation. Documenting the exceptional and extremely unusual hardship that removal of an alien will have in the life of a U.S. citizen or LPR is not easy, because exceptional and extremely unusual hardship are terms with specific legal meanings. The INS is an agency that interprets the meaning of the law, and it does not necessarily understand psychological hardship as providers of mental health services do. Therefore, the evaluations should provide detailed information about why forcing the alien to leave the country will be a serious threat to a U.S. citizen's or permanent resident's physical and mental health. Likewise, the impact in education and physical or mental health needs to go beyond reporting the emotional pain of a separation or financial burden that the alien's deportation may cause. Is the U.S. citizen or lawful resident receiving special education or treatment for a medical or mental condition? What are the resources available in the alien's country of origin for those conditions?

Background information about the applicant's home country is relevant when educational and clinical conditions exist; however, the testimony and report should be limited to references of pertinent information. This means that the evaluator must consider the historical, political, and economic factors in the psychological evaluation, but the lawyer will use the information to make the arguments in the court.

Clients are the first source of information, and their narratives are helpful to understand how they construct the meaning of an immediate relative's deportation. Cultural competence skills and cross-cultural knowledge are essential to help these clients sort out the information that they need to provide. Finally, the provider's cultural competence is an essential skill needed to assess the client's credibility. The report or testimony should specify whether the findings of the psychological examination are consistent with the client's descriptions of the exceptional and extremely unusual hardship that he or she will suffer with the removal of his or her alien relative.

RECOMMENDATIONS, REFLECTIONS, AND CONCLUSIONS

The laws of immigration are complicated, and legislative initiatives and actions are changing them constantly. Understanding the individual's history of efforts and quality of experiences with the legal system are vital. Prior to giving clients information, providers of services should obtain legal consultation and always encourage clients to meet with immigration law specialists to explore their concerns and possible avenues to adjust their status. Never should an undocumented client be encouraged to disregard an INS request (e.g., responding to a letter or attending a hearing); and when responding to a request, it is best to obtain legal representation or consultation.

Providers should use caution and avoid generalizations. What may have been true in the case of one person may not be the same for another. For example, a U.S. citizen who emmigrated to another country had several children. When they were adults, three of them applied to become LPRs. The INS denied one application and granted two. The laws that were in effect in the year in which the individuals were born and the laws in the year in which they applied made the difference.

It is necessary to keep in mind that illegal immigrants tend to develop culturally based survival behavior patterns that may be misleading, remembering or paying attention only to what is meaningful to them. They may also use multiple documents, and their date of birth may change according to how the information will be used. A client explained, "It is better not to remember the address because if the *migra* stops me then I cannot report where I live. INS officers know that in my residence they will probably find other undocumented individuals. One only needs to know how to go back to one's home."

Although their parents arrived or stayed unlawfully, children born in this country are citizens, and the U.S. Constitution protects them. However, the exercise of their rights is limited because their parents have become, in a sense, modern slaves. Most children in immigrant families (78%) are citizens (Capps, 2001). Therefore, it is also a myth that they use public resources of education without having a legal right. The acculturation rates and legal status of immigrant parents influence children's success. Children of immigrants are the fastest-growing segment of the U.S. population under age 18 (Van Hook & Fix, 2000). One in five children in the United States is the child of an immigrant. In addition, one in four low-income children is an immigrant's child (Fix, Zimmermann, & Passel, 2001).

The freedom of undocumented individuals is a social delusion. Oppression has taken a new form. The chains are invisible. Economic structures and ideology have replaced the iron. However, the new social chains are equally efficient. The individual believes he or she is exercising his or her own will in choosing to immigrate. As slaves, undocumented workers and their families live in substandard housing and their children have inadequate education and health care. Socially, we tend to think that their needs should not be included in social planning. Ideology helps us to ignore and be indifferent to social injustices: "It was their choice to be here illegally." However, as a society, we know that undocumented individuals are doing our undesirable jobs, which often are the hardest, most underpaid, and dangerous (e.g., housekeeper with no benefits or job security). Furthermore, many undocumented aliens report working in agriculture with harmful chemicals or in factories under unsafe labor conditions.

As a society, we tend to believe that in the United States, the protection of the human rights of the illegal person is not a social concern. Our trend is to remember that the United States dominates the world's economy and to forget the consequences of this domination. Social thinking is ideology dictated by economic structures. The relationship of the United States with the individual's country of origin also shapes the experience of the immigrant. For example, a Mexican's experience with the INS system is different from that of a Vietnamese or a Spaniard. The United States' economic and political strategies determine the temporary privileges as well as the quality of interaction that individuals of different countries (e.g., El Salvador, Guatemala, Nicaragua, and so on) will receive.

Professionals must consider, respect, and protect the individual's human rights, even when the holder of those rights is an unlawful resident. Providers of legal, social welfare, and health services are not powerless to help the situation of undocumented individuals in the United States. Cultural competence, the development of awareness, knowledge, and skills, will empower them to serve this special population. An emancipatory perspective that questions the double standard of U.S. society will increase the effectiveness of services and lead to community activism.

General mistrust, uncertainty about the future, and anxiety about the present are affective components in the cultural practice and daily life of most illegal immigrants. Culture is activity cultivating psychological phenomena. The psychology of undocumented immigrants emerges from cultural practices. The undocumented migratory status dictates behavioral and emotional patterns, ways of relating to the external and internal world, and in a sense becomes a subculture of the dominant cultures that coexist in both the host country and the individual's country of origin. Understanding the individual's psychological functioning requires knowledge of how the cultures and subcultures interact and construct the individual's reality. Human compassion and good intentions are not enough; cultural competence and political consciousness are requirements to serve this population effectively.

NOTES

1. Prior to October 1994, most illegal residents were required to leave the United States and acquire a visa abroad from the Department of State, as they are again required to do. Beginning in October 1994, illegal residents who were eligible for immigrant status could remain in the United States and adjust their permanent resident status by applying at an INS office and paying an additional penalty fee. This provision is no longer available unless the alien is the beneficiary of a petition under section 204 of the Immigration Act or of an application for labor certification under section 212(a)(5)(A), filed before January 15, 1998.

2. The Violence Against Women Act (VAWA) was passed by Congress in 1994. With this law, the spouses and children of United States citizens or LPRs may self-petition to obtain lawful permanent residency. The immigration provisions of the VAWA

allow certain battered immigrants to file for immigration relief without the abuser's assistance or knowledge, in order to seek safety and independence from the abuser. Help is available to victims of domestic abuse through the National Domestic Violence Hotline: 1-800-799-7233 or 1-800-787-3224 [TDD]. These hotlines provide information about shelters, mental health care, legal advice, and other types of assistance, including information about self-petitioning for immigration status.

REFERENCES

Capps, R. (2001). *Hardship among children of immigrants. Findings from the 1999: national survey of America's families* (Assessing the New Federalism Policy Brief B-29). Washington, DC: The Urban Institute.

Fix, M. E., Zimmermann, W., & Passel, J. S. (2001). *The integration of immigrant families in the United States.* Washington, DC: Urban Institute.

Passel, J. (2002). New estimates of the undocumented population in the United States. *Migration Information Source,* May 2002. Accessed October 1, 2003, from http://www.migrationinformation.org

U.S. Census Bureau. (2000). *The Hispanic population: Census brief.* Accessed October 1, 2003, from http://www.census.gov/prod/2001pubs/c2kbr01-3.pdf

U.S. Department of Justice. (2002). *Annual report, #5, January 2002.* Accessed October 1, 2003, from http://www.usdoj.gov/

Van Hook, J., & Fix, M. (2000). A profile of the immigrant student population. In Jorge Ruiz-de-Velasco, Michael Fix, & Beatriz Chu Clewell (Eds.), *Overlooked and underserved: Immigrant children in U.S. secondary schools* (pp. 9–33). Washington, DC: The Urban Institute.

INDEX

ABOUT THE EDITORS

Kimberly Holt Barrett, EdD, MFCC, is Senior Lecturer in the Department of Psychology at the University of Washington in Seattle. She teaches classes on cultural psychology, racism and minority groups, developmental psychopathology, and on the psychological assessment and treatment ethnic minority groups, immigrants, and refugees. She supervises doctoral students in clinical psychology as they provide clinical and assessment services through the department's cross-cultural psychology resource program. Barrett completed her bachelor's degree at the University of Washington, her master's degree at the University of Oregon, and her doctorate degree in counseling and educational psychology at the University of San Francisco. She completed a 2-year NIAAA post-doctoral training fellowship in addictive behaviors at the University of Washington. She was formerly Adjunct Faculty Member and Research Psychologist in the Department of Family and Community Medicine at the University of California–San Francisco, and Instructor for the Graduate Program in Counseling at the University of San Francisco. She was also a consulting psychologist in special education programs for the San Francisco and San Jose public schools. She has maintained a private practice counseling children, adolescents, and families since 1981. Barrett's research has focused on adolescent substance abuse, family and cultural influences in addictive behaviors, and more recently on children and racism. She is bilingual in English and Spanish, which led to the development of her providing forensic consultation services for various court systems with clients forming diverse backgrounds and nationalities. She lives in Mexico several months each year teaching for the University of Washington's international studies program. She has also taught in Zimbabwe and Northern Ireland. She is the author of *Changing Racial Consciousness* (forthcoming).

William H. George, PhD, is Professor of Psychology at the University of Washington in Seattle. He teaches undergraduate courses on abnormal psychology and clinical psychology, and graduate courses on theories of psychotherapy, minority mental health, cross-cultural competence, and alcohol and sexual behavior. George supervises doctoral students in clinical psychology as they provide clinical services through the department's psychology training clinic and the cross-cultural psychology resource program. He provides research mentoring for several doctoral students and postdoctoral fellows. George is also Director of the University of Washington's Institute for Ethnic Studies in the United States, which funds intramural grants for faculty research on ethnicity. He was raised on Chicago's Southside and attended Lindblom Technical High School. George completed his bachelor's degree at Rockford College and worked as a correctional counselor for the Illinois Department of Corrections in Rockford. He completed his doctoral training in clinical psychology, his clinical internship, and his postdoctoral training in addictive behaviors at the University of Washington. He served as Assistant to Associate Professor of Psychology at the State University of New York at Buffalo, where he also directed a graduate externship program at Attica Correctional Center. Much of his research and scholarship focuses on sexual deviance and understanding the effects of alcohol and alcohol expectancies on sexuality (sexual perception and disinhibition, sexual coercion and assault, HIV-related sexual risk-taking). He has authored over 50 book chapters and peer-reviewed scientific articles. George has served as Principal Investigator or Co-Principal Investigator on federal and state funded research grants concerning sexual disinhibition and sexual assault, and periodically provides forensic consultation. He has taught in Zimbabwe, traveled to Cuba, and commutes frequently to Mexico.

ABOUT THE CONTRIBUTORS

Rudolph Alexander Jr., PhD, is Professor in the College of Social Work at Ohio State University and Director of the Undergraduate Social Work Program. He has an AS degree in criminal justice, a BS degree in criminology and corrections, a master's degree in social work, and a PhD in social work. He has published over 50 articles in peer-reviewed journals and four books, *Counseling, Treatment, and Intervention Services With Juvenile and Adult Offenders* (2000), *Race and Justice* (2000), *Understanding Legal Concepts That Influence Social Welfare Policy and Practice* (2002), and *To Ascend Into the Shining World Again* (2002). His scholarly interests are in the areas of mental health, juvenile justice, and legal issues in social work and criminology.

Anthony V. Alfieri is Professor of Law, Founder and Director, Center for Ethics and Public Service at the University of Miami School of Law. The Center has won the American Bar Association 1998 E. Smythe Gambrell Professionalism Award, the Florida Bar Seventh Annual 1999–2000 Professionalism Award, and the Miami-Dade County Commission on Ethics and Public Trust 2001 ARETE Award for nonprofit of the year. He teaches civil procedure, community lawyering, and professional responsibility and has published 28 widely cited works. He is recipient of the 2000 Richard Hausler Professor of the Year Award, the Class of 2000 Amicus Curiae Dedication, and the Florida Supreme Court 1999 Faculty Professionalism Award. He is a member of the American Law Institute and the University of Miami Circle of Omicron Delta Kappa Honor Society.

Patty Bardina, MS, is a doctoral candidate in clinical psychology at the University of Washington. She has conducted forensic psychological evaluations for the Cross Cultural Psychology Resource Program. Her interests include working with adolescents of color.

Sutapa Basu, PhD, is Executive Director of the Women's Center and Assistant Professor of Women's Studies at the University of Washington. She received her doctorate from Fielding Graduate Institute and was a CSI fellow at Stanford Graduate School of Business for Nonprofit Leaders. She specializes in women and international development, working extensively with women's groups in India and the U.S. She speaks nationally and internationally on women in development and violence against women. She studied trafficked women in the state of Kerala and has worked with Washington State Representative Velma Veloria to pass legislation to protect trafficking survivors. Her awards include Soroptomist International Women Helping Women, the Florence Merrick Award, the Woman of the Year Award, the International Examiner Community Voice Award, and the United Nations Human Rights Award.

Breean Beggs is Executive Director at the Center for Justice in Spokane, Washington. The Center is a nonprofit law firm that seeks to bring justice to the disenfranchised in our society. Breean graduated from Whitworth College in 1985 with a degree in international studies. He graduated from University of Washington School of Law in 1991. He has focused on representing victims of government abuse and people who have been injured in their claims against insurance companies. He has been an adjunct instructor at Fairhaven College and is a frequent speaker on the topics of Constitutional rights and lawyer satisfaction.

Susan Bryant, JD, LlM, is Director of Clinical Education and Professor of Law at the CUNY School of Law. She received her JD and LlM from Georgetown University Law Center, where she was Prettyman Fellow for 2 years. She began her practice as a lawyer at the Defender Association of Philadelphia. An early advocate of clinical education as a pedagogical program for teaching students the practice of law, Bryant has served as a consultant and trainer for the Association of American Law Schools, the Legal Services Corporation, and the United States Department of Education. She works with the Battered Women's Rights and Immigrant and Refugee Rights Clinic and teaches family law courses. She also works with lawyers, judges, teachers and law students to improve cross-lingual work and cross-cultural competence.

Angela Burnett is a general practitioner at the Sanctuary Practice, London, UK, developing primary health care for asylum seekers and refugees, and at the Medical Foundation for the Care of Victims of Torture. She has provided career advice for refugee doctors, assisting them to return to work, and runs training workshops on refugees' health needs. Previously she worked in Zambia, providing health care for people affected by HIV/AIDS and developing collaboration between traditional healers and formal health workers, and with Oxfam in Ethiopia with people affected by drought and famine.

Dori Cahn is an adult educator and community activist in Seattle, Washington. She has taught English as a Second Language and Adult Basic Education at community-based organizations in the Seattle area. She has been on the faculty of the University of Washington, Evergreen State College, and South Seattle Community College, where she worked with first-generation immigrant students. Since the signing of a repatriation agreement between the United States and Cambodia, Cahn and her coauthor have been advocates for Cambodian refugees facing deportation. They traveled to Cambodia in 2003 and 2004, where they met with returnees, their supporters, and Cambodian officials.

Sonia Carbonell, MA, has over 20 years of experience as an English/Spanish speaking clinician in inpatient and outpatient hospitals, community agencies, and private practice where she focused on assessment and treatment of Latinos. Additional experience includes forensic psychology, participation in numerous workshops and conferences as a speaker and trainer, publications, and teaching. She has worked for the North County Health Services in San Marcos, California, doing community work while providing culturally competent mental health and training services. She completed her doctorate in cultural psychology from the California School of Professional Psychology. Her research focuses on exploring disparities in Latino mental health services. She also holds a Master of Arts in psychodynamic psychotherapy and a specialization in adolescent treatment from Antioch University, Ohio.

Felipe González Castro, PhD, is Professor of Psychology at Arizona State University. He received his MSW from the UCLA School of Social Welfare and his PhD in clinical psychology from the University of Washington. His research focuses on two major areas regarding drug abuse prevention and treatment: (a) measurement of *cultural variables,* and their analysis via multivariate models for understanding the relationship of these cultural variables to health-related outcomes, and (b) the study of *intervention adaptations* to improve the intervention's cultural relevance and effectiveness when applied to members of special subpopulations, including Hispanics/Latinos, and other racial/ethnic and cultural groups. He has served on several federal and state grant review panels and currently chairs the University of California Tobacco-Related Disease Research Program's Social and Participatory Research Review Committee.

Tamara C. Cheshire, MA, is Adjunct Faculty in the Department of Anthropology at Sacramento City College. She is Lakota, and her interests lie in American Indian education, American Indian families, and tribal sovereignty issues. She also teaches courses in Native American studies.

Dana Chou, MA, is a marriage and family therapist licensed in Colorado. She completed an undergraduate degree in child development and family relations, and a master's degree in marriage and family therapy at Brigham Young University. Her career experiences include over a decade of private practice, counseling immigrant children and youth detained in the United States, and coordinating provision of forensic medical and psychological examinations to child and adult survivors of torture and other human rights abuses in the southwestern United States for Doctors of the World–USA.

Deborah Freed, PhD, is in private practice and volunteers with Doctors of the World, evaluating people seeking political asylum, and continues her work with people living in New York affected by the terrorist attacks of September 11, 2001. She received a bachelor of fine arts degree from the Philadelphia College of Art (she continues to paint to this day) and a master's degree in art therapy from Pratt University, and she completed training as a registered animal nurse at the Royal College of Veterinary Surgeons in the United Kingdom. She later received a PhD from the California School of Professional Psychology in clinical psychology followed by postdoctoral training in psychotherapy and psychoanalysis from New York University. The treatment of trauma and stress has been a part of her work throughout her career.

Christina Garcia is a doctoral student in clinical psychology at the Long Island University–Brooklyn Campus in Brooklyn, New York. Her current research includes assessing attitudes and the utilization of mental health services in Latinos with Dr. Elizabeth Kudadjie-Gyamfi. She formerly worked with Dr. Gordon Nagayama Hall during a summer training program, formulating a literature review of ethnic issues in sexual aggression, including risk and protective factors, and presenting research demonstrating the necessity of an accurate picture of Latino sexual abuse. She also completed undergraduate research at Texas A&M University–Corpus Christi, primarily with Dr. Paula Biedenharn, studying barriers and ethnic differences in attitudes toward mental health care providers and perceptions of nursing homes in the Mexican American older adult community.

Rachel E. Goldsmith has worked at San Francisco General Hospital and Stanford Medical Center, and completed her graduate work at the University of Oregon. Her work focuses on relations among trauma and recovery, culture, and health. Her research has included designing studies with Allison Ball and Gordon Hall that examine correlates of trauma among American Indians and among Asian Americans. She has collaborated with Jennifer Freyd on research investigating links between trauma, memory, disclosure, alexithymia, and health. She has taught Introductory Psychology and Psychology of Trauma, and has worked as a therapist and assessment specialist for adults and children.

Gordon N. Hall, PhD, is Professor of Psychology at the University of Oregon. He is interested in the sociocultural context of psychopathology, particularly sexual aggression. He has found that the behavior of ethnic majority persons tends to be influenced by intrapersonal determinants, whereas the behavior of ethnic minority persons tends to be influenced by both intrapersonal and interpersonal determinants because ethnic minority persons often are bicultural. Hall is currently investigating culture-specific models of sexual aggression among Asian American and European American men. He is also interested in the development of effective research training programs for ethnic minority students.

Marian S. Harris, PhD, ACSW, LICSW, is Assistant Professor at the University of Washington, Tacoma, Social Work Program. She completed a 2-year, NIMH Postdoctoral Fellowship Training Program at the University of Wisconsin–Madison, School of Social Work. Her areas of research and writing include mothers and children in the child welfare system, mental health, substance abuse, extended family support, and children who witness domestic violence. She has a special interest in the disproportionality of children of color in the child welfare system. She is currently the principal investigator for the following research studies: (a) The Relationship Between Alcoholism, Attachment Typology, Child Maltreatment, and Parental Stress; and (b) The Effect of TANF: Birth Parents, Mental Illness, Substance Abuse, and Parental Stress.

Sandra Ibarra, BA, received her bachelor's degree from the University of Washington in Seattle. She worked as a legal advocate for the King County Sexual Assault Resource Center in Washington State.

Tedd Judd, PhD, is currently in private practice in Bellingham, Washington. He received his undergraduate psychology degree from Princeton University. He completed his PhD in psychology from Cornell in 1979, including 2 years of training in neuropsychology at the Boston VA Medical Center, and had postdoctoral training in neuropsychology at the University of Washington. He has taught in 16 countries, including a Fulbright Senior Lectureship in Spain, and courses in Costa Rica and Nicaragua. In 1996 he taught what may have been the first course in Latin America on forensic neuropsychology. His specialties and interests include cross-cultural neuropsychology and development of culturally appropriate neuropsychology in developing countries. He has published 14 articles and book chapters and his 1999 book, *Neuropsychotherapy and Community Integration: Brain Illness, Emotions, and Behavior.*

Walter T. Kawamoto, PhD, is with the County of Sacramento, California, Department of Human Assistance where he has a Native American Culture Special Skill certification. His graduate work featured a study sponsored by the National Institute of Mental Health and conducted with the assistance of the Confederated Tribes of Siletz Indians of Oregon. He launched a course focusing on indigenous families in the Spring of 2001 at CSU Sacramento. He was also a member of the American Indian–Alaska Native Head Start Research and Outcomes Assessment Consultant Panel.

Ellen G. Kelman, PhD, is a licensed psychologist in private practice in Glendale, Arizona. She currently works with children, adolescents, and adults on issues such as anxiety, depressive disorders, all types of abuse, grief, and relationships. She holds a doctorate and master's in psychology from Arizona State University and a bachelor's degree in psychology from Pomona College. Kelman is actively involved in a number of volunteer projects. She serves as a group facilitator for Camp Paz, a retreat for bereaved children and their families. In addition, she conducts psychological evaluations for Doctors of the World–USA, Inc., an organization devoted to evaluating torture survivors from all over the world who are applying for asylum in the United States.

Robin A. LaDue, PhD, is a clinical psychologist in private practice in Renton, Washington. She works with people in recovery from trauma. She has specialized in the field of fetal alcohol syndrome (FAS), and has provided national and international training in the areas of FAS and Native American mental health. She was visiting professor at Waikato University in Hamilton, New Zealand, and is the author of the award-winning books and videos "Journey Through the Healing Circle."

Kim Moore is a MPH student at the University of Washington (UW) School of Public Health and Community Medicine and a Health and Environmental Investigator at Public Health–Seattle and King County. She graduated from the UW, majoring in psychology, minoring in public health. She has worked for the Washington State Department of Health, interned for the Washington Board of Health, advocated for domestic violence victims in the Tacoma City attorney's office, and assisted in research at the Northwest Center for Public Health Practice. She has served as Chair of the Health Justice Network where she has organized community forums and raised awareness about social justice issues and cultural competency in health care.

Madeline Wordes Noya was Research Associate with the National Council on Crime and Delinquency (NCCD), where she worked on projects concerning the juvenile justice system, juvenile offenders, and juvenile victims.

Anne Nurse, PhD, is Assistant Professor of Sociology at the College of Wooster in Ohio. She has MA and PhD degrees in sociology from the University of California at Davis. She has published a number of articles and book chapters on incarcerated juvenile fatherhood as well as authoring *Fatherhood Arrested: Parenting From Within the Juvenile Justice System* (2002). Her current longitudinal project follows 40 first-time male admissions to the Ohio Department of Youth Services. The project seeks to understand juvenile prison culture as well as prison's effects on social network ties.

Jean Koh Peters, JD, is Clinical Professor of Law and Supervising Attorney at the Yale Law School. She received her AB from Radcliffe in 1979, and her JD from Harvard in 1982. She specializes in refugee and asylum law, advocacy for children, children and the law, and advocacy for parents. She is admitted to bars in New York and Connecticut. She clerked for the Hon. William P. Gray, U.S. District Court, Los Angeles, 1982 to 1983, was a staff attorney with the Juvenile Rights Division, Legal Aid Society of N.Y., 1983 to 1985, and Assistant Clinical Professor and Associate Director, Child Advocacy Clinic, Columbia, from 1986 to 1989. She has been Clinical Professor at Yale since 1989. She is the author of *Representing Children in Child Protective Proceedings: Ethical and Practical Dimensions, Second Edition* (2001).

Eileen Poe-Yamagata, MA, was Senior Research Associate with the National Council on Crime and Delinquency (NCCD), where she worked on several projects evaluating programs for youthful offenders in both San Francisco and Alameda counties. Previously, she worked at the National Center for Juvenile Justice for 7 years. Her work has involved conducting analyses of national data on juvenile offending and victimization and preparing reports, and evaluation of court systems and programs for young offenders. She holds a master's degree in public policy and management from Carnegie Mellon University. She has authored and coauthored several publications and reports concerning the juvenile justice system, juvenile offenders, and juvenile victims.

Maria P. P. Root, PhD, resides in Seattle, Washington, and is self-employed as a clinical psychologist. Her publications cover the areas of trauma, cultural assessment, multiracial identity, and eating disorders. One of the leading authorities in the field of multiracial identity and families, Root has edited two award-winning books. For more than 15 years, she has served as an expert witness in forensic settings for work discrimination cases involving ethnic, racial, national origins, and sexual harassment.

Bahira Sherif-Trask, PhD, is Associate Professor of Individual and Family Studies at the University of Delaware. She has an undergraduate degree in political science from Yale University and a PhD in cultural anthropology from the University of Pennsylvania. Her research centers on issues of cultural diversity, gender, work, and intergenerational relations. She has conducted fieldwork on these topics in the United States, Europe, and the Middle East and has published extensively on these issues. Sherif-Trask recently edited a volume on the lives of Middle Eastern women for the Greenwood Encyclopedia of Women's Issues Worldwide. She is currently working on a new study on cross-cultural perceptions of the marriage and work intersection.

Ada Skyles, PhD, JD, is Research Fellow and Associate Director at the University of Chicago's Chapin Hall Center for Children. She received her PhD in social welfare policy from the University of Wisconsin and her JD from Northwestern University School of Law. Her research focuses on child welfare systems—especially regarding children of color, juvenile justice and family courts, community participation, and capacity building in community-based agencies. Her legal practice emphasized family law. She coedited a special issue of *Children & Youth Services Review* focusing on children of color in child welfare systems. She chairs the Inspector General's Ethics Board for Child Welfare Professionals of the Illinois Department of Children and Family Services. Formerly, she directed the Wisconsin Bureau of Child Support Enforcement.

Jay Stansell is Assistant Federal Public Defender in Seattle, Washington. He has represented over 600 noncitizens, including many Cambodian Americans, facing indefinite detention by the Immigration and Naturalization Service. During that litigation, Stansell argued before the United States Supreme Court on behalf of Kim Ho Ma, resulting in the decision in Zadvydas v. Davis, 533 U.S. 678 (2001), in which the Supreme Court held that the INS could not indefinitely detain noncitizens who have been ordered deported and who cannot be returned to their countries of origin. He continues to work with refugees and immigrants facing deportation.

Kari A. Stephens, MS, is a doctoral candidate in Clinical Psychology at the University of Washington. She has conducted forensic psychological evaluations for the Cross Cultural Psychology Resource Program. Her research interests include sexual aggression, addiction, and cultural issues.

David Sue, PhD, is Professor of Psychology and an Associate of the Center for Cross-Cultural Research at Western Washington University. He has served as the director of the mental health counseling program and director of the psychology training clinic at Western Washington University and received his PhD in clinical psychology at Washington State University. *Counseling the Culturally Different* and *Understanding Abnormal Behavior* are books that he has coauthored, and he has published a number of articles on Asian Americans.

Kate Thompson, a counselling psychologist, has done extensive aid work in Africa: with Médecins sans Frontières (1993–1995) in Liberia and the Ivory Coast, and in refugee camps in Tanzania. She was a delegate for the International Committee of the Red Cross in Rwanda (1996–1997). She is the Refugee Support Psychologist for the North East London Mental Health Trust, providing services that combine individual clinical work, community development, and training. The project has been cited as an example of good practice and judged effective by external reviewers. She has also worked with Sudanese women's activists through the British Council in Khartoum on strategies for community coping. Her interests include the social meaning of war, political oppression, and exile, and emphasize the community as a tool for healing.

Rachel Tribe is a senior lecturer, chartered psychologist, and course director in the School of Psychology at the University of East London. She is an experienced clinician, who has extensive experience working with different cultural, racial, and religious groups in the UK and other countries. Her work has involved consultancy to individual clients and teams as well as the evaluation of program on behalf of a range of organizations. She has also undertaken substantial training and organizational development work, and has also worked as a forensic psychologist. She has had a number of academic articles published and presented papers at international conferences. Her most recent coedited book is *Working With Interpreters in Mental Health* (2003).

Joseph E. Trimble, PhD, is Professor of Psychology at Western Washington University and a Senior Scholar at the Tri-Ethnic Center for Prevention Research at Colorado State University. His is formerly a Fellow at Harvard University's Radcliffe Institute for Advanced Study, and has held offices in the International Association for Cross-Cultural Psychology and the American Psychological Association. He has generated over 130 publications on cross-cultural and ethnic topics in psychology and received numerous teaching and mentoring awards for his work in this area, including the APA's Division 45 Lifetime Achievement Award, the Janet E. Helms Award for Mentoring and Scholarship in Professional Psychology at Teachers College, Columbia University, and the Washington State Psychological Association Distinguished Psychologist Award for 2002. He earned his PhD from the University of Oklahoma, Institute of Group Relations, in 1969.

Stacy Shaw Welch, MS, is currently a graduate student in the Clinical Psychology Program at the University of Washington. Her interests include working with people with borderline personality disorder, and in particular, their physiology. She completed her clinical internship at the Seattle Veterans Affairs Hospital.

Jennifer Wheeler, PhD, received her doctorate in Clinical Psychology from the University of Washington. She is currently the Research and Assessment Team Coordinator with the Department of Corrections Sex Offender Treatment Program in Monroe, Washington. She is also in private practice in clinical and forensic psychology in Seattle, Washington.

Jean C. Yi, MS, is currently a graduate student in the Clinical Psychology Program at the University of Washington. She obtained bachelor's and master's degrees from the University of Washington. Her interests include couple therapy and intimate relationships, ethnic minorities in treatment outcome studies, and ethnic identity and acculturation.

Jeanette Zanipatin, JD, is a statewide policy analyst for the California Immigrant Welfare Collaborative in Sacramento and focuses on health, welfare, and immigrant rights. She has worked on several campaigns for immigrants including the statewide driver's license coalition and efforts to ensure access to healthcare. She received her BA in legal studies from the University of California at Berkeley and her JD from the Seattle University School of Law. She has worked as an immigration attorney for the Northwest Immigrant Rights Project in Seattle and at La Raza Centro Legal in San Francisco. She has worked on various immigrant rights issues, including representing victims of domestic violence, political asylum, and detained immigrants. She is licensed to practice law in California and Washington State.